ALMANACS OF AMERICAN WARS

KOREAN WAR ALMANAC

Paul M. Edwards

Facts On File
An imprint of Infobase Publishing

Dedicated to Gregg Edwards: friend, colleague, son.

If the best minds in the world had set out to find us the worst possible
location in the world to fight this damnable war, politically and
militarily, the unanimous choice would have been Korea!

—Dean Acheson

Quoted in Michael E. Hass, *In the Devil's Shadow*
(Annapolis, Md.: Naval Institute Press), p. 1.

Korean War Almanac

Copyright © 2006 by Paul M. Edwards

Facts On File, Inc.
An imprint of Infobase Publishing
132 West 31st Street
New York NY 10001

Library of Congress Cataloging-in-Publication Data
Edwards, Paul M.
    Korean War almanac / Paul M. Edwards—1st ed.
        p. cm.—(Almanacs of American wars) Includes bibliographical references and index.
    ISBN 0-8160-6037-1 (hardcover : alk. paper)
    1. Korean War, 1950–1953—Chronology. 2. Korean War, 1950–1953. 3. Korean War,
1950–1953—United States. 4. United Nations—Armed Forces—Korea I. Title II. Series.
    DS918.E365 2008
    951.904'2—dc22   2005009374

Facts On File books are available at special discounts when purchased in bulk quantities for businesses, associations, institutions, or sales promotions. Please call our Special Sales Department in New York at (212) 967–8800 or (800) 322–8755.

You can find Facts On File on the World Wide Web at http://www.factsonfile.com

Text design by Erika K. Arroyo
Cover design by Pehrsson Design
Maps by Dale Williams

Printed in the United States of America

VB FOF 10 9 8 7 6 5 4 3 2 1

This book is printed on acid-free paper.

 Contents

PREFACE

Most of those involved in the Korean War, whether in the military or the political arena, seem to feel that it was the wrong war. While both the decision to go to war and the interpretation of what happened during the war will be argued for decades to come, it is clear that it was a war that America was not prepared to fight, either psychologically or militarily. Coming as it did so close to the victories of World War II, it was a war that America did not want. At the same time, pressed with a fear of the expansion of communism and well aware of the increasing role played by the United States in international affairs, it was a war the administration of President Harry S. Truman believed had to be fought. And, as it turned out, it was a highly significant war. In many respects it was a watershed in the flow of both American and international history.

Today, after more than a half-century, it is still difficult to understand all that happened during the Korean War. Arguments continue among respected historians about the causes, the fighting, and the outcome of the war and most certainly about the legacy of the war. New information that has become available from the archives of our onetime enemies has shed new light on our inquiries and sometimes provided new evidence for our established theories. To those studying the cold war (when it was important enough to be capitalized), the outcome of the Korean War often seems to be more interesting and significant than the war itself. Most of us, however, without acknowledging the source of the condition, live out our lives in the shadow of decisions made and goals accomplished during those often desperate days.

Since the 1950–53 conflict, the United States as well as the rest of the world has been involved in many struggles. The blood of the men and women of many nations has soaked the earth in the defense of international peace and the pursuit of localized ideologies. Americans continue to fight and die in the continuation of national policies established and doctrines accepted during the days of the Korean War.

Veterans of the Korean War do not seem to speak out as much as other veterans. They call their war the "Forgotten War." They do not hold as many unit reunions; they do not produce a lot of unit newsletters. They have not written as many memoirs, novels, poems, or songs to commemorate their service. They are not inclined to identify themselves as quickly by personal automobile plates or stickers in car windows. The reason for this behavior is one of many questions that remain about the war. But when seeing the extent of this conflict laid out on a daily basis, it is possible to recognize the American commitment and the personal courage that appear day after day.

We still do not know a great deal about the war. Some parts of it seem immune to inquiry and understanding. The war was a very complex venture at an extremely complicated time in American and world history. The simple answers provided by orthodox and revisionist historians do not always apply. Often called a "police action," a "conflict," the "Korean Question," a "limited action," "Truman's War," the "war before Vietnam," and traditionally the "forgotten war," the action in the Korean War was warlike. It was a war in every sense and meaning of the word. It embraced all the political turmoil, the national pride, the military aggression, the dying, and the suffering that are reflected in any war.

It was not, however, a popular war, nor was it a war that most persons, certainly most Americans, really understood. Following on the heels of the vastly popular and dramatically concluded World War II—during which nearly every American was deeply and personally involved—events in Korea seemed an unwelcome breech of a peace so dearly bought. The coming of the war was an interruption in the economic growth of the nation and an inconvenience to those who were called upon to fight once again and so quickly. The war was not personally felt by most other Americans. The draft, weakened by an elaborate deferment system, left the burden to only a few, generally lower-income families. There was no rationing and few shortages to be faced. Nothing happened, or was attempted, to impress on the American people the seriousness of what was occurring in that distant Asian nation. Later, the war in Korea was lost in the military and political turmoil of the growing conflict in Vietnam, and its memory faded quickly from the American mind.

There is still a great deal to be learned from the Korean War, as well as about the war. It was a war that was waged on land, at sea, and in the air. It was a war of combined operations, of military unpreparedness, of fierce controversies and prolonged negotiations. It was a war that reflected much of the major confrontation between the Free World and the communist world—between East and West. It witnessed a significant shift in American policy and strategy. And, it was a war during which limited objectives became both necessary and advantageous.

ACKNOWLEDGMENTS

I wish to acknowledge the major sources used for this work. Because of the scope of the task and the wide variety of entries, it has been necessary to rely heavily on many secondary sources from which the bulk of the information presented here has been gleaned. The last few years have seen an increase in the scholarly work done, and a growth in the materials produced, about the Korean War. But there is still a considerable limitation as to what is available. In comparison to the information now on-hand about World War II, or even about the more debated war in Vietnam, the number of sources remains small. There are not yet nearly enough of the monographs or narrative histories that are so important to the researcher. But fortunately there have been some excellent documentary works, as well as official histories produced in the last decade or so. A large number of books, articles, and papers have been referenced in the *Almanac,* and they are referenced in the attached bibliography. Some sources, however, require special mention. These are Kathryn Weathersby, coeditor, *Cold War International History Project Bulletin* (Korean Initiative); Walter G. Hermes, *Truce Tent and Fighting Front* (Office of the Chief of Military History, 1988); Roy E. Appleman, *South to the Naktong, North to the Yalu* (Chief of Military History, 1960); Donald Knox, *The Korean War: Uncertain Victory* (Harcourt Brace Jovanovich, 1988); David Rees, *The Limited War* (1964); Lee Ballenger, *The Outpost War: U.S. Marines in Korea, 1953* (Brassey, 2001); Lee Ballenger, *Final Crucible: U.S. Marines in Korea, 1952* (Brassey, 2000); Charles Whiting, *Battleground Korea: The British in Korea* (Sutton, 2003); Ted Barris; *Deadlock in Korea: Canadians at War, 1950–1953* (Macmillan, 1999); William C. Russell, *The Days at White Horse* (Arlington, 1988); Lynn Montross and Nicholas A. Canzona, *U.S. Marine Operations in Korea,* 5 vol. (Historical Branch, 1954–72); T. R. Fehrenbach, *This Kind of War* (Brassey, 2000 ed.); James I. Matray, *Historical Dictionary of the Korean War* (Greenwood Press, 1991); Roy E. Appleman, *Escaping the Trap* (Texas A & M University Press, 1990); Roy E. Appleman, *Disaster in Korea* (Texas A & M University Press, 1989); Billy C. Mossman, *Ebb and Flow: November 1950–July 1951* (Center of Military History, 1990); James A. Field, Jr., *History of United States Naval Operations, Korea* (1962); and *The Marines in the Korean War Commemorative Series,* published during the 50th anniversary of the Korean War. This series, written by reliable historians from primary sources, is an excellent tool for anyone studying the war, but the various titles lack an index. Also of considerable value is the series of pamphlets produced by the United States of America Korean War Commemoration Committee (U.S. Army). Also to be mentioned, with thanks, are the individual contributors, with offerings in dictionaries and encyclopedias; among these I would acknowledge the contributions of Clay Blair, Stanley Sandler, Allen Millett, James Matray, and Roger Dingman.

Among the primary sources consulted were those found at the archive and library at the Center for the Study of the Korean War, located at Graceland University's campus in Independence, Missouri; Central Plains Region National Archives and Records Administration (Kansas City, Missouri); the Dwight D. Eisenhower Presidential Library (Abilene, Kansas); the Harry S. Truman Presidential Museum and Library (Independence, Missouri); and the Allied Forces Command and Staff College Library (Fort Leavenworth, Kansas). Appreciation is also expressed for the librarians and staff of the University of Missouri at Kansas City and of Park University, in Parkville, Missouri. Special thanks to the staff and administration of Graceland University, essentially to those at the Independence campus, where so often the seeds of inquiry grow into blossoms of understanding. And to the history faculty at Graceland University, even to those who do not think it is important.

For aid in the work-up of the photographs used I am most grateful for the help of Lisa Hecht of the Center for the Study of the Korean War. Special thanks go to Megan Bethel for help with the maps and to Joni Wilson for her professional eye.

Personal acknowledgment goes to my long-suffering wife, Carolynn; to Paula, Jeff, Gregg, DeAnne, Alison, Courtney, Megan, and McKenzie, now all delightful adults. Thanks to colleagues and friends Lisa Hecht, Leroy (Jack) Eller, Judith Charlton, Greg Smith, Cindy Roberts, and Nancy Eisler. And, of course, to Bailey, who is never absent.

Introduction

The war in Korea (1950–53) is perhaps best understood if recognized as being fought in four phases. Each phase is fairly distinct. Initially, following the North Korean invasion of South Korea, there was a period of retreat in the face of overwhelming odds. The Communist drive was met with increasing resistance as first the Republic of Korea Army and then the United States and finally United Nations (UN) forces, began to fight back. Yet even after the effort was boosted by the political and military support of many nations, the United Nations Command was forced to withdraw in the face of the aggressive enemy. Soon the UN was driven inside a defensive perimeter running in an arc some 28 miles inland from the port city of Pusan. There the Eighth Army held fast in the southeasternmost part of the beleaguered nation.

The second phase is represented by the dramatic end-around accomplished when General Douglas MacArthur's X Corps landed at the port of Inchon, caught the North Korean Army unprepared, cut off its supplies, and began a drive north. At the same time, Eighth Army broke free from the desperate defense at Pusan and moved north to join with X Corps, after which the two units pushed inland. The North Korean Communist forces were driven back across the 38th parallel. At this point the United Nations halted only briefly. Then the decision was made to complete the job by crossing the arbitrary division between the Koreas. The objective was to destroy the North Korean Army and return all of Korea to UN control. From the 38th parallel the United Nations Command began its move toward the Manchurian border at the Yalu River. The North Korean Army was initially shattered by the drive of the attacking forces and moved ever northward. In late October, troops of the advancing army reached their northernmost point, some even to the Yalu River. By November 1950, a conclusion to the war appeared imminent. The efforts to unite the Korean people under one government—friendly to the United States—seemed to be near fulfillment.

The third phase of the war began when soldiers of the Chinese People's Liberation Army—defined by the Chinese as volunteers—crossed the Yalu River and intervened in the war. The massive impact of these combat-seasoned Chinese troops caught the United Nations off guard and turned the once proud advance into a massive retreat. The UN forces were driven back, both on the east coast, where X Corps was caught at the Chosin Reservoir, and on the west coast, where Eighth Army was involved in a widespread withdrawal. The Chinese soldiers who poured into Korea overwhelmed the UN troops, and their involvement completely changed the nature of the war. Fighting in the awful cold and over vastly difficult terrain, the split forces of General MacArthur's command were simply overwhelmed. The flight was fierce and the retreat demoralizing. Within a month, the UN forces had withdrawn to positions well below the 38th parallel. By the end of 1950, the war had already resulted in a terrible loss of men and equipment.

The fourth and final phase of the Korean War lasted until an armistice was signed in July of 1953.[1] This period is sometimes defined as a stalemate. During this phase, both armies dug in. Suffering with exhaustion and increasingly cautious, they waited for the outcome of the negotiation efforts that began in July of 1951. The war had reached a point where neither side was willing to risk major forces or to commit to any heroic effort to acquire massive land gains. It was a war in which the goal no longer seemed to be victory but rather perseverance. This phase was later to be identified as the "limited war" or the "hill war."

The first year of the war was characterized by movement. During this time, there were dramatic changes in the battlefront as the fighting swept up and down the length of the Korean Peninsula. As efforts at negotiation began, and dragged on, it became evident that the two opposing groups—the Democratic People's Republic of (North) Korea and the Republic of (South) Korea—were determined to fight to the death for the unification of the nation under their respective governments. But the cold war participants were not so willing. The governments of the People's Republic of China, the Soviet Union, and the United States were less anxious to make a stand in Korea and began to realize that it was not in their best national interests to seek total victory in Korea. Behind this attitude lay several important considerations, not the least of these being that the cost, in terms of men and materiel, was simply too great to be sustained for any length of time. Significant, also, was the fear that the war in Korea might escalate into a global confrontation—even World War III—and that was not the goal of either the United Nations or the Communist countries involved.

It was equally true that, while seeking an end to the war, none of the major nations involved were willing to simply pull out. Each had its own principles to defend and objectives to be gained or maintained. Neither side was interested in much compromise. The vast differences in both expectation and style made the negotiations difficult. The Communists saw the armistice discussions as yet another means to fight a war, while the United States—the primary nation in establishing the basic requirements for a settlement—faced conflicting goals at home and disagreement with the other nations involved in the confrontation. For the Chinese, there was the question of national identity and the need to present themselves as a self-sufficient nation and to be recognized among world powers. For the Democratic administration at home, still suffering from the charges that it had "lost China" and dealing with the increasing fear generated by the fire-breathing senator Joseph McCarthy, there was a constant awareness of the dangers of a worldwide Communist conspiracy.

---

[1] Actually the war never ended. What was accomplished was a cease-fire between warring parties. The war that was never declared in the beginning ended with no declared peace.

THE NATION

In 1950, Korea was a small nation of about 30 million people. The mountainous Korean Peninsula dangled from the Asian mainland, where it touched on two great powers, China and the old Soviet Union. It was so located as to be easily dominated by its proximity to Japan. With more than 5,400 miles of coastline, it is nearly an island. Its northern boundaries are at the Yalu (Amnokgang) and Tumen (Duman-gang) Rivers, its eastern, the east the Sea of Japan—Koreans of today prefer East Sea—and its southern, the Korean Strait. On the west is the Yellow Sea. The Yalu River runs about 350 air miles, and approximately 500 ground miles, before enter-ing the northeastern corner of the Yellow Sea. The Tumen River, which emerges from the same mountain areas as the Yalu, makes a hundred-mile inverted "V" before it reaches the East Sea.

Slightly more than 575 miles in length, Korea ranges from 90 to 200 miles in width. On the east the sea is met by sharply rising mountains. In contrast the west is a place of many islands and deep inlets that provide numerous harbors. The total area, including islands, is 222,154 square miles, 45 percent of which (99,313 square miles) is in the south. The country is about the size of Hungary. There about 3,000 islands, most of which are on the west and south coasts. The Taebaek Mountains on the east side nearly isolate the narrow east coast from the remainder of Korea. In the summer the weather is hot and humid, with a high of 104°F, aggravated by a four-month monsoon season. In the winter it is cold and raw, sometimes going as low as –40°F. Though Seoul is on the same general parallel as the state of Indiana, the winds driven down from the interior of Asia make Korea, particularly North Korea, harsh and devastatingly cold in the winter.

During the long occupation of 1905–45, the Japanese built an extensive railway system to connect the cities at the northern and southern ends, primarily following a military rather than an economic agenda. After the Korean War broke out, the UN took control of and operated the railway system in South Korea. Both the economy and the terrain influenced the number and location of the roads and railways. The location of the mountain ranges meant that most roads ran north and south and transportation across the land was generally difficult. Railways, many narrow-gauge, were limited and followed trade routes but were totally inadequate for the move-ment required by a modern army.

In 1945, Korea had an average of 0.17 miles of road for every square mile. This is in comparison with an average 4.6 miles of road per square mile in Japan. In 1950, there were fewer than 20,000 miles of road on the peninsula, and only a few miles (primarily from Inchon to Seoul) were paved. Most of the roads consisted of packed dirt and were immediately affected by the weather.

During the Japanese occupation, air travel had been encouraged, but when World War II ended, so did much of the service. The Korean Air Transport company flew limited routes to Hong Kong, Taipei, and Tokyo. The only international flights avail-able were provided by the U.S.-based Northwest Airlines, which flew into Seoul. Dur-ing the war, Northwest shifted its landing destination to Pusan. Perhaps the easiest transportation was provided by the abundance of waterways of all sizes that checker the land as they roll toward the sea. It was often far easier to go around Korea than it was to go across Korea. Telephone communication was provided, up until 1949, by the Radio Corporation of America, after which the government took control and managed to keep about 50,000 phones in operation. On January 11, 1952, the Republic of Korea was granted admission into the International Telecommunications Union.

The Korean people are the inheritors of a long and creative culture but in 1950 were primarily agricultural, relying on rice crops and fish from the waters to provide their basic needs. At the time of the war, about 15 million people, about 50 percent, were farmers who lived and worked on family farms that averaged 2.5 acres. These farms produced a significant amount of rice, barley, rye, wheat, and soybeans, in addition to vegetables, fruits, and 15,000 tons of tobacco. The majority of animal protein was provided by a fishing industry that employed more than a million Koreans on both sides of the border. During the war, the fishing actually improved as the presence of UN vessels prevented Japanese fishermen from infringing in Korean waters.

Most of the population lived in small villages scattered among the mountains. Seoul, the capital city, had an estimated population in 1949 of about 1.5 million. By December 1952 the population had dropped to about 700,000. Pusan, the second city and the temporary capital during the Communist occupation of Seoul, had an estimated population of 820,000 in 1952.

The light industry of South Korea was not adequate to meet local needs. The industry consisted primarily of textile production and food processing, but rubber shoes, bicycle tires, cement, paper, and coke were also manufactured. Mineral production consisted primarily of copper ore, gold, graphite, kaolin, lead ore, nickel, tungsten, and zinc ore. The struggling industrial effort was nearly halted when, in May 1948, North Korea cut off the supply of electric power that it had been selling to the South for years. To meet the need the United States provided power barges and helped in the construction of domestic facilities. But it was not until 1952 that South Korea was producing the power it needed.

When World War II ended, it was necessary to reorganize the entire Korean educational system. The Japanese had not encouraged education among the Koreans. Nevertheless about a quarter of the Korean people attended the missionary schools, and some of them were able to go on to study in secondary and professional schools. Compulsory elementary education was established in South Korea in June 1950. The poor timing meant that it would not be implemented as quickly as desired, but even during the war, primary and secondary education was pushed and provided when possible. In 1948, the literacy rate in South Korea was between 70 and 80 percent; it is higher today.

The Korean people have been influenced by a wide variety of religions over the years. Six of these need to be mentioned. Sinkyo is a mixture of shamanism and animistic nature worship and is the oldest religion recorded in Korea. Its influence is seen even in the practice of other religions in Korea. Confucianism was introduced to Korea in the first century and is considered second only to Sinkyo in terms of influence. In 1392, it overcame Buddhism in popularity to become the state religion.

Buddhism, while it has been a part of the Korean culture since the fourth century, had a sudden burst of popularity during the Japanese occupation. Korean Buddhism and Japanese Buddhism differ somewhat in their essential concepts and maintain separate identities. In 1940, there were an estimated 300,000 Buddhists of the Japanese variety and 200,000 of the Korean variety. Christianity grew slowly, primarily through the influence of a series of individual missionaries who came to Korea. After the West opened Korea to international commerce, the spread of Christianity increased rapidly by means of missionary schools. In 1940, there were an estimated 600,000 Protestants and Catholics in Korea.

Chondokyo came late to Korea. It is an eclectic religion that incorporates some of the more traditional beliefs from Buddhism and Confucianism. It was founded by a man named Choe who may have had as many as 2 million followers in the early 20th century. By 1940, however, the number of followers had dropped to less than 100,000. Shintoism, which had a brief popularity, flourished primarily as a Japanese belief and was maintained during the period of occupation. It nearly died out after the close of World War II. In 1940, the estimated number of Korean followers of Shintoism was given at less than 30,000.

BRIEF HISTORY

Until the 11th century, the nation of Korea included most of what is today Manchuria. During repeated conflicts with the Chinese, the Koreans retreated until the Yalu and Tumen Rivers became the northern boundary. After a long history of conflict and occupation, Korea was annexed by Japan in 1910. The Japanese ruled the nation harshly and completely until the end of World War II. Anticipating unification at the end of the war the Korean people were vastly disappointed by the Allied decision to divide the nation. The line for the acceptance of the Japanese surrender at the end of World War II was located at the 38th parallel. It cut Korea in half. The Soviet Union, just entering the Pacific war, agreed to occupy the north while the United States took responsibility for the south. Lieutenant General John R. Hodges, in command of XXIV Corps, was to administer the southern half for the United States. Meeting in Moscow in December 1945, the foreign ministers of the United States, Great Britain, and the Soviet Union had considered plans for a four-power trusteeship to lead Korea to independence within five years. Then, in August 1947, the United States, Great Britain, and China (Nationalist) agreed to reconsider the trusteeship idea in the hope of Korean unification, but the Soviet Union blocked the effort. Partition became inevitable when efforts to create a unified government fell apart.

Therefore, by 1948 two different governments had been inaugurated on the Korean Peninsula—two nations divided along the 38th parallel. Both North and South Korea held elections that gave birth to two new governments: the Democratic People's Republic of Korea and the Republic of Korea. Both governments—the DPRK under Kim Il Sung and the ROK under Syngman Rhee—claimed jurisdiction over all Korea. The original occupation plan was for both the United States and the Soviet Union to pull their troops out of Korea, and both parties did so in time. However, both the Soviet Union and the United States left behind advisory groups to help train the armies of the respective nations. The U.S. Korean Military Advisory Group consisted of about 500 men.

Using the Almanac

This almanac is an attempt to provide a day-by-day account of the war and to make available basic information about equipment, nations, and individuals that played significant roles in the Korean War. For the sake of clarity, events on a given day are divided into five, and sometimes six, subheadings. They are:

Political/Administrative: All activities that are related to politics, administration, legal matters, logistics, command, strategy, or equipment and were of concern to the war in general.

Eighth Army: All events in which the Eighth Army was the primary unit involved. This includes the Allied nations as well as the ROK.

Tenth Corps: During that period in which X Corps operated as an independent command, the activities of the corps are listed separately.

Sea War: This heading lists activities that were primarily naval in execution. Because of an agreement reached on July 9, 1950—that all air/ground targets, except those that were specifically naval operations, would be directed by the U.S. Air Force and the Joint Service Target Analysis Group—it seemed best to list naval air activity, with the same exceptions, under Air War rather than Sea War.

Air War: All events in which the primary activity was conducted by aircraft—either Air Force, Navy, or Marine—against assigned targets.

Partisans: Throughout the war much of the activity behind enemy lines or on the many coastal islands was conducted by groups of partisans. At first they were unorganized but later became more official. These activities, though they were often executed in cooperation with regular land, sea, or naval forces, are listed under this general heading.

In considering these entries it will be helpful to keep the following things in mind.

Inclusion: It is not possible to include everyone or every event; therefore, a selection process has been necessary. An effort has been made to include everything possible. Yet while the selection of inclusions has not been arbitrary, it has certainly been subjective. I am to blame for any omissions, as I am for any mistakes of commission.

Dates: There will be some disagreement about dates. First of all, there are a variety of ways in which various sources determine when an event begins or ends. For example, does a reconnaissance flight begin when the planes leave the field or carrier, or when they are over the target, or even when the raid is first reported? Selecting dates is also complicated by the fact that various units (as well as the varied services) sometimes recorded different dates. Thus, some flexibility is required in assigning "exact dates."

Time: The almanac is first of all a chronology, and every effort has been made to list the most significant events as they occur. However, Korea and the

United States are in different time zones and are a half-day apart. Thus events are happening at different local times—on some occasions, even on different calendar days. As much as possible, the dates presented are listed at the time the event is taking place *in the place* where it is happening. This means that events will sometimes appear to be out of order. For example, Washington, D.C., may appear to have heard about the North Korean invasion before it happened.

Language: Some areas and events are best remembered by their Japanese name (as they appeared on the Japanese maps being used) rather than by the more proper Korean name. This is most obvious in the use of the Japanese name of Chosin Reservoir. When this applies, an attempt is made to provide both names. The Korean language is written in Hangul, meaning great letters, and is very different from the Romance languages. Because the sounds of the letters are not the same, many multiple spellings are available in the various sources (Pusan/Busan). Because consistency is most helpful in identification, and there are different spellings for most of the persons or places identified, an effort has been made for consistency. Nevertheless, there is some redundancy. Though it is clear that *ri* means village and *do* means an island, it is helpful in some cases to be redundant and say "the island of Wolmi-do" or the "village of Sinto-ri."

Numbers and Estimations: The numbers reported by many primary sources, foreign sources, standard secondary works, and after-action reports are often vastly different. For example, the Soviet record of the number of UN planes shot down is considerably different from the figures offered by the United States. In these cases, every effort has been made to arrive at a reasonably accurate figure, but be forewarned that exact numbers may never be known and others are still being determined. In selecting numbers, the national sources (Soviet, etc.) have been used whenever possible.

Disagreement: While it has been more than 50 years since the Korean War was fought, there are still hundreds of events not yet clearly understood. Every month or so, highly competent and totally trustworthy historians discover new challenges to the prevailing understanding.

CHRONOLOGY

★ PRELUDE TO WAR ★

The people of Korea are of the Tungusic branch of the Ural-Altaic family. They migrated into the area from the northwestern regions of Asia. As a people they are racially and linguistically homogeneous, speaking a Uralic language only remotely related to Japanese, Finnish, and Mongolian.

2333 B.C.

October 3

This exact date is usually given to the founding of the Kingdom of Old Choson (Chosan)—"The Land of the Morning Calm"—when a god named Hwanung transformed a bear into a woman and mated with her. Their son, Dangun, established the Korean nation with a capital at Asadal (Pyongyang) that was called Choson. A more scientific suggestion is that the Go-Chosun people, called Dongyi, inhabited Manchuria, east China, and the Korean Peninsula sometime before this date.

1122 B.C.

Some historians writing of the Korean nation are inclined to date the official beginning of civilization to a semi-mythical leader known as Ki-ja who brought Chinese culture to Korea.

109–108 B.C.

Wu-ti, the Han emperor of China, invades the estuary of the Biao River and, after winning an impressive victory against the Korean people, sets up provinces of control in the northern part of the Korean Peninsula. In time this will evolve into the Han dynasty.

57 B.C.

Korea's recorded history begins as several tribes of Koreans occupying the area organize themselves into three kingdoms that, during the early years, wage rather constant warfare among themselves. Finally, with the aid of the Chinese, one of the kingdoms, Silla, is able to unite the country.

A.D. 370

Buddhism emerges as the primary religion of Korea. It was brought to the land by missionary monks from India and China who found a fertile ground.

660–686

A prominent monk, Wonhyo, is believed to be the first to systematize Buddhism and to make it popular among the common people. His works, primarily commentaries on Mahayana Sutras, are a major influence on Chinese, Japanese, and Korean Buddhists.

682

The year given for the official sanction of Confucianism.

935

The kingdom of Silla is overthrown by Wang Kon who founds the Koryo dynasty.

1231

The Mongols invade and occupy Koryo and finally establish some kind of control by 1259. The Koryo leaders govern under Mongol control and establish a Mongol pattern for the court and for government.

1267

The Golden Horde—the armies of Genghis Khan and his successor Kublai (also Qubilai, Khubilai) Khan—attempt to cross the Sea of Japan (East Sea) and conquer Japan. A sudden and awesome storm destroys their ships and prevents the invasion. The Japanese believe the storm to be a divine intervention and immortalize the event in their culture. This kamikaze (divine wind) will give its name to the Japanese suicide pilots of World War II.

1364

Yi Song Gye leads an army in the defeat of the Mongol occupiers and drives out the "Red Turbans," thereafter emerging as a leader among the Korean people. Expanding his army after the Mongol defeat, he turns his attention to controlling the Japanese pirates who have been attacking the coast of Korea for decades.

1389

General Yi Song Gye, who has gained power by way of his victories over the Mongol invaders and against Japanese pirates, begins an internal revolt to depose King Kong-yang and take power. The new leader soon pushes for a series of land reform programs that greatly expand his support among the people.

1392

The internal revolt led by Yi Song Gye overthrows the government, and he becomes king by popular acclaim. Yi Song Gye establishes a new dynasty. The Supreme Council, the highest organization in the Koryo government, formally declares that the Koryo dynasty has come to an end and that the Joseon/Chosen (Korean name) or Yi (Japanese name) dynasty has begun. Titled Taejo, or king, Yi Song Gye establishes the capital at present-day Seoul. He is able to maintain his independent control primarily because of the recognition he receives from the Ming emperor of China. The Yi dynasty will rule Korea for two centuries. He removes all influences of Buddhism and adopts Confucian teachings.

1418–1450

Under King Sejong the Joseon dynasty enters its greatest period of cultural activity and economic growth. Sejong sponsors the creation of the Korean alphabet (Hangul). It is during his reign that the Confucian classics are printed using a movable, metal type machine.

1582

A white man whom the Koreans record as Pingni, lands with some Chinese sailors on the island of Cheju-do. Pingni is the first white man known to be in Korea. He eventually makes his way back to China, where he spreads the news about his Korean adventures.

1592

The Japanese warlord, Hideyoshi, successfully invades Korea, coming by sea with 150,000 men armed with muskets. The goal of the invasion is to secure a base on the Asian mainland in order to more effectively conquer China. Once in Korea, he will remain in occupation for several years.

1593

One of Hideyoshi's officers, Konishi Yukinaga, is a Roman Catholic, and he is accompanied in the invasion by a Jesuit priest, Gregorio de Czspedes. Within a few years there will be a growing interest in Catholicism among the Koreans.

1597

The Japanese are driven from Korea following a naval battle in which the Koreans, led by Admiral Yi Sun-shin, destroy enemy transports. Yi Sun-shin had under his command several Turtle ships, the first iron-clad warships acknowledged to have been used in battle.

1627

Some Manchu armies with the intention of occupying Korea try an invasion but are repulsed before any effort can take hold.

1637

A second Manchu army successfully invades Korea. Under its harsh rule the area is driven into an extended period of economic desolation. The citizens rise up and form the Ui-Bying (the righteous armies) to combat the enemy, which eventually wins out.

1730s

The initial series of "ginseng trade wars" begins as the first recorded contact between Korea and the people of North America. Overplanting and widespread use have made the root scarce in Korea, and the best source of supply is to be found in the Americas, where the root has been a staple of the Native American diet.

1770

When Chon Du-won, a diplomat in China, brings back a copy of Father Matteo Ricci's book, *The True Doctrine of the Lord of Heaven,* it influences a small group of Korean reformists, called Shilhak, who seek to learn more about contemporary Catholic theology.

1777

The founder of modern Korean Christianity is identified as Yi Pyok, a scholarly young nobleman who, having read about Christianity as a result of a philosophical discussion, decides to become a Christian.

1783

The Shilhak reformers send Yi Sung-Hun to China to learn more about Catholicism. While there Yi Sung-Hun becomes the first legally baptized Korean Catholic. He returns to Korea in an effort to proselytize his religion. The young man is responsible for the first formal converts.

1784

February 22

The *Empress of China* leaves New York harbor loaded with American ginseng roots and begins a trade with the Orient that will produce a more than 300 percent profit for its American investors. Shortly after, a number of Korean ginseng growers are brought to the United States to aid in the trade. They are believed to be the first Koreans in America.

Christianity begins to spread rapidly—and begins to cause considerable stress with native institutions and values.

1785

A Jesuit missionary, Father Peter Grammont, begins baptizing converts to Christianity and moves the church to the next step by ordaining Catholic priests.

1794–1866

There are repeated efforts to uproot the "barbarian foreigners" who, Korean officials believe, are involved in an imperialistic Western effort to turn Korea into a European nation. The primary method being used, they believe, is the expansion of Christianity.

1839

The Korean king, fearing the influence of the growing Catholic religion, orders the extermination of the Catholic Church in Korea. The order leads to the execution of more than 200 Catholics, including two French priests and a French bishop.

1840

A resolution is passed by the U.S. Congress to open trade with Korea.

1847

The French, greatly upset at the insult to both church and state, dispatched a fleet and troops to Korea to seek revenge for the killing of the French clergy. The task force is frustrated by a storm that sinks two of its warships and forces the fleet to return to France.

1854

America's Commodore Perry forces Japan to open its shores to world trade. Once established, an effort is made to extend this trade to Korea, but the Koreans resist. The "Hermit Kingdom" is able to defeat a series of attempts by the French, Americans, and Japanese to force the issue.

1866

March 11

Father Simon François Berneux, a French missionary who has been preaching in Korea illegally since the attempted eradication in 1839, is arrested. He and about 8,000 of his followers are put to death.

June

An American schooner, *Surprise,* flounders in the Yellow Sea off Korea's northwest coast. Some members of the crew make it to shore and work their way to Manchuria. Two months later they return to the United States with many exaggerated tales of the land they had visited so briefly.

August

The American schooner, *General Sherman,* sails from Chefoo, Japan, to Korea's Tae-dong River in an effort to establish trade with the Koreans. The ship is sailing under a British charter. On arrival the ship tries to move upstream toward Pyongyang but is quickly stuck in the mud. A crowd of local people, suspicious and afraid of the foreigners, attack the ship. The crew fights well, but after four days the Koreans are able to take the ship, and they burn the *General Sherman.* When the devout Buddhist regent, Daewongun, comes to power, he decides to wipe out Christianity; during his reign, he murders numerous believers, including the king's wife and nurse.

1867

January

In an effort to answer questions about the mysterious disappearance of the *General Sherman,* Commander Robert W. Shufeldt takes the USS *Wachusett* from its base in China to the west coast of Korea; foul weather forces him to return without an answer to his question.

1868

March

Commander John C. Febiger of the USS *Shenandoah* sails from China to the mouth of the Taedong River. Once there he manages to communicate with the local authorities. He eventually receives the information that Commander Robert W. Shufeldt had requested. He is informed that a crowd of locals destroyed the *General Sherman* and killed the entire crew.

1870

President Grant's secretary of state, Hamilton Fish, instructs the U.S. minister in China to procure a treaty with Korea for the protection of stranded seamen and, if possible, to negotiate a commercial treaty with Korea.

1871

May

The American minister to China, Frederick F. Low, boards the USS *Colorado* at the Japanese port of Nagasaki. Accompanied by a squadron of gunboats and warships, Low heads for Korea. They land at Chemulpo (Inchon), where they are told that the Koreans want friendly relations but are not interested in a commercial treaty.

May 31

The 1,200-man Low-Rodgers expedition arrives off Kanghwa Island, Korea.

June 1

A surveying party sent out by the expedition is fired on by a Korean shore battery. The Americans return fire and, in a short engagement, inflict rather serious damage on the Korean battery. Despite the fact that no Americans are hurt, Admiral Rodgers feels it necessary to punish the Koreans and to project American strength.

June 10

Four steam launches and two gunboats proceed up the Yom-ha (Salee), the narrow stretch of water that separates the mainland from Kanghwa, to make soundings. The American gunboats silence the batteries and return to anchorage. The conflict results in the death of three Americans and approximately 259 Koreans. The authorities at Seoul still refuse to enter into negotiations. Six Americans are awarded the Medal of Honor for their actions during this involvement. Despite the effort, the United States comes away without the treaty the expedition had gone to secure.

July 3

Having failed in his efforts to establish some sort of trading agreement, Ambassador Low and the U.S. flotilla leave Korea and return to China.

1875

March 26

Syngman Rhee, who will later become president of the Republic of Korea, is born. The son of Yi Kyung-sun, a devoted follower of the Yangban, he is a descendant of the Yi dynasty. He is named Yi Seung-man and in his youth is known as Yongi, the Korean term for dragon. Western missionaries rename him Syngman Rhee because of their difficulty in translating his name into English. It will remain Rhee ever after.

1876

February 26

The Japanese complete negotiations with Korea and sign the first trade agreement. The agreement, as limited as it is, is the first move in the Japanese effort to wean Korea away from its traditional dependence and loyalty to China. It is also the beginning of Korean's willingness to deal with the outside world.

1878

December

A fleet of American warships under Commodore Shufeldt begins a round-the-world cruise. When the fleet reaches the Far East, the commodore, with the assistance of the Japanese, sets out to establish a treaty with Korea. While there is no immediate reaction, the effort does set the stage for future treaty negotiations.

1882

Progressive elements within the Korean court, often aided and encouraged by the Japanese, lead a series of ill-founded and unsuccessful revolts.

May 22

After further discussions with China and Korea, and with the approval of the United States, a treaty of "Peace, Amity, Commerce, and Navigation" is eventually signed with Korea. The agreement is reached with the efforts of the Chinese viceroy Li Gung Tiensten in return for U.S. help in building up the Chinese navy. The agreement is called the Korean American Treaty, and in it the United States formally recognizes the nation of Korea. The United States is the first Western nation to conclude a treaty with Korea and the first to send a minister to the Korean court.

1883

The first American minister to Korea is Lucius M. Foote. In an effort to encourage mutual friendship Foote arranges for a delegation of Korean dignitaries to visit the United States. They meet with President Chester A. Arthur.

1884

While Christianity is often seen as a threat, government officials no longer interfere. The arrival of Protestantism sets off a new round of Christian converts. The first recorded Protestant (denomination unknown) missionary arrives in Korea in 1884.

1885

April 5

The Reverend Horace G. Underwood (Presbyterian) and the Reverend Henry G. Appenzeller (Methodist) arrive at Inchon to begin missionary work in Korea.

1887

September 12

The first Presbyterian church is organized in Seoul with a congregation of 14 charter members.

October 9

Under the leadership of Reverend Henry G. Appenzeller, the first Methodist church, the Chong Dong, is established in Korea.

1894–1895

Kim Ok-kuin, a Korean statesman who fled the country after causing some political disturbance and who was living in exile in Japan, is assassinated. He was decoyed to Shanghai and murdered by Korean emissaries. Because the Chinese take no action against the murderers, Japan considers the Chinese to be responsible for the assassination. The Sino-Japanese War is the result of Chinese and Japanese struggle for control of Korea, often in plots that originate in Seoul among pro-Chinese and pro-Japanese factions. In the war the Japanese, with an army and navy trained by European powers, will emerge victorious. During the conflict the Chinese forces are quickly beaten and driven across the Yalu to the Liaotung Peninsula, site of Port

Arthur. Recognizing defeat, China sues for peace. For the victory the Japanese demanded possession of the Liaotung Peninsula in perpetuity, a huge indemnity, and a guarantee of Korean independence. The Treaty of Shimonoseki declares the independence of Korea but in fact proclaims uncontested Japanese control.

1894

July 28
A group of revolutionaries aided by rebellious members of the Qing (Ch'ing) dynasty declare the formation of the Taiwan Republic. The island government is the first republic in East Asia. The Japanese crush the movement within a few weeks, although several other attempts are made to establish breakaway governments.

1895

October 8
In an effort to expand Japan's political influence in Korea and to increase its cultural impact, a group of Japanese murder the hostile Korean queen, Min, on the suspicion that she is anti-Japanese. They then seize King Tae-wang, forcing him to accept a cabinet of Korean ministers who are friendly with the Japanese.

1896

February 11
King Tae-wang, with his son, manages to escape from the Japanese and flees to the Russian legation in Seoul. Tae-wang has taken the great seal of Korea with him and is able to rule the nation from inside the legation. While there, he grants the Russians significant mining and lumbering rights in Korea.

June 15
A tidal wave 80 feet in height and 300 miles wide hits the coast of Japan, killing some 28,000.

1897

Horace N. Allen, a Presbyterian medical missionary who was the first of several American ministers sent to Korea to convert the people to Christianity, is named U.S. minister to Korea.

1898

February 15
The USS *Maine* blows up in Havana. The American response sets off a war with Spain.

March 27
The United States goes to war with Spain and enters the Asian arena with the annexation of the Philippines. China agrees to Russia's right to build the Trans-Siberian Railroad across Manchuria to Vladivostok.

1899

Ahn Chang-ho, a leader in the Korean independence movement, arrives in the United States to set up residency. He establishes the Chinmok-hoe Friendship Society and, 10 years later, the Young Koreans Academy (Hung Sa Dang).

1900

May

Chinese anger over the growing intervention of Western culture leads to the outbreak of a short-lived rebellion by the secret society of I-Ho-Chuan (The Righteous and Harmonious Fists), called Boxers by foreigners because they believed that the performance of ritual calisthenics would protect them from bullets. An 18,000-man European relief force will arrive in Peking on August 14, 1900, and put down the revolt. China will make several commercial concessions.

1902

December 22

The first of several groups of Korean emigrants leave Korea for Hawaii aboard the SS *Gaelic*. While slow, the flow of Korean immigration is continuous. As their numbers grow in the United States, so does their influence.

1903

The Russians make an effort to avoid confrontation with Japan over Korea by suggesting that Korea be divided along the 39th parallel, with Japan recognized as the dominant influence in the south and Russia in the north.

1904

February 6

Japan breaks off diplomatic relations with Russia over a dispute about control of Manchuria and Korea. Considerable effort is extended in an attempt to negotiate a division of the area into spheres of influence. However, the Russian belief that they can defeat Japan in battle means that Russia is willing to take an inflexible position.

February 8

Imperial Japan and czarist Russia go to war (Russo-Japanese War). Without a declaration of war, the Japanese attack Port Arthur and bottle up the Russian fleet stationed there. A series of Russian defeats in several land battles follows as the Japanese appear far stronger than the Russians had anticipated. Japanese troops land at the Korean port of Inchon and move north, defeating Russian troops. In the meantime, the Japanese sign a treaty with Korea that guarantees the Hermit Kingdom its independence in return for permission to use a portion of its land in their war against Russia. In the war, the Japanese have the moral support of the United States and Great Britain, which have been increasingly frightened by Russian expansion in the

Pacific. As planned, Japanese forces move through Korea to attack Manchuria, but actually never leave Korea.

Syngman Rhee arrives in the United States, where he will later earn a Ph.D. in international law from Princeton University.

August 24–September 4

During the Battle of Liaoyand, the Japanese force the Russians to retreat to an area of the Sha Ho River near Mukden.

1905–1910

During the early period of the Japanese occupation of Korea, there are numerous uprisings and rebellions, all of them crushed by the Japanese. An estimated 14,566 "rebels" are killed during this period.

1905

January 2

Russia's Port Arthur falls to the Japanese.

February 20–March 10

The last major land battle of the Russo-Japanese War is fought at Mukden in Manchuria (the current Shenyang). It lasts for three weeks and leads to the total defeat of the Russian forces.

May

The final destruction of the Russian fleet under Admiral Rozhdestvenski at Tsushima Strait by Admiral Togo brings an end to the war. This defeat soon led to a Russian surrender. As a part of its victorious response Japan declares Korea its virtual protectorate (dependent state).

July 29

President Theodore Roosevelt's secretary of war, William Howard Taft, signs the Taft-Katsura Memorandum in Tokyo, by which the United States sanctions the Japanese takeover of Korea. Despite active treaties that guarantee the U.S. protection of Korea, the United States recognizes Japanese control over the Korean nation. President Roosevelt expresses the view that Japanese strength in the area will add to the peace and security of the Orient. In return for America's acceptance, the Japanese are willing to avoid taking any aggressive action against American expansionist interests in the Philippines. This move violates the intent, if not the legal implications, of the Treaty of Peace, Amity, Commerce and Navigation and greatly increases Korean bitterness toward the United States.

September 5

The Treaty of Portsmouth, signed in New Hampshire (USA), ends the Russo-Japanese War. In the agreement Russia cedes the southern part of Tsushima Island to Japan and acknowledges Japan's "paramount" interests in Korea. It clears the way for Japanese annexation in 1910.

November 11

In light of political unrest and a limited relationship with Korea, the United States withdraws its legation from Seoul.

November 17

A battalion of Japanese troops enters the Korean capital at Seoul and pressures the Korean cabinet into passing a treaty of protection with the Empire of Japan.

1906

February 10

The Korean Evangelical Society is organized in San Francisco by Koreans who converted to Christianity before leaving Korea. Korean churches serve as community meeting halls where Korean independence is stressed. The Mutual Assistance Society, which publishes the first Korean-language newspaper, is also established at this time.

1907

At the Peace Conference at The Hague Emperor Kojong of Korea accuses Japan of aggression. However, a third Japanese-Korean agreement is forced on the Koreans. As a result of the treaty, the Korean armed forces are disarmed and disbanded. Japan quickly takes over the judicial branch of the government.

September 2

Representatives from 24 Korean cultural, religious, and political organizations meet and create the United Korean Society, headquartered in Honolulu. It begins publication of the nationalist newspaper, *The United Korean News.*

1908

March 28

Chang In-hwan, a Korean patriot, shoots and kills an American, Durham Stevens, who supported the Japanese takeover of Korea as a protectorate.

1909

February 1

California's Mutual Assistance Society and Hawaii's United Korean Society merge. The new organization, the Korean National Association, is dedicated to working with emigrants toward Korean independence.

1910–1945

Japan declares Korea a colony, making the virtual takeover a reality. Korea remains in this status until it is liberated by American and Russian troops at the close of World War II.

For 35 years the Japanese rule Korea with an iron hand, exploiting the people and raping the land. While the Japanese make a good many improvements, most of them are done with military priorities in mind. During these years, Korea becomes almost totally dependent on the Japanese for manufactured products.

1910

October 22

Japan formally annexes Korea when the last ruler of the House of Yi signs away the remainder of the nation's rights to Japan. Syngman Rhee returns to Korea briefly after receiving his Ph.D. from Princeton University. He is quickly pressured to leave.

1911

Syngman Rhee flees from Korea and goes to Hawaii, where he organizes the Korean Methodist Church and the Korean Christian Institute. Both organizations have, as an underlying purpose, the freedom of the Korean people.

1912

Kim Il Sung, later the leader of the Democratic People's Republic of Korea—and first called Kim Song Ju—is born near Pyongyang.

September 16

The Korean Youth Corps is established as a part of the rapidly growing move toward Korean independence among immigrants. The Corps offers a voluntary program of military training at a camp in Hastings, Nebraska, under the leadership of Park Yong-man. He and his Corps believe that Korea can achieve independence only by defeating Japan militarily.

1913

The name of the Korean Boarding School in Hawaii is changed to the Central Institute and Syngman Rhee is named as principal. The school, as well as a community organization known as the Tongjihoe (Comrade Society), is established by Rhee as a part of a political base he is creating among Korean expatriates.

1918

January 8

President Woodrow Wilson's Fourteen Points announce the principle of national self-determination, and the Korean government in exile seeks ways to capitalize on the point. Wilson denies the Korean memorial (request for aid in self-determination); when Syngman Rhee tries to go to Paris to deliver his appeal, he is denied a passport on the grounds that he is now a Japanese citizen.

1919

A brief rebellion is staged by Koreans, but the Japanese put it down quickly and harshly. The Japanese do, however, substitute civilian courts for military courts, an improvement of questionable value.

February 20

Kim Chong-nim founds the School of Aviation in Willows, California. He donates three airplanes to train future pilots to fight against the Japanese. Like the Korean Youth Corps, Kim Chong-nim's trainees believe in the necessity of a war against Japan.

March 1

When the former Yi dynasty (1392–1910) ruler, Emperor Kojong, dies it is said that he was poisoned by the Japanese. Two days before the funeral of the man who is considered a symbol of national independence, Korean nationalists issue a "Proclamation of Independence" that is read at a rally in Seoul. This action initiates a massive nationwide protest effort, later known as the March First Movement or Manse (Long Live Korea). As many as 500,000 people join in the protest, which is violently put down. An estimated 2,000 Korean leaders are killed and numerous others imprisoned during the violent Japanese response. The effort has to be considered a failure but it does mark the beginning of a renewed effort for Korean independence.

April

A series of nationwide demonstrations and riots protest the Japanese rule of Korea. The purpose of the riots is to prevail on the United States to live up to the Treaty of 1882 and force the Japanese to accept Korean independence.

April 10

Several leaders from the March First Movement, operating out of Shanghai, China, create the Korean Provisional Government. At a secret session in Seoul, they elect exiled Syngman Rhee as president of the Korean Provisional Government. The nationalist exiles are determined to free Korea from foreign involvement. The provisional government is supported by persons in Korea, albeit secretly, and by several individuals and organizations in the United States. During World War II, the Korean Provisional Government will fail in its effort to gain widespread support in the United States and will turn toward the more sympathetic Soviet Union, providing an input for Communist revolutionary ideology.

1920

October 20

A gallant force of about 400 Korean men fight a four-day battle at Chuongsan-ri. The Koreans are attempting to set off an armed struggle for independence, but they do not succeed.

1921

June

A Korean army estimated at 3,000 is cut off by the Russian army at the "free city" of Braweschensk in June of 1921. Only about 1,700 survive, and they are taken to Irkutsk and absorbed into the Red Army.

1925

April 18

The Korean Communist Party is established in Korea and grows, particularly among the anti-Japanese underground; it is linked with the Russian Communists through the Communist International (Comintern). Many Korean Communists flee to Manchuria.

1928

According to North Korean records, Kim Il Sung, at age 16, leads a violent demonstration in the Manchurian city of Kirin against the expansion of the railroad into Manchuria. He is jailed briefly and then retired to the countryside to continue encouraging Korean resistance to the Japanese.

1929

December 29

Fifty Koreans register with the California National Guard for training. In response to a growing interest, a separate Korean National Guard unit is formed.

1931

The Japanese army invades Manchuria and carves out a puppet state they call Manchukuo. Kim Il Sung, then called Kim Song Ju, enters a guerrilla band organized to fight the Japanese. He changes his name, adopting the nom de guerre of a legendary Korean hero, Kim Il Sung.

1933

Japan proclaims its plan for the Greater East Asia Co-Prosperity Sphere. The plan is the first official indication of Japanese expansion efforts and is intended to appeal to Asian nationalism.

1934

October 8

Exiled Korean leader Syngman Rhee marries Francesca Donner, an Austrian woman. Rhee is criticized by the Korean community for marrying a white woman and suffers a brief decline in his influence.

1937

The Japanese army attacks the mainland of China in the opening stages of what will become the Pacific phase of World War II.

1937–1945

The war (in the early stages called the China Incident) between Japanese and Chinese forces for control of the mainland continues for eight years. While conflicting forces in China will merge to meet this new threat, the war will suck the strength out of the Nationalist government. It will also allow the Communists to gain control over large segments of the mainland by the organization and control of guerrilla units. When the civil war resumed in 1946, the Communists will have gained considerable strength.

1939

In Los Angeles, Korean Americans picket against the sale of U.S. scrap iron and aviation fuel to the Japanese. Syngman Rhee moves from Hawaii to Washington, D.C., to begin his effort to gain American support for Korean independence.

1940

September 7

Haan Kil-soo, a leader of the Sino-Korean People's League, urges all Koreans in Hawaii to change their immigration status and to insist that they are Korean, and not Japanese subjects as their passports indicate. At the time Korea is considered by most foreign powers to be a part of the Japanese Empire rather than a separate nation.

1941

Syngman Rhee publishes his book *Japan Inside Out,* in which he warns of the coming Japanese aggression. Most of his predictions are surprisingly accurate, but the book, and its theories, are generally ignored.

December 7

The Japanese Imperial Navy attacks the American bases at Pearl Harbor on Oahu. This surprise attack brings the United States into World War II. The Korean government in exile promises its support to America in the war against Japan. The American government considers the Koreans to be victims of the war rather than a part of the aggressor force.

December 10

General Douglas MacArthur sends a cable from the Philippines urging his superiors to find a way to bring the Soviet Union into the emerging war in the Pacific. He feels that the opportunity is ripe for a master stroke against Japan.

1942

Kim Il Sung is recruited by Soviet intelligence for an independent sniper brigade, a multiracial body of about 600 men who are to gather military information about the Japanese in Manchuria and Korea. Syngman Rhee loses the support of the Korean Provisional Government and is voted out as president and replaced by Kim Ku, a moderate living in exile in Nationalist China.

February 19

President Franklin D. Roosevelt signs Executive Order 9066, which authorizes the internment of more than 120,000 Japanese Americans and Japanese nationals. While most of those interned are completely loyal to the United States, Roosevelt is under considerable pressure by anti-Japanese groups to take some action. (On December 4, 1943, Koreans living in the United States will be exempted from "enemy alien status" and declared Korean rather than Japanese.)

1943

March 27

Foreign Secretary Anthony Eden of Great Britain suggests that Korea be placed under an international trusteeship—with China, the United States, and one or two other countries participating.

December 1

In the declaration resulting from the Cairo Conference, U.S., British, and Chinese leaders state that Korea should become "free and independent" in due course, implying some continued period of supervision. President Franklin Roosevelt feels that the Koreans are not capable of maintaining independence and are not ready for self-government. This decision signals the U.S. reentry into Korean affairs. The declaration is greatly resented and soundly condemned by Korean nationalists who claim there are no words in Korean for "in due course."

December 4

After some delay, Korean nationals living in the United States are exempted from "enemy alien status" by Military Order No. 45. Thereafter they are recognized as Korean rather than Japanese citizens.

1944

May

A State Department planning document warns that if the Soviet Union attempts to occupy Korea on its own, the United States will consider this to be a threat to the future security of the Pacific.

1945

February 4–11

A long-delayed meeting of Franklin D. Roosevelt, Winston Churchill, and Joseph Stalin is held at Yalta in the Crimea (because Stalin refuses to leave Russia) to discuss the end of World War II. Stalin promises to enter the war in the Pacific just as soon as victory is secured in Europe. In return he is to receive rather extensive compensation. On February 8, 1945, a temporary agreement is reached concerning the occupation of Korea.

February 8

At the Yalta Conference, Soviet leader Joseph Stalin confirms his earlier promise to enter the war in the Pacific. He has troops ready at the border to move into Korea. He also suggests that the trusteeship for Korea should consist of the United States, China, and the Soviet Union.

June

As the War Department is considering the invasion of Japan, General Douglas MacArthur sends a cable that pleads for support from the Soviet Union. His invasion plan calls for the Red Army to attack from Siberia. These plans, and the need for them, will be outdated by the dropping of the atomic bomb. MacArthur will later understate this appeal for Russian support but the content of the cables is quite clear.

July

The Democratic People's Front and the North Korean Labor Party are both formed, drawing their membership from the Korean Communist Party and strengthening Communist control over much of Korea.

August 6

The United States drops the first atomic bomb on Hiroshima, changing dramatically the picture of the war in the Pacific. The realization that it will not be necessary to invade Japan alters the political as well as military situation and gives the Soviet Union an unexpected windfall in terms of sharing the fruits of victory but not the costs of the Pacific war.

August 8

The Soviet Union enters the war against Japan, fulfilling the intent of its pledge made at Yalta. The involvement will be far too late to be of any practical value. The Soviets begin assembling troops in Manchuria for a march into Korea.

August 9

A U.S. Army Air Force B-29 bomber drops an atomic bomb (Fat Man) on the Japanese city of Nagasaki. This second act of destruction has been ordered to prove to the Japanese that the United States has additional resources and also to speed up the surrender of Japanese forces.

August 10

Two U.S. officials, Colonel C. H. Bonesteel and Colonel Dean Rusk (who later becomes the secretary of state), working with the State-War-Navy Committee, identify the 38th parallel as a potential dividing line across Korea. The Allied Command issues orders that the United States will accept Japan's surrender south of the 38th, and the Soviet Union will accept it north of the 38th. After landing at Rashin, Soviet troops move quickly south against extremely light Japanese resistance.

August 12

Just two days before the Japanese collapse, and with the 38th parallel still to be officially approved as a dividing line, a force of 100,000 soldiers from the Soviet Union, under General Ivan Christiakov, crosses the Siberian border into northern Korea. Upon arrival, Soviet occupation troops create an entirely new complexity in the military and political situation in Asia.

August 14

General Stilwell tells the U.S. occupation commander, General John R. Hodge, that he should consider the occupation as "semi-friendly." But in his address to his officers Hodge tells them to treat the Koreans as enemies of the United States. When asked for additional guidance from General MacArthur, Hodge is told to use his own judgment.

Korea's infamous 38th parallel crossing *(NARA Still Photos Division)*

August 15

President Harry Truman approves General Order Number 1, sending copies to Moscow and London. The order fixes the 38th parallel as the temporary dividing line between occupying forces of the United States and the Soviet Union. Stalin does not object. Japan agrees to an unconditional surrender, thus ending World War II. As Japan surrenders, Korean leaders headed by Yo Un-hyong and Pak Hon-yong begin to prepare an interim government. They form the Committee for the Preparation of Korean Independence (CPKI). By the end of the month, 145 branches of the CPKI, called "people's committees," will be set up as local governments.

August 29

A directive issued by General Douglas MacArthur's headquarters determines that the Japanese army headquarters should continue to function in order to aid the demobilization. He secures the property rights of Japanese citizens. This decision leaves a high number of Japanese officials at their jobs while the American troops land.

August 30

General Douglas MacArthur arrives by plane at Atsugi airdrome in Tokyo. The FEAF ADV lands the 11th Airborne Division at Atsugi. Eighth Army headquarters closes at Okinawa and opens at Yokohama. Lieutenant General Eichelberger assumes command of the Tokyo area. The 4th Marine Regiment of the 6th Division lands at Yokosuka simultaneously with Eighth Army's arrival.

September 2

In the surrender agreement that ended World War II, the Japanese Empire is stripped of all its overseas holdings, including Korea. It is stipulated that the surrender of Japanese forces north of the 38th parallel will be made to the Soviet Union.

September 3

Lieutenant General Yoshio Kozuke, the Japanese commander, radioes Lieutenant General James Hodge that Soviet troops have arrived at the 38th parallel and are waiting for the Americans to arrive.

September 6

The Communist-controlled Committee for the Preparation of Korean Independence (CPKI) elects 55 leaders to head the new Korean People's Republic. They hope to create an independent Korean government. The U.S. military refuses to recognize the Korean People's Republic.

September 8

The U.S. occupation force, which consists of elements of the 7th Infantry Division led by Lieutenant General John R. Hodge, reaches the port of Inchon. He establishes his headquarters at the Banda Hotel. The movement of the occupation troops has the code name "Black List Forty." When the ships are still 20 miles from Inchon, three men in a small boat approach and present themselves as representatives of the Korean government. Hodge sends them away as he does all those who claim a political authority. The United States is not willing to recognize either the People's Republic that has been set up by Yo Un-hyong nor the provisional government led by exiled Kim Ku.

September 9

Lieutenant General Hodge of XXIV Corps accepts the surrender of Japanese forces in South Korea.

September 11

General MacArthur sends Hodge a cable saying that Japanese officials must be removed from public office. Many, however, retrain their influence as unofficial advisers.

October

Syngman Rhee receives some unexpected support from General Douglas MacArthur, who wants a national leader in Korea that he can trust. American officials had always been more comfortable with leaders than with ideology or political movements. MacArthur's inquiries include a series of questions he asks of Nationalist Chinese leader Chiang Kai-shek (Jiang Jieshi), questions that lead MacArthur to select Rhee as that man. Rhee's strong anticommunist position is a major point in Chiang Kai-shek's consideration. At MacArthur's direction, both Syngman Rhee and Kim Ku (the Provincial president) are returned to Seoul.

October 1

President Harry Truman disbands the Office of Strategic Services (OSS) and transfers most OSS agents, as well as their functions, to the State Department and the army.

October 10

There is a great deal of pressure among the political parties in Korea to establish a "legitimate government" as quickly as possible. This leads Major General A.

V. Arnold to issue a statement to the Korean press that there is only one government in Korea south of the 38th parallel—the government established by General Douglas MacArthur. The pressure does not lessen, however, as political unrest gathers.

October 14

Kim Il Sung returns to Wonsan as a major in the Soviet Twenty-fifth Army. He is introduced to the Korean people as a national hero. He was a leader of a Chinese Communist guerrilla unit between 1932 and 1940 and was a member of the Chinese Communist Party that participated in the Korean national liberation movement. The Soviet Army backs Kim Il Sung in making Pyongyang the political center of the Communist Party and in cutting links with Seoul. A compromise is reached with Pak Hon-yong (leader in the south) that allows for the formation of the North Korean bureau of the Korean Communist Party in Pyongyang.

October 16

Exiled Korean leader Syngman Rhee, at this time perhaps the most important figure in recent Korean history, arrives in Seoul on the plane used by MacArthur. The State Department has been concerned about Rhee's influence, primarily his militant nationalism, and makes Rhee promise that his return to Korea will be as a private citizen and not as a member of the Korean Provisional Government. It proves to be an empty promise.

October 20

Frustrated by the lack of Soviet cooperation, the State-War-Navy Coordinating Committee announces that the American policy affirming the current Soviet-U.S. occupation of Korea should, at the earliest possible date, be turned over to a trusteeship appointed by the United Nations.

November

President Harry Truman meets with Prime Ministers Clement Attlee of Great Britain and Mackenzie King of Canada, in Washington, D.C. They agree that affairs in Korea should be turned over to a trusteeship consisting of the four powers.

November 25

General Hodge cables General MacArthur that he intends to denounce the Korean People's Republic (KPR). It is the more liberal of the two parties growing in South Korea. The other, the Korean Democratic Party (KDP), is far more conservative and considered less of a threat. What Hodge has in mind will constitute a declaration of war against Communist elements in Korea. As a first step, General Hodge shuts down the KPR's newspaper, its most prominent Seoul sympathizer, for "accounting irregularities."

November 29

American officials in Korea oppose the trustee plan strongly. In response, Secretary Byrnes replies that if an assurance of Korean independence can be gained from the Russians at the Moscow Conference, the United States will drop the idea of a trusteeship.

December 7

Lieutenant General John R. Hodge announces that Russian forces are building fortifications along the 38th parallel.

December 16

The Moscow Conference on the future of Korea begins. At the conference the Soviet Union agrees to a joint Soviet-American commission to prepare Korea for the election of a provisional government and to provide a continuing trusteeship that will last as long as five years. General Hodge recommends that the United States give serious consideration to seeking an agreement with the Russians to simultaneously leave Korea. Afterward, Korea can develop its own political agenda.

December 27

The Moscow conference ends in Moscow with a significant agreement. The Russians accept the U.S. proposal that Korea be governed for five years by a Four-Power international trusteeship.

December 29

In response to the Moscow Declaration, Syngman Rhee and a variety of Korean political organizations organize mass demonstrations in the streets of Seoul.

1946

The Peace Preservation Officers Training Schools, the nucleus of the North Korean People's Army, are activated.

January 1

General MacArthur asks for permission to arm the newly formed Korean National Police by giving them surplus U.S. weapons.

January 9

The Joint Chiefs of Staff authorizes General MacArthur to arm the Korean National Police with U.S. weapons held in surplus. It is decided that the formation of a Korean armed force should wait until independence has been established.

January 14

The 1st Battalion, 2nd Regiment, Korean Constabulary is activated and begins training at a former Japanese army barracks northeast of Seoul. By April 1946, other regiments will be established at Pusan, Kwangju, Taegu, Iri, Taejon, Chongju, and Chunchon.

January 22

President Harry Truman signs a bill that creates the Central Intelligence Group, with 100 employees reassigned from the State Department. It has been created by Congress, not the president, and is designed as an independent agency with a director who will report directly to the president. The group will operate under the control of the National Security Council, to be created in July 1947, and have access to the intelligence information collected by all other agencies. The first director is Rear

Admiral Roscoe H. Hillenkoetter, but it will not grow powerful until it comes under General Walter Bedell Smith and Allen W. Dulles. Its mission is to coordinate all intelligence information and to make reports ready for, and directly to, the president. The Korean War, and the growing concern over national security that it sets off, will be responsible for a huge expansion of the CIA, whose failure to predict the North Korean invasion of 1950 will be used as an example of a system that does not have wide enough powers.

Moving out of a U.N. base camp, near Seoul, Korea *(Center for the Study of the Korean War, Graceland University)*

January 28

General Hodge offers to resign in protest of State Department experts who have set up the Moscow trusteeship agreement, thus causing major riots in Seoul. His resignation is not accepted.

February

The Provisional People's Committee of North Korea establishes the Security Bureau, which will soon become the Interior Ministry. The ministry includes the Secret Police under Pang Hak Se. It is formed in response to the Moscow Agreement that calls for the establishment of a Korean interim government to last for five years under an Allied trusteeship. It is the forerunner of the government headed by Kim Il Sung.

February 14

In accordance with General Hodge's proposal that a political body should be developed before the first meeting of the Soviet-American Joint Commission, the Representative Democratic Council holds its first meeting in Seoul. Of the 28 members, 24 are drawn from the rightist position.

February 16

Korean Communists who had been exiled in China form their own party, the New People's Party (Sinmindang), with Kim Tu-bong as the leader.

March 20

The Soviet-American Joint Commission holds its first meeting at the Duk Soo palace in Seoul, Korea. From the very beginning, the Soviet and American delegates clash over the future of Korea.

May 6
The Soviet-American Joint Commission breaks up after 24 sessions—and no tangible results. Seeing no point in any future meetings, the commission is adjourned.

July 22
The New People's Party joins with the Communist Party of North Korea to form the United Democratic National Front.

August 28
The United Democratic National Front adopts the name of North Korean Worker's Party.

November
The Provisional People's Committee of North Korea holds elections for representatives who will establish a government for the northern half of Korea.

November 1
A group called the Representative Democratic Council of South Korea, headed by Syngman Rhee, sends an appeal to the United Nations calling for the freedom and independence of the Korean people. They want all American and Soviet troops withdrawn and the admission of an interim Korean government to the United Nations. No UN member is willing to sponsor the bill, and it dies.

December 12
The first meeting of the provisional South Korean legislature is held. The group is dominated by right-wing parties.

1947

May
Recognizing a decline in military manpower, President Harry Truman's Advisory Commission on Universal Training is established to consider ways in which to maintain the American armed forces.

May 27
In one more effort to settle the Korean question, and in the face of what appears to be a change in the Soviet mind, the Soviet-American Joint Commission reconvenes in Seoul. But the old issues reappear quickly, and the meetings are adjourned permanently.

July
The U.S. military hopes to form a moderate coalition that can gather a broad base of political support. But the assassination of a prominent leftist in the coalition, and a decision by a coalition moderate to enter into unification talks with North Korea, undermine any possible success of the movement and it is dropped.

July 26
The National Security Act creates the National Security Council to coordinate security policy, renames the Central Intelligence Group as the Central Intelligence

Agency, giving it statutory recognition, and provides the same recognition for the
Joint Chiefs of Staff. Because there is considerable concern over civilian control of
the armed forces, limits are placed on the size and structure of the JCS and the power
of its chairman. The act also recognizes the U.S. Air Force as an independent service
separate from the U.S. Army. The navy retains its own aviation unit and manages
to block an effort to have the army absorb the marines. The act also establishes the
National Security Council as the primary body concerned with American security,
but it does not unify the armed forces. The issue of armed forces unity will lose much
of its steam, especially after the 1949 amendment that creates a far stronger Defense
Department, under which the Joint Chiefs will be subsumed, and provides congressional oversight of the CIA.

August 4

The first report of the State-War-Navy Coordinating Committee's (SWNCC 176/30)
subcommittee on Korea outlines ways by which the Soviet-U.S. deadlock over
Korean reunification can be broken. The group does not recommend that American troops be pulled out because that will give the Soviet Union a publicity advantage. It also recommended that a way be found to spend as little money as possible
in Korea.

August 28

Recognizing that the Soviet-American Joint Commission has been a failure, the U.S.
State Department proposes at the United Nations that a Four-Power conference be
convened to consider the Korean problem.

September

South Korean Communists establish the Kang Dong Political Institute, a cadre
school for the training of guerrillas.

September 4

The Soviet Union rejects the American proposal for a Four-Power conference on
Korea to discuss unification of the nation.

September 17

Concerned over the Soviet Union's response to the joint meetings and its refusal to
consider a Four-Power conference, Secretary of State George C. Marshall informs
the General Assembly of the United Nations that America is turning the Korean
question over to the United Nations. The trustees concept has pretty well disappeared by this time.

September 18

When President Truman's effort to establish a coalition of the warring elements in
China fails, Lieutenant General Albert C. Wedemeyer is sent to report on conditions
in Asia. In his report, General Wedemeyer will recommend the eventual withdrawal
of American troops from Korea. But he will be clear that the United States needs to
provide "moral, advisory, and material support."

September 26

The Soviet Union, responding to America's referral of the Korean question to the United Nations, offers a counterproposal. It calls for the withdrawal of all foreign troops beginning in 1948, after which the Korean people will be allowed to work out their own government. In the meantime, the Joint Chiefs send Secretary of Defense Forrestal the following message: "From the standpoint of military security, the United States has little strategic interest in maintaining the present troops and bases in Korea." The message goes on to say, "Enemy interference from Korea could be neutralized by air action, which would be more feasible and less costly than large-scale ground operations."

September 29

The U.S. Joint Chiefs of Staff comes to the conclusion that South Korea has no strategic military significance to the United States. It is neither militarily nor politically advantageous for America to be involved to any significant degree. South Korea does not warrant the stationing of 45,000 troops of occupation. The Soviet-American Joint Commission is not working and Truman, lacking any real alternatives under the circumstances, accepts the intent of SWNCC 176/30 that calls for referring the whole matter to the United Nations. The President's Committee on Civil Rights issues a landmark report by taking a stand against continued segregation anywhere, but especially in the Armed Forces.

October 22

In response to a War Department inquiry, General Hodge replies that a South Korean army capable of defending itself can be raised within one year, if trained and armed by the United States.

November

Making no effort to hide the general attitude of the occupation forces, General Hodge reportedly tells a replacement depot in Yongonpo that there are only three things the troops in Japan are afraid of, "they're gonorrhea, diarrhea, and Korea."

November 14

By a vote of 43 to zero, with six abstentions, the United Nations creates the United Nations Temporary Commission on Korea to deal with the Soviet-U.S. dispute. It accepts an American plan, despite USSR opposition, which calls for a general election to be held in Korea that would eventually lead to the formation of a united Korea.

December 19

The first meeting of America's National Security Council passes NSC 4/A that empowers the CIA to perform a broad range of covert actions (at the time, in Italy).

1948

In an effort to overcome the lack of money and equipment for maintaining U.S. forces, Operation Roll-Up is begun. The U.S. Far Eastern Command begins scavenging World War II vehicles and military equipment left behind on the battlefields.

These items are taken to Tokyo where they are refurbished. The impact of this decision is apparent during the first 60 days of the Korean War, when more than 4,000 of these vehicles will be sent into action against the North Koreans.

January 12

The United Nations Temporary Commission on Korea meets for the first time in Seoul. The Russians and the North Koreans completely reject UN participation in any decisions about the future of Korea. The opposition parties in South Korea warn against holding elections without including the Communists. Such an action, they decree, would doom national unity for decades to come. Canada and Australia agree, but the majority of the commission—France, the Philippines, Nationalist China, El Salvador, and India—support the call for elections.

January 14

The State-War-Navy Coordinating Committee document 176/35 focuses on Korean policy and identifies several points of consideration: the reduction of men and money directed toward Korea, an acknowledgment that there is little interest in Korea as a military or political asset, and that a settlement of the Korean problem should be sought so that troops can be withdrawn. This seems to contradict the earlier idea that South Korea can become self-sufficient and that elections would help to form a provisional government.

January 24

The Soviet commander in North Korea denies entry permission to members of the United Nations Temporary Commission on Korea. This action effectively prevents a Korea-wide election and leads to the eventual formation of separate governments.

February

The Prague coup, in which the Russians seize control of the government, is often given as the opening date of the cold war.

February 2

President Harry Truman, addressing Congress, says that he has instructed the secretary of defense to eliminate racial discrimination in the Armed Forces as quickly as possible.

February 8

The North Korean Provisional Government announces the birth of the Democratic People's Republic of Korea Army, with the organization and activation of the 1st, 2nd, and 3rd Infantry Divisions. The army is known as the Inmingun.

Army personnel resting on a trip into the hills; note the pack and bedroll on the man with his back facing front (*Center for the Study of the Korean War, Graceland University*)

February 28

The United Nations Temporary Commission on Korea adopts a resolution calling for an election in that part of Korea that is still available to the commission. At the same time, the Joint Chiefs of Staff recommends that all U.S. troops in South Korea be pulled out, even if this means the eventual Soviet domination of Korea.

March 17

President Harry Truman calls on Congress to provide an immediate increase in the strength of the armed forces.

March 22

The United States military government announces a land reform plan for South Korea.

April 1

The Berlin Airlift begins as the Soviet Union cuts off all land access to the defeated capital. The blockade will continue until September 30, 1949. During the crisis, the United States, aided by the British, manages to airlift more than 2.3 million tons of food and coal. This action by the Soviets greatly increases the tension of the expanding cold war.

April 2

The U.S. National Security Council document NSC 8 establishes the position that the United States should take responsibility to build up the ROK economy and its armed forces. But it reaffirms the belief that the defense of South Korea should be left to the Koreans. President Harry Truman accepts this position as U.S. policy, agreeing that it provides for the withdrawal of troops without appearing to abandon Korea. Choosing a middle ground in Korea, the U.S. position would be to support South Korea as a self-sufficient nation.

April 8

President Harry Truman requests that every effort be extended that will allow the United States to withdraw its troops from Korea before the close of the year.

May 1

A new constitution is promulgated in North Korea, forming the basis of a new government.

May 4

Major Pyo Mu-won, commander of the 1st Battalion of the 8th Regiment (ROK army), which is stationed in Chunchon, defects to North Korea along with 456 of his men. The major, it is reported, is a member of a secret cell of the Communist-based workers party.

May 5

Major Kang Tae-mu, commander of the 2nd Battalion of the 6th Regiment (ROK army), stationed at Hongchon, defects to North Korea along with his 294 men. Major Kang Tae-mu, like Major Pyo Mu-won, is identified as a member of a secret Communist-based workers party.

May 10

The United Nations Temporary Commission on Korea (UNTOCK) observes the voting for the election of convention delegates leading to the formation of the Republic of Korea's first national assembly. Despite efforts to hold an election in the north, there is no other choice but to move ahead without the participation of North Korea and in opposition to the views held by Syngman Rhee. The reports of the commission state that 95 percent of the registrants (about 75 percent of eligible voters) voted.

May 27

Newly elected delegates of the South Korean National Assembly meet in Seoul and elect Syngman Rhee as temporary chairman.

May 31

At 2 P.M. the National Assembly meets and Syngman Rhee proclaims a sovereign government, the Republic of Korea.

June 12

The Republic of Korea National Assembly establishes a constitution that provides for a democratic republic.

June 18

National Security Council document 4/A is replaced by NSC 10.2, outlining the policy that authorizes covert action all over the world.

July 17

The first Korean constitution goes into effect and nationalist leader Syngman Rhee is elected to a four-year term as president. Despite the election, the political situation in Korea is not clear.

July 24

Syngman Rhee delivers his inaugural address as first president of the ROK. After he has stated as his goal the unification of Korea, he calls on the Democratic People's Republic of Korea to join with him.

July 26

President Harry Truman signs Executive Order 9981, which calls for an end to racial discrimination in the Armed Forces. It will take some time to implement.

July 29

Because of some confusion in the interpretation of his order, President Harry Truman clarifies Executive Order 9981 by saying that the intent is to end segregation in the Armed Forces.

August

During this time, the Department of Defense redirects a significant number of its Far East air-power strength to support of the Berlin Airlift. General Douglas MacArthur objects to the transfer of over half the medium bombers and a large number of fighters and transports.

August 14

The Republic of Korea (Taehan Mingok) is formally established at ceremonies in Seoul. Sovereignty is transferred from the U.S. military government in Korea to the Republic of Korea. The American flag is lowered and the new flag of the Republic of Korea raised over the South Korean capitol building. The ROK claims sovereignty over all of Korea. John J. Muccio is appointed special representative to Korea as head of the U.S. Diplomatic Mission in Seoul.

August 25

In North Korea, the People's Congress elects representatives to a Supreme People's Congress.

September 3

The North Korean government adopts a constitution for the newly established Democratic People's Republic of Korea.

September 9

North Korean leader Kim Il Sung proclaims that the Democratic People's Republic of Korea has been established, suggesting that the DPRK government represent the entire nation.

September 19

Moscow acknowledges its recognition of the DPRK as the legitimate government of Korea. It announces that, with a government established, all Russian occupation troops will be withdrawn from Korea by the end of December 1948.

September 26

President Harry Truman assures President Syngman Rhee that the United States will leave the Korean Military Advisor Group (KMAG) in Korea and that it will continue to recommend equipment and support for the ROK army when Congress appropriates more military funds.

October 6

Lieutenant General Earle E. Partridge assumes command of the Fifth Air Force in the Far East.

October 12

Moscow sends General Terenty Shtikov as the first Russian ambassador to the Democratic People's Republic of Korea. Several other Communist nations in Europe also recognize the DPRK. A UN resolution establishes the United Nations' commitment to South Korea.

October 19

Only two months after Syngman Rhee takes office, the 14th Regiment of the Republic of Korea Army, which has been sent to control Communist rebels on the island of Cheju, rebels in the southern port city of Yosu. While the rebellion is put down within a few days, it creates a serious sense of insecurity among the people of South Korea. In response, and at the request of President Rhee, the United States defers the withdrawal of its occupation forces. President Rhee imposes martial law over the southern sections of the country and expands his purge of Communists within the armed forces.

December 6
A vast majority of the UN Political and Security Committee rejects the Democratic People's Republic of Korea's claim to legitimacy. They invite the newly formed ROK to send delegates to the United Nations.

December 10
Congress agrees to send $300 million in military aid to the Republic of Korea.

December 12
The United Nations passes a resolution that recognizes the Republic of Korea as the only legitimate government in Korea, and establishes the UN Commission on Korea (UNCOK).

December 28
The United States announces that it is withdrawing a full American division from occupation duty in Korea. It is the first stage of the planned withdrawal.

December 31
The Soviets announce that all their troops have been withdrawn from Korean soil and immediately challenge the United States for keeping troops still in Korea, suggesting that this is part of a continuing U.S. policy of imperialism.

1949

January
General Douglas MacArthur informs the Joint Chiefs of Staff that the ROK army will not be able to defend Korea. He agrees, however, that the United States should not commit more American troops. In case the North Koreans invade the south, General MacArthur believes that the United States should evacuate its troops from South Korea. Dean Acheson is appointed secretary of state. He is committed to the Truman Doctrine and its containment policy.

January 20
President Truman begins his second term of office with the U.S. policy in Asia under considerable criticism. Truman announces that the United States will not seek bases on Taiwan, nor will it become involved in China's continuing civil war.

March
America raises the status of its Korean Embassy to ambassador rank, and John Muccio becomes the first ambassador.

March 3
The National Security Council recommends that the United States encourage the rift between the Soviet Union and China by restoring normal economic relations

with the Communist-controlled regions of China. President Harry Truman approves the recommendation.

March 5
Kim Il Sung meets with Joseph Stalin in Moscow and asks for Soviet military and economic aid against the potential threat imposed by the ROK and the United States. Stalin suggests that it is possible to render assistance.

March 23
National Security Council document 8/2, a revision of previous plans, establishes U.S. policy toward Korea. President Harry Truman, in response to the political instability in Korea, decides to postpone the withdrawal of the remaining American troops until June 1949.

March 28
Louis Johnson is sworn in as secretary of defense and announces that he plans to speed up the reforms and unification of the armed forces. He has not been in office a month when he cancels the experimental flush-deck supercarrier the USS *United States,* which is under construction. He believes that the carrier simply duplicates functions performed by the air force in strategic bombing. His decision angers the navy and causes a congressional investigation. He is committed to the idea of strategic nuclear air power.

April 8
The Soviet Union casts a veto on the vote to admit the ROK, as the legitimate Korean government, to the United Nations. Lieutenant General George E. Stratemeyer is assigned as commanding general Far East Air Force.

April 24
The Communist Chinese occupy Nanjing (Nanking), the Nationalist capital.

May 2
The Korean Military Advisory Group (KMAG) is activated as a training mission, with 500 officers and men commanded by Brigadier General William L. Roberts.

May 3
Early in the morning, a reinforced battalion of the NKPA under Choe Hyun attacks elements of the South Korean army on Mt. Songak. They then occupy a large area of land near the city of Kaesung. Mt. Songak hugs Kaesung and straddles the 38th parallel. Mt. Songak has two major peaks, Hills 485 and 488, and both will see significant action during the Korean War. While caught unaware, the South Korean army under Brigadier Kim Suk-won is able to beat back the onslaught and, with fresh troops brought in as reinforcements, retakes the area. The battle lasts several days, during which the ROK army suffers mass desertions.

May 10
South Korean warship *#508* defects, sailing into Wonsan harbor in North Korea with all its crew.

May 24
The U.S. flag freighter *Kimball R. Smith,* on a loan to the ROK, is surrendered to the North Koreans at Chinnampo by its captain.

June 19
The CIA determines that North Korea is capable of seizing and holding at least the upper reaches of South Korea without either Chinese or Soviet help.

June 27
The State Department recommends that the United States should deal with North Korea, if it invades, by working through the United Nations.

June 29
According to previous agreements the last of the U.S. occupation force is withdrawn. The United States leaves behind the 500-man Korean Military Advisory Group.

July
The Central Intelligence Agency reports that the "inefficiency and shortsighted authoritarianism" of the government of the ROK will most likely induce "a public reaction favoring Communism."

July 11
Dr. Pyung Ok Chough, a representative of Syngman Rhee, talks with Secretary of State Dean Acheson in Washington, seeking a specific guarantee that the United States will defend South Korea if it is attacked. Acheson says that such a guarantee is out of the question.

August
General of the Army Omar N. Bradley is named the first permanent chairman of the Joint Chiefs of Staff (1949–53). In this position, he becomes the principal military adviser to the president and the secretary of defense. Although the chairman does not have the deciding vote on issues that divide the JCS, he does have considerable influence on the manner in which the agency functions.

August 26
Vice Admiral C. Turner Joy assumes command of Naval Forces Far East.

September 8
The United Nations Commission for Korea issues a report warning that there is danger of a civil war in Korea and that China might come to the aid of the North Koreans by invading the south.

September 10
Letters from three U.S. Navy admirals critical of U.S. Air Force and Department of Defense policy become public. They criticize the underemphasizing of naval air power and the excessive reliance on strategic air power for national defense.

September 24
The Soviet Union recommends to Kim Il Sung that any attack on the ROK be put off until he has more time to prepare for the battle.

September 30
After U.S. and British planes fly more than 2.3 million tons of food and fuel into the blockaded city, the Soviet Union lifts the Berlin blockade after more than a year.

UN soldiers in Korea fought in all kinds of weather *(Center for the Study of the Korean War, Graceland University)*

October 1

In the traditional capital of Beijing, Mao Zedong proclaims the founding of the People's Republic of China. He and his Communist army have defeated the Nationalist Chinese leader Chiang Kai-shek (Jiang Jieshi), whose forces have withdrawn to the island of Taiwan. General Albert Wedemeyer later accuses U.S. policymakers of pushing China over the brink and comments that if China had remained friendly there would have been no war in Korea, nor in Vietnam.

October 2

The Soviet Union is quick to recognize the People's Republic of China.

October 10

The Republic of Korea Air Force becomes a separate and independent service branch of the ROK armed forces. The Chinese Air Transport (CAT) was originally owned by Claire Chennault and Whiting Willauer and was designed to provide air transportation in China. The cargo business is primarily a cover, however, and the airline covers covert CIA missions beginning on this date. The airline will be ejected from China in January 1950 and follow Chiang Kai-shek to Taiwan.

October 14

The North Korean government, in a letter to UN Secretary General Trygve Lie, states openly its intention to unite Korea by force, if necessary.

October 21

The United Nations approves the U.S. resolution to provide a continuing mission and presence in Korea to report on conditions there.

December

Intelligence units of the Far East Command report to General Douglas MacArthur that Pyongyang has set March or April 1950 as the date for its attack on South Korea.

December 29

General Charles Willoughby, head of MacArthur's G-2 Intelligence, reports to Washington, D.C., that in his opinion the suggestion of a North Korean attack during April 1950 is extremely unlikely.

1950

January

Joseph Stalin informs Kim Il Sung that he will support a military offensive against South Korea and suggests that Kim meet him in Moscow to discuss the situation.

January 5

In a public address, President Harry S. Truman says that the United States has no "predatory" designs on any Chinese territory—a phrase that Joseph Stalin apparently understands to mean that the time is ripe to push for Communist China's entry into the United Nations.

January 12

Dean Acheson makes his famous Aleutians speech at the National Press Club in Washington, D.C. He draws an Asian defense perimeter for the United States that excludes Korea. He defines the U.S. position in the Far East as a line that "runs along the Aleutians to Japan and then goes to the Ryukyus and from the Ryukyu to the Philippine Islands."

January 13

Soviet delegate Yakov A. Malik walks out of the UN Security Council, saying that Russia will not participate in any proceedings until the Nationalist Chinese are removed from the United Nations.

January 16

Following instructions, the U.S. Army issues its new integration policy in Special Regulations No. 600–629.1.

January 19

The House of Representatives defeats the Korean Aid Bill, which calls for a three-year, $385 million economic aid program, by a vote of 191–192. Under Secretary of State James E. Webb had urged its approval while military experts testified that the chances of a Communist invasion were unlikely. The bill will be resubmitted in altered form as the Far Eastern Economic Assistance Act.

January 26

The United States and the Republic of Korea sign a military assistance agreement. The agreement authorizes significant aid to Korea and formally recognizes the Korean Military Advisory Group (KMAG).

January 31

President Harry Truman announces that he has ordered the Atomic Energy Commission to proceed with the development of a hydrogen bomb.

February 14

The Sino-Soviet Treaty of Friendship and Alliance is signed. The Soviets promise China mutual assistance against aggressive action by Japan or by any state that is united with Japan. In the United States, Congress passes the Far Eastern Economic Assistance Act of 1950. The Senate version authorizes $60 million in aid to Korea and extends the China Aid Act until June 30.

March

Brigadier General William L. Roberts writes a 300-page personal letter to Lieutenant General Charles Bolte of the JCS staff, warning that the ROK army cannot hold out in any significant military conflict.

March 2

The CIA sends Lt. Col. Jay Vanderpool (later to become commander of Guerrilla Division 8240 Army Unit) into North Korea to determine whether the British claim about the size of the North Korean forces (set at 136,000 men) is more accurate than MacArthur's claim of 36,000. About the time the North Korean army crosses the 38th parallel, MacArthur reports to the CIA that the figure is 140,000.

March 8

Far East Command intelligence warns that the North Koreans have constructed five new airfields, four of them within a few miles of the 38th parallel; all are designed to give North Korea an advantageous position for offensive action against the south.

March 10

General Douglas MacArthur's intelligence branch reports to the JCS that there are indications the north will invade the south in June of that year. At the same time, the South Korean defense minister tells the press that the North Koreans are moving toward the 38th parallel and will attack. However, both MacArthur and the Pentagon believe that an attack is not imminent.

March 15

The commanding officer of the Korean Military Advisory Group warns that North Korea can defeat the South Korean army, that civilians will accept North Korean rule, and that the Republic of Korea will be quickly assimilated into the Communist block.

Spring intelligence discovers that elements of the Russian air force have been sent to the coastline of mainland China, setting off a fear that the Chinese may attack Taiwan.

March 24

CAT is purchased outright by the CIA. On President Harry Truman's approval, a Provisional American Military Advisory Group to South Vietnam is established.

April 10

Major General Chae Byung Chae is named chief of staff of the ROK army.

April 10–25

In three meetings between Kim Il Sung and Joseph Stalin, the latter sets preconditions for his support of military action in South Korea. He wants to be assured that the United States will not enter the war and that China will support Kim Il Sung. Stalin emphasizes the point that the Soviet Union is not prepared to become directly involved in any war in Korea, especially if the United States is to invest troops.

April 14

National Security Council document 68 recognizes the Soviet threat, recommending a military and economic strengthening of the free world and also a triple increase in the defense budget. General Douglas MacArthur provides a memorandum that emphasizes Taiwan's strategic importance to the United States.

April 25

President Truman approves National Security Council document 68 as the basis of the American defense policy. It will remain so, primarily unchanged, for the next 40 years. It calls for up to 20 percent of the gross national product to be spent for defense and states that it would be U.S. policy to resist Communist threats to non-Communist nations "wherever they may be."

April 28

A P-38 belonging to the ROK air force is fired on and crashes.

May

In the national election conducted in the Republic of Korea, the independents win 110 seats in the National Assembly, much to the satisfaction of many of the American critics of ROK president Syngman Rhee.

May 1

Over the strong objections of General MacArthur, the Central Intelligence Agency (CIA) establishes its initial presence in Tokyo, Japan. It is a minuscule intelligence team consisting at first of only a few operators.

May 2

Senator Tom Connally of Texas, chairman of the Senate Foreign Relations Committee, concedes that the Republic of Korea will be abandoned if it is attacked.

May 6

Vice Admiral A. D. Struble assumes command of the Seventh Fleet.

May 13–15

North Korean leader Kim Il Sung secretly visits Beijing to inform Chairman Mao of his plans to invade South Korea. Mao is interested in support if it is to be a quick and decisive war. Mao agrees to establish troops on the northern border and, if requested, to supply ammunition. Kim rejects this offer. Mao also promises that China will send troops if the United States enters the war.

May 17

In its weekly report, the CIA forecasts that if President Rhee's power is reduced during the coming election, this will lessen the chances of Communist exploitation of South Korea.

May 25

Having been warned of a North Korean buildup, General Willoughby, MacArthur's intelligence officer, claims in the daily intelligence summary that the warnings are exaggerated, stating that the North Koreans cannot assemble such a large force.

June 1

The intelligence section of the Far East Air Force agrees that South Korea will fall if there is a North Korean invasion. According to captured North Korean documents, the plan is for small groups of North Korean intelligence agents to land and gather information in advance of the invasion.

June 7

The Democratic Fatherland Front makes a unification proposal calling for general elections in North and South Korea on August 5, 1950.

President Truman asks Congress to appropriate $150 million in economic aid for the Republic of Korea, which, he says, has become a testing ground for the practical validity of the idea of democracy.

June 8

The newspapers of the North Korean capital of Pyongyang print a manifesto of the Central Committee of the United Democratic Patriotic Front, which announces as its goal an election to be held throughout Korea to elect a parliament. The parliament is to be held in Seoul no later than August 15, 1950.

June 10

The Pyongyang government announces a new plan for unification and peace and brands the top ROK leaders as traitors. The Russian news service reprints the Manifesto of the Central Committee of the United Democratic Patriotic Front, first printed in Pyongyang, calling for Korea-wide elections and the seating of a parliament in Seoul by August 15, 1950.

June 11

The three North Korean representatives who come to South Korea with the proposed unification and peace manifesto are arrested.

June 14

General Douglas MacArthur informs Washington of the dangers of a Communist takeover of Taiwan. Besides the obvious military reasons to support the Nationalist Chinese, MacArthur feels that the United States has a moral commitment to aid this non-Communist country.

June 15

KMAG warns the State Department that supplies are so limited for the ROK army that it subsists on bare necessities. They predict that the army can withstand an invasion for only 15 days and warn that the same thing will happen in Korea that happened in China.

June 15–24

The DPRK moves its army into a belt north of the 38th parallel from which all civilians have been vacated.

June 19

President Syngman Rhee presses John Foster Dulles, adviser to the State Department, for assurance that the United States will come to the aid of the ROK in case of either Chinese or North Korean aggression.

The CIA reports that the chief aim of the Soviet Union and the DPRK is the unification of Korea under Communist control. However, such action can be prevented by the use of U.S. economic and military aid.

Despite the superiority of the Communist armed forces and the fact that North Korean civilians are being evacuated from an area two miles from the 38th parallel, the CIA predicts there will be only "limited military action" in Korea.

June 20

The CIA warns that if the North Koreans attack they can quickly control the northern part of South Korea, including the capital city of Seoul. The agency says that there is no assurance the Chinese will enter the war, but if they do all of South Korea will be lost. At this time, the CIA maintains that there is no evidence that a major war is inevitable. Ironically, at this same time, the North Korean People's Army divisions are issued their orders: The 1st, 3rd, and 4th Divisions, with armor in the lead, are to attack South Korea, moving down the Uijongbu Corridor toward Seoul. Other divisions are to attack toward the east.

June 23

Nearly 90,000 NKPA soldiers are assembling near the 38th parallel. They have in support 150 medium tanks and 200 aircraft, as well as 122-mm and 76-mm self-propelled guns. The force is composed of seven infantry divisions, an armored brigade, an unattached infantry division, a motorcycle regiment, and a brigade of the Bo An Dae (the Border Constabulary).

June 24

A UN commission sent to observe along the 38th parallel is unable to find any evidence that the ROK is using its military forces for any "illegal purposes." They report that ROK troops are engaged solely in rounding up guerrillas.

June 25

Major General Earl E. Partridge, who is commander of the Fifth Air Force and also serves as acting commander of Far East Air Forces, orders his wing commanders to prepare for an air evacuation of U.S. citizens from South Korea. He also orders an increase in aerial surveillance of the Tsushima Strait between Korea and Japan. The Twentieth Air Force places two squadrons of the 51st Fighter-Interceptor Wing on air defense alert in Japan.

★ WAR BEGINS ★

June 25

POLITICAL/ADMINISTRATIVE: At 0900 Korean time, John J. Muccio, America's ambassador to Korea, notifies the State Department that troops of the Democratic People's Republic of Korea (North Korea) have crossed the 38th parallel in force. President Harry S. Truman is notified of the invasion while at the summer White House in Independence, Missouri, and decides to return to Washington the next morning. At U.S. request, the UN Security Council identifies North Korea as breaking the peace, calls for the end of all aggression, and orders the withdrawal of North Korean troops from South Korea. President Truman provides a press release assuring the American people that the American response is being conducted under international authority and will be limited to whatever military action is needed to protect the evacuation of American personnel. General Douglas MacArthur states that it is "probably only a reconnaissance in force." At 1100 hours local time, North Korea announces the war. Sensing the crisis in Korea, American ambassador John Muccio communicates the Republic of Korea (South Korea) request for much-needed ammunition and air power.

EIGHTH ARMY: At 0400 (Korea time) on a rainy morning, the military force of the Democratic People's Republic of Korea invades the Ongjin Peninsula of the Republic of Korea with 135,000 men. The invasion is preceded by heavy artillery and led by Soviet-made T-34 tanks. At the same time, North Korean troops land at Kangnung on the east coast and slightly south of the 38th parallel. By 0930, Kaesong, the ancient capital of Korea, becomes the first city to fall to the advancing troops.

SEA WAR: At the time, all American naval vessels are located on southern and western coasts, but an ROK navy patrol craft (PC 701) under the command of Nam Choi Yong fires on and sinks an armed 1,000-ton North Korean freighter with about 600 troops on board. The limited sea battle occurs about 18 miles off the port city of Pusan.

AIR WAR: North Korean fighters attack the airfields at Seoul and Kimpo, destroying a U.S. Air Force (USAF) C-54 on the ground. Major General Earle E. Partridge, commander of Fifth Air Force, puts two squadrons of the Twentieth Air Force's 51st Fighter Interceptor Wing on alert in Japan to prepare for evacuation.

U.S. fighter planes from the 8th Fighter Group attack a small North Korean convoy off the coast of South Korea at about 1700 hours. VP (Patrol Squadron) 46 under Commander M. F. Weisner begins its first tour of duty in Korea.

Far East Air Force cargo planes begin the evacuation of 700 U.S. State Department and Korean Military Advisory Group personnel and their families. Air Group Five under Commander H. P. Lanham arrives aboard the USS *Valley Forge* (CV 45). North Korean leader Kim Il Sung speaks to the North Korean people over radio, telling them they need to "liquidate" the menace identified as South Korea.

June 25–29

POLITICAL/ADMINISTRATIVE: The evacuation of American personnel begins as authorized by Ambassador Muccio. By June 28, all civilians have either escaped by air or crossed over the Han River and begun the process of leaving. Many are evacuated by a Norwegian boat, the *Reinholt,* which sails from Inchon. By June 29, more than 1,500 have been evacuated.

June 26

POLITICAL/ADMINISTRATIVE: U.S. ambassador John Muccio orders all nonessential personnel and dependents out of Korea.

The Blair House meeting on the war in Korea reveals that President Harry S. Truman still maintains the hope that ground forces will not be needed in Korea. President Truman authorizes General Douglas MacArthur, the U.S. commander in the

Far East, to send ammunition and equipment, to provide ships and aircraft to protect the evacuation of American citizens, and to send an investigation team to determine how best to help the ROK government.

Later in the afternoon, Truman expands his orders to permit General MacArthur to use air force and navy facilities in his command to hit North Korean targets south of the 38th parallel.

As the enemy advances, President Syngman Rhee calls General Douglas MacArthur but is told that he is asleep. Rhee and his cabinet then abandon the capital at Seoul and move south to Taejon.

The UN Committee on Korea reports that North Korean troops have moved across the 38th parallel in force.

EIGHTH ARMY: In their rapid advance, the North Korean army captures the towns of Chunchon, Pochon, and Tongduchon in South Korea.

On the second day of the war the capital city of Seoul is under siege.

Uijongbu quickly falls to North Korean forces.

SEA WAR: The U.S. Seventh Fleet sails north from the Philippines. Seven hundred Americans and foreign nationals are evacuated from Seoul through Inchon. They are escorted by USS *Mansfield* (DD 728) and USS *DeHaven* (DD 727).

AIR WAR: The ROK government requests 10 F-51s to provide support to its limited air defense. They have only a few AT-6s.

SB-17s of the USAF fly rescue cover for those U.S. citizens fleeing Seoul. Twin Mustang fighters from the 68th All-Weather Squadron provide air cover.

Far East Air Force trades C-54s for C-47s because the latter plane can land on smaller and undeveloped air fields. The Fifth Air Force flies escort and surveillance missions over both the capital at Seoul and the straits separating Japan and Korea.

June 27

POLITICAL/ADMINISTRATIVE: The United Nations adopts a U.S. resolution proclaiming that the North Korean attack is a breach of the peace. The resolution asks member nations to assist the Republic of Korea in repelling the invasion.

President Harry Truman addresses the American people about the conditions in Korea; he not only discusses the invasion of Korea but also indicates that there will be an increase in military support for the French in their fight against Ho Chi Minh's forces in Vietnam.

Brigadier General John Church is sent to Korea by General Douglas MacArthur to survey the situation. On arrival, he is to take command of the newly established Advance Command and Liaison Group in Korea.

Ambassador Muccio and his staff leave Seoul for Suwon. The ROK army headquarters leaves Seoul for Sinhung-ni without informing its U.S. advisers in KMAG. Personnel from KMAG headquarters follow soon afterward.

Nationalist Chinese leader Chiang Kai-shek (Jiang Jieshi) offers to provide a division of (33,000) troops for the war in Korea. President Truman is originally interested in the idea, but his staff points out that a variety of military and political problems are involved in the offer. The offer is rejected, much to the disappointment of those in the China Lobby.

GI in a communications bunker heating up C-rations *(Center for the Study of the Korean War, Graceland University)*

The American embassy is deserted, leaving unprotected more than 5,000 personnel records of loyal Korean employees for the Communists to find.

President Harry Truman orders naval and air forces in the Far East to support Korean forces and directs the Seventh Fleet to take steps to prevent the invasion of Taiwan. The president is also concerned that Chiang Kai-shek might use the situation to attack the mainland. Zhou Enlai, premier and foreign minister of the People's Republic of China, brands this action as an armed invasion of Chinese territory and a violation of the UN charter. It is the basis, as least politically, for China's entry into the war. This difficulty lies behind any potential cease-fire and must be left out of the discussions.

President Harry Truman sends a dispatch to Soviet leader Joseph Stalin, assuring him that U.S. objectives in Korea are limited and expressing the hope that the Soviet Union will help in the restoration of peace.

General Walter Smith, director of the CIA, appoints an old OSS operative, Hans Tofte, to head CIA operations in the Far East.

The fact that Washington immediately links the invasion of the Republic of Korea to a threat on the Nationalist stronghold of Taiwan has an immediate effect on China's view of the situation. President Truman's comments on this subject make matters worse. He says that the occupation of Taiwan by Chinese Communist forces would be seen as a direct threat to the U.S. performance of its lawful and necessary activities to assure the security of the Pacific area.

Zhou Enlai adopts a far more belligerent public attitude toward the American blockade of the Taiwan Strait than was displayed concerning American and UN intervention in Korea.

EIGHTH ARMY: Under fighter cover from Japan, civilians and KMAG staff begin to fly out of Suwon Airfield for Japan. A group of YAK-9 fighters of the Korean People's Air Force try to stop the evacuation and are intercepted by American F-82 twin Mustangs. Four twin Mustang, propeller-driven night fighters and several F-80 Shooting Star jet fighters cover the evacuation and shoot down three YAK-9. These are the first planes to be destroyed in aerial combat during the war. During the night, the North Korean 3rd Infantry Division enters Seoul.

General Douglas MacArthur establishes GHQ Advanced Command Group at Suwon under the command of Brigadier General John H. Church. Church's primary mission is to reorganize the demoralized ROK army.

SEA WAR: The flagship USS *Juneau* (CLA 119) leaves Sasebo on nearby Kyushu to investigate reports of an enemy landing on the island of Koje-do. The rumor proves to be unfounded.

The U.S. Seventh Fleet is ordered to neutralize Taiwan.

AIR WAR: With presidential authorization, General Douglas MacArthur instructs Far East Air Force (FEAF) to attack units of the North Korean military located south of the 38th parallel.

Kimpo and Suwon airfields are used for the air evacuation of 748 dependents in USAF C-54s, C-46s, and C-47s. When North Korean planes approach the airfields at Kimpo and Suwon, they are engaged by USAF planes. Major James W. Little, commander of the 339th FAWS, fires the first shot. Six American planes shoot down seven North Korean aircraft. The pilots involved are William Hudson and Carl Fisher, who share one kill; James W. Little, Charles Moran, and Fred Larkins, who share a kill; Robert Wayne, who gets two; Robert Dewald; and Raymond E. Schillereff.

Fifth Air Force B-26s, flying from Ashiya Air Base in Japan, attack enemy targets in South Korea, but bad weather makes the raids ineffective.

Lieutenant General George E. Stratemeyer, commander FEAF, returns to Japan after being caught in Washington when the war broke out.

June 28

POLITICAL/ADMINISTRATIVE: Brigadier General John Church, who has been sent to Korea to survey the situation, reports to General Douglas MacArthur that extreme measures are needed to stabilize the war. He suggests that at least two regimental combat teams will be necessary to hold a line along the 38th parallel. In the meantime, President Harry Truman goes public, addressing a meeting of the American Newspaper Guild about events in Korea.

EIGHTH ARMY: After a day of street fighting, North Korean forces capture the city of Seoul. Only a few men hold the south shore of the Han River. At approximately 0215 ROK army engineers prematurely blow the Han River bridge, thereby destroying the last escape route available and trapping nearly three divisions of ROK army troops still fighting in Seoul. An estimated 500 to 800 people are killed in the explosion. Later, KMAG personnel manage to escape using still operable ferries. The ROK army can muster only 22,000 men. A new attempt to consolidate is made at Suwon.

Detachment X, about 35 men of the 507th Antiaircraft Artillery Automatic Weapons Battalion, are the first ground forces to arrive in Korea.

The capital city of Seoul falls to the North Koreans.

SEA WAR: The British commander of naval forces in the Far East places his ships under the control of the senior naval commander, Admiral C. Turner Joy. The British force includes the light carrier HMS *Triumph,* the cruisers HMS *Jamaica* and HMS *Belfast,* as well as two destroyers and three frigates. The British ships rendezvous at Buckner Bay, Okinawa.

AIR WAR: North Korean YAK fighters strafe Suwon Airfield, destroying one F-82 and one B-26 on the ground.

More than 20 B-26s, members of the 3rd Bombardment Group, attack the railroad yards near the town of Munsan-ni, not far from the 38th parallel. The first B-29 medium bombers, the 19th Bomber Group flying from Kadina Air Force Base on Okinawa, focus on targets of opportunity along the route being taken by the North Korean army. Bad weather over Japan limits the Fifth Air Force, but some fighters are able to provide close air support. C-54s and C-47s, escorted by fighters, take out 851 dependents. More than 150 tons of ammunition and supplies are flown into Korea.

June 29

POLITICAL/ADMINISTRATIVE: Responding to a reporter's question on the status of what is happening in Korea, President Harry Truman agrees to the suggestion that it is a UN *police action*. The term is not used by the president, but it is quickly adopted by those who are critical of how President Truman is handling the war.

The Soviet Union tells the United States that it has no intention of becoming involved in the Korean civil war but declares that the UN resolutions on Korea are illegal.

President Harry Truman orders U.S. air-sea units to support the ROK army and instructs the Seventh Fleet to maintain peace in the Taiwan Strait.

Congress approves the Deficiency Appropriations Act that increases the economic aid provided to the ROK to $110 million.

General Douglas MacArthur flies to Suwon, Korea, to confer with General John Church and to get a firsthand look at what is happening. His initial report gives President Truman reason to believe that U.S. troops will not be needed.

EIGHTH ARMY: Detachment X, a recent arrival in Korea, shoots down a YAK fighter with an M-55 machine gun at Suwon Airfield. The detachment sustains five wounded men. The first U.S. casualties of the Korean War.

North Korean troops take Kapyong and mass on the north shore of the Han River.

SEA WAR: The USS *Juneau* (CA 119) fires at shore targets in the vicinity of Samchok, probably the first significant naval gunfire support mission. Antisubmarine warfare patrols are established off the Sasebo area.

AIR WAR: Far East Air Force B-29s successfully bomb Kimpo Airfield and the main Seoul railway terminal. The Fifth Air Force, 3rd Bombardment Group, sends 18 B-26 Invader light bombers against Heijo Airfield near the North Korean capital of Pyongyang: Twenty-five enemy aircraft are destroyed on the ground and one YAK-9 fighter is shot down. North Korean planes bomb and strafe Suwon Airfield, destroying a parked C-54.

While approaching the battlefields, General Douglas MacArthur's plane is attacked by North Korean YAK-3 fighters, but they are driven away. Aboard the *Bataan,* Major General Earl E. Partridge receives a radio message from General MacArthur that he is to take out North Korean airfields quickly and with as little publicity as possible.

The FEAF concentrates its attacks on the Han River bridge.

U.N.C. Commander General of the Army Douglas MacArthur (right) at the front lines in Suwon, Korea, with Lieutenant General Matthew B. Ridgway (third from right) *(Library of Congress, Prints and Photographs Division)*

F-82s drop napalm for the first time.

Photo reconnaissance flights begin over North Korean airfields as the 8th Tactical Reconnaissance Squadron begins reconnaissance flights over North Korea. As well, RB-29s of the 31st Strategic Reconnaissance Squadron flying from Japan, begin operations over Korea.

During the day, six enemy fighters are shot down; William T. Norris gets an La-7, Orrin R. Fox downs two Il-10s, Harry T. Sandlin downs a YAK-9, and Roy W. Marsh destroys an Il-10.

June 29–July 3

EIGHTH ARMY: In the Han River operation, General MacArthur tries to establish a defensive line at the Han River south of Seoul. His forces there are immediately challenged by North Korean forces, the main attack coming on July 1. The Han River defense crumbles, forcing MacArthur to reconsider the military situation and to call for four more U.S. divisions.

June 30

POLITICAL/ADMINISTRATIVE: General Douglas MacArthur provides a more detailed report on the military situation in Korea. This time he calls for the authority to send a regimental combat team into Korea and to introduce two divisions for a counterattack. President Harry Truman meets with officials at State and Defense, and they recommend sending the RCT and two army infantry divisions to Korea from Japan. It is also determined that North Korea should be blockaded.

President Truman receives congressional authority to order into active service any or all reserve components for a period of 21 months. For political reasons, President Truman officially rejects the Nationalist Chinese offer of 33,000 troops to fight in Korea. The president gives General MacArthur permission to send U.S. ground troops to Korea and to engage the enemy at sea. In authorizing the wider use of American ground forces, President Truman does so with the prediction that "we have met the challenge of the pagan wolves." However, MacArthur is ordered to stay clear of the Manchurian and Soviet borders.

Later in the day, President Truman authorizes General MacArthur to send a regimental combat team to Korea. Shortly thereafter, the order is expanded to include two combat divisions, with permission to use American troops in the area of Suwon. At this point the United States is committed to participation in the Korean War.

Lieutenant General Chung Il Kwon is assigned as the ROK army's chief of staff.

The Chinese Communist Party's Military Committee informs its naval forces that the timing for the liberation of Taiwan has changed and must be postponed as the government prepares for dealing with the United States in Korea.

EIGHTH ARMY: Major General William F. Dean, commanding the 24th Infantry Division, is ordered to deploy to Korea. The first deployment consists of the 24th's 1st Battalion of its 21st Infantry Regiment (less two companies) and a rifle platoon sent from Itazuki Air Base to Pusan, Korea. This group is identified as Task Force Smith.

General Church, who has gone out to report on the increasingly desperate situation, meets retreating troops on the road from Suwon and orders them back. When he discovers that all communication equipment has been destroyed, he authorizes a fall-back to Taejon.

AIR WAR: The Royal Australian Air Force 77th Squadron arrives to support UN troops.

North Korean troops who have crossed the Han River now threaten Suwon airfield. FEAF begins the evacuation of the airfield and starts work on improving a secondary field at Kumhae, 11 miles northwest of Pusan.

The Fifth Air Force Tactical Air Control Party arrives at Suwon. Fifteen planes, B-29s, hit railroad bridges, tanks, and troop concentrations along the north bank of the Han River.

Two YAK-9 fighters are shot down, one by John B. Thomas in an F-80C and one by Leonard H. Plog in an F9F-3.

July 1

EIGHTH ARMY: The first U.S. infantry unit (Task Force Smith) arrives in Korea. It is composed of the 1st Battalion, 21st Infantry Regiment, of the 24th Infantry Division, along with Able Battery of the 52nd Field Artillery Battalion.

The transfer of the army's ocean shipping to the Military Sea Transportation Service is accomplished smoothly.

General Dean is named to command U.S. Army Forces in Korea (USAFIK).

Advance Command and Liaison group (ADCOM) establishes a headquarters at Taejon.

SEA WAR: The commander in chief, Pacific Fleet, forms Task Force Yoke under Rear Admiral Boone. These ships are assembled on the West Coast and at Pearl Harbor for service in Korea.

Commander Naval Forces Far East (COMNAVFE) discontinues routine anti-submarine patrols off Sasebo.

AIR WAR: North Korean forces occupy Suwon, preventing use of the airstrip.

The Fifth Air Force is given control of the 77th Royal Australian Squadron. The 374th Troop Carrier Wing (TCW) begins the job of airlifting the U.S. 24th Infantry Division from Itazuki to Pusan. These are the first combat troops to enter the war.

July 2

EIGHTH ARMY: Task Force Smith arrives at Taejon at about 0800 and is ordered north to the towns of Pyongtaek and Ansong. Arriving after dark, Charlie Company digs in at Pyongtaek and Company Baker digs in at Ansong. The 34th Infantry Regiment of the 24th Infantry Division arrives at Pusan.

General Douglas MacArthur requests the immediate detachment of a Marine Regimental Combat Team (RCT) with supporting air. Acting on the same day, the Joint Chiefs of Staff (JCS) approves the request and Admiral Radford is instructed to comply.

SEA WAR: The only U.S. naval battle of the war occurs when USS *Juneau* (CA 119) and two British ships destroy three of four North Korean torpedo boats near Chumunjin. The fourth boat escapes.

AIR WAR: Planes of the Seventh Fleet and British ships begin carrier operations off the west coast of North Korea.

PARTISANS: Colonel John McGee is ordered to form a base for guerrilla operations in Korea as quickly as possible.

July 3

EIGHTH ARMY: General William F. Dean arrives at the Taejon Airport to take command of U.S. Army Forces in Korea.

Leaving the men of Task Force Smith to rest, Colonel Smith and his staff move forward to locate a blocking position north of Osan in a line of low rolling hills, the most dominant of which command the main railroad line to the east.

North Korean troops take Inchon and Yongdungpo

SEA WAR: U.S. Navy operations begin as carriers USS *Valley Forge* (CV 45) and HMS *Triumph* send fighters against airfields in the Pyongyang-Chinnampo area.

President Harry Truman's orders calling for a blockade of the Korean coast are implemented.

YMS 513 (a minesweeper) catches and sinks three enemy boats unloading military supplies at Chuldo.

HMS *Black Swan* receives the first air attack against a UN ship.

AIR WAR: Flying C-46s and C47s, the 374th TCW continues airlifting the 24th Infantry Division from Japan. They use the smaller planes to prevent further destruction of the airfield at Pusan.

A Royal Australian Air Force F-51 mistakenly attacks a UN ammunition train that has stopped at the Pyongtaek railroad station. The train explodes and the station is destroyed.

Aircraft from USS *Valley Forge* (CV 45) and HMS *Triumph* attack airfields in the Pyongyang-Chinnampo area on the west coast. Two YAK-9s are shot down, one by Eldon W. Brown in an F9F-3 and one by Robert A. Coffin flying an F-80C.

July 3

SEA WAR: The New Zealand frigate, HMNZS *Tutira,* arrives in Korean waters as one of the first Commonwealth contributions to the war effort. She is quickly assigned to the Blockade and Escort Group.

The frigate HMNZS *Pukaki* is the second New Zealand ship to begin a tour with the UN Korean waters.

July 4

POLITICAL/ADMINISTRATIVE: General MacArthur asks for the U.S. 2nd Infantry Division, a regimental combat team from the 82nd Airborne Division, and the First Marine Division to be sent to Korea.

General Douglas MacArthur informs Communist commanders via radio that the United Nations expects all prisoners of war to be well treated.

EIGHTH ARMY: Task Force Smith gathers at Pyongtaek, where it is reinforced by elements of the 52nd Field Artillery Battalion (six 105s) under the command of Lieutenant Colonel Miller O. Perry as well as members of the Headquarters and Service Batteries, a total of 73 vehicles and 134 men. The combined force moves out of Pyongtaek by truck and arrives at its position about 0300.

The 2nd and 3rd Battalions plus regimental support troops of the 21st Infantry Regiment arrive at Pusan. Far East Command establishes the Pusan Base Command as a subordinate command to furnish logistical support for combat services under the UN flag.

July 5

POLITICAL/ADMINISTRATIVE: Chairman Joseph Stalin wires Premier Mao Zedong of Soviet agreement with the Chinese plan to concentrate their divisions along the border with North Korea. The plan is that they will be used in the event U.S. forces cross the 38th parallel. There is still some disagreement about what Joseph Stalin is offering when he says that air cover will be available.

EIGHTH ARMY: The battle for the city of Wonju begins. The small city is a railway and road hub near the center of the peninsula and about 50 miles south of the 38th parallel. During the initial North Korean drive, the city is lost to the enemy on July 5.

Private Kenneth Shadrick of Skin Fork, West Virginia, becomes the first (some reports say the second—an unknown machine gunner was reported killed somewhat earlier) American to die in the Korean War.

The Battle of Osan begins as the first U.S. ground action of the war. Colonel Smith orders his artillery to conduct registration fire. Early in the day a column of eight Korean People's Army T-34 tanks, part of the NKPA 107th Tank Regiment, 105th Armored Division, approaches. At 0800, the artillery fire opens up. The high-explosive rounds have no effect on the tanks, but there are heavy casualties on the infantry. The artillery has only six antitank rounds (a third of all those in the Far East Command). The 75-mm recoilless rifle fire, held to the last minute, is also inef-fective. The 3.5 bazookas, later to prove effective, are not yet in country. By 1015, the last of the 33 T-34 tanks drive through the U.S. positions and nearly destroy them. At 1100, three more tanks appear. Smith holds the position as long as he thinks pos-sible, but his casualties are high and his men nearly out of ammunition. At 1630, Smith orders a withdrawal, a planned leapfrogging effort, but in the confusion the casualties continue to mount. Colonel Perry and his artillerymen disable their how-itzers and then withdraw into Osan where they are met by NKPA tanks. On the return to Chonan, only 250 men of the Task Force are located; later a few more drift in. The cost of the battle is 150 KIA. The Battle of Osan, fought by Task Force Smith, holds up the NKPA advance for about seven hours.

Sea War: Service Squadron 3 is established as the principal logistics agent for Sev-enth Fleet. COMNAVFE (Commander Naval Forces Far East) implements President Harry Truman's orders for a blockade of the Korean coast.

Air War: In Taejon, a Joint Operations Center is set up to provide close air sup-port for troops battling the North Koreans near Osan.

July 6

Political/Administrative: Fifty-seven U.S. Army nurses arrive at Pusan for assignment in Korea.

President Harry Truman approves a request to increase the authorized strength of the army from 630,000 to 680,000.

Eighth Army: North Koreans continue their offensive against the 24th Infantry Division. They force the 24th to withdraw from its second blocking position at Pyongtaek that was being held by the 34th Infantry Regiment. The 34th manages to hold up the advance somewhat, as does the 21st Regiment when it delays the NKPA slightly at Chochiwon. General William Dean's 1st Battalion falls back below Chonan and his 3rd Battalion soon follows, having retreated nearly 30 miles. The 34th blows the highway and railroad bridges north of its position, a move that stops the advancing tanks but not the North Korean infantry. In order to prevent encir-clement, the 1st Battalion of the 21st Infantry Regiment retreats and takes up block-ing positions at Chonui. The battalion withdraws south to Chonan and sets up a new defensive line about two miles from the city.

Air War: B-29s hit the Rising Sun Oil Refinery at Wonsan and a chemical plant in the area of Hungnam. It is the first strategic air attack of the Korean War.

Several tanks are destroyed by B-29s that strike advancing armored units.

July 7

Political/Administrative: Acting on a resolution sponsored by Great Britain and France, the UN Security Council authorizes formation of the UN Command to consolidate the forces in Korea. The United States is asked to act as UN executive agent and to name the commander who will report to the United Nations. After this date the war in Korea is fought under the blue and white flag of the United Nations.

Major General Earle E. Partridge resumes active command of Fifth Air Force.

The 1st Provisional Marine Brigade is activated at Camp Pendleton under Brigadier General Edward A. Craig. The force is built around the 5th Marine Regiment.

Zhou Enlai chairs a meeting of the CCP Military Committee that decides to form the Northeast Defense Army (NDA) immediately. Su Yu, the CCP general who had been designated to liberate Taiwan, is appointed commander of the NDA, which will eventually include four infantry armies and three artillery divisions.

General Douglas MacArthur is named to command UN forces.

General MacArthur changes his mind about the needs in Korea and tells the JCS that he is now confronted by an aggressive and well-trained professional army under excellent leadership. In order to hurl back this formidable enemy, he will require a force of from four to four-and-a-half full-strength American divisions, supported by an airborne regimental combat team and an armored group. A minimum of 30,000 men needs to be sent immediately or success will be extremely doubtful.

EIGHTH ARMY: With Task Force Smith, the 3rd Battalion of the 34th makes an attempt to retake some ground, or at least to provide some delaying action, but is forced to retreat. The general retreat begins with the 3rd Battalion continuing south of Chonan and eventually taking up positions at the railroad station on the west and northern edges of the town. Elements of the 21st Infantry Regiment arrive at Taejon and are ordered to advance toward Chochiwon and Chonui.

The 63rd Field Artillery arrives in support.

AIR WAR: FEAF is assigned command control of the Australian 77th RAAF Fighter Squadron. VP Squadron 6 under Commander A. F. Farwell begins its tour of duty in Korea.

SEA WAR: The destroyer HRMS *Evertsen* begins its cruise in Korean waters in support of the UN Command.

July 8

POLITICAL/ADMINISTRATIVE: President Harry Truman names General Douglas MacArthur as Commander in Chief, United Nations Command. Lieutenant General Walton Walker flies to Taejon to meet with General William Dean, promising him the Eighth Army. Dean is assured that elements of four divisions are on the way. General Dean sends a message warning his commanders that the equipment of the North Korean Army and the training of the North Korean soldier have been vastly underestimated.

EIGHTH ARMY: General Dean issues the order that the Kum River Line is to be held at all costs and stresses that maximum delay is essential. Rations arrive and all troops have a hot meal, the first in four days. In the morning, North Korean tanks and supporting infantry break into Chonan. Remnants of the 3rd Battalion have been reduced to fighting in the streets. The NKPA pushes hard, and it looks as though the

American battalion may be destroyed. Fortunately, friendly artillery units provide a white-phosphorus screen and several of the men are able to escape by heading down the road to Taejon. General Dean orders the remainder of the 34th Infantry Regiment to fight a delaying action as it moves south and heads toward the Kum River. A road block is prepared by 3rd Engineer Combat Battalion to cover the 34th Infantry withdrawal.

Twelve army nurses move forward to the battle front at Taejon to set up a MASH unit.

SEA WAR: Chief of Naval Operations authorizes the activation of several ships from the mothball fleet. Ships, from destroyers to minesweepers and from cruisers to carriers, are released.

AIR WAR: Bomber Command (Provisional) is established at Yokota, with Major General Emmett O'Donnell, Jr., as commander.

Lieutenant Frank Chermak and Lieutenant Oliver Duerksen, using radio equipped jeeps, become the first forward air controllers to direct air-to-ground attacks in Korea.

An unidentified U.S. destroyer being refueled from a carrier while at sea *(Center for the Study of the Korean War, Graceland University)*

July 9

EIGHTH ARMY: The 1st Provisional Marine Brigade reaches a component of 192 officers and 4,503 men.

General Dean's Able and Dog Companies, still north of the Kum River, come under heavy shelling but hold out until evening, when they are ordered back out of rifle range. By mid-afternoon, T-34 tanks and 200 to 300 enemy troops appear on the road north of Chonui. Air strikes are called in as North Korean patrols enter Chonui and begin probing the blocking position held by the 1st Battalion. A short exchange of small arms fire sets ablaze the village of Chonui.

Chonui falls to the Communists.

SEA WAR: Commander M. J. Luosey (USN) takes command of the ROK navy.

AIR WAR: An agreement concerning air missions is worked out between U.S. air and naval forces. Naval aircraft will be under navy control when on specifically naval missions. For all other missions, however, their activities will be coordinated by U.S. Air Force. The assignment of targets is placed under the control of the Joint Service Target Analysis Group. The first forward airborne air control, directing air-to-ground attacks, is established by using L-5G and L-17 liaison airplanes.

Responding to the call for air support, planes hit enemy tanks and troops north of Chonui, leaving five tanks burning and the North Koreans in a limited retreat.

July 10

POLITICAL/ADMINISTRATIVE: General Douglas MacArthur officially becomes Commander in Chief, United Nations Command, adding this assignment to his positions as Supreme Commander of the Allied Powers, Commander in Chief, Far East, and Commanding General U.S. Army Forces, Far East. MacArthur requests that the Joint Chiefs of Staff expands the Marine Brigade to a full, war-strength Marine Division.

EIGHTH ARMY: The 27th Infantry Regiment, 25th Infantry Division, begins to arrive in Korea from Japan. Walker anticipates the establishment of a line of defense at the Kum River just north of Taejon.

At Chonui, North Korean infantry come out of the fog to begin a frontal attack, and one is beaten off. Dealing with both North Korean infantry and friendly fire, the 1st Battalion withdraws back to Chochiwon. They are able to hold for a short time but have to withdraw to a position north of Chochiwon. Here the first tank battle of the war is fought, and it is quickly discovered that the American M-24 is not a good match for the Soviet-built T-34. The Americans come off better in the second battle, later in the afternoon, during which two T-34 tanks are destroyed.

Task Force Smith, with more than 200 replacements, is ordered to join the 21st Infantry Regiment at Chochiwon.

The 27th Infantry Regiment, 25th Infantry Division, lands at Pusan and is sent north to Uisong, about 25 miles north of Taegu.

The battle for Chochiwon begins.

SEA WAR: The naval blockade of Korea is extended to include the ports of Wonsan and Chinnampo.

Task Force Yoke is ordered to sail when ready.

AIR WAR: Four North Korean YAK fighters bomb and strafe the U.S. 19th Infantry Regiment at Chongju.

Air Force planes catch an enemy convoy near Pyongtaek and destroy 117 trucks, 38 tanks, and seven half-tracks. Discovering that the liaison planes are not fast enough to avoid the enemy, the FEAF begins using the Texan T-6 trainer, known as the Mosquito, for forward air control.

July 11

EIGHTH ARMY: In preparation for the landing of the 1st Cavalry Division, a crew of officers flies into the Pohang (or Pohang-dong) area to consider the harbor as a potential landing point.

Task Force Smith moves into position about two miles north of Chochiwon as its 3rd Battalion finds itself engaged with enemy tanks. Surrounded by a North Korean double envelopment, the 3rd Battalion is overrun as individuals and small groups try to make it south to join their forces. Of the 667 involved only 322 make it back.

On the Chonan-Taejon highway, the 1st Battalion fights some delaying actions as it withdraws. It crosses the south bank of the Kum River during the afternoon.

A 10-man demolition team of sailors and marines under Commander William B. Porter conducts the first organized commando operation of the war.

SEA WAR: A captured North Korean soldier tells intelligence officers that mines have been planted in the vicinity of Chongjin.

July 11–22

EIGHTH ARMY: During this period, the Kum River line of defense is established near Taejon.

July 12

POLITICAL/ADMINISTRATIVE: The United States and the ROK army sign the Taejon agreement that concerns the status and rights of U.S. armed forces personnel stationed in Korea.

Lieutenant General Walton H. Walker, one of Patton's officers during World War II, is named Commander, Eighth Army, in Korea. General Walker officially assumes command and establishes his headquarters at Taegu.

Photographs of seven American soldiers who have been shot in the head are released to the public.

Rear Admiral R. W. Ruble is named Commander Naval Air Japan with responsibility for providing logistical support to all naval aircraft in the theater.

EIGHTH ARMY: The 1st Provisional Marine Brigade begins embarkation for Korea.

At dawn the North Koreans begin probing the 1st Battalion, 21st Regiment. By noon the 1st Battalion and then the 21st Infantry Division pull back in a general withdrawal to the Kum River line. General William Dean orders all his troops to Taepyong-ni on the south bank of the Kum River. Army engineers blow the bridges across the Kum River. Dean places the three regiments he has available—34th Infantry, the 19th, and the 21st—in an arc along the horseshoe bend made by the river at Taejon.

The 24th Infantry Regiment, 25th Infantry Division, arrives at Pusan. The 27th Infantry is sent to Yonk Airfield to provide security.

SEA WAR: Naval Air Japan is established as the temporary organization for all naval aeronautical activities in Japan.

AIR WAR: In the first of many emergency flights, the Military Air Transport Service delivers 58 large, 3.5-inch rocket launchers and shaped charges to Korea. They are urgently needed as North Korean tanks move forward.

Flying on its first mission, the 92nd Bomber Group leaves its base at Yokota, Japan, and bombs the marshaling yards at Seoul. During the day North Korean fighters shoot down a B-26, a B-29, and an L-5 liaison plane.

July 13

POLITICAL/ADMINISTRATIVE: Lieutenant General Walton Walker assumes command of all ground forces in Korea.

On President Harry Truman's orders, General J. Lawton Collins, army chief of staff, and General Hoyt S. Vandenberg, air force chief of staff, visit MacArthur in Japan to access current and future needs of men and materiel. They leave the following day recommending a prompt deployment of reinforcements, including the 1st Marine Division, an infantry division, and three regimental combat teams.

The Joint Chiefs of Staff recommends a second increase in the strength of the army, setting the new goal at 740,500 men. Both Eighth Army and ROK army headquarters move to Taegu.

EIGHTH ARMY: The first day of the Battle of the Kum River. On July 12 and 13, the engineers destroy all the bridges over the Kum. All ferries and flat-bottom boats are destroyed. The U.S. 21st Regiment is in reserve. The North Korean 4th Infantry Division crosses the river downstream on barges and overruns the 34th defensive position, pushing it back toward Taejon.

The 21st Regiment is now down to fewer than 1,100 men. They have lost 1,433 men during the first week of the fighting. At Kongju, the 3rd Battalion, 34th Infantry Regiment, holds the high ground around the town, on both sides of the Kongju-Nonsan road. The North Korean 5th Division enters Pyonghae-ri only 22 miles north of Yongdok and 50 miles above Pohang.

SEA WAR: The considerable flooding of USS *Fort Marrion*'s cargo well destroys a good deal of the ammunition and equipment of the 1st Marine Brigade as it prepares to land at the port at Pusan.

The reconnaissance party that flies into Pohang to see if the 1st Cavalry Division can land there returns with detailed plans on the beaches, depths of water, unloading facilities, and the general ability of the port to accept incoming troops.

AIR WAR: Seventy-one B-29s of the 22nd and 92nd Bomber Groups conduct a major strike against the marshaling yards in North Korea near Wonsan. B-29s from Bomber Command hit the oil deposits at Wonsan.

Airborne control is forced to move south from Taejon to Taegu as the enemy advances.

Flying SB-17s, the 3rd Air Rescue Squadron (ARS) begins the practice of dropping rescue boats to downed B-29 crews.

FEAF-Bomber Command takes control of the 19th Bombardment Group and the 22nd and 92nd Bombardment Groups, transferred from SAC bases in the United States. They are to be used in tactical attacks.

July 13–16

EIGHTH ARMY: Dates given for the Battle of Kum River, which opens up the first defensive phase of the war. Hoping to defend the temporary ROK capital at Taegu, Lieutenant General Walton H. Walker, commander of Eighth Army, establishes a defensive line to run along the Kum River north of Taegu. The U.S. 24th Infantry Division is in defense.

July 14

POLITICAL/ADMINISTRATIVE: President Syngman Rhee places all ROK military forces under the UN commander, General Douglas MacArthur. This makes legal what has in effect already been accomplished. On several occasions, Rhee will threaten to remove troops from UN control, but he never does so.

EIGHTH ARMY: At daylight North Korean artillery begins to bombard the Americans on the south bank of the Kum River. A large force crosses on the left of the 34th Regiment and attacks the artillerymen of the 63rd Field Artillery Battalion. The North Koreans overrun the position and the artillery battalion ceases to exist. The news comes that Kongju has fallen. The enemy pours through, driving the retreating UN toward Taejon. Instead of attacking the enemy, 3rd Division continues its move south of the river. The enemy soon overruns the 63rd Field Artillery Battalion that is set up near the village of Samyo. The 63rd loses all its 105-mm guns and 163 officers and men. The 555th Field Artillery Battalion (Triple Nickel) is overrun with the loss of 300 soldiers. On the south bank of the Kum River, the 19th Infantry Regiment is stretched for nearly 30 miles, its main defense astride the Seoul-Pusan highway where the road crosses the Kum at Taepyong-ni. Meanwhile, ROK army forces on the east coast withdraw to develop new positions between Yonghan and a fishing port 20 miles north of the port of Pohang. On the east coast, planning begins for the landing of the 1st Cavalry Division at Pohang.

AIR WAR: The first air group to be based in Korea, the 35th Fighter Interceptor Group, flies into Pohang airfield (K-3). The 6132nd Tactical Air Control Squadron under Colonel Joseph D. Lee is activated at Taegu as the first such unit of the war. The unit is available to control close air support for UN forces.

The Fifth Air Force activates its advance headquarters at Itazuki, Japan.

VP Squadron 28 under Commander C. F. Skuzinski begins its first tour of sea-based duty in Korea.

SEA WAR: The cruiser USS *Juneau* (CA 119) and the destroyer USS *DeHaven* (DD 727) on the Korean east coast use an army liaison plane to spot naval gunfire for the first time.

Attacks on unidentified submarines are authorized, as is self-defense or offensive action, when indicated.

The minesweepers USS *Pledge* (AM 277), *Kite* (AMS 22), *Mockingbird* (AMS 27), *Osprey* (AMS 28), *Partridge* (AMS 31), *Redhead* (AM 378), and *Chatterer* (AMS 40) begin sweeps in Yongil Man (Pohang) in preparation for the landing force.

July 14–20

EIGHTH ARMY: Battle of Kum River continues as the 19th and 34th Infantry Regiments, 24th Infantry Division, delay the advancing North Korean forces at the Kum River line. Total U.S. costs are 650 casualties among 3,401 men deployed.

July 15

POLITICAL/ADMINISTRATIVE: President Rhee sends a letter to General Douglas MacArthur in which he formalizes the agreement that assigns the forces of the ROK army to serve under the UN Command for the period of hostilities.

EIGHTH ARMY: The 19th Infantry (the Rock of Chickamauga) holds the primary crossing point on the Kum River, near the village of Taping-ni. The survivors of the 21st reorganize a defense as the 1st Battalion digs in astride the main highway between Okchon and Taejon.

The assault force for the Pohang landing gets underway from the Tokyo-Yokosuka area, with the strains of an army band playing "Anchors Aweigh." At this time, they do not know if there will be opposition to the landing.

SEA WAR: Task Force 90 transports two regimental combat teams of the 1st Cavalry from Tokyo Bay to P'ohang-dong.

The frigate activation program begins at Yokosuka.

AIR WAR: The call sign "Mosquito" is given to the T-6 planes serving as airborne controllers.

The 51st Fighter Squadron (Provisional) launches the first F-51 Mustang mission during the war.

Carrier aircraft, assigned missions over Korea, report to the Joint Operations Center at Taegu.

Robert A. Coffin downs an enemy YAK-9 fighter.

July 16

EIGHTH ARMY: At 0300, a North Korean plane drops a flare and then directs artillery at the 19th Regiment, opening up on it with a massive barrage.

At 0558, the ship carrying the first contingent of the 1st Cavalry Division enters Yongil Bay under heavy fire.

North Korean soldiers of the 3rd Division begin to cross the river by every means available and challenge the 19th Regiment. The UN center begins to break when a conglomerate force of cooks, drivers, and staff moves in and holds the line briefly, then the retreat begins, with Americans troops leaving their dead and equipment behind them. With the loss of Taping-ni, the 34th Infantry pulls back from Nam-san to about three miles west and south of the city of Taejon.

Chaplain Herman G. Felhoelter is posthumously awarded the Distinguished Service Cross after he volunteers to stay behind with wounded men and is overtaken by the Communists.

July 17

POLITICAL/ADMINISTRATIVE: General Douglas MacArthur tells the Joint Chiefs of Staff that he sees a "unique use" of the atomic bomb. Apparently he is considering the possibility that China might enter the war and sees a potential use of the atomic weapon to strike a blocking blow.

EIGHTH ARMY: The 1st Cavalry Division begins to arrive in Korea, landing at P'ohang-dong. Meanwhile, at the Battle of Kum River, two North Korean divisions assault the city of Taejon. The U.S. 34th is forced to withdraw to establish a line north and east of Taejon. General William Dean relieves the 19th Regiment with a company of the 34th Regiment and moves the Rock of Chickamauga 25 miles southeast of Taejon to reorganize and reequip.

AIR WAR: Friendly civilians in Andong, South Korea, are accidentally bombed by three B-29s, reaffirming the danger of bombers being used to provide close air support.

Francis B. Clark, flying an F-80c, downs an enemy YAK-9 fighter.

July 18

POLITICAL/ADMINISTRATIVE: The Joint Chiefs of Staff requests a third increase in the size of the army, to a total of 834,000. The request is approved by President Harry Truman.

General Walker flies to Taejon to ask General Dean to hold the city one more day so that the 1st Cavalry can take up positions at Yongdong.

EIGHTH ARMY: The Pohang attack group arrives after managing to dodge most of the havoc of capricious typhoon Grace. At this time, the battle line is still north of Pohang. By midnight 10,270 troops, 2,027 vehicles, and 2,729 tons of equipment of the 1st Cavalry Division have landed under General Hobart Gay. The 1st Cavalry will be deployed by July 22.

SEA WAR: Carrier-based planes from the Seventh Fleet's USS *Valley Forge* (CV 45) hit and destroy North Korean airfields, railroads, and refineries at Wonsan. They also hit transportation targets at Hungnam, Hamhung, and Numpyong.

Rear Admiral James Doyle's ships take on the danger of sailing in typhoon Helene and enter a murky Pohang harbor with the men of the 8th Cavalry.

AIR WAR: Some B-29s of the 19th Bomber Group are modified in order to launch radio-guided bombs (Razon) in hope of improving the accuracy against enemy bridges.

July 19

POLITICAL/ADMINISTRATIVE: President Harry Truman authorizes the Department of Defense to call up reserve units. The president addresses Congress and the nation on the emergency in Korea. He urges Congress to remove limitations on the size of the armed forces and to provide the authority to allocate the necessary materials. General MacArthur makes his second request for the 1st Marine Division.

EIGHTH ARMY: The U.S. 24th Infantry Division begins the Battle of Taejon. The 24th Reconnaissance Company tries to defend the town against the North Koreans after it is asked to "hold it for two more days." The Communists, with the 16th and 18th Regiments in the lead, begin a two-pronged assault on the city of Taejon. In the attack, the newly arrived 3.5 bazookas are used with considerable success in destroying enemy tanks. Nevertheless, within two hours the enemy's overwhelming armor and infantry move through the 24th and the survivors are soon in full retreat.

The 1st Battalion, 34th Regiment, comes under heavy attack in the Yusong area. The 1st Battalion is able to hold most of its forward position, but the headquarters is withdrawn to Taejon. A few thousand yards to the west of the 34th Regiment, elements of the 19th Regiment are attacked by significant units of North Korean troops, which they manage to repel. But, during the night, DPRK troops and tanks move south through a gap between companies of the 19th Regiment.

SEA WAR: The first navy plane is shot down by a North Korean pilot.

AIR WAR: North Korean YAK planes bomb the railway bridge northwest of Okchon. Three YAK fighters are shot down by Fifth Air Force F-80s in a dogfight near Taejon. In the meantime, seven F-80s of Lieutenant Colonel William T. Samway's 8th Fighter/Bomber Group destroy 15 airplanes on the ground near Pyongyang.

Three enemy YAK-9 fighters are shot down, one by Robert D. McKee, one by Charles A. Wurster, and one by Elwood A. Kees, all flying F-80Cs.

July 20

POLITICAL/ADMINISTRATIVE: Major General Otto P. Weyland arrives to become Vice Commander FEAF, for Operations.

Taejon, the temporary ROK capital, is captured by North Koreans.

Believing that the conflict in Korea is but the first step in the outbreak of World War III, 14 U.S. reserve aviation squadrons are sent to bolster the Sixth Fleet and the Atlantic defense of Western Europe.

EIGHTH ARMY: At early dawn the North Koreans boil across the Kum River, where the 24th Infantry Division is left to fight on its own. Tanks and troops enter the city of Taejon. Soon Major General William Dean orders a withdrawal using the Taejon-Okchon road to move his group to Yongdong. But by this time the North Korean army is already astride the road. As various units pull back, they are stopped by enemy road blocks and forced to leave their vehicles behind in order to escape into the mountains. During the battle, Major General William F. Dean is separated from his men. After eluding his captors for some time, he will be taken prisoner.

In the central sector, elements of the 24th Infantry Regiment, 25th Division, meet North Korean forces at Yachon. The Communist strike at 0300 with infantry and armor coming down both sides of the road, pushing the American right flank and driving the 1st Battalion of the 34th Regiment into the hills. The 24th Regiment, 25th Division, an all-black command, breaks and runs at the first appearance of the enemy at Yachon. By nightfall Taejon is surrounded, and the enemy has cut off the main route of escape. The area becomes a graveyard for the men of the 34th Infantry.

Sergeant George D. Libby (USA) is posthumously awarded the Medal of Honor for service near Taejon.

AIR WAR: Two more enemy aircraft are shot down by Fifth Air Force's F-80s. The pilots are Robert L. Lee and David H. Goodnought. Enemy air opposition seems to be getting considerably thinner.

July 21

POLITICAL/ADMINISTRATIVE: National Security Council document 76 suggests that if the Soviet Union enters the war, the United States should minimize its commitment to Korea and prepare general war plans that include mobilization.

EIGHTH ARMY: The battered 24th Division ends its 15-day conflict and turns over its positions at Yongdong to the 1st Cavalry Division. After that the 24th Infantry Division goes into reserves. The division has lost nearly 30 percent of its original 12,200 men and most of its equipment.

Engineers blow the bridges and tunnels north of Okchon, including the last bridge across the Kum River east of Okchon. The 21st Infantry Regiment, supported by the 52nd Field Artillery Battalion, withdraws from Okchon and takes up defensive positions nearly four miles northwest of Yongdong. Survivors make their way across the mountains from Taejon to join the forces at Yongdong.

The 2nd Battalion, 25th Infantry, 25th Infantry Division, takes up positions northwest of Hamchang on the Yachon-Sangju road.

For action at Taejon during July 20–21, Major General William F. Dean (USA) is awarded the Medal of Honor.

SEA WAR: A British merchant vessel reports seeing between 500 and 1,500 junks in the Taiwan Strait, which leads to an investigation by Fleet Air Wing One.

USS *Juneau* (CA 119) provides a naval bombardment for the ROK army attack on Yongdok. Supported by HMS *Belfast,* the ships fire more than 800 shells.

July 22

POLITICAL/ADMINISTRATIVE: Major General John H. Church assumes command of the 24th Infantry Division.

The Department of the Army asks reserve officers to volunteer for active duty.

The Pentagon authorizes the expansion of the 1st Marine Brigade to a full war-strength division.

EIGHTH ARMY: A North Korean unit hits the 1st Battalion, 8th Cavalry Regiment, north of Yongdong, but it is repulsed. The North Koreans attack four times, and an enemy battalion infiltrates and establishes a roadblock to the rear.

The 2nd Battalion, 35th Infantry, withdraws to new positions north of Sangju. The 2nd Battalion, 24th Infantry Regiment, 25th Infantry Division, encounters fire from the North Koreans as it moves up along a dirt road. ROK army units on both sides of the U.S. forces withdraw without telling the Americans, leaving them to receive fire on both flanks. Companies Easy and Fox withdraw under fire. At noon those elements of the 24th holding at Yongdong are relieved by the 1st Cavalry Division. The 1st Battalion, 8th Cavalry, takes up the defense on the Taejon road northwest of Yongdong. The 2nd Battalion is southwest of Yongdong. At this time, these regiments, like many others deployed in Korea, consist of only two battalions.

This is the original date set for a landing at Inchon, called Operation Bluehearts, but the invasion has to be postponed because there are simply not enough troops to launch an invasion while defending Pusan.

AIR WAR: The first helicopter, an H-5, is deployed to Taegu with the 3rd ARS and given the mission of locating downed fliers.

July 23

POLITICAL/ADMINISTRATIVE: Maggie Higgins becomes the only female reporter in Korea when she returns to Taegu after MacArthur rescinds the order that had barred her from Korea.

EIGHTH ARMY: The Battle of Yongdong begins at dawn when the North Koreans attack the 1st Battalion, 8th Cavalry, northwest of Yongdong. It takes four frontal attacks to do so, but the North Koreans are able to occupy the American position, while an enemy battalion infiltrates around the 2nd position to establish a road block. The 2nd Battalion, 35th Infantry, retreats to a point about five miles from Sangju. The U.S. 25th Division holds its position on the Seoul-Pusan highway to Sangju.

The ROK army's 1st Infantry Division and the 17th Infantry Regiment conduct a series of successful ambushes at Kallyong Pass.

SEA WAR: The submarine USS *Remora* goes out on patrol of the La Pérouse Strait.

The carrier USS *Boxer* (CV 21) makes a transpacific run in eight days to bring 145 F-51 propeller planes for deployment by the Far East Air Force.

AIR WAR: Air reconnaissance indicates that the NKPA is swinging south and east, behind the Eighth Army left flank.

A Tactical Air Control Center is established at Taegu by the 6132nd Tactical Air Control Group (Provisional). It is located near the Joint Operations Center.

July 24

POLITICAL/ADMINISTRATIVE: As General Douglas MacArthur establishes his UN Command, he places the responsibility for the Far East Air Force on General Stratemeyer. Naval Forces Far East are under the command of Vice Admiral C. Turner Joy. General Walton Walker maintains command of Eighth Army in Korea.

EIGHTH ARMY: During a heavy fog, North Korean troops approach the 1st Battalion position, and soon a seesaw battle is going on. Several tanks appear, only to be stopped by bazookas or air strikes. When darkness falls, the 1st Battalion withdraws through the 2nd Battalion and establishes a position behind it. At Yongdong, 2nd Battalion, 8th Cavalry, fails to dislodge the North Koreans. The enemy keeps the attack going as several smaller units begin to infiltrate.

The 24th Infantry Regiment relieves the ROK army's 1st Division in the area of Sangju.

At Pusan, the 29th Infantry Regiment arrives. It is filled primarily with new and untrained men. The unit has never fought together, and the heavy weapons are untested. Yet the regiment is ordered to proceed immediately to Chinju.

SEA WAR: The Escort Element, consisting of HMS *Black Swan,* HMAS *Hart,* and HMAS *Shoalhaven,* is established.

At midnight the Seventh Fleet weighs anchor and moves out to the east coast of Korea to participate in the first close air support strikes of the year.

AIR WAR: Fifth Air Force moves its advance headquarters to Taegu, South Korea, from Japan. It is located next to the U.S. Eighth Army headquarters.

July 25

POLITICAL/ADMINISTRATIVE: The Far East Command requests winter clothing and equipment, an indication that the war will continue through the winter.

EIGHTH ARMY: The 24th Infantry Division is ordered to defend Chinju in order to prevent flanking operations.

The independent 29th Regiment is ordered to seize the road junction at Hadong more than 35 miles southwest of Chinju. On the way, the 3rd Battalion is caught in an ambush; 313 are killed and 100 captured.

At Sangnyong-ni, the North Koreans are caught unawares under the guns of the 2nd Battalion of the 27th (including quad-fifties), and a "turkey shoot" takes place. There are only a few survivors from the Hadong ambush. Nevertheless, the North Koreans keep the pressure on and finally the regiment is ordered to the high ground near Hwanggan.

At Kimchon near Nogun-ri (where U.S. troops will later be accused of killing civilians), the 7th Cavalry Regiment and 2nd Battalion take up positions. By morning the 1st Cavalry Division is in Yongdong, and it comes under fire by infiltrating North Koreans. Major General Hobert Gay orders the town abandoned. To the southwest, the 2nd Battalion is caught in a roadblock that traps Fox Company, 16th Reconnaissance Company, and the 1st Platoon of Able Company, and the 71st Tank Battalion. Only four of the tanks are able to break through; the others are abandoned as crews and troops move into the mountains. Fox Company runs into an ambush and is badly mauled; only 26 men return. On the other side of the enemy roadblocks, the 5th Cavalry Regiment is unable to keep the road open after it is caught in an ambush and hurt badly.

SEA WAR: The mothballed carrier USS *Princeton* (CV 37) is ordered reactivated and scheduled for service in Korea.

AIR WAR: Carrier-launched planes remain over the front lines, but the success is limited.

July 26

EIGHTH ARMY: Acting on an erroneous report of enemy advances, the 7th Cavalry withdraws, scattering in panic and leaving weapons and headquarters equipment behind. Later, a group of NCOs and truck drivers recovers most of the equipment. While the 7th is regrouping, other elements of the 1st Cavalry Division hold on to their positions near Yongdong. The attack is stopped despite the fact that the North Koreans drive hundreds of refugees ahead of them to break through the American minefields. By dawn the 27th Regiment, 25th Infantry Division, completes its withdrawal and holds its position near Hwanggan. The 34th Regiment fills in on the right flank of the 27th, but there is still a gap between the UN forces. To the south, the 3rd Battalion, 29th Infantry (attached to the 24th Division), meets a truckload of wounded ROK soldiers who inform them that the enemy is holding Hadong. Ordered on despite this information, the unit advances to the village of Hongchon-ni about three miles from Hadong.

SEA WAR: Having received a very positive submarine report, carrier planes go to investigate. However, little of value is accomplished other than the destruction of some trucks caught on a coastal road. In addition, some Corsairs hit troop concentrations at Yongdong.

Air War: A VP-28 plane is attacked by enemy planes that are identified with North Korean markings as it flies over the northern part of the Taiwan Strait. The attack causes no damage.

July 27

Political/Administrative: The National Security Council authorizes aerial reconnaissance over all North Korea. However, no reconnaissance flights are permitted in Manchuria or over the territory of the Soviet Union.

President Harry Truman signs Public Law 624 that extends enlistments in the armed forces for an additional period of no more than 12 months.

Australia, New Zealand, and Turkey all offer ground troops to the UN command in Korea.

Eighth Army: As dawn breaks, the 1st Battalion of the 27th Regiment, 29th Infantry Division, comes under attack but manages to fight off each of the enemy's probes. At Hongchon-ni, the 3rd Battalion, 29th Regiment, moves toward the pass that separates it from Hadong. A group of high-ranking officers who have come to watch an air-strike called against Hadong are struck by fire from North Korean troops located to the north of the pass. General Chae Han-kook is killed and several others wounded. At noon the battalion is ordered to withdraw, but the only escape route is cut off by North Koreans who have dug in at the rear. Few are able to make it out. The 3rd Battalion loses so many men that it is no longer considered a legitimate fighting unit. The 1st Battalion of the 29th goes north to relieve units of the 19th near Chinju. To the north, the 34th Regiment of the 24th Division digs in at Kochang.

Sea War: Carrier Task Force 90 conducts harassing and demolition raids using UDT and marine reconnaissance personnel against selected North Korea military objectives on the east coast.

The USS *Toledo* (CA 133) fires its eight-inch guns on troop concentrations along the battle line on the east coast. This is the first use during the Korean War of this size weapon in this manner. The successful bombardment continues for 11 days.

Air War: The Fifth Air Force embarks on a mission to establish air superiority in order to cover evacuation efforts and to defend the South Korean mainland. When the enemy appears over Kimpo and Suwon airfields, the USAF engages the enemy in the first air battle of the war. Major James W. Little, commander 339th FAWS, fires the first shot.

July 28

Eighth Army: At Chinju, the 3rd Battalion of the 29th is reorganized with the 354 officers and men who have escaped from previous actions. They are organized into companies King and Love of the 2nd Battalion, 19th Regiment, and Love of the 1st Battalion of the 19th. By midmorning, the North Koreans penetrate the positions at Hwanggan being held by 1st Battalion, 27th, and the regiment is ordered to withdraw through the 1st Cavalry position. At Anui, Baker and Dog Companies of the

29th Regiment are pushed back by a superior force. They try to head for the high ground but the route is cut off. The remainder of the group finds itself engaged in street fighting that lasts nearly until midnight. Those who are able to get away slip into the hills and head for their own lines. Almost half the strength of the two companies are either killed or missing.

AIR WAR: SA-16 Albatross aircraft, the first to arrive in Korea, are made available for air rescue missions off the Korean coast. They are stationed in Japan.

Burton E. Thayer of the 80th Fighter-Bomber Squadron shoots down an Il-10 enemy fighter. A B-29 is credited with shooting down a Seafire.

July 29

POLITICAL/ADMINISTRATIVE: Great Britain, Australia, and New Zealand commit troops to Korea under the United Nations Command.

Major General John H. Church assumes command of the 24th Infantry Division.

EIGHTH ARMY: UN troops form a 150-mile-long Pusan Perimeter.

Lead elements of the 2nd Infantry Division begin to arrive in Korea. The last elements of the 1st Cavalry Division and its equipment are unloaded after having been delayed by typhoon Grace.

An unexplained panic takes hold of the 1st Battalion, 24th Regiment, following an incoming Chinese barrage. As a result, a roadblock is set up to halt deserters and turn them around.

The 1st Cavalry, its forward units outflanked around Yongdong, begins to retreat toward Kumchon.

At Kochang, the 34th Regiment comes under attack in the early morning as a unit of NKPA soldiers strikes from the north, cutting out Item Company. The other unit circles the town and cuts the road east of the city. The 1st Battalion halts the attack and then begins to withdraw to a defensive position three miles east of Kochang. At first light, the 1st Battalion returns and rescues most of those from Item Company. One platoon, however, loses most of its men. The regiment then withdraws to the east about 15 miles, to a place near Samje. As they do, engineers destroy all bridges and blow some of the overhanging cliffs in order to block the road.

Responding to the loss at Kochang, Eighth Army orders the 17th Regiment of the ROK army to Sanje, and the 1st Battalion, 21st Infantry, from Yongdok-Pohang to a position where it can provide backup for the 34th. Leaving Umyang-ni, the 1st Battalion, 29th Infantry, also withdraws after dark. The 2nd Battalion, 35th Infantry, must also withdraw and takes up new positions two miles north of Anju. The 27th Infantry is ordered into reserves. The 1st Cavalry withdraws to a position near Kumchon and the 8th Cavalry sets up along the Sangju road. The 5th Cavalry Regiment locates on the Chirye road, and the 7th Cavalry takes up positions astride the Yongdong road to the northwest.

July 30

EIGHTH ARMY: North Korean units flank the 2nd Battalion, 19th Infantry, sometime during the night, and cut the Chinju-Hadong road. Other units hit the battalion from the front. By nightfall the 2nd Battalion, and the attached survivors of the 3rd Battalion, 29th Regiment, are on the east bank of the Nam River, a little less than two

A South Korean soldier with a wounded colleague *(Harry S. Truman Library)*

miles from Chinju. The 24th Infantry Regiment withdraws to the last high ground about three miles west of Sangju, while the 2nd Battalion, 35th Infantry, takes up new positions to the south of the city.

General Walton Walker establishes a new defensive line along the Naktong River.
SEA WAR: Ships of Carrier Task Force 90 finally complete the Pohang landing of the 1st Cavalry Division.
AIR WAR: B-29s hit the Chosen Nitrogen Explosive Factory at Hungnam. Forty-seven bombers take part in this raid on the east coast of North Korea.

July 31

POLITICAL/ADMINISTRATIVE: General Douglas MacArthur visits Taiwan to discuss measures for the defense of the Nationalist island.

The 5th Regimental Combat Team, reactivated in Hawaii, arrives in Korea.
EIGHTH ARMY: The 1st Marine Brigade arrives at Pusan.

The battle for Chinju begins with an artillery barrage that lasts about 45 minutes. North Korean soldiers attack Easy and Fox Companies of the 19th Infantry Regiment. Fox Company breaks out and the survivors head for the Easy Company positions. The two units fall back to Chinju as daylight arrives. George Company is also ordered to fall back. It becomes obvious that they cannot hold the town, so they withdraw and move back across the Nam River to the east, picking up wounded men and stragglers from Easy, Fox, and How Companies as they move.

At San Chong, 1st Battalion, 29th Infantry, becomes aware of the loss of Chinju, and joins the withdrawal, heading for Harman. First Battalion moves 10 miles to the east toward Masan and sets up positions in the Chinju Pass. In support the 27th Infantry Regiment is taken out of reserves and ordered to Mansas. The 35th also withdraws, relocating eight miles south of the city of Sangju.
SEA WAR: The carrier USS *Badoeng Strait* arrives at Kobe, Japan, with Marine Fighter Squadrons VMF 214 and VMF 323.

July 31–September 16

EIGHTH ARMY: The dates given for the Battle of the Pusan Perimeter, the dramatic stand to protect the southeastern port city of Pusan. The battle begins as General Walton Walker's retreating army finally crosses the Naktong. As an obstacle, the Naktong is less than perfect; while it runs nearly a mile wide at some points, it is very shallow. This period includes some of the most desperate fighting of the war.

August 1

POLITICAL/ADMINISTRATIVE: Soviet delegate Jacob Malik ends the Russian boycott of the United Nations and assumes the presidency of the Security Council. The Soviets introduce Malik's resolution to invite Communist China and North and South Korea to discuss the war. The resolution is defeated.
EIGHTH ARMY: The Battle of the Notch begins. The 1st Battalion, 19th Regiment, is turned around and goes into a blocking position on the Masan road near Chindong-ni. A North Korean division bypasses Taejon and its leading elements are nearing Masan just 30 miles from Pusan. Under pressure, the 1st Battalion abandons its posi-

tion at Chinju Pass and relocates to "the Notch," a few miles east of Chungam-ni. The 27th Infantry arrives and occupies the high ground at Chungam-ni. Able Company of the 8072nd Medium Tank Battalion arrives at Mansas, equipped with rebuilt World War II M4E8 tanks. As evening approaches, the 1st Battalion, 29th Regiment, forms a tank/infantry task force to make a reconnaissance west of the Notch.

General Walton Walker calls for an orderly withdrawal across the Naktong River, the last natural barrier at which to defend the port of Pusan. At this point, they are less than 55 miles from the sea.

In anticipation of a prolonged war, shipments of cold weather gear are sent to Korea. The 2nd Infantry Division lands at Pusan.

SEA WAR: Two carriers, USS *Sicily* (CVE 118) and USS *Badoeng Strait* (CVE 116), are assigned, along with destroyers, to provide close air support to UN land forces in Korea.

The USS *Philippine Sea* (CV 47) reports for duty.

Admiral W. G. Andrewes takes HMS *Belfast* and HMAS *Bataan* to Haeju-man to bombard shore batteries guarding the approaches.

AIR WAR: Forty-six B-29s, in a second raid, hit the Chosen Nitrogen Explosive Factory at Hungnam. Planes from the 22nd and 92nd Bomber Groups take part. Considerable damage is caused to the site, which is identified as the largest chemical plant in the Far East. Flying T-6 aircraft, the 6147th Tactical Control Squadron is established at Taegu.

Air Wing One under Commander R. W. Vogel comes aboard the *Philippine Sea.*

August 2

POLITICAL/ADMINISTRATIVE: Major General John B. Coulter assumes command of I Corps.

One hundred and thirty-four National Guard units are sent activation notices for service in Korea.

EIGHTH ARMY: At Chungam-ni, a tank/ infantry force heads for the Notch at 0615, led by a platoon of tanks. Locating the North Korean infantry, the tanks open fire until the lead tank is knocked out by a mortar round. Then a second tank is hit. The remaining tanks are halted where they are and the engagement turns into an infantry fight. The 1st Battalion of the 29th and the 1st Battalion of the 19th become intermingled but hold their positions until the North Koreans eventually withdraw. This allows for the recovery of most of the trapped tanks and the evacuation of the wounded.

At the same time, the 1st Battalion of the 27th Infantry sends a tank/infantry force down the Chinju road. Leaving at 0400, they get several miles before they run into light opposition. After that they move on again to where they catch some North Korean armor and supply trucks. They are warned that North Korean troops are closing the road behind them, so they turn the tanks around, mount the infantry, and manage to make it back to the 27th Infantry's lines by midnight.

U.S. I Corps is activated at Fort Bragg, North Carolina, and ordered to Korea.

SEA WAR: The *Clymer,* first of the ships carrying U.S. marines to war in Korea, arrives at Pusan harbor. It is carrying the first contingent of the 1st Provisional Marine Brigade.

AIR WAR: During a 24-hour period, planes of the 374th Troop Carrier Group airlift 300,000 pounds of supplies from Ashiya Air Base in Japan to Korea. This establishes a new lift record for the war.

August 3

POLITICAL/ADMINISTRATIVE: The U.S. Congress removes the existing limitation on the size of the U.S. Army. The army issues involuntary recalls for 30,000 enlisted men.

EIGHTH ARMY: The 27th Regiment, in fighting off an attack at Chindong-ni, manages to kill or wound some 600 NKPA troops with a unit loss of 14 KIA and 40 WIA.

A wrecked sampan on the barrier rocks of Pusan harbor, December 1950 *(Center for the Study of the Korean War, Graceland University)*

The understrength 2nd Infantry Division and the 5th Regimental Combat Team (RCT) land at Pusan.

At this point, all of Eighth Army is withdrawn south of the Naktong with the exception of the 8th Cavalry Regiment, which serves as a rear guard. Withdrawing across the remaining bridge, the retreating troops are followed by the enemy Immun Gun, forcing Major General Hobart Gay to blow the bridge while several hundred Korean refugees are still crossing.

SEA WAR: The ROK *YMS 502* sinks seven sailboats as the enemy tries to unload men and supplies off Kunsan.

AIR WAR: The first marine air strike is launched from USS *Sicily* (CVE 118) as VMF-214 flies out in a rocket attack on Chinju.

SA-17 amphibious rescue craft begin flying along the Korean coast to pick up downed U.S. pilots.

The 18th Fighter/Bomber Group headquarters moves from Japan to Taegu in order to expand operations of the F-51.

August 3–5

SEA WAR: Experimenting with the use of the helicopter, rations and water are delivered to marines in the area near Masan-Chan. The helicopters bring back wounded personnel on the return trip.

August 4

EIGHTH ARMY: The defense of the Pusan/Naktong Perimeter begins at a line just 50 miles from the sea. The UN troop strength is 141,808, a number that includes 82,000 ROK army. Many of the NKPA divisions facing them are at half-strength, an estimated 70,000 men.

The U.S. 25th Infantry Division occupies positions from the south coast at Chindong-ni to the Notch overlooking the Nam River at Chungam-ni. To the north, the 24th Infantry Division, supported by the 17th Regiment of the ROK army, holds the east bank of the Naktong from the point where it joins the Nam River to the Koryong-Taegu road. From there north, the area is occupied by the 1st Cavalry Division. The 9th Infantry Regiment of the 2nd Infantry Division is in reserve.

SEA WAR: Fleet Air Wing 6 is commissioned and given operational control over all U.S. and British patrol squadrons in the Japan-Korea area.

AIR WAR: As the first FEAF interdiction campaign begins, B-29s bomb bridges north of the 38th parallel. This is the first step in Interdiction Campaign No. 1.

The first aerial evacuation of casualties by a marine VMO-6 helicopter unit is completed.

August 5

POLITICAL/ADMINISTRATIVE: Intelligence suggests a major buildup of Communist forces north of Taegu, in an area occupied by the 1st Division of the Republic of Korea Army and the U.S. 25th Infantry Division.

At a meeting of his command, General Walton Walker announces that the period of trading space for time is over, and he orders all commands to make a stand. This is often misquoted as the "Stand or Die" message.

EIGHTH ARMY: UNC takes up defensive positions along the Naktong River after failing to hold the North Koreans at the Battle of Kum River. At this point, General Walton Walker's position extends from Taegu to Masan on the south coast and to the east coast.

Across from the 1st Cavalry Division and the ROK army's 1st Division position near Taegu, a North Korean buildup is identified. The same is true to the west of the 25th Division. And, though undetected, there is also a buildup on the far side of the Naktong and across from the 3rd Battalion, 34th Infantry, 24th Infantry Division. The North Korean 4th Infantry Division mounts one of the first massive attacks against the U.S. 24th Infantry Division and successfully pushes forward across the river with tanks and guns, overrunning the UN posts. The area is known as the Naktong Bulge and is seven miles north of where the Nam River joins the Naktong. Realizing that it will be nearly impossible to defend, the 3rd Battalion nevertheless sets up a rough triangle with King Company on the high ground at the southern end of the bulge, Item Company at the northern end on high ground north of the Ohang ferry crossing, and Love Company at the far western end on high ground. The problem is that wide gaps remain between the companies and endanger the defense.

SEA WAR: In conjunction with an international sea effort USS *Sicily* (CVE 118) steams into the Yellow Sea. Its onboard marine squadrons' planes descend on Inchon, Seoul, and Mokpo, hitting airfields, factories, supplies, and harbor facilities.

The USS *Philippine Sea* (CV 47) arrives as the second U.S. carrier in the war.

The navy attempts an amphibious sabotage mission as two frogmen go ashore from the fast transport USS *Diachenko* (APD 123). The men are detected and the mission fails.

Planes from *Philippine Sea* and USS *Valley Forge* (CV 45) are engaged in close air support.

AIR WAR: The first USAF Medal of Honor to be awarded during the Korean War is given to Major Louis J. Sebille, posthumously. Commander of the 67th Fighter/Bomber Squadron, he dived his damaged plane into an enemy position.

Captain Charles E. Shroder's crew rescues a USN pilot who is shot down off the Korean coast.

Reinforcements become a problem. The airlift bringing troops to Korean delivers about 340 replacements a day, but this amount does not allow UN forces to stay ahead of the casualty rate.

August 6

POLITICAL/ADMINISTRATIVE: W. Averell Harriman and Lieutenant General Matthew B. Ridgway visit General Douglas MacArthur in Tokyo, seeking some clarification on the future of the war in Korea.

EIGHTH ARMY: The 1st Provisional Marine Brigade is attached to the 25th Infantry Division and given orders to move forward to Chindong-ni. A North Korean force of nearly a thousand makes a bridgehead across the Naktong River and breeches the last natural barrier protecting the lifeline from Pusan to Taegu. The 1st Battalion is ordered out of reserve, but, as it moves north of town, it is stopped at a place known as Cloverleaf Hill. The 19th Infantry Regiment is ordered to the Naktong Bulge. Fighting continues near Cloverleaf Hill during most of the day. The 9th Infantry Regiment, 2nd Infantry Division, is attached to the 24th Division and moves toward the Naktong Bulge. Orders are given to the 25th Infantry to attack toward Chinju on the following morning. The 5th Regimental Combat Team is to continue west along the Masan-Chinju road and the 1st Provisional Marines is assigned the job of attacking south down the Kosong road. The 35th Regiment is to move from the area near the Notch, head toward Muchon-ni, and link up with the 5th RCT. The 24th Regiment is assigned to clean up the enemy pockets.

PFC William Thompson (USA) is posthumously awarded the Medal of Honor for services rendered near Haman.

AIR WAR: Operating from the deck of USS *Badoeng Strait* (CVE 116), VMF-323 flies 30 sorties in deep support of Eighth Army's forward lines. Nightly visual reconnaissance flights begin over North Korean supply lines.

August 7

EIGHTH ARMY: East of Masan the newly arrived 1st Provisional Marine Brigade is committed to combat with the 5th Regimental Combat Team (RCT), and elements of the 25th Infantry Division, in the first major counterattack of the war. Overnight the 16th regiment of the NKPA seizes both Cloverleaf Hill and Oblong-ni Ridge and thereby is able to control the road to Yongsan. The counterattack launched by the United Nations during the morning fails to gain any significant ground.

To the south, the 35th Regiment is making progress until it runs into a North Korean battalion, supported by tanks, that is preparing for an attack. In a five-hour battle, the North Korean unit is routed, and the 35th Regiment is freed to move forward, taking the high ground above the Muchon-ni road fork.

The 24th Regiment is not having the same success and as night arrives the enemy force still holds its positions in the Sobuk Mountain area.

The 5th RCT has also run into trouble. Instead of continuing west, it moves down a road the combat team believes is in the area of attack assigned to the marines. In doing so, the 5th leaves the area unoccupied. The North Koreans take advantage of the situation and launch an attack. The enemy attack is beaten off, but UN forces quickly find that they must now fight a second NKPA contingent that has circled around Chindong-ni and now blocks the main supply route from Masan. A counterattack is launched but it fails.

A column of men believed to be ROK soldiers are passing by Hill 255 when they are finally identified as North Koreans. A brief fire fight results, but little damage is suffered.

AIR WAR: The first phase of new runway construction is concluded at Taegu by the 822nd Engineer Aviation Battalion.

The 98th Bomber Group flies its first mission of the war after 20 B-19s land at Yokota.

VP Squadron 28 under Commander C. F. Skuzinski ends its first tour of sea-based duty in Korea. VP Squadron 1 under Commander J. B. Honan begins its sea-based tour of duty in Korea.

August 8

POLITICAL/ADMINISTRATIVE: A full-page advertisement is run in Australian newspapers calling for volunteers to fight in the Korean War. The response is good, and Australia begins to put together its land support for the United Nations.

EIGHTH ARMY: At dawn the 5th Marine Regiment attacks the enemy on Fox Hill and routs them, breaking through to the trapped 1st Battalion. Elements of the 24th Infantry Division and marines try to break the roadblock east of Chindong-ni but are unable to do so. At the Naktong Bulge, the 34th, fighting on Cloverleaf Hill and the Oblong-ni Ridge, is relieved but that evening the unit is driven back off. That night the 15th North Korean Division comes ashore along the front held by the 5th Cavalry Regiment at Waegwan. The North Koreans then move on toward the Yuhak Mountains.

SEA WAR: USS *Perch,* a submarine especially equipped for clandestine work, arrives in Korea.

Fleet Air Japan is established, replacing Naval Air Japan.

AIR WAR: The continued pressure applied by the North Korean advance forces the 18th Fighter-Bomber Group to evacuate its base to Ashiya, Japan.

The 307th Bomber Group flies its first mission from its base on Okinawa.

August 9

POLITICAL/ADMINISTRATIVE: The Pentagon officially complains that U.S. soldiers lack the aggressive spirit of their World War II counterparts. Unofficially, the problem is identified by the increasing number of cases of "Bug-Out Fever."

EIGHTH ARMY: Very early in the morning, the North Korea's 3rd Division begins to cross over the Naktong in the area maintained by 5th Cavalry. Encountering heavy losses, the Communists take Hill 268 (Triangulation Hill) on the east bank of the Naktong. But the attack is slowed and they are finally held. At midmorning the 1st Battalion of the 7th Cavalry comes forward and mounts an unsuccessful attack on Hill 268. At the Naktong Bulge, the 9th Infantry Regiment moves against its former positions on Cloverleaf Hill and Oblong-ni Ridge and takes them after a short fight.

To the south, the 3rd Battalion, 5th Marines, and elements of the 24th Infantry Regiment finally break though the North Korean roadblock east of Chindong-ni. Within a few hours, the 5th Regimental Combat Team successfully moves up the Chinju road, breaking the enemy defensive positions south of Chindong-ni and along the road. The 5th RCT advances on Muchon-ni.

SEA WAR: U.S. carriers are west of Mokpo, flying air strikes against targets in the area of Inchon and Seoul.

August 10

POLITICAL/ADMINISTRATIVE: Major General Frank W. Milburn assumes command of IX Corps.

EIGHTH ARMY: Shortly before noon, the 3rd Battalion, 5th Marines, and elements of the 24th Infantry Division overrun the North Korean roadblock east of Chindong-ni and move up the Chinju road. The 1st Cavalry artillery pounds Hill 268 while a tank column circles the hill, leading to a combined attack toward the crest of the hill. After a short engagement Hill 268 is taken. The 2nd Battalion, 19th Infantry, is able to capture several key hills, the most significant being Ohang Hill. At first, F-51s bomb and strafe the regiment of North Koreans that is defending the hill, and then the 1st Battalion, 7th Cavalry Regiment, attacks and manages to drive the few survivors off the crest.

At the Naktong Bulge, the North Koreans launch an attack on Cloverleaf Hill and portions of the Oblong-ni Ridge, hitting at dawn. They are able to drive the defending 9th Infantry from both positions. The NKP army turns east, hoping to expand its victory by taking even more territory. But the effort runs into UN units and fails to gain more ground. The forward movement stops and the NKP army is held there. To the north of Cloverleaf Hill, the 2nd Battalion, 19th Infantry, manages to capture several smaller areas, including Ohang Hill, then digs in for the night with orders to attack again in the morning. The 2nd Battalion of the 5th Regimental Combat Team takes and holds the southern ridge of a pass at Pongam-ni, located to the south of Cloverleaf. On the north side of the pass, the land is held by Baker and Charlie Companies, 1st Battalion. The North Koreans hold the rest of the northern ridge from positions that allow them to fire on UN troops. During the day the fighting continues for the ridges; as night approaches, the North Koreans launch a final counterattack. The attack is focused and the troops seem determined but in the end they are beaten off. During the morning, artillery bombards Hill 255, after which the softening-up process continues with marine aircraft dropping napalm. Following these attacks the marines take the peak with very little opposition.

Elements of North Korean units work their way through the mountainous areas and cut the road behind the ROK 3rd Infantry Division. The ROK has already been pushed back through Yongdok to Changsa. Under considerable pressure, the 3rd Division is successfully evacuated by sea.

The Communists take the town of Phonang.

The 2nd Battalion, 5th Marine Regiment, presses forward from the tangled mess at Tosan junction where it has been held up for two days.

SEA WAR: The Marine Corps' helicopter unit, VMO-6, recovers a downed pilot. Task Force 77 moves up the Korean west coast to begin the interdiction of targets in North Korea.

AIR WAR: Operating from the deck of USS *Badoeng Strait* (CVE 116), the VMF-323 flies 30 sorties in deep support of Eighth Army's forward lines. Planes from USS *Philippine Sea* (CV 47) hit the Inchon-Seoul complex in four groups of six-plane formations that are sent to attack at three-hour intervals.

Two reserve units, the 437th Troop Carrier Wing (TCW) and the 452nd Bombardment Wing, are called up and placed on active duty.

The 22nd, 92nd, and 98th Bombardment Groups, with 46 B-29s, hit oil storage tanks and railroad shops near Wonsan.

Flying off USS *Philippine Sea,* a four-plane attack against enemy barracks is effective.

August 10–20

EIGHTH ARMY: In the Battle of Pohang, North Korean forces are able to drive the defenders out and to seize the city. American naval units evacuate stranded ROK army forces.

August 11

EIGHTH ARMY: At the Naktong Bulge, the U.S. 19th, 34th, and 9th Infantry Regiments launch an attack but are stopped. During the night, the North Koreans bring tanks and artillery, and elements of the 4th North Korean Division come across the river on underwater bridges. The U.S. 27th Infantry Regiment is pulled out of reserves and is sent to take the bridge over the Naktong. As they approach, they run into a massive movement of refugees some of whom are North Koreans, which jams the roads and makes movement nearly impossible. After a short fight with about 200 North Koreans, the 27th advances during the night to take the bridge and establishes itself on the north side of the river.

Near the town of Kosong, the 3rd Battalion, 5th Regiment, catches a motorized North Korean unit. As the unit tries to escape, it is hit by Marine Corsairs. The marines are in position by nightfall, about four miles west of Kosong. At Pongam-ni the marines' 2nd Battalion, 5th Regiment, drives the defending North Koreans from the north side of the ridge, in what is known as the "Kosong Turkey Shoot." Hill 88, located in the western suburbs of Kosong, becomes momentarily significant as George Company moves onto the hill, taking the crest at 1330. There they found evidence that the North Koreans have beaten a hasty retreat.

NKPA troops surprise and destroy a U.S. squad guarding the Namji-ri bridge, cutting the only road between the 24th Infantry and 25th Infantry Divisions.

SEA WAR: HMS *Warrior* and HMS *Ocean* join the British and American forces in Korean waters. UN Task Force 77 moves up Korea's west coast to conduct interdiction flights in North Korea.

AIR WAR: Flying Boxcars begin transporting trucks from the air base at Tachikawa, Japan, to Taegu.

Marine air and artillery units conduct the "Kosong Turkey Shoot" as planes from USS *Badoeng Strait* (CVE 116) discover a column of enemy vehicles making a dash for safety. VMF-323 and marine artillery concentrate fire on the column, destroying 100 vehicles of the NKPA 83rd Motorcycle Regiment, including jeeps and trucks.

PARTISANS: North Korean guerrillas attack the VHF radio relay stations on Hill 915, eight miles south of Taegu. About 100 men drive off the defenders and the unit disappears after the attack.

August 12

POLITICAL/ADMINISTRATION: Planning for an invasion behind the enemy lines resumes. Earlier efforts, called Operation Bluebeards, were stalled in July 1950 due to the lack of available troops. General MacArthur's second plan, Operation Plan 100-B, is named Operation Chromite. It is produced by Far East Command's Joint Strategic Plans and Operations Group while working on a very strict timetable.

EIGHTH ARMY: At the Naktong Bulge near Miryang, the North Koreans infiltrate during the night and set up a strong roadblock about three miles from the city on the Yongsan-Miryang road. They construct several underwater bridges and use them to bring heavy equipment and vehicles across. When the U.S. 19th, 34th, and 9th Infantry Regiments attack, they find the enemy stronger than expected and have to hold up. As this is happening, North Korean troops are moving south in an effort to cut the main Yongsan-Masan road at the Naktong River. The 27th Infantry Regiment is pulled out from reserve and sent to retake the bridge. After a short fight with enemy soldiers that have collected just a short distance from the Naktong bridge, the 27th retakes its objective.

Just before noon, in the 25th Infantry Division sector, the leading 3rd Battalion of the 5th Regimental Combat Team flushes out a hidden motorized North Korean unit. The North Koreans try to escape but are caught by Marine Corsairs and USAR F-51s that destroy a good many in a series of bombing and strafing runs. In the afternoon the 2nd Battalion, 5th Regimental Combat Team, near Pongam-ni, attacks the North Koreans. They manage to drive the enemy away from the area and in the evening the 2nd Battalion and a battery of artillery are able to get through the pass. Later the remains of the 555th Artillery and other troops of the 5th Regimental Combat Team are heading through the pass when they are ordered to stop.

In the 25th Infantry Division sector, elements of the 1st Battalion, 5th Regimental Combat Team, are attacked and driven from their position. The commander decides the best action is to move through the pass at that time. Unfortunately, some of the vehicles slip on the road and must be pulled back into the column. As dawn arrives some of the vehicles are still in the gulch. With the breaking sun, enemy tanks and self-propelled artillery appear on a trail north of the gulch and open fire. In just a few minutes, the 555th Field Artillery and the 90th Field Artillery Battalions are overrun and all of their vehicles destroyed. The few remaining survivors head west. The 3rd Battalion of the 5th Regimental Combat Team is advancing toward Muchon-ni when it links up with the 35th Regiment that has already occupied the town. In the 7th Cavalry sector, the North Koreans move across the Naktong in the Hyongpung area and take Hill 265, the northern knob of Hill 409. Then a second regiment of the enemy crosses over a partly ruined bridge and engages the 2nd Battalion, moving through Yonpo and then to Wichon. In a series of counter-attacks, the UN force is able to stop the advance and drive the enemy from Hill 265 and out of the Wichon area. The enemy retreats back over the Naktong. At the Naktong Bulge, the enemy infiltrates and sets up a roadblock about three miles east of Yongsan. An ad hoc force from the 24th Infantry Division, made up of clerks, cooks, military police, and the men from the reconnaissance company, takes up the challenge and stops the enemy advance. To the south, the 27th Infantry continues to advance toward Yongsan but is held up by accurate fire from enemy mortars. With the help of an air strike, the 27th continues north.

The 1st Battalion, 23rd Infantry Regiment, arrives at Miryang. The marines are ordered to clean up the remaining positions that have been bypassed during the main drive. The cleanup is halted when an enemy unit is spied near the crest of Hill 202. The marines dig in and prepare an ambush that, once executed, causes an estimated 39 deaths among the North Korean group. After securing the high ground, the marines are evacuated, their escape covered by slow-moving tanks.

Enemy troops, from fortified positions on Hill 409, ambush an I & R patrol from the 21st Infantry.

Sea War: USN Task Force 77 stops flying close air support and interdiction strikes over South Korea. The belief is that North Korean supply units need to be taken out. The Task Force moves to the west coast to hit interdiction targets in North Korea.

Air War: The withdrawal of Task Force 77 from close air support assignments leaves all air targets in South Korea to the FEAF.

More than 40 B-29s bomb the port city of Rashin, a manufacturing and a transportation hub located only 19 miles from the Soviet Union. The question about the wisdom of bombing so close to the Russian border continues during much of the war.

August 13

Eighth Army: To the south of Yongsan, the 27th Infantry Regiment makes progress as it moves toward the city. On the east the 1st Battalion, 23rd Regiment, advances from Miryang. Both columns reach the assigned objectives, the high ground north and east of Yongsan, by mid-afternoon. There they defeat a North Korean unit that has set up a roadblock.

In the 25th Division sector, the 5th Marines are ordered to abandon the attack and pull back to positions around Chindong-ni. The same order is given to the 25th Division's regiments. The trouble lies in the southern end of the area held by the 1st Cavalry Division. Enemy regiments are crossing the Naktong and have established themselves on Hill 409 near Hyongpung. Elements of the 21st Infantry are sent to meet the threat.

The North Koreans that had been driven off Hill 202 the day before, return to retake the much disputed area. Elements of the NKPA 6th Division rush ahead and quickly overrun the 3rd Platoon that was defending the hill. After a considerable exchange of fire, orders come through that the 3rd Platoon is to disengage at 0630 hours.

AIR WAR: Two squadrons of F-51s from the 35th FIG (Fighter Interceptor Group) are forced to return to their original air base at Tsuiki, Japan, as the enemy advances on Pohang. The move increases the distance that must be traveled to deliver ordnance and gives the planes considerably less time over the target.

August 14

POLITICAL/ADMINISTRATIVE: General Douglas MacArthur is ordered not to authorize any attack against mainland China by Nationalist Chinese troops on Taiwan. This issue has been a long-standing contention between MacArthur, the JCS, and President Harry Truman. The Truman administration believes that the political implications of allowing the Nationalist Chinese to become involved are far more costly than whatever good could be accomplished by the engagement. MacArthur sees the potential of a Nationalist raid against the mainland creating a diversion against possible Red Chinese intervention in Korea.

EIGHTH ARMY: In the early morning, the 10th North Korean Division crosses over the partially destroyed bridge at Yonpo and advances toward Wichon. About half a mile from the bridge it is hit by air attacks, artillery, mortar, and small arms fire coming from the 2nd Battalion, 7th Cavalry. The advance continues to make some progress but by noon the enemy unit is stopped. Held in position, it becomes badly mauled by artillery fire directed against it. Only a few survivors are able to get back across the river.

At the Naktong Bulge, Baker Company, 34th Infantry, is briefly successful in taking the Oblong-ni Ridge. But their success is short-lived, and the 34th is quickly driven off by a fierce counterattack. The same experience occurs when two battalions of the 9th Infantry attack Cloverleaf Hill. The 19th Infantry is able to make some progress toward the crest, but, when the enemy counterattacks, they are unable to hold.

Hill 303, which rises to a 1,000-foot crest on the northern outskirts of Waegwan, provides a good view of the city and surrounding areas. A North Korean infantry regiment, with tanks from the NKPA 105th Armored Division, moves quickly across the Naktong and sets up at the base of Hill 303. The hill is defended by the George Company, 2nd Battalion, 5th Regiment. By 0830 George Company is completely surrounded. A relief column made up of Baker Company, 5th Cavalry, attempts to reach the surrounded men but is unable to get through.

SEA WAR: A hastily assembled UDT (Underwater Demolition Team) marine reconnaissance force—Special Operations Group—conducts the first successful amphibious sabotage mission after it is launched from the fast transport USS *Horace A. Bass* (APD 124).

August 15

POLITICAL/ADMINISTRATIVE: Eighth Army begins the recruitment of Korean personnel into its divisions. The plan, called Korean Augmentation to the United States Army (KATUSA), is seen as a means to strengthen the vastly under-strength divisions. The plan allows for an incorporation of up to 100 ROK soldiers in each company or battery. The prime difficulty is that KATUSA is not usually of regular army but instead of men and boys picked off the streets and pressed into military service.

EIGHTH ARMY: At Hill 303, the coming of dawn shows that T-34 tanks and North Korean infantry have surrounded the eastern base of the hill. The enemy has overrun the How Company mortar platoon and captured most of the men and equipment. By 0800 hours, the hill is surrounded, and the North Koreans begin to move up. George Company pulls back into a tight defense. A relief column made up of men from Baker Company, 5th Cavalry Regiment, and a platoon of tanks tries to reach George Company. The relief column is driven back.

The Marine Brigade completes its move to Miryang by rail, LST, and truck. At the Naktong Bulge, attacks and counterattacks continue with neither side gaining much ground. Casualties are heavy and both sides exhausted. Eighth Army order the 1st Provisional Marine Brigade north to the Naktong Bulge with instructions to attack on August 17. The 1st Battalion of the 23rd Infantry is ordered to Hill 409 to help the 21st Infantry, located near Hyongpung, deal with an enemy regiment. The North Koran thrust arrives at a point within 15 miles of Eighth Army headquarters.

SEA WAR: During the night, one of only a few raids is conducted on the Korean east coast by a landing party composed of a navy underwater demolition team and several U.S. marines. They embark from USS *Horace A. Bass* (APD 124) and in the raid destroy a railroad bridge and demolish the entrance to a tunnel.

August 18–25

EIGHTH ARMY: The Bowling Alley is a one-mile stretch of road north of Taegu where a fierce battle is fought between the 27th Infantry Regiment (Wolfhounds) and units of the Korean People's Army. The ROK's 1st Division holds the high ground while the Wolfhounds deploy along the road. For a week the NKPA attacks down the 200-yard valley. The balls of fire streaming from the enemy tank turrets are reminiscent of the sound of bowling balls moving down an alley. Night after night the North Koreans attack and are stopped. Later, after the Wolfhounds have withdrawn and the 8th Cavalry Regiment is in position, NKPA forces manage to overrun the 2nd Battalion. The breech allowed the enemy to advance about 10 miles. The U.S. 23rd Regiment, 2nd Infantry Division, and the 27th Regiment, 25th Infantry Division, halt the North Korean People's Army. The fight causes the NKPA a high toll of casualties.

August 16

POLITICAL/ADMINISTRATIVE: The USS *Consolation* (AH 15), America's first hospital ship in the area, arrives at Pusan. Up to this point the hospital ships available had been provided by allied or neutral nations.

The first KATUSA join the badly understrength 7th Infantry Division, as every effort is made to ready the 7th for its role in the invasion of Inchon.

EIGHTH ARMY: Hill 303 is lost after tanks and infantry try to reach George Company, which is still barely holding the crest. The North Korean unit is able to resist all attacks. Sensing that the hill cannot be taken without unacceptable losses George Company is ordered to fight its way off during the night and work its way back to friendly lines.

The 5th Marines move forward from Miryang in preparation for an attack on the Naktong Bulge. The 34th Infantry and the 19th Infantry are assigned to support the Naktong attack on the left and right flank respectively.

The 27th Infantry Regiment goes into Eighth Army reserve at Kyongan.

Twenty miles to the northeast of Waegwan and 15 miles north of Taegu, North Korean forces break through the ROKA lines and advance south down the Sangju-Tabu-dong-Taegu road.

Private Seiju Nakandakarc and Private Ralph Saul operate a 3.5-mm bazooka on the front lines of Korea, 1950. *(Library of Congress, Prints and Photographs Division)*

Hill 208, a long landmass that begins its rise near the Mabang-ri highway, is the target of the 2nd Battalion, 38th Infantry Regiment. The attack is supported by strikes by a flight of F-51s. The group reaches the hill and by 1200 Fox and Dog Companies secure it.

X Corps:* X Corps is organized in preparation for the anticipated attack to be launched at Inchon.

An order to General Kean dissolves Task Force Kean.

Air War: Hoping to save Seoul, General Douglas MacArthur calls for carpet bombing against NKPA troops located on the west side of the Kaktong-ni. In a unique effort, nearly 100 B-29s make a carpet bombing attack on enemy troop concentrations near Waegwan. They drop more than 800 tons of bombs in an area about 7,000 yards wide and 13,000 yards long. Enemy losses are minimal, however, because most of the North Korean troops have already withdrawn.

Facing enemy pressure at Taegu, the Fifth Air Force advance headquarters is moved to Pusan.

Four F4Us and eight Ads from USS *Philippine Sea* (CV 47) hit troop concentrations at nine separate villages. Four F4Us from USS *Valley Forge* (CV 45) hit a gasoline dump and four villages near Taegu.

The ROK army's 3rd Division is rescued by sea after it was surrounded and cut off by North Korean forces near Yonghae. The rescue is accomplished by the cruiser USS *Helena* (CA 75), escorting destroyers, and four landing ships.

---

* Note: During the brief period when X Corps serves as an independent command, the activities of the corps are listed separately from Eighth Army.

August 17

EIGHTH ARMY: A second relief column tries to drive through to George Company, still holding on to some portions of Hill 303, but fails to accomplish its mission. During the night, members of George Company, following orders, escape from Hill 303.

A massive artillery barrage and a series of air attacks are launched against the enemy bridgehead at the Naktong. These are followed up by an attack by Easy and Fox Companies, which by 0430 are able to take the hill. Near Hill 303 at Waegwan, 25 men of the 5th Cavalry Regiment are found bound and executed by the NKPA.

In the Naktong Bulge, the 2nd Battalion, 5th Marines, moves out at 0800 to attack the Oblong-ni Ridge. They gain the ridge twice but do not have enough men to hold it and counterattacks drive them back both times. The 2nd Battalion, which has suffered 60 percent casualties, is replaced by the 1st Battalion.

At 1600, U.S. artillery units fire barrages on Cloverleaf and Oblong-ni Ridge. Following the barrage the 9th Infantry and 5th marines attack. The 1st Marine Provisional Brigade is committed. The 9th Infantry is able to retake Cloverleaf Hill and its reverse slope. The marines capture the northern end of the ridge at about 1700, then take the next two knobs to the south. They cannot take the third peak (Hill 145). As the marines hold, the North Koreans send in four tanks to break a gap between the ridge and Cloverleaf Hill. In the battle that follows marine M-26 and 3.4 bazookas are able to destroy three of the tanks.

West of Masan, North Koreans conduct a series of probes. The most serious is an attack on the 1st Battalion, 35th Infantry, located on Sibidang Ridge. The initial attack is successful but a counterattack at the end of the day returns control of the hill to the United Nations.

The Republic of Korea ships 7,000 Koreans out of Pusan who are "trained"; they are attached to the 7th Infantry Division.

SEA WAR: Navy Task Element 96.51 successfully evacuates the entire ROK army's 3rd Division from a position south of Yongdok.

August 17–October 20

PARTISANS: Operation Lee is undertaken. The plan is to attack the island of Tokchok in the Yellow Sea and occupy it for the purpose of future intelligence gathering.

August 18

POLITICAL/ADMINISTRATIVE: A CIA report acknowledges the advantages to the United Nations and ROK if Korea can be unified. But it argues that the value received will be outweighed by the risks involved. They support the belief that the Soviet Union might enter the war if any U.S. act is seen as an invasion of North Korea.

The Korean Relief Center is established in Pusan to aid refugees of the war.

General Walton Walker requests authority to activate and equip five new ROK army divisions. However, only the 1st and 7th are organized.

EIGHTH ARMY: The first tank-to-tank battle of the Korean War occurs at the beginning of the Battle of the Bowling Alley, when NKPA armor moves down a narrow valley northwest of Taegu and is met by the 23rd Infantry Regiment and the 27th's Wolfhound.

At the Naktong Bulge, the 5th Marines survive a North Korean counterattack and continue down the Oblong-ni Ridge. To the north, the 9th Infantry and the 19th and 34th Regiments move forward against moderate opposition. By dusk the enemy's 4th Infantry Division has been defeated and the few survivors are trying to escape across the river. The Battle of the Naktong Bulge is over.

Far to the north, two battalions of the 27th Infantry attack along the Sangju-Tabu-dong-Taegu road. As they do, two ROK army regiments from the 1st ROK Division advance up both sides of the ridges on the flanks of the 27th. When the ROK regiments on the flanks are stalled, the advance stops and a defensive line is set up near the village of Soi-ri. The road they are defending is a valley between two mountains. Shortly after dark, the North Koreans launch attacks, led by T-34 tanks and Su-76 self-propelled guns. During a fierce engagement, the tanks are destroyed and the infantry begins to retreat. The 3rd Platoon drives against the Koreans that hold Hill 147 and, after concentrated fire, drive the Communists away. Seeing Communist troops moving in an orderly retreat, a spotter calls in artillery fire that is quickly delivered and causes a large number of casualties. While the 1st Battalion of the 9th Infantry is moving up the southern tip of Oblong-ni, the 3rd Battalion prepares to attack the next ridge and take Hill 206. In less than an hour, the 9th Regiment is on the hill after discovering that the enemy has already begun to retreat. Artillery catches a good many of the North Korean troops who were forced out of the trenches and into the open.

Air War: Planes from USS *Sicily* (CVE 118) attack the ridges that lie ahead of the marine advance near a bend in the Naktong River. After they strike two tanks, they turn their fire power against a large number of retreating North Koreans who are trying to swim to safety. The strikes cause a lot of casualties among the NKPA.

Marine Able Company hears the sounds of enemy soldiers on Hill 117 and prepares for an attack. It is quick in coming, and the enemy forces move against Able Company and then Company Baker on nearby Hill 109. The enemy comes up the gully between the two hills. Able Company finds itself engaged in a fight with a group three times as large. At about 0300, the men of Able Company are overrun and the enemy penetrates the brigade line. Company Baker holds firm.

August 19–25

Political/Administrative: General J. Lawton Collins and the navy's chief of staff, Admiral Forrest P. Sherman, visit General Douglas MacArthur to discuss the proposed Inchon landing. They are also there to consider the relief of General Walton Walker. There has been some criticism of Walker, and there are a few in leadership positions who believe he is not tough enough for the assignment he has been given. While in Japan, the officers reach a consensus on the eventual need to cross the 38th parallel; following their visit, President Harry Truman authorizes General MacArthur's plan. There is no action taken in regard to General Walton Walker.

August 19

Political/Administrative: Operation Flushout begins. It requires all military units in Japan to reassign a part of their troop strength to be used as replacements for badly mauled units in Korea.

A meeting is called in Tokyo to discuss the plans for the Inchon landing. Present are General J. Lawton Collins, the army chief of staff; Admiral Forrest P. Sherman, chief of naval operations; General Douglas MacArthur; Major General E. A. Almond, MacArthur's chief of staff; Lieutenant General G. F. Stratemeyer, MacArthur's air commander; Lieutenant General Shepherd, commander of marines (Pacific); Rear Admiral J. Doyle and Vice Admiral A. D. Struble. Most reports from the meeting suggest that General Douglas MacArthur is able to bring them all onboard with his plans for the invasion. Despite the group's willingness to go ahead, there is considerable concern expressed by those who will be given the job of landing the invasion force.

EIGHTH ARMY: South Korean troops recapture Pohang and Kigye. In the Bowling Alley, North Korean troops launch another attack against the 27th Infantry positions. Two ROK army regiments on the flanks make some small advance. The 23rd Infantry Regiment, 2nd Infantry Division, moves behind the 27th Infantry and establishes a defensive position. The 1st Provisional Marine Brigade after two days of fighting is able to push the Communists back across the Naktong River. The marines are then released from the 24th Division and sent into Eighth Army reserve at Masan. The 38th Infantry Regiment, 2nd Infantry Division, arrives at Pusan and is ordered to Miryang.

SEA WAR: The Canadian destroyer HMCS *Athabaskan* escorts a South Korean vessel to Yonghung-do, an island located some 14 miles from Inchon, to check out an area where troops have been sighted.

AIR WAR: The northeast port area of Chongjin and its surrounding industrial area are hit hard by 63 B-29s.

Thirty-seven USN dive bombers from two aircraft carriers follow up on the USAF attack on Chongjin. Nine Superfortresses of the 19th Bomber Group drop 54 tons of 1,000-pound bombs on the railway bridge at Seoul. The bridge, called the "elastic bridge," is located at the west end of Seoul and has been unsuccessfully bombed several times before.

The Joint Operations Center is moved from Taegu to Pusan as the enemy advances southward.

August 20

POLITICAL/ADMINISTRATIVE: General Douglas MacArthur's message to the VFW is released. In it he is bitterly critical of President Truman's policy in the Far East. He restates his belief in the extreme military significance of the Chinese Nationalist forces on Taiwan.

The British War Office announces it is sending an infantry force, consisting of two battalions, for participation in the Korean War.

General Douglas MacArthur sends his second message to the Communists, warning about the consequences of their mistreatment of prisoners.

EIGHTH ARMY: UNC forces cross the Naktong River on a bridge built by the engineers in only 36 hours. In the Bowling Alley, the day passes quietly, but during the night, the North Koreans launch a new attack down the valley. It begins with a barrage of 120-mm mortar fire and then direct fire from T-34 tanks. The 27th holds its fire until the last minute and then opens up with combined fire. Five of the tanks are destroyed and the enemy retreats.

In the vicinity of Sobuk Mountain, an area identified as Battle Mountain is held by the 35th Infantry, 25th Infantry Division. A large enemy force locates their position and fires on them. In the return fire, the enemy suffers significant losses and moves back.

Able Company of the 29th Infantry and Charlie Company of the 35th move into blocking positions behind the 1st Battalion of the 35th Infantry. Probing attacks continue during the night and units of the 24th Infantry are eventually forced to abandon their positions. The 2nd Infantry Division is ordered to relieve the 24th Infantry in the Naktong Bulge.

August 21

Eighth Army: In the Bowling Alley a patrol from the 27th Infantry advances up the Alley where it discovers five disabled T-34 tanks and destroys them. The patrol then withdraws from the area without taking any casualties.

The 5th Cavalry Regiment fights against heavy enemy resistance along the Waegwan-Taegu road and then links up with the 8th Cavalry attacking north from Taegu. There they cut off elements of the NKPA 1st, 3rd, and 13th Divisions.

At Sibidang Ridge, the 1st Battalion, 35th Infantry, is harassed by enemy probes, but no significant gains are made.

The 1st Battalion of the 5th Regimental Combat Team is ordered to take Sobuk Mountain. After a massive air attack, the unit accomplishes the mission but is driven off after dark by a North Korean counterattack. The unit is ordered to launch a counterattack in the morning of the next day.

Sea War: Planes from USS *Valley Forge* (CV 45) and USS *Philippine Sea* (CV 47) set a new record, with 202 sorties flown in one day. The majority of these sorties are against Pyongyang.

Air War: VP Squadron 42 under Commander G. F. Smale begins its first tour of duty in Korea.

August 22

Political/Administrative: Chief of Naval Operations Admiral Forrest P. Sherman takes his flag aboard USS *Rochester* (CA 124) at Sasebo.

Soviet ambassador Malik warns the United Nations that any continuation of the Korean War will inevitably lead to a widening conflict.

Eighth Army: On Sibidang Ridge, North Koreans infiltrate through the 1st Battalion, 35th Infantry. A heavy battle of small arms and grenades develops, but the enemy attack against the ridge fails and the North Korean units withdraw.

The North Koreans launch an attack down the Bowling Alley and against the ROK army regiments that are holding the high ground on both sides of the position occupied by the 27th Infantry Regiment. The attack, which is led by nine T-34 tanks, runs into an American minefield in front of the 27th Infantry position. Then it is met by M-24 tanks and supporting artillery. The Americans are able to stall the column, trapping the tanks while small arms and artillery fire cut deep into the infantry.

By dawn the fight ends after the North Koreans lose seven of their nine tanks, three Su-76 SP guns, and several trucks. However, as the battle is going on, a North Korean regiment infiltrates around the positions held by the 27th Infantry and the ROK 1st Division troops and ahead of the 23rd, which is guarding the artillery.

AIR WAR: An RB-29, flying reconnaissance along the border near the Yalu River, is shot at by Chinese antiaircraft gunners from across the Yalu. This attack is considered to be the first hostile Chinese action in the Korean War.

August 23

POLITICAL/ADMINISTRATIVE: An additional 77,000 members of the U.S. Army Organized Reserve Corps are called to involuntary active duty.

France offers ground troops to the UN Command despite the fact it is busily engaged in its own war in Indochina.

EIGHTH ARMY: On Sobuk Mountain, in the area held by the 5th Regimental Combat Team, Able Company of the 1st Battalion tries to take the crest southwest of Sobuk, but is unable to do so.

To the north, at what is called Battle Mountain, the 24th Infantry manages to gain a toehold on an area that is to be known by its primary feature, Old Baldy.

The North Koreans attack down the Bowling Alley once again but are stopped with the loss of two T-34 tanks and significant numbers of infantry. At dawn the enemy is behind the 23rd, but the 23rd pulls together a counterattack and drives the enemy from the ridge. The UN regiment then moves on to sweep up what is left of the enemy on the ridge.

The ROK army's 1st Division relieves the 27th Infantry, which is ordered back to 25th Infantry Division control at Masan. The 23rd Infantry completes the job of cleaning out pockets along the ridge. The Battle of the Bowling Alley is considered to be over.

General Douglas MacArthur sets September 15, 1950, as the date for the invasion at Inchon.

SEA WAR: In an unusual occurrence, North Korean YAK fighters attack and damage a British destroyer off the west coast.

AIR WAR: An attempt to use radio-guided bombs (Razon) against a bridge at Pyongyang bridge results in only one hit. The experiment is considered unsuccessful. The value of the guided bomb is still in question.

August 24

EIGHTH ARMY: The northwestern thrust of the NKPA appears to have burned out, and the section is left primarily in ROK hands. The U.S. 25th Infantry Division is withdrawn. The remaining enemy pockets on the ridge (leading to Old Baldy) are cleaned out by elements of the 23rd Infantry.

SEA WAR: The USS *Helena* (CA 75) and four destroyers arrive off the northeast coast at Tanchon and, with the help of a helicopter spotting for them, they work over the marshaling yards.

The USS *Toledo* (CA 133) manages to place an eight-inch shell into one end of a tunnel that is holding a supply dump. The resulting explosion creates considerable damage.

August 25

POLITICAL/ADMINISTRATIVE: Secretary of the Navy Francis P. Matthews suggests the possibility of initiating a war with the Soviet Union to secure peace. His comments further ignite an underlying American fear of "a preventive war." He is not reflecting American policy, and President Harry Truman disavows the concept immediately.

Admiral Arthur D. Struble is replaced as commander, Fast Carrier Task Force, by Read Admiral Edward C. Ewen.

President Harry Truman orders the seizure of American railroads on August 27 to prevent a nationwide strike.

The U.S. Army organizes the Japan Logistical Command to provide logistical support to Eighth Army.

The first shipment of whole blood for combat forces in Korea is loaded at the American Red Cross Regional Blood Center in Japan.

China formally charges the United States with strafing its territory across the Yalu.

EIGHTH ARMY: General William Dean, who has avoided capture for more than a month, is taken prisoner by the Communists and will spend the rest of the war as a POW.

At Battle Mountain, elements of Company Easy, 2nd Battalion, 24th Infantry, repel several counterattacks against their positions. Charlie Company accomplishes the same mission on Old Baldy.

SEA WAR: ROK naval units are involved in seven engagements with North Korean junks trying to land troops and/or supplies on Namhae Island off the southern coast. The ROK ship YEMS *504* damages 14 out of 15 sail junks it encounters.

AIR WAR: Aware of enemy movement and afraid of potential enemy adjustments prior to the anticipated landing at Inchon, Fifth Air Force is ordered to provide constant surveillance against a possible enemy buildup. While the anticipated invasion is considered to be top secret, there is every indication that there are many leaks concerning it.

August 26

POLITICAL/ADMINISTRATIVE: The public release of General Douglas MacArthur's statement to the Veterans of Foreign Wars, urging the defense of Taiwan and criticizing Harry Truman, causes considerable unrest within the administration and adds fuel to the fire growing there.

General MacArthur assigns his chief of staff, Major General Edward Almond, to command X Corps.

EIGHTH ARMY: On Battle Mountain, the North Koreans continue their attacks against Easy Company of the 24th Infantry but fail to dislodge the defenders. On Old Baldy, Charlie Company manages to hold on against several counterattacks. The 34th Infantry is disbanded and its men and equipment used to form the 3rd Battalion, 19th Regiment. Of the more than 2,000 men of the regiment who arrived on July 3, only 184 are left. The 5th Regimental Combat Team is transferred to the 24th Infantry Division, where it becomes its third regiment.

For action on August 25–26 near Sobuk Mountain, Master Sergeant Melvin O. Handrich is posthumously awarded the Medal of Honor.

X Corps: X Corps is assigned the 7th Infantry Division and the 1st Marine Division, along with supporting artillery and engineers, to execute the Inchon landing. Command is given to Major General Edward Almond. He holds this commission in addition to his other responsibilities at General MacArthur's headquarters.

Sea War: Lieutenant Eugene F. Clark's (USN) plan to use irregular forces to capture islands near Inchon and to spy on Inchon harbor is approved.

Air War: C-46s from all over the Far East are formed into the 47th and 48th Troop Carrier Squadron (TCS) (Provisional) Wing at Tachikawa to provide what air transport is needed to assemble UN resources for the September offensive. The 1st Troop Carrier Task Force (Provisional) is formed as the prime organization of the new Combat Cargo Command (Provisional). Major General William H. Tunner, who organized the Hump airlift of World War II and the cold war Berlin Airlift, is assigned to the command.

August 27

Political/Administrative: Chairman Mao Zedong orders an increase in Chinese forces along the Sino-Korean border, expanding the four armies already located in that area.

Eighth Army: At Battle Mountain and Old Baldy, the North Korean infantry continues to attack but again fails to make any gains.

On the east coast, the North Korean 5th and 12th Divisions attack ROK positions in the Kigye–Pohang-dong area, driving the ROK's 3rd and Capital Divisions back below Pohang. The 21st Infantry Regiment is ordered to their aid and by afternoon it arrives and takes up position. It hopes to prevent the loss of the airfield at Yonil below Pohang-dong. On arrival, it moves in behind the Capital Division at Angong. During the night, elements of the North Korean force penetrate the ROK lines west of Pohang.

The 65th Infantry (later to be 3rd Infantry Division's third regiment) sails from Puerto Rico.

Air War: Mistaking Andong airfield in China for Sinuiju airfield in North Korea (on the left bank of the Yalu River), two Mustang pilots strafe the airstrip. The Chinese protest the incident, making it a major diplomatic event.

B-19s from the 92nd Bomber Group bomb Kyomipo's steel plants. The FEAF uses the occasion to test some delayed action bombs against rail lines. The delayed action bombs are designed to discourage immediate repairs. The largest problem with the interdiction campaign is the speed with which the North Koreans are able to repair the damage done.

August 28

Political/Administrative: The Joint Chiefs of Staff approves General Douglas MacArthur's plan for an Inchon landing. Intelligence warns of an impending attack.

Eighth Army: The ROK's Capital Division regains the land lost the day before but is unable to hold it when the North Koreans counterattack just after dusk.

The 1st Cavalry Division is directed to shift east to include the Taegu-Sangju road in its area. The 7th and 8th Cavalry Regiments are sent to the mountains north and west of Taegu, while the 23rd Infantry, 2nd Division, is ordered to fill the positions on the Naktong left by the 7th Cavalry Regiment.

Eighth Army intelligence warns that a general attack is expected along the line being held by the 2nd and 25th U.S. Infantry Divisions. It is assumed that the attack is designed to break the Taegu-Pusan railroad and highway and improve the chances of capturing Masan.

August 29

Eighth Army: Elements of the British Argyll and Sutherland Highlanders, the 1st Battalion of the Middlesex Regiment, and the headquarters of the British Commonwealth's 27th Brigade, arrive in Korea from Hong Kong.

The NKPA offensive opens up on the west side of the Pusan Perimeter. The 21st Infantry's Company Baker, supported by tank platoons from the 73rd Tank Battalion, launches a counterattack against the North Korean forces at Pohang. ROK army troops take over the recaptured area and U.S. troops move back to Pohang. The ROK's Capital Division regains the town of Kigye, but loses it after an aggressive enemy counterattack.

August 30

Eighth Army: The give-and-take battle in the area of Pohang–Kigye continues. The 714th Transportation Railway Operations Battalion arrives in Korea and takes responsibility for operating the nearly 500 miles of railway within the Pusan Perimeter. The trains are about the only resource Walker has to move troops quickly to where they are needed.

Air War: Planes from the fast carrier task force attacks bridge, docks, shipping, and the water works at Chinnampo and Pyongyang.

Searching for a hidden pontoon bridge, an experiment is conducted by B-29s that drops illuminating flares at the Han River area around Seoul. The intent is to make a B-26 strike against the enemy pontoon bridge more successful. But the hidden bridge is not located, and the B-26s attack the permanent bridge.

August 31

Political/Administrative: Zhou Enlai chairs a meeting in which it is decided to strengthen the Chinese border establishment to include 11 armies with 700,000 men.

Eighth Army: After a lull in the fighting, North Korean troops strike again, beginning the Second Battle of the Naktong Bulge. In the 2nd and 25th Division sectors, North Korean troops cross the lower Naktong. North Korea breaks through the defenses of the 25th Infantry Division and threatens Masan. The 2nd Infantry Division farther north is almost cut in half by NKPA troops overrunning their position. The 1st Cavalry loses Waegwan, and General Walker is required to transfer his own headquarters to Pusan. The 35th Infantry Regiment holds the northern part of the line, but there is a three-mile gap between Fox Company's main position and its platoons guarding the bridge at Namji-ri. Baker Company of the 35th Infantry is on the 1,100-foot Sibidang-san (Hill 278) when enemy artillery units begin a barrage that lasts past midnight. The 24th Infantry Regiment holds the high ground, including Battle Mountain, and the 5th Infantry controls the southern spur of Sobuk Mountain. ROK marine units hold the line from Chindong-ni to the coast. The battle for the Pohang–Kigye area continues as the North Korean 5th and 13th Divisions make some small gains.

Corporal William F. Lyell (USA) is posthumously awarded the Medal of Honor.

Hill 209, which is located five miles north of Agok and overlooks the Paekchin ferry, is the next target of the 2nd Infantry Division. The plan is to take the hill during the night. But, at this same time the North Korean I Corps begins moving across the river. How Company, 9th Infantry Regiment, moves up to the hill and establishes its heavy weapons. On reconnaissance they discover that the North Koreans are moving across the river unmolested. At 0200, the men of How Company make their final attack. It is strong and well directed, but the North Koreans are able to prevent the men of the 9th from taking the high ground.

SEA WAR: Lieutenant Eugene F. Clark arrives at Tokchonk-kundo, the island group that rests at the mouth of Flying Fish Channel. There he meets with local officials of the national police and plans are made to clear the islands all the way to the channel.

AIR WAR: Seventy-four B-29s hit mining and industrial targets—including aluminum and magnesium plants—and railway marshaling yards at Chinnampo.

Planes from USS *Valley Forge* (CV 45) and USS *Philippine Sea* (CV 47) sweep airfields in the Seoul-Suwon area.

September 1

POLITICAL/ADMINISTRATIVE: President Harry Truman authorizes the mobilization of four National Guard units to active duty: 45th Infantry (Thunderbird from Oklahoma), 40th Infantry (Grizzly from California), and the 28th and 43rd Infantry Divisions. The 40th and 45th will see action in Korea. The army initiates an involuntary recall for reserve officers, and 7,862 reserve captains and lieutenants are ordered to report for duty in September and October.

The 196th and 278th Regimental Combat Teams are called into federal service.

President Harry Truman goes on radio and television to explain to America "why we are there." He relates the situation in Korea with that in Nazi Germany in 1939 and tells America that the events in Korea require a forceful response. He announces his intention of doubling the size of the armed forces from 1.5 to 3 million.

National Security Council document 81 acknowledges that any movement north of the 38th parallel will require UN authorization. UN approval will serve the best interests of the United States and will do little to encourage either China or the Soviet Union to enter the war. The document insists that the United States must not approach the Manchurian border nor engage in a war with China.

EIGHTH ARMY: At the Naktong, across from the Bulge area, men of the 9th Infantry Regiment are attacked by North Korean infantry and forced to move back. They establish a line in the hills west of Yongsan. To the north of the 9th Regiment, North Korean troops advance against the 23rd Regiment breaking the line between the division headquarters and 9th Infantry and the 23rd and 38th Infantry. A counterattack fails, and by midmorning two North Korean regiments are moving through a gap nearly three miles wide. A decision is made to commit the 5th Marines in the Bulge. The Koreans also attack the 25th Infantry Division sector, where they break through the 2nd Battalion, 24th Regiment, and enter Haman, forcing the 24th northeast of Haman. The 1st Battalion is ordered to counterattack to restore the line, but most of the unit has already fled to high ground east of Haman. With about 60 men the 1st Battalion makes the effort to advance but the attempt fails and the rest of the men withdraw rapidly.

The North Koreans have also moved across underwater bridges to attack UN positions near Sibidang Mountain. In the early stages of the attack, they manage to circle the 1st Battalion, 35th Infantry, bringing it under considerable fire. As the artillery lifts, tanks begin to cross the Naktong River using the hidden bridges and encircle the 1st Battalion. The attack is stopped by small and heavy weapons fire, however, and by dawn the enemy has withdrawn. The situation is still very dangerous as many of the North Korean troops have moved in behind the UN lines.

At the battle for Yongsan, to the east, a unit made up of combat engineers, a reconnaissance company, and supported by the 72nd Medium Tank Battalion, holds the enemy forces for a while, but then has to withdraw to the hills north and west of town.

At Taegu, elements of the 7th Cavalry Regiment attack at Hill 518. Once the hill is secure, the UN troops move on to try and take Hill 314. As they fight, the North Koreans begin to gather three divisions that are being prepared for an attack against the 7th and 8th Cavalry position.

To the south, in the 35th Infantry area, the regiment holds the position that overlooks the point where the Nam River joins the Naktong. However, it has to deal with significant North Korean forces on its rear. It takes up positions across the North Korean supply route, forcing enemy troops to its west where, without additional supplies, they will need to maintain contact. After Hill 278 (Sibidang-san) has been bombarded all night, two battalions of the North Korean 13th Regiment, 6th Division, advance to within 150 yards of the UN position. Anti-personnel mines halt the advance but before long the defenders begin to run short of ammunition. Nevertheless, with the help of Charlie Company, 35th Infantry, Baker Company is able to hold the hill against several counterattacks.

Concerned over the North Korean penetration in the 2nd and 25th Infantry zones, General Walton Walker orders the 1st Cavalry to create a diversion for some of the enemy forces. The focus of the attack is Hill 518, five miles northeast of Waegwan. The attack is to occur in the morning of the next day.

Sergeant Charles W. T. Turner (USA) is posthumously awarded the Medal of Honor for services near Yongsan. First Lieutenant Frederick F. Henry (USA) is posthumously awarded the Medal of Honor for services near Am-Dong. Master Sergeant Ernest R. Kouma (USA) is awarded the Medal of Honor for actions taken near Agok. PFC Luther H. Story (USA) is posthumously awarded the Medal of Honor for service near Agok. Joseph R. Ovellette receives the Medal of Honor posthumously for action near Yongsan. David M. Smith is posthumously awarded the Medal of Honor for courageous activities near Yongsan.

SEA WAR: A U.S. Navy team under Lieutenant Eugene F. Clark commences Operation Trudy Jackson. The mission is to gather intelligence on Inchon and the surrounding waterways. The operation commences as Lieutenant Clark, some Royal Marines, and members of the South Korean police force arrive at the island of Yonghung-do. A small ROK army reconnaissance team goes ashore. Royal Marines and South Korean police retake Yonghung-do and Taemui-do, both located near Inchon, from the North Koreans.

AIR WAR: All the air power available, including heavy bombers, is directed to support the defensive fight at the Pusan Perimeter along the Naktong River. Planes from Task Force 77 provide close air support to those forces holding positions within the Perimeter.

In Operation Summit, a company of 228 marines is airlifted by 12 Sikorsky S-55 helicopters.

The 21st TCS airdrops rations and ammunition to UN troops that have been cut off.

September 2

EIGHTH ARMY: The breech caused by the North Korean advance, after the relief of the Wolfhounds at the Bowling Alley, allows two divisions of the NKPA offensive effort to drive through the ROK lines that run about 30 miles north of Yongchon. The NKPA 8th Division attacks from the northwest while the 15th Division is assaulting from the northeast. The ROK, however, fights the NKPA 8th Division to a halt near a region known as Hwajong. The NKPA 15th fights its way forward and reaches the city of Yongchon and then moves slightly south of it. They cut the roadway link with Pohang and Taegu.

At Naktong, the 9th Infantry continues the fight. Company Baker, with heavy weapons from Companies Dog and How, is on Hill 209 overlooking where a ferry crosses the Naktong River. The enemy continues the attack most of the night but fails to take the hill. Ammunition becomes a problem, and the infantry defenders strip the dead. When the North Koreans fail to get the hill, they bring in heavy mortar fire. Despite the effective artillery fire, the North Korean units are still unable to take the hill. At Yongsan, where the UN holds most of the hills, the North Koreans move forward (clad in white outfits) but fail to take the areas defended by Dog Company. Following that, the North Koreans launch a tank attack against Dog Company (2nd Engineers). The assault continues until 1100 when it is driven off. Four hours later Fox and George Companies, 9th Infantry, set off in a tank attack and retake the town. By evening most of the North Koreans have retreated.

In the Changnyong area, 2nd Infantry Division's 1st Battalion, 38th Infantry, while cut off, is ordered to hold and defend its positions astride a road the North Koreans need if they are to sustain any prolonged advance. The 35th Infantry Regiment holds its blocking position as one North Korean attack after another tries to dislodge it. Around midnight, 29 of the original 41 men are finally able to make it back to the George Company positions. On Hill 518, after nearly an hour of bombing, strafing, and napalm attacks by UN aircraft, the 1st Battalion, 7th Cavalry, attacks the hill, but it is held up just short of the crest. The attack has had little success right from the beginning, and the 7th Cavalry is ordered to pull out and move on to attack Hill 490 (in the Walled City area) from where NKPA artillery units are shelling them. In response, a renewed attack allows the North Koreans to overrun the 2nd Battalion, 8th Cavalry Regiment, on Hill 448, about two miles west of the Bowling Alley. The UN troops withdraw through the 3rd Battalion line at Tabu-dong.

King Company, 2nd Battalion, of Colonel Stephens' 21st Infantry, attacks northwest from Pohang-dong in an effort to help the ROK army recapture Hill 99; despite several tries they are unable to take the hill.

The 2nd Battalion, 5th Marines, arrives and is given the assignment to cover positions on the road leading to Yongsan.

As night approaches on September 2–3, 1950, the Communists delay the United Nations' aggressive plans when they attack and smash through the 9th Infantry line.

September 3

EIGHTH ARMY: Perhaps the most difficult day of defense along the Pusan Perimeter occurs as General Walton Walker faces five threats from the enemy. The NKPA breaks through at Pohang and cuts off the corridor between Taegu and Pohang. In the Pohang area North Korean forces launch a determined attack against the ROK army's Capital Division, driving it back so that the enemy can penetrate the east-west road three miles east of Anyang-ni. The Capital Division is basically collapsed. The break forces the ROK 18th Regiment on the left and the 17th Regiment on the right of Hill 334 to withdraw. To meet the attack, the 3rd Battalion, 9th Infantry, and batteries from the 15th Field Artillery Battalion, 865th Anti-Aircraft Artillery (AAA) Battalion, and 933rd AAA Battalion are put in support.

In the Naktong Bulge area, on Hill 209, enemy attacks are repulsed by Companies Baker, Dog, and How of the 9th Infantry Regiment.

At Yongsan, the 5th Marines advance about two miles while, to the north, the 38th Infantry takes on an enemy unit that crosses the Naktong and moves into the hills that overlook the command post. At dawn it is run off, though the fight for the base of the hills will go on for several days.

At Tabu-dong a North Korean unit supported by T-34 tanks attacks the 3rd Battalion. The attack moves toward the south but still manages to take the town, while another segment launches an attack on Hill 902. Aware that the North Korean position at Kasan gives the enemy a perfect view of UN behavior, Dog Company, 8th Combat Engineers, is sent to retake it. In preparation they move to the base of Hill 902. A coordinated attack against Hill 518 fails.

At Sibidang Mountain, an all-night fight occurs over positions lost by George Company, 3rd Platoon. The action comes to a standstill by dusk, at which time the 3rd Battalion holds the high ground along the Masan highway, called the "Horseshoe."

General Walker withdraws the 23rd and 27th Regiments to patch the line, and the NKPA 1st, 3rd, and 13th launch an attack against them. The size of the force used in this limited effort suggests that the NKPA is planning an even greater attack at the "bulge."

The NKPA is fighting in the mountains north of Taegu and makes penetrations to the south behind the 25th Infantry Division.

Master Sergeant Travis E. Watkins is posthumously awarded the Medal of Honor for service rendered near Yongsan.

In the afternoon, Company Able's platoon leaders work out a plan to take Hill 91. The plan is to feint an attack some 200 yards off and then allow all of Fox Company to circle around to the south and move up from the enemy's right. A delay in execution, however, means that the North Koreans had time to get back in the trenches after the artillery bombardment. Despite a determined enemy defense, the aggressors take their objective at 1630 and dig in, expecting immediate counterattacks.

SEA WAR: The carriers of Task Force 77 are required to withdraw from Pusan for replenishment at sea.

AIR WAR: Carrier-based marine planes provide close air support from Ashiya Air Force Base. Because of the withdrawal of TF 77 for replenishment in order to strike communications targets to the north, the FEAF is given all close air support assignments.

September 4

EIGHTH ARMY: The plans for Operation Chromite are finalized.

At Hill 209, the company defenders from Baker, Dog, and How hold out against repeated attacks. But as the afternoon passes, they are down to their last ammunition and decide to withdraw. At about 2000 hours, all those who are able to travel make it down off the hill and slip into the mountain areas to the east.

As daylight comes to the Anyang-ni area, George Company finds itself all alone and nearly surrounded. It holds its position until about 1600, when it withdraws from the town and relocates to the east, near the bridge over the Hyongsan River. The 2nd Battalion is fighting its way toward Kyongju but, after it destroys an enemy roadblock, it joins up with George Company. Once united they fight their way south toward Kyongju. As they withdraw, the North Koreans destroy three M-46 Patton tanks and establish roadblocks on the Kyongju–Anyang-ni road. Instead of heading for Kyongju the North Koreans turn to the east for the airfield at Yonil.

At the Naktong Bulge area, the North Koreans again attack the 9th Infantry, but are beaten back. The advance continues, however. The 5th Marines begin pulling back to Pusan. The 9th is eventually able to join up with the 38th Infantry to make contact with the 2nd Battalion at Changnyong. At Pohang, the North Koreans break through the ROK lines and take the town.

At Waegwan, the 1st Cavalry Division's 5th and 7th Regiments are ordered to withdraw to the south, leaving the town and the surrounding hills to the enemy.

At Kasan, the 8th Cavalry is attacked by the North Koreans as Dog Company, 8th Combat Engineer Battalion, holds its position on Hill 755. Easy Company, 2nd Battalion, 8th Cavalry, arrives at the summit of Hill 755 to support the engineers, but by early afternoon it is forced to withdraw.

Melvin L. Brown is posthumously awarded the Medal of Honor for action near Kasan.

By now enemy units have established road blocks along the Kyongju–Anyang-ni road, causing a two-mile gap between the ROK 3rd Division and its Capital Division. Late in the evening, the 9th Infantry moves on to higher ground next to the 3rd Battalion, 5th Marines, completing the "advance phase line." The 2nd Battalion, 5th Cavalry, attacks and captures Hill 303.

SEA WAR: U.S. Navy fighters shoot down a Soviet aircraft in the Yellow Sea and announce that a Soviet pilot was found in the plane.

The USS *McKean,* a destroyer, manages to blow up four mines.

Task Force 77 is approached by a Soviet bomber flying out of Port Arthur. Corsair fighters from USS *Valley Forge* (CV 45) intercept. The Soviet planes turn toward Korea and open fire. The F4U's return fire and shoot down the Soviet twin-engine plane. A destroyer picks up the body.

AIR WAR: The first of many rescue missions is undertaken to pick up a U.S. pilot from behind enemy lines. The mission is accomplished when Lieutenant Paul W. VanBoven rescues Captain Robert E. Wayne in an H-5 helicopter.

Three squadrons of C-119 Flying Boxcars arrive at Ashiya, Japan, for assignment to Korea.

Edward V. Laney, Jr., shoots down an enemy Ilyushin-4. He was flying an F-4U-4B from the 67th Fighter/Bomber Squadron.

September 5

POLITICAL/ADMINISTRATIVE: Pressured on every front and unable to get troops where he needs them most, General Walton Walker begins to consider a general withdrawal when, rather suddenly, it becomes apparent that the North Korean offensive drive is running out of energy. In nearly every section, half-hearted probes by the enemy are easily repulsed. The invader's supply lines have become far too long to maintain the attack.

EIGHTH ARMY: The British enter the battle for the first time when they join the defense of Taegu. The battle begins for the city of Yongchon, a significant transportation center, which is the last defense of the road between Taegu and Kyongju. The North Korean 15th Division starts the offensive as it sends a company against the 9th Infantry flank. The attack is unsuccessful, and most of the North Koreans are killed or wounded. The right flank of the area is held by the 21st Infantry Regiment; on the central front, however, the ROK's 8th Division collapses in the face of the NKPA main thrust.

Sergeant First Class Loren R. Kaufman, for actions taken near Yongsan, is posthumously awarded the Medal of Honor.

Marines of the 3rd Battalion, 5th Marines, successfully defend Hill 125 at the cost of 15 casualties.

The 2nd Battalion, 5th Cavalry, on Hill 303 is told to cover the 7th Cavalry withdrawal and then to pull off the hill.

SEA WAR: A twin-engine Russian bomber is shot down by aerial fire near the location of Task Force 77. Elements of the Inchon attack force sail from Yokohama.

September 5–13

EIGHTH ARMY: Near dawn the North Korean 15th Division follows up on its strike at the ROK 8th Division north of Yongchon. Moving through the center front, the NKPA reaches the edge of town. On September 6, the North Korean troops forced the ROK army units to retreat west of the Kumho River. On September 7, however, the 19th Regiment of the ROK's 6th Division recaptures the town. Heavy fighting continues for several days, with the town changing hands four times. A major coun-

A T-6 Mosquito observer plane waits to gas-up as rocket is fired in the distance. *(Center for the Study of the Korean War, Graceland University)*

terattack is launched on September 10, and the North Korean forces withdraw. By the 13th, all the territory taken by the enemy has been retaken.

September 6

POLITICAL/ADMINISTRATIVE: The U.S. Congress approves a fiscal budget that includes more than $13 billion for defense. As a result of Operation Flushout, calling in soldiers from Japan and reassigning a part of those troops for replacement duty in Korea, 229 officers and 2,201 enlisted men are reassigned.

EIGHTH ARMY: In the battle for Yongchon, the NKPA 15th Division moves into town, forcing the 8th ROK Division to retreat to the west bank of the Kumho River. The NKPA moves on to take control of the railroad station. Commander Yu Jai Hyung, ROK II Corps, releases the 19th Regiment from the 16th Division and the 11th Regiment from the 1st Division, in addition to five tanks from the 1st Cavalry Division. The North Koreans also advance against and occupy Hill 570, which overlooks the Taegu Road. At the same time, the North Koreans establish a roadblock just three miles south of Tabu-dong. By mid-afternoon, the roadblock is destroyed and the hills cleared of North Koreans. The Eighth Army headquarters is withdrawn to Pusan.

At dawn the marines who were in defense of Hill 125 are pulled out and follow the rest of the brigade out of the Pusan area.

Hill 303 is turned over to the enemy after 2nd Battalion, 5th Cavalry, is ordered to withdraw.

The 3rd Battalion, 8th Cavalry Regiment, is ordered to take Hill 334, located about 2,200 yards from Hill 418. By the end of the day, and after two attempts, they clear the hill. During the night, there are two counterattacks, but the defenders are able to hold.

X Corps: Pulled out of the fighting at Pusan, the 1st Marine Brigade, now assigned to X Corps, prepares for debarkation.

Air War: Aircraft, including the T-6 Mosquitoes of the 6147th Tactical Control Squadron, are moved southward to Pusan as North Korean forces approach Taegu.

September 7

Eighth Army: Hill 464 is deserted by George Company, 7th Cavalry, which moves to Hill 380 to join the rest of the battalion. Together they withdraw to the southwest to an area held by the 5th Cavalry Regiment. The 1st Cavalry Division, lacking the 1st Battalion, is ordered, along with the 1st ROK Division, to retake Kasan.

At the Kyongju-Yongchon Road, the 21st Infantry, 24th Infantry Division, is attacking up the road when it comes to a halt about noon after it has advanced several miles. An ROK battalion relieves the 21st Infantry.

At Battle Mountain and Sobuk Mountain, North Korean artillery and mortars probe but are turned back. Early in the morning a battalion of North Koreans drives the ROK and American defenders from Battle Mountain. The 3rd Battalion, 27th Infantry, is ordered to retake it.

The 1st Provisional Marine Brigade is withdrawn from combat at the Naktong Perimeter and regroups at Pusan in the first stage of preparation for the Inchon invasion.

Air War: Twenty-four B-29s of 22nd Bomber Command attack the ironworks at Chongjin in the extreme northeast corner of North Korea. There is an increased effort to cut the enemy supply lines as the North Korean offensive slows for lack of a steady source of replacements and materiel.

September 8

Political/Administrative: The Defense Production Act passes Congress. It gives President Harry Truman broad discretionary powers over the economy.

The NKPA loses one of its most significant leaders when a land mine kills Lieutenant General Kang Kon.

Eighth Army: On Battle Mountain, the 27th Infantry fails to recapture the hill in a battle that will continue until September 14.

At Waegwan, the 5th Cavalry is forced out of its position three miles east of the town and retreats to Hills 203 and 174. While the enemy advance is stopped at that point, the battle will continue for several days, with each side winning and losing.

The 3rd Battalion of the 8th Cavalry launches a drive against Hill 570; while they are able to take a good portion of the base, the crest remains in North Korean hands.

The North Koreans launch a fierce attack against the 23rd Infantry defending the area around Changnyong. In the fighting that follows, the 23rd holds on to its position and wreaks havoc on the North Korean 2nd Infantry Division.

During the night, King Company, 3rd Battalion, 19th Infantry, is hit by enemy forces that manage to drive them from Hill 300.

SEA WAR: Elements of the 1st Marine Brigade begin to load at Pusan for the amphibious assault against Inchon.

Lieutenant Eugene Clark, with members of the Royal Marines and irregulars, retakes Taemuui-do. Several other small islands in the Flying Fish area are taken by members of the National Police. The North Koreans are aware that Clark and his men are there, and launch a few counterattacks, but there is no serious effort to drive them from the islands.

AIR WAR: The 18th Fighter-Bomber Group, which had been removed to Japan, returns to Tongnae, Pusan East.

September 9

POLITICAL/ADMINISTRATIVE: The Chinese Military Committee orders the 9th Army Corps near Shanghai and the 19th Army Corps in the northwest to congregate along the railway lines in order to move quickly when called on. While no final decision has been made, the Chinese are obviously redirecting their fighting units from a focus on Taiwan and bringing them closer to the war in Korea.

EIGHTH ARMY: In the east, the North Korean military takes up positions on three sides of Yonil Air Field. To take back the area, Task Force Davidson is established. The unit includes elements of the 19th Infantry, the 3rd Battalion of the 9th Infantry, the 9th Regimental Tank Company, two batteries of antiaircraft weapons, Able Company, 3rd Combat Engineer Battalion, and parts of several other groups. Task Force Davidson departs Kyongju around dawn and arrives at a small hamlet just south of Yonil.

During the night, ROK troops attack and take Hill 131 in the culmination of an advance eight or nine miles up the road toward Yongchon.

At Taegu, the 1st Cavalry Division is driven back in all sectors. But the 8th Combat Engineer Battalion, holding the bridge across the Kumho River near the Naktong, and the 1st ROK Division, defending the hills to the east of Yongchon, are able to hold.

After the North Korean 3rd Division forces the 1st Battalion, 5th Cavalry, off Hill 345 west of Waegwan, it moves forward to attack Hill 203. The enemy unit is able to take the hill. Efforts at a counterattack are not successful.

On Hill 300, the 3rd Battalion, 19th Infantry, makes a second effort to take the crest, but the North Korean defenders are able to hold the hill.

AIR WAR: Medium bombers concentrate on rail and marshaling yards in an interdiction campaign that is launched north of Seoul. The effort is extended in the hope that it will slow the movement of enemy reinforcements.

Bomber Command sends its planes to cut the rails at numerous points along the major routes to interrupt enemy movement.

September 10

POLITICAL/ADMINISTRATIVE: General Douglas MacArthur is informed that he is no longer to authorize bombing the city of Rashin because of the political implications involved. Rashin is so close to the Soviet Union that there is a fear that any mistakes that might be made would encourage the Russians to enter the war. On the other hand, Rashin is a major supply center from which ammunition is distributed. A major disruption at Rashin would speed victory.

EIGHTH ARMY: At Yongchon, the ROK begins to regroup and six regiments are sent into an attack along all fronts. An ROK training battalion holds Hill 321, southeast of Hill 570, against the North Koreans. The untried unit is able to prevent the Communists from breaking through. In the meantime confusion reigns as the 8th Cavalry tries to take Hill 570 and fails. North of Kyongju an ROK unit and the 3rd Battalion, 19th Infantry, complete a weeklong battle to take Hill 300.

On this date, for action at Kasan, Corporal Gordon M. Craig (USA) receives the Medal of Honor, posthumously.

SEA WAR: The first in a series of air raids begins against Wolmi-do in Flying Fish Channel, as carrier-based Corsairs begin dumping thousands of tons of napalm. The AMS of MinDiv 51 heads for Wonsan.

Elements of the Inchon Attack Force sail from Kobe.

AIR WAR: The need for better coordination of close air support is emphasized by the unexpected withdrawal of the planes of Carrier Force 77. The air force lacked the resources to cover all the assignments. It soon became apparent that when there were more requests than could be handled by the Fifth Air Force, the extra needs should be coordinated through the commander of Naval Forces Far East. In an effort to solve the confusion, General Douglas MacArthur orders all close air support requests to be routed through Fifth Air Force headquarters.

September 11

POLITICAL/ADMINISTRATIVE: Major General Frank W. Milburn assumes command of I Corps, replacing Major General John B. Coulter.

EIGHTH ARMY: The prolonged battle for Hill 300 comes to an end when a regiment of the ROK's 3rd Division finally captures the hill. After the crest is taken, the 3rd Battalion, 19th Infantry, relieves the ROK on the hill. During the prolonged fight for Hill 300, the 3rd Battalion has lost eight lieutenants and 29 enlisted men.

X CORPS: The main body of the amphibious task force puts to sea a day ahead of schedule, after being pounded by the 125 mph winds of Typhoon Jane. In a calculated risk, Admiral J. H. Doyle orders the Transport Movement Group at Kobe to put to sea. He and his staff leave aboard USS *Mount McKinley* (AGC 7). The 7th Infantry Division sails from Yokohama to Korea.

September 12

POLITICAL/ADMINISTRATIVE: Secretary of Defense Louis A. Johnson resigns, to be replaced by General George C. Marshall. Johnson, who had once considered running for the presidency, has been controversial since the moment of his appointment and leaves the government bitter over his experiences.

The Women's Temperance Union stops the army "beer ration."

Major General John B. Coulter relieves Major General Frank Milburn as commanding officer of IX Corps.

EIGHTH ARMY: The day when the North Korean offensive ends. After months of continuous fighting, the North Korean 12th Division has been virtually destroyed. As it begins to retreat, it is followed and harassed by the ROK's Capital Division. The North Korean units that have been on the attack heading for Yongchon has been stopped and were in full retreat. The ROK is finally able to seal the breech created in the line by probing North Korean forces. Their success at Yongchon aids UN Command in its advance following the Inchon invasion.

Hill 314 is attacked and in a bloody battle is secured by 8th Cavalry Regiment, supported by 3rd Battalion, 7th Cavalry.

The ROK's Division moves forward in the direction of Kasan.

Hill 482 is bombed and napalmed by South African F-51s. Following up, the 2nd Battalion, 19th Infantry, is able to secure the hill by 1200.

The 3rd ROK Division takes the offensive and occupies the towns to the west of Pohang. At the same time the Capital Division advances on Kigye.

The 2nd Battalion of the 5th Cavalry joins with the 1st Battalion in an effort to take Hill 174 from the North Koreans. After the enemy puts up a stiff defense, they finally drive them back from the ridge that includes Hills 179, 175, and 174. In this fight, First Lieutenant Samuel S. Coursen, a platoon leader, performs in such a manner as later to be awarded the Medal of Honor.

The order is given to move through the 8th Cavalry lines and take Hill 314, a location some call the key to Taegu. For the first 500 yards, Love Company, 3rd Battalion, 7th Cavalry, which is leading the attack, is able to move forward with only slight resistance. Then, in a quick reverse, a counterattack halts forward movement. An air strike is called in; after the bombardment the battalion moves ahead. A few men gain the crest but are pushed off again. On the third attack, and after another air strike, the hill is secured at 1530.

X CORPS: The organization of X Corps is completed under the command of Major General Edward M. Almond. The Corps consists of the 1st Marine Division and the 7th Infantry Division. X Corps had originally gone to Japan as a part of the U.S. occupation force and was deactivated on January 31, 1946. The command is reinstated for the Inchon landing.

The Advance Attack Group heads out from Pusan with the 5th Marine Battalion, recently refitted after the Battle of the Pusan Bulge. The plan for the landing at Inchon includes two regiments of the 1st Marine Division (the 7th Regiment has not yet arrived), the U.S. 7th Infantry Division, 21 air squadrons, amphibious engineers, and logistics and underwater demolition teams. All the invaders are Americans.

Sergeant Frederick W. Mausert III (USMC) is posthumously awarded the Medal of Honor for services performed at Songnap-yong. First Lieutenant Samuel S. Coursen is posthumously awarded the Medal of Honor for actions near Kaesong.

SEA WAR: The UN Blockade and Escort Force (Task Force 95) is organized. It is composed of the West Coast Group (95.1), East Coast Group (95.2), the Minesweeping

Group (95.6), and the Republic of Korea Navy (95.7). The force includes ships from several nations.

AIR WAR: Navy planes from Task Force 77 continue their attacks on both the island of Wolmi and the nearby harbor at Inchon.

PARTISANS: A diversionary landing is made at Kunsan, a small port about 50 miles south of Inchon, in hope of distracting the defense of Inchon. The raiders, made up of partisans, British commandos, and 1st GHQ Raider Company, land on Robb Island, make a lot of noise, and then withdraw about dawn.

September 13

POLITICAL/ADMINISTRATIVE: The 1st Marine Provisional Brigade is formally deactivated and absorbed by 1st Marine Division for the Inchon landing.

EIGHTH ARMY: The ROK has regained lost territory in the Battle of Yongchon, and in a series of attacks, they are able to push the line more than 11 miles north of the Yongchon-Pohang road.

Between midnight and 0400, the North Koreans attack and take Hill 174 from Love Company of the 5th Cavalry. The area had been won only the night before. In a counterattack launched in the afternoon, the 5th is unable to retake the position.

X CORPS: In the Inchon Approach, all the islands other than Wolmi-do (attached to Inchon by a causeway), Yongchong-do (about three miles west of Wolmi-do), and the lighthouse island of Palmi-do are in UN hands.

SEA WAR: Douglas Skyraiders continue to attack the island of Wolmi-do. The destroyers USS *Mansfield* (DD 728), *DeHaven* (DD 727), *Lyman K. Swenson* (DD 729), *Collett* (DD 730), *Gurke* (DD 783), and *Henderson* (DD 785), in addition to the United Kingdom's HMS *Jamaica* and *Kenya* and the cruisers USS *Rochester* (CA 124) and USS *Toledo* (CA 133), move up the narrow Flying Fish Channel toward Inchon. The *Swenson* is damaged by two near-misses, during which one man is killed and one wounded. The *Gurke* receives minor damage from three hits but with no casualties. The *Collett* is hit by seven shells that wound five of the crew.

Remaining elements of the Inchon Attack Force sail from Pusan.

AIR WAR: The fury of typhoon Kezia, which hits southern Japan hard, limits nearly all air operations and requires some aircraft to move to Pusan and Taegu.

September 14

EIGHTH ARMY: In an exchange of hills, the 8th Cavalry launches an attack and takes part of Hill 570. The ROK 1st Division takes Hill 755; south of Kasan advance elements of the South Korean division enter the Walled City at the crest.

Item Company of the 5th Cavalry tries once again to take Hill 174, which has now changed hands three times. During the fight they suffer 82 casualties, but, by its conclusion, they have managed to take and hold at least one side of the hill.

SEA WAR: The naval bombardment continues from ships in Flying Fish Channel.

The USS *Missouri* (BB 63) arrives in Korea just in time to join USS *Helena* (CA 75), three destroyers, and a minesweeper in battering the port of Samchok on the Sea of Japan.

The Transport and Tracker Group approaches the invasion objective, and carrier-borne aircraft are on call along the entire west coast of South Korea.

September 15

EIGHTH ARMY: The UN defensive campaign ends. Heavy fighting continues north and west of Taegu as the 1st Cavalry Division holds against enemy counterattacks. To the south, seesaw fighting continues at Sibidang Mountain, Battle Mountain, and the Sobuk Mountain area west of the city of Munsan-ni. The North Korean advance is stopped along the mountains near Yongchon.

X CORPS: At 0508 hours, USS *Mt. McKinley* (AGC 7), the command ship, hoists the U.S. Navy signal "Land the landing force." Operation Chromite begins as the first elements of X Corps (70,000 men) land on the beaches of Wolmi-do and Inchon. The first wave of Marines lands on the north arm of Wolmi-do almost unopposed. Once Wolmi-do is secure, the 3rd Marines take up defensive positions. At 1500 hours, the 5th Marines land on the mainland against resistance centered at the seawall. Within half an hour, however, and despite the opposition, Cemetery Hill is taken. The 5th Marines land on the right side of Red Beach. By midnight all first-day objectives have been taken.

For action during the Inchon landing, First Lieutenant Baldomero Lopez (USMC) is posthumously awarded the Medal of Honor.

Item Company is given the task of taking Observation Charlie, the seaward tip of Hill 233.

SEA WAR: Shortly after midnight, the Gunfire Support Group begins a 45-minute naval and air bombardment of Inchon. At 0633, the first troops are ashore.

The USS *Missouri* (BB 63) continues the bombardment of Samchok.

The aircraft carrier USS *Boxer* (CV 21) reports for duty with Task Force 77.

Minesweepers sweep the inner anchorages of Inchon harbor but find no mines.

AIR WAR: USN and USMC carrier-based planes provide air cover during the amphibious assault.

FEAF raids in South Korea prepare for the Eighth Army's breakout from the Pusan Perimeter.

Air Group Three under Commander W. F. Madden comes onboard USS *Leyte* (CV 32).

PARTISANS: At Changsha, about 20 miles north of Pohang, a second landing is taking place. The Miryang Guerrilla Battalion, which is made up primarily of men from North Korea, is ordered to set up a roadblock on the only supply road available for the North Korean 3rd Division. At first the landing is successful, but by noon the partisans are forced to withdraw.

September 16

EIGHTH ARMY: The UN offensive campaign begins. The breakout from the Naktong Perimeter begins slowly as Eighth Army tries to advance along several fronts. Four U.S. divisions—the 1st Cavalry, 2nd Infantry, 24th Infantry, and 25th Infantry—participate. The 15th Regiment, 1st ROK Division, advances to the Walled City north of Taegu. To the south, the U.S. 2nd Cavalry Division begins to advance on the city of Waegwan. In the Masan area, however, the 25th Infantry Division is under attack and cannot get started.

In the continuing battle for Hill 174, the 1st Battalion of the 5th Cavalry Regiment attacks the North Korean–held hill, but the UN troops are no more successful.
X Corps: The marines leave Cemetery Hill and head for Seoul. They pass through the southern sections of Inchon where the KMC is mopping up. The North Koreans attempt a counterattack when 16 T-34 tanks move down the main road to Inchon to challenge the United Nations Forces. All of the Korean tanks are destroyed either by marine Corsair strikes or marine Pershing tanks, in one of the few tank-to-tank battles of the war. By midnight, the 5th Marines hold the forward positions overlooking the Seoul highway west of Ascom City.

At 1900 hours, Baker Company approaches its assignment—Hill 233. Within a few minutes, they take the western slope of the hill. Then the 2nd Platoon of How Company passes through the Item Company line to reach the summit of Hill 233.
Sea War: With the coming of the early tide, all available LSTs are retracted, beginning the placement of 15,000 men, 1,500 vehicles, and 1,200 short tons of supplies. LSTs *799, 857, 859, 883, 898, 914, 973,* and *975* are all awarded the Navy Unit Citation for their action at Inchon.

September 16–27
Eighth Army: The battle of the Naktong Perimeter breaks out. Eighth Army pushes out of the perimeter as the 1st Cavalry Division and the 2nd, 24th and 25th Infantry Divisions participate. It is estimated that casualties will be 790 U.S. KIA with 3,544 WIA.

September 17
Political/Administrative: General Oliver Smith, as landing force commander, is ordered to establish civilian control in the city of Inchon.
Eighth Army: At Masan, a battalion task force from 35th Infantry Regiment, 25th Division, attacks the North Koreans at Battle Mountain but fails to take the area.

At Pusan, the area to the east of the Naktong River, known as the Bulge, is retaken by elements of the 2nd Infantry Division who take Oblong-ri. By evening, the areas captured in the early August assault are retaken. The North Koreans are moving out quickly and are making no efforts to counterattack.

Once again trying to take the North Korean–held Hill 174, the 1st Battalion of the 5th Cavalry and the 2nd Battalion of the 7th Cavalry join up in an unsuccessful attempt to get to the crest of the hill.
X Corps: The 7th Infantry Division begins to debark at Inchon and prepares to advance toward Suwon. Marines move rapidly toward Kimpo Airfield, reaching the southern edge by afternoon. The 1st Marines advance along the Seoul highway toward Yongdungpo and, after a clash with a North Korean regiment, halt at Sosa-ri.

PFC Walter C. Monegan (USMC) is posthumously awarded the Medal of Honor for action near Sosa-ri.

Just before dawn, the advance platoon of Dog Company, 5th Marines, spots six T-34 tanks and their accompanying infantry. Bazooka teams knock out one of the tanks, and the other five are quickly set on fire by M-26s and recoilless rifles. By night most of Kimpo Airfield has been taken and the UN assault on the city of Seoul begins.

SEA WAR: HMS *Jamaica* shoots down one of two single-engine YAK fighters that attack USS *Rochester* (CA 124).

Task Force 77 flies 304 sorties, destroying more than 200 vehicles north of Inchon.

Two YAK fighters from North Korea make a rare appearance and catch USS *Rochester* (CA 124) and HMS *Jamaica* unaware. A Royal Navy seaman is killed and others wounded in the strafing attacks.

On the east coast, the ROK army crosses the Hyongsan with the support of 298 16-inch shells launched from USS *Missouri* (BB 63).

AIR WAR: The Fifth Air Force's F-51s and F-80s drop napalm in support of the Eighth Army offensive. Reports indicate that more than 1,200 enemy soldiers are killed. The FEAF begins to drop four million psychological warfare leaflets calling for the enemy troops to surrender.

PARTISANS: The attempted landing at Changsan is a failure and the battalion is withdrawn by ships of Task force 77.

In an effort to secure Tokchok Island in the Inchon approach, Operation Lee uses two YEMS to put a 110-man force ashore.

September 18

EIGHTH ARMY: The ROK's 3rd Infantry Division attacks and recaptures the east coast port of Pohang.

Coming out of the Pusan Perimeter, elements of the 2nd Division cross the Naktong and find the high ground clear. The North Koreans are pulling back.

The 2nd Battalion takes Hill 206 after a long fight.

Near Waegwan, the 5th RCT and the 5th and 7th Cavalry Regiments fight bloody battles on Hills 174, 188, and 903 (Kasan). All attempts fail as the North Koreans fight a desperate battle.

To the east, the ROK's 1st Division forces a gap in the North Korean lines and moves forward to the Tabu-dong-Kunwi road, only 10 miles from Tabu-dong. The 27th Infantry-tank force once more drives toward Battle Mountain but is unable to take the hill from its defenders.

After several days of trying, the 1st Battalion, 5th Cavalry, is finally able to take Hill 203 from the defending North Koreans.

X CORPS: Kimpo Airfield and its surrounding villages are occupied and secured by 1000 hours, and Objective Dog (Hill 131), which is the high point overlooking the Han River north

A helicopter delivering supplies to forward areas *(Center for the Study of the Korean War, Graceland University)*

of the airfield, is taken by 1145. During the evening, ROK marines move up to take their positions near the 5th Marines. The 1st Marines go around Sosa-ri, seize Hill 123, and continue their advance toward Yongdungpo, despite taking heavy losses from enemy artillery fire.

The 7th Infantry Division's 32nd Infantry Regiment lands at Inchon and moves along the Seoul highway to join the marines.

SEA WAR: The British ship HMS *Kenya* delivers 300 six-inch shells on Hill 123, where the North Koreans are dug in. The North Korean forces counterattack, starting with a long mortar barrage.

AIR WAR: An HO3S-1 helicopter is the first American plane to land at Kimpo Airfield since the retreat.

Bombers of the 92nd and 98th Bomber Group, a total of more than 40 B-29s, hit the marshaling yards near Waegwan, where 1,600 bombs are dropped. The effort destroys enemy troop concentrations that are blocking the Eighth Army offensive.

PARTISANS: Survivors from the Miryang Guerrilla Battalion are pulled off the beach of Changsan, on the east coast, by the U.S. Navy.

In support of Operation Lee, on Tokchok, HMCS *Athabaskan* backs up the effort and the island is secured.

September 19

EIGHTH ARMY: Eighth Army finally crosses the Naktong River. Serious delay arises at the crossing of the Kumho River near Taegu, primarily from enemy positions across the river on Hill 174. By midnight most units are across. Hills 253 and 300 are still occupied by North Korean troops who hang on as long as they can, until elements of the 7th Cavalry take them both. After several days of trying, and supported by an air strike called in on Hill 174, the attacking battalion finally succeeds in capturing it but they do not take Hill 371, a mile north. The fall of Waegwan allows the attack to continue up the Waegwan-Tabu-dong road.

In the face of mounting pressure, the North Koreans abandon Battle Mountain sometime during the night. The 24th Infantry occupies the mountain while the 35th Infantry advances toward Chungam-ni.

The 10th Philippine Infantry Battalion Combat Team arrives in Pusan.

Sergeant William R. Jecelin (USA) is posthumously awarded the Medal of Honor for actions near Saga. Captain John W. Collier (USA) is posthumously awarded the Medal of Honor for actions near Chindong-ni.

X CORPS: The 5th Marines have now cleared the entire south bank of the Han River.

General Douglas MacArthur visits the front-line troops.

The 5th Marine Regiment reaches its assigned positions on the south side of the river with little resistance, thus occupying the high ground on Hills 118, 80, and 85. Late that night a patrol crosses the Han River eight miles west of Seoul. Just before midnight, eight LVPs start across the Han but North Korean mortars and machine guns open up immediately, causing them to withdraw.

The Third Logistical Command is activated in Japan to provide logistical support to X Corps.

The 32nd Infantry Regiment of the 7th Infantry Division takes its place with the 1st Marines on the south side of the Seoul highway. In the meantime, the rest of 7th

Division is landing at Inchon. The marines continue their attack and advance to Kalchon Creek just west of Yongdungpo.

Just before dawn, the marines discover that the North Koreans are moving on to Hills 80 and 85. It is not an attack because the NKPA, having discovered that the hills were unoccupied, simply moved in.

SEA WAR: In the continuation of Operation Lee, Yonghung-do, an island located in the Inchon approach, is finally taken. On the afternoon of this date, the marines move beyond the range of the guns on the light cruisers and destroyers, and USS *Missouri* (BB 63) is made available for fire missions.

AIR WAR: The Fifth Air Force flies a series of close air support missions to cover the 24th Division crossing at the Naktong River near Waegwan.

Thirty-two C-54s and C-110s of Cargo Combat Command transport 208 tons of equipment and supplies to Kimpo Airfield.

September 20

EIGHTH ARMY: The 3rd ROK Division, on the east coast, captures Pohang and then moves on toward Hungnam. The 35th Infantry takes the high ground overlooking Chungam-ni. By midnight the 1st and 2nd Battalions are across the Naktong and on the move toward Waegwan.

During the day, the British 27th Brigade crosses the river and, in the south, the 24th Infantry Division crosses at the Sangpo ferry site. By noon the 24th Infantry has captured Hill 227, the dominant terrain feature. After losing Hill 303 on September 6, the 2nd Battalion, 5th Regimental Combat Team, now moving through the area east of the Naktong River, is able to attack and retake Hill 303.

X CORPS: The 1st Marine Division crosses the Han River on LVTs with little to no resistance. The Baker Ferry, set up by Baker Company, First Shore Party Battalion, establishes a supply route across the Han. It is reinforced by elements of the 7th Infantry Division, ROK army units, and the 7th Marine Regiment that arrived too late for the invasion.

On the south side of the Han River, Able Company, 1st Marines, takes up positions on Hill 118, but is unable to prevent the North Koreans from occupying Hills 80 and 85. Shortly before dawn, however, they launch a counterattack that allows them to take Hills 80 and 85. In response, a battalion-sized North Korean force comes out of Yongdungpo, headed by five T-34 tanks, and engages the marines east of the city. In the battle most of the North Korean force is annihilated. By 1000 hours, the marines occupy the ground west of the city. The 7th Infantry Division protects the flanks, with the 32nd Infantry Regiment capturing Tongdok Mountain two miles south of Yongdungpo.

For action near Yongdungpo, Second Lieutenant Henry A. Commiskey (USMC) is awarded the Medal of Honor.

SEA WAR: A landing party from HMCS *Athabaskan* destroys the radio gear at Palmi-do lighthouse.

The USS *Missouri*'s (BB 63) guns are unable to reach Seoul and it is released for other assignments.

AIR WAR: Using night-lighting equipment flown in the previous day, Combat Cargo Command expands the Kimpo airlift to an around-the-clock operation.

Supporting the marines, B-29s attack three barracks in and around Pyongyang, where reinforcements are collecting.

September 21
POLITICAL/ADMINISTRATIVE: General George C. Marshall is sworn in as U.S. secretary of state, the only military officer, to that time, to hold the office.
EIGHTH ARMY: At Waegwan, the 3rd Battalion, 5th Regimental Combat Team, is relieved of its hold on Hill 300 and crosses over the Naktong before dark.

To the northeast of Waegwan, the 1st and 3rd Battalions advance to the Tabu-dong-Taegu highway. The ROK 1st Division advances south and is able to prevent the enemy from withdrawing in that direction. The North Korean 1st, 3rd, and 13th Divisions are cut off at Kasan.

The 35th Infantry captures Chungam-ni and the "Notch," then advances past the Muchon-ni road to the high ground at Chinju Pass. The enemy is in full retreat to the west.
X CORPS: Elements of the 1st Marine Division continue to cross the Han River. North Korean troops try another counterattack with a drive against ROK and marine units northeast of Kimpo. The effort at a counterattack is driven back by highly accurate naval gunfire.

Joint Task Force 7 is dissolved and operational control of the advance party is given to Major General Almond at 1700, when, in a small ceremony, the Commander of X Corps establishes his headquarters at Inchon. Command at Inchon receives word of a pending counterattack by the North Koreans but the attack never materializes.

At dawn the 32nd Infantry Regiment takes Copper Mine Hill and the 7th Division Reconnaissance Company arrives at Anyang-ni.
AIR WAR: Marine aircraft begin to fly sorties from Kimpo Airfield.

Combat Cargo Command, flying C-119s, initiates the airdrop of food and supplies to UN troops on the front line. T-6 spotters prevent an ambush of the advancing 24th Infantry Division when they call in air and artillery strikes on a group of 30 enemy tanks lying in wait of the advance.

In another incident Combat Cargo Command, with C-54s, airlifts more than 65 tons of rations to the recently captured airfield at Suwon, south of Seoul.
SEA WAR: Naval gunfire, primarily from the cruisers USS *Toledo* (CA 133) and *Rochester* (CA 124), is put to maximum use against targets in the Kimpo area.

September 22
POLITICAL/ADMINISTRATIVE: Omar Bradley, chairman of the Joint Chiefs of Staff since August 1949, is promoted to General of the Army (five stars).

The Chinese Foreign Office announces that China will stand in defense of North Korea and not allow it to be occupied by the Americans. Little notice is taken of this latest Chinese pronouncement.

EIGHTH ARMY: The 1st Battalion, Argyll and Sutherland Highlanders, moves across the Naktong River to support the left flank of the new offensive against North Korean forces. At the Pusan area, the 1st Battalion, 23rd Infantry, is counterattacked on the Siban-ni road. The battle ends in a stalemate.

To the north, the 38th Infantry takes Chogye.

The Walled City on Kasan (Hill 903) is taken by the ROK's 1st Division and units of the National Police. The units then move out to continue cleaning out pockets of resistance.

On the east coast, the ROK Capital Division takes Kigye as its 3rd Division captures Hungham.

A task force composed of units from the Cavalry Division drives toward the river crossing at Sonsan Ferry and on to Kaktong-ni where it discovers hundreds of enemy soldiers and vehicles. The concentration is attacked, and as a result, a large number of casualties are inflicted on the enemy force.

X CORPS: The 1st Marine Regiment runs into resistance from the NKPA 18th Division before it reaches the Han. Approaching from the west, Seoul is assaulted by marines who run into strong NKPA resistance. At this time, the 1st Marine Division issues the plan for the capture of Seoul. The marines are to attack across the Han River and deploy north. Shortly after midnight, T-34 tanks attack the 7th Division Reconnaissance Company three miles south of Suwon. Later in the afternoon, the 7th Division's 31st Regiment arrives at Suwon Airfield. A discussion between General Walker and General MacArthur results in scrapping the plan to invade at Kunsan in favor of the breakout at Pusan. An earlier consideration had anticipated a second amphibious landing but at this point it has become unnecessary.

AIR WAR: B-29s drop flares over rail lines to light the landscape so following B-26s can locate and destroy enemy trains traveling at night.

Flying a Mosquito (T-6), Lieutenant George W. Nelson flies over a group of about 200 enemy soldiers. He drops a note telling them to surrender to the nearest UN troops, and they do so. The connection between the two events has not really been established.

September 23

EIGHTH ARMY: By 0900, the Argyll achieve their objective and take over a series of abandoned enemy gun positions. Late in the day they and the Sutherland Highlanders come under friendly fire as a flight of three USAF P-51 Mustangs pours streams of 20-mm shells on the hill. After three passes, the planes return and drop napalm on the Argyll position; the commander, Major Kenneth Muir, tries to wave them off. After the unfortunate attack, what is left of the battalion is still able to fight off the North Korean aggression that follows.

The 2nd Battalion, 23rd Infantry Regiment, crosses the Naktong River and passes through the stalled 3rd Battalion to take Siban-ni after a hard fight. The 1st Battalion passes through and takes Chogye. The 1st Battalion, 7th Cavalry, advances to Songju, which has been abandoned by the North Koreans.

IX Corps becomes operational at Miryang under Lieutenant General John B. Coulter, with the 2nd Infantry and 25th Infantry Divisions.

Sweden's Red Cross field hospital arrives in Pusan.

By this date, the North Korean People's Army is retreating all along the Pusan Perimeter.

Elements of the North Korean 1st Division force the 8th Cavalry's I & R Platoon, and a detachment of South Korean police, off the crest of Hill 902 (Ka-Kan). The 1st Cavalry is ordered to counterattack, capture Hill 902, and hold it. As they approach, they come under heavy fire from adjacent Hill 755 and so believe it best to take that hill first. They make progress at first but are unable to take the hill. Feeling they have slowed, if not stopped the artillery, the I & R Platoon returns to Hill 902. Easy Company is joined by Dog Company, but the two units are still unable to dislodge the defenders. General Hobart Gay finally orders 8th Cavalry to call back its men. Unfortunately, Easy Company does not get the message; by the time they are able to head back, the unit has suffered significant casualties.

X Corps: The 1st Korean Marine Battalion attacks Hill 104 to straighten out the line. It makes a valiant effort but the attack is stopped cold. The 1st Battalion, 32nd Infantry, captures Hill 290, a high point that dominates the southeastern approaches to Seoul. The 2nd Battalion of the 32nd Regiment takes the hills south of the railroad. North of the Han River, U.S. and ROK marines attack Hills 66 and 88, which are standing in the way of their advance on the capital. However, only small gains are made.

Sea War: Intelligence reports that more than 3,500 new enemy mines have been sown in Korean waters. Sweeping operations begin immediately.

Air War: SB-17s of the 3rd ARC play a significant role in the first special operations mission of the Korean War.

Fifth Air Force Headquarters is moved from Pusan to Taegu.

September 24

Eighth Army: The 27th Infantry advances toward Chinju along the southern coast road, and the 35th moves forward to the Nam River. Near Suwon the 31st Infantry, located two miles from the city, defeats a North Korean counterattack. In a double envelopment the 23rd Infantry and 38th Infantry hit Hyopch'on from two directions. Enemy survivors of the attack, in trying to escape, move through a preregistered kill zone and more than 300 men are lost.

The 24th Infantry Division fights a well dug-in enemy as it advances up the Taegu-Taejon highway. The advance is finally stopped just short of Kimchon. The 1st Cavalry Division's point is stopped at Songju to allow the division to catch up.

The 25th Infantry Division's 35th Infantry attacks across the Nam River, taking Chinju.

The 187th Airborne Regimental Combat Team arrives at Kimpo from Japan.

X Corps: The marines continue to attack against the hills. The 2nd and 3rd Battalions join when they reach the base of Hill 66. There they run into enemy forces that occupy the lower trenches. After being supported by an air strike, an attack group of about 35 men moves to the top, driving the North Koreans off. The survivors repel several counterattacks. The engagement cost, 176 casualties among the original 206 men.

The marines move against Hill 79, which is located in the southwest section of Seoul itself. After dealing with some small-arms fire, the marines take the hill at 1500. **PARTISANS:** Lieutenant Eugene Clark receives orders to liberate the major islands south of the 38th parallel.

September 25

EIGHTH ARMY: The 2nd Infantry Division's 38th Infantry starts northwest from Hyopch'on toward Kochang. It is slowed by abandoned vehicles but manages to advance 38 miles, halting only a few miles from Kochang. Coming in on a parallel road north of the 38th parallel, the 23rd Infantry works its way toward Kochang. By late evening the 1st Cavalry Division, concentrated in and around Sangju, is given permission to link up with X Corps near Suwon. Protecting the right flank of the 1st Cavalry is the ROK's 1st Division.

X CORPS: At 0700, the 1st Marine Division launches the final phase of the attack on Seoul. There is heavy resistance from Hill 105 but a flame-throwing tank breaks up the enemy units, and the marines move onto Hill 88 as other marines enter the western edge of the city. The 32nd Regiment, 7th Infantry Division, crosses the Han River only three miles from the heart of Seoul. It is followed by the ROK's 17th Infantry. The two units take Hill 120 and wait for a counterattack. On the east, the 17th Infantry Regiment advances toward Hills 348 and 292.

SEA WAR: The British light carrier HMS *Theseus* arrives off Korea to replace HMS *Triumph*. The USS *Perch* (SS 313) under Lieutenant Commander Robert Quinn carries a 63-man detachment of the 41 Royal Marines to a demolition raid along the Korean coast.

AIR WAR: During a bad day, three squadron commanders are shot down.

In order to defend X Corps's flank, Combat Cargo Command delivers a battalion of the 187th Airborne Regimental Combat Team to Kimpo.

As North Korean troops begin to flee from Seoul, USAF planes drop flares all through the night so that USMC night fighters can fire on the retreating enemy.

September 26

POLITICAL/ADMINISTRATIVE: General Douglas MacArthur prematurely announces that the capital city of Seoul has been liberated. It is considered politically important to register this success as occurring just three months after the initial invasion.

EIGHTH ARMY: South of Suwon the 31st Infantry moves toward the area where Task Force Smith first encountered the enemy.

The 38th Infantry, 2nd Division, takes Kochang and the 23rd Infantry takes Anui by 2200 hours.

The 19th Infantry, 24th Division, enters Yongdong and moves on to Okchon. Elements of the 1st Cavalry move out of position and take Chongju by mid-afternoon after they encounter little resistance.

The 5th Cavalry Regiment crosses the Naktong to Songju.

X Corps: The North Koreans fail as they attack the 32nd Infantry at South Mountain, an effort that results in the death of nearly 400 and the capture of 174 of the enemy. In its position to the east, the 3rd Battalion of the 32nd Regiment catches a large force on the highway and attacks, killing nearly 500 of the enemy.

The ROK's 17th Regiment takes Hills 348 and 292, and by evening the regiment has cleared the area of the enemy.

In Seoul, the Battle of the Barricades moves through the city; after heavy fighting, the marines hold more than half the capital by nightfall.

PFC Eugene A. Obregon (USMC) is posthumously awarded the Medal of Honor for services at Seoul.

Sea War: USS *Brush* (DD 745) is damaged after hitting a mine off Tanchon; nine men are killed and 10 wounded.

Air War: The 22nd Bomber Group launches 20 B-29s against the munitions factory at Haeju. The attack destroys the power plant and four or five other buildings. The 92nd Bomber Group, flying B-29s, attacks the Pujon hydroelectric plant near Hungnam.

The Fifth Air Force establishes the 543rd Tactical Support Group (Provisional) at Taegu to manage tactical reconnaissance squadrons.

September 27

Political/Administrative: General Douglas MacArthur receives his directions concerning the crossing of the 38th parallel. The instructions provide the authority to move north, where he is to engage and destroy the North Korean forces and bring about the unification of Korea. But these orders are dependent on a continuing non-indication that neither the Soviet Union nor China's Communists will inject major forces into the war. This decision has not yet been approved by the United Nations.

The U.S. Congress authorizes an additional defense budget of more than $11.7 billion and an increase in the number of men and women in the armed forces, raising it to a total of 2.1 million. The secretary of defense authorizes the army to plan for 17 divisions and 1,263,000 troops.

British intelligence says it has evidence the Chinese are planning to enter the Korean War. At this point, British sources are closer to the pulse

North Korean prisoners captured as 1st Marine Regiment moved into Seoul, South Korea, September 27, 1950 *(Harry S. Truman Library)*

of the Chinese Communists, but the United States either ignores the information or does not take it seriously.

EIGHTH ARMY: At dawn the 1st Cavalry (Task Force 777) enters Osan, where it meets up with the 31st Infantry. The advance cuts off the 105th North Korean Armored Division. The 25th Infantry Division reaches Hadong at about 1700 hours.

The 24th Infantry fights a desperate battle as the North Koreans take the defensive action necessary to allow their forces to escape from Taejon. A major setback occurs at Anui as the 3rd Battalion, 23rd Infantry, 2nd Division, is caught in a bombardment that kills several of the battalion command. But, later in the afternoon, the 9th Infantry Regiment enters Hyongpung-ni and overcomes the last resistance in the Naktong Bulge area.

X CORPS: The Battle of the Barricades continues as the marines capture Seoul. X Corps and Eighth Army link up south of Seoul. The 31st Infantry inflicts heavy casualties on the North Korean 105th Armored Division to the south. Brigadier General Edwin K. Wright, MacArthur's operations officer, presents Operation Plan 9-50 that outlines a two-pronged attack north of the 38th parallel. Following a landing at Wonsan, on the Sea of Japan the 1st Marines are to cross over the waist of Korea and surround Pyongyang. The U.S. flag is raised over the capitol building.

AIR WAR: The Joint Chiefs of Staff orders a halt to further strategic bombing in North Korean territory.

The final element of the 187th Airborne Regimental Combat Team is delivered to Kimpo Airfield by the Combat Cargo Command.

September 28

POLITICAL/ADMINISTRATIVE: General Douglas MacArthur informs JCS that he is moving west and will begin his drive with an amphibious landing at Wonsan.

EIGHTH ARMY: Led by a single tank, vehicles of the 25th Reconnaissance Company—called Task Force Matthews, which got stuck crossing the river south of Namwon—liberate 86 Americans being held there. They move to Chonju. Also heading for Chonju is the 38th Infantry, 2nd Infantry Division, that arrives just after noon.

Following a series of air attacks west of Okchon, the 19th Infantry enters Taejon at 1630 hours.

Third Battalion of the Royal Australian Regiment arrives in Pusan.

X CORPS: The 31st Infantry, 7th Infantry Division, fights all day with North Korean troops trying to escape to the north. The battle is fought mainly with artillery and air strikes that break up the enemy concentration without a single UN casualty.

Private First Class Stanley R. Christianson (USMC) is posthumously awarded the Medal of Honor, for service near Seoul.

SEA WAR: The American submarine USS *Tilefish* (SS 307) begins her patrol duties in Korean waters. She is assigned to running reconnaissance patrols off La Perouse Strait to inform UN Command on the movement of Soviet ships.

AIR WAR: Air force strikes continue on enemy troops that are retreating from Taejon and heading for Chochiwon. The 7th Fighter-Bomber Squadron moves from Itazuki to Taegu to become the first jet fighter/bomber squadron to operate from a base in Korea. The first reconnaissance jets arrive in the Far East as three RB-45 Tornadoes are assigned.

September 29

POLITICAL/ADMINISTRATIVE: General Douglas MacArthur flies into Kimpo Airfield to make a celebration out of the return to Seoul of Syngman Rhee. General MacArthur presides over an emotional ceremony during which he returns the government and its capitol to ROK president Syngman Rhee. Secretary of State George Marshall communicates with General MacArthur, telling him that he should not feel hampered from a move north across the 38th parallel.

MacArthur holds a meeting to discuss the landing at Wonsan (Operation Tailboard) to be directed by Rear Admiral James H. Doyle's Amphibious Forces Far East. There is some controversy over the economy of moving by sea or by land, and eventually, X Corps will move by both land and sea.

EIGHTH ARMY: Elements of the 25th Infantry Division take the town of Iri, and the port city of Kunsan on the Kum River falls to the 1st Battalion, 24th Infantry. The 35th Infantry encircles the Chiri Mountain area—a 6,000–7,000-foot forested mountain area marked by Chinju, Hadong, and Namwon.

ROK marines land at Yosu, on the southern coast of Korea and take the city.

On the east coast, and in the central sectors, the ROK army is advancing and quickly approaching the 38th parallel all along the line. Although a good number of Communist guerrillas have remained behind, the NKPA appears to have disintegrated, or at least ceased to be an effective fighting force.

X CORPS: In the first American battle north of Seoul, the 2nd Battalion, 17th Regiment, 7th Division is attacked by the enemy, causing 79 American casualties and losing more than 400 of their own.

SEA WAR: USS *Magpie* (AMS 25) strikes a mine and sinks while sweeping near Pohang. The result of the explosion is that 21 men are listed and presumed death. There are 12 survivors.

AIR WAR: An attempt is made to utilize aircraft for antimine operations by establishing daylight patrols along the west coast of Korea. The plan calls for an extensive use of helicopters.

September 30

POLITICAL/ADMINISTRATIVE: The Soviet Politburo, considering the changing war in Korea, focuses on ways to avoid a direct confrontation with the United States. As of this day, all South Korea is back under control of the Republic of Korea.

Chinese premier and foreign minister Zhou Enlai warns that the Chinese people will not tolerate foreign aggression, nor will they allow their neighbors to be invaded by imperialist forces.

EIGHTH ARMY: ROK troops are in North Korea. Under UNC orders, the ROK 3rd Division crosses the 38th parallel. At this point, General MacArthur has available about 165,000 ground troops.

X CORPS: The 1st Marine Division assumes responsibility for Seoul. UN forces clear up the few remaining pockets of the enemy that remain in Seoul.

Sea War: USS *Mansfield* (DD 728) strikes a mine in the vicinity of Changjon while searching for a downed airman. Twenty-seven men are wounded and five are listed as missing.

October 1

Political/Administrative: Soviet leader Joseph Stalin directs Kim Il Sung to talk with Mao Zedong about the timing of a Chinese intervention. Meeting that night with the Chinese ambassador, Kim requests intervention by the 13th Army Corps and calls for support for the North Korean war effort. Stalin affirms his belief that if Chinese troops enter Korea they should be commanded by Chinese officers.

General Douglas MacArthur calls for the North Korean commander in chief to surrender in order to prevent the complete and total destruction of his armed forces.

Once again Zhou Enlai warns against "foreign aggression," saying that China will not allow the "imperialists" to invade North Korea. MacArthur issues UNC Operations Order 2, the plan that orders troops to North Korea.

Eighth Army: The 3rd Division of ROK's I Corps, commanded by Brigadier General Kim Baik Yil, is the first unit to cross the 38th parallel. Forces in Taejon find the bodies of more than 1,000 South Koreans and 30 Americans killed as the North Koreans retreated from the city.

The 27th British Commonwealth Brigade is attached to the U.S. I Corps.

Sea War: The USS *Missouri* (BB 63) bombards installations on the east coast of Korea. During the night, USS *Perch* sends her raiders ashore to where two rail tunnels join at the coast. The attack is protected by USS *Thomas* (DD), which launches a bombardment on an adjacent target as a diversion, and by USS *Maddox* (DD 731).

The minesweeper USS *Magpie* (AMS 25) strikes a floating mine two miles off Chuksan and sinks with 33 casualties.

Near the port of Mokpo the ROK's *YMS 504* sets off a mine with her screw; five crew members are injured.

October 2

Political/Administrative: General Douglas MacArthur orders the bulk of his troops across the 38th parallel.

Andrei Y. Vyshinsky, Soviet foreign minister, introduces a seven-point proposal to the UN General Assembly's Political and Security Committee, calling for a cease-fire and the removal of all foreign troops in Korea. The resolution is defeated.

Premier Zhou Enlai summons K. M. Pannikkar, the Indian ambassador, and informs him directly that, if the UN crosses the 38th parallel, China will intervene in the war. When President Truman is informed, he dismisses it as a bald attempt to blackmail the United Nations.

Mao Zedong convinces his colleagues that the People's Republic of China should send troops to fight in Korea as volunteers. At a meeting of the Politburo, it is agreed that, in order to aid North Korea, Chinese volunteers would cross the Yalu on October 15.

Stalin agrees to send elements of the Soviet air forces to cooperate with a ground force. The aim is the total destruction of U.S. forces in Korea, especially Eighth Army.

EIGHTH ARMY: Eighth Army orders U.S. I Corps to cross the 38th parallel and seize a line west of the Imjin River. The main effort is led by the 1st Cavalry Division, with the U.S. 24th Division and the ROK 1st Division assigned to protect I Corps' flanks.

SEA WAR: Vice Admiral A. D. Struble orders Joint Task Force Seven to prepare for an assault on Wonsan and instructs all available sweepers in the Far East to the port of Wonsan. The 41 Independent Commandos, Royal Marines, traveling on the USS *Perch*, converted to a troop carrying ship, raided the east coast railroad, placing anti-tank mines under the rails. Explosions are heard as the commandos depart.

AIR WAR: Twenty-two B-29s from Bomber Command strike near Nanam in the northeast, where concentrations of North Korean troops are in training. The result is the destruction of 75 percent of the buildings and a large number of enemy personnel.

The 8th TRS, the first day-reconnaissance squadron in Korea, moves to Taegu from its base in Japan.

PARTISANS: Lieutenant Eugene Clark begins to act on orders to liberate the islands in the Yellow Sea north of the 38th parallel.

October 3

POLITICAL/ADMINISTRATIVE: Premier Zhou Enlai again warns Indian ambassador K. M. Panikkar that China will enter the war if the United States crosses the 38th parallel. Secretary of State Dean Acheson continues to believe that the Chinese are bluffing.

AIR WAR: Air and naval forces begin a three-day bombing attack on Wonsan as well as on the main road between Andong and Pyongyang. Air crews report that they have knocked out a 100-mile-long convoy.

October 4

POLITICAL/ADMINISTRATIVE: Chinese leader Mao Zedong makes the final decision to intervene in the Korean War. The Chinese leader tells his colleagues that if China can stand by and watch while North Korea is invaded, there is every reason to expect that the Soviet Union would stand by while China is being invaded. He stresses the fact that, if China does not act, then the commitment to internationalism is empty talk.

The ROK government charges North Korea with the murder of more than 10,000 civilians in Seoul.

General Edmond Almond issues X Corps Operations Order #4, ordering the 7th Infantry Division to go overland to Pusan for the landing at Wonsan. The 1st Marine Division to report to Seventh Fleet as a landing force for the Wonsan amphibious assault.

X CORPS: After taking the city of Uijongbu, some 10 miles south of the 38th parallel, the 1st Marine Division is ordered to Inchon for redeployment to Wonsan. The 7th Infantry Division is ordered to Pusan, a distance of 360 miles, also for redeployment to Wonsan. These two units will make up the amphibious assault on the east coast.

SEA WAR: Task Force 77 reports that carrier-based planes have flown 3,330 sorties during the 13-day period of the Inchon assault. COMNAVFE announces that more than 65 floating and moored mines have been destroyed in the past 30 days. Air strikes are ordered and shore bombardment begins in the Chinnampo and Haeju areas.

AIR WAR: FEAF takes operational control of all land-based aircraft in Korea. This includes the marine squadrons at Kimpo. The 2nd South African Squadron (SAAF) arrives in the combat area and is assigned to the FEAF.

In anticipation of later use, a command decision is made to stop most of the air attacks on airfields in South Korea.

October 5

POLITICAL/ADMINISTRATIVE: Communist Chinese radio calls for a drawn-out war against the foreign aggressors. It appears that Mao Zedong has already decided to enter the war.

EIGHTH ARMY: The ROK 3rd and Capital Divisions move toward Changjon on the east coast, 55 miles north of the 38th parallel, with little resistance. To the west, the 6th and 8th ROK Divisions wait at the 38th parallel for resupply.

X CORPS: Movement of elements of the 1st Marine Division begins as the 1st, 5th, and 11th Marines move to a staging area in the vicinity of Inchon in anticipation of transportation for the assault on Wonsan.

SEA WAR: Joint Task Force 7 is reactivated under command of Admiral Arthur Struble, in preparation for the movement against Wonsan.

October 6

POLITICAL/ADMINISTRATIVE: The Chinese high command meets to work out the details of the coming intervention. There is still some indecision about the date for entering the war.

EIGHTH ARMY: The ROK 6th and 8th Divisions cross the 38th parallel in central Korea, advancing toward Chorwon and the area known as the Iron Triangle.

X CORPS: The 1st, 5th, and 11th Marines complete the move to Inchon for redeployment.

SEA WAR: The ROK navy is authorized to operate on the east coast of Korea as far north as possible in support of advancing ROK ground troops. The USS *Horace A. Bass* (APD 124) works with British commandos to make the first combined attack against North Korean rail lines.

AIR WAR: The enemy arsenal at Kan-ni, North Korea, is hit by 18 B-29 bombers.

The USAF takes charge of Kimpo Airfield, relieving the USMC, which has held it since its capture. The FEAF cancels the attacks on bridges south of Pyongyang and Wonsan.

October 7

POLITICAL/ADMINISTRATIVE: The General Assembly of the United Nations passes a vaguely worded resolution that instructs UNC to ensure "stability throughout Korea." This resolution does not direct the invasion of North Korea, but gives implicit authority to cross the 38th parallel.

The Commission for the Unification and Rehabilitation of Korea appears to have emerged as the result of the optimistic reports from the fighting. It was designed to fulfill the UN mission to unite Korea under the UN.

President Harry Truman fires Admiral Roscoe H. Hillenkoetter, the director of the CIA, for alleged intelligence failures.

General Walton Walker, Eighth Army, takes over command of the Inchon-Seoul area from General Almond's X Corps.

Mao Zedong issues an order to change the identity of the Northeast Border Defense Army to the Chinese People's Volunteers and to move it into Korea immediately. General Peng Dehuai decides to go to Korea to meet Kim Il Sung.

EIGHTH ARMY: Eighth Army relieves X Corps on the line above Seoul. The U.S. 16th Reconnaissance Company, 1st Cavalry Division, is the first significant American force to enter North Korea as it crosses the 38th parallel near Kaesong. It heads for Pyongyang. The ROK 6th Division joins the American force in the drive.

X CORPS: The 1st Marine Division command post at Inchon is transferred aboard USS *Mount McKinley.* The 7th Marine Regiment, the last of the 1st Marine Division to leave the Inchon area, is relieved for redeployment.

Staff Sergeant Lewis Watkins, 7th Marine Regiment, is awarded the Medal of Honor for giving his life in an effort to shield his companions.

AIR WAR: USAF planes drop food and supplies to 150 POWs who escaped from their captors during the North Korean retreat.

October 7–November 28

The official dates given for the invasion of North Korea. The invading army consists of the U.S. I Corps (Eighth Army) in the west and X Corps in the east. The I Corps attack from Kaesong is composed of the 1st Cavalry and 24th Infantry Division. In the east, the ROK I Corps is pushing ahead of X Corps. The 1st Marine Division command is transferred to USS *Mount McKinley* (AGC 7).

October 8

POLITICAL/ADMINISTRATIVE: When Peng Dehuai and Gao Gang leave for Manchuria to begin carrying out their orders, Zhou Enlai flies to the Soviet Union to discuss Soviet military aid, particularly the participation of the Soviet air force.

EIGHTH ARMY: North of Kaesong the 7th and 8th Cavalry Regiments, 1st Cavalry Division, secure the I Corps area. The 8th Cavalry moves up the Kaesong-Kumchon road, while the 7th Infantry Division heads toward Hanpo-ri. The 8th establishes a roadblock where the main Pyongyang-Seoul highway crosses the Yesong River.

X CORPS: First elements of the USMC 5th Regiment board the *Bayfield, George Clymer,* and *Boxar* for the trip to Wonsan.

SEA WAR: The aircraft carrier USS *Leyte* (CV 32) reports for service with Task Force 77 after sailing from the Atlantic.

Minesweepers begin the task of clearing mines from Wonsan harbor for the 250-ship force bringing the 1st Marine Division.

AIR WAR: Two USAF pilots flying F-80s strafe a Soviet airfield near the Russians' major Asian seaport of Vladivostok, inside the Soviet Union. The pilots report it as a navigational error. This, and UNC reconnaissance fights conducted over Siberia, might well have caused a political uproar. However, the lack of Soviet response to these events suggests to some that a Chinese or Soviet intervention is unlikely.

A second attempt to use radio-guided bombs (Razon), delivered recently from the United States, is somewhat more successful. The 162nd TRS moves from Itazuki to Taegu. It is the first night-reconnaissance squadron stationed in Korea.

PARTISANS: The ROK activates its 1st, 2nd, 3rd, 5th, and 6th Guerrilla Battalions in the formation of the 1st Guerrilla Group.

October 9

POLITICAL/ADMINISTRATIVE: General Douglas MacArthur demands that North Korea surrender immediately. The ultimatum is given after the UN offensive takes his command across the 38th parallel. MacArthur is advised by Washington that he is not to recognize South Korea's authority over occupied areas for which it has no legal claim.

The United States apologizes to the Soviet Union for the raid on its airfield and agrees to pay for all damages. No Soviet response is recorded.

Zhou Enlai meets Stalin in the Crimea. Several significant Russian leaders are involved, including Malenkov, Beria, Mikoyan, and Molotov. In a meeting that lasts all night, Stalin agrees to immediately send arms for 20 divisions to Manchuria. But he is not ready to allow the air force to participate directly.

Mao Zedong issues an official directive turning the Northeast Border Defense Army into the Chinese People's Volunteer Army (CPVA). This enables the People's Republic of China (PRC) to enter the war with the United States without formally avowing it. The Chinese People's Volunteers are ordered to move into Korea immediately to assist the "Korean comrades in their struggle."

EIGHTH ARMY: Two ROK Divisions, the 3rd Infantry and the Capital, reach the outskirts of Wonsan, more than 100 miles north of the 38th parallel. Major units assemble north of the 38th parallel.

Private First Class Robert H. Young, 8th Cavalry Regiment, is awarded the Medal of Honor for leadership and courage in the face of the enemy.

X CORPS: While the 7th Infantry Division is marching to Pusan, its headquarters convoy is ambushed at Mungyong Pass, resulting in several casualties. The 17th Regiment clears the way and the movement continues.

SEA WAR: The carriers USS *Leyte* (CV 32) and USS *Philippine Sea* (CV 47) leave Sasebo with USS *Manchester* (CL 83) and 11 destroyers, heading to Wonsan to provide air support for the anticipated amphibious assault.

AIR WAR: Air Group Two, under Commander D. M. White, comes aboard USS *Boxer* (CA 21).

October 10

POLITICAL/ADMINISTRATIVE: In a radio broadcast, North Korean leader Kim Il Sung rejects General MacArthur's surrender demand—thus, it is assumed, justifying Eighth Army's continuing offensive drive toward the Yalu River. In contradiction of UN instructions, President Syngman Rhee tries to exercise control over captured areas of North Korea. Cho Pyong-ok, home minister, announces that the National Police control nine towns north of the 38th parallel.

President Harry Truman announces he will meet with General Douglas MacArthur somewhere in the Pacific.

Zhou Enlai telegraphs Mao Zedong and informs him of Stalin's decision. This is apparently a shock to Mao, who was counting on Soviet air power to cover the invasion. However, plans for the Chinese intervention go ahead.

EIGHTH ARMY: The ROK 3rd Infantry and Capital Divisions enter Wonsan, an east coast port near the 39th parallel. The ROK 6th Division takes the central transportation area at Kumhwa. The 1st Cavalry Division's 8th Regiment is slowed by roadblocks and mines.

ROK troops enter the outskirts of the North Korean capital city of Pyongyang. General Paek Sun Yup leads the 1st ROK Division into the city, many of the infantry riding triumphantly on the hulls of American armored vehicles.

SEA WAR: A force under Captain Richard T. Spofford begins the process of clearing a sea lane through the minefields at Wonsan. The amphibious force is greatly surprised at the large number of mines it encounters.

AIR WAR: Medical treatment, including the use of blood plasma, is applied on board an H-5 while in flight. The crew members who initiate this first-time response receive the Silver Star for their actions.

October 11

EIGHTH ARMY: The ROK I Corps has pushed ahead of the U.S. X Corps and, after two days, takes the city of Wonsan. The 3rd and Capital Divisions move north along the east coast and enter Wonsan, securing both the city and its airfield.

The ROK army 8th Division and the 7th Regiment, 6th Division, arrive at Pyongyang at the west end of the iron triangle. The 27th British Commonwealth Brigade, with Baker Company, 6th Medium Tank Battalion, and followed by the 5th Cavalry, crosses the Imjin River northeast out of Kaesong. They soon slow down as the trail disappears.

The 7th Cavalry crosses the Yesong River and closes the western escape route for the North Koreans.

General Peng Dehuai meets with Kim Il Sung to make the final arrangements for China's entry into the war. Mao Zedong telegraphs Peng to proceed.

SEA WAR: Planes from Task Force 77 destroy North Korean vessels off Songjin and Wonsan and north of Hungnam. Planes from British carriers hit the west coast port of Chinnampo (now, Nampo), near Pyongyang.

October 12

POLITICAL/ADMINISTRATIVE: The UN Interim Committee on Korea passes a resolution stating that the United Nations will recognize no government as having legal control over North Korea. The UNC will administer affairs in North Korea until the UNCRK is prepared to fulfill its mission.

President Harry Truman leaves for his Wake Island meeting with General Douglas MacArthur.

Mao Zedong apparently has second thoughts and, early in the morning, orders Peng to keep the troops where they are and to wait for further instructions.

EIGHTH ARMY: In the west, the 5th Cavalry runs into a strong roadblock but is able to break through. Elements of the 24th Infantry Division, with the 7th and 1st Cavalry, run into fierce resistance near Kumchon, finally taking the battered town. The 8th Cavalry, however, is halted by roadblocks about halfway to Kumchon, and cannot break through. The ROK 6th Division destroys a primary Communist triangle by taking Kumhwa, Pyongyang, and Chorwon.

First Lieutenant Samuel S. Coursen, 1st Cavalry Division, is awarded the Medal of Honor for defending his own men at the cost of his life.

SEA WAR: The minesweepers USS *Pirate* (AM 275) and USS *Pledge* (AM 277) sink after hitting mines in Wonsan harbor. Six crew members are killed and 43 wounded. An attempt is made to destroy the mines when 39 carrier planes are sent in to drop more than 50 bombs. It is discovered that even a 1,000-pound bomb will not set off a mine.

The USS *Missouri* (BB 63) bombards the Tanchon marshaling yards and USS *Helena* (CA 75), *Worcester* (CL 144), and UK *Ceylon* Commonwealth destroyer hit bridges in the Chongjin area.

AIR WAR: Following the capture of Wonsan by advancing ROK forces, U.S. Combat Cargo Command begins to airlift supplies there. The group also begins the transportation of more than 600 tons of bridge sections to the airfield at Kimpo.

October 13

POLITICAL/ADMINISTRATIVE: Despite the failure of the Soviet Union to supply the air power it had promised, the Chinese People's Volunteers are ordered to go ahead with the planned intervention.

Joseph Stalin calls for the abandonment of all North Korea and the relocation of Kim and his forces either to the Soviet Union in the northeast or to China in the north and northwest. China's Politburo meets again to discuss if the CVA should cross the border without Soviet air cover. It is decided to do so, and Moscow is informed.

EIGHTH ARMY: At the Yesong River, the North Koreans cross over and their 19th and 27th Divisions try to push back the 5th and 8th Cavalry, but fail.

At Wonsan, 530 anticommunist political prisoners are found executed.

SEA WAR: In the Yellow Sea, ships under Admiral William Andrewes bombard Haeju and HMS *Theseus* delivers hits at Chinnampo.

On the west coast, Admiral C. C. Hartman's group, joined by USS *Toledo* (CA 133) and the destroyer *H. J. Thomas* (DD), hits targets along a 120-mile stretch south from Chongjin.

October 13–25

POLITICAL/ADMINISTRATIVE: In a situation unparalleled in modern warfare, the intellectual staff of General MacArthur's headquarters and the civilian agencies assigned to provide such information, fail to discern any significant evidence of the movement of more than 130,000 Chinese troops and supporting services.

October 14

POLITICAL/ADMINISTRATIVE: Joseph Stalin reverses his order to abandon North Korea when he is informed that Chairman Mao Zedong and the Chinese Communist Party Central Committee have determined they will enter the war in Korea. Mao Zedong and Peng draw up a military plan together and decide that the Chinese Volunteers should cross the Yalu on October 19. Mao, however, is no longer certain that they can achieve a quick victory. He again hesitates and telegraphs instructions to the army's IX Corps to leave Shanghai but not to move into Manchuria.

EIGHTH ARMY: The ROK 6th Division closes in on Yangdok. The Battle of Kumchon continues, but the North Koreans are unable to withstand the close air support that kills more than 500 of the enemy and destroys a good number of their vehicles. Near the close of day Kumchon falls to the 1st Cavalry Division as its regiments link up.

Operation Showdown begins as the 7th Infantry Division and the ROK's 2nd Infantry Division move forward in an effort to seize Sniper Ridge. The idea is to improve the IX Corps defensive line north of Kumhwa.

SEA WAR: Marine Air Squadron VMF 312 begins its operations in the Wonsan area.

AIR WAR: Two Communist planes, probably from Sinuiju, North Korea, conduct raids on Inchon harbor and Kimpo Airfield. Only minor damage is done.

PARTISANS: Lieutenant Eugene Clark's mission is concluded, and he and his force are ordered to Japan's home islands to be disbanded.

October 15

POLITICAL/ADMINISTRATIVE: President Harry Truman and General Douglas MacArthur meet on Wake Island to discuss the Korean War and the possibility of China's entry. President Harry Truman understands MacArthur to say that the Chinese will not enter the war.

Mao Zedong telegraphs Gao Gang at 0100 to order the CPV to cross the Yalu on October 18, or at least no later than the 19th.

EIGHTH ARMY: When ROK troops enter Yonghung-do, they find that large numbers of South Korean prisoners have been executed.

AIR WAR: Headquarters Fifth Air Force is opened in Seoul.

Antiaircraft fire from the Chinese Communists shoots down an F-51 at the Yalu River near Sinuiju. This is the first downing of a UN plane by Chinese ground forces.

October 15–31

SEA WAR: Naval forces focus their attention in the Wonsan area in an effort to support minesweeping in anticipation of an amphibious landing. The USS *Missouri* (BB 63), *Helena* (CA 75), *Toledo* (CA 133), USS *Manchester* (CA 83), and destroyer escorts make up a blockading force patrolling the approaches to Wonsan.

October 16

POLITICAL/ADMINISTRATIVE: A Foreign Missions Conference in New York estimates that 30 Korean Christian leaders were killed by the Communists while they held Seoul.

Mao Zedong changes his mind again and cables Gao Gang saying it would be better to cross the Yalu on the 17th so that all troops could be in Korea within 10 days. A regiment of the 42nd Army, however, has already acted on the October 15 orders and is in the process of moving across. Further instructions come, selecting October 19 as the day to cross. Peng and Gao are ordered back to Beijing at once. The finalizing of the date for the intervention will be made on the 18th. UN Intelligence announces that Chinese army units have crossed the Yalu River. Beijing radio calls them volunteer forces.

EIGHTH ARMY: The ROK III Corps is activated with the 5th and 11th Divisions. Its primary mission is to locate and destroy enemy troops that have been cut off in the Seoul-Chunchon-Inje-Yangyang area.

X CORPS: Most of the marines identified for the Wonsan landing are onboard as ships sail from Inchon in the late evening. A small advance staff for X Corps operations is taken to Wonsan by air.

October 17

POLITICAL/ADMINISTRATIVE: Peng Dehuai receives a telegram from Deng Hua and Hong Xuezhi, the commanders of the army's XIII Corps, who recommend that perhaps the invasion should wait until spring, since they will have no air cover. But Mao Zedong is now determined. After a brief meeting at 2100, the decision is to go.

EIGHTH ARMY: The 1st Cavalry, supported by the 27th British Commonwealth Brigade, secures the cities of Sariwon and Hwangju, while the 24th Infantry Division moves up the west coast toward the Haeju-Chaeryong-Chinnampo highway. The ROK's 1st Division advances up the highway and enters Suan during the afternoon. Meanwhile, the 1st Cavalry Division advances up the Kaesong-Pyongyang highway, reaching Sariwon and Hwangju south of Pyongyang. The 24th Division advances until it reaches Chaeryong. The ROK Capital Division occupies Hamhung, the port of Hungnam, and Yonpo Airfield.

The Turkish Brigade under Brigadier General Tahsin Yazici arrives in Korea.

X CORPS: The USS *Mount McKinley* (AGC 7), with General Oliver P. Smith on board, heads for Wonsan.

SEA WAR: The Wonsan Amphibious Attack Force, TF 90, sails from Inchon with marines of the X Corps.

The USS *Helena* (CA 75) and USS *Worcester* (CL 144) bombard transportation targets at Songjin.

One of the Japanese minesweepers being used at Wonsan hits a mine and sinks. This creates a political problem, and the Joint Chiefs of Staff urges MacArthur to keep it quiet, knowing the Communists will take advantage of the information.

AIR WAR: Aeromedical evacuation begins from newly captured Sinmak as casualties head for Kimpo. They are followed by planes of Combat Cargo Command delivering fuel and rations to support the UN offensive moving toward the North Korean capital.

October 18

EIGHTH ARMY: The date given for the capture of Pyongyang. In the race to take the city the 1st Cavalry Division and the ROK 1st Division, supported by U.S. tanks, push toward the enemy capital. The ROK 1st Division is closer but is being slowed by pockets of NKPA resistance.

The ROK's Capital Division completes the occupation of the east coast cities of Hamhung and port city of Hungnam.

SEA WAR: The attack headquarters ship USS *Mount McKinley* (AGC 7) arrives off Wonsan.

AIR WAR: Tension increases when more than 75 enemy fighters are spotted at the Anthung Airfield in China by the crew of an RB-29 reconnaissance plane. Such a buildup is seen by many as a warning of a pending Chinese intervention.

October 19

POLITICAL/ADMINISTRATIVE: Before evacuating the city of Hungnam, North Korean forces execute civilians who are identified as traitors and political enemies.

EIGHTH ARMY: The ROK 6th, 7th, and 8th Divisions drive to the west to join in the fighting around Pyongyang. Company Fox, 5th Cavalry, is the first UN unit to reach the capital. The ROK 2nd Battalion, 12th Regiment, reaches the southern edge of the Taedong River. The ROK 11th Regiment takes and holds Pyongyang Airfield.

The Chinese People's Volunteer Army begins to move across the Yalu.

In what is known as "The Twin Tunnels Massacre," 68 Americans are killed by North Korean soldiers after being taken off a train north of Pyongyang. Twenty-one of the soldiers survive.

Fox Company, 2nd Battalion, 5th Cavalry, troops enter the North Korean capital city of Pyongyang, and the city falls to the U.S. 1st Cavalry Division and the 1st ROK Division. To the south the 24th Infantry Division and British units close in on Chinnampo.

SEA WAR: The Wonsan Amphibious Attack Force arrives off Wonsan. The scheduled landing is delayed by mines that remain in the harbor. The Korean minesweeper *YEMS 516* hits a mine at Wonsan and disintegrates.

AIR WAR: Fighters of Fifth Air Force provide close air support for the U.S. 1st Cavalry Division during the Battle of Pyongyang.

October 20

POLITICAL/ADMINISTRATIVE: The Chinese Communists continue the movement of 30,000 men across the Yalu River into Korea. Three armies face the UN troops and the ROK soldiers in the west, while Fourth Army is moving in the east. CINCFE issues Operational Plan 202 outlining the procedures to be followed after the fighting is over in Korea. It is based on the assumption that, once North Korea is occupied, neither China nor the Soviet Union will interfere.

General MacArthur orders "all concerned" to prepare for a maximum effort to advance rapidly toward the northern border of North Korea. Charles Willoughby circulates the following information: "organized resistance on any large scale has ceased to be an enemy capability." He goes on to suggest that the North Korean military and civilian government leaders have probably already fled to Manchuria.

EIGHTH ARMY: In the first airborne operation of the war, the 1st Battalion, 187th Airborne Regimental Combat Team, and 674th Field Artillery Battalion make a parachute assault (2,860 troops) on Sukchon. The 2nd Battalion lands at Sunchon, north of Pyongyang. The mission is to cut off the North Korean escape route. Forty-six are injured in the jump and there are 65 battle casualties.

Seventy-five soldiers are found executed in Sunchon.

General Edward Almond takes command of all UN and ROK forces east of the Taebaek Mountain Range and north of the 39th parallel.

The survivors of the "Death March" from Seoul to Pyongyang tell their liberators that most of the 283 Americans who were captured died in the march.

Private First Class Richard G. Wilson, 187th Airborne Regimental Combat Team, is awarded the Medal of Honor for courage defending the wounded in his care.

SEA WAR: Task Force 98 arrives off Wonsan. The landing is delayed for six days because minesweeping is still not complete.

AIR WAR: Seventy-one C-119s and 40 C-47s of the Combat Cargo Command drop the 187th Airborne Regimental Combat Team 30 miles north of Pyongyang. They drop 2,800 troops and 300 tons of the unit's supplies and equipment at Sukchon and Sunchon. After that, supplies are dropped to UN troops wrapping up the occupation of Pyongyang.

October 21

POLITICAL/ADMINISTRATIVE: Premier Kim Il Sung of North Korea establishes a temporary capital at Sinuiju on the Yalu River, opposite the Chinese city of Andong.

The Joint Chiefs of Staff informs General MacArthur that military demands in other parts of the world will require that the 2nd and 3rd Infantry Divisions be withdrawn from Korea as soon as the fighting ends.

EIGHTH ARMY: More than 1,800 men of the 187th Airborne Regimental Combat Team move into the area north of Pyongyang in hope of capturing North Korean leaders fleeing from Pyongyang, in addition to rescuing some of the UN prisoners being taken north. They engage the enemy and then make contact with friendly troops. They miss their goal, however, as the North Korean leaders have move out ahead of them. But they are able to take the high ground toward Yongju at the cost of heavy casualties.

PFC Richard G. Wilson (USA) is posthumously awarded the Medal of Honor.

The U.S. 24th Infantry Division and British Commonwealth Brigade move north out of Sukchon.

AIR WAR: Following the link-up of ground and airborne troops near Sukchon, the 3rd ARS, flying H-5s, evacuates 35 paratroopers. It is the first use of helicopters in support of an airborne operation. They also evacuate seven POWs found in the area. The wounded, in turn, are evacuated to Pyongyang. C-47s cover most of the area, broadcasting an appeal to isolated North Koreans to surrender.

October 22

EIGHTH ARMY: Soldiers of Charlie Company, of the Australian 3rd Battalion, in a mad hand-to-hand fight, kill some 270 NKPA troops and take 200 prisoners. The

Australian casualties are seven WIA. The 187th Airborne's 3rd Battalion reports killing 805 and capturing 681 of the enemy.

The vanguard of the ROK 6th Division veers to the northwest and approaches Kunu-ri, about 45 miles north of the North Korean capital.

Charlie Company, 6th Medium Tank Battalion, identified as "Task Force Elephant," heads out from Pyongyang to block the railway at Kujang-dong. The ROK's 1st Division follows them.

British troops relieve the 187th Airborne at Sukchon and the paratroopers move into Pyongyang.

SEA WAR: Two high speed minesweepers (DMS), USS *Thompson* and USS *Carmick* (DMS 33), reach Japan for service in Korea. PBMs are reassigned to the west coast for mine-sweeping duties.

AIR WAR: Combat Cargo Command continues its airborne support of the 187th Airborne Regimental Combat Team.

Air Group Two under Commander D. M. White ends its first tour of duty onboard the USS *Boxer*.

A VMF-312 flight surprises a group of retreating enemy soldiers near Kojo, south of Wonsan, and inflicts a significant number of casualties.

October 23

POLITICAL/ADMINISTRATIVE: At a joint meeting in Washington, D.C., of the British and American chiefs of staff, General Omar Bradley is reported to have said "we all agree that if the Chinese Communist come in to Korea we will get out."

EIGHTH ARMY: A large number of American soldiers are found executed at the Sunchon tunnel.

At dawn ROK's 1st Division advances through the Chongchon Valley to Anju, near the Yellow Sea. Engineer units arrive at Anju just behind the ROK and begin work on the bridge across the Chongchon River.

AIR WAR: Combat Cargo Command completes the job of airlifting the 187th Airborne Regimental Combat Team, as it spends the day delivering the last 4,000 troops and materiel.

October 23–30

EIGHTH ARMY: British and Australian units are involved in the fight for Chongju.

October 24

POLITICAL/ADMINISTRATIVE: General Douglas MacArthur removes all restrictions on still separated UN forces from moving to provinces bordering on the Yalu River.

President Harry S. Truman tells General MacArthur that the capture of Pyongyang will have a "profound influence for peace."

EIGHTH ARMY: The ROK 6th Division occupies Huichon. Engineers complete repairs on the Chongchon River bridge and wheeled traffic begins to move across. A tank ford is found about three miles east of the brigade, and the 6th Medium Tank Battalion crosses the river there. By night the ROK's 1st Division is on the north side of the river and moving toward Unsan. At Sinanju, west of Anju, the 27th British Commonwealth Brigade crosses using assault boats. The 24th Infantry Division also moves toward Anju. To the east, the 6th and 8th ROK Divisions move out of Kunu-ri. When the ROK 8th Division reaches Tokchon it turns toward the Chongchon River at Kujang-dong.

Advance parties of the Netherlands Battalion and the British 29th Brigade arrive in Korea for assignment.

X Corps: Bob Hope and Marilyn Maxwell, who have flown into Wonsan to put on a USO show, poke fun at the frustrated marines still onboard the assault ships.

Sea War: The minesweepers USS *Chatterer* (AMS 40), *Incredible* (AM 249), *Kite* (AMS 22), *Merganser* (AS 26), *Mockingbird* (AMS 27), *Osprey* (AMS 28), *Partridge* (AMS 31), *Pirate* (AMS 275), *Pledge* (AM 277), and *Redhead* (AM 378) all receive the Presidential Unit Citation for service rendered from October 10 to 24, 1950.

Air War: A VMF-312 flight catches a column of enemy troops near Kojo, 39 miles south of Wonsan, and scatters them, inflicting serious losses.

October 25

Political/Administrative: General Douglas MacArthur is informed that replacement fillers will not be shipped, as planned, in October and November, except for 17,000 NCO grades. Regular replacement shipments to Europe will begin on January 1, 1951.

Eighth Army: The first ROK forces reach the Yalu River. They send a bottle of river water to Syngman Rhee. The ROK II Corps, which is driving north on the western axis of the UN advance, is attacked by a large force and nearly destroyed. The ROK 1st Division finds itself heavily engaged. It captures a soldier who tells his captors that he is Chinese and that there are many other Chinese in the fight. UNC forces meet stout resistance just about everywhere along the front. The first involvement of Chinese Communist forces in the war occurs. The 3rd Battalion, 2nd Regiment, of the ROK's 6th Division is nearly destroyed when it is trapped by the Chinese Communist forces near Onjong, south of Chosin on the Yalu River. The ROK 6th Division reaches Kujang-dong, just 18 miles to the south. South of the crossroad village of Onjong, the ROK's 3rd Battalion, 2nd Regiment, 6th Division, comes under fire. The probe soon turns into a major battle with Chinese troops. The battalion is nearly wiped out, losing 350 of its 750-man strength. The ROK 2nd Battalion of the 2nd Regiment moves to support its 3rd Battalion, only to run into a trap. However, it escapes and returns to Onjong. In the area of Unsan, elements of Dog Company, 6th Medium Tank Battalion, and the 16th ROK Infantry Regiment, run into heavy resistance from Chinese troops waiting for them. The ROK 15th Regiment, with elements of Dog Company and the U.S. 6th Medium Tank Battalion, advances north to Unsan where it runs into a Chinese roadblock. The 11th Regiment, which is following, is stopped on the road south of Unsan.

X Corps: X Corps, which had been sent to Wonsan under Operation Tailboard (called Operation Yo Yo by the marines), is finally able to land on the Kalma Peninsula. Despite the fact that the navy has cleared the harbor of more than 2,000 mines, the inner harbor is still not clear enough for a landing. Command orders the 1st

Marines to locate one regimental combat team at the Hamhung area and to relieve ROK elements at the Chosin (Changjin) and Fusen (Pujon) Reservoirs. The ROK I Corps (a part of X Corps) captures Chinese soldiers near the reservoir. They tell their captors that Chinese Communist forces are in the area.

SEA WAR: The USS *Endicott* (DMS 35) and USS *Doyle* (DMS 34), along with an AMS, sweep the 18-mile channel at Kunsan (the port of Iwon), but no mines are discovered.

At dusk it is reported to Captain Spofford that Wonsan harbor has been cleared of all mines.

AIR WAR: Bomber Command suspends combat missions against North Korean targets because it is becoming difficult to identify significant targets that have not already been bombed. At the same time, FEAF withdraws orders that restrict close air support near the Yalu River. Pilots are now allowed to fly all the way to the Chinese border.

Combat Cargo Command sets a new record by delivering 1,767 tons of equipment within Korea.

October 25–26

EIGHTH ARMY: The "Battle of the Broken Bridge" is the second major action at Pakchon. The 3rd Royal Australian Regiment pushes across a half-destroyed bridge and drives the North Korean defenders back.

October 26

POLITICAL/ADMINISTRATIVE: In anticipation of a complete victory in North Korea, President Harry Truman announces to a press conference that South Koreans will man border posts along the Yalu. American, British, and Australian forces will hold positions in the western area; while the ROK army will control the central and eastern parts of North Korea.

EIGHTH ARMY: A South Korean reconnaissance regiment from the 6th Division pushes far ahead of other units and reaches the Yalu River. Chinese troops attack the ROK near Onjong and the ROK withdraws, only to discover that the Chinese are waiting for them in a roadblock three miles to the east. The unit breaks, with everyone heading for the hills. Two of the three KMAG advisers make it to safety.

The 15th Infantry Regiment, north of Unsan, is forced to fall back in the face of Chinese attacks. The 6th Medium Tank Battalion withdraws to higher ground near Unsan. During the day, the 11th Regiment is forced to withdraw to the edge of Unsan.

The first significant groups of Chinese prisoners of war are taken.

X CORPS: The 1st Marine Division lands at Wonsan (administratively), thanks to the port's earlier capture by the ROK. The marines were scheduled to make a landing similar to the one at Inchon, but it was unnecessary.

AIR WAR: Combat Cargo Command, flying C-119s, drops supplies to ground troops that are cut off in North Korea. The supply drops focus on a location near Onjong. CCC delivers more than 28 tons of ammunition, fuel, and rations.

Tanks off-loading from LST at Wonsan, Korea *(Center for the Study of the Korean War, Graceland University)*

October 27

POLITICAL/ADMINISTRATIVE: Political opinion at the UN strongly objects to allowing the Republic of Korea to automatically assume political control over the north. The Joint Chiefs of Staff directs General Douglas MacArthur that political questions regarding sovereignty over North Korea must wait for the United Nations to act.

India expresses its regret that China has decided to enter the war, even though many UNC officers have not yet fully accepted their presence. China replies to India that the problem in Korea is a domestic problem. China uses the occasion to acknowledge that it has invaded Tibet and is advancing on the capital, Lhasa.

EIGHTH ARMY: The ROK's 6th Division is forced to withdraw and it, along with the 7th and 8th Divisions, sets up defensive positions.

Chinese Communist troops numbering as many as 20,000, plus North Korean troops, attack UN forces in a region stretching from Unsan to Huichon. A regiment of the 1st Cavalry Division is trapped near Unsan. The ROK 6th Division withdraws from the position near the Yalu River, which it had set up the day before.

X CORPS: The 17th Infantry Regiment, 7th Division, departs in seven LSTs for Iwon, about 150 miles north of Wonsan.

It has been fairly quiet near Hill 185, about 700 yards in front of the dike, when at 1600 hours a wire team is fired on. Then the men on Hill 185 receive word that Hill 109 has been deserted, with 30 men missing. The marines on Hill 109 have been unexpectedly hit by North Korean forces, estimated at two platoons, that overrun the position and kill seven marines—some of them caught in their sleeping bags and killed. At 2215, the 3rd Platoon of Baker Company suffers a second attack, and it becomes necessary for them to withdraw. A slow, position-by-position withdrawal leaves the enemy in charge of Hill 109.

AIR WAR: Airdrops by 10 C-119s provide fresh ammunition and supplies that allow the 11th and 12th ROK Regiments to regain some of their lost ground.

Taking seriously the presumptive idea that there is little left to bomb, General George Stratemeyer considers sending home the 22nd and 29th Bombardment Groups.

Less than a month after its original call-up, the 452nd Bomber Group flies its first B-26 combat mission in Korea.

October 28

POLITICAL/ADMINISTRATIVE: The Joint Chiefs of Staff reaffirms its position, telling General MacArthur that the question of political sovereignty over Korea must await UN action. North Korea is to be occupied in the name of the United Nations. MacArthur's job is to dispose of the Communist government but not to create, or allow to be created, any government. The Rhee government is to have no authority over the occupied areas of North Korea. Rhee protests to President Harry Truman about these instructions but it is to no avail.

EIGHTH ARMY: The area around Unsan is unusually quiet, but General Walton Walker sends the 1st Cavalry Division to the area to provide support. Australian and U.S. tanks break up a Communist attack and destroy three tanks.

The 2nd and 19th ROK Regiments reach a point near Onjong but then are cut off and defeated by a superior Chinese force. The survivors head into the mountains.

The 7th Regiment is cut off as well and requires an airdrop of supplies in order to complete a withdrawal.

X CORPS: The 3rd Battalion of the 1st Marines arrives at Majon-ni, relieving the ROK 26th Regiment. Majon-ri is very important for it sits at the headwaters of the Imjin River and is at the junction of roads leading east to Wonsan, south to Seoul, and west to Pyongyang.

The ROK's Capital Division sends a "flying column" into the far northeast area to capture Songjin (Kimchaek).

October 29

EIGHTH ARMY: The 8th Cavalry Regiment begins its move on Unsan, while to the west the 24th Infantry Division and the British 27th Commonwealth Brigade enter Chongju on the Anju-Sinuiju highway. Chongju is about 40 miles from the Yalu.

The 7th Infantry Regiment (ROK) begins to move south at dawn but runs into a roadblock 20 miles south of Kujang-dong. After fighting all day the ROK is able to withstand the Chinese attacks, but as night falls and air cover is restricted, the regiment is overrun.

X CORPS: The 17th Regiment of the 7th Infantry Division comes ashore without opposition at Iwon, about 60 miles north of Hungnam, after the area is reported to be clear of all mines. The rest of the 7th Infantry Division is to follow in the next nine days. The 7th Marines, given the job of spearheading the drive north, begins moving to Hamhung. Movement is slowed by determined Communist forces.

AIR WAR: The capture of Sinanju allows C-47s to take out the wounded. Sinanju is the northernmost Korean airfield used by the FEAF during the war.

October 30

EIGHTH ARMY: The 1st Battalion of the 8th Cavalry Regiment arrives at Unsan as ROK army units are being pushed from their positions about 8,000 yards to the north. After the collapse of ROK's II Corps, the 8th Division withdraws to form a defensive line.

X CORPS: The First Marines are ordered to relieve the ROK's I Corps around the Changjin (Chosin) Reservoir. The 7th Marines move to Hamhung to begin operations north. The ROK Capital Division's 18th Regiment arrives at the south end of the Pujon Reservoir.

October 31

POLITICAL/ADMINISTRATIVE: Eight Russians, apparently connected with biological warfare, are taken into custody by the army after they indicate that they do not want to return to Russia.

From this date to November 8, 1950, the so-called Death March occurs, during which more than 100 military and civilian prisoners perish.

EIGHTH ARMY: During a series of ongoing battles, 25 prisoners are taken who admit to being Chinese and who talk about there being thousands of others in the area.

The ROK army's 12th Regiment is relieved by the 2nd and 3rd Battalions of the 8th Cavalry Regiment. Chinese forces break through the ROK's 16th Regiment (8th Division), where the regiment joins with the ROK 1st Division.

X CORPS: After three weeks at sea, the majority of X Corps is again on land. The 7th Infantry Division's 17th Regiment headquarters and 1st Battalion move to Pungsan. The ROK army's Capital Division has cleared the road.

SEA WAR: Transports are sent to Moji, Japan, to begin shipping the first units of the U.S. 3rd Infantry Division to Korea.

November 1

POLITICAL/ADMINISTRATIVE: President Harry Truman escapes an attempted assassination by two Puerto Rican nationalists who fire at him.

EIGHTH ARMY: In what is probably the first conflict between the Chinese People's Volunteer Army and U.S. forces, the Chinese attack at Unsan from the north and west. The U.S. 8th Cavalry Regiment is rushed to Unsan to replace the mauled ROK units fighting there. They barely arrive when they are assaulted by the 115th and 116th Chinese Divisions—an estimated 20,000 Chinese troops—driving the exposed 1st and 2nd Battalion apart. The 3rd Battalion is sent in relief, but it is too late. By afternoon the Chinese move against the ROK's 15th Infantry Regiment and then on to the west where 8th Cavalry is located. By late afternoon, the 15th is no longer a fighting unit. Tanks guard the bridge and allow a significant number of men to escape to the south.

Under extended pressure, the 8th Cavalry Regiment is ordered to withdraw, but it is too late for a good many. By nightfall the 8th Cavalry is no longer combat-effective.

South of the Chongchon River the Chinese push the ROK 7th back to Won-ni, leaving a gap that threatens the Eighth Army at Unsan. The U.S. 2nd Division is ordered in to plug the gap. The 24th Infantry Division and the British 27th Commonwealth Brigade are ordered to retreat to the Chongchon River. Eighth Army intelligence identifies the Chinese Communist units fighting alongside North Korean troops.

X CORPS: The U.S. 17th Infantry Regiment and the ROK 1st Regiment fight off a strong North Korean attack two miles north of Pungsan. The 7th Marines are trucked out of Hamhung to an area near Majon-dong.

AIR WAR: Six MiGs, the first to appear in Korea during the war, fire on a T-6 and a flight of F-51 Mustangs in the area of the Yalu River. In another incident, three YAK fighters attack USAF planes, including a B-29, over North Korea. The bomber crew is able to shoot down one of the YAKs, and two F-51 pilots guarding the formation destroy the other two. A flight of F-80s attacks Sinuiju Airfield and manages to destroy several YAK fighters on the ground. However, antiaircraft artillery from across the Yalu hit and destroy one FEAF jet.

An F-51 is shot down near Singisyu, an F-80 near Andong, and one near Bihen.

For the first time in the war, a confirmed report of a MiG-15 is provided.

November 2

EIGHTH ARMY: Out of ammunition and vastly confused, survivors of the 8th Cavalry unit at Unsan manage to escape and retreat on foot through a Chinese roadblock. With more than 600 men killed or captured, the 8th Cavalry is no longer capable of holding a position. At this point, the UN Offensive Campaign comes to an end. Following two days of fighting around Unsan against the 8th Cavalry Regiment, the Chinese 19th Division withdraws to the hills.

The 24th Infantry Division completes its withdrawal from the Chongju area and takes up positions along the Anju-Pakchon area.

X CORPS: The 1st and 2nd Battalions of the 7th Marines meet up with the Chinese (as they move to relieve ROK's I Corps) along the road to the Chosin Reservoir, at about the same spot where the ROK 3rd Division suffered its defeat in late October. It is one of the few battles in which Chinese tanks are involved.

Staff Sergeant Archie Van Winkle, 7th Marine Regiment, is awarded the Medal of Honor for courage shown when his unit is attacked by the Chinese.

The Chinese 124th withdraw into the mountains after a stiff fight with the 7th Marines.

AIR WAR: The first jet reconnaissance mission of the war is flown by an RB-45 Tornado.

Two enemy YAK-9 are shot down by pilots flying F-51Ds. The pilots are Alma R. Flake and James L. Glessner.

SEA WAR: The port of Wonsan is open for operations. An temporary strip is completed on the east side of the Majon-ni perimeter. Kosong is swept prior to a landing scheduled for November 3–8, 1950.

November 3

POLITICAL/ADMINISTRATIVE: The United Nations creates the Collective Measures Committee and asks it to study any means to strengthen international peace, including the use of armed forces.

General MacArthur's headquarters acknowledges that some 34,000 Chinese troops have entered Korea and that about 415,000 regular troops are located in Manchuria and ready to cross.

EIGHTH ARMY: The CCF Intervention Campaign begins. Less than an hour after the British 27th Commonwealth Brigade leaves Taechon, Chinese troops enter. The ROK

1st Division begins withdrawing through the lines of the 19th Infantry Regiment, 24th Division, to defensive positions northeast of Anju.

The 5th Regimental Combat Team, 24th Infantry Division, backs up the ROK II Corps at Kunu-ri, which has been forced to consolidate into a small area.

X Corps: The ROK Capital Division "flying column" moves up the west coast road to capture Kilchu, then heads for Chongjin. The 7th Marine Regiment moves toward Hamhung and then on to Chosin and becomes engaged in its first fight with the Chinese. The U.S. 17th Infantry battles two miles to the north of Pungsan.

The remainder of the 65th Infantry Regiment, 3rd Infantry Division, lands at Wonsan.

November 4

Eighth Army: The ROK 1st Division's withdrawal to the south of the Chongchon River is accomplished by noon. The Chinese try to capture Kunu-ri and Hill 622, the largest mountain northeast of Kunu-ri, which dominates the Chongchon River Valley. During the battle, Hill 622 changes hands several times but the ROK army holds on.

The 19th Infantry's 1st Battalion is overrun but most troops are able to escape across the Chongchon River. The 3rd Battalion, 19th, tries to retake the 1st Battalion position but enemy resistance is too strong.

The enemy forces hit in great strength against the Eighth Army flank at Kunu-ri and against the Commonwealth Brigade at the western end of the bridgehead, but the attacks are repulsed.

The North Koreans drive hard against Hill 622 (aka Kunu-ri), a large area that dominates the valley of the Chongchon.

A strong CCF attack breaks the ROK 3rd Regiment and sends the South Koreans reeling back through the 5th Regimental Combat Team area. They are sent back into the fight and, with help from the 8th ROK Regiment, are able to take the hill after it has changed hands several times.

X Corps: When the Reconnaissance Company of the 7th Marines moves out at 0800, it is surprised by CCF troops on the edge of Sudong. In a 30-minute fight the marines kill three and captured 30. The 31st Infantry Regiment, 7th Infantry Division, lands at Iwon and moves northwest to protect the 17th Infantry flank.

Sergeant James I. Poynter (USMC) is posthumously awarded the Medal of Honor for service near Sudong. Corporal Lee H. Philips (USMC) is posthumously awarded the Medal of Honor.

Several tanks of the North Korean 344th Tank Regiment are destroyed by 7th Marine Regiment north of Chinhung-ni near the Chosin Reservoir.

Sea War: Admiral C. Turner Joy is ordered to extend immediate and maximum close air support to X Corps.

Air War: Approximately 500 enemy soldiers are killed when hit by B-26s providing close air support for the retreating Eighth Army near Chongju.

November 4–5

Eighth Army: During the night, the North Koreans make a coordinated attack all along the line. The enemy achieves surprise against George and Easy Company of the 19th Infantry who are caught, and many killed, in their sleeping bags. The UN troops pull back about 1,000 yards to a point where they are finally able to hold.

November 5

POLITICAL/ADMINISTRATIVE: In Pyongyang, a germ warfare laboratory is discovered. There is no evidence of the production or distribution of weapons of germ warfare.

EIGHTH ARMY: In hand-to-hand fighting, the Commonwealth Brigade beats back a Chinese attack on its positions at Pakchon on the Taeryong River. The 21st Infantry is sent across the Chongchon River to take the lost 19th Regiment position; after it is taken, the Chinese mount a coordinated attack against all defensive positions. The attack on Hill 123 catches two companies by surprise and several men are shot in their sleeping bags. The remnants of the battalion withdraw.

Corporal Mitchell Red Cloud (USA) is posthumously awarded the Medal of Honor.

The final element of the 65th Regimental Combat Team arrives at Wonsan.

X CORPS: During the night, more than 200 Korean laborers move supplies forward and take casualties out. At How Hill (891) marines run into a heavy fight. For 45 minutes, a platoon from the 7th Marine Regiment is held up and finally forced to withdraw. During the night, plans are made for entering Funchilin Pass.

The Chinese have established fortifications on Hill 987 and the 5th Marines are ordered to silence them. But the enemy is well entrenched, and the marines make only a few yards toward their goal; as night falls the Chinese still hold Hill 987.

AIR WAR: VMF-312 flies 37 sorties in 90 hours between Chinhung-ni and the Chosin Reservoir. The 19th Bomber Group launches an attack on Kanggye. Twenty-one B-29s drop 170 tons of fire-bombs on the provincial capital, about 20 miles from the Chinese border.

Bomber Command authorizes incendiary bomb attacks on North Korean towns and villages.

General MacArthur orders a heavy air offensive over North Korea that includes the Yalu River bridge at Sinuiju. The order is a violation of the JCS instructions that he is not to drop bombs within five miles of the Yalu.

General MacArthur orders General George Stratemeyer to fly his men to exhaustion, if necessary, in a two-week effort to knock out the North Koreans and their new allies.

November 6

POLITICAL/ADMINISTRATIVE: MacArthur condemns the Chinese intervention, saying that it "was one of the most offensive acts of international lawlessness of historic record."

The Joint Chiefs of Staff reconsiders and decides this is not the time to cut troops in Korea. All previous actions to do so are rescinded.

EIGHTH ARMY: All along the front, the CCF abruptly halts all of its activities in most sectors. The 19th Infantry is able to move forward as the Chinese appear to have withdrawn. After dark an enemy guerrilla force ambushes a convoy south of Kowon and 35 miles north of Wonsan, destroying the trucks and most of the equipment. At

0130, on a foggy night, flares announce the arrival of NKPA troops, from the 15th Division, at Majon-ni. When their ammunition runs out, the marines are forced to withdraw, only to recapture the area after the fog lifts.

X CORPS: In the morning, the Chinese, who were on the line in front of the Marine 7th Regiment, have disappeared. Many wonder if the earlier attacks were simply a warning of the Chinese willingness to act. Others presume optimistically that the 124th CCF Infantry Division was so badly mauled in the initial attacks that it is not capable of continuing the fight.

The 7th Marine Regiment occupies the southern tip of Hill 891 without opposition. The marines decide that it is necessary to take How Hill (Hill 750) if they are going to move through Funchilin Pass. They attack the hill, making several efforts, but by night the men from How Company withdraw. The marines try again to take Hill 987 and are beaten off in the first attack. The second attack gets them to within 300 yards of the crest, but the resistance is so strong they are still unable to take the crest.

Second Lieutenant Robert Dale Reem (USMC) is awarded the Medal of Honor posthumously.

SEA WAR: Minesweeping operations begin at the North Korean port city of Hungnam.

Task Force 77 returns to Korean waters in response to the arrival of Chinese forces.

AIR WAR: Two F-51s are attacked and destroyed near Andong.

Two enemy YAK-9s are shot down by USAF pilots. Howard Price gets credit for one and shares a credit with H. Reynolds.

November 7

POLITICAL/ADMINISTRATIVE: The Interim Committee of the UN Korean Commission votes to exclude the Yalu River and Manchuria as parts of the combat zone. It acts on the assumption that China will withdraw its troops from North Korea if it is assured that it will not be attacked in these areas.

General Douglas MacArthur confirms his original opinion that the Chinese will not make a full-scale intervention into the war.

EIGHTH ARMY: Almost mysteriously, the Chinese forces vanish from the Kunu-ri bridgehead.

Adding to the UN Command, the first Canadian troops, the 2nd Battalion, Princess Patricia's Canadian Light Infantry Regiment, land at Pusan. The Thailand Battalion also arrives.

X CORPS: After a bitter clash between the 7th Marine Regiment and the CCF 124th Division, the CCF withdraws from the Chosin Reservoir area and seems to fade away. After failing to take How Hill (Hill 750) on the previous day, patrols from the Marine 3rd Battalion move forward, only to discover that the enemy has withdrawn during the night. The marines move forward toward the village of Pohujang. After three days of trying to take Hill 987, the 7th Marines finally reach the top to discover that the Chinese have pulled back.

SEA WAR: The landing of the 7th Infantry Division at Iwon is completed.

After 10 days of minesweeping, the first shallow-draft vessels begin to enter the port of Chinnampo. The LSU *1402* is the first to enter the port, bringing Eighth Army much needed supplies.

AIR WAR: Howard Tanner, flying an F-51D for the 36th FBS (Fighter/Bomber Squadron), shoots down a MiG-15.

November 8

POLITICAL/ADMINISTRATIVE: The UN Security Council invites the People's Republic of China to attend the UN discussion of a charge against the United States pertaining to aggression against Taiwan.

The Korean Service Medal is authorized.

President Harry Truman lifts the ban on bombing within five miles of the Yalu River.

X CORPS: Third Infantry Division joins X Corps at Wonsan. The U.S. 31st Infantry Regiment moves up on the east side of the Pujon Reservoir and encounters Chinese troops on Paek-San, a 7,700-foot-high peak about 12 miles from the southern end of the reservoir. After a lengthy firefight, the Chinese withdraw.

A volunteer scouting patrol led by First Lieutenant William F. Groggin, 2nd Battalion, 7th Marines, leaves Chinhung-ni at noon and moves forward 25 miles to the Chosin Reservoir plateau somewhat southeast of Koto-ri. They find the area to be clear of enemy forces.

A Communist unit of about 250 men tries to encircle How Company's 2nd Platoon at Majon-ni, but it is scattered by well-directed artillery fire.

The 5th Marines in the area of Huksu-ri, on the west of the advance, conduct a running fight with North Korean troops until the marines are recalled.

SEA WAR: A new priority is issued to Task Force 77, now maneuvering to avoid snowstorms: destroy the southern span of all bridges over the Yalu River.

AIR WAR: More than 70 Superfortresses unload 580 tons of fire-bombs on Sinuiju. This is probably the largest fire-bomb raid of the war.

In one of the first jet-to-jet dogfights, Lieutenant Russell J. Brown, of the 16th Fighter Interceptor Squadron, shoots down the opposing MiG-15.

Two F-51s are fired on by enemy fighters and downed near Andong.

November 9

POLITICAL/ADMINISTRATIVE: The UN Security Council fails to take action on the British proposal to establish a buffer zone around the Yalu River. Great Britain is worried that the conflict with the Chinese will expand the war and is receiving a great deal of pressure from a variety of pro-Chinese groups at home.

X CORPS: The 5th Marine Regiment is ordered to concentrate along the main supply route leading to the Chosin Reservoir. The 7th Infantry Division's 7th Reconnaissance Company moves east of Pungsan.

SEA WAR: Soviet MiG-15s attack F9Fs from USS *Philippine Sea* (CV 47). Lieutenant William Amen shoots down an enemy jet.

The last of the 29,000 men of the 7th Infantry Division have been put ashore.

AIR WAR: Corporal Harry J. LeVene of the 91st Strategic Reconnaissance Squadron scores the first RB-29 victory over an attacking MiG-15, shooting it down as his damaged plane returns to Japan. William T. Amen shoots down a MiG-15. Two F-80s are shot down near Andong, and a B-29 bomber near Sinuiju.

November 10

POLITICAL/ADMINISTRATIVE: The British, in fear of an all-out war with China, propose halting MacArthur's advance at a line between Hungnam and Chongju and creating a DMZ from there to the Yalu. They believe that such defensive positions will expedite Korean unification. Canada and India support the idea, but the United States and most of the UN member nations do not support the resolution. Russia vetoes a discussion of North Korean troop removal unless the North Koreans are represented at the UN discussions that considered such a removal.

X CORPS: The 7th Marines occupies the area of the Chosin Reservoir and Koto-ri Plateau. On this date, the temperature drops by 40 degrees to –8°F accompanied by a 35-mph wind.

Concerned over attacks on Majon-ni, the 3rd KMC Battalion arrives as reenforcements.

At 0830, on the Marine Corps birthday, the 1st Battalion of the 7th Marines moves into Funchilin Pass, moves through the 3rd KMC position, and emerges into the area of Koto-ri. The 3rd Division receives orders to relieve all marine units in the Wonsan area and to take over all their responsibilities for the antiguerrilla mission.

Charlie Company of the 1st Battalion, 5th Marines, is ambushed near Chigyong, and the survivors have to be rescued by a battalion attack on the next day.

AIR WAR: A B-29, assigned to the 307th Bomber Group, is shot down by a MiG-15 near the Yalu River and the crew taken captive.

The 437th TCW uses C-46s to begin airlifting cargo to Korea, less than 36 hours after the unit arrives in Japan.

Two F-51s are shot down by enemy fighters near Andong. Clyde J. Whaley, flying an F-80C, downs a MiG-15.

November 11

X CORPS: X Corps command issues orders for an advance to the border. The ROK army's I Corps is on the right, the 1st Marine Division on the left, and the 7th Infantry Division in the center. Remaining elements of the U.S. 3rd Division's 15th Regiment land at Wonsan. Other than a brief fight with a unit reported to be Chinese, the area is quiet.

SEA WAR: The USS *Buck* (DD 761) and USS *Thompson* (DMS 203) are damaged in a ship-to-ship collision.

AIR WAR: An F-80 and an F-84 are shot down by enemy fighters near Andong.

November 12

EIGHTH ARMY: The ROK 18th Regiment is halted at Orang-chon when it runs into a North Korean force supported by tanks. The enemy is prevented from a breakthrough by naval gunfire and air support that break up the troop concentrations.

X CORPS: First Battalion, 15th Infantry, 3rd Division, heads out for Majon-ni to take over the perimeter and relieve the marines and the ROK army. The 7th Division is ordered to advance to the Chinese border: The 17th Regiment's assignment is to take Kapsan, the 31st Infantry is to advance on the left flank, and the 32nd Infantry to seize the southeast shore of the Pujon Reservoir. Weather becomes an increasing problem. Over the next few days, hundreds of cases of frozen feet will be recorded.

November 13

POLITICAL/ADMINISTRATIVE: The U.S. State Department seeks the opinion of the governments at London, Delhi, Wellington, Canberra, Ottawa, Moscow, and The Hague, on what the reaction would be if the United States conducted overflights of Manchuria when in hot pursuit. All areas reported that the reaction would be highly unfavorable. Such flights will be prohibited throughout the Korean War, giving the Communists an advantageous sanctuary.

X CORPS: X Corps, now based at Hungnam, North Korea, begins to move northward as it advances into the Changjin (Chosin) Reservoir area. While operating out of Majon-dong, a patrol of the 1st Battalion, 5th Marines, runs into an enemy unit that kills seven and wounds three before retiring.

November 14

EIGHTH ARMY: The battle in the Orang-chon area continues with the North Korean units having the support of T-34/85 tanks. Despite the odds, elements of the ROK's 18th Regiment are able to contain the advance.

X CORPS: Following orders, the 2nd Battalion, 17th Infantry, attacks across the Ungi River on a floating footbridge. Upstream, the 3rd Battalion tries to cross at a shallow point, but the North Koreans open the floodgates of a dam, causing the water to rise. The battalion has to move to the footbridge. Temperature along some areas of the front drops −20°F.

AIR WAR: While 18 B-29s are attacking the bridges at Sinuiju, they are jumped by 15 Communist MiG-15s. Gunner Richard W. Fisher shoots down one of the attacking MiG-15s. The enemy damages two of the 18 B-29 bombers as they attack the bridges at Sinuiju. VP Squadron One, under Commander J. B. Honan, ends its first tour of duty in Korea. VP Squadron 22, under Commander R. J. Davis, begins its first tour of duty in Korea.

November 15

POLITICAL/ADMINISTRATIVE: A meeting is held by NKPA and CVA officers to settle questions of command structure. The Soviets bring a Chinese complaint to the United Nations concerning the United States' repeated violation of Manchurian air space. The Korean *Times* describes life in liberated Seoul as returning to normal. The Sino-Soviet Treaty of Friendship signed in Moscow provides some relief for the tension that exists between Chairman Mao and Joseph Stalin. But in reality it provides very little of the material support China needs.

EIGHTH ARMY: The Battle at Orang-chon continues as newly reinforced North Korean units force the ROK's 18th and 1st Regiments to withdraw.

X CORPS: General Douglas MacArthur directs X Corps to reorganize to the west on reaching Changjin and to move to cut the Chinese main supply route, the Manpojin-Kanggye-Huichon Road and railway lines. General Oliver P. Smith warns of significant and imminent Chinese intervention and suggests that it is necessary for someone to "make up their minds" about what the military goals are. General Smith writes to the commandant of the Marine Corps that General Edward Almond's orders are wrong and that the 1st Marines will not press forward too rashly. The 17th Infantry crosses the Ungi River as both 1st and 2nd Battalions make small gains. The

31st Infantry reaches the eastern shore of the Pujon Reservoir. The ROK Capital Division advances to within 35 miles of Manchuria after a long march over snow-covered mountains.

SEA WAR: Minesweeping begins at Songjin (Kimchaek). The tactical organization of Escort Carrier Task Group (TG 98.6) is established under the command of Rear Admiral R. W. Ruble. The first of the ships that arrive to support the troops, and that will later take part in the evacuation of X Corps, arrives in Hungnam. After the sweeping is complete, ships enter the harbor at Hungnam.

November 16

POLITICAL/ADMINISTRATIVE: President Harry Truman announces that he has no intention of fighting in China. The Italian Red Cross Hospital Unit 68 sets up to receive UN casualties.

EIGHTH ARMY: After four days of fighting, the North Koreans in the Orang-chon area are finally turned, and the ROK's 18th Regiment regains some ground that it had previously lost.

X CORPS: The 17th Infantry advances nearly eight miles toward Kapsan during the day.

SEA WAR: USS *Saint Paul* (CA 73) commences operations with the Fast Carrier Task Force (TF 77) at Kojo. The USS *Rochester* (CA 124) sails off Songjin to provide fire support.

November 17

POLITICAL/ADMINISTRATIVE: Peng Dehuai (P'eng Te-huai) sends a telegram to the Central Military Commission saying he will release 100 POWs before the start of its campaign. Mao Zedong replies that releasing prisoners is a good idea, and they should continue to do so from time to time.

X CORPS: The U.S. 3rd Infantry Division's 7th Regimental Combat Team lands at Wonsan. Its first assignment is against isolated North Korean guerrilla units.

SEA WAR: After extensive sweeping, the harbors at Hungnam, Chinnampo, Inchon, and Kunsan are declared open and safe for all shipping. However, the minesweepers continue to make regular sweeps.

November 18

X CORPS: Being sure their rear is covered, the 31st and 32nd Regiments of the 7th Infantry Division move north to the Pungsan-Kapsan area behind the 17th Infantry. The units then plan to advance to Singalpajin on the Yalu River. However, they make it no further than a point west of Hyesanjin before they run into resistance.

SEA WAR: Eight F9F jets of the Fast Carrier Task Force (TF 77) engage eight to 10 MiG-15s. During the fight, one MiG-15 is shot down and five are damaged.

AIR WAR: The 35th Fighter-Interceptor Group settles at Yonpo Airfield near Hungnam and becomes the first USAF group to be based in North Korea. Two MiG-15s are shot down, one by the combined efforts of W. Lamp and R. Parker, and one by Frederick C. Weber.

November 19

EIGHTH ARMY: Turkish soldiers begin guarding UN supply lines against guerrilla units that are increasingly active in the area between Seoul and Pyongyang.

X CORPS: Acting on General Oliver Smith's orders, work starts on a small airfield located in the "Bean Field" just a few miles below the Chosin (Changjin) Reservoir. The marine general is worried about the protection of his advancing units. In a quick fight, the 17th Regiment captures Kapsan and moves on until it is only 23 road miles from the Chinese border.

AIR WAR: Fifty B-26s, flying from Japan, drop incendiary bombs on Musan, North Korea, located on the Tumen River border with China. The attack destroys about 75 percent of a barracks area.

November 20

POLITICAL/ADMINISTRATIVE: General Edward Almond, acting on General MacArthur's orders, warns that only small units should move in the vicinity of the Manchurian border and that no troops or vehicles are to cross into Manchuria.

EIGHTH ARMY: India's 60th Field Ambulance and Surgical Unit arrives in Korea, the neutral nation's contribution to fighting the war.

X CORPS: The 17th Infantry, marching in a column of battalions, advances another 19 miles to a point only a few miles from Hyesanjin. The 41 Independent Commando, Royal Marines, joins the 1st Marine Division at Hungnam.

SEA WAR: The deepwater port at Chinnampo is finally cleared of mines, allowing Captain Charles H. Perdue's hospital ship the *Repose* to enter.

AIR WAR: Combat Cargo Command supplies the 7th Infantry Division at Kapsan, some 20 miles south of the Yalu River, with rations and gasoline.

November 21

POLITICAL/ADMINISTRATIVE: The air force chief of staff, General Vandenberg, and the chief of naval operations, Admiral Forrest P. Sherman, in a joint meeting of State and Defense Departments, urge that, if General MacArthur's advance to the Yalu is stopped by any form of Chinese interference, Beijing should be warned. If the Chinese do not withdraw, then the United States should hit them in Manchuria. Washington takes the Chinese warning of an attack, and the fact that the CPVA seemed to have withdrawn right after the attack, as a sign of weakness and an overall reluctance to fight.

X CORPS: Elements of the 17th Regimental Combat Team, 7th Infantry Division, reach the Manchurian village of Hyesanjin, the northernmost penetration by Allied troops during the Korean War. Hyesanjin is known as the "ghost city of broken bridges." General Edward Almond orders that the road to the Chosin Reservoir be developed as a corps supply road and that an RCT from the 7th Infantry Division be instructed to guard it. Sergeant First Class Archie Van Winkle (USMC) is awarded the Medal of Honor for service near Sudong. Along the eight-mile gap between Majon-ni and Tongyang, enemy guerrilla units attack a convoy, killing 28 and destroying most of the convoy.

SEA WAR: The USS *New Jersey* (BB 62) is recommissioned after being laid up since 1948. She is scheduled for service in Korea.

November 22

POLITICAL/ADMINISTRATIVE: Chinese Communist Forces in North Korea announces that it does not want to fight the United States. At the same time, it releases 27 wounded prisoners of war.

November 23

EIGHTH ARMY: The NDVA or "Van Heutsz Battalion," established in October of 1950 by enlisting volunteers, arrives in Korea and is attached to the Eighth Army. Far East Command Intelligence finally agrees that there are up to 12 Chinese Communist divisions in Korea. History will show that there were probably 30 or more Chinese divisions in Korea at the time. Thanksgiving dinner of turkey and trimmings is served to the troops in the field.

X CORPS: The 1st Battalion leads the advance as X Corps begins to move toward the border.

SEA WAR: The East Coast Blockade and Patrol Task Group (TG. 95.2) reverts to the operational control of the United Nations Blocking and Escort Task Force (TF 95).

AIR WAR: Air Group Five under Commander H. P. Lanham ends its first tour of duty onboard USS *Valley Forge* (CV 45). Two B-29s are hit and destroyed near Andong. The crew members are captured.

November 24

POLITICAL/ADMINISTRATIVE: The British proposal for a DMZ and cease-fire is turned down by Washington. General Douglas MacArthur announces his "win the war" and "home by Christmas" offensive. A Chinese Communist special delegation arrives at the UN Security Council to participate in discussions concerning the war in Korea.

EIGHTH ARMY: Thanksgiving Day arrives bleak and blustery as General Walker's Eighth Army moves out in the final assault. The U.S. 2nd Infantry Division approaches Hill 219 on the east bank of the Chongchon River when it is hit by artillery and small arms fire. At Kunu-ri, located about 50 miles north of Pyongyang, George Company, 9th Infantry Regiment, is one of the first to be hit by the new Communist offensive. This is the evening when the Chinese cross the Chongchon and ambush the 25th Infantry Division spread out on both sides of the river. The U.S. 24th and ROK 1st Divisions attack toward Taechon. Both are able to move forward with little resistance so that by night the 24th Division is near Chongju and the 1st Division is just four miles from Taechon. The Turkish Brigade is left in reserve, while the 25th Infantry Division advances on Unsan and the 2nd Infantry Division on Huichon. The 35th Regiment, 25th Division, moving on the west side of the Kuryong River, and the 24th Infantry on the east side, make four and seven miles respectively. The ROK's II Corps moves north along mountain roads in an effort to keep pace with Eighth Army. The Gloster Battalion, concentrated at Sibyon-ni, mounts sweeps and raids on villages. One patrol runs into, and fights off, a North Korean battalion on the road to Tosan.

X Corps: X Corps strikes northwest to cut the enemy supply line at the Manpojin-Kanggye-Huichon axis. Men of the 1st Battalion, 7th Marines, have a late Thanksgiving dinner (the last full meal for 17 days) and take Yudam-ni against little resistance.

Sea War: The USS *Doyle* (DMS 34) and *Endicott* (DMS 35) sweep and buoy the channel into Kojo.

Air War: B-29s attack communication centers, supply depots, and bridges at the Yalu River. FEAF fighters increase close air support missions and fly protection for the planes of the Combat Cargo Command as it continues to supply frontline troops.

November 25

Political/Administrative: The Chinese release 57 American POWs without any explanation. The release of a prisoner from time to time is seen as an incentive for trapped UN soldiers to surrender.

Eighth Army: The 21st Infantry enters Chongju only to find that it is empty; the Chinese Communists have withdrawn. Behind the 21st Regiment, the 19th Infantry advances to Napchoongjon. The ROK 1st runs into heavy resistance in the Taechon area and a CCF counterattack drives it back. By nightfall it is still three miles short of its target. The 25th Division holds the line centered in the Chongchon Valley, with the 9th Infantry Regiment on the left and the 38th Infantry on the right, along the Paengnyong River. Baker Company of 1st Battalion, 9th Infantry, 2nd Division, fights a disjointed battle for Hill 219. The 14 men defending the spot spent most of the night fighting off grenades being thrown into the area. The 1st Battalion of the 23rd Infantry holds on to a short gap between the 9th and 38th Infantry. As the day comes to an end, the 25th Infantry Division is near Unsan. In the 2nd Infantry Division area, two CCF regiments attack the 9th Infantry at the Chongchon Valley while another hits the 38th Infantry. George Company of the 2nd Battalion is sent in relief of Charlie Company of the 1st Battalion, which is occupying the crest of Hill 291. Once on the hill, they are vulnerable to Chinese units that seem to be gathering on both sides of the hill. Then a strange thing happens: Three Chinese soldiers appear to play a flute and dance. Both sides watch for a while and then, just as suddenly, firing opens up. The defenders try to move out but, misdirected, march right into an air strike. One of the men escapes, but the rest are not heard of again. This unexplained event is followed by a second, when the Chinese choose not to follow up on their potential victory. A carrying party, bringing supplies and bed rolls to men on Hill 356, is ambushed and loses several men.

X Corps: Marine operations east of the Chosin Reservoir come to an end at noon as the marines are relieved by the 5th Regimental Combat Team.

Air War: The Greek air contribution to the UN action, the Royal Hellenic Air Force, arrives. The C-47 detachment is assigned to FEAF.

November 26

Political/Administrative: Intelligence comes in from the 7th Marines that three captured soldiers have been identified as members of the 60th CCF Division.

EIGHTH ARMY: Despite the heavy CCF assault against the 2nd Division, the attack is stopped and the Chinese withdraw to an area known as Chinaman's Hat Hill. By noon it becomes apparent that two divisions of the ROK's II Corps, the 7th and 8th, have been overrun and are retreating. The 1st Cavalry Division advances to hold Sunchon and the road. The Turkish Brigade is ordered to move toward Tokchon. The 24th Division and the ROK 1st Division are ordered to halt and begin a withdrawal to Chongchon. Sergeant John A. Pittman (USA) is awarded the Medal of Honor for actions near Kujang-dong. The enemy launches another attack on Hill 219, defended by men from the 9th Regiment. More than half the men become casualties, and they are soon out of machine gun and BAR ammunition. Finally, an air strike is called in and covers Hill 219 with napalm and rockets, but this is not enough to prevent continuing enemy attacks. The men on Hill 219 are finally ordered down. This leaves the 23rd fighting desperately to maintain a foothold near Chinaman's Hat Hill. Easy and George Companies of the 24th Infantry Regiment reach the base of Hill 273. With George Company on the hill and Easy on the ridge, they are cut off from the 3rd Battalion. Waiting for supplies, George Company is attacked and forced to withdraw to the positions held by Easy Company. Using a ruse to confuse the Chinese, Major George A. Clayton, the 2nd Battalion commander, orders the survivors to head south toward the 9th Infantry line. The enemy is left with Hill 272. By nightfall the 2nd Infantry Division has been driven back two miles southwest of the Chongchon River. The command posts of the 9th Infantry Regiment's 1st and 3rd Battalion are overrun.

X CORPS: The 5th and 7th Marine Regiments are in defensive positions near Yudam-ni, at the west side of the Changjin Reservoir. The remainder are strung out along the supply route for 45 miles. The 3rd Battalion, 1st Marine Regiment, arrives at Hagaru after dark. First Lieutenant Frank N. Mitchell (USMC) is posthumously awarded the Medal of Honor for service near Hansang-ni. The temperature drops to 0°F.

AIR WAR: B-26s fly their first close air support mission at night under TAC direction. In an effort to slow the enemy advance, B-26s from the 3rd Bomber Group fly 67 missions during a five-hour period. Marine Fighter Squadrons 214 and 323 receive the Presidential Unit Citation.

November 27

EIGHTH ARMY: The ROK's 6th Division and the 1st Cavalry Division manage to stop the Chinese at Sinchang. On the west coast, the U.S. 23rd, ROK 1st, and British 27th Commonwealth Brigade withdraw to below the Chongchon River near Anju. The 25th Infantry Division crosses the river at Anju. The Turkish Brigade and the 2nd Division are able to maintain the area northeast of Kunu-ri. Sergeant First Class Robert S. Kennemore (USMC) is awarded the Medal of Honor posthumously for action near Yudam-ni. For action near Ipsok, Captain Reginald B. Desiderio is posthumously awarded the Medal of Honor.

X CORPS: On General Edward Almond's orders, the marines launch an attack at 0800 against the Chinese, to relieve pressure on the Eighth Army that is under attack farther to the west. The decision will be called "the most ill-advised and unfortunate operation of the Korean War." The CCF counterattacks with major elements of the 120,000-man Ninth Army Group. Seventh Division's Task Force McLean and the 1st Marine Division are ordered to attack north on both sides of the Chosin Reservoir. At 2125, mortar fire begins dropping on the marine area. A wave of Chinese soldiers, moving south on a broad field covering the two-mile front of Northwest Ridge, begins an attack. Task Force McLean becomes Task Force Faith when McLean is captured, and Lieutenant Colonel Don C. Faith takes command. To the rear of the UN forces, the CPA 59th Division cuts the UN supply line. The temperature drops to −20°F. A general calm results near Yudam-ni after the marines advance about 1,500 yards. The 3rd Battalion, 7th Marines, about 1,200 strong, are able to take Southwest Ridge and Hill 1403. The 225th Infantry Regiment, Chinese Communist Forces, attacks Hill 1282; by daylight they have taken the crest and driven off the defenders.

PARTISANS: Kim Ung Su, ROK army intelligence agent and onetime schoolmaster, forms a partisan unit from former students. Supplied by Eighth Army, several units are formed to protect refugees; they move to Ae-do, an island off Sinanju.

November 28

POLITICAL/ADMINISTRATIVE: Great Britain votes against General MacArthur's UN request to bomb targets in Manchuria. The British blame MacArthur's offensive for drawing the Chinese into the war. Acknowledging their presence in the conflict, China tells the UN Security Council that it will drive all UN troops out of Korea. General Douglas MacArthur informs Washington that he is faced with an entirely new war.

EIGHTH ARMY: Divisions that have moved north of the Chongchon River are ordered to retreat south of the river. As IX Corps is trying to hold the Chinese back, I Corps organizes a defensive line south of the river. The 2nd Infantry Division and Turkish Brigade are ordered to withdraw to Wawon. The 38th is able to reassemble a mile to the south of Kunu-ri after completing a withdrawal.

X CORPS: UN Command positions begin to crumble. At dawn, faced with a determined enemy and a temperature of −20°F, every man goes on line with a weapon. During the night, troops of the 1st Marine Division are surrounded at the reservoir by a superior Chinese force. The fighting is aggravated by temperatures that continue to drop and a wind that increases. A series of marine counterattacks commences on Yudam-ni, taking pressure off the units in the valley. For action during November 28–December 2, Captain William E. Barber (USMC) is awarded the Medal of Honor. Staff Sergeant Robert S. Kennemore, 7th Marine Regiment, is awarded the Medal of Honor for action near Yudam-ni. Private Hector A. Cafferata, Jr., 7th Marine Regiment, is awarded the Medal of Honor for courageous action against the advancing enemy. During the night, the Chinese slip to the southeast and cut the remaining marine supply line. During the early morning, elements of the 7th Marine Regiment lead an attack to retake Hill 1282. In fighting that becomes hand-to-hand, the marine unit retakes the hill.

AIR WAR: Combat Cargo Command begins a two-week airlift of ammunition and supplies for those troops that are cut off. The supply problem becomes intense as UN troops begin to work their way out of the Changjin (Chosin) Reservoir area. Drops are made at extremely low levels to ensure that they are dropped on marine positions. The cargo planes suffer from heavy ground fire. The 35th Fighter/Interceptor Group flies intense close air support missions for the surrounded UN troops. Using an improved radar system, the planes are able to bomb to within 1,000 yards of the front line. Small Communist aircraft drop bombs on the U.S. air field at Pyongyang, damaging 11 P-51 Mustangs that are on the ground.

SEA WAR: COMNAVFE alerts Admiral J. H. Doyle of the possible need to redeploy all ground forces from Korea to Japan. Task Force 90 is placed on six-hour notice in anticipation of an evacuation order.

November 28–December 23

EIGHTH ARMY: Eighth Army withdraws to the Imjin River defense line on the west coast. During the withdrawal, evacuation to Japan is considered several times; while it is not ordered, the sea alert is valuable. At several locations during the general withdrawal, troops are evacuated by sea.

November 29

POLITICAL/ADMINISTRATIVE: The Joint Chiefs of Staff tells General MacArthur that he needs to close the gap that exists between X Corps and Eighth Army in an effort to form a continuous defense line across Korea. The feat will be far more difficult than it sounds for the terrain in the gap is most desolate.

EIGHTH ARMY: General Walton Walker orders Eighth Army to withdraw to new defensive lines near the North Korean capital of Pyongyang. The 1st Cavalry Division is deployed east of Sunchon to man a series of roadblocks when enemy troops, passing as refugees, infiltrate. However, the 1st Cavalry and elements of the ROK II Corps manage to block this movement enough to allow the 2nd Infantry Division to escape through Sunchon and to prevent the enemy from encircling the UN forces. The 1st Cavalry holds despite its lack of the necessary rations and still, in the freezing weather, being dressed in summer clothing. The Turkish forces, fighting with bayonets, are able to stop the Chinese advance near Kunu-ri. The UN forces on the west coast fight to keep from being surrounded. Near the village of Kunu-ri, the Eighth Army locates its right flank, where they are getting pressure from the 130,000-man, Chinese Communist 13th Army Group. Holding Kunu-ri is the key to the planned withdrawal. While the rest of Eighth Army pulls back down the main Sinanju-Pyongyang highway, the 2nd Infantry Division moves to block the Communists from attacking the flank of the withdrawal. General Laurence Keiser is threatened by enemy troops approaching his front, flank, and rear. He fights a desperate rearguard action in the Kunu-ri area in order to protect the right flank of the retreating army.

X CORPS: ROK and Eighth Army engineers at East Hill defend the area against heavy Chinese attacks. Of the 77 service personnel holding the hill, 10 are killed, 25 wounded, and nine listed as missing in action. Of the 90 ROK troops involved, 50 are casualties. In a relief effort, elements of the 1st Battalion, 5th Marines, and the 1st and 3rd Battalions, 7th Marines, as well as the 41 Independent Commandoes of the Royal Marines, fight their way through from Koto-ri to bring supplies. There they run into considerable Chinese fire, and the marines, with the aid of artillery, are forced to break off the engagement. The bulk of the convoy, however, is overrun by the Chinese and 130 UN troops captured. Fear of a second Chinese attack on the highly significant East Hill causes the marines to counterattack with a composite unit of reserve and support troops. Nearly 55 units are represented in the company-size force. Reaching the dividing line near the top of the hill they move onto the crest of the hill and hold it during the night. Major Reginald R. Myers (USMC) is awarded the Medal of Honor for service near Hagaru-ri. Private First Class William B. Bauch, 1st Marines, is awarded the Medal of Honor for action along the Koto-ri road.

SEA WAR: Seven Corsairs and five Ads are sent to aid in the defense against the attacking Chinese.

November 29–December 1

EIGHTH ARMY: During the fierce Battle of Kunu-ri, the Chinese Communists inflict heavy casualties on the U.S. 24th Infantry Division.

X CORPS: It starts to snow just before midnight as enemy shells announce the Chinese attack at Hagaru-ri. At one point the enemy breaks through deep enough to fire on the bulldozers still trying to enlarge the airfield. Soon the marines are nearly surrounded, but the enemy, unexpectedly, does not take advantage of their success. For action on these dates along the road from Koto-ri to Hagaru-ri, PFC William B. Bauch (USMC) is posthumously awarded the Medal of Honor.

November 30

POLITICAL/ADMINISTRATIVE: At a press conference, President Harry Truman refuses to reject the possible use of atomic weapons against China. He says that the United States will use every weapon available and that the commander in the field will have charge of the use of the weapons. There is worldwide reaction to this statement. Great Britain strongly objects.

EIGHTH ARMY: When the 2nd Infantry Division withdraws from Kunu-ri, its men are faced with a gauntlet that stretches for six miles along the road from Kunu-ri south to Sunchon. The area, unknown to General Keiser, is occupied by two regiments of Chinese who hold the high ground looking down on the road. At 1330, he orders his men to run the road, where they come under horrible mortar and machine gun fire. For six miles, the unit pushes through the deadly bombardment. The rush through the pass below Kunu-ri becomes one of the more desperate sagas of the Korean War. In this one afternoon, the 2nd Infantry Division loses nearly 3,000 men and most of its equipment. The Glosters arrive south of Pyongyang but approaching snowstorms prevent them moving on. The line moves through mountain passes that are to be a disaster for the 2nd Infantry Division. The 9th and 38th Infantry Regiments are decimated, and most of the division artillery is lost to the Chinese.

Marine tanks at rest after being held up by a heavy snowstorm *(Center for the Study of the Korean War, Graceland University)*

X Corps: Lieutenant General Edward Almond orders X Corps to withdraw south to Hungnam. During subfreezing temperatures, the 5th and 7th Marine Regiments begin to fight their way back to the division command post at Hagaru-ri. The marines on Fox Hill hold on against a heavy attack. Captain Carl L. Sitter (USMC) is awarded the Medal of Honor for his actions near Hagaru-ri on November 29–30. Company Item, 3rd Battalion, 5th Marines, is able to hold off another attack by Chinese forces trying to retake Hill 1282.

Sea War: All units of the Amphibious Task Force (TF 90) are ordered to Korea in response to the increasingly critical situation. Air cover from USS *Badoeng Strait* (CVE 116) pushes through the bad weather to drop napalm on Chinese troops. Thirty-nine sorties are sent to report on any and all enemy movement. All ships are put on a two-hour notice.

Air War: More than 4,300 casualties are flown out of Hagaru-ri. Marines also receive 537 replacements by air.

December

Air War: USAF Combat Cargo Command diverts 15 cargo planes to ferry approximately 1,000 war orphans from Inchon to Cheju-do. "Operation Little Orphan Annie" takes over when anticipated South Korean navy ships do not arrive.

December 1

Political/Administrative: General Douglas MacArthur explains, via a *U.S. News and World Report* interview, that the UNC retreat is a result of the prohibition that has been placed on air strikes in Manchuria. These limitations are an "enormous handicap without precedent in military history." A UN resolution establishes the UN Korean Reconstruction Agency, which is to provide relief and rehabilitation for the Korean people. At the earlier Wake Island conference, General MacArthur had said that it would cost $500 million to reconstruct Korea. By a vote of 51-0, with five abstentions, the UN resolution is approved. The Joint Chiefs of Staff (JCS) recommends to General MacArthur that X Corps be withdrawn from the Changjin Reservoir. The JCS recommends once again that he coordinate with Eighth Army as quickly as possible to prevent the enemy from moving through the gap that separates them.

EIGHTH ARMY: The British Commonwealth Brigade moves north from Sunchon to help the 2nd Infantry Division withdrawal, but it is stopped on the mountain road by the Chinese. The 23rd Regimental Combat Team of the 2nd Division, with the 15th Field Artillery, serves as the rear guard for the division's withdrawal. The 23rd RCT has to retreat to escape the slaughter experienced by the 9th and 38th Regiments on their retreat route. Nearly a third of the 2nd Infantry Division's strength—about 5,000 soldiers—is lost by the time they reach the British lines.

X CORPS: The 3rd and 7th Infantry Divisions are ordered to withdraw south to Hungnam. Task Force Faith (7th Division) begins to fight its way out from the east bank of the Chosin (Changjin) Reservoir to Hegari at the south end, in hopes of joining with the 1st Marine Division. Moving out on its own, in temperatures of −35°F, TF Faith continues moving south. Air force fighters, unaware they are U.S. Army, drop napalm at the front of the column. The desperate column reaches Hadong only to discover that the regimental tank company has already retreated to Hegari. Trying to move on, the task force is hit by a major Chinese offensive. Colonel Don Faith is killed along with most of his wounded. When the unit finally makes it to UN lines, only 385 from a 3,200-man task force have survived. Colonel Don C. Faith is posthumously awarded the Medal of Honor. The breakout from Yudam-ni begins at 0800 with the 1st and 3rd Battalions. Runs of Corsairs help keep Communist heads down. The rear guard, Baker Company of the 115th, finally sneaks off Hill 1240. Taking Hill 1419 and 1930 gives the marines the area they need for an advance across the mountain tops. Staff Sergeant William G. Winrich (USMC) is posthumously awarded the Medal of Honor for service at Yudam-ni. The 3rd Battalion, 5th Marines, is ordered off Hill 1282 that it had taken and defended the day before. A column of the 1st Battalion, 7th Regiment, comes up against Hill 1520, where the Chinese have fortified positions on the eastern and western slopes. It is considered necessary for the exhausted men to take the hill, so Baker and Charlie Company, supported by heavy machine guns and 81-mm mortars, move out. As it turns out, the Chinese defense is fairly weak and the men from Baker and Easy Companies are able to clear the eastern slope.

SEA WAR: Primary air-ground support for X Corps is assigned to the 1st Marine Air Wing by Fifth Air Force. The first C-37 lands at the Nagaru-Ri airstrip and begins the evacuation of casualties. Many flights have to be canceled because of the bad weather. The USS *Valley Forge* (CV 45) returns to San Diego. A naval air station is commissioned at Atsugi, Japan.

AIR WAR: Casualties are so heavy it is decided to try landing planes at the new strip, ordered by General Smith, that is only about 40 percent complete. Two FEAF C-47s make the landing and are able to take out about 85 casualties. On the last round they bring in ammunition. First Marine Division receives its first C-119 airdrop from Japan. Six MiG-15s attack three B-29s, damaging them despite the presence of an F-80 escort. More than 1,500 casualties from the Pyongyang area are evacuated by Combat Cargo Command. The 4th Fighter Interceptor Wing arrives in Japan. Fifth Air Force headquarters is moved to Seoul. The recently activated 314th Air Division takes responsibility for the air defense of Japan. The U.S. Air Force establishes the Tactical Air Command under Lieutenant

General John K. Cannon to train and develop tactical aviation in cooperation with the army.

December 1–24

X Corps: During this period, the U.S. X Corps, composed of the 1st Marine Division, the 7th Infantry Division, and the 3rd Infantry Division, conducts one of the most famous withdrawals in American history. While certainly a retreat, it has all the earmarks of a victory as the units withdraw against the extremes of weather and enemy action.

December 2

Political/Administrative: The CIA reports that China, lacking air and naval forces, might influence but cannot decisively alter the war. The agency doubts that the Soviet Union has any intention of participating in any significant way.

Eighth Army: At Pyongyang, elements of Eighth Army establish a defensive perimeter, but they are ordered out. Retreating troops burn the supplies at Chinnampo. The 7th Cavalry Regiment and the 3rd Battalion of the 8th Cavalry are hit by concentrated Chinese fire when they approach a roadblock set up at Hill 335. It is necessary for the units to swing wide and out of range of any fire from Hill 335.

X Corps: A company-size task force, known as Task Force Anderson, moves out of Hagaru to locate and bring back any survivors of the three, nearly destroyed battalions. It runs into CCF fire but continues its mission until it has located and rescued about 1,050 of the original 2,500 troops. The 385 able-bodied men left are assembled into a provisional battalion and given marine equipment. Sergeant James E. Johnson (USMC) is posthumously awarded the Medal of Honor for actions near Yudam-ni. Captain William Barber, 7th Marines is awarded the Medal of Honor for leading his men in a desperate rearguard action. At daybreak the 1st Battalion, 7th Marines, attacks toward Hill 1653 north of Fox Hill. After taking Hill 1520, the 7th Regiment must defend it against a Chinese counterattack. The marines lose control of the crest of the hill, but are able to create a defensive line. By 1200, however, the marines return; after considerable difficulty, and six inches of new snow, the hill is taken, and the marines are free to move on.

Sea War: The USS *Princeton* (CV 37) arrives at Sasebo en route to Korean operations. Task Force 90, Amphibious Force, starts the evacuation process by taking out UN soldiers and sailors at Wonsan and Chinnampo. Task Force 77 flies more than 80 sorties of ground support at the reservoir.

Air War: The air force flies 827 sorties in support of the retreating troops. Fourteen planes from fast carriers hit the Chinese at Chosin while observation planes cover the area, locating the enemy and relaying the information to the marines.

December 3

Political/ Administrative: The UN General Assembly resolves that the fate of non-repatriated prisoners must be determined by a political conference held three months after an armistice agreement is signed.

EIGHTH ARMY: U.S. 3rd Infantry Division begins to withdraw into the Wonsan-Hamhung area. The 7th Infantry Division's 17th Regiment withdraws toward Hungnam. UN soldiers begin an evacuation by the Task Force 90 Amphibious Force at Chinnampo, and 1,800 Americans and 5,900 ROK soldiers are taken from Wonsan on the east coast. General Walker orders the evacuation of Pyongyang and the destruction of any war materiel that cannot be evacuated quickly. On the east coast, the order is given to evacuate Wonsan.

X CORPS: Six inches of snow cover the ground and give the Toktong Pass a peaceful look. Darkhorse is on the move again, its mission to break through the Chinese soldiers that are blocking the pass in order to allow the 5th and 7th Marines to move through and reach Hagaru-ri. The first elements of the 5th and 7th Marine Regiments begin arriving within the Hagaru-ri perimeter after their breakout from Yudam-ni. Reunited within the perimeter, the division is supplied by air and more than 4,000 casualties are withdrawn by the returning planes. At 1300, after the enemy has been cleared from Toktong Pass, the 3rd Battalion, 5th Marines, and 1st Battalion, 7th Marines, join hands. At 1359, X Corps directs the 1st Marine Division to withdraw all elements to Hamhung as rapidly as possible. Nearly 300 soldiers of the 7th Infantry Division, the survivors of an ambush on the shores of the Chosin Reservoir, are rescued.

December 3–5

SEA WAR: United Nations Blockading and Escort Task Element (TE 95.1) provides escorts in addition to gun and air support for the emergency redeployment of Eighth Army troops from Chinnampo to Inchon.

December 4

POLITICAL/ADMINISTRATIVE: National Security Council document 92 urges complete control of all strategic materials that might be of any use to the PRC and the freezing of China's assets in the United States. As of December 16, 1950, the United States denies permission to any American-registered ship to enter Chinese Communist ports. In Operation Pink, General Larkin, G-4, orders a division's worth of equipment to be shipped as quickly as possible to replace items lost during the Eighth Army retreat.

EIGHTH ARMY: Pyongyang is recaptured by the Chinese without a fight. Thousands of refugees swarm south and interfere with UN retreat and evacuation plans.

President-elect Dwight D. Eisenhower inspects the living quarters of troops of the ROK's Capital Division, December 4, 1952. *(Dwight D. Eisenhower Library and Museum)*

X Corps: The Yudam-ni column successfully takes Hagaru-ri at a cost of nearly 1,500 casualties. General Oliver Smith begins flying out his casualties (nearly 4,316) and bringing in a few replacements. General Smith makes his famous statement about "advancing in another direction." On this date, Lieutenant Colonel Raymond Davis (USMC) is awarded the Medal of Honor for his actions near Hagaru-ri.

Sea War: Several units of the Far East Naval Force arrive at Wonsan to provide a sea lift for U.S. Army forces there. The USS *St. Paul* (CA 73) assumes the duties as gun fire support coordinator. Lieutenant (J.G.) Thomas Jerome Hudner is awarded the Medal of Honor.

Air War: A MiG-15 shoots down a USAF reconnaissance plane. Efforts to rescue the pilot, Lieutenant Jesse L. Brown, fail. Brown is the first African-American naval aviator. He was shot down near the Chosin Reservoir. An RB-45 on reconnaissance near Sensen is shot down. Two F-84s are hit and crash near Teju.

December 4–8

Political/Administrative: Prime Minister Clement R. Attlee's first day of a four-day visit to the United States. He has hastily arranged the trip in response to President Harry Truman's news conference at which Truman suggested he was considering atomic weapons in Korea. Attlee is afraid that the war in Korea may well turn into a wider conflict with China. While he is able to express the British point of view, he is not successful in that President Truman is unwilling to put into writing the oral promise he has given that atomic weapons will not be used in Korea without prior consultation with the British.

December 5

Political/Administrative: President Harry Truman takes steps to quiet General Douglas MacArthur. The general is ordered to issue no press releases or make any speeches on foreign policy without clearance from the Department of State. The Joint Chiefs of Staff recommends an accelerated expansion of the army, with a goal of 18 divisions created by June 1952.

Eighth Army: Pyongyang is abandoned, leaving behind vast quantities of stores and equipment. During the first phase of this retreat Eighth Army suffers nearly 11,000 casualties and is in full retreat by land, sea, and air. Much of the city of Pyongyang is on fire as enemy troops enter the outlying areas of the city.

X Corps: The 41 Independent Commandoes, Royal Marines, make an abortive foray to recover nine 155-mm howitzers that had been abandoned when their tractors ran out of diesel fuel. The equipment has to be demolished.

Sea War: The carrier USS *Princeton* (CV 37) arrives on station. UN forces, Task Force 90, evacuate more than 2,000 army and navy personnel and 6,000 ROK soldiers from small inlets and harbors running from Chinnampo to Inchon. The *HMCS Cayuga, HMCS Athabaskan, USS Bataan,* and *USS Forest B. Royal* are at anchor with guns trained at the Chinnampo waterfront. The USS *Princeton* and four destroyers join Task Force 77 and begin the launching of 284 sorties directed toward support of the troops at the reservoir. The *Noble* is detached from Wonsan and sent to Songjin to evacuate elements of the retreating ROK I Corps.

AIR WAR: The Combat Cargo Command evacuates 3,925 patients from Korea to Japan, most from the frozen strip at Hagaru-ri. Newly arrived Greek C-47s join in the airlift of supplies to UN troops still struggling in northwest Korea. The USAF suspends attacks on bridges over the Yalu as the growing depth of the winter ice provides another route across the river. Air Group 19 under Commander Richard C. Merrick begin its first tour of duty aboard USS *Princeton* (CV 37). Two F-80s are hit and crash.

December 6

POLITICAL/ADMINISTRATIVE: The Joint Chiefs of Staff directive prohibiting unauthorized public statements by public officials regarding the war in Korea becomes effective. Although a blanket statement, it is directed at General Douglas MacArthur. The United Nations issues a call to the Communists to halt their advance at the 38th parallel. General J. Lawton Collins flies to Hamhung to meet with General Edward Almond. General Almond informs him that the area can be held and, if necessary, the forces can be successfully withdrawn.

EIGHTH ARMY: The Chinese Communist Forces complete the liberation of the city of Pyongyang.

X CORPS: The fight from Hagaru-ri to Koto-ri begins with elements of the 7th on the road. Marines start the trip from Hagaru-ri to the Marine positions at Koto-ri. By dusk the 7th Marines has advanced only 5,000 yards but has not taken many casualties. As they move forward toward Hell Fire Valley—the same place where Task Force Drysdale had been ambushed—they are stopped by fire from a machine gun. An army tank finally takes out the machine gun. The route is 11 miles and takes 38 hours, during which time there are more than 600 casualties among the 10,000 marines and nearly 1,000 vehicles are lost.

SEA WAR: After the morning fog lifts, USS *Princeton* (CV 37) and USS *Leyte* (CV 32) launch 100 effective sorties. The USS *Valley Forge* (CV 45) is ordered back to Korea in response to the increased danger imposed by the Chinese intervention.

AIR WAR: The 27th Fighter Escort Wing, flying F-84 Thunderjets, arrives and begins operations from Taegu. Strong air support is provided for the retreating marines. Three B-29s are downed by Soviet pilots and crash near Anju. An F-80 is shot down near Singisyu.

December 7

POLITICAL/ADMINISTRATIVE: General Douglas MacArthur returns X Corps to Eighth Army.

EIGHTH ARMY: Task Force 90 continues the evacuation of UN troops and materiel out of Inchon. The relocation of these troops is determined by plans to create a defensive line.

X CORPS: The marines reach Koto-ri. At 1700 hours, the first elements of the 7th Regimental Combat Team are at the perimeter of Koto-ri. By 2000 hours, the marine column from Hagaru-ri manages to fight its way into Koto-ri. Task Force Dog, primarily the 3rd Battalion, 7th Infantry Division, supported by tanks and artillery, starts north and reaches Chinhung-ni by late afternoon. The port city of Wonsan is abandoned to the Chinese. General Smith orders that the height overlooking

Funchilin Pass be taken. This requires taking Hill 1328, located about 2,500 yards from Koto-ri, and Hill 1081, three miles to the north. The assignment is given to the 3rd Battalion, 7th Regiment.

SEA WAR: The USS *Philippine Sea* (CV 47), USS *Princeton* (CV 37), and USS *Leyte* (CV 32) put 125 sorties in the air directed against Koto-ri. The sea evacuation from Wonsan is completed. The navy moves 7,009 refugees, 3,834 military personnel, 1,146 vehicles, and 10,013 bulk tons of cargo.

AIR WAR: In an effort to relieve pressure on the units trying to break out from Koto-ri and Hagaru-ri, B-29s bomb towns in the Changjin Reservoir area. Combat Cargo Command is able to bring in food and supplies via a crude airfield. Eight C-119s drop bridge spans (M-2 steel tramway) to the retreating troops to cross a 1,500-foot gorge blocking the escape route. Air Force C-47 and C-19 transports continue the daisy-chain of resupply and evacuation of wounded all night. Three F-80 are shot down by enemy planes in aerial combat near Singisyu. H. Herrmann and W. Hegwood shoot down an enemy MiG-15.

December 8

POLITICAL/ADMINISTRATIVE: A joint Truman-Attlee memo is issued at the end of their talks, affirming the two nations' agreement to seek a negotiated peace; however, there is to be no appeasement. The talks also link the conditions in Korea with a need for an increase in the military strength of NATO. Neither leader is yet convinced that the assault in Korea is not a diversion for some sort of Soviet action in Europe.

EIGHTH ARMY: All Eighth Army units are continuing their move south below the 38th parallel.

X CORPS: The withdrawal from Chosin continues, with the retreat slowed by the blown bridge at the Funchilin Pass. The 1st Battalion, 1st Regiment Marines, with elements of the U.S. Third Army, holds the approaches to Hungnam in order to provide some protection at the bridge site. After evacuating the wounded during the night at Koto-ri, the units move out with 1,400 vehicles. Two battalions of the 1st Regiment stay behind to fight the rear-guard action. The 41 Independent Commandoes, Royal Marines, moves out in a snowstorm during the night to guard against infiltration. Ordered to take Hills 1081 and 1328, the 7th Regiment is committed and Easy and Fox Companies advance. Then, the attack is held off until morning.

AIR WAR: Combat Cargo Command continues to airlift supplies for the troops during the withdrawal at Changjin Reservoir.

December 9

POLITICAL/ADMINISTRATIVE: Eight ships leave from American west coast ports carrying emergency resupply items for the troops in Korea. General Douglas MacArthur requests commander's discretion to use atomic weapons in the struggle. There is no evidence that any atomic weapons are available in Korea.

X CORPS: Schmuck's battalion attacks and takes the Big Hill, killing the enemy to the last man. At the site of the blown bridge in Funchilin Pass, the column is stopped. Task Force Dog, which includes a self-propelled 155-mm howitzer, covers the position as engineers work to bridge the gap. By early evening, a tramway bridge is in place and men and vehicles begin to move south again. The tramway bridge had been dropped in sections at Koto-ri. Hills 1081 and 1328 are attacked after a day's delay, and Easy and Fox Companies move up against limited opposition and take the hills as the dawn comes up.

SEA WAR: Elements of the ROK army's I Corps are evacuated by sea from Songjin (Kimchaek) by units of Amphibious Task Force (TF 90).

AIR WAR: An F-80 and an F-84 are shot down by enemy planes near Sensen.

December 10

X CORPS: The last of the 1st Marines leave the Koto-ri sector and relieve the 7th as rear guards for the division train. For actions from November 29 to December 10, Lieutenant Colonel John D. Page is posthumously awarded the Medal of Honor.

SEA WAR: The 1st Marine jet squadron to fly in combat becomes active as 12 F9Fs of Marine Squadron 311 arrive. The embarkation of X Corps personnel and equipment begins at Hungnam. The evacuation of U.S. and ROK troops, in addition to some civilians, is completed at Wonsan.

AIR WAR: The Combat Cargo Command concludes a two-week airlift to support surrounded U.S. troops. During this time it has delivered 1,580 tons of supplies and equipment, and evacuated nearly 5,000 sick and wounded troops. More than 350 flights by C-47s and C-119s are involved. An F-84 is shot down in aerial combat near Sensen.

December 11

POLITICAL/ADMINISTRATIVE: X Corps is returned to the command of Eighth Army.

EIGHTH ARMY: Eighth Army sets up a defensive line north of Seoul just below the 38th parallel. General Walton Walker promises President Rhee that Seoul will be defended. A defensive line is established between Seoul and the 38th parallel.

X CORPS: At 1300 hours, elements of the 1st Marine Division pass through the army perimeter around Hungnam and prepare for departure. The final firefight of the breakout occurs near Sudong, when the 1st Marines drive though an attempted ambush. X Corps complete its move to Hungnam and the whole of the 1st Marines are clear. American and ROK troops begin the evacuation to Pusan.

SEA WAR: As the marines begin to reach Hungnam, MSTS ships are arriving. X Corps begins loading on ships in Hungnam harbor as the evacuation gets under way. A gunfire support group (TG 90.8) is established for Hungnam evacuation. It consists of USS *St. Paul* (CA 73), Destroyer Division 162, LSR Division 11, and a few other ships.

December 12

POLITICAL/ADMINISTRATIVE: Thirteen Asian and Arab nations submit a draft proposal requesting that a committee be formed to investigate how a cease-fire might be accomplished. The United Nations General Assembly establishes the United Nations Service Medal.

EIGHTH ARMY: Most units of Eighth Army and the ROK Army are south of the 38th parallel. The Battle of Koto-ri results in 143 UN fatalities. General MacArthur informs the Department of the Army that X Corps is being withdrawn, and the ROK 3rd Division is already heading toward Pusan by ship.

X Corps: 1st Marine Division closes into Hungnam, having successfully retreated through six Chinese divisions.

Sea War: First Anti-Submarine Hunter Killer Group commences exercises in the area off Honshu. The group consists of USS *Bairoko* (CVE 115) and destroyers of Destroyer Division 32. The East Coast Korea Blockade Patrol Element (TE 95.22) is formed. It is later changed to TG 95.5.

Air War: According to Soviet sources, three F-80s are shot down in aerial combat near Singisyu.

December 13

Political/Administrative: National Security Council document 95 suggests that the UN General Assembly appoint a committee for the purpose of setting up conditions for a cease-fire. The UN cease-fire proposal includes an end to the fighting, a DMZ across Korea, and a restriction on the introduction of new men or more equipment into Korea after the cease-fire.

Eighth Army: Royal Australian Regiment encounters North Korean guerrillas near Hill 924, called Unak San.

X Corps: General Oliver Smith closes his command post ashore and goes onboard the USS *Bayfield.*

Sea War: Divers at Wonsan, covered by USS *Zellars* (DD 777) and USS *Charles S. Sperry* (DD 697), are unable to salvage the sunken minesweepers *Pirate* (AM 275) and *Pledge* (AM 277), so the demolition of the two ships is completed.

Air War: F-84 Thunderjets attack an enemy convoy near Sariwon, causing considerable damage. Marine Fighter Squadron VMF-212 embarks aboard USS *Bataan* (CVL 29).

December 14

Political/Administrative: The UN General Assembly passes a resolution appointing a group of three representatives to determine on what basis a cease-fire might be negotiated. The UN cease-fire group is considered illegal by the Communists because there is no PRC representative present during its creation. The resolution is in response to an Arab-Asian effort to prevent the spread of the war from Korea to a larger field. The Soviet Bloc opposes the resolution and Russia votes against it. China begins to reaffirm what it requires if a cease-fire is to be considered.

X Corps: The evacuation of those forces that remain in Hungnam continues. The remnants of the First Marine Division, the 3rd Infantry and 7th Infantry Divisions, British Commandoes, the Puerto Rican 65th Regimental Combat Team, and the 3rd and Capital Divisions of the Republic of Korea, prepare to disembark. Marines begin loading on a variety of small ships. Plans are made to withdraw as many North Korean refugees as they can carry.

Sea War: The navy announces that approximately 7,000 soldiers and civilians have been successfully withdrawn from the Pyongyang area.

Air War: Combat Cargo Command begins an aerial evacuation from Yonpo Airfield near Hamhung. The Tarzon bomb (a six-ton version of the Razon bomb) is used on a tunnel near Huichon, with limited effect. Marine Fighter Squadrons VMF-312, 513, and 542 are evacuated from Yonpo, Korea, to Itami, Japan. An F-80 is shot down near Singisyu.

December 14–15

AIR WAR: Allied bombers set out to flatten Pyongyang as they drop 75 tons of bombs and vast amounts of napalm. The bombers continue to drop bombs set to explode 72 hours later in the hope of catching incoming troops. These are primarily retaliation efforts, and there will be little evidence that they have accomplished much militarily.

December 15

POLITICAL/ADMINISTRATIVE: President Harry Truman addresses the nation, telling the people that he will, on the morning of the next day, declare a national emergency.
EIGHTH ARMY: Operation SNAP, to receive and store in Japan supplies evacuated from Korea, begins. Eighth Army moves to protect Seoul and to develop a coast-to-coast defense centered at the Imjin River line north of Seoul.
X CORPS: On this date, 22,215 marines from the 1st Division sail from the Sea of Japan port of Hungnam for debarkation at Pusan further south. The cost of this withdrawal is 718 killed or died of wounds; 3,508 wounded in action; and 7,313 non-battle casualties, primarily from frostbite.
SEA WAR: Naval gunfire support, which has covered the evacuation at Hungnam, begins night harassing barrages fired by USS *St. Paul* (CA 73). Air control passes from 1st Marine Air Wing Tactical Air Direction Center to USS *Mount McKinley* (AGC 7). Wing Command Post moves to Itami Air Force Base in Japan.
AIR WAR: The 4th FIG starts conducting F-86 Sabre operations in Korea. Air Force Bomber Command launches the first mission in a new zone-interdiction plan. An F-84 is shot down by Soviet pilot Nikolai V. Sutyagin.

December 15–18

SEA WAR: The USS *Doyle* (DMS 34), *Endicott* (DMS 35), *Incredible* (AM 249), *Curlew* (AMS 8), and *Heron* (AMS 18) sweep the Hungnam harbor to clear the way for the bombardment and evacuation ships coming into the harbor.

December 16

POLITICAL/ADMINISTRATIVE: President Harry Truman signs a declaration of a state of a national emergency in the United States. He also signs Executive Order 10193, creating the Office of Defense Mobilization.
EIGHTH ARMY: The U.S. 24th Infantry Division receives the Distinguished (Presidential) Unit Citation for heroism.
X CORPS: The few remaining forces at Hamhung withdraw to Hungnam. About 12 North Korean and Chinese divisions attack Hungnam but are held back by heavy naval gunfire and waves of carrier-based aircraft that maintain a gap between the opposing forces.
SEA WAR: The light carrier USS *Bataan* (CVL 29) with Marine Fighter Squadron 212 joins Task Force 77. ROK navy intelligence groups land behind enemy lines on the east coast of Korea.

AIR WAR: Air Group 2 under Commander R. W. Rynd begins its first tour of duty on USS *Valley Forge* (CV 48). Bruce H. Hinton, flying an F-86A, downs a MiG-15.

December 17

POLITICAL/ADMINISTRATIVE: Communist General Peng Dehuai, in his report to Mao Zedong, acknowledges that some 40,000 men have died in the fighting and from the cold.

X CORPS: The Chinese occupy Hamhung. At the Hungnam evacuation, the ROK Regiments are taken off. Flights of Sabrejets fly from Kimpo to the Yalu, where they meet MiGs coming from Manchuria.

AIR WAR: Lieutenant Colonel Bruce H. Hinton, 4th Fighter/Bomber Group, scores the first F-86 aerial victory by destroying a MiG-15. Combat Cargo Command is forced to abandon Yonpo Airfield to Communist forces. Before leaving, it withdraws 2,088 tons of cargo, 228 patients, and 3,891 other passengers in four days.

December 18

X CORPS: The 1st Marine Regiment is back at Pusan where it goes into position as a part of the 1st Marine Division in Eighth Army reserve. Here it is allowed to rest and reorganize for three weeks.

SEA WAR: The battleship USS *Missouri* (BB 63) brings her 16-inch guns to the fight at Hungnam keep the Communist troops from getting too close.

December 19

POLITICAL/ADMINISTRATIVE: General Douglas MacArthur's headquarters claims that 30,000 to 40,000 casualties have been imposed on the enemy during the Chosin retreat. The Chinese do not follow up on the retreat as quickly as expected, and General Charles A. Willoughby expresses his puzzlement as to why the Chinese have remained out of continuous contact.

X CORPS: The 7th Infantry Division completes out-loading at Hungnam. The 3rd Infantry Division assumes responsibility for defending the beachhead. General Edward Almond closes his command post on shore and joins Admiral J. H. Doyle on USS *Mount McKinley* (AGC 7). The United States abandons the airbase at Yonpo near Hamhung and positions southwest of the Sungchun River.

December 20

POLITICAL/ADMINISTRATIVE: Press censorship is imposed on all news media after a leak appears concerning the arrival of the F-86 jets in Korea.

X CORPS: First Marine Division is transferred from X Corps to Eighth Army.

SEA WAR: USS *Bataan* (CVL 29) is detached from Fast Carrier Task Force (TF 77) to Escort Carrier Group (TG 96.8).

AIR WAR: Twelve C-54s of the 61st TCG are used to airlift 806 orphans from Kimpo to Cheju-do in Operation Christmas Kidlift.

December 21

POLITICAL/ADMINISTRATIVE: Chairman Mao Zedong orders General Peng Dehuai, commander of the Chinese People's Volunteer Army, to cross the 38th parallel. General MacArthur's headquarters announces the continuation of full military censorship. Also, military briefings are to be held daily.

X Corps: The Chinese attacks against the port city of Hungnam stop. The 7th Infantry Division sails for Pusan. Refugees begin loading.

Sea War: The 7th Infantry Division completes embarkation at Hungnam and heads south.

Air War: FEAF conducts Operation Kiddie Car, transporting some 1,000 Korean war orphans to the island of Cheju-do to keep them safe from the advancing Chinese. An F-84 is shot down by enemy planes near Bihen. Glenn T. Eagleston, flying an F-86A, shoots down a MiG-15.

December 22

Political/Administrative: Chairman Mao Zedong formally rejects the 13-nation resolution calling for a cease-fire. The Joint Chiefs of Staff informs General Douglas MacArthur that no additional troops will be sent to the Far East until the Truman administration decides on the future course of action.

Eighth Army: The Eighth Army Command post is moved from Seoul to Taegu.

Air War: Five USAF pilots and one U.S. Navy pilot shoot down six MiG-15s in the highest daily total since June. The pilots are Paul E. Pugh, Glenn T. Eagleston, John C. Meyer, John M. Odiorne, James Roberts, and Arthur L. O'Connor. A MiG-15 shoots down an F-86 for the first time. The headquarters for the Joint Operations Center moves to Taegu. Five F-86s are shot down in aerial combat by Soviet pilots near Sensen.

December 23

Eighth Army: General Walton Walker is killed in a head-on collision with a civilian truck near Uijongbu. Major General Frank W. Milburn assumes temporary command until his replacement, Lieutenant General Matthew B. Ridgway, army deputy chief of staff, can arrive.

Sea War: The USS *Valley Forge* (CV 45) comes on station. The USS *Charles S. Sperry* (DD 697) is damaged by three hits from a shore battery while conducting interdiction and harassing fire from the harbor at Songjin. The USS *Ozbourn* (DD 846) is damaged by Wonsan shore batteries, causing two casualties. The first 50,000 Korean refugees are loaded on three victory ships and two LSTs and head out of Hungnam. China Air Task Force planes fly 161 sorties in defense of the harbor.

Air War: Eleven U.S. and 24 South Koreans are rescued from a field nearly eight miles behind enemy lines by three H-5 helicopters that conduct the withdrawal as fighter escorts protect the operation.

December 24

Political/Administrative: The ROK National Assembly votes to withdraw the capital to Pusan. General Douglas MacArthur sends a list of targets to the Pentagon and asks for 34 atomic bombs to create a "belt of radioactive cobalt" across the neck of Manchuria, thereby assuring that there will be no invasion from there for at least 60 years.

EIGHTH ARMY: The "rear guard," the 3rd Infantry Division, completes its mission and is pulled out and sets sail for Pusan. The Hungnam operation is completed: 105,000 U.S. and ROK troops and 100,000 refugees have been evacuated. As the navy pulls out, engineers destroy the docks and facilities at Hungnam.

SEA WAR: Naval gunfire keeps the Chinese from advancing too close to the evacuating troops just out of Hungnam. Evacuation is complete with the out-loading of 3rd Infantry Division at 1436 hours.

AIR WAR: FEAF B-26s join with naval bombardment ships to keep the enemy away from the dock areas as the evacuation continues. Naval gunfire maintains a barrage along a 3,000-yard perimeter. The 3rd ARS flies 35 liberated POWs from enemy territory. Captain Stepen Naumenko, 29th Guards Fighter Aviation Regiment, is the first reported Communist ace. Four F-86s are shot down, three near Sensen and one near Tsio-To.

December 25

EIGHTH ARMY: Chinese forces cross the 38th parallel, moving into South Korea. General Edward Almond arrives at Pusan along with the last of the evacuees.

SEA WAR: The USS *Noble* (APA 218) and USS *Henrico* (APA 45) are awarded the Navy Unit Citation.

December 26

POLITICAL/ADMINISTRATIVE: Chinese Radio Peking announces that Chinese forces will drive the United States out of Korea if it does not pull out of Korea and Taiwan. When Lieutenant General Matthew B. Ridgway arrives and makes his initial inspection of Eighth Army, he is quickly convinced that the force he has inherited is not ready "mentally or spiritually for the sort of war I was planning."

EIGHTH ARMY: Lieutenant General Matthew B. Ridgway, as he takes command of Eighth Army, arrives in Tokyo to meet with General MacArthur. Ridgway is in Taegu by 1600 hours. His command is in poor shape.

December 27

POLITICAL/ADMINISTRATIVE: Lieutenant General Matthew B. Ridgway assumes command of all ground troops in Korea.

EIGHTH ARMY: The Chinese move in and occupy the port of Hungnam.

SEA WAR: USS *Cacapon* (AO 52) is awarded the Navy Unit Citation.

AIR WAR: Three UN F-80s are shot down in aerial combat near Teiju.

December 28

POLITICAL/ADMINISTRATIVE: The Australian government announces that it will continue to send replacements, but no additional troops, to Korea.

SEA WAR: Fast Carrier Task Force (TF 77) resumes air operations on the east coast of Korea. It is to furnish close air support on the eastern flank of Eighth Army and conduct interdiction strikes in North Korea.

AIR WAR: VP Squadron 47 under Commander J. H. Arnold ends its first tour of duty in Korea. The USS *Mount Katmai* (AE 16) is awarded the Navy Unit Citation. Two F-84s are shot down by Soviet pilots near Sensen.

December 29

AIR WAR: RF-51s from Taegu begin flying tactical reconnaissance in Korea for the first time. This craft has a longer range than the RF-80.

SEA WAR: The USS *Rochester* (CA 124) arrives at Inchon to assume duty as Amphibious Task Element.

December 30

EIGHTH ARMY: General Douglas MacArthur warns the Joint Chiefs of Staff that the Chinese Communist can drive the United Nations from Korea if they want to do so. At 0759 on a bitter cold morning, North Koreans holding an area known as Gibraltar, are attacked and the area taken by UN troops. The North Koreans return, probing, but are unable to retake any of the area. At 0300, Northumberland troops move out to take an area called the Hump.

AIR WAR: USAF F-86 Sabres engage MiG-15s over northwest Korea in an area known to the United Nations as "MiG Alley" and to the Soviets as "The Sausage." An F-86 is shot down by an enemy plane near Singisyu. Paul E. Pugh, flying an F-84E, downs an enemy MiG-15.

December 31

EIGHTH ARMY: During the night, Chinese troops begin their Third Phase Offensive with a general offense all along the 38th parallel from Kaesong on Ridgway's left flank to Chunchon on the right. The main effort is focused on the Yongchon-Uijongbu-Seoul area, with the intent to take Inchon and Seoul.

1951

January

POLITICAL/ADMINISTRATIVE: At the beginning of the year, a series of cables between General Douglas MacArthur and the Joint Chiefs of Staff (JCS) further aggravate the growing tension between them. In a reply to a JCS request about the state of the war in Korea, General MacArthur point out that the American forces are not being used as they should and that the denial of the use of Chiang Kai-shek's Kuomintang troops (as well as denial of permission to conduct guerrilla warfare on the Chinese mainland) means that it is time for the United States to declare a de facto state of war with the Chinese Communists. This would allow the blockade of Chinese ports, the bombardment of supply points, and the dual advantages to be gained from Chiang's delivery of troops to be used in Korea and his willingness to launch diversionary raids on the Chinese mainland.

January 1

POLITICAL/ADMINISTRATIVE: Taking command of a dispirited Eighth Army, General Matthew B. Ridgway writes a "Letter to the Men of Eighth Army," in which he describes the greater principles that he believes are involved in the war in Korea, and those for which the American GI is fighting. Two additional National Guard units are mobilized into national service. Australian troops are involved in a battle for Uijongbu. A B-29 is shot down by enemy fighters near Anju. Rear Admiral William

G. Andrewes (RN) is knighted and promoted to vice admiral. For six weeks, the British vice admiral will continue to serve under the American rear admiral. Both men agree to the arrangement.

EIGHTH ARMY: On General Ridgway's orders, the western divisions pull back from the Imjin River to a line just north of the Han River, forming a bridgehead around Seoul. The 3rd Royal Australian Regiment is responsible for blocking positions at Tokchon.

AIR WAR: The Fifth Air Force embarks on a campaign of air raids to slow the advancing enemy columns, as a suspected half-million Chinese Communist Forces and North Korean troops launch a new ground attack.

January 2

POLITICAL/ADMINISTRATIVE: The United Nations reports that the Communists have rejected its proposals. The United Nations reaffirms the non-forcible repatriation of prisoners of war on both sides as a condition for any potential cease-fire.

EIGHTH ARMY: The U.S. 2nd Infantry Division holds Wonju against two Chinese Communist divisions. When the ROK II Corps collapses on the east flank, General Matthew Ridgway orders Wonju abandoned. For action near Changbong-ni, Sergeant First Class Junior D. Edwards (USA) is awarded the Medal of Honor.

AIR WAR: C-47s drop flares, for the first time, to light an area in order to increase the efficiency of the B-26 and F-82 night attacks. The flares also help to keep the enemy from attacking U.S. troops. It becomes necessary for the 4th Fighter Interceptor Wing to withdraw its F-86s from Kimpo Airfield to Johnson Air Base in Japan, as enemy units advance rapidly.

January 3

POLITICAL/ADMINISTRATIVE: The UN Cease Fire Group acknowledges its failure to come to any kind of agreement with the Chinese Communists. President Syngman Rhee and his cabinet are the first civilian officials to leave Seoul as they flee ahead of advancing enemy troops.

EIGHTH ARMY: Matthew Ridgway orders his divisions to move south of the Han River and abandon Seoul. Eighth Army begins evacuating Seoul as massive numbers of Chinese Communist troops cross the frozen Han River, east and west of the capital, taking Uijongbu.

AIR WAR: Sixty or more B-29s drop 650 tons of incendiary bombs on Pyongyang. Planes of the FEAF fly 958 combat sorties during the day, establishing another daily record. It is necessary to destroy more than 500,000 gallons of fuel and 23,000 gallons of napalm as the UN troops leave Kimpo Air Field.

January 4

EIGHTH ARMY: General Matthew Ridgway orders his forces to concentrate at Line Dog, below the Han River from Pyongtaek on the west, in order to buy time to regroup the Eighth Army. The Eighth has retreated about 60 air miles in seven days. UN forces abandon the South Korean capital at Seoul, which is quickly taken over by Chinese Communist Forces. Eighth Army regroups behind the Pyongtaek-Wonju-Samchok line. The British 27th Commonwealth Brigade covers the withdrawal, and then blows the Han River bridges. With little to stop them, the CCF moves on toward Pyongtaek and Wonju.

SEA WAR: Task Force 90 manages to hold back the advancing Chinese Communist line with bombardments as 69,000 troops are withdrawn by sea from the port of Inchon.

AIR WAR: While Seoul changes hands again, the last USAF aircraft leave Kimpo as the enemy advances on the area.

January 5

POLITICAL/ADMINISTRATIVE: Senator Robert Taft (R-Ohio) launches an attack on President Truman for taking America to war in Korea without getting congressional approval.

SEA WAR: Amphibious Group 3, aboard USS *Eldorado* (AGC 11), completes the partial redeployment of UN troops from Inchon to Taechon.

AIR WAR: The 18th Fighter-Bomber Group launches its final mission from Suwon Airfield. After the planes leave, the buildings are burned behind them. Fifty-nine B-29s drop some 672 tons of incendiary bombs on Pyongyang.

January 6

POLITICAL/ADMINISTRATIVE: General MacArthur complains to the JCS that the ROK is unable to hold ground under pressure even when integrated with American forces. He believes that his command should be evacuated to Japan. Congress provides a supplement of $16.7 billion for Korean aid. This is in addition to funds allocated for defense.

AIR WAR: Much of the day is spent with the FEAF airlifting supplies to the U.S. 2nd Infantry Division, which is fighting to keep the enemy from breaking through the most recent defensive line that has been established across Korea. C-119s of the 314th TCG drop 460 tons of supplies to the division. Twenty-one C-47s land 115 tons of cargo at Wonju in central Korea.

January 6–11

POLITICAL/ADMINISTRATIVE: Under censorship rules announced on January 6, 1951, reporters are not allowed to report on the low morale among UN troops. Eighth Army headquarters in Korea says on January 9 that future pullbacks must be called withdrawals not retreats. Reportedly, anyone who embarrasses the UN forces can be expelled from the country, or even face court-martial. Members of the British press, openly displeased with the rulings, call the UN Command reports of battles and casualties fairy tales. Beginning on January 11 individual commands are responsible for briefing reporters, and Tokyo will deal with questions of theater development as well as human interest stories.

January 7

POLITICAL/ADMINISTRATIVE: London's *Sunday Express* runs an editorial asking if General Charles Willoughby is really General Douglas MacArthur's "publicity officer." The question arises because of Willoughby's rather "precise," but questionable, estimates of the number of Chinese soldiers involved in Korea.

SEA WAR: The Thai frigate HTMS *Prasae* goes aground. Unable to get it unstuck, the *Prasae* is destroyed. The USS *Philippine Sea* (CV 47) and USS *Leyte* (CV 32) return to action.

AIR WAR: Massive blizzards sweep Korea, preventing any potential air action.

January 8

POLITICAL/ADMINISTRATIVE: In his State of the Union address, President Harry S. Truman identifies the Soviet Union as the greatest threat to freedom around the world. Anti-communist North Korean refugees on islands located off the western coast of North Korea, ask for arms from Eighth Army to fight the Communists. At this time they are totally disorganized.

EIGHTH ARMY: UN forces withdraw to new positions about three miles south of Wonju.

AIR WAR: The continuing blizzard forces the carriers of Task Force 77 to curtail close air support. Because of this it becomes necessary for the Fifth Air Force to take over as much of the task as possible. Superfortresses bomb the Kimpo Airfield, leaving it full of craters in order to limit its use to the enemy.

PARTISANS: Eighth Army is informed by ROK Navy Task Group 95.7 that semi-organized groups of friendly partisans are still active in North Korea's Hwanghae Province. However, enemy raids have forced most of them to withdraw to offshore islands. Partisans again request Eighth Army to arm them.

January 9

POLITICAL/ADMINISTRATIVE: The Joint Chiefs of Staff (JCS) informs General Douglas MacArthur that if he can hold Korea, two partly trained National Guard divisions can be sent to defend Japan. If Korea cannot be defended, then those military units evacuated from Korea will need to be withdrawn to defend Japan. The JCS defines General MacArthur's mission as holding a succession of defensive lines in Korea, inflicting as much damage as possible on the enemy and, in the final analysis, defending Japan. President Truman presents the first Medals of Honor to wives and parents of those awarded up until September 1950. The *Chicago Daily Mail* reports that General MacArthur has recommended that American troops be withdrawn from Korea. General MacArthur's headquarters denies the report.

January 10

POLITICAL/ADMINISTRATIVE: After the JCS suggests to General Douglas MacArthur that his requests are inappropriate, they ask him to defend Korea by withdrawing to defensive positions or, if absolutely necessary, to withdraw to Japan. MacArthur asks for clarification. His position is not strong enough, he tells them, to maintain a position in Korea while at the same time guaranteeing the security of Japan. Joseph Stalin expresses his belief that the Chinese Volunteer Army should stay north of the 38th parallel in order to avoid international condemnation. The North Korean army should carry the war to the south. Brigadier General James E. Briggs replaces General Emmett O'Donnell as commander of FEAF Bomber Command. The bomber command plans to change commanders every four months in order to give senior officers experience. Major General John T. Selden succeeds Major General Gerald C. Thomas as the 1st Marine Division commander.

EIGHTH ARMY: The Chinese are once again outrunning their ability to supply their troops and halt along a line that runs from Pyongtaek to Wonju to Chechon.

X CORPS: The 1st Marine Regiment leaves Masan for the Pohang-Andong area to aid in neutralizing a North Korean guerrilla division that has infiltrated the area. The 1st, now reinforced, concentrates at Andong to secure the city.

AIR WAR: The bad weather continues, preventing Fifth Air Force from flying its usual close air support missions. FEAF, also hampered, flies the smallest number of missions since July 1950.

January 11

POLITICAL/ADMINISTRATIVE: In a report to the Joint Chiefs of Staff the CIA warns against any belief that the United States can eliminate the "China problem" at any reasonable cost. The Chinese Communist regime will, they conclude, control mainland China for some time to come. The report expresses doubt that any direct economic aid on naval or air assault will be effective. In effect it challenges General MacArthur's plan for victory. Truman appoints a mission headed by John Foster Dulles to go to Japan to confer with General Douglas MacArthur and Japanese leaders, in a first step leading to a peace treaty. President Truman says the "New Deal" must take second place behind winning the Korean War. The United Nations makes a five-point proposal for a cease-fire.

EIGHTH ARMY: Wonju falls to Chinese Communist Forces.

SEA WAR: As weather clears, aircraft from Task Force 77 hit a large troop concentration southwest of Wonju and Kangnung on the east coast and as far south as the headwaters of the Naktong River.

AIR WAR: During the day, the weather improves, allowing Fifth Air Force and FEAF Bomber Command to resume close air support, primarily for X Corps in north-central Korea.

January 11–13

POLITICAL/ADMINISTRATIVE: Some elements in the U.S. Congress continue to express the opinion that President Truman should not have sent troops to Korea without a declaration by Congress. Senator Howard Taft (R-Ohio) leads the criticism. Senator Henry Cabot Lodge provides some defense for the move.

EIGHTH ARMY: Some 70 miles east of Seoul, in the Battle of Hoengsong, 2nd and 7th Infantry Divisions, along with the 187th Airborne Regimental Combat Team, suffer 2,018 casualties.

January 12

POLITICAL/ADMINISTRATIVE: The Joint Chiefs of Staff (JCS) rejects General Douglas MacArthur's plan for ending the war in Korea. In a clarification of the January 9, 1951, directive, the JCS emphasizes the significance of holding a position in Korea for as long as possible and the accomplishment of whatever can deflate the Chinese Communist prestige. It also acknowledges that it might not be possible to hold Korea indefinitely. The Communists reject the UN five-point peace proposal. The ROK's President Syngman Rhee announces he would rather fight the Japanese than the Chinese.

EIGHTH ARMY: Chinese Communist troops drive UN forces out of Inchon after a 12-hour attack.

AIR WAR: The 98th Bomber Command's B-29s attack the city of Wonju just after it is taken by the Communists. They drop 500-pound bombs fused to explode above the ground. The attack slows the advance but does not stop it. An experimental short-range navigation system (SHORAN) is used by the B-29s for the first time.

January 13

POLITICAL/ADMINISTRATIVE: The United States supports a UN resolution agreeing to a discussion of a wide range of Asian issues. In a letter to General Douglas MacArthur, President Harry Truman mentions the possibility of withdrawing UN forces from South Korea to nearby islands for a last defense. The secretary of commerce establishes the National Shipping Authority (NSA) to provide for necessary military transportation.

EIGHTH ARMY: Chinese Communist Forces extend their attack to its farthest point within South Korea when they take Wonju.

AIR WAR: A six-ton radio-guided bomb (Tarzon) is dropped on the center span of a bridge at Kanggye, destroying the span and proving the precision of the emerging system.

PARTISANS: Fourteen ROK navy vessels withdraw civilians from Upcho-ri while the partisans fight a delaying action to cover the withdrawal. North Korean troops close in on a group of partisans fighting in the northwestern quadrant at Hwanghae.

January 14

EIGHTH ARMY: General Matthew Ridgway criticizes the laxity he perceives on the part of unit commanders that has resulted in the reckless abandonment of essential equipment. Having been warned of the extended Chinese Communist entrenchments near Seoul, General Ridgway must decide if he should try to advance or withdraw to defensive lines at Osan. In order to make this decision he executes an in-depth reconnaissance called Operation Wolfhound, named after the regiment of the same nickname.

PARTISANS: As North Korean troops close in, navy vessels withdraw hundreds of refugees from Upcho-ri on the southwest coast. Partisans fight a delaying action as the withdrawal progresses. A second partisan group in the northwest quadrant of Hwanghae Province defends refugees awaiting withdrawal.

January 14–17

EIGHTH ARMY: Operation Mousetrap is a test of the ability of the marines, with an HMR-161 helicopter, to launch an antiguerrilla attack on short notice. With only minor problems, the machines transport 500 marines to a site cleared by the Air Delivery Platoon.

January 15

POLITICAL/ADMINISTRATIVE: U.S. Army Chief of Staff General J. Lawton Collins and Air Force Chief of Staff General Hoyt S. Vandenberg visit with General Douglas MacArthur in Tokyo. They express the belief that it is best to continue operations in Korea, and the Far East commander is told to hold out as long as possible without risking the destruction of Eighth Army or endangering the security of Japan. MacArthur is informed that two additional infantry divisions are being sent to Japan to bolster the defenses there. While there is little talk among the officers about evacuation, there is a surprisingly broad discussion about which Koreans should be evacuated in order to prevent a reign of executions. After a risky inspection near the front lines in Korea, the two officers return to Washington, saying that Eighth Army can hold.

EIGHTH ARMY: Operation Wolfhound begins as a reenforced regiment of the U.S. 24th Infantry Division drives north, meeting little resistance. The orders are to kill as many of the enemy as possible and then withdraw. The enemy begins a limited withdrawal in some areas within South Korea.

PARTISANS: The 15th Attrition Section is organized under the Miscellaneous Division of Eighth Army's G-3, to direct partisan operations and to organize, equip, and train refugees into a partisan combat force. The Pyongyang Partisan Regiment in northwest Hwanghae Province is ambushed by its North Korean pursuers.

January 16

POLITICAL/ADMINISTRATIVE: Brigadier General Erwin Wright, reconsidering his previous position, begins to speculate that an evacuation of Korea may not be necessary. Nevertheless, General Douglas MacArthur is informed that, if an evacuation is required, President Harry Truman wants all members of the ROK government, military, and police to be taken out also. *Look* magazine reporter Homer Bigart says that General Douglas MacArthur committed a momentous blunder in his movement toward the Yalu and that he should be relieved.

EIGHTH ARMY: Operation Wolfhound runs into machine-gun fire and a Communist attempt to cut them off. The 31st and 47th Infantry Divisions, National Guard, enter federal service.

PARTISANS: The Pyongyang Partisan Regiment stops a North Korean attack north of Changnyong.

SEA WAR: Marine Fighter Squadron 323 withdraws from USS *Badoeng Strait* (CVE 116) for Itami.

January 17

POLITICAL/ADMINISTRATIVE: The Chinese reject a five-point cease-fire proposal issued by the United Nations.

EIGHTH ARMY: Operation Wolfhound sets up defensive positions near the Chinwichon River. Eighth Army reenters Suwon.

SEA WAR: The USS *Bataan* (CLV 29) relieves HMS *Theseus* and screening destroyers as Carrier Task Element (TE 95.11).

PARTISANS: The Pyongyang Partisan Regiment, after retaking Changnyong, holds it briefly and then is forced to withdraw to the coast.

AIR WAR: The continuation of Tarzon bombing missions is canceled because of a shortage of the bombs. Three of the guided bombs are kept for emergencies. Operating from Taegu, a detachment of the 4th FIG returns to Korea and restores F-86 operations in country. Sabres fly against enemy planes while conducting armed reconnaissance while on missions.

January 17–18

AIR WAR: In a major effort, Combat Cargo Command, using C-119s, launches 109 sorties during which they drop more than 550 tons of supplies to troops along the front line.

January 18

POLITICAL/ADMINISTRATIVE: Communist China rejects new UN cease-fire proposals as Eighth Army enters Wonju without opposition.

EIGHTH ARMY: A patrol of the 3rd Battalion, 1st Regiment, 1st Marine Division, is assigned a three-pronged mission: the protection of the Pohang-Kyongju-Andong main supply line, to secure Andong and the two airfields that are in the area, and to prevent the penetration of Chinese forces south of the Andong-Yongdok road.

January 19

POLITICAL/ADMINISTRATIVE: The U.S. Congress approves a resolution that calls for the United Nations to declare China as the aggressor. Refugees complain to UN officers that the U.S. military is indiscriminately burning houses and villages to deny them to the Communists.

SEA WAR: USS *Leyte* (CV 32) is detached from Fast Carrier Task Force 77. Escort Task Group (TG 95.5) is activated. Seven U.S. patrol frigates are added to the United Nations Blockading and Escort Force (TF-95). Members of Underwater Demolition Team 1, from USS *Horace A. Bass* (AD 124), are attacked by the enemy while on a beach survey operation. Two are killed and five wounded. The USS *Leyte* (CV 32) receives the Navy Unit Citation for service from October 9, 1950, to this date.

AIR WAR: FEAF begins a 13-day intensive air campaign, using fighters in addition to medium and light bombers, against supply and reenforcement lines. These flights are able to supply the ground troops with much of their immediate needs. Air Group Three ends its tour of duty aboard USS *Leyte*.

PARTISANS: The Pyongyang Partisan Regiment leaves the mainland and retreats to the island of Cho-do.

January 20

POLITICAL/ADMINISTRATIVE: General Matthew Ridgway issues a directive designed to convert his reconnaissance operation into a deliberate attack. The operation is called Thunderbolt. His goal is to discover enemy intentions and to drive the enemy forces north of the Han River. The United States demands that the Chinese Communists be condemned as an aggressor. The secretary of state speaks in New York and say that the United States must be willing to confer and negotiate, even with Red China.

EIGHTH ARMY: The Royal Australian Regiment occupies Inchon. The 16th Regiment Royal New Zealand Artillery joins the 27th Commonwealth Brigade. A Seabee detachment arrives with graders and bulldozers to begin work on an airfield at Bofu in Japan.

SEA WAR: Amphibious Task Force 90 conducts a sea-lift of POWs from South Korea to Joje Do and Oheju Do islands.

AIR WAR: Suddenly, after more than two weeks of absence, Communist MiGs show up again, leading to an air battle. It is the first encounter between F-86s and MiG-15s. Two F-84s are shot down by Soviet pilots near Kaisen.

January 21

POLITICAL/ADMINISTRATIVE: A Gallup poll shows that 66 percent of Americans favor a U.S. withdrawal from Korea. Nearly 50 percent disapprove of America ever sending troops to Korea in the first place.

EIGHTH ARMY: Conferring with his I and IX Corps commanders General Ridgway orders them to begin strong combat reconnaissance in the areas bounded by the Suwon-Inchon-Yoju road and the Han River. The goals are to disrupt hostile concentrations and to inflict maximum destruction on the enemy.

AIR WAR: A large flight of MiG-15s attacks USAF jets and is able to shoot down one F-80 and one F-84. Two other F-84s are shot down near Bihen. Flying an F-84 Thunderjet, Lieutenant Colonel William E. Bertram, of the 27th FEG, destroys a MiG-15. It is the first aerial victory by an F-84 Thunderjet. Paul E. Pugh, from the 4th FIW, destroys a MiG-15.

January 22

POLITICAL/ADMINISTRATIVE: The U.S. Senate votes 91-0 to pass a resolution demanding that the United Nations declare the Chinese Communists as the aggressor in Korea, and that the Communists not be allowed to represent China at the United Nations.

EIGHTH ARMY: I and IX Corps begin a limited offensive to probe Communist positions and strengths. The marines meet and flush out a group of Chinese soldiers at Mukkye-dong in the Andong area.

AIR WAR: The airfield at Bofu is completed enough to allow Lieutenant Colonel Fontana to set up the MAG 33 command post there. An F-80 and F-84 are shot down near Singisyu by Soviet pilots.

January 23

POLITICAL/ADMINISTRATIVE: The British prime minister informs the House of Commons that the British government will not support the U.S. desire to have China branded the aggressor. India takes the same position. Secretary of State George Marshall tells the House of Representatives that 18-year-old men must be made eligible for the draft in order to ensure national security.

EIGHTH ARMY: General Matthew Ridgway organizes a move against the Chinese defensive line along the Seoul-Chipyong-ni-Hoengsong area. His plan calls for I, IX, and X Corps to advance abreast northward along the Han River. First Marine Division elements attack guerrilla concentrations near Andong.

Sea War: The Anti-Submarine Warfare Hunter Killer Task Group (TG 96.7) is formed.

Air War: During an unusually heavy day for air battles, a half-hour fight between MiG-15s and 33 F-84s occurs when the MiGs emerge from across the Yalu after the F-84s attack Sinuiju. Three MiGs are shot down by members of the 523rd FES, one by William W. Slaughter, Jr., and two by Jacob Kratt, Jr. Seven F-84s are shot down by enemy fighters, five near Singisyu and three at Sinuiju. In the meantime, 46 F-80s move in to suppress antiaircraft guns around Pyongyang as 21 B-29s create huge craters in the enemy capital's airfield.

January 24

Political/Administrative: Rear Admiral I. N. Kiland relieves Rear Admiral J. H. Doyle as commander of Amphibious Group, Far East (TF 90).

Eighth Army: The Chinese Communist intervention phase of the campaign ends. General Matthew Ridgway and Lieutenant General Earl Partridge fly over the front lines trying to determine if the Chinese have, in fact, withdrawn or if they are setting a trap.

Sea War: Marine Fighter Squadrons, VMF-214, -312, and -323 begin operating from Bofu Air Base in Japan.

January 25–February 10

Eighth Army: General Matthew Ridgway's offensive begins. In Operation Thunderbolt, Eighth Army moves out on the first UN offensive of the year. The operation is to clear the area south of the Han River and retake the port of Inchon and the airfield at Suwon. This will lead to the capture of Seoul; I Corps is to take Inchon and Kimpo, X Corps to advance against Hoengsong via Wonju, and IX Corps is to move forward to attack Chipyong-ni.

Air War: In support of Operation Thunderbolt, 68 C119s drop 1,162 tons of supplies—fuel oil, sleeping bags, wire, and rations—at Chinju.

January 25

Eighth Army: Operation Thunderbolt begins with I and IX Corps, led by the 25th Infantry and 1st Cavalry. The purpose of the operation is to determine the enemy's disposition and to reestablish contact. In the action, Thunderbolt's I and IX Corps advance to the Han River, where they find Wonju deserted. The 7th Infantry Division is assigned to hold the area. At this point, Operation Wolfhound comes to a close. The result of the campaign is the belief that the Chinese strength has been overestimated. General Matthew Ridgway responds and the Western phase of the first UN counteroffensive begins.

Air War: In a major change, the Combat Cargo Command (Provisional) is replaced by the 315th AD (Combat Cargo) that reports directly to FEAF. The unit no longer depends on administrative or logistical support from Fifth Air Force.

January 26

EIGHTH ARMY: Chinese Communist Forces continue their counterattack on Wonju. Suwon, the large airfield complex north of Osan, is recaptured by the Turkish Brigade. Task Force Puller moves quickly to Chouja, seven miles northeast of Uisong, to investigate a report that 300 enemy troops are occupying the area. On arrival they discover the hills are empty.

SEA WAR: USS *St. Paul* (CA 73) is fired on by shore batteries at Inchon. Korean Marine Commandos raid Inchon.

AIR WAR: In an early manifestation of the later "early warning system," a C-47 aircraft is loaded with communications equipment and connected by radio to all T-6 Mosquitoes, Tactical Air Control Center, to coordinate close air support. The first combat flights from the new airfield at Bofu begin. USAF pilot Jacob Kratt, Jr., destroys an MiG-15, his third in two days.

January 27

EIGHTH ARMY: As Operation Thunderbolt continues and 3rd Infantry Division is joined with I Corps, the Corps captures the town of Suwon. UN forces continue to build as a 1,000-man, New Zealand artillery regiment reaches the front and it is assigned to the 27th Commonwealth Brigade. The U.S. 3rd Division joins Eighth Army.

January 28

EIGHTH ARMY: Operation Thunderbolt continues with the 24th Infantry Division added to IX Corps. As they move, the forces become aware that they are dealing with an increase in Communist resistance. A patrol from the 1st Battalion, 23rd Infantry, 2nd Division, returns from the Twin Tunnels area east of Chivying-ni with a report of an enemy buildup there.

January 29

EIGHTH ARMY: The Korean Marine Corps regiment opens its command post on Yongdok. An estimated 3,000 Chinese soldiers attack the Greek Battalion on Hill 381. After several attacks, lasting most of the night, the Greeks hold on to the hill. A patrol from the 1st Battalion, 23rd Infantry, 2nd Infantry, is sent to the Twin Tunnels area to investigate an enemy buildup, but it is attacked by two North Korean battalions. The patrol calls for help and Fox Company, 2nd Battalion, fights its way through and rescues the patrol.

SEA WAR: The carriers of Task Force 77 commence the interdiction of east coast bridges. As the bitter winter with low temperature, snow, sleet, and ice progresses, it becomes a major problem for the Task Force. The TF 77's Operation Ascendant consists of two AKAs, two LSTs, and some smaller ships with rockets attached with assistance from Task Force 95. It is involved in an amphibious feint in the Kansong-Kosong area some 50 miles behind the front line.

January 30

EIGHTH ARMY: In Operation Thunderbolt, Ridgway responds to Communist resistance by converting his "reconnaissance in force" to a major attack, including an increase in air support. Sergeant Leroy A. Mendgnca (USA) is posthumously awarded the Medal of Honor for service near Chich-on. First Lieutenant Robert McGovern (USA) is awarded the Medal of Honor for action near Kamyang-jan-ni. Enemy resistance stiffens and the Chinese begin to counterattack in battalion strength. In the continuing battle for the Twin Tunnels area, the 3rd Battalion, 23rd Infantry, along with the French Battalion, is sent to counter the developing thrust.

SEA WAR: The deceptive landing directed toward Kosong and Kansong begins with a bombardment from USS *Missouri* (BB 63) and USS *Manchester* (CL 83) and their screening destroyers. Throughout the day, the activities of an invasion continue. The action involves pre-landing deception operations, including minesweeping.

AIR WAR: Bringing 270 tons of supplies, USAF aircraft, C 54s of the 61st TCG, are the first to be allowed to land at the recaptured Suwon Airfield.

January 30–31

EIGHTH ARMY: To take advantage of the enemy's sensitivity to amphibious assaults, an amphibious demonstration is made on the east coast near Kansong, just north of the 38th parallel. RADM A. E. Smith in USS *Dixie* (AD 14) supervises the feint, which includes minesweeping and bombardment. The USS *Montague* (AKA 98) and USS *Seminole* (AKA 105), along with several LSTs, simulate the fake landing.

January 31

POLITICAL/ADMINISTRATIVE: Major General Bryant E. Moore relieves Major General John B. Coulter as commanding officer of IX Corps. The truck driver involved in the crash that killed General Walton Walker, Eighth Army Commander, is sentenced to three years in prison. Three other soldiers who were involved are acquitted.

EIGHTH ARMY: For his actions on January 30–31 near Sobuk, First Lieutenant Carl H. Dodd (USA) is awarded the Medal of Honor. Belgian troops under Lieutenant Colonel Ven Crabay arrive in Korea to join with Eighth Army. A two-battalion offensive begins at the Battle of the Twin Tunnels, with the French moving in from the left and the 3rd Battalion on the right. They gain control of the area and set up tight perimeters for the anticipated night attacks.

SEA WAR: Amphibious Task Force 90, including USS *Seminole* (AKA 105), USS *Montague* (AKA 98), and LSTs, simulate landings at Kosong and Kansong for a second day in an effort to cause enemy redeployment. The USS *Dixie* concludes the operation by firing more than 200 rounds at the beaches at Kosong.

AIR WAR: In the first special operations mission recorded, a unit of the 21st TCS implants an UN agent behind enemy lines near the town of Yonan, on the west coast of South Korea but still south of the 38th parallel.

February 1

POLITICAL/ADMINISTRATIVE: The Political Committee of the UN General Assembly votes to accept the January 30, 1951, resolution to end the war in Korea by peaceful means. The United Nations names the People's Republic of China as the aggressor nation in Korea, and calls for the cessation of all hostilities. The UN Additional Measures Committee is established to consider sanctions that can be taken against the Chinese Communists.

EIGHTH ARMY: In Operation Thunderbolt, I Corps reaches its objective, taking Inchon and Kimpo airfield. The 23rd Infantry Regiment, 2nd Infantry Division, the French Battalion, and the 347th Field Artillery Battalion confront several CCF regiments, killing at least 1,300 Chinese in the Battle of the Twin Tunnels. Master Sergeant Hubert Lee (USA) receives the Medal of Honor for his actions near Ipori.

February 2

EIGHTH ARMY: In continuing Operation Thunderbolt, armored elements of X Corps reach Wonju, in the central section, 50 miles southeast from Seoul. They are held up by CCF positions on Hill 180. Easy Company, 27th Infantry Regiment, 25th Division, is given the job of taking the hill. Led by Captain Lewis L. Millett, they attack the hill in a dramatic grenade and bayonet assault, driving the enemy off the hill. The units move forward to capture Hoengsong. The French Battalion, which is attached to the 23rd Infantry Regimental Combat Team of the 2nd Infantry Division, is hit by a Chinese counterattack north of Yoju, but it holds and stabilizes the UN position. Elements of X Corps capture Hoengsong against light resistance.

SEA WAR: The USS *Partridge* (AMS 31), a minesweeper, hits a mine off Sokcho-ri while sweeping and sinks within 15 minutes. Ten men are killed or missing, and six are wounded.

February 3

POLITICAL/ADMINISTRATIVE: In response to the United Nations, which has branded China as an aggressor nation, Premier Zhou Enlai calls the decision "an insult to the Chinese people." In his radio speech, he also indicates that the action has blocked any peaceful settlement.

EIGHTH ARMY: In Operation Thunderbolt, IX Corps moves against the hill areas around Chipyong-ni, and the 23rd Regimental Combat Team, 2nd Division, along with elements of the 1st Cavalry Division, occupies Chipyong-ni. This is the first phase of the 2nd Division plan to occupy a new Line QQ that will begin in Chipyong-ni and run east through Hoanhung-ni. Hill 321 is in the possession of Chinese troops when men of the 3rd Battalion, 1st Marines, attack. The move toward the crest is delayed by the difficult terrain but, when the Marines arrive, they discover the Chinese have withdrawn. The 187th Airborne Regimental Combat Team launches an attack and establishes the defense of a sector near Wonju, until February 21. In the Battle for the Twin Tunnels, the 23rd Regimental Combat Team moves west of the tunnels and toward the town of Chivying. The U.S. losses are 45 KIA, four MIA, and 207 WIA.

SEA WAR: USS *Leyte* (CV 32) ends its first tour of duty in Korean waters.

AIR WAR: Three F-80s are shot down near Sinuiju by enemy fighters.

February 4

EIGHTH ARMY: An unusual tactic is used against North Korean soldiers fleeing through the area held by the 7th Marine Regiment. Loudspeakers attached to planes, speak to them in their own language, demanding a surrender. Reports state that 150 NKPA soldiers surrender. For action this date at Sesim-ni, Sergeant First Class Stanley T. Adams (USA) is awarded the Medal of Honor. Turkish troops meet and defeat the Communists on Hill 431, somewhat north and west of Suwon. During the battle, the hill changes hands five times. X Corps begins Operation Roundup, a plan calling for the ROK's 5th and 8th Divisions to strike south of Hongchon-ni. UN troops moving north of Wonju discover North Koreans defending Hill 289 and Hill 300. The men of the 187th Airborne Regimental Combat Team manage to take the hills by 2030.

AIR WAR: It is necessary to modify some B-26s in order to enable them to drop flares. The C-47s usually assigned to the job are having trouble keeping up with the faster bombers.

February 5

EIGHTH ARMY: Operation Punch begins in conjunction with Operation Roundup. An extension of the I and IX Corps drive on Seoul, it consists of a task force made up of the 24th Division and heavy artillery and armor support. Its mission is to destroy the enemy in the vicinity of Hill 440 just south of Seoul. Operation Roundup is launched as UNC forces advance northward from Hoengsong toward Hongchon-ni.

AIR WAR: Strong air support is provided to X Corps as it moves near Hoengsong, north of Wonju. Major Arnold Mullins, 67th FBS, flying an F-51 Mustang, destroys a YAK-9 fighter seven miles north of Pyongyang. VP Squadron 46 under Commander M. F. Weisner completes its first tour of sea duty in Korea. VP Squadron 731, a reserve squadron under Commander H. S. Wilson, begins its sea-based tour of duty in Korea.

February 5–9

EIGHTH ARMY: Operation Punch is implemented, the same day as Operation Roundup in the area of Hongchon-ni. It consists of a task force made up of the 25th Division—reinforced with heavy artillery and armored units and air support—whose mission is to destroy all enemy troops at Hill 440, just south of Seoul, and make way for the liberation of the capital. For four days, it pounds Hill 440, and by February 9, the CCF retreats across the Han River, leaving a casualty count of 4,200 Chinese killed and 70 UN deaths. The operation clears the way for I Corps to assault Seoul. A platoon-size patrol from a KMC battalion runs into a CCF unit southwest of Yongdok; the KMC unit is scattered, losing one killed, eight wounded, and 24 missing.

February 5–11

EIGHTH ARMY: Operation Roundup is a limited offensive in central Korea to follow up on Eighth Army control of the Han River. The mission is to advance at the center of the line in preparation for the attack on Seoul. X Corps and the ROK III Corps move forward. It is executed in conjunction with I Corps and IX Corps advances under Operations Thunderbolt and Exploitation. X Corps under General Almond presses forward despite evidence that a counterattack is building. On the night of

February 11, 1951, Chinese troops, organized into four armies, counterattack in force, break through the ROK at the head, and establish roadblocks. X Corps manages to retreat toward Wonju, but the ROK 8th Infantry is nearly destroyed and several U.S. units are cut off and suffer heavy casualties. It develops into a desperate battle centered at Hoengsong, but X Corps is forced to retreat south. They halt the retreat. General Matthew Ridgway orders defensive positions established at a line north of Wonju. But the CCF launch a new attack west of Wonju at Chipyong-ni, on the X Corps left flank. The 23rd Infantry and French Battalion hold their position until relief comes.

February 6

EIGHTH ARMY: Operation Roundup continues, but Communist resistance is growing. Then, suddenly, the Chinese pressure gives way. As it does, the UN forces are racing northward while the U.S. 25th Division secures Inchon.

AIR WAR: In an effort to catch up on medical evacuations, the C-47s of the 315th AD airlift 343 patients from Chungju to Pusan. The B-26 crews are equipped with the new MPQ-2 radar that gives them an advantage, especially at night, in identifying enemy targets. The 91st Strategic Reconnaissance Squadron performs its first night photographic mission. In an effort to destroy enemy morale at Kwangdong-ni, six C-119s drop 32 booby-trapped boxes that will blow up when opened. Eight C-54s airlift a 40 ton 310 foot Treadway bridge, in 279 pieces, from Tachikawa Air Base in Japan to Taegu.

February 7

POLITICAL/ADMINISTRATIVE: The General Assembly Political and Security Committee of the United Nations decides against acting on the Soviet Union charge that the United States has been bombing targets in Manchuria. It also tables a Soviet claim that U.S. protection of Formosa against potential Chinese attack is an act of aggression.

EIGHTH ARMY: Operation Punch continues, with heavy artillery bombardment of Hill 440 and vicinity. Captain Lewis L. Millett (USA) is awarded the Medal of Honor for services rendered near Soam-ni.

February 8

POLITICAL/ADMINISTRATIVE: Brigadier General John P. Henebry replaces General Tunner as commander of the 315th AD and airlift operations in Korea.

AIR WAR: B-29s and B-26s, as well as fighters, carry out a major attack on rail lines between Hoeryong and Wonsan.

February 8–10

SEA WAR: The USS *Missouri* (BB 63) and amphibious ships under the command of the West Coast Blockading and Patrol Task Group, coordinate a pre-invasion deception at Inchon. The enemy retreats.

February 9

EIGHTH ARMY: Operation Punch finally dislodges the Communists from the area near Hill 440. The Chinese retreat across the Han River, opening the way for I Corps to assault Seoul. Estimated Chinese losses are set at 4,200 and the UNC's at 70. Operation Roundup continues to move toward Hongchon-ni while intelligence warns of a counterattack. U.S. troops reach the Han River about seven miles from Seoul. The 1st Regiment, ROK Capital Division, enters Chumunjin on the Sea of Japan near the 38th parallel.

SEA WAR: UN ships acting together bombard the east and west coasts of Korea. Prelanding operations are carried out at Inchon by the USS *Missouri* (BB 63) and amphibious ships as part of a planned deception.

February 10

EIGHTH ARMY: Operation Thunderbolt achieves its mission, with most of the Eighth Army at the Han River. ROK units move across the frozen Han to attack the lower areas of Seoul, but are repulsed by the Chinese who still control the city. The U.S. 24th Division moves forward 11,000 yards to occupy Inchon and Kimpo Airfield. South Korean National Guard units kill citizens at Koch whom they claim are stragglers and Communist guerrillas. A fake landing is planned for the Inchon area. The USS *Missouri* begins the feint with a bombardment on February 8, but the rest of the feint is canceled because the advancing UN forces are flanking Inchon.

AIR WAR: The airfield at Kimpo is again in UN hands; however, it has been so badly cratered that it will require extensive renovation before it can be used. Three F-80s are shot down by enemy fighters.

February 10–15

EIGHTH ARMY: Operation Clam-Up is carried out. It was designed to decrease UN activity along the main line of resistance (MLR) in the hope of luring enemy troops out in the open.

February 11

EIGHTH ARMY: During the night, two Chinese armies and a North Korean corps attack along the central front, scattering three ROK divisions and forcing the troops in the sector to abandon Hoengsong and withdraw southward toward Wonju. Operation Roundup is halted as Chinese and North Korean troops counterattack, beginning their Phase Four Offensive, and set up roadblocks behind UN lines. This forces X Corps to retreat to relative safety near Wonju, but the ROK 8th Infantry, located near Hoengsong, suffers 7,500 casualties and near-annihilation. The 1st Marine Division is ordered to Chongju to participate in Operation Killer. General Douglas MacArthur reportedly informs the Joint Chiefs of Staff that the Chinese have lost the advantage.

AIR WAR: VP Squadron 5 under Commander A. F. Farwell ends its land-based tour in Korea. VP Squadron 772 (Reserve) begins its tour of duty in Korea.

February 11–13

EIGHTH ARMY: The battle for Hoengsong begins when the ROK army tangles with advancing Communist forces in central Korea, some 50 miles east of Seoul. Chinese and North Korean forces attack the South Korean 3rd and 8th Divisions. Facing overwhelming forces, the ROK withdraws, leaving the 15th Field Artillery unprotected.

The Communist forces swarm over the position, resulting in serious losses among the Americans. Soon the Chinese control the only escape route, a twisting road through the valley toward Hoengsong. The Chinese rain fire down on the Americans from the hills on both sides of the road. Those Americans who are able finally reach Hoengsong, newly captured, in time to join the general retreat. During the fight, more than 500 members of the 15th and 503rd Field Artillery Battalion are killed or wounded, one of the largest single losses of the war.

February 12

POLITICAL/ADMINISTRATIVE: Representative Joseph Martin (Republican) renews his call for opening a second front in Asia by using Chiang Kai-shek's Nationalist soldiers against mainland China. He is critical of President Truman for not using Nationalists troops in Korea. Lieutenant Colonel M. P. A. den Ouden, commander of the Netherlands Battalion, is killed in action.

EIGHTH ARMY: Sergeant Charles R. Long (USA) is posthumously awarded the Medal of Honor for service near Hoengsong. UN forces regroup along Han River. The ROK Capital Division takes Yangyang.

AIR WAR: Cargo aircraft airdrop supplies to the X Corps command-post strip at Wonju. A C-47 that is dropping leaflets, which encourage the enemy to surrender, is struck by anti-aircraft fire and crashes on its return to Suwon. An F-80 fighter is shot down by enemy pilots. While B-26s hit enemy positions at night, using the light of flares to illuminate the target, two enemy aircraft use the same light to attack two UN positions.

February 12–15

EIGHTH ARMY: The 1st Detachment, NDVA, receives the Presidential Unit Citation for service during the Hoengsong-Wonju period.

February 13

POLITICAL/ADMINISTRATIVE: The British 27th Brigade passes under the command of X Corps to provide badly needed reinforcements. The previous two weeks have been spent guarding the IX Corps headquarters and the Brigade is anxious to move out.

EIGHTH ARMY: Chipyong-ni is the scene of a major Chinese Communist counterattack, and becomes the area where General Matthew Ridgway makes the decision to hold the line. Withdrawing south toward Wonju, UN troops abandon Hoengsong. By nightfall three Chinese divisions open the attack on Chipyong-ni, a key road junction in the central zone. The U.S. 23rd Infantry, 2nd Division, and its attached French Battalion form a perimeter around the town and the surrounding low ring of hills. Here they hold off three Chinese divisions for three days while their food and ammunition are supplied by air. During the night, however, the enemy launches a powerful counterattack from its bridgehead and moves toward Suwon. The attack is quickly contained. After relieving a U.S. Cavalry battalion, the Gloster Battalion is attacked by the Chinese shortly after midnight; the attack is repulsed. An attempt to bring reinforcements in by C-47s proves unsuccessful when these groups run into heavy resistance, and Chipyong-ni is surrounded by elements of six CCF divisions.

The 9th Infantry Division, which had not received the order to hold the advance, moves out in an attack on Hill 414, only to run into advance forces of the Chinese Communist 116th Infantry, which are in the lead of the Chinese counterattack. The order is given to disengage and withdraw to positions west of Wonju.

AIR WAR: C-47s of the 315th AD airlift more than 800 sick and wounded from forward airstrips, like the one at Wonju, to Taegu and Pusan. The size of the airlift uses so much equipment that it limits the ability make drops in other locations.

February 13–15

EIGHTH ARMY: The battle for Chipyong-ni (northwest of Wonju) begins when Chinese forces strike toward Wonju/Chipyong-ni. The British Commonwealth Brigade and the 3rd Battalion, 9th Infantry, as well as the 2nd Reconnaissance Company, run into heavy enemy resistance from elements of the six CCF divisions that surround the village. On the night of February 13, nearly 18,000 CCF soldiers, supported by mortars and artillery, try to overrun the perimeter but are not successful. The 23rd Infantry Regimental Combat Team, 2nd Division, still holds on. They are reinforced by air drops. On February 15, the 5th Cavalry Regiment, 1st Cavalry Division, is ordered to break through; it manages to do so by that evening. The defending group suffers 52 killed, 259 wounded, and 42 missing in action.

AIR WAR: In support of the surrounded U.S. 23rd Regiment and the French Battalion, and in the presence of heavy enemy antiaircraft fire, 93 transports drop more than 420 tons of food and ammunition. Over the night C-119s drop supplies on locations lit up by burning, gas-soaked rags. H-5 helicopters land, bringing in medical supplies and taking out more than 40 wounded men. Fifth Air Force continues to fly numerous close air support missions until the 23rd is relieved.

February 14

POLITICAL/ADMINISTRATIVE: General Matthew Ridgway blames the leaders on the excessive numbers of men and pieces of equipment that have been lost. He promises to take severe action against commanders who lose equipment. The army announces that National Guard draftees will be given 14 weeks of training and be shipped to Korea. The Senate Armed Services Committee approves a bill to lower the draft age to 18. However, every eligible man in the 19–25 bracket will be drafted before the selection of 18-year-old men.

EIGHTH ARMY: Marines are assigned to IX Corps. As the battle for Chipyong-ni continues, the Chinese break through the perimeter but are held at the high ground by artillery and mortar fire. UN forces are aided by air drops of supplies and close air support sorties. Heavy fighting breaks out around an objective known as Hill 578, as the 5th Cavalry takes the hill against stiff Chinese resistance. By evening the Chinese withdraw. For action at Chipyong-ni, Sergeant First Class William S. Sitman is posthumously awarded the Medal of Honor. Operation Roundup officially ends and the battle for Wonju begins. Elements of China's XIII Army Group open an attack on the 23rd Regimental Combat Team on and near Hill 397. The attack lasts all night.

Sea War: The navy is asked to take responsibility for interdiction on the northeast coastal route until February 25, because of the extreme distance the 9th Air Force has had to fly to complete such missions.

Air War: A B-20, flying near Hityasi, is shot down.

February 14–17

Eighth Army: The battle for Wonju begins. In central Korea, about 65 miles southeast of Seoul, the battle breaks out at the same time that other UN forces are engaged at Chipyong-ni. At daylight Communist forces attack from along the Som River to the west. The defending artillery opens up on the Communists, catching the enemy in the open and creating a near-slaughter. After making an attempt against Wonju, the remains of the enemy advance shift toward Chipyong-ni.

February 15

Political/Administrative: General Douglas MacArthur seeks permission to resume bombing the port city of Rashin, near the Russian border, but the request is denied by the Joint Chiefs of Staff. The Department of Defense announces that American casualties, as of February 9, 1951, are 8,154 dead, 30,569 wounded, and 8,289 missing. President Truman announces that the United Nations has authorized General MacArthur to move beyond the 38th parallel.

Eighth Army: At Chipyong-ni, the Chinese continue their attack through the night. The 1st Cavalry Division's Fifth Cavalry Regiment, as Task Force Crombez and reinforced by tanks from the 24th Division, is ordered to break through in support of the besieged UN forces. By evening the task force breaks through the perimeter of Chipyong-ni and ends the siege. The command loses 52 KIA, 259 WIA, and 42 MIA. In the face of the long retreat, Chipyong-ni is a vital tactical victory. Hoengsong falls to the Communists in a limited effort that goes as far south as the outskirts of Wonju. The 23rd Regimental Combat Team, defending Hill 397 from elements of the Chinese XIII Army Group, is forced from its positions and pulls back to more defensible grounds. The counterattack, extended by Lieutenant Colonel James W. Edwards's 2nd Battalion, moves against the area and, after taking a large amount of fire, the Chinese begin to withdraw. As they do, they present themselves as targets and fire is poured in on them.

Sea War: Training programs for the ROK at Chinhae begin with USS *Wiseman* (DE 667). A significant number of boats and rafts are lost in heavy storms that hit Tokyo and Yokosuka.

Partisans: Task Force William Able (soon to be identified as Leopard Base) conducts its first mission, directing partisan operations on the island of Paengnyong-do on the 38th parallel off the coast of North Korea. Baker section is established at Kijang-ni near Pusan to train partisans for airborne operations. They are commanded by Major William Burke and based in Paengnyong-do.

February 16

Political/Administrative: Soviet leader Joseph Stalin says in *Pravda* that the United Nations is being used as a weapon of aggression. He also says that he will be talking with President Truman about the possibilities of peace.

EIGHTH ARMY: After three days of fighting at Chipyong-ni, the enemy advance is stopped. For action taken near Kamil-ni, Second Lieutenant Darwin K. Kyle is posthumously awarded the Medal of Honor. The Gloster Battalion moves to take Hill 327. After a long fight against a shower of grenades and the loss of two ranking officers, the battalion is able to take the hill.

AIR WAR: The L-19 Bird Dog, an army plane, is used for the first time by the army to provide forward air control, artillery spotting, and other frontline duties. This relieves the Fifth Air Force of providing this service.

PARTISANS: Attrition Section activates a partisan headquarters on the island of Paengnyong-do, about 126 miles behind enemy lines, in order to support future raids against the North Korean mainland.

SEA WAR: As Task Force 95 starts its blockade of Wonsan harbor, the U.S. Navy begins a siege of the city of Wonsan and the Hungnam-Songjin (Kimchaek) steel complex. The siege of Wonsan will last for 861 days. It is the longest effective siege of a port in U.S. naval history.

February 17

EIGHTH ARMY: A squadron of Centurion tanks and elements of the Gloster Battalion patrol forward of the Han River without making contact.

SEA WAR: United Nations Blockade and Escort Task Group 95.2 begins the bombardment of Wonsan.

February 17–18

AIR WAR: Overnight, B-26s from Bomber Command fly the first bombing mission during which they use SHORAN. This is an airborne radar device that provides a ground beacon for precise bombing. It proves successful.

February 18

EIGHTH ARMY: General Matthew Ridgway is informed that the enemy is withdrawing. A UN patrol confirms reports that enemy forces have withdrawn along the entire central front. The Gloster Battalion moves to the Han River. In the Wonju area, the Chinese counterattack, which has lasted nearly 20 days, is finally withdrawn. It is the last of several battles for the railway and road hub.

February 19

POLITICAL/ADMINISTRATIVE: Vice Admiral William G. Andrewes (Royal Navy) relieves Rear Admiral Allen E. Smith as commander, United Nations Blockading and Escort Forces. Task Group 95.9 is formed with Rear Admiral A. E. Smith as commander.

EIGHTH ARMY: The 2nd Battalion of the Princess Patricia's Canadian Light Infantry enters combat. Taking advantage of the enemy withdrawal, Ridgway orders X Corps to complete the destruction of the North Koreans on the eastern flank of Chechon, while IX corps is to seize positions running from Hajin to Yangpyong. During the day the initiative passes into UN hands. An effort to take and control Hill 687 is delayed as enemy troops maintain strong resistence.

SEA WAR: Shore batteries at Wonsan fire on USS *Ozbourn* (DD 846) but do no damage to the ship.

February 20

POLITICAL/ADMINISTRATIVE: General Douglas MacArthur announces that he has accepted the air force thesis concerning aerial interdiction. Under consideration is a drastic and rapid withdrawal to lengthen the Chinese supply lines, advancing their logistical support difficulties and making them vulnerable to air attacks. Much to General Ridgway's amazement, General MacArthur announces, from his headquarters in Japan, the forthcoming Operation Killer.

EIGHTH ARMY: Operation Thunderbolt comes to an end. Hill 687 is finally taken and held.

SEA WAR: The Royal Navy cruiser *Belfast* and the Australian destroyer *Warramunga* join the UN forces off Wonsan.

AIR WAR: A "Special Air Mission" detachment is organized under the 315th AD to provide transportation for important officials. It is also called on to perform psychological warfare missions, including aerial broadcasting and leaflet drops over enemy territory.

February 21–March 6

EIGHTH ARMY: Despite the premature announcement, Operation Killer begins. It is directed at the destruction of a salient of North Korean troops near Chechon. The immediate goal is to kill the enemy east of the Han River and south of Line Arizona. The 1st Marine Division is to lead the attack along Route 29. The 7th Infantry Division will attack north and the British Commonwealth Division, U.S. 1st Cavalry, and 24th Infantry Divisions will approach from Yonju. From the beginning, there is trouble. Bad weather holds the advance and restricts air support. On February 23, however, the marines reach Hoengsong just south of Line Arizona, and move on to complete its portion of the operation by March 6. The X Corps, after heavy contact, close up on the 7th Division.

February 21

POLITICAL/ADMINISTRATIVE: The Communists continue their charges of germ warfare, but this time claim that the American artillery is firing typhus-infected animals into four known locations.

EIGHTH ARMY: Ridgway launches Operation Killer, an advance by the U.S. IX and X Corps, the former including the 1st Marine Division, to deny significant positions to the enemy and, in keeping with his general directive, to kill as many enemy troops as possible. The objective is the creation of a line running eastward from Yangpyong to the Han River east of Seoul, then north of Chipyong-ni and Hwangson-ni, and east to portions of the Wonju-Kangnung road between Wonju and Pangnimni. Operation Killer is the first successful counteroffensive following the Chinese intervention. It is directed against the Communists in the eastern section who, in their assault, have outrun much of their logistics. X Corps, supported by elements of IX, is sent on a kill or destroy mission against the enemy just above the town of Hoengsong.

February 22

EIGHTH ARMY: Operation Killer continues.

PARTISANS: Two CIA agents are dropped into North Korea, one at Yonan and the other near Chinnampo.

February 23

POLITICAL/ADMINISTRATIVE: The secretary of state assumes the position that neither the United Nations nor the United States is under any obligation to unify Korea by military means. Secretary Acheson asks Secretary Marshall if it would be wise to revise the September 27, 1950, directive to allow General MacArthur to cross the 38th parallel, in case Eighth Army reaches the border. The Joint Chiefs of Staff believes that the military situation demands the freedom to pursue.

EIGHTH ARMY: Operation Killer continues.

AIR WAR: In one of the early missions using the more accurate MPQ-2 radar, a B-29 mission flown by Bomber Command hits selected targets. The more precise targeting allows the bombing of a highway bridge seven miles northeast of the South Korean capital. An F-80 is shot down by enemy fighters near Anju.

February 24

POLITICAL/ADMINISTRATIVE: General Bryant E. Moore, commander of IX Corps, dies of a heart attack shortly after he is involved in a helicopter accident; he is succeeded by General Oliver P. Smith. This is the only case where a marine officer commands a major multi-force unit during the Korean War.

EIGHTH ARMY: In a significant helicopter troop-and-supply action, helicopters relieve the 2nd Battalion, 7th Marines, by airlifting troops and supplies of the 1st Battalion onto the bleak and roadless heights of Mount Helicopter (Hill 884) in Operation Rotate. The 1st and 3rd Battalions of the 5th Marines take two objectives designated as goal one.

SEA WAR: ROK amphibious troops capture Sindo-Ri Island in Wonsan harbor. They are supported by two destroyers and two patrol craft.

AIR WAR: The 315th Air Division, using 67 C-119s and two C-46s, drops more than 333 tons of cargo to front-line troops.

February 24–27

EIGHTH ARMY: Royal Australian Regiment captures Hill 614.

February 25

POLITICAL/ADMINISTRATIVE: General Stratemeyer, Far East commander, announces that interdiction raids have prevented the Communists from exploiting their initial momentum.

X CORPS: Operation Killer continues, slowed by bad weather and logistics problems.

AIR WAR: Four B-29s are shot down by enemy fighters.

February 26

EIGHTH ARMY: Corporal Einar H. Ingman, Jr. (USA), is awarded the Medal of Honor for courageous service near Maltari.

February 27

POLITICAL/ADMINISTRATIVE: The *People's Daily* and Beijing radio report that Koreans have seen the United States airdrop cholera-infected insects.

EIGHTH ARMY: The last deliberate bayonet charge in American history is led by infantryman and Medal of Honor winner Captain Lewis L. Millett.

SEA WAR: The minesweeper USS *Carmick* (DMS 33) and frigate HMS *Alacrity*, and two Korean minesweepers sweep northward along the coast into the ice-filled waters of Taedong Estuary.

February 28

EIGHTH ARMY: Operation Killer has been hampered by bad weather but manages to drive the Communists out of the town of Hoengsong. UN ground command eliminates the last Communist presence south of the Han River. A two-span "Swiss boat bridge" is constructed over the river Som allowing the marines to cross. On the eighth day of Operation Killer, all UN forces finish the job of taking their assigned objectives.

March 1

POLITICAL/ADMINISTRATIVE: Douglas MacArthur is denied permission to bomb the power complexes along the Yalu. The Joint Chiefs of Staff tells him that it is a political rather than a military decision. Mao Zedong predicts that the United States will not withdraw from Korea unless a significant part of its troops are eliminated. He suggests that his people should be prepared for a war lasting two years. Intelligence reports that the enemy is unloading Soviet sea mines from freight cars in the vicinity of the Kalmagak railroad station.

EIGHTH ARMY: Operation Killer draws to a close as X Corps battles a rearguard contingent left behind near Hoengsong to cover the Chinese retreat. While its primary objective of killing the enemy falls short of expectations, the prolonged action does establish the UN line along the Yangpyong-Hoengsong line. The 2nd Battalion, 7th Marine Regiment, encounters stiff opposition from Chinese forces as the marine advance is halted by the enemy, sheltered in log-covered bunkers.

SEA WAR: The enemy is reported unloading Soviet sea mines from freight cars in the vicinity of Kalmagak railroad station.

AIR WAR: MiGs attack unescorted B-29s over Kogunyong, North Korea. The 22 F-80s that were to support the bombers arrived too early and had to return to base for more fuel. When the unescorted bombers arrive at Kogunyong, North Korea, they are attacked by a flight of MiG-15s. Ten planes are damaged but manage to get back to South Korean territory. One of the B-29 gunners, William H. Finnegan, is able to bring down a MiG fighter. The first mission of the new interdiction campaign begins. Two B-29s and an F-80 fighter escort are shot down by enemy planes.

PARTISANS: Task Force William Able is instructed to initiate partisan operations in support of Eighth Army's Operation Killer. The Able Base is organized into Donkey units (clandestine groups) of about 20 men and women.

March 2

POLITICAL/ADMINISTRATIVE: Ambassador at large Philip C. Jessup leaves for the Big Four deputy foreign ministers conference that begins on March 4, determined not to be fooled by Soviet efforts to control the agenda.

EIGHTH ARMY: The 2nd Battalion, 7th Marines, makes an effort to continue the assault but is able to move forward only a few yards in the face of heavy enemy artillery. Elements of the 1st Marine Division capture Hoengsong.

AIR WAR: Three F-84s are shot down by enemy fighter planes.

SEA WAR: The HMNZs *Hawea* is in Korean waters.

March 3

EIGHTH ARMY: A regiment of the ROK Capital Division is ambushed near Soksa-ri. The South Korean unit is cut off and suffers 59 killed, 119 wounded, and 801 missing. The 7th Marines moves out toward Hill 303; before any significant advance can be made, the movement forward is halted.

SEA WAR: Working at Wonsan, the Gunfire Support Element (TE 95.21) is fired on by shore batteries but no hits are recorded. Transport Squadron 1, with 3 APA (attack transport) and 2 AKA (attack cargo), makes an amphibious demonstration off Cho-do near Chinnampo. The Danish hospital ship *Jutlandia* joins the UN forces in Korea.

AIR WAR: After the arrival of a new shipment of Tarzon bombs, the FEAF restarts the precision raids that have been suspended since January 17, 1951. Two F-86s are shot down by enemy planes near Andong.

March 4

POLITICAL/ADMINISTRATIVE: At the Deputy Foreign Ministers Conference in Paris, Andrei Gromyko, the Soviet delegate, accuses the United States of arming West Germany in violation of postwar agreements. Major General William Hoge arrives at Yoju and takes command of I Corps, relieving Major General Oliver P. Smith, who returns to the 1st Marine Division, allowing General C. Puller to resume his duties as assistant division commander.

EIGHTH ARMY: The 2nd Battalion, 7th Marines, moves forward slowly and prepares to attack the Chinese on Hills 536 and 333. Moving to the crest in the snow, they discover that the Chinese have pulled out during the night. Operation Killer comes to an end at this point except for mopping up exercises.

AIR WAR: Fifty-one C-119s drop 260 tons of much needed supplies to the 1st Marine Division.

PARTISANS: William Able's Donkey 4 launches Operation Shining Moon.

Mobile Army Surgical Hospital helicopter landing on the hospital ship *Jutlandia (Center for the Study of the Korean War, Graceland University)*

March 5

POLITICAL/ADMINISTRATIVE: The French Battalion receives its third U.S. Presidential Citation for its action at Hongchon-ni and at Hill 1037 (March 3–5, 1951).

EIGHTH ARMY: The Greek Battalion is able to hold back a Chinese offensive southeast of Yongdu. Elements of the U.S. 2nd Infantry Division, supported by the French Division, capture and hold several Communist positions near Pangnum.

SEA WAR: Marine Fighter Squadron 212 is located on board USS *Bataan* (CVL 29). Intelligence reports suggest a buildup of Chinese Communist junks and other forces in ports opposite Formosa.

AIR WAR: The air force establishes a Special Activities Unit Number One, a hybrid intelligence and special operations unit designed to perform behind the enemy lines on missions ranging from airfield surveillance to airborne ranger assaults on high priority targets.

PARTISANS: Operation Virginia I is supported by four U.S. rangers who join Baker Section's K-3 Detachment.

March 5–28

SEA WAR: Out of the more than 70 mines sighted during this period, 36 are destroyed by sweepers.

March 6–21

EIGHTH ARMY: Operation Ripper begins. It is an extension of Operation Killer, but in this case it covers the entire front. The mission is to cause as many casualties as possible and, in doing so, to prevent a Communist offensive. Also a goal is the retaking of Seoul. The advance is to move as far as Phase Line Idaho. Launched on March 7 with the 25th Division crossing the Han, elements of the combined forces reach Line Albany on March 12, and by March 13, the ROK unit has moved beyond Line Idaho. By March 15, they will have outflanked Seoul only to discover that the Communists have withdrawn to about five miles north of the city. By March 19, most units are on the Buster/Buffalo Line. They seize Chunchon on March 21.

March 6

EIGHTH ARMY: The Belgium-Luxembourg battalion of elite infantry is placed in a combat position.

SEA WAR: Marine Fighter Squadron 312 goes aboard USS *Bataan* (CVL 29).

AIR WAR: After an absence of several months, F-86s of the 334th FIS, using the base at Suwon, begin flying raids near the Yalu River.

March 7

POLITICAL/ADMINISTRATIVE: General Douglas MacArthur's "Die for Tie" statement is made at a Suwon press conference. In it, he is critical of President Truman's policies and informs the group that if the war continues without any attack on the military elements in China, it can result only in a stalemate. General MacArthur had flown to Suwon to be present at the jump-off of Operation Ripper.

Eighth Army: Operation Killer is followed up by Operation Ripper. Ripper is to take UN forces to a new base line, Idaho, on the central front. Only the flooding of the Han River has delayed the UN advance until this date when Ridgway launches Ripper. Operation Ripper begins after one of the largest artillery bombardments of the war. The 25th Division crosses the Han and establishes a beachhead on the north bank. The 7th Marine Regiment reenters Hoengsong more than three weeks after the 15th Field Artillery was cut off. They find most of the bodies still there, frozen in the positions of their death. As Operation Ripper begins, the Chinese are forced to retreat north of the 38th parallel, where they try to establish a bulge at what is to be called Line Idaho. I Corps, which has just taken Kimpo, is waiting to the west and south of Seoul for the final assault on the capital. X Corps and IX Corps are in position to sweep westward until Seoul is surrounded. Near Yonggong-ni, Sergeant First Class Nelson V. Brittin (USA) is posthumously awarded the Medal of Honor.

Sea War: Acting on information from a Korean agent, USS *Manchester* (CL 83) bombards a train on the Kalmagak railroad siding, creating a massive explosion assumed to be the reported cargo of Soviet mines.

Air War: Fifth Air Force continues to fly close air support missions to aid the launching of Operation Ripper. An attack on a six-span bridge drops the northern-most span.

March 7–12

Eighth Army: Australian troops are involved in the Battle of Maehwa-San.

March 7–25

Eighth Army: I Corps retakes Kimpo Airfield and Inchon and is to remain in a defensive position as Operation Ripper sends IX and X Corps to form a bulge east of the city of Seoul at Line Idaho. The idea is to surround Seoul with three U.S. corps. By the 14th, Seoul is taken, and on March 15, Hongchon is captured by elements of X Corps. The U.S. 1st Cavalry and U.S. 187th Airborne Regimental Combat Team manage to complete the exercise by taking Chunchon on March 21.

March 8

Political/Administrative: In Washington, D.C., the minority leader of the House of Representatives, Joseph W. Martin, sends General Douglas MacArthur a copy of a speech calling for the use of Chiang Kai-shek's Nationalist troops to open a second front. He asks General MacArthur for his opinion.

Eighth Army: Operation Ripper continues. Company Able of the 7th Marines runs into a most difficult action against a hill mass just left of Oum San. Several Marines are killed by artillery fire as they advance. Despite the resistance, the unit eventually takes its goal. The Philippine 10th Battalion Combat Team takes objectives in the area of Chamsili Island.

Sea War: Siege of Songjin (Kimchaek) begins with HNLMS *Evertsen* (DD), USS *Manchester* (CL 83), USS *Frank E. Evans* (DD 754), and USS *Charles Sperry* DD 697).

March 9

EIGHTH ARMY: As Operation Ripper continues, the advance of the 1st Marines is held up while units of the 1st Cavalry, on the right, catch up. Patrols go out to see if lateral contact can be made. For action near Taemi-dong, Captain Raymond Harvey (USA) is awarded the Medal of Honor.

March 10

EIGHTH ARMY: Operation Ripper continues.

March 11

POLITICAL/ADMINISTRATIVE: The first 51 bodies of the U.S. KIA from Korea leave for Yokohama, Japan, and then to the United States for burial.
EIGHTH ARMY: In Operation Ripper, the advance resumes as the first element of the 24th Infantry Division gains Line Albany. A patrol from George Company, 3rd Battalion, 1st Marines, has a hot fight over Hill 549, where one marine is killed and nine are wounded before the marines withdrew. IX Corps reaches the first phase line of Operation Ripper.
SEA WAR: Marine Night Fighter Squadron 41 is pulled out to be equipped with new all-weather jet aircraft.

March 12

EIGHTH ARMY: In Operation Ripper, additional elements of the 24th Infantry Division reach Line Albany shortly after dark. Third Division patrols cross the Hongchon River to locate Chinese shore positions that might have been vacated.
AIR WAR: Two MiG-15s are shot down by planes from the 36th FBS.

March 13

POLITICAL/ADMINISTRATIVE: General Matthew Ridgway issues the following statement to the press: "It would be a tremendous victory if the war ended with our forces at the 38th parallel. However there are no such plans now that I know of." Brigadier General Crawford Same, General Douglas MacArthur's surgeon general, is escorted by a CIA guerrilla team, launched from a navy destroyer, to behind the lines south of Wonsan. He is seeking conclusive evidence to discredit the Communist propaganda claims that the United Nations is using germ warfare.
EIGHTH ARMY: Enemy opposition to Operation Ripper is noticeably weakened. In Operation Ripper, the ROK III Corps is meeting little opposition, and the III and I Corps move beyond Line Idaho, which is their objective.

March 14

EIGHTH ARMY: The second phase of Operation Ripper begins as the U.S. 2nd Division and ROK 5th and 7th reach Line Albany. Eighth Army forces in the west push across the Han River near Seoul. Five patrols from the ROK 1st Division enter Seoul without opposition. Moving into the outskirts of Seoul, they discover a devastated city, a metropolis of ruins in which only the capitol building and the railway station remain standing. There they move quickly toward Phase Line Buffalo. All units are dug in along Phase Line Albany. In the center section, X Corps moves forward rapidly to the north and takes the key junction and supply depot at Chunchon. The second phase of Operation Ripper is over.

SEA WAR: The battleship USS *Missouri* (BB 63) begins a five-day bombardment during which it is credited with the destruction of eight railroad bridges and seven highway bridges.

AIR WAR: At night several B-26s begin dropping tetrahedral tacks on highways around the north side of Seoul to puncture the tires of enemy vehicles. They use a specially designed tack because the roofing nails, used earlier, had not been all that effective.

March 15

POLITICAL/ADMINISTRATIVE: General Douglas MacArthur argues in a press interview that the UNC should not halt short of the unification of Korea.

EIGHTH ARMY: The city of Hongchon-ni falls without a fight to the 7th Marines. Patrols move into Seoul during the night. This will be the fourth time the capital city changes hands.

SEA WAR: Task Element of Task Group 95.2 bombards troops assembled near Wonsan. The USS *Wallace L. Lind* (DD 703) is fired on at Singi.

PARTISANS: In Operation Virginia I, Eighth Army Liaison Group parachutes a sabotage team made up of U.S. Army Rangers and Korean guerrillas into North Korea. The mission is not well planned and fails, with heavy casualties.

March 16

EIGHTH ARMY: In Operation Ripper, the enemy begins to disengage its troops and begins a series of withdrawals. The 1st Battalion, 7th Marines, under Major Sawyer, runs into harsh resistance from the CCF on Hill 339. The fight becomes a matter of moving from bunker to bunker and tossing grenades. The engagement lingers on during the night.

SEA WAR: Wonsan shore batteries fire on the East Coast Blocking and Patrol Task Group with no significant damage.

AIR WAR: The FEAF flies 1,123 support sorties, setting a new daily record. An F-86 is shot down by an enemy plane.

March 17

POLITICAL/ADMINISTRATIVE: Concerned that he has not been given the details of Operation Ripper, General Douglas MacArthur raises the question of the independent operations conducted by Eighth Army.

EIGHTH ARMY: In Operation Ripper, X Corps and the ROK III Corps reach Line Idaho. The Greek Battalions, often fighting with bayonets, fight off four Communist attacks against their position. They then drive northwest of Hongchon-ni, killing 220 of the enemy and capturing 12. IX Corps is ordered to make for Line Baker and Line Buffalo.

AIR WAR: In a midair collision that kills both pilots, Lieutenant Howard J. Landry of the 36th Fighter/Bomber Squadron, flying an F-80, hits a MiG-15 fighter and both planes go down.

March 18

POLITICAL/ADMINISTRATIVE: The Department of Defense announces that all basic training units located within the United States are now integrated.

EIGHTH ARMY: The city of Seoul is once more in the hands of troops from Eighth Army.

March 19

POLITICAL/ADMINISTRATIVE: The Joint Chiefs of Staff (JCS) meets with the secretaries of state and defense concerning the future course of action in Korea and drafts a presidential declaration on matters of defense. A cable is sent to General MacArthur, in strict secrecy, telling him to expect a forthcoming statement from President Truman, concerning efforts to begin cease-fire talks. He is informed that no more advances are to be made until a political solution has been attempted.

EIGHTH ARMY: In Operation Ripper, most elements of IX Corps reach their goal at the Buster/Buffalo Line only to find most Communist troops already withdrawn.

March 20

POLITICAL/ADMINISTRATIVE: The JCS informs General Douglas MacArthur of President Truman's decision to begin a cease-fire initiative. But before it is put into effect, General MacArthur makes his own announcement. It amounts to sending the Chinese leaders an ultimatum. General MacArthur writes to Representative Joseph Martin (R-Massachusetts) continuing his criticism of the manner in which the war is being fought. He disagrees vehemently with Truman's handling of the war in Korea.

EIGHTH ARMY: In Operation Ripper, the IX Corps takes Chunchon unopposed. Follow-up marine units reach Line Buffalo after encountering only moderate opposition. The 1st Marine Division and with the KMC move toward Hill 975 where they receive an ammunition drop. Eighth Army jumps off from Line Buffalo toward Line Cairo.

AIR WAR: Fifteen F-94Bs, all-weather jet fighters, arrive in the Far East to provide night escorts for B-29 bombers.

PARTISANS: Under code name Donkey, partisans act on a report of a meeting of communist officials in a village police station. They arrive at night, and in the morning are able to observe several high-ranking political officers arriving at the spot. When the meeting has begun, the partisans cut the telephone lines to the village and attach explosives to the windows and doors. After the explosion, they move inside and kill off those remaining, killing 27 officials.

March 21

POLITICAL/ADMINISTRATIVE: General MacArthur's response to the JCS is abrupt, stating that no more military restrictions should be placed on his command, nor should those already imposed be implemented. Responding with less force than might be expected, the JCS amends its previous orders to say that the aggressor should not be pushed back any farther than the 38th parallel, claiming at that point that the UN will have accomplished its goal. Chief of Staff General George C. Marshall reports to the

American people that the size of the U.S. military has reached 2.9 million because of the Korean War.

March 22

POLITICAL/ADMINISTRATIVE: General MacArthur approves the plans submitted by General Matthew Ridgway for a drive across the 38th parallel. In what is to be called Operation Courageous, Ridgway plans to move forward and occupy positions generally along the 38th parallel. Ridgway is warned, however, that he is not to cross to the north of the 38th parallel until specifically ordered to do so.

SEA WAR: Marine Air Control Group 1 and Marine Ground Control Interceptor Squadron 3 arrive in the Far East to be attached to the 1st Marine Air Wing. Fleet Activities Group, the Military Sea Transport Services, and Naval Control Shipping Office are assigned to oversee all naval functions at Inchon.

March 23

EIGHTH ARMY: The last airborne drop of the war is executed. In Operation Tomahawk, the 187th Airborne Regimental Combat Team (2nd and 4th Ranger Companies attached), 3,447 men, makes an air assault on Munsan-ni, 20 miles northwest of Seoul. The hope is to cut off the Communists who are fleeing in the face of Operation Courageous. The Communists, however, are able to withdraw fast enough so that the operation is not very effective. The American costs include 84 who are injured in the jump, one KIA, and 18 WIA. Task Force Growden moves forward to make contact with airborne troops.

AIR WAR: The second airborne operation of the war, Operation Tomahawk, involves 120 C-119s and C-46s and 16 escorts. The 314th TCG and the 437th TCW air transport take the airborne troops from Taegu to Munsan-ni, which is, at the time, behind enemy lines. It is about 20 miles northwest of Seoul. There they drop the 187th Airborne Regimental Combat Team, two Ranger companies, and 220 tons of supplies. Helicopters evacuate 68 wounded men from the drop zone. The raid by five AD fighters eliminates a significant portion of the ground fire, but one C-199 is hit by ground fire and crashes on the return trip. Elsewhere, 22 bombers of the 19th and 307th Bomber Groups, escorted by 45 F-86s, manage to destroy two bridges in the northwestern section of Korea. An F-86 is shot down by enemy fighters near Bihen.

March 24

POLITICAL/ADMINISTRATIVE: General Douglas MacArthur demands that the Chinese meet with him to discuss the terms of their surrender. General MacArthur issues a "Pronunciamento" in which he clearly states that the United States must act against Communist China without regard to the politics of the United Nations and suggests that such military action might not be limited to Korea. In doing so he postpones, if not destroys, President Truman's forthcoming peace proposal. MacArthur further imposes his will by saying in Tokyo, after returning from a visit to the front, that he has authorized General Ridgway to take Eighth Army as far across the 38th parallel as is tactically advisable.

EIGHTH ARMY: Task Force Growden reaches Munsan-ni to join up with the 187th Airborne Regimental Combat Team that was dropped earlier. ROK forces cross the 38th parallel.

SEA WAR: The USS *Tilefish* (SS 307) ends its period of patrols in Korean waters where she has kept tabs on the movement of Soviet vessels.

AIR WAR: An H-19 helicopter is used for the first time to evacuate wounded. This copter is considerably larger and more powerful than the utility H-5. It was already in Korea being service tested. Richard S. Becker from the 334th FIS shoots down a MiG-15.

March 24, 26–27

AIR WAR: More than 50 C-119s and C-46s drop more than 264 tons of additional supplies for UN troops near Munsan-ni. This massive drop, conducted over several days, is necessary because surface lines have become undependable.

March 25

EIGHTH ARMY: Operation Courageous continues in an effort to inflict maximum destruction on the withdrawing Communist forces.

SEA WAR: Rail traffic along the northeast coast of Korea is greatly curtailed by the destruction of key bridges and the cutting of railway lines.

PARTISANS: British naval units agree to support partisan operations by providing naval gunfire and aerial strikes when called on.

March 26

EIGHTH ARMY: Operation Courageous continues as the Communists withdraw to positions just south of the 38th parallel.

SEA WAR: The USS *Philippine Sea* (CV 47) ends its first tour of duty in Korean waters.

March 26–April 7

POLITICAL/ADMINISTRATIVE: The Ministers of Foreign Affairs in American States meet in Washington to discuss Latin America's contribution to the war in Korea. The United States receives rhetorical support; only Colombia sends even a token force to Korea.

March 27

EIGHTH ARMY: Elements of Eighth Army cross the 38th parallel. The first UN troops, the ROK's I Corps, once more cross into North Korea.

SEA WAR: The USS *Boxer* (CV 21) replaces USS *Valley Forge* (CV 45). The first all-reservist Carrier Group, Group 101, enters the war aboard USS *Boxer*.

AIR WAR: Air Group 101 begins its tour of duty on USS *Boxer* (CV 21).

March 28

POLITICAL/ADMINISTRATIVE: Vice Admiral H. M. Martin relieves Vice Admiral A. D. Struble as commander, Seventh Fleet. The Canadian foreign minister criticizes U.S. military policy in Korea and says that the easy relationship between Canada and the United States is over.

SEA WAR: Efforts begin to reopen Inchon as a supply port. USS *Philippine Sea* (CV 47) begins its second tour of duty in Korean waters. Air Group 5 on USS *Philippine Sea* ends its first tour of duty in Korea and is transferred to USS *Valley Forge* (CV 45) for the trip home. Air Group 2 ends its tour aboard USS *Valley Forge* and is transferred to USS *Philippine Sea*.

March 29

POLITICAL/ADMINISTRATIVE: China uses a radio broadcast to reject MacArthur's ultimatum and to promise a renewed military effort in Korea.

EIGHTH ARMY: Operation Courageous is completed. Communist forces have withdrawn to just south of the 38th parallel.

AIR WAR: B-29s with heavy fighter escorts bomb the bridges across the Yalu. The winter ice is beginning to thaw and it is becoming important to prevent movement by bridge. The Fifth Air Force light bombers were unable to destroy the bridges during the winter. An enemy twin-jet bomber is spotted over central North Korea, suggesting that the NKPA is improving its airfields.

March 30

SEA WAR: The USS *Philippine Sea* (CV 47) receives the Navy Unit Commendation for service from August 4, 1950, to this date.

AIR WAR: B-29 gunners of the 28th Bombardment Squadron, Staff Sergeant Norman S. Green and Technical Sergeant Charles W. Summers, shoot down two MiGs in one day. The C-119s are pulled off line for modification.

PARTISANS: Virginia I (a clandestine unit) reestablishes contact with 7th Infantry Division liaison aircraft.

March 31

POLITICAL/ADMINISTRATIVE: General MacArthur informs the Joint Chiefs of Staff that a massive Chinese counterattack is expected at any time after April 1.

EIGHTH ARMY: An evaluation at the end of Operation Courageous suggests that, while it advanced, it failed in the effort to trap gathering North Korean troops. Advancing ROK I Corps takes the town of Yangyang.

SEA WAR: Two Panther VF 191 jets from USS *Princeton* (CV 37) hit enemy railway bridges at Songjin (Kimchaek).

AIR WAR: The first aerial victory recorded by an F-86 since 1950 is scored by Flight Lieutenant J. A. O. Levesque of the Royal Canadian Air Force. He is flying with the 334th FIS in an F-86 when he destroys a MiG-15. The 3rd ARS uses an H-19 helicopter to retrieve 18 UN personnel from behind enemy lines. This is the first use of this plane in a special operations mission. The C-119s of 315th Air Division are grounded for modifications.

PARTISANS: Three of the Virginia I Rangers, who had been caught behind enemy lines, are ex-filtrated by a navy helicopter from a hot landing zone. All of the others have been killed or captured.

April 1

POLITICAL/ADMINISTRATIVE: General Matthew Ridgway requests permission for the army to integrate all units within his command.

AIR WAR: RAAF pilots from the 77th Squadron down two MiG-15s. Bruce Gogerly is responsible for one, and officers Scannel, Thorton, and Cadan share the credit for another.

April 2

EIGHTH ARMY: The 1st Marine Regiment is ordered into reserves near Hongchon-ni while the 5th Marines and the 1st KMC Regiment move forward to bring relief to the 1st Cavalry Division north of Chunchon.

AIR WAR: Planes from Task Force 77 strike the bridge at Carlson Canyon, hitting it so hard that none of the original spans are left standing.

April 3

POLITICAL/ADMINISTRATIVE: Rear Admiral A. E. Smith returns to command of United Nations Blockading and Escort Force, relieving Vice-Admiral William G. Andrewes, Royal Navy.

EIGHTH ARMY: Under the name Operation Rugged, Eighth Army advances and begins an effort to move forward to an area that will later become the Kansas-Wyoming Line. The U.S. 187th Airborne RCT, 1st Cavalry Division, and 3rd, 24th, and 25th Divisions are assigned to advance north across the 38th parallel from their positions near Munsan-ni. The 2nd Australian Battalion arrives in Korea. General Ridgway orders Operation Dauntless, designed to destroy the enemy and its equipment, to keep enemy units in front of I and IX Corps off-balance, and to advance the two corps toward the Utah Line. If attained, it will create a salient of about 12 miles. The advanced troops would then be about six miles from Chorwon. In the U.S. I Corps sector, a rail bridge over the Han River toward Seoul is completed and supplies begin to arrive by rail.

SEA WAR: Logistic Support Force, including Service Squadron 3 and Service Division 31, are placed under Commander Seventh Fleet for operational control.

AIR WAR: The 3rd ARS, using a service test (performance test under combat conditions) YH-19 helicopter, is struck by small-arms fire as it picks up a downed F-51 pilot southeast of Pyongyang. An F-86 is shot down by enemy fire near Tetsuzan. James J. Jabara of the 334th FIS and Benjamin H. Emmert each shoot down a MiG-15 fighter. R. McLain and W. Yancey combine efforts to shoot down a third MiG-15.

April 3-16

EIGHTH ARMY: Dates for the Battle of Kapyong-Chon, in which the British are heavily involved.

April 4

EIGHTH ARMY: UN forces move forward to establish a defensive line at Kansas. Achieving some success, Matthew Ridgway extends his reach to include Line Utah, a bulge in Line Kansas, to occupy the area south of Chorwon in the southwest corner of the Iron Triangle. The 7th Infantry Division completes it move westward, establishing its command post in the Yangye area.

AIR WAR: Edward C. Fletcher, 336th FIS, shoots down a MiG-15 enemy fighter.

April 5

POLITICAL/ADMINISTRATIVE: In Washington, D.C., House of Representatives Minority Leader Joseph W. Martin (R-Massachusetts) reads a letter from General Douglas MacArthur on the floor of the House. On February 12, Martin had sent a copy of a speech calling for the use of Chiang Kai-shek's Nationalist troops to open a second front. He asked MacArthur for his opinion. MacArthur's answer is highly critical of President Truman. General Douglas MacArthur concludes his letter with "there is no substitute for victory." The Joint Chiefs of Staff (JCS) tells the secretary of defense and President Truman that in their opinion if the Russians enter the war in Korea, with regular troops or volunteers, all UN forces should be withdrawn from Korea. The JCS calls for atomic retaliation against 200 Soviet bombers at air bases in Manchuria, in the event of a major attack on UN forces. In reporting to the JCS, General MacArthur informs them that Operation Rugged will move troops across the 38th parallel and occupy the land to the south of Line Kansas. Following up with Operation Dauntless, Eighth Army will move an additional 20 miles into North Korean territory and occupy Line Wyoming. These moves are based on the assumption that, after the positions have been established, they will be maintained by patrols and probes but that there will be no major aggressive move. There is on the part of the JCS an increasing fear that the Chinese will bring their air power to bear in ways they have not done before. The fear is that the enemy will begin bombing and strafing UN troops. This would require a response by bombing the bases in Manchuria. The JCS asks for, and receives, presidential approval for this action in case it is necessary. This knowledge is deliberately withheld from General MacArthur, as consideration of his dismissal is already in the wind.

EIGHTH ARMY: Eighth Army moves forward in Operation Rugged as the U.S. 3rd, 24th and 25th Divisions and the ROK 1st Division of I Corps advance in the west. The goal of the exercise is to establish a line roughly 20 miles above the 38th parallel where UN forces can entrench, fortify, and prepare for the anticipated Chinese attack. In the center, IX Corps, made up of the 1st Marine Division, the 1st Cavalry Division, and four Ranger companies of the 187th Airborne RCT, is to advance. The advance is assigned so that X Corps, with the 2nd, 7th, and ROK 5th Divisions, can go up one coast and the ROK I and II Corps, the other. Seventh Division relieves elements of the 1st Marines and attacks toward Line Kansas. Corpsman Richard David Dewert (USN) is posthumously awarded the Medal of Honor.

SEA WAR: During the night, the destroyers *Zellars* and *Hank* fire 297 rounds of five-inch shells on vehicular traffic at Wonsan.

AIR WAR: VP Squadron 28, under Commander C. S. Minter, begins its tour of land-based duty in Korea.

April 5–9

EIGHTH ARMY: General Matthew Ridgway calls for Operation Rugged, which will consist of an Eighth Army advance to what will become the Kansas-Wyoming Line.

April 5–15

Eighth Army: The enemy is entrenched in the Chorwon-Kumhwa-Pyongyang areas (Iron Triangle). Six U.S. divisions, 1st Cavalry, 2nd, 3rd, 7th, 24th, and 25th Infantry, are advancing. The cost of the battle for the United States is 156 KIA, 1,056 WIA.

April 6

Political/Administrative: President Truman meets with his advisers to consider the dismissal of UN commander General Douglas MacArthur. Truman believes that MacArthur has been insubordinate and that it is necessary to remove him in order to maintain civilian control over the war. President Truman orders the transfer of "nuclear capsules" to Guam in fear of a new major offensive by the Chinese in Korea. A major UN cemetery is dedicated at Pusan by General Matthew Ridgway.

Eighth Army: Operation Rugged is completed as troops reach and set up defensive lines across the 38th parallel at Line Kansas. X Corps is reorganized with the 2nd U.S. Infantry Division and the 2nd ROK reassigned and the U.S. 3rd, 7th, and ROK 5th and 8th Divisions assigned. Eighth Army is instructed to move into the Iron Triangle, thus establishing a bulge in the line and an advance above the Wyoming Line. There it will link up with IX and X Corps, which are already established on the Kansas Line. The operation is called Dauntless.

Air War: An F-86 is shot down by enemy fighters near Sensen. The U.S. I Corps moves its command post forward to Uijongbu and the X Corps moves closer to Chungju.

April 6–11

Eighth Army: I Corps, along with other elements of Eighth Army, is to move into the area known as the Iron Triangle to develop an offensive bulge. The directions are that, after clearing the enemy from the triangle, I Corps is to advance to the Kansas-Wyoming Line. This effort, known as Operation Dauntless, reaches the Wyoming Line, but I Corps develops a supply problem. It is then determined that I Corps should line up with IX and X Corps on the Kansas Line and link with them.

April 7

Eighth Army: Operation Dauntless continues. The 41st Independent British Royal Marine Commandoes destroy rail installations south of Sorye dong. The 7th Infantry Division reaches the 38th parallel. Heavy resistance is encountered along the Kansas Line as reconnaissance patrols run into more and more roaming units of enemy soldiers.

Sea War: The USS *Saint Paul* (CA 73), USS *Wallace L. Lind* (DD 703), USS *Massey* (DD 778), USS *Fort Marion* (LSD 22), and USS *Begor* (APD 127) support a commando raid. USS *Valley Forge* (CV 45) ends its second tour of duty in Korean waters. The USS *Saint Paul*, USS *Massey*, USS *Lind*, and the USS *O'Brien* (DD-725) fire on and destroy enemy shipping in the port of, and damage rail junctions in, Songjin.

Air War: Aerial observers sight 2,000 enemy vehicles moving south. Two B-29s and an F-84 fighter are shot down by enemy planes near Andong.

PARTISANS: A commando and guerrilla raid is launched against Chongjin in the far northeast. Under command of Admiral Roscoe E. Hillenkoetter, it is supported by the cruiser USS *Saint Paul* (CA 73) and the destroyers *Wallace L. Lind* (DD 703) and USS *Massey* (DD 778) and 250 men of the 41st Independent Royal Marines, who land from USS *Fort Marion* (LSD 22) and USS *Begor* (APD 127). The attack destroys the exposed coastal rail line eight miles south of Chongjin.

April 8

EIGHTH ARMY: Operation Dauntless continues against increasing resistence.

SEA WAR: Command reports that cooperation between air force night heckler planes and besieging ships has greatly reduced enemy traffic at Wonsan and nearby. British Royal Commandoes land under the support of naval gunfire and blow up more than a hundred feet of rail track and a key railroad bridge.

AIR WAR: An RB-45 is shot down near Andong and crashes into the gulf.

April 8–15

SEA WAR: Task Force 77 is employed in operations at the Formosa Strait, during which time it makes no interdiction flights over Korea.

April 9

POLITICAL/ADMINISTRATIVE: The Joint Chiefs of Staff unanimously recommends that President Truman relieve General Douglas MacArthur on the charge of insubordination.

EIGHTH ARMY: Operation Rugged reaches its goal. With limited resistance from the Communists, the U.S. I and X Corps, along with the ROK III Corps, all reach Line Kansas. Resistance has been the greatest in the central section and had slowed the progress of the X Corps and the ROK III Corps. As Eighth Army moves north, enemy troops open the dam gates and flood the Pukhan River area, taking out some of the smaller bridges. The effort is generally unsuccessful. At about 0430, the 1st Battalion, 17th Regiment, 7th Infantry Division, begins to cross the Soyang River. By nightfall they have secured a crossing site on the river and hold the high ground on Hill 512 that overlooks the crossing.

AIR WAR: A B-26 and an F-80 fighter are shot down by enemy planes near Tetsuzan, seven B-29s and an F-84 near Andong, and two F-80s near Sinuiju. USAF pilot Arthur L. Connor, with the 336th FIS, shoots down a MiG-15.

April 10

POLITICAL/ADMINISTRATIVE: Secretary of Defense George Marshall approves the program called the Qualitative Distribution of Military Manpower. It requires the other services to assume their share of the responsibility for the "less gifted inductees" with the army.

EIGHTH ARMY: An extended Operation Rugged moves to Line Utah. The occupation of Line Utah is the objective of Operation Dauntless, which will run until April 22, 1951. General Ridgway's plan is for I and X Corps to move toward the Iron Triangle with the intention of harassing, rather than defeating, the enemy.

AIR WAR: An F-86 is shot down near Tetsuzan and an F-84 near Sinuiju. James J. Jabara, a USAF pilot from the 334th FIS, shoots down an enemy MiG-15 fighter.

April 11

POLITICAL/ADMINISTRATIVE: President Truman relieves General Douglas MacArthur, replacing him with General Matthew B. Ridgway, who assumes command of all UN forces. Truman states that "military commanders must be governed by the policies and directives issued to them." Due to a press leak, the dismissal order is released before General MacArthur is notified. There is an immediate reaction from members of Congress and the American people. The Joint Chiefs of Staff issues a directive to prepare plans to identify targets for atomic bombardment in Korea.

EIGHTH ARMY: UNC forces reach the Wyoming Line in Operation Dauntless (the last military operation in which General MacArthur played a part), but because they have overextended both supplies and lines of supply, they are held up at Wyoming Line. Hastily commissioned, a force of Rangers and cavalrymen attempts to capture the Hwachon Dam but fails.

SEA WAR: Carrier Task Force 77 begins air operations in the Straits of Formosa, flying outside the three-mile limit of the Chinese mainland.

April 11–22

EIGHTH ARMY: An attempt is made by I and IX Corps to establish a 25-mile bulge toward the Iron Triangle. The advance is planned to move to Line Utah, then Line Wyoming. They reach Utah on April 21 and move slowly toward Wyoming. A Chinese counterattack, however, displaces them from their position and delays the plans.

April 12

POLITICAL/ADMINISTRATIVE: The Eighth Army commander, General Matthew Ridgway, officially replaces General Douglas MacArthur, who has been relieved by President Truman.

EIGHTH ARMY: The Gloucestershire Battalion of the British 29th Brigade moves out to seize the high ground around Cheesing. Anticipating a massive Chinese counterattack, Eighth Army completes the primary plan for Operation Audacious. It calls for the orderly withdrawal of the army in the face of a successful enemy attack in force. The withdrawal is to consist of a series of phase lines south of Line Kansas. They are: Delta, Golden, and Nevada. Line Golden is a heavily fortified defense line around Seoul.

AIR WAR: Forty-six B-29s, and approximately 100 escorting fighters, run into a flight of MiGs estimated at from 100 to 125. The bombers, on a mission to attack the Sinuiju bridge over the Yalu, are caught unaware. During the raid, three bombers are shot down and seven damaged by enemy fighters. Four F-80s are shot down. The cost to the enemy is 11 planes. Gunners from the B-29s, Lyle R. Patterson, Robert A. Winslow, E. S. Dye, and David R. Stime, shoot down four of the MiGs, and F-86 pilots John C. Meyer, James J. Jabara, Bruce H. Hinton, and Howard M. Lane destroy four more. It is one of the heaviest concentrations of B-29s against a single bridge during the war, and it ends up being one of the largest aerial duels. While there are several recorded hits, the Sinuiju bridge across the Yalu River remains standing. The 1st Marine Air Wing flies its first night close air support mission.

April 13

POLITICAL/ADMINISTRATIVE: General Matthew Ridgway completes his plan for the rotation of troops based on six months of combat. It will go into effect on April 22, 1951. There is a huge backlog of men eligible for rotation.

April 14

POLITICAL/ADMINISTRATIVE: Lieutenant General James A. Van Fleet arrives at his new command and relieves General Matthew Ridgway of Eighth Army.

EIGHTH ARMY: The British 29th Brigade, with Belgian forces attached in addition to tanks of the 8th Hussars, engages an enemy patrol four miles north of the Imjin River and attacks the enemy-occupied Hill 826.

PARTISANS: General James Van Fleet, the new Eighth Army commander, is a firm believer in the role of partisan units and intends that there will be support for, and the use of, increased partisan participation.

SEA WAR: The ROK frigate *Apnok,* returning from a mission in the gulf of the Yalu, is attacked by three propeller-driven aircraft. The frigate shoots down one plane but suffers numerous casualties among its crew.

April 16

POLITICAL/ADMINISTRATIVE: General and Mrs. MacArthur depart from Haneda Airport. Nearly half-a-million Japanese citizens come to see them off.

EIGHTH ARMY: The X Corps moves beyond Line Utah and takes control of the Hwachon Dam, which overlooks the reservoir. On the east coast, South Korean forces capture Taep'o-ri, as other ROK troops cross the Imjin River. The British 29th Brigade takes Hill 826. The Northumberland Fusiliers and the British Centurions conduct a nine-mile reconnaissance patrol into no-man's-land without meeting any enemy forces.

SEA WAR: Task Force 94, Naval Forces Marines, reverts to operational control of CINCPAC.

AIR WAR: An F-80 is shot down near Sinbi-do by enemy planes.

April 16–20

AIR WAR: Bomber Command flies an average of 10 B-29 sorties each day against several North Korean airfields, including the ones at Pyongyang, Kangdong, and Yonpo. Believing that control of the air is an essential, the United Nations Command begins a week during which it focuses its Superfort attacks on North Korean airfields. Naval and marine aircraft join the attack. The raids will continue on a more limited base until mid-June of 1951.

April 17

POLITICAL/ADMINISTRATIVE: In an executive order, President Truman extends involuntarily the enlistments of all U.S. personnel by nine months. The drain on manpower in Korea is creating a serious shortage in the military services. General Matthew Ridgway asks the Joint Chiefs of Staff for permission, on his own discretion, to withdraw UN forces from Korea if the Soviet Union enters the war. His request is denied.

EIGHTH ARMY: The 24th and 25th Infantry Divisions continue to advance against softening Chinese resistance.

AIR WAR: Anxious to get information about the MiG fighter, a YH-19 helicopter transports a U.S. and South Korean team to a site south of Sinanju, North Korea, where a MiG has reportedly crashed. While escorts are warding off enemy fighters, the party is able to extract some components and take photographs. During the mission, the helicopter is hit by ground fire but returns safely.

April 18

EIGHTH ARMY: A KMC patrol crossed the Pukhan River into the town of Hwachon and finds that it is deserted except for a few dozen Chinese soldiers.

AIR WAR: The 3rd ARS, using H-5 helicopters, evacuates 20 wounded soldiers from aid stations on the front lines. During the 10 trips required, the helicopters are fired on several times by enemy ground troops. Two F-86s are shot down near Tetsuzan by enemy planes.

PARTISANS: A unit called Donkey attacks an army vehicle park and takes the town of Sinchon, where the North Koreans have 1,700 citizens imprisoned on the charge of aiding the United Nations. The partisan group is able to free most of them and to get away.

April 19

POLITICAL/ADMINISTRATIVE: General Douglas MacArthur, given the privilege of addressing a joint session of Congress, delivers his "old soldiers never die" speech, calling for an economic and naval blockade of China, the removal of limitations on overflights of China, and the use of Nationalist Chinese troops in the war against communism. "The object of war is victory," he said, "not prolonged indecision." Matthew Ridgway informs General James Van Fleet that he is not to send any strong forces farther north than Line Wyoming without permission from his office.

EIGHTH ARMY: Units of I and IX Corps reach Utah Line in the area south of the Iron Triangle. Marine engineers install a floating bridge across the Punhan River for the advancing KMC.

AIR WAR: The first of the newly modified and reconditioned C-119s return to service.

April 20

EIGHTH ARMY: A patrol of the 8th Hussars encounters and skirmishes with a Chinese patrol. The U.S. 7th Infantry Division and the ROK 3rd Division (X Corps) reach Line Kansas.

April 21

EIGHTH ARMY: The first UN Counteroffensive Campaign ends. Canada sends the three battalions of the 25th Infantry Brigade to join the UNC in Korea. The first to enter combat is the Princess Patricia's Light Infantry. An ROK regiment seizes the Hwachon Dam but has to pull out as the Chinese break through the line, regaining control of the dam. The 1st Marines resumes the attack toward Line Quantico. They are able to advance against little resistance. General James Van Fleet establishes Line Alabama to secure Route 24 at the junction with the coastal highway near Kansong.

SEA WAR: Marine Air Group 12 begins operating from Seoul City Airport.

AIR WAR: An SA-16 from 3rd ARS fails in its attempt to pick up a downed YAK fighter pilot. The pilot, who went down near Chinnampo, is wanted by intelligence for questioning, but heavy enemy fire makes the pickup impossible. Three YAK-9 enemy planes are shot down by USMC pilots Philip C. DeLong (who gets two) and Harold D. Daigh.

April 22

POLITICAL/ADMINISTRATIVE: Truce talk negotiators reassemble. The new Eighth Army commander, General James Van Fleet, during his first press conference has to reply "I don't know" to a question about what his goals are in Korea. While other nations continue to rotate their troops home by units, the United States initiates a "Rotation Plan" that allows personnel to return to the United States individually after a specified number of months in Korea. While the idea improves morale among the troops, it does create a rather significant problem in terms of unit unity and the effectiveness of commands.

EIGHTH ARMY: The CCF Spring Offensive Campaign begins and the renewed Communist aggression is able to stop the advancing UN forces just short of Line Wyoming. The attack is launched along the entire Eighth Army front. During the night the Communists penetrate UN lines as the 3rd Division gives up about 10 miles. The Gloster Battalion, primarily the men of Charlie Company, 7th Platoon, stop the Chinese advance four times until they run out of ammunition and must withdraw. After fierce fighting for Hill 148 (Castle Hill), the CCF is able to take the highest point of the defensive line. The 1st Marine Division is in the Iron Triangle between Chorwon, Pyongyang, and Kumhwa. They receive two hours' notice of a major Chinese assault that begins during the night. The ROK 6th Division on their left collapses and starts to head for the rear. In doing so, they impede the advance of supplies and replacements. The marines hinge back on their line to cover the flank. Chinese forces attack the Kapyong valley. Patrols of the Gloucester and Northumberland Fusiliers north of the Imjin River report that the majority of the enemy forces are on the move. By 0600, the Belgian Battalion also reports contact. At 1000, the Ulster battle patrol is sent hastily forward in Oxford Carriers to secure the bridges at Ulster Crossing, the ford by which the Chinese have been crossing for several days. The South Korean and New Zealand troops are forced into retreat. All other troops are ordered to halt the attack. The Australians are pushed back, but after a night of fighting they recapture their position. For this action, they are awarded a U.S. Presidential Unit Citation. UN forces are halted just short of their goals on Line Alabama and Line Wyoming. The 29th British Infantry Brigade occupies a position near the Imjin and Hantan Rivers, holding the hinge between the 29th and the ROC 1st Division. The Chinese begin their assault at night but the 29th holds its ground. PFC Herbert A. Littleton (USMC) is posthumously awarded the Medal of Honor for his action near Chunchon. Line Nevada is designated as the second withdrawal line, to be used if enemy pressure forces elements of Eighth Army to retreat from Line Delta.

AIR WAR: Four Communist MiG-15s are shot down by USAF pilots Glenn T. Eagleston, William B. Yancey, Richard S. Becker, and James J. Jabara.

April 22–24

EIGHTH ARMY: The British 27th Brigade is ordered to block the Kapyong River valley to prevent the Chinese from cutting Route 17. The Royal Australian Regiment is set up on Hill 504, which is located to the right of the valley. During the fight for Hill 504, three Australian companies lose and then retake the hill. On the 24th, the Chinese return in force and the Australians are ordered off.

Aerial view of deep trench line cut into a hill, 1951 *(Center for the Study of the Korean War, Graceland University)*

April 22–25

EIGHTH ARMY: Battle of Imjin River. At about 2200 hours, a reported 27 divisions of the CPA hit Eighth Army across a 40-mile front. The position of the 29th Infantry Brigade is at the junction of the Imjin and Hantan Rivers at a natural approach to the capital city of Seoul. The low water makes it possible for the Chinese to cross. The enemy advances, and the withdrawal of the flanking units requires the majority of the brigade to seek new positions north of Seoul. The cutoff Gloucester Regiment suffers major casualties in the effort to retain the hill. Fighting continues on the 23rd, with many areas changing hands several times. On the 24th, the battle reaches its most aggressive point as the fighting rages all along the front. By the 28th, the United Nations pulls back below the river to Line Golden. While at a heavy cost, the stand slows the Chinese attempt to push into Seoul.

April 22–25

EIGHTH ARMY: The Battle of Gloucester Hill occurs (Hill 235) as Chinese forces surround and cut off the 1st Battalion of the Gloucestershire Regiment at the Imjin River. The area is a part of Eighth Army's defensive line along the Imjin. The Gloucestershires hold the left flank of the 29th British Brigade's defensive. The Chinese Communists launch their spring offensive with nearly a quarter-million men and hit the front ahead of the British units. Air supply proves to be ineffective under the conditions. After three days of bitter fighting, the order goes out to abandon the Hill 235 and withdraw. The Fusiliers, Ulsters, and the Belgian battalions manage to fight their way out in good order, but the Gloucester cannot. On April 25, it is ordered to abandon its position and get back the best way it can. The costs of the battle were high, as 681 men of the 850 who had begun the fight are killed or wounded.

April 23

EIGHTH ARMY: Elements of the 24th and 25th Divisions on the edge of the Iron Triangle are slowly withdrawing, as the Chinese move toward their objective, Seoul. The battle for the Imjin River enters a second day as fighting continues and some elements of the UN Command are forced to withdraw to the east. The marines draw back to the Pendleton Line. Fortunately, the Chinese do not take full advantage of some of the gaps left by the move. The Battle of Kapyong gains momentum as the Chinese attack the 3rd Battalion, Royal Australian Regiment. The Australians manage to repulse several attacks. The forward battalion of the 29th British Brigade is required to concentrate its position or be wiped out. They are later awarded the U.S. Presidential Unit Citation for this action. Company Baker of the Gloster Battalion fights off seven Chinese attacks until its forward section is overwhelmed by sheer numbers. Fighting with bayonets and entrenching tools, the men concentrate into one area on Hill 235 (renamed Gloster Hill) where, totally alone, they are told to hold on. The Chinese reach Hill 194 that is held, in part, by the Belgian Battalion. Facing a fierce fight, the Chinese take two key bridges. Major General Robert H. Soule sends elements of the 1st Battalion, 7th Infantry, and two platoons of the 7th Tank Battalion to reclaim the bridges. Then it is decided to pull the division back but no plan is in place by which to withdraw the Belgians. Finally, the Belgian battalion moves off the backside of Hill 194 and escapes, losing a good many vehicles in the withdrawal.

SEA WAR: In an invasion feint, USS *Saint Paul* (CA 73), USS *Helena* (CA 75), and USS *Manchester* (CL 83), as well as four destroyers, bombard Ko Song.

AIR WAR: The 336th FIS moves to Suwon Airfield in order to give its F-80s more time over the target in MiG Alley, located near the Manchurian border. An estimated 340 close-air support missions are flown by planes from the FEAF. It is, to date, the heaviest daily total. Marine aircraft fly 205 sorties on this date.

April 23–25

EIGHTH ARMY: The Battle of Kapyong takes place around the town of Kapyong, located at the junction of the Kapyong and Pukhan Rivers. Chinese forces hit the right flank of the ROK 6th Division, causing some ROK elements to withdraw. The 27th Commonwealth Brigade is sent to plug the gap and moves to the northern approaches to the town, along the hills at the Kapyong River. What follows is a series of defensive actions played out by the 3rd Battalion, Royal Australian Regiment. The Australians give ground on April 24 but prevent the Chinese breakthrough; the enemy cuts off the engagement on the third day. Losses among the Canadian and Australian troops are 42 KIA, 82 WIA, and several missing. The failure of the Chinese, despite the valor of the defenders, seems to indicate that the enemy's resources are being pushed to the brink.

April 23–26

EIGHTH ARMY: The Battle of Horseshoe Ridge begins with a four-hour attack as the CCF moves against the men of George Company. The attack continues through the night of April 23. In the morning, all units are ordered to pull back to Line Kansas. They withdraw under the cover of marine sorties. Throughout the night of April 24, the CCF continues to probe but is unsuccessful. By April 25 and 26, all UN units have made it back to Line Kansas. There they are ordered farther back to the defense of Chunchon, along the south bank of the Soyang River.

AIR WAR: During these days, more than a 1,000 combat sorties are flown daily by FEAF. Their mission is to destroy supplies needed to sustain the communist offensive.

April 23–25

EIGHTH ARMY: British, Australian, and Canadian battalions fight an excellent defensive battle against repeated attacks by the Chinese 118th Division. For 24 hours, they are surrounded and cut off. Twenty-five miles to the west, on the I Corps front, the British 29th Brigade's three infantry battalions and a fourth Belgian command are holding position along the line of the Imjin River, 30 miles south of Seoul. The Imjin River bows north in front of the British lines. Much of the area is under observation from the high ground. The ROK 1st Division is on the west and the American 3rd Division on the east.

April 24

EIGHTH ARMY: The third day of the Battle of Imjin River. The Chinese commit a second division and are able to surround the Gloucestershire Regiment. Efforts to relieve the Gloucestershires fail, and the brigade is ordered to new positions north of Seoul. At Kapyong, the Australians are forced to give ground but are finally able to prevent the Chinese from breaking through their area. Technical Sergeant Harold E. Wilson (USMC) is awarded the Medal of Honor.

AIR WAR: In two rather daring rescue attempts, with friendly fighters keeping the enemy at a distance, an H-5 helicopter from the 3rd ARS rescues a pilot and then the navigator of a downed B-26. They are near Chorwon about 15 miles north of the 38th parallel in the central section. Two F-86s are shot down by enemy planes near Sensen. William J. Hovde from the 4th FIW shoots down a MiG-15.

April 24–25

EIGHTH ARMY: Australians withdraw under pressure and expose the 2nd Prince Patricia Canadian Light Infantry (PPCLI) position to enemy attack. Patricias maintain their position at the cost of 10 killed and 23 wounded. The marines are forced to give up some ground but they manage to break the impulse of the Chinese attack.

April 25

POLITICAL/ADMINISTRATIVE: The U.S. Senate unanimously adopts a resolution calling for an inquiry into policies regarding the military situation in the Far East. It is primarily an investigation into the firing of General Douglas MacArthur and meant to be a political embarrassment to the president.

EIGHTH ARMY: Getting increased pressure from the Chinese Communists, General Frank W. Milburn orders a pullback to Line Delta, which is west and below Line Kansas. By 0800, the retreat begins during a thick ground fog. The Fusiliers begin to disengage with the Chinese who are still on the high ground. The infantry, after more than 72 hours of combat, are in no shape to do anything. The 24th and 25th Divisions begin their withdrawal at 0800 as the ROK 1st stays behind to cover the retreat. The fourth day of the Battle of Imjin River, the UN is forced to pull back about 20 miles. The Gloucestershires are advised to get out on their own. The brigade tries to withdraw to its own lines, but many are killed or captured by the Chinese in the process. The brigade suffers 25 percent casualties. The battle is successful in that it prevents the Chinese from breaking through to Seoul. At Kapyong, the Chinese, unable to break through, call off the action. For action on this date near Popsu-dong, Corporal John R. Essebagger, Jr. (USA), is posthumously awarded the Medal of Honor. Also in the area, Corporal Clair Goodblood (USA) is posthumously awarded the Medal of Honor. Near Tong-mang-ni, PFC Charles L. Gilliland (USA) is posthumously awarded the Medal of Honor. For action near Taejon, Corporal Hiroshi H. Miyamura (USA) is awarded the Medal of Honor.

SEA WAR: The Joint Operations Center in Korea requests the navy to assist in the interdiction of western rail routes.

PARTISANS: Task Force Kirkland is formed at P'ohang-dong and moves to Samchok for training. Kirkland is named for the Harvard University fraternity made up exclusively of World War II, airborne-qualified personnel. Eighth Army (Miscellaneous) G-3 assumes control of the east coast partisans formerly under control of the ROK army.

April 26

EIGHTH ARMY: The port of Hungnam is placed under siege by UN warships. The siege will not be lifted until after the armistice is signed. Near Mugok, Sergeant First Class Ray E. Duke is awarded the Medal of Honor posthumously.

SEA WAR: Fearing a breakthrough by the Communists near Seoul, USS *Toledo* (CA 133) returns to Inchon in anticipation of a potential enemy move.

AIR WAR: During the night, a B-29 on close air support is able to break up a concentration of troops who are preparing to assault a unit of the U.S. IX Corps in the western section.

April 27

EIGHTH ARMY: Munsan-ni falls to advancing Chinese Communist forces as the spring offensive continues. Eighth Army continues to withdraw in order to establish a new defensive line.

April 28

POLITICAL/ADMINISTRATIVE: The Joint Chiefs of Staff authorizes UN Command to fire on air bases in Manchuria, if CCF planes threaten UNC ground forces. First Battalion, King's Own Scottish Borders, arrives in Korea to relieve the 1st Battalion, Argyle and Sutherland Highland Regiment.

EIGHTH ARMY: Eighth Army completes its withdrawal and establishes a new line. No more withdrawals are anticipated.

April 29

EIGHTH ARMY: General Matthew Ridgway establishes a new UN line. It begins just north of Seoul and runs through Sabangu in central Korea and to the coastal village of Taep'o-ri north of the 38th parallel. It is called "No Name Line."

SEA WAR: The USS *Helena* (CA 75), USS *Manchester* (CL 83), USS *Bausell* (DD 845), USS *Rogers* (DDR 876), USS *Agerholm* (DD 826), and USS *Anderson* (DD 786) all strike targets in the Kojo-Tongchon area. It is a part of an amphibious demonstration by USS *Okanogan* (APA 22), USS *Telfair* (APA 210), and USS *Winston* (AKA 94) designed to divert Chinese forces pressuring Eighth Army. The USS *Princeton* (CV 37) begins its third tour of duty in Korean waters.

PARTISANS: One hundred and four members of Unit Y go ashore in North Korea, while the White Tiger Brigade, Charlie Company (12 men), led by Kim In Sik goes ashore near Chongjin.

April 30

EIGHTH ARMY: The 1st Marine Division is transferred from operational control of IX Corps to X Corps. Holding new defensive lines, UN forces are able to halt the Chinese offensive drive north of Seoul and the Han River.

AIR WAR: At 1600 hours, six Ads (skyraiders) set off with two 2,000-pound bombs, accompanied by five Corsairs for flack suppression. They bomb the Hwachon Dam and are able to produce a hole in one gate. Three F-51s are shot down by enemy

aircraft near Sinmak, suggesting that the enemy is using some sort of radar-controlled antiaircraft guns. A new record of daily sorties is established when 50 air force planes fly 960 missions. Two H-5 helicopters on separate missions pick up downed UN pilots behind enemy lines. The helicopters are hit by small-arms fire.
PARTISANS: Unit Kirkland is removed to Samchok.

May 1

EIGHTH ARMY: The 1st Marine Division is once again assigned to X Corps.
SEA WAR: The USS *Helena* (CL 74) is the target of more than 100 rounds of shore fire at Wonsan, but none of the shells score a hit. The USS *Toledo* (CA 133) is stationed at Inchon for gunfire support of I Corps, Eighth Army. As redeployment shipping begins to arrive, nearly 20,000 refugees gather at Inchon hoping to escape.
AIR WAR: Eight Ads are launched with torpedoes to attack Hwachon Dam. Six of the eight torpedoes run true and one gate is destroyed while a second is damaged. The 315th AD begins the delivery of nearly 15 tons of fresh vegetables on a daily basis to various Eighth Army supply points. The produce, while welcome, is always a secondary cargo. VP Squadron 892, a reserve unit, under Lieutenant Commander E. R. Swanson, begins its sea-based tour of duty in Korea. Navy pilot Simpson Evans, from the 336th FIS, shoots down an enemy MiG-15 fighter.
PARTISANS: The 12-man unit of Charlie Company, Yellow Dragon Brigade, arrive at the staging area at Yo-do. Kim Jung Wahn's team lands at Ahn-byon.

May 2

POLITICAL/ADMINISTRATIVE: The National Security Council confirms the concept that the United States will seek what is essentially a restoration of the status quo ante bellum. While the government is willing to pay continued lip-service to the concept of a unified and independent Korea, it is now willing to push this only as a political, rather than a military, goal.
AIR WAR: VP Squadron One, under Commander W. M. Ringness, begins its second land-based tour of duty in Korea. VP Squadron 22, under Commander R. J. Davis, ends its land-based tour of duty in Korea.

May 3–June 25

POLITICAL/ADMINISTRATIVE: The Senate's "Great Debate" begins before the Joint Committee of the Armed Services and the Foreign Relations Committee. The hearings last until June 25. General Douglas MacArthur, General George Marshall, Dean Acheson, and member of the Joint Chiefs of Staff, among others, testify. The hearings lose steam very quickly as it becomes apparent to most members that General MacArthur had overstepped his authority. The meetings are terminated.

May 3

POLITICAL/ADMINISTRATIVE: The first contingent of the Canadian 25th Infantry Brigade arrives in Korea.
SEA WAR: Twelve Corsairs and eight Skyraiders from USS *Princeton* (CV 37) make inland torpedo attacks on Hwachon Dam, somewhat north of Yangyang.

May 5

SEA WAR: The ROK minesweeper *JML 306* strikes a mine and sinks.

AIR WAR: A 3rd ARS H-5 rescues a downed F-51 pilot north of Seoul. The rescue is complicated by the fact that the helicopter is hit several times by small-arms fire.

PARTISANS: TD unit G-3, Miscellaneous Group, 8086th Army Unit, takes control of partisan operations on the islands of the Han River Estuary. Previously, the islands were under the control of U.S. I Corps.

May 6

POLITICAL/ADMINISTRATIVE: Once again the National Security Council confirms that the United States will seek a restoration of the political situation that existed before the outbreak of the Korean War. The idea of Korean unification and independence is to receive lip service, but it is no longer a recognized goal for the outcome of the war. Rear Admiral G. R. Henderson relieves Rear Admiral R. A. Ofstie as commander of Task Force 77.

EIGHTH ARMY: The 1st Cavalry Division captures Uijongbu. Ethiopian troops arrive in Korea.

SEA WAR: The USS *Helena* (CL 75), USS *Orleck* (DD 886), USS *Fiske* (DD 842), USS *Buck* (DD 761), and HMS *Cockade* (DD 34) provide pre-D-day bombardment for ROK troops at Kosong and Kansong.

May 7

POLITICAL/ADMINISTRATIVE: President Harry Truman addresses a dinner at a Civil Defense Conference, during which he speaks about the potential for an atomic war resulting from a widening conflict in Korea.

EIGHTH ARMY: The front has been fairly quiet after the Communist forces pull back about 10 miles. They leave few resources to prevent the United Nations from a counterattack. The 1st Marines are thus able to fight their way back into Chunchon and several other key areas. Uijongbu falls, at the same time, to elements of the U.S. 1st Cavalry Division.

SEA WAR: The USS *Hoquiam* (PF 5) is hit by shore fire at Songjin, and one of the crew is seriously wounded.

May 8

POLITICAL/ADMINISTRATIVE: The Communists renew the charge that UN Command is using germ warfare in Korea.

AIR WAR: A H-5 helicopter picks up two U.S. soldiers who are located north of Seoul. The helicopter encounters small-arms fire.

May 9

AIR WAR: The U.S. Far East Air Force and the 1st Marine Air Wing launch a 306-plane strike against Sinuiju Airfield in extreme northwest Korea on the Yalu River. The raid is a response to reports that 40 enemy fighter planes are on the airfield. Two F-84s are shot down by enemy fighters near Sensen.

May 10–June 5

POLITICAL/ADMINISTRATIVE: General Matthew Ridgway officially requests authority to abolish segregation in Eighth Army.

EIGHTH ARMY: The second Chinese Communist Forces spring offensive begins with the May Massacre.

SEA WAR: Amphibious Task Force (TF 90) completes the transportation of air force personnel and equipment from Naha, Okinawa, to Inchon.

May 10

EIGHTH ARMY: The Battle of Bunker Hill begins as the 38th Infantry Regiment, 2nd Infantry Division, is involved.

SEA WAR: USS *Bon Homme Richard* (CV 31) begins its tour of duty in Korean waters.

May 11

EIGHTH ARMY: The Chinese attack several segments of the Zebra Line before the defenders are able to block them. As the attacks continue, several ROK units pull out without orders, leaving gaps through which the Chinese move. At first, UN tanks force the attacking units off the road, but elements of the 103rd Regiment of the Chinese 35th Division quickly push Able Company back, and the battle moves to Hills 975 and 1051.

SEA WAR: USS *Orleck* (DD 886), on the east coast, kills 140 enemy troops and aids an ROK army unit in its successful withdrawal.

AIR WAR: Thirty-two Ads, carrying two 2,000-pound bombs each, and an escort of 32 F4Us for flack suppression and 16 F4Fs for cover, respond to an air force request and attack four rail bridges on the west coast. The attack destroys three spans of the bridge.

PARTISANS: Donkey attacks a mining complex and frees hundreds of Koreans who were working there as forced labor.

May 12

POLITICAL/ADMINISTRATIVE: General Matthew Ridgway reports to Washington that the Chinese Communists are in the advance stages of preparing a new offensive. Intelligence suggests that it will most likely occur within the next 76 hours.

May 13

AIR WAR: Planes from the USAF 58th Fighter Bomber Wing attack Toksan Dam in North Korea and destroy a major irrigation system.

May 14

EIGHTH ARMY: General Van Fleet anticipates a renewal of Chinese pressure during the early weeks of May and so he orders defensive stockpiling of ammunition, fuel, and supplies at and closely behind the front.

May 15

POLITICAL/ADMINISTRATIVE: The British 1st Battalion, Middlesex Regiment, is relieved by the King's Shropshire Light Infantry.

EIGHTH ARMY: During the night, the area around the assembling Chinese divisions shakes as they are hit by a long and heavy bombardment. Twenty-one Chinese divisions, supported by three North Korean divisions on the east flank and six more on the west flank, begin to advance. Hit the hardest is X Corps, located in the center of the line, and the ROK III Corps on the right. The sector at the front is an area where the terrain should provide the United Nations a distinct defensive advantage. It is maintained by the ROK. The Chinese plan is to move through the ROK in order to flank the remainder of Eighth Army. Chinese Communist Forces penetrate No Name Line in central Korea, creating a 35-mile bulge in the line. All in all, however, the attack is a failure. Despite the fact that the Chinese spearhead breaks through the ROK section, they then run into a barrier made up of U.S. Marines and ROK units north and east of Chunchon. The ROK also stops a Communist feint toward Seoul. The 2nd Infantry Division suffers 3,700 casualties.

SEA WAR: The helicopter rescue ship, *LST 799,* rescues Lieutenant J. A. Winterbotham, a British pilot.

AIR WAR: Lieutenant James H. Kasler (USAF) becomes the war's 15th ace after downing two MiGs.

PARTISANS: At Chumunjin, a small east-coast port city seven miles south of the 38th parallel, Task Force Kirkland (Rear) is established to support the headquarters. Advance elements of Task Force Kirkland (Forward) move out to Nan-do, an island on the 39th parallel.

May 15–26

AIR WAR: Providing a week of maximum effort, the 315th AD cargo aircraft deliver a daily average of 1,000 tons of supplies from Japan to Korea. The flights are necessary in order to provide the ammunition and rations needed.

May 16

POLITICAL/ADMINISTRATIVE: The UN Security Council officially states that the war in Korea must be brought to a close and that it is seeking an acceptable armistice. This is their "substitute for victory."

EIGHTH ARMY: The Chinese spring offensive takes five Chinese armies into the line along the Chunchon-Hongchon-ni axis. UN forces are reenforced at the center of the line, and with heavy artillery support (38th Field Artillery fires 12,000 rounds of 105-mm shells in 24 hours) the line manages to hold. The Chinese begin the second phase of their 1951 spring offensive, hit Bunker Hill in the afternoon, and by night manage to push soldiers of the 38th Infantry Regiment, 2nd Infantry Division, off the hill.

AIR WAR: Air force fighter/bombers kill an estimated 5,000 enemy troops on the roads leading from Chunchon and Inje in a two-day period that is identified as the May Massacre. Captain Manuel J. Fernaddez, Jr., becomes the war's third-ranking ace with 14 $^1/_2$ aerial victories.

May 16–18

EIGHTH ARMY: Anticipating an attack since mid-April, Bunker Hill has become one of the most fortified positions constructed during the Korean War. The somewhat warmer weather has allowed for additional digging and timber and sandbag reinforcement.

May 16–19

EIGHTH ARMY: The UN defensive position atop Bunker Hill is one of the best constructed during the war. It is at this point that the Chinese plan to drive a wedge into the main line of resistance (MLR). The attack begins in the afternoon with an estimated 125,000 men in the section held by the ROK I and II Corps and the 24th Infantry. By evening the Chinese take Bunker Hill. On May 17, the United Nations counterattacks and regains the hill; but the Chinese still hold major positions. On May 18, the United Nations is in command, and on May 19, the Chinese withdraw.

May 16–22

EIGHTH ARMY: 1st and 2nd Detachments of the NDVN (Netherlands Detachment United Nations) receive the Presidential Unit Citation for services at Soyang River.

May 17

POLITICAL/ADMINISTRATIVE: National Security Council document 48/5 represents a hardening of American policy toward the PRC, specifically encouraging resistance to Communist China by protecting Taiwan and recognizing the ROK. At the same time, it acknowledges that it is very necessary to limit the war in Korea and to avoid any expansion of the war. It recommends that whatever outstanding questions remain between the parties be solved by political means. President Truman, therefore, in approving the recommendations of the NSC, calls for a cease-fire initiative. Rear Admiral R. A. Ofstie relieves Rear Admiral A. K. Morehouse as chief of staff, COMNAVFE.

EIGHTH ARMY: After being been pushed off most of Bunker Hill the day before, the 38th Regiment, 2nd Infantry Division, retakes the crest and much of the hill complex. For the next several hours they fight. The 2nd Infantry stops the Communists at the Soyang River. Supported by the French and Dutch battalions, they take the heart out of the Communist drive on the east-central front and are responsible for the deaths of an estimated 10,000 enemy soldiers.

SEA WAR: The battleship USS *New Jersey* (BB 62) arrives on the east coast of Korea for the first of two tours of duty in Korea.

May 17–20

EIGHTH ARMY: The battle of the Soyang River.

May 17–22

EIGHTH ARMY: Five U.S. Army divisions are involved in trying to hold the new Chinese offensive: the 2nd, 3rd, 7th, 24th, and 25th Infantry Divisions. The battle for Soyang River begins and will last for three days.

AIR WAR: B-29s from Bomber Command fly 94 sorties against enemy ground forces. The size and number of these raids appear to increase daily. Most of these missions are flown at night as the Communists are trying to avoid the impact of daylight raids by delivering their attacks at night. The bombers not involved in this effort are involved in other support missions.

May 18

POLITICAL/ADMINISTRATIVE: Secretary Acheson asked George Kennan to contact the Soviets' chief UN delegate, Jacob Malik, and inform him that the United States was ready to negotiate with the Chinese Communists if they would be reasonable. The UN General Assembly approves a resolution by the UN Additional Measures Committee calling for UN members to impose an embargo on the shipment of arms, ammunition, and other materials of strategic value for Communist China and North Korea. The vote is 47-0, with eight abstentions, including the USSR. The assistant secretary of state for far eastern affairs describes the government in Peking as "a Slavic Manchukuo on a large scale" and not the true government of China.

EIGHTH ARMY: The Communist offensive is still in progress, but General James Van Fleet orders a counterattack. King Company of the 38th Regiment takes the Hill 800 complex and then fights off counterattacks. By morning the 38th Regiment, 2nd Infantry Division, has cleared most of the Communist troops from the pockets of resistance they held. By noon the hill belongs to the 2nd Division. The Netherlands Battalion, attached to the 2nd Infantry Division defending Hill 738 (Sobuk-san), is called off to help plug a gap created by the advance of the Chinese 44th Division. The battle focuses around Hill 724 and Hill 710. Easy Company from Hill 710 and George Company from Hill 975 try to clear the area but soon find they are ringed by Chinese. Units of the 2nd and 3rd Battalions of the 2nd Infantry Division go to their aid, and the three companies return to friendly areas.

SEA WAR: The USS *Duncan* (DDR 874), USS *Leonard F. Mason* (DD 852), and USS *Brinkley Bass* (DD 887) conduct interdiction and are fired on by shore batteries from Kalma Gak. None of the ships are damaged.

AIR WAR: Captain Joseph C. McConnell qualifies as the top ace of the war after shooting down another three MiGs. He completes his tour with 106 missions and 16 MiG kills. Task Force 77 suffers its heaviest single-day casualties as six planes (five F4Us and one AD) are lost to enemy action.

May 19

EIGHTH ARMY: Along No Name Line, the heavy Communist attack begins to peter out, and the Chinese are forced to slow the advance because of the heavy opposition provided by UN forces. By daylight the Chinese are beginning to disengage and are withdrawing. After winning the battle, the 38th Regiment, 2nd Infantry Division, is called off the hill. It has been decided that the hill is too far north for it to be supplied and defended. The Chinese have suffered more than 800 casualties. The Chinese are beginning to face the difficulties caused by the extension of their supply lines that cannot carry the load of further operation. Believing that the enemy has overextended itself, General Matthew Ridgway orders General James Van Fleet to counterattack immediately, not only through the Uijongbu-Chorwon corridor, but also along the entire front. The Chinese withdraw from Bunker Hill. The U.S. 2nd Infantry Division, along with Dutch and French battalions, fights its way out of a trap set by the Chinese in the central Korean mountains.

AIR WAR: A downed F-51 pilot is rescued southwest of Chorwon by an H-5 helicopter that sustains some damage from small arms fire.

PARTISANS: The main body of Kirkland (Forward) arrives on Nan-do.

May 20

POLITICAL/ADMINISTRATIVE: General George E. Stratemeyer, FEAF commander, suffers a severe heart attack.

EIGHTH ARMY: At the front near No Name Line, the Chinese attack comes to a standstill and UN forces begin to stabilize. The Eighth Army counterattack moves up the western sector as far as Kumhwa. The advance toward Seoul, which came on the heels of General James Van Fleet's arrival, halts after the enemy has penetrated UN lines for more than 30 miles. UN forces begin a counterattack, leaving No Name Line behind. Operation Detonate, the third return to Seoul and the effort to retake Phase Line Kansas, begins. Sergeant First Class Donald R. Moyer (USA) is posthumously awarded the Medal of Honor for action near Seoul.

SEA WAR: Shore batteries at Wonsan hit USS *Brinkley Bass* (DD 887), killing one and wounding nine. The USS *New Jersey* (BB 62) arrives and begins shelling Wonsan. The ship is slightly damaged after being hit by shore batteries. There are four casualties.

AIR WAR: The USAF launches Operation Strangle. Fifty MiG-15s attack the 4th FIG. The 334th Fighter Interceptor Squadron's Captain James Jabara destroys his fifth and sixth MiGs in aerial combat to become the world's first jet-to-jet ace. Milton E. Nelso, from the 335th FIS, also gets a MiG-15. Four F-86s are shot down by enemy planes near the area of Tetsuzan.

May 20–21

SEA WAR: British commandos are involved in a landing raid and demonstration on Korea's west coast opposite Cho-do. Air spotting and gunfire is provided by USS *Bataan* (CVL 29) and USS *Toledo* (CA 133).

May 21

POLITICAL/ADMINISTRATIVE: Lieutenant General Earle E. Partridge assumes acting command of FEAF, replacing Lieutenant General George Stratemeyer. Major General Edward J. Timberlake, Jr., takes over as Fifth Air Force commander.

EIGHTH ARMY: The 187th Airborne Regimental Combat Team comes back on line between the 1st Marines and the 2nd Infantry Division on the left. PFC Joseph C. Rodriguez (USA) is awarded the Medal of Honor for action near Munye-re. General John R. Hodge's troops enter the Munsan-ni area and close in on Line Topkwa.

May 22

POLITICAL/ADMINISTRATIVE: Major General William K. Harrison replaces Admiral C. Turner Joy as the senior UN command delegate at the armistice talks.

Eighth Army: General William Hoge, disappointed with his four divisions' performance, orders them to move forward at least six miles, which will take them beyond the Georgia Line. They get no farther than the Georgia Line, however. The Battle of Soyang River ends after 406 UN fatalities.

Air War: In close air support, Fifth Air Force fighters are the source of an estimated 1,700 casualties among enemy troops.

May 23

Political/Administrative: Brigadier General Robert H. Terrill assumes command of the FEAF Bomber Command, replacing General Ellis Briggs.

Eighth Army: Eighth Army moves from the Kansas and Wyoming Lines to the area known as the Iron Triangle. Enemy resistance is beginning to stiffen. The 1st Marines begin their drive on Yanggu.

Sea War: Feeling that the danger is over, Admiral Thackrey begins to release shipping from Inchon. As a part of the coordinated operation called Fireball, near Wonsan, 4,903 rockets are fired by *LSMR 409* and *LSMR 412*. The USS *New Jersey* (BB 62) fires on targets near Yangyang.

Partisans: The presence of army officers Major Burke, commanding Leopard, and Captain Robert Channon, is required to stop internecine war between ROK army irregulars and partisans from mainland Hwanghae Province.

May 24

Eighth Army: The 1st Marine Regiment reaches a line about five-and-a-half miles north of Sango-ri. There it is relieved. The 187th Airborne Regimental Combat Team, with the 72nd Tank Battalion attached, attacks to the north above Inje.

Sea War: Shelling by USS *Manchester* (CL 83) and USS *Brinkley Bass* (DD 887) breaks up a fleet of smaller ships heading toward Rei-To Island in the Wonsan area. Forces recovered by the *Manchester* include four sampans, modified to carry four M-26 sea mines. Eleven enemy are killed and one wounded.

Air War: The 136th Fighter-Bomber Wing, one of the two Air National Guard organizations called up for service in Korea, launches its first combat sortie of the war.

Partisans: Operation Kirkland establishes several coast watchers on Song-do, an island close to the North Korean coast.

May 25

Political/Administrative: Nineteen POWs, captured by the Chinese during the Chosin campaign, are released and returned to UN officials. There is no reason given for the release.

Sea War: The evacuation alert is lifted and USS *Toledo* (CA 133) is the last ship to be relieved.

Partisans: Captain Robert Channon, on TDY to Miscellaneous Group from the 3rd Ranger Infantry Company, arrives at Kanghwa-do to study partisan tactics.

May 26

Political/Administrative: Chairman Mao Zedong, in a telegram to Pen Dehuai, acknowledges that it is impossible for the CVA to encircle and eliminate a U.S. army, and probably not a division, so he suggests that the enemy be destroyed one company at a time.

EIGHTH ARMY: The marines moving toward the Soyang River are two-thirds of the way to their goal by noon.

SEA WAR: Rocket-bearing LSMRs 409 and 412 loose a heavy rocket barrage on gun emplacements at Wonsan.

May 27

AIR WAR: C-47s, belonging to Unit 4/Special Air Mission, fly a leaflet drop and make a voice broadcast that encourages the enemy to surrender to elements of IX Corps. Thereafter, about 4,000 enemy soldiers surrender, some of them carrying the leaflets. POWs report that the constant UN aerial attacks are causing morale problems among the enemy.

May 28

POLITICAL/ADMINISTRATIVE: The UN negotiation team presents a set of "final terms" and threatens to break off the talks if they are rejected.

EIGHTH ARMY: Eighth Army takes Hwachon and Inje. The Chinese attack outposts along the 25th Infantry Division line and overrun Outposts Carson and Outposts Elko and Vegas, which had been abandoned.

SEA WAR: Marine Fighter Squadron VMF-214 begins flying aircraft from Hoengsong.

May 29

POLITICAL/ADMINISTRATIVE: Brigadier General Thomas J. Cushman relieves Major General Field Harris as commander, 1st Marine Aircraft Wing. Brigadier General W. O. Brice assumes duty as the deputy commander.

EIGHTH ARMY: Private First Class Whitt L. Moreland (USMC) is awarded the Medal of Honor, posthumously, for action near Kwagchi-dong. The 187th Airborne Regimental Combat Team reaches Inje and moves into the high ground surrounding it.

SEA WAR: Three steel-decked junks are destroyed and two guards killed when USS *Stickell* (DD 888) and USS *Burlington* (PF 51) land a raiding party near Songjin.

AIR WAR: Air Group 19 from USS *Princeton* (CV 37) ends its tour of duty in Korea. They are replaced by Air Group Nineteen "X Ray."

PARTISANS: Able Company (about 15 men) of Y unit, White Tigers, led by Lee Nam Soo, and Baker Company, led by Han Chnag Duk, land near Chongjin.

May 30

POLITICAL/ADMINISTRATIVE: The Joint Chiefs of Staff makes it clear to General Ridgway that he is no longer free to pursue the Communists but reluctantly agrees to allow him to go ahead with Operation Piledriver, which has the primary objective of seizing as much as possible of the Iron Triangle.

EIGHTH ARMY: The Communist offensive comes to a halt. Eighth Army advances to Line Kansas. The 1st Marine Division moves forward from the Hwachon Reservoir toward the Punchbowl. Canadian troops are forced to withdraw during an attack on Chail-li. It was the brigade's first serious engagement. During the battle, six men are killed and 54 wounded. The Chinese hold Hill 467 (aka Kakhul-Bong), which overlooks the UN staging area known as the Iron Triangle. Dog Company of the 2nd Royal Canadian Regiment is assigned to take the hill and after a heavy fight manages to take the western peak. The eastern peak, however, remains with the Chinese. By 1900, the attack is recalled and the men return to the line. Six men have been killed and 54 wounded.

AIR WAR: Air Group 102 begins its tour of duty on USS *Bon Homme Richard* (CV 31).

May 31

POLITICAL/ADMINISTRATIVE: First meeting between Jacob A. Malik and George F. Kennan about a possible cease-fire agreement. In a directive to General Matthew Ridgway, the Joint Chiefs of Staff redefines the mission in Korea. In effect it denies his request to launch retaliatory raids on China and authorizes him to withdraw Eighth Army to Japan, if he feels that this is necessary for the defense of that nation. In addition, General Ridgway is encouraged to inflict a maximum of materiel and personnel costs on the Chinese. Major General O. P. Weyland replaces Lieutenant General Earle E. Partridge as commander of the Far East Air Force. Rear Admiral A. A. Burke arrives to assume command of Bombline Element TE 9.28.

EIGHTH ARMY: The 7th Division arrives at Yanggu, breaks through a heavily contested pass, and takes control by nightfall. For service near Wontong-ni, Corporal Rodolfo D. Hernandez (USA) is awarded the Medal of Honor.

SEA WAR: The USS *Philippine Sea* (CV 47) receives the Navy Unit Citation for service from March 31, 1951, to this date. The USS *Princeton* (CV 37) begins a second tour of duty in Korean waters.

AIR WAR: Operation Strangle continues as the Fifth Air Force launches more interdiction flights against enemy supply lines in North Korea. Two USAF pilots destroy enemy MiG-15 fighters. Bobbie L. Smith and Otis Gordon from the 335th FIS each get a MiG. Michael R. Martocchia, a gunner on a B-29A, shoots down a MiG-15.

June 1

POLITICAL/ADMINISTRATIVE: Major General Frank F. Everest assumes command of the Fifth Air Force, replacing General Edward J. Timberlake. Secretary of State Acheson states that America is willing to accept a truce line near the 38th parallel if other agenda items can be settled satisfactorily. During the testimony at the MacArthur hearing, Secretary of State Acheson says that he has not understood the unification of Korea to be one of the aims of the war in Korea.

EIGHTH ARMY: Operation Piledriver is launched with the objective of seizing the Iron Triangle in order to solidify the UNC defensive position along the Kansas-Wyoming Line. The 5th and 7th Marines are heavily engaged with CCF in defending Hill 651, which the Marines took after four VMF-214 planes bombed and strafed the target.

SEA WAR: Eighth Army requests a program of highway interdiction south of the 39th parallel, to be called Operation Strangle. USS *Bon Homme Richard* (CV 31) and USS *Los Angeles* (CA 135) enter Korean waters.

AIR WAR: A flight of F-86s from the 336th Fighter/Bomber Squadron are escorting a flight of B-29s when they are engaged by 18 MiGs and destroy two of them. B-29s from the 343rd Bomber Squadron flying near Sunchon defend themselves against 22 MiGs and are able to destroy two of the enemy planes while suffering one B-29 destroyed and one damaged. In the meanwhile, C-47s from the FEAF Special Air Mission drop 15 Koreans into enemy territory in an effort to retrieve parts from a downed MiG. Communist forces waiting in the area capture all 15 of the investigators. FEAF places the area known as MiG Alley off-limits for unescorted bombers. Enemy aviators shoot down an F-52 at Rikaho and an F-86 at Sensen. Samuel Pesacreta and Richard Ransbottom, flying F-86s for the 336th FIS, each destroy a MiG-15 fighter.

June 1–13

EIGHTH ARMY: Called Operation Piledriver, it is Eighth Army's last major effort to complete its control of the Kansas-Wyoming Line in the area known as the Iron Triangle, as well as the last major offense prior to the "defensive" order. I Corps moves forward to capture and hold the towns of Chorwon and Kumhwa and enters the nearly destroyed town of Pyongyang. IX Corps is to take the area from Hwachon north to Samyang-ni. The X Corps attack will move north from the east side of the reservoir. The ROK I Corps is assigned Kojin-ni. But the high ground over Pyongyang is controlled by Chinese forces, and I Corps is forced to withdraw. The Iron Triangle, from this point on, is basically a no-man's land, held by neither side.

June 2

POLITICAL/ADMINISTRATIVE: Dean Acheson agrees with Trygve Lie, who believes that, since the Chinese Communists have been pushed back, a cease-fire line can be established along the 38th parallel. This would, in effect, satisfy the Security Council resolutions of June 25, June 27, and July 7, 1950. Acheson admits that there are two problems facing the United States, one military and one political. While the political issues are important, it is the shooting war that has to be stopped. The United States has come a full circle and the goal, once more, is containment rather than victory.

EIGHTH ARMY: Marines of the 1st Battalion, 5th Regiment, secure the ridge line that provides the approach to Taeam-san on the southern end of the Punchbowl. They take and hold Hill 610. Sergeant Cornelius H. Charlton (USA) is posthumously awarded the Medal of Honor for service near Chipo-ri.

SEA WAR: Underwater Demolition Team 3, supported by USS *Begor* (APD 127), lands ROK guerrillas on Song-do Island near Kojo.

AIR WAR: Air Group 2 on USS *Philippine Sea* (CV 47) is recalled at the end of its Korean tour. An F-86 is shot down by enemy fighters near Sensen. It crashes near Gaisio-To.

June 3

EIGHTH ARMY: Operation Piledriver, the securing of Phase Line Wyoming and the Iron Triangle, begins. The advance immediately hits unexpected Communist resistance. The marines move against Hills 680 and 692 and, after napalm attacks are delivered in support, are able to take and hold both hills.

AIR WAR: UN antiaircraft mistakenly shoot at and destroy two C-119s from the 315th FBS, which were trying to resupply ground troops. The incident results in the development and adoption of new procedures (Friend or Foe) for identifying friendly aircraft during a drop.

PARTISANS: In its first raid against mainland Korea, Kirkland moves forward. The raid against the North Korean mainland is to provide the unit its first combat experience and to gather intelligence. It also hopes to draw troops away from the front.

June 4

POLITICAL/ADMINISTRATIVE: Eighth Army opens a forward command post in Seoul. Eighth Army Main is still located in Taegu.

EIGHTH ARMY: In Operation Piledriver, X Corps resumes the battle. The KMC moves out against Hill 1122 with the hope of then moving on toward Hill 1218 and Hill 1316. The battle will continue for five days.

SEA WAR: The USS *New Jersey* (BB 62) fires on targets at Wonsan.

AIR WAR: General Otto P. Weyland directs FEAF Bomber Command to keep up the attacks against the most significant enemy airfields, in order to prevent them from being used. Intelligence reports suggest that the enemy is trying to reconstruct the fields and to improve them to receive more aircraft.

PARTISANS: After a successful raid on Kojo, Kirkland withdraws.

June 5

POLITICAL/ADMINISTRATIVE: State Department representative George Kennan and Soviet leader Jacob Malik meet again. Kennan presents the U.S. desire for an armistice. Malik tells Kennan that the United States should approach the Chinese and North Koreans, pleading that the Soviet Union is not a belligerent in the war.

EIGHTH ARMY: First Battalion, 65th Infantry Regiment, takes Hill 466 after a two-day battle. It finds more than 200 enemy dead on the crest of the hill. Master Sergeant Benjamin F. Wilson (USA) wins the Medal of Honor near Hwachon-Myon.

PARTISANS: Captain Channon leaves the Han River islands after helping to end the dispute between partisans and regulars.

June 5–7

EIGHTH ARMY: For reasons probably related to supplies, CCF resistance in the area in front of I Corps at the Iron Triangle begins to diminish.

June 5–September 20

EIGHTH ARMY: Operation Strangle divides Korea into areas and makes separate units responsible for preventing enemy supplies from moving in their areas.

June 6

EIGHTH ARMY: Artillery is fired for more than two hours to soften the defenses on Hill 729. The follow-up assault by 1st Marines is successful and by 2100 the 2nd and 4th Battalions, 5th Regiments, are in possession of their first assigned advance.

SEA WAR: The USS *Los Angeles* (CA 135) and USS *New Jersey* (BB 62) bombard enemy positions at Kosong.

June 7

POLITICAL/ADMINISTRATIVE: As the result of vigorous grilling by a Senate Committee, Acheson clarifies that any reliable armistice based on the 38th parallel will be acceptable.

EIGHTH ARMY: Operation Piledriver is initiated by the 7th Infantry Division. The 31st Regiment takes the east side of the Hwachon-Kumhwa road; the 32nd Regiment the west side of the road; and the 17th Regiment, held in reserve, blocks the area around Hwachon. The enemy fights this penetration almost to the last man. Near Pachi-dong, PFC Jack G. Hanson is awarded the Medal of Honor posthumously.

SEA WAR: USS *Rupertus* (DD 851) puts a small raiding party ashore at Songjin (Kimchaek). The raid captures three enemy prisoners.

AIR WAR: An F-86 is shot down by enemy fighters near Taisen.

June 7–10

AIR WAR: During this period, FEAF B-26 and B-29 operations focus on radar bombing attacks against the area known as the Iron Triangle. This is in preparation for a ground assault against the important Chorwon-Kumhwa-Pyonggang communications and supply area. The planes drop 500-pound bombs designed to explode over the heads of the enemy troops. The problem of protecting the bombers against MiG attacks leads to the decision to operate almost entirely at night.

June 8

EIGHTH ARMY: Two battalions of the 7th Regiment advance up the valley of the Sochon River toward Hill 420. Operation Piledriver continues as Operation Detonate, the plan to return to Seoul and the retaking of Phase Line Kansas, comes to an end.

June 9

EIGHTH ARMY: Enemy resistance is light as UN forces approach the base of the Iron Triangle. The 7th Marines, advancing along the Sochon River valley, meet heavy resistance but, during the night, manage to take and hold Hill 420. The NKPA conducts a brief counterattack that first bombards and then moves against the 2nd Battalion 1st Marine, position. The enemy is finally beaten off.

SEA WAR: The USS *Helena* (CA 75) fires 10,000 major caliber rounds against enemy sites. The first test of an air drop station on Yo-do (Yodo) is executed. The USS *Philippine Sea* (CV 47) ends its second tour of duty in Korean waters. The USS *Tiru* (SS 417) sets out on her first patrol assignment in Korean waters.

AIR WAR: VP Squadron 892 (Reserve), later identified as VP-50, under Commander W. H. Chester, ends its tour of duty in Korea.

June 10

ADMINISTRATIVE: Lieutenant General Otto P. Weyland assumes command of FEAF, replacing General Partridge.

EIGHTH ARMY: The UN counterattack continues to move north. In Operation Piledriver the 17th Regiment, 7th Infantry Division, passes through the 31st Regiment and attacks to the north. The base of the Iron Triangle, the Chorwon-Kumhwa line, falls to a combined force of Americans, Filipinos, ROKs, and Turks who take the high ground south of Chorwon. For action near Hangnyong, Corporal Charles G. Abrell (USMC) receives the Medal of Honor posthumously. After five days of fighting for Hill 1122, the ROK army catches the North Koreans in a surprise night attack and takes the hill. Then the ROK moves on to take Hill 1218. Both areas are secured.

AIR WAR: Fifty miles northeast of Seoul, and about 10 miles south of the 38th parallel, Chunchon Airfield is opened for cargo traffic, and the 315th AD begins landing there to help meet the growing need for supplies.

SEA WAR: Two PB4Y-2s start working as flare-dropping planes for night attacks. Marine Fighter Squadron VMF-312 begins operations from Pusan as VMF-323 embarks on USS *Sicily* (CVE 118).

June 11

EIGHTH ARMY: I Corps moves in to capture the towns of Chorwon and Kumhwa, driving farther into the area called the Iron Triangle. Taking the enemy by surprise in a night attack, which results in a near-slaughter of the enemy, I Corps is able to move on toward the Punchbowl. Just before noon a patrol sent out by Baker Company, 1st Battalion, 7th Regiment, 3rd Division, enters Chorwon and captures five prisoners. Later the 1st Battalion enters Kumhwa from the southeast and is held up by enemy resistance at Hill 566. At this point, the 1st Battalion is forced to withdraw from the attack. A Turkish patrol enters the southeast edge of Kumhwa but locates no enemy troops. The Royal Marines stage a hit-and-run mission far behind Communist lines in North Korea.

AIR WAR: Two pilots earn the Distinguished Service Cross when they rescue a downed F-51 pilot from the Taedong River near Kyomipo, North Korea. Flying an SA-16 of the 3rd AFS, they pick up the pilot despite enemy fire coming from both sides of the river.

June 12

EIGHTH ARMY: In Operation Piledriver, UN patrols enter Chorwon only to discover that the CCF withdrew two days before. The 1st Battalion of the 17th Regiment, which had been denied victory on Hill 566 the day before, sends Able and Charlie Companies against the hill from different directions. They then take the hill. Both the U.S. 3rd Division and the 25th Infantry Division are on Line Wyoming at the base of the Iron Triangle, the 3rd at Chorwon and the 25th at Kumhwa. The two divisions order a tank/infantry patrol to go to Pyonggang. Operation Piledriver, the securing of Phase Line Wyoming and the Iron Triangle, ends.

SEA WAR: The destroyer USS *Walke* (DD 723) is hit by a mine off Hungnam and suffers 26 KIA and 35 WIA—the largest ship loss during the Korean War and the highest number of casualties suffered at sea.

PARTISANS: Agents of Blueboy (five young men and three older Koreans) are dropped 20 miles inland. All are able to return and bring out considerable information.

June 13

EIGHTH ARMY: As Eighth Army advances, two tank/infantry task forces enter the ruins of Pyonggang. Pyonggang is significant because the hills around it are held by large Chinese forces who built defensive systems as they withdrew from the city. Task Force Hamilton from Kumhwa crosses the line of departure at 0815 and engages the enemy, inflicting 21 casualties and taking 21 prisoners. At Pyonggang, they meet up with Task Force Hawkins. At this point, Hawkins withdraws and returns to Kumhwa where it is dissolved. Task Force Hamilton returns to Chorwon. I Corps is ordered to take the area north of the Hwachon-Pyonggang road and to move about six miles north of Line Wyoming. The ROK 2nd Division and the 32nd Regiment of the U.S. 7th Infantry Division move forward after meeting stiff resistance on Hill 1073. They eventually capture the hill. The Turkish Brigade is given the assignment to take Hill 507. A Triple-Single Bailey, M-2 Panel Bridge, 772 feet in length, is completed by the 185th Engineer Combat Battalion across the Soyang River.

June 14

POLITICAL/ADMINISTRATIVE: In a telegram from Mao Zedong to Kim Il Sung, Chairman Mao advises that it is best to wait for the United Nations to make an appeal for armistice talks.

EIGHTH ARMY: By late in the afternoon, the 1st Marines are in position along Brown Line, an extension of the Kansas Line. The Turkish Brigade attacking Hill 507 is able to take it and hold it briefly but loses it again during night attacks.

SEA WAR: The USS *Thompson* comes to within 3,000 yards of the beach near Songjin. Out of camouflage appear four three-inch batteries that begin to fire on the ship. The *Thompson* increases speed and returns fire. The ship manages to break clear but only after she has been struck 13 times and suffered three killed and three wounded. The hits destroy much of her radio equipment.

AIR WAR: A Communist Polikarpov PO-2 biplane drops several bombs on Suwon Airfield. These attacks mark the beginning of a nightly harassment called "Bedcheck Charlie."

June 15

EIGHTH ARMY: UN Command consolidates its forces in a defensive position along the Kansas-Wyoming Line. Eighth Army reaches its terrain objective defined in Operation Piledriver.

AIR WAR: Fifth Air Force headquarters is moved back to Seoul from Taegu.

June 16

EIGHTH ARMY: The Turkish Brigade, which has been denied occupancy of Hill 507 for two days, attacks and occupies the hill. They hold during several counterattacks.

SEA WAR: UNC marks the 100th consecutive day of the siege at Songjin.

PARTISANS: Twenty coast watchers take up positions at Song-do (listed as Sal-Sam on army maps).

June 17

EIGHTH ARMY: In Operation Piledriver, the 17th and 32nd Regiments of the 7th Infantry Division reach Line Kansas and begin to prepare for the anticipated counterattack. Communist troops strike back in a limited counterattack and are able to retake Pyonggang.

AIR WAR: Samuel Pesacreta, from the 4th FIW, shoots down a MiG-15. Three F-86s are lost to enemy fighter planes, one near Ju-Son and two at Sensen.

June 18

SEA WAR: There are four injuries on USS *Frank E. Evans* (DD 754) after it is hit by shore batteries firing from Wonsan.

AIR WAR: Six enemy planes are shot down. Ralph D. Gibson gets two MiG-15s and Richard D. Creighton, Erwin A. Hesse, James E. Heckman, and William D. Crone each get a MiG-15. Six F-86s are shot down by enemy fighters, two at Anju and four at Sensen.

PARTISANS: Operation Spitfire, a group that operates primarily with American and British members, begins as teams parachute into North Korea. Their mission fails and the group suffers heavy casualties. It is decided that, for the remainder of the war, only Korean nationals will be sent on deep penetration missions into Communist territory. With some brief exceptions, that will hold true.

June 18-20

PARTISANS: Members of Choe Yun Chan's 61 operative team parachute safely at Mount Paik.

June 19

POLITICAL/ADMINISTRATIVE: President Harry Truman signs the Universal Military Training and Service Act, thereby lowering the draft age to 18. The bill also increases service time from 21 to 24 months and extends the draft until July 1, 1955.

AIR WAR: Two F-86s are shot down by enemy fighter planes near Andong.

June 20

POLITICAL/ADMINISTRATIVE: Rear Admiral G. C. Dyer relieves Rear Admiral A. E. Smith as commander, United Nations Blockading and Escort Force.

SEA WAR: The USS *Brinkley Bass* (DD 887), the first ship to control bombing aircraft, directs a B-26 at it hits the Wonsan area. The coordinated effort proves successful and becomes the model for future action.

AIR WAR: For the first time, the Communists use fighter and ground attack aircraft in a combined combat operation. In the battle, F-51s and F-85s clash with planes of both types along the west coast of Korea. Two Il-10s are shot down, one by Ralph H. Saltsman and one by John Coleman. A YAK-9 is also destroyed by John B. Harrison. Four F-51s are shot down by enemy fighters near Sibito.

June 21

POLITICAL/ADMINISTRATIVE: A Big Four foreign minister conference in Paris collapses in anger after the Soviet delegates try to push through an anti-NATO tactic.

EIGHTH ARMY: 1st Marine Division begins the defense of the Hwachon Reservoir and surrounding areas. The 5th Marine Regiment sends patrols into the Punchbowl area and to Hill 792 without coming up on any enemy troops. The ROK 1st Division sends a reconnaissance in force that enters Kaesong without opposition; it does run into opposition at Korangpo-ri.

AIR WAR: A detachment of the 600th Air Intelligence Service Squadron spends a week near Cho-do (Cho Island) in an attempt to recover components from a downed MiG-15. The Fifth Air Force provides high cover, and planes from British carriers provide low support. Charles O. Reister, flying an F-86A, shoots down a MiG-15.

PARTISANS: A semi-independent sub-command of Leopard, Task Force Perry, arrives at Kyodong-ni to establish command as well as control of Donkeys along the southern coast of Hwanghae Province. This includes the Han River Estuary islands.

June 22

POLITICAL/ADMINISTRATIVE: The Voice of America calls on Jacob A. Malik to give some word concerning the armistice talks, suggesting the Communists are awaiting some sign from the Soviet Union.

EIGHTH ARMY: The 24th Infantry Division relieves the 7th Infantry Division, which then goes into IX Corps reserve.

AIR WAR: Three F-86s are shot down by enemy fighters near Sinuiju.

June 23

POLITICAL/ADMINISTRATIVE: After another meeting with American diplomat George F. Kennan, Soviet ambassador Jacob Malik broadcasts a message on UN radio, saying that the Soviet people believe a cease-fire and an armistice can be arranged through a mutual withdrawal of troops. It is just about a year since the North Koreans invaded the Republic of Korea. In his talk, "The Price of Peace," Malik urges the warring parties to begin consideration of an armistice and recommends a cease-fire based on the separation of the armies along the 38th parallel. Major General Lee Chong Shan is named ROK chief of staff.

EIGHTH ARMY: A marine regiment is ordered to establish Badger Line, about two miles ahead of Kansas Line. Two dogs and their handlers accompany each rifle company of 1st Battalion, 15th Infantry, as they set out toward the Sobang Hills. The battalion-strength probe is to move seven or more miles. The dogs are to warn of any enemy hiding along the approach. The interesting experiment is a failure, however, as some of the dogs grow so tired that they have to be carried. The battalion arrives at the foot of Hill 717 and takes it later in the afternoon.

AIR WAR: Two F-86s are shot down by enemy fighters, one near Bihen and one at Teiju.

June 24

EIGHTH ARMY: The Communist troops on Hill 717 launch a counterattack at about 0200. They penetrate the 1st Battalion perimeter, but the defenders hold on long enough for the unit to make an orderly withdrawal. For actions at Sobangsan, PFC Emory L. Bennett (USA) is posthumously awarded the Medal of Honor.

AIR WAR: USAF pilot Richard M. Heyman shoots down a Po-2. Four F-86s and one F-84 are shot down by enemy fighters near Anju. Two F-86s are destroyed in aerial combat, one at Teiju and one at Bihen. According to Soviet sources, five F-80s are shot down by enemy planes, three at Bihen, one at Sensen, and one at Teiju.

June 25

POLITICAL/ADMINISTRATIVE: Chinese radio reports that the People's Republic of China is in favor of a peace effort and supports the idea of a cease-fire.

SEA WAR: The USS *Bataan* (CVL 29) ends its first tour of duty in Korean waters.

AIR WAR: The 8th Fighter-Bomber Group returns and begins operations out of Kimpo Airfield. Repairs have been made on the short runway, and work continues on an expansion of the main runway. Four F-86s are shot down by enemy fighters near Anju and one F-80 near Chinnampo. Milton E. Nelson, from the 136th FBW, shoots down a Po-2.

June 26

POLITICAL/ADMINISTRATIVE: Generals Matthew Ridgway and James Van Fleet tour the battlefield and decide against any attempt to advance beyond Line Wyoming. It is their belief that the cost in casualties would far out-distance the value of additional land gains.

EIGHTH ARMY: The Marine 3rd Battalion of the 1st Regiment moves forward to establish a base on Hill 761, but it is hit by such a powerful bombardment of Chinese artillery that it finds it necessary to pull back early the following day.

AIR WAR: Two USAF pilots, A. Olinger and H. Underwood, lay claim to the destruction of a MiG-15.

PARTISANS: An Operation Spitfire augmentation team, consisting of one Briton, one American, and nine Koreans, is dropped. This is in violation of the previous decision not to send non-Koreans on deep penetration missions.

June 26–28

EIGHTH ARMY: Operation Cat and Dog begin with the primary goal of capturing as many enemy prisoners as possible.

June 27

POLITICAL/ADMINISTRATIVE: Alan G. Kirk, the American ambassador in Moscow, meets with Deputy Minister of Foreign Affairs Andrei A. Gromyko, who confirms Jacob Malik's attempts to help the cease-fire. Gromyko asserts that negotiations should be conducted by field commanders, thereby limiting the talks to strictly military questions. It is necessary, he suggests, to avoid any political questions or territorial agendas.

PARTISANS: A large South Korean guerrilla raid on Chong Ye-Re, on the west coast, is supported by naval gunfire. Several of the enemy are killed or captured.

June 28

EIGHTH ARMY: The 1st Commonwealth Division is formed through the unification of the 25th Canadian, 28th Commonwealth, and the 29th British infantry brigades. Operation Cat and Dog, to capture prisoners and destroy enemy positions in the IX Corps area, comes to an end.

SEA WAR: Shore batteries at Wonsan harbor fire on USS *Tucker* (DDE 875), hitting the ship and causing some superficial damage.

AIR WAR: Three F-51s are shot down by enemy fighter planes, near Anju.

A member of the Korean Service Corps (KSC) getting ready to load up his A-frame *(Center for the Study of the Korean War, Graceland University)*

June 29

POLITICAL/ADMINISTRATIVE: Sounding confused, Kim Il Sung wires Chairman Mao Zedong asking how he should respond if the United States suggests negotiations. America's allies in the Korean War are informed by Assistant Secretary of State Dean Rusk that there will be a statement forthcoming in which General Matthew Ridgway will make an appeal for cease-fire discussions. Following the statement, plans are made, via Armed Forces radio, for General Ridgway to propose the idea of armistice talks.

June 30

POLITICAL: On instructions from Washington, General Matthew Ridgway announces that the UNC is willing to discuss an armistice. He suggests that representatives from the participating nations meet in Wonsan harbor aboard the Danish hospital ship *Jutlandia*. The South Korean government publically announces its opposition to armistice negotiations.

EIGHTH ARMY: Preparations for Operation Doughnut define that it will begin with the taking of Hill 717 and the subordinate high ground in the Sobang Hills and Mountains that lie to the northwest of Kumhwa. The 3rd Battalion, 7th Infantry, is to attack and take Hill 717; the 1st Battalion, 7th Infantry, to attack and take Hill 682; and the 3rd Battalion, 65th Infantry, to take Hill 581.

SEA WAR: The naval bombardment and siege of Wonsan enters its 134th consecutive day, suggesting it might not be a good place for the hostile parties to meet.

July–August

PARTISANS: During these two months, the South Korean partisans carry out 158 attacks in which they kill 1,200, wound 2,000, and capture 150 of the enemy. They also destroy several trains deep in North Korean territory, blow up 150 trucks, and ruin several bridges.

July 1

POLITICAL/ADMINISTRATIVE: North Korean premier Kim Il Sung and the CPVA commander, General Peng Dehuai, respond to Ridgway's suggestions of a meeting and agree to participate in armistice talks. They are not happy with the *Jutlandia,* and, establishing a pattern of always offering a counterproposal, they suggest the meeting be held at the old capital city of Kaesong. General James Van Fleet admits that he feels it is imperative for Eighth Army to remain actively involved in the fight in order to prevent the softening process that accompanies stagnation.

EIGHTH ARMY: Operation Doughnut, an effort to seize the dominant terrain features in the Sobang Hills, begins as the 7th Infantry attacks but takes only a part of the southern slope of Hill 717. The 3rd Battalion of the 65th Infantry moves from Chorwon along the Pyonggang road in preparation for an attack on Hill 717.

SEA WAR: Night fighters from the 1st Marine Air Wing shoot down a MiG-15. It is the first enemy aircraft shot down in night combat during the Korean War.

AIR WAR: An RF-51, flown by Colonel Karl L. Polifka, commander of the 57th Tactical Reconnaissance Wing, and a leading proponent of aerial reconnaissance, is shot down. Colonel Polifka is killed. Edwin Long and Bob Buckingham of VMF-513, working together, shoot down a Po-2.

PARTISANS: Choe Che Bu leads a party of 52 men of the White Tiger Brigade who land near Chang Duk and line up with Charlie Company, already in place.

July 2

POLITICAL/ADMINISTRATIVE: Kim Il Sung, as commander of the North Korean People's Army, and Peng Dehuai agree to a preliminary meeting of the liaison officers, suggesting July 8 as the date for a meeting. The CIA joins the Office of Special Operations and the Office of Policy Coordination to form the Joint Advisory Commission, Korea (JACK) to take overall control of operational and intelligence activities on the Korean Peninsula.

EIGHTH ARMY: The U.S. 3rd Infantry Division moves out on Operation Doughnut, a sequence of attacks on the hills of the Iron Triangle.

SEA WAR: Typhoon Kate hits the area and forces the suspension of all operations by the planes of Fast Carrier Task Force 77.

July 3

POLITICAL/ADMINISTRATIVE: General Matthew Ridgway sends the Communists, via Armed Forces radio, his approval of Kaesong as a negotiation site, and accepts July 8 as the date.

EIGHTH ARMY: In Operation Doughnut, the 7th Infantry, aided by the 10th Philippine Battalion Combat Team, seizes Hills 717 and 682 against a strongly entrenched enemy. During the night, they repulse several counterattacks. During the day, the 3rd Battalion of the 65th Infantry takes Hill 608. Lieutenant (j.g.) John Kelvin Koelsch (USN) is awarded the Medal of Honor posthumously, for his courageous actions near Wonsan.

SEA WAR: USS *Everett* (PF 8) is hit by shore fire at Wonsan. The hit causes some minor damage, and one crewman is killed and seven wounded.

July 4

EIGHTH ARMY: The 7th Infantry is able to repulse a series of predawn counterattacks. Under the cover of the last attack, the Chinese withdrew their forces from the hills and retreat into the area of Pyonggang. Operation Doughnut, to seize the dominant terrain features in the Sobang Mountains, comes to a successful end. Sergeant Leroy A. Mendonca (USMC) is posthumously awarded the Medal of Honor for action near Chichon.

SEA WAR: The USS *New Jersey* (BB 62) begins a series of bombardments on Kansong that will last until July 12. Intelligence reports that the enemy forces in the Wonsan area have increased considerably. Believing that the Communists are quickly gaining the ability to challenge the UN in the area, TE 95.21, the bombardment element, concentrates its fire on scattering the enemy forces.

July 5

SEA WAR: Planes from Fast Carrier Task Force 77 fly 247 sorties against selected targets in the Wonsan area. More than 600 ROK troops, supported by naval gunfire, raid the Wonsan area mainland opposite Cho-do.

PARTISANS: Planes assigned to drop supplies for Operation Spitfire are unable to find the drop zone at night and so wait until dawn. This time they drop the supplies directly over the hideout but, in the process, expose the partisan location to the enemy. The partisans are required to scatter.

July 6

SEA WAR: SFCP members are landed on the island of Hwangto-do in southern Wonsan harbor from USS *Evans* (DD 754). Following the raid there is a three-destroyer bombardment of buildings in the area.

AIR WAR: A KB-29M tanker, assigned to the 43rd Air Refueling Squadron, Air Materiel Command, conducts the first in-flight refueling over enemy territory under combat conditions. The tanker, crewed by men from the Strategic Air Command, refuels four RF-80 Shooting Stars that are flying air reconnaissance missions over North Korea.

PARTISANS: The advance scouts for Operation Spitfire are ambushed in a dawn attack. Delaying action by Sergeant Miles and 3rd Lieutenant (cadet) Ho allows the others to escape. Both men are MIA, and only half of the eight members of the group manage to get away. The mission is considered a failure.

July 7

POLITICAL/ADMINISTRATIVE: CINCFE approves the request to allow small groups of ROK midshipmen at Chinhae to sail aboard U.S. ships for training.

EIGHTH ARMY: The 1st Marine Division is ordered to construct secondary defense positions against an attack that is anticipated, based on the increasing buildup of enemy troops.

SEA WAR: The USS *Blue* (DD 744) lands SFCP and ROK Marine Forces on Kukto Island in Wonsan harbor and establishes a listening post.

AIR WAR: Three F-86s are shot down by enemy planes in the area near Sensen.

July 8

POLITICAL/ADMINISTRATIVE: When the U.S. negotiation team drives into Kaesong, white flags flying from their vehicles to "make them more identifiable," they come to deal with the Chinese on an equal basis. The Communists, however, want to make this aspect of the discussions difficult in any way they can. And it begins immediately. After a successful meeting between liaison officers, the cease-fire negotiation talks officially begin. The Communists agree to a cease-fire if the UN repatriates all Chinese prisoners. This first offer is declined. New York governor Thomas E. Dewey visits Korea, traveling as a private citizen, during the negotiation of the Japanese Peace Treaty. The CCF spring offensive campaign begins.

EIGHTH ARMY: The attack to take Taeu-san jumps off only to be met by crushing artillery and mortar fire from the enemy. A composite battalion created from the Korean Marine Corps is set up to meet the immediate problem developing near Taeu-san. The composite force is ordered to Hill 1100. The KMC digs in for the night during which time they repulse a series of Chinese attacks.

AIR WAR: Two F-86s are shot down by enemy fire near Sensen. Francis S. Gabreski, Richard S. Becker, and Franklin L. Fisher each shoot down a MiG-15.

July 9

POLITICAL/ADMINISTRATIVE: General Matthew Ridgway names Vice Admiral C. Turner Joy as chief of the UN delegation to the truce talks at Kaesong. Others include Major General L. C. Craigie, Major General H. I. Hodges, Rear Admiral A. A. Burke, and Major General Paik Sun Yup. A special operations element under CTF 90 begins its duties in support of the UN delegation at Kaesong.

EIGHTH ARMY: The UN summer-fall offensive campaign begins. The KMC commits its 1st Battalion to an attack on Taeu-san but with no more success than on the previous day. The KMC has taken Hill 1100 but is unable to move on to take Taeu-san at the time. They are finally driven off the hill by Communist forces. During the battle, the KMC suffers 222 casualties.

AIR WAR: An F-86 fighter is shot down by Soviet pilots near Teiju. USAF pilot Milton E. Nelson shoots down a MiG-15, and a B29A gunner, Gus C. Opfer, gets two.

July 10

POLITICAL/ADMINISTRATIVE: The cease-fire talks begin at the old Korean capital at Kaesong. The site is about 30 miles northwest of Seoul and just south of the 38th parallel. Admiral C. Turner Joy leads the American delegation. That night newsmen at Munsan-ni set up a betting pool on the length of the armistice talks. The most pessimistic bet is for six weeks. Vice Admiral C. Turner Joy (USN), Major General Henry I. Hodes (USA), Rear Admiral Arleigh A. Burke (USN), Major General Laurence C. Craigie (USAF), and Major General Paik Sonyup (ROKA) join the UN armistice negotiation team. The Communist negotiation team consists of Lieutenant General Nam Il (NKPA), General Teng Hus (CPVA), Major General Lee Sang Cho (NKPA), and Major General Hsieh Fang (CPVA).

AIR WAR: The Fifth Air Force diverts all available aircraft to attack a bridge where F-80s report that a long line of an enemy convoy is stalled. During the strike, more than 150 enemy vehicles are destroyed.

PARTISANS: The "Die for Tie" campaign is reported to be demoralizing partisan troops, many of whom are fighting for the unification of their homeland. Among the partisans, Colonel McGee is replaced by Colonel Jay Vanderpool of the CIA.

July 11

SEA WAR: The USS *Blue* (DD 744) and USS *Evans* (DD 754) are fired on near Yo-do. There is no damage to the ships. Overnight, naval forces execute Operation Cave Dweller. The USS *New Jersey* (BB 62) and USS *Leonard F. Mason* (DD 852) hit troop concentrations in the Kansong area as a part of Operation Cave Dweller. The bombardments result in the deaths of an estimated 129 enemy troops.

AIR WAR: Four F-86s are shot down by enemy planes, three of them near Sibi-do and one at Sinbi-do. An F-80 is shot down in aerial combat near Teiju-Anju. Milton E. Nelson and Ralph D. Gibson, flying F-86As and from the 335 FIS, each down a MiG-15.

General Matthew B. Ridgway standing at checkpoint on the road to Kaesong, where, on July 11, 1951, the Communist Chinese tried to prevent UN correspondents from attending the armistice talks *(Center for the Study of the Korean War, Graceland University)*

July 12

POLITICAL/ADMINISTRATIVE: Chief negotiator C. Turner Joy breaks off talks at Kaesong, telling the Communists that the United Nations must receive the same press coverage as the CCF or they will not continue to meet.

EIGHTH ARMY: The Special Aviation Inspection Group reports that the air strikes of the previous three months have resulted in the major destruction or disruption of most of the essential enemy airfields.

AIR WAR: Donald L. Fenton, flying an F4U-5NL, shoots down a Po-2.

PARTISANS: Task Force Perry moves from Kyodong-do to Kanghwa-do in order to maintain better control of the partisans on the Han River islands.

July 14

POLITICAL/ADMINISTRATIVE: The Communist negotiators at Kaesong agree to allow equal press coverage of the cease-fire talks.

EIGHTH ARMY: At the request of Eighth Army, the ROK organizes the Korean Service Corps to provide general manual labor for U.S. units to which it is attached.

Site of the first armistice talks at Kaesong, Korea, July 16, 1951 *(Center for the Study of the Korean War, Graceland University)*

Units of the 41st Independent Commandoes arrive at Wonsan from an LST and disembark on Yo-do.

AIR WAR: A B-26 of the 452nd Bomber Group discovers two enemy convoys north of Sinanju. In the early morning hours, the bombers attack and claim 68 vehicles destroyed or damaged.

July 15

POLITICAL/ADMINISTRATIVE: Major General Clovis E. Byers replaces Major General Edward Almond as X Corps commander.

July 17

POLITICAL/ADMINISTRATIVE: After more administrative adjustments, the cease-fire talks begin again at Kaesong.

SEA WAR: The shore batteries at Wonsan harbor are unusually active. Continuous and well directed fire scores hits on two rocket-launching ships, LSMR *409* and LSMR *525*, but no personnel are hurt. The USS *O'Brien* (DD 725) suffers one minor injury from the gunfire. Task Element 77.11, USS *New Jersey* (BB 62), and Task Element 77.14, USS *Helena* (CA 75), return fire.

PARTISANS: Donkey Eight partisans raid the North Korean mainland where their boats are stranded by the outgoing tide. Navy gunfire and naval air support allow them to escape but only after they suffer heavy casualties.

July 18

SEA WAR: Operation Kickoff begins. It is an operation that will become standard tactics for those ships active in Wonsan harbor. The plan is for ships to steam clockwise at five knots, firing at known battery positions in each enemy sector. The firing is to begin at 1500 hours and continue until dark. The USS *New Jersey* (BB 62) arrives off Wonsan in the early morning and begins bombardment.

July 19

POLITICAL/ADMINISTRATIVE: Major General John W. O'Daniel is assigned as commander of the U.S. I Corps.

July 21

POLITICAL/ADMINISTRATIVE: General James Van Fleet directs X Corps to develop a plan for taking the western ridge of the area known as the Punchbowl.

SEA WAR: Naval forces complete a salvage operation on a crashed MiG-15 off the Korean coast, but they are unable to collect very much.

AIR WAR: A combined force of British carrier planes flying low, and Fifth Air Force planes flying high, allows a detachment of the 6004th Air Intelligence Service Squadron to complete a weeklong effort to recover parts of a downed MiG near Cho-do Island.

July 22

POLITICAL/ADMINISTRATIVE: Admiral William M. Fechteler assumes the role as chief of naval operations (CNO) following the death of Forrest P. Sherman.

July 24

POLITICAL/ADMINISTRATIVE: Radio Pyongyang broadcasts the most current Communist demand that all foreign troops be withdrawn from Korea as a precondition of any cease-fire agreement.

AIR WAR: The second Air National Guard wing to be called up and deployed to Korea, the 116th Fighter Bomber Wing, arrives at Misawa and Chitose Air Bases in Japan. They fly F-84 Thunderjets.

July 25

SEA WAR: HMS *Cardigan Bay* (PF), HMAS *Murshison* (PF), ROKN *Apnok* (PF 62), and three minesweepers commence bombardments on the enemy coast in the Han area.

AIR WAR: An air defense system is established for South Korea, utilizing the resources of the 502nd Tactical Control Group.

July 26

POLITICAL/ADMINISTRATIVE: At the truce talks the long controversy over agenda items finally results in both sides agreeing to five agenda items. The U.S. Army announces that it will integrate all units in Japan, Korea, and Okinawa. Integration will be complete in six months.

PARTISANS: The survivors from Operation Spitfire begin to return through the 35th Infantry Regiment line.

July 27

POLITICAL/ADMINISTRATIVE: Major General Christian F. Schilt, USMC, assumes command of the 1st Marine Aircraft Wing.

July 28

SEA WAR: To show the Communists that UN forces are in control of the area, USS *Los Angeles* (CA 135) enters the channel of Haeju-man and, using the directions from a spotter plane, delivers a long bombardment of enemy front-line positions. The UN aircraft returns undamaged. Other naval units bombard the north bank of the Han River.

July 29

AIR WAR: Reconnaissance planes discover a group of MiGs near Pyongyang. They are flying much farther south than usual. The UN planes, which are vastly out-numbered, are able to evade action and return to safety. Four F-86s are shot down by enemy fighters, three at Anindo and one at Teiju. Three F-80s are shot down by Soviet pilots near Etsuhori. USAF pilot William W. McAllister shoots down a MiG-15.

July 30

EIGHTH ARMY: General James Van Fleet decides to deepen his defensive field and orders Line Wyoming to become a permanent line. This means establishing fortifications.

AIR WAR: Addressing targets in the Pyongyang area, 91 F-80s suppress the enemy air defense systems while a record 354 USMC and USAF fighter-bombers hit specified military targets. The scope of the mission, and its success, is withheld from the media because of the fear it might affect the ongoing peace negotiations. VP Squadron 6, commanded by Commander G. Howard, begins its second tour of land-based duty in Korea.

July 31

SEA WAR: The USS *Helena* (CA 75) is hit on its main deck by fire from shore bat-teries at Wonsan. The result is some damage to the ship and two crewmen slightly wounded.

August 1

EIGHTH ARMY: General Matthew Ridgway tells the Joint Chiefs of Staff (JCS) that reconnaissance has discovered large military stockpiling at the city of Rashin and asks permission to resume bombing in the area. This time the JCS and President

Truman agree to the action. Admiral Joy, at the cease-fire meetings, proposes that, in addition to no augmentation of troops or equipment after the cease-fire, there should also be an agreement that no new airfields be constructed or old ones rehabilitated.

SEA WAR: The USS *Badoeng Strait* (CVE 116) receives the Navy Unit Citation for duty from August 3, 1950, to this date. The USS *Princeton* (CV 37) receives the Navy Unit Citation for service from August 3, 1950, to this date. The USS *Badoeng Strait* (CVE 116) is awarded the Navy Unit Citation.

PARTISANS: Aviary Section, Combined Command Reconnaissance Activities, Korea (9240th AU), is established at K-6, the Seoul City Airport. Its formal name is Far East Command Liaison Detachment, Korea, 8240 Army Unit.

August 2

AIR WAR: Determining that the Communist logistical system will break down if the railroads are destroyed, Operation Strangle (a repeat of the June and July operation) is reestablished and the FEAF increases its fighter/bomber campaign against the rail lines. Numerous flights, mostly at night and using SHORAN, are composed of bombers concentrating on bridges and fighter planes on rail cuts. The role of the B-25s is shifted from daylight interdiction to night time truck-hunting operations.

August 3

EIGHTH ARMY: Operation Cow Puncher, the plan to move Phase Line Utah forward to Phase Line Wyoming, comes to an end.

August 4

POLITICAL/ADMINISTRATIVE: A company of North Korean troops is reported to be in the area of the Kaesong truce talks, threatening the discussions.

SEA WAR: British Royal Marines install mortars on Hwangto-do at Wonsan.

August 4–8

EIGHTH ARMY: Heavy rains cause a lull in the fighting during July and the early part of August, particularly at this period. When patrols probe the Punchbowl area, they run into more difficulty dealing with swollen rivers and streams than with the enemy. Fortunately, the same weather conditions greatly reduce the Communist activity.

August 5

POLITICAL/ADMINISTRATIVE: UN negotiators suspend the cease-fire talks at Kaesong because North Korean troops have, contrary to the agreement, marched through the area.

August 6

SEA WAR: The USS *Carmick* (DMS 32) captures 13 enemy fishermen and destroys four sampans near Chongjin.

August 7

AIR WAR: Patrol Squadron 772 (Reserve), under Commander D. D. Nittinger, ends its tour of duty in Korea.

PARTISANS: The partisan group Kirkland loses Song-do (aka Sol-sam) to an enemy aggressor force.

August 8
PARTISANS: Coast watchers from the Kirkland group return to Song-do (aka Sol-sam) after the Communists withdraw from the area.

August 9
AIR WAR: Four F-80s are shot down by enemy fighter planes, one at Ryugampo and three at Teiju.
PARTISANS: Lieutenant Colonel Samuel Koster takes command of the Partisan Miscellaneous Group.

August 10
POLITICAL/ADMINISTRATIVE: The cease-fire talks resume at Kaesong. The North Korean delegates, without admitting to any violation, promise to respect the neutrality of the zone where talks are being held.
SEA WAR: The USS *Princeton* (CV 37) is detached for routing to the United States.
AIR WAR: Air Group Nineteen "X Ray" ends its tour aboard USS *Princeton* (CV 37). The USS *Princeton* receives the Navy Unit Commendation for service from December 5, 1950, to this date.

August 11
SEA WAR: The USS *Dextrous* (AM 341) and USS *Redstart* (AM 378) are fired on while conducting a sweep near Hodo Pando. The *Dextrous* suffers two hits; during the engagement, one crewman is killed and three are wounded. The *Dextrous* suffers minor damage. HMCS *Cayuga* (DDE) fires on shore batteries located near the Han River estuary, continuing the naval bombardment of enemy shore installations.
PARTISANS: Friendly guerrillas are supported by HMCS *Cayuga* (DDE).

August 12
EIGHTH ARMY: Major General Clark L. Ruffner, U.S. 2nd Division commander, is ordered to attack Bloody Ridge. The importance of the ridge is that it is being used by the enemy to direct artillery fire against UN supply lines.

August 13
AIR WAR: VP Squadron 731 (Reserve) under Commander H. S. Wilson ends its sea-based tour of duty in Korea. VP Squadron 47 under Commander W. T. Hardaker begins its second tour of sea-based duty in Korea.

August 14
POLITICAL/ADMINISTRATIVE: All divisions are notified that cold war clothing and equipment have been requisitioned. The announcement serves as a warning that the war will continue through the coming winter.
EIGHTH ARMY: A group of North Koreans tries to cross the mud flats in an effort to take the island of Sunni. The attempt fails and the enemy forces suffer heavy casualties.

Sea War: Nine occupants of enemy fishing sampans are captured by USS *William Seiverling* (DE 441) off Tanchon.

August 15

Eighth Army: The Battle of Bloody Ridge begins with units of the ROK 36th Regiment, attached to the U.S. 2nd Infantry Division in the attack. After a fight that declines at one point to hand-to-hand combat the regiment takes some of the high ground on Bloody Ridge and is able to hold it. They cannot take it all, however, and the Chinese dig in for a long fight. The Ethiopian infantry battalion, raised from Emperor Haile Selassie's bodyguard, enters combat attached to the U.S. First Cavalry Division.

Sea War: Marine Helicopter Transportation Squadron 161 begins to move to Korea. In Operation Strangle, air attacks continue against Pyongyang.

August 15–September 5

Eighth Army: Bloody Ridge is a group of hills located about 17 miles north of the 38th parallel. They consist of Hills 980, 940, and 773. The primary advantage of holding the ridge, which is parallel to the line of battle, is that the holder will have better observation. Beginning on August 15, the ROK 36th Regiment attempts to take most of the high ground. The battle to do so continues until August 26, when the NKPA counterattacks and takes Hills 980 and 940 and the ridge between. The 9th Regiment, 2nd Infantry Division, is ordered to retake them. Attacking on August 30, they fail in the attempt, but are successful when they counterattack on August 31. In early September, the 23rd Regiment will join the fight and take Hill 754, located north of the ridge, along with hill 660. By the September 4, the 9th Infantry will take and hold Hill 940, which is the central peak. The cost of the ridge will be 2,700 UN casualties and an estimated CCF loss of 15,000.

Air War: USAF renews Operation Strangle in order to interrupt communication lines. The attacks begin on Pyongyang.

August 16

Eighth Army: In the Battle of Bloody Ridge, the 36th ROK Regiment is unable to capture the ridge.

August 17

Political/Administrative: Communists claim that some of their troops have been ambushed near the cease-fire site at Kaesong and demand a UNC apology. The request is denied.

Eighth Army: The ROK 36th Regiment, 7th Infantry Division, again attempts to take the hills of Bloody Ridge.

Sea War: The USS *New Jersey* (BB 62), USS *Toledo* (CA 133), HMNS *Van Galen* (DD), and USS *Agerholm* (DD 826) are formed into a special bombardment group to provide gunfire support for UN troops. HMAS *Murchison* (PF), HMS *Cardigan Bay* (PF), and HMS *Morecambe Bay* (PF) combine to shell a concentration of 400 enemy troops in the Han River area.

AIR WAR: Okinawa-based B-29s are unable to operate because of a typhoon that hits the area.

August 18

EIGHTH ARMY: The area of the fighting consists of Hills 983, 940, and 773 as well as the connecting ridges and valleys known as the Punchbowl. Eighth Army tries to straighten out its line. The ROK 5th Division attacks Bloody Ridge, west of the Punchbowl, where it continues to meet stubborn resistance from elements of the 45th, 13th, and 2nd North Korean Divisions. Attacking are elements of the ROK 7th Infantry Division, 72nd Tank Battalion, and 2nd Infantry Division artillery. Operation Citadel, to move the MLR forward to the then existing Outpost Line of Resistance, begins. General James Van Fleet orders all X Corps commanders to eliminate significant enemy outposts that might be capable of directing artillery fire against the UN Line Kansas. Elements of the ROKA I Corps attack Hill 1031. The North Koreans are deeply dug in with well-built fortifications along the ridge. The attack will continue for 11 days. Elements of the North Korean 45th, 13th, and 2nd Divisions launch a counterattack against an area known as J-Ridge. The battle for the ridge will last nine days.

SEA WAR: Aircraft of the 1st Marine Aircraft Wing evacuate to Itami Air Base because of the threat of typhoon Marge. The USS *Volador* (SS 490) leaves Yokosuka for a period of special reconnaissance.

AIR WAR: The FEAF begins the second phase of Operation Strangle, directed toward the North Korean railway system. An F-86 is shot down near Teiju by enemy fighter planes.

August 18–August 29

EIGHTH ARMY: ROK troops from the 8th, 11th, and Capital Divisions attack a J-shaped ridge northeast of the Punchbowl. They meet with stubborn resistance from elements of the 45th, 13th, and 2nd North Korean Divisions. The battle continues for 11 days. The pattern of attack and counterattack continues until August 27 when the ROK seizes the hook of the ridge and then on August 29 takes the stem.

August 18–September 5

EIGHTH ARMY: A mountain range 17 miles to the north of the 38th parallel and 30 miles east of Kumhwa, is known as Bloody Ridge. The apex of the area is called the Iron Triangle and consists of Hills 983, 940, and 773. This area is the focus of the Eighth Army movement.

August 19

EIGHTH ARMY: Battle of Bloody Ridge continues. Operation Citadel, to move the MLR toward the Outpost Line of Resistance, ends successfully.

SEA WAR: Near Tranchon USS *Thompson* (DMS 38) captures two prisoners in a sampan.

AIR WAR: Richard S. Becker from the 334th FIS shoots down two MiG-15s.

August 20

EIGHTH ARMY: Battle of Bloody Ridge continues.

Sea War: USS *Uhlmann* (DD 867) is taken under fire by seven guns off Hondo-Pando, Wonsan. There are no hits or personnel lost, though the *Uhlmann* is bracketed by 117 splashes. Counter-battery fire reduces the enemy gunfire to two guns.

August 21

Eighth Army: Battle of Bloody Ridge continues.

Sea War: The 5th Marine Aircraft Wing returns its planes to combat fields. The contract is awarded for the first nuclear-powered submarine. It is to be called the *Nautilus*.

August 22

Political/Administrative: Communists suspend the truce talks after a discussion of the demarcation line and DMZ fails to come to any satisfactory agreement.

Eighth Army: Battle of Bloody Ridge continues.

Sea War: In supporting the ROK's I Corps and U.S. X Corps operations, USS *Toledo* (CA 133) expends more than 700 rounds. The USS *Essex* (CV 9) replaces USS *Princeton* (CV 37) and joins Fast Carrier Task Force 77. The USS *Essex* is the first jet-capable carrier to arrive in the Korean operations area.

Air War: Air Group 5 (VFs 51, 53, 54, 172) begins its tour of duty onboard USS *Essex* (CV 9).

August 23

Political/Administrative: The Communists suspend the cease-fire talks at Kaesong after claiming that U.S. planes have bombed the truce talk area. This ends the period of the Kaesong truce talks.

Eighth Army: Battle of Bloody Ridge continues.

Sea War: The USS *Los Angeles* (CA 135) relieves USS *Toledo* (CA 133) on the east coast bombline.

Air War: F2H Banshee jet fighters from USS *Essex* (CV 9) fly in combat for the first time in Korea. Benjamin S. Preston and Jack A. Robinson, flying F-86As, each shoot down a MiG-15.

August 24

Eighth Army: Battle of Bloody Ridge continues.

Air War: An F-86 is shot down near Teiju by enemy fighter planes.

August 24–25

Air War: Overnight a flight of B-26s reports destroying more than 800 trucks during a new campaign directed at nighttime attacks on trucks moving supplies.

August 25

Eighth Army: During the battle for Bloody Ridge, the ROK 36th Regiment takes the ridge after heavy fighting.

Sea War: For the first time in aviation history, navy fighters, 12 F2H-2 aircraft, escort USAF B-29 medium bombers on a raid. The USS *Helena* (CV 75), USS *Harry E. Hubbard* (DD 748), and USS *Rogers* (DDR 876) perform Bird Dog duties for B-29s striking Rashin.

AIR WAR: Thirty-five B-29s, escorted by U.S. Navy fighters, drop more than 300 tons of bombs on the marshaling yards at Rashin in the extreme northeastern corner of Korea. The bombing of Rashin, with its large supply depots, had been suspended because it was located within 20 miles of the Soviet border. The B-29 raid is conducted with excellent results and no loss of aircraft. Two Meteors are downed by enemy fighters near Sensen.

PARTISANS: Choe, with the White Tiger unit, establishes contact with the CIA and requests 31 replacements and supplies.

August 26

POLITICAL/ADMINISTRATIVE: The 77th Engineer Combat Company is the last combat unit in Korea to lose the asterisk, the army way of designating a black unit.

EIGHTH ARMY: In the Battle of Bloody Ridge, pressure from significant North Korean troops, forces the 36th Regiment, ROK, to withdraw. The NKPA counterattacks and at first surrounds, and then captures, Hill 983 as well as the saddle between it and Hill 940.

August 27

EIGHTH ARMY: The 3rd Battalion of the 9th Infantry hits Hill 983 but is stopped short of victory. The 3rd Battalion launches an attack on Hill 773 but is unable to take the hill. The ROK 36th Regiment finally takes the ridge but is able to hold it through the night only. Some units of the ROK 36th break under pressure at the defensive line near Hill 983, which causes panic among troops of the 9th Infantry. The units are unable to take their objective. After 11 days of fighting, elements of the ROK I Corps take the hook and the stem of Hill 1031, and finally the crest. After nine days of fighting, troops of the ROK I Corps and the U.S. X Corps take J-Ridge. For action near Sobangsan First Lieutenant Lee R. Hartell of the U.S. army is posthumously awarded the Medal of Honor.

August 28

POLITICAL/ADMINISTRATIVE: Delegates reassembled at the peace talks agree to a cease-fire line that will be the line of contact at the time of the agreement.

EIGHTH ARMY: The battle for Bloody Ridge continues as the 36th is once again forced off the ridge.

SEA WAR: Near Changjon on the Sea of Japan an amphibious demonstration is conducted by Transport Division 13 in an effort to limit enemy resistance to the UN advance. The USS *Helena* (CA 71), destroyers, minesweepers, and amphibious ships take part. The USS *New Jersey* (BB 62) joins the group for a short time.

August 29

EIGHTH ARMY: Battle of Bloody Ridge continues.

AIR WAR: Two F-86s are shot down by enemy fighters near Hinchen, and two Meteors are lost, one at Kaisen and one at Kusen.

August 29–September 5

SEA WAR: The HMNZS *Taupo* is in Korean waters.

August 30

EIGHTH ARMY: At the battle for Bloody Ridge, the 9th Regiment's 1st and 2nd Battalions are given the responsibility for taking Hills 933 and 950 of the Bloody Ridge complex. They launch another attack. It is supported by artillery units that fire nearly a half-million rounds in preparation. The fight goes on all day; by nightfall all of Bloody Ridge is still in Communist hands.

August 31

EIGHTH ARMY: The 9th Regiment counterattacks at Bloody Ridge. After days of fighting, the 2nd Infantry Division attack in the early morning. The assault is supported by heavy artillery, armor, and fighter strikes. In order to keep the advancing team supplied, rear area personnel are pressed into service as carriers. The 9th is finally able to drive the Communists off Hill 773, but the other hills and the saddle remain in Communist hands. The battle continues as General James Van Fleet determines to renew the offensive to drive the Communists back north from the Hwachon Reservoir. This is the reservoir that provides Seoul's water supply. The 1st Marine Division, with the attached 1st ROK Marine Regiment, begins attacking the northern rim of the Punchbowl. The KMC objectives are Hills 924 and 1026. The KMC moves out and, as night approaches, they are within 1,000 yards of Hill 924 and halt for the night. The 1st KMC moves through the 3rd KMC line to begin a drive against Hill 702 but quickly discovers that the slopes are heavily mined. Corporal William F. Lyell (USA) is posthumously awarded the Medal of Honor for his service near Chupa-ri.

AIR WAR: Four F-80s are shot down by enemy fighters near Teiju.

September 1

POLITICAL/ADMINISTRATIVE: The Soviet Union conducts its first atomic bomb test—"Semipalatinsk." The ANZUS (Australian, New Zealand, United States) Treaty is signed to be effective April 1, 1952. It reflects concerns over the security of Korea and the Australia–New Zealand fear that any peace treaty with Japan will strengthen Japan's role in Asia.

EIGHTH ARMY: In the vicinity of Hill 702, the 3rd Battalion, 7th Marines, clashes with the NKPA in several attacks against the hill. Four counterattacks fail to dislodge the North Koreans. Renewing the attack on Hill 924, the 2nd Battalion, KMC Regiment, takes Hill 924 and elements pass through toward Hill 1026.

SEA WAR: In the Han River area, HMAS *Murchison* (PF) is hit above the water line by 75-mm antitank fire, machine gun, and mortar fire. One seaman is seriously injured and two are wounded. The ship loses its 40-mm gun.

AIR WAR: VP Squadron 1 under Commander W. M. Ringness ends its land-based tour of duty in Korea. VP Squadron 2 under Commander R. Turner, Jr., begins its tour. Twenty air force cargo planes from Japan successfully drop rations and ammunition to supply frontline troops. USAF pilot Winton W. Marshall shoots down a MiG-15. Communist sources report an F-86 is shot down by its fighters near Linsen.

PARTISANS: Mustang II (a plan to rescue POWs, including General William Dean) is approved by Headquarters Far East Command. Mustang I, planned for July 1951, had been canceled at the last minute.

September 1–2
Sea War: The USS *Hopewell* (DD 681) controls FEAF aircraft on bombing and strafing runs in the Wonsan area.

September 1–4
Eighth Army: The 23rd Regiment of the U.S. 2nd Infantry Division joins the continuous assault on the adjacent hills of Bloody Ridge. Despite the new effort, the Communists maintain control.

September 2
Eighth Army: In the continuing battle for Bloody Ridge, the 2nd U.S. Infantry Division, west of the advancing marines, moves north against Bloody and Heartbreak Ridges. At Hill 1026, marines and the KMC repulse counterattacks to a point 800 yards from the crest, but the lines are not penetrated. George Company, supported by How Company, resumes the marine attack against Hill 602. Supported by heavy machine guns, the 3rd Battalion, 7th Marines, sweep the crest of Hill 602. There is an immediate counterattack, but the North Koreans are repulsed and withdraw to the north. After winning the battle for Hill 924, the 2nd Battalion of the KMC fights off several counterattacks and, as day breaks, is still in control of the area. The North Koreans withdraw.
Sea War: Marine Helicopter Transport Squadron 161 arrives at Pusan, Korea.
Air War: The Communists report nine F-86s downed by their fighter planes, seven at Teiju and two at Syukusen. Four MiG-15s are shot down by USAF pilots Winton W. Marshall, Francis S. Gabreski, Ralph D. Gibson, and Richard S. Johns.

September 3
Political/Administrative: Commander Amphibious Group 1, Rear Admiral T. B. Hill, relieves Vice Admiral I. N. Kiland as Commander Amphibious Force Far East.

Eighth Army: The 1st Marine and 1st ROK Divisions enter the Punchbowl. The KMC constructs bunkers on Hill 603 and continues the attack toward Hill 1026. The North Koreans counterattack just after noon, but after two hours of desperate fighting they withdraw. By midmorning, the ROK is in full possession of Hill 1026, and the 1st Marine Division is in control of the Hays Line that dominates the northern rim of the Punchbowl. The marines had caught the North Koreans involved in a replacement change. Captain Edward

Headquarters Company squad tent being used as a mess hall in a temporary camp outside of Seoul, Korea *(Center for the Study of the Korean War, Graceland University)*

C. Krzyzowski (USA) is posthumously awarded the Medal of Honor for service near Tondul.

September 4

Eighth Army: With the 23rd Regiment, 2nd Division, joining the fight, UN troops are finally able to take and occupy Hills 754 and 660, just to the north of Bloody Ridge. The UN control of these hills makes the Communist positions on Bloody Ridge nearly untenable. It takes until 1400 for the 9th Regiment to take the crest of Hill 490, the dominant peak of the ridge. The Communist forces begin to withdraw and move quickly to avoid the trap being developed for them. UN casualties (primarily 2nd Infantry Division) are 2,700. PFC Melvin L. Brown is posthumously awarded the Medal of Honor for action near Kansas Line. During the night, the marines assault along their sector of the Kansas Line but are unable to make any significant progress. The 7th Marines is sent against Hill 812, which it is able to take.

Sea War: Fast Carrier Task Force 77 loses three planes to enemy fire and one from operational failure. Three pilots are killed.

September 5

Eighth Army: Bloody Ridge is finally secured after more than a month of fighting. The U.S. 2nd Division is ordered to continue the attack. After retreating, the NKPA begins to reorganize, and the 2nd Infantry Division is ordered to maintain the pressure along Heartbreak Ridge to prevent the CCF from using the valley to attack X Corps positions at the Punchbowl. The battle cost the UN nearly 3,000 casualties; the enemy, 15,000.

Sea War: New sweeping operation orders from the commander, United Nations Blockading and Escort Force (CTF 95), call for a minesweeping group (CTG 95.6) to begin sweeping operations from Wonsan to Hungnam. The goal is to clear the area of mines so that the Wonsan-Songjin patrol can be within gun range at all times. The port city of Hungnam is under fire for the first time since the December 1950 withdrawal.

Air War: Soviet pilots, Grigorii U. Ohay and Ivan Tjuliyaew, each claim a Meteor fighter downed in air-to-air combat, and another Meteor is downed by an unknown pilot near Teiju.

September 6

Partisans: North Korean troops attack Yuk-do and Yongwi-do in an attempt to dislodge the partisans. The partisans are able to successfully defend Yuk-do, but the other island falls. During the battle, Captain David Maus is killed on Yongwi-do.

September 7

Political/Administrative: After intelligence reports unusual Chinese Communist activity, unit commands are warned that the CCF is about to launch an attack on key terrain features. This appears to be in response to continued disagreements at the armistice talks. General Pollock determines that Bunker Hill and Outpost Bruce must be held.

EIGHTH ARMY: For actions on September 6–7 near Chorwon, Corporal Jerry K. Crump (USA) receives the Medal of Honor. Private Billie G. Kanell (USA) is posthumously awarded the Medal of Honor for service near Pyongyang.

September 8

POLITICAL/ADMINISTRATIVE: General James Van Fleet issues a directive to his corps commanders instructing them to emphasize limited objective attacks, reconnaissance, and patrols. Forty-eight nations sign a peace treaty formally ending World War II with Japan. The treaty puts into effect the Cairo Declaration that requires Japan to release all claims that it might have on Korea and to recognize the independence of Korea. As well, Japan signs a security treaty with the United States.

EIGHTH ARMY: Operation Minden begins. It extends the Wyoming Line from Sanggorangpo to Chung-gol, to remove salients created by curves in the Imjin River. The Commonwealth Brigade establishes a firm bridgehead in no-man's-land on the north bank of the lower Imjin.

SEA WAR: The USS *Seiverling* (DE 441) is hit three times by shore batteries at Wonsan. The fire room is flooded but there are no casualties.

PARTISANS: Units composed of about 200 ROK regulars make an amphibious raid on the west coast of Korea under the support of naval gun fire. The raid results in an estimated 105 enemy killed.

September 8–12

EIGHTH ARMY: Operation Ohio-Sloan is launched to gain new positions along Phase Line Wyoming.

September 9

POLITICAL/ADMINISTRATIVE: General Pollock, in further consideration of an attack warning, adds eight more areas to his defense requirement. They are, from east to west, Hills 86 and 38 in the Korean Marine sector, Hills 56 and 48A in the center sector, and the Outposts then known as Allen, Clarence, Felix, and Jill.

EIGHTH ARMY: The 7th Marines jump off in the attack against Hills 812, 980, and 1052 near the Kanmubong Ridge. They have orders to take the hills and the ridge line and to move on and occupy Hill 602.

AIR WAR: Twenty-eight Sabre-jets flying between Sinanju and Pyongyang are attacked by at least 70 MiGs. During the air duel, two F-86 pilots, Captain Richard S. Becker from the 334th FIS, and Captain Ralph D. Bigson of the 335th FIS, each add a downed MiG to their tallies and increase the number of jet aces from one to three. Seven F-86s are shot down by Soviet pilots, according to the Communist claims.

September 9–10

EIGHTH ARMY: Operation Clean-Up, an attempt to sweep enemy forces from the front facing I Corps, begins.

September 9–12

EIGHTH ARMY: The focus of the battle moves to Heartbreak Ridge.

September 10

EIGHTH ARMY: Operation Clean-Up comes to an end.

SEA WAR: Enemy shore batteries at Wonsan hit both USS *Redstart* (AM 378) and USS *Heron* (AM 18) while they are checking a newly swept area. There are no casualties.

AIR WAR: A H-5 helicopter from the 3rd ARS rescues F-80 pilot Captain Ward M. Millar of the 7th Fighter-Bomber Squadron. He is located south of Pyongyang after escaping from two months of captivity and then avoiding recapture for more than three weeks. The rescue group also brings out a North Korean army sergeant who aided the downed pilot and wanted to defect. Communist sources claim three F-86s, five F-84s, and a Meteor are shot down by their planes near Kaisen and Anju.

September 11

POLITICAL/ADMINISTRATIVE: Dean G. Acheson, secretary of state, meets with the British foreign secretary, Herbert S. Morrison, to discuss the future of Korea if the suspended truce talks (August 23, 1951) do not resume. Acheson outlines a fairly aggressive view, while Morrison is concerned that whatever is done must not lead the United Nations into a war with China.

EIGHTH ARMY: Elements of the British Commonwealth Brigade leave their bridge-head on the Imjin River and move out in Operation Minden, an effort to extend the line from Sanggorangpo. The 3rd Battalion, 8th Cavalry, tries again to take Hill 570. Despite several attempts they fail to do so. The 7th Marines moves out against Objectives Able and Baker, Hills 673 and 749. They are stopped at Hill 673, where the enemy is deeply dug in. The fighting lasts through the night. The battle for Kanmubong Ridge begins. The 10-day engagement is the scene of the first tactical use of helicopters by the marines. During the night of June 11, the 7th Marines moves out, pushing toward Hill 749 and Hill 812. Within three hours the hills are in its possession.

AIR WAR: In Communist claims, Mijail S. Ponomarieu, flying a MiG-15, shoots down two F-84s. N. Volkov shoots down an American F-84, Grigorii U. Ohay gets an F-80C, and I. Semenenko and Aleksandr S. Kumanichkin each get an F-80 in air combat.

PARTISANS: Volunteers find and return the body of partisan leader Captain David Maus.

September 12

EIGHTH ARMY: The 1st Marine Regiment relieves the 7th Marine Regiment east of the Punchbowl. Second Lieutenant Jerome A. Sudut (USA) is posthumously awarded the Medal of Honor for action near Kumhwa. Sergeant Frederick Mausert III (USMC) is posthumously awarded the Medal of Honor for courage in action near Songnap-yong. Second Lieutenant George H. Ramer (USMC) is posthumously awarded the Medal of Honor for heroic service. The planned attack on Hill 570 has to be canceled because enemy forces begin to move toward Hills 314 and 660. After maneuvering all night, the 1st Battalion, 7th Marine Regiment, attacks Hill 673 from two directions, and by 1445 the marines take the summit.

AIR WAR: According to Communist claims, Soviet pilots Mijail S. Ponomarieu shoots down an F-84F and three F-80s. Ivan V. Suchkow gets two F-80s. N. Kvartzov, Georgii A. Lobov, and Mijail A. Zykov each get an F-80.

September 13

EIGHTH ARMY: The U.S. 2nd Division attacks the ridge line north of Bloody Ridge, later to be called Heartbreak Ridge. At 0530, the artillery bombardment begins to pound Heartbreak Ridge. Then the 23rd Regiment of the 2nd U.S. Infantry Division sets off, with the 3rd Battalion leading the way. When they moved north from Hill 702, the North Koreans spot them. Heavy fire from Heartbreak soon follows, causing a large number of casualties. When the 3rd Battalion reaches the spur and heads up the hill, in an effort to split the forces on Heartbreak Ridge, it runs into a determined enemy. Elements of the NKPA 6th Division are holed up in a series of concealed bunkers; the 23rd Regiment is halted. At 1600, Operation Windmill I is set in motion. It consists of moving one day's supply to the 2nd Battalion, 1st Marines, over a distance of seven miles. The landing team clears an area, and by 1610, the first helicopters begin releasing cargo by net and then drop off troops. In two-and-a-half hours the helicopters deliver 18,848 pounds of cargo and evacuate 74 casualties. Operation Minden is successfully completed with little opposition or casualties. The attack of the 1st Marines, scheduled for Hill 749, is postponed because of a serious ammunition shortage.

SEA WAR: The first mass-helicopter resupply operation (Operation Windmill I) is conducted by Marine Helicopter Squadron 161.

AIR WAR: According to Soviet sources, V. Verduish shoots down an F-51D, and three F86As are downed by unknown Soviet pilots. A. F. Plitkin gets an F-51D.

September 13–October 15

EIGHTH ARMY: The Battle of Heartbreak Ridge. The fight begins with an artillery barrage followed by an assault by the 23rd Regiment, 2nd Division; it is an effort to round out the defensive positions on the Punchbowl. The 2nd Infantry Division is assigned to take a line of rough hills running north and south. The North Koreans are deeply dug in on the ridge following their defeat at Bloody Ridge. Heartbreak is a 3,000-foot-long ridge line that consists of three peaks designated Hill 894, Hill 931, and Hill 851. In effect, it is an extension of Bloody Ridge three miles to the south. Satae-ri is to the east and Mundung-ni to the west, creating a critical area for maneuvers. The plan calls for a three-pronged attack by the 23rd Regiment. Almost immediately it runs into heavy North Korean opposition. After more than two weeks, the plan will be revised, and UN troops will include some adjacent hills in their area of attack. The effort is designed to spread the North Korean forces. A road will be prepared by the engineers to provide tank support. On October 13, elements of the 23rd, including the French Battalion, will succeed in taking Hill 851 on the north, and two days later the ridge is taken. The U.S. 2nd Infantry Division will suffer 3,700 casualties. It is estimated that the participating North Korean 16th, 12th, and 13th Divisions, as well as the Chinese 240th Division, will have lost as many as 25,000.

The artillery bombardments during this time are so heavy that they create an ammunition shortage in Eighth Army. The 2nd Battalion of the 1st Regiment is delayed in its progress toward Hill 751 by enemy forces firing from Hill 749. The decision is made to redirect the attack.

September 14

EIGHTH ARMY: The 2nd Battalion, 1st Marines, finally moves against Hill 749 and takes it with the support of the 11th Marines, who fire 3,029 rounds. The battle for Heartbreak Ridge continues as the 23rd Regiment tries to split North Korean forces between Hills 931 and 851, but as night falls the units have moved forward only a few yards from their previous positions. The 9th Regiment is directed to take Hill 894 in an effort to pull pressure from the units engaged on Bloody Ridge. By nightfall the 9th has reached to within 600 yards of the crest. PFC Edward Gomez is posthumously awarded the Medal of Honor. The marine assault on Hill 751 is slowed and the regimental objective is denied by the enemy, which still occupies portions of Hill 749. An attack on the latter finally takes the rest of Hill 749, but the fighting takes most of the day to accomplish this. In renewed fighting for Hill 570, the 3rd Battalion, 8th Cavalry, supported by fire coming from the newly occupied Hill 314, sets out to push the North Korean troops off the hill.

AIR WAR: Captain John S. Walmsley (USAF) of the 8th Bomber Squadron is posthumously awarded the Medal of Honor after he is shot down and killed by ground fire near Yangdok. Flying a B-29, he attacked and destroyed an enemy train. Then, after expending all his ammunition, he spotted another target. He stayed around long enough to light the area with an experimental spot on his wing, in order that another B-29 could continue the attack.

PARTISANS: Kim Myong Ryon leads an attack on an enemy cavalry unit, killing 83 enemy soldiers as well as 13 horses. However, Kim and Commander Lee Yi Sup are both captured.

September 15

EIGHTH ARMY: Three companies of the 3rd Battalion continue the battle at Heartbreak Ridge and by late evening secure Hill 894. The marines on Hill 749 are still in a fight where consolidated enemy forces respond from scattered pockets of resistance. Marines of the 5th Regiment are called on to pass through the 3rd and carry on the assault. The battle continues for Hill 570 as the 2nd Battalion, 8th Cavalry, makes some gains but is still not able to control the hill. The 9th Regiment, sent to take Hill 894 in an effort to relieve pressure on Bloody Ridge, finally succeeds in its mission late in the afternoon. Several efforts by the enemy to counterattack fail. The hope that this will relieve pressure on Bloody Ridge does not materialize.

September 16

EIGHTH ARMY: The 23rd Regiment is still trying to take control of Bloody Ridge and is still pinned down on the lower levels. The Communist location is such that it is possible to resupply and reinforce the units on the ridge. The North Korean 13th Regiment is sent in to replace the 1st NK Regiment in the defense. Facing focused

artillery fire on Heartbreak Ridge the North Koreans push forward in a brief counterattack against the small UN position, rushing ahead with burp guns, but the
assault is unsuccessful. Just after midnight the enemy launches a vicious four-hour
attack against Hill 749. The first waves are stopped by the marines, but the enemy
keeps coming. It is noon when the attacks subside. Hill 749 is finally secured. Casualties are 90 KIA, 714 WIA, and one man is listed as missing. The Chinese losses are
estimated at 771 KIA. Fox Company of the 2nd Battalion, 5th Marines, moves on,
attacking toward Hill 980. Corporal Joseph Vittori (USMC) is posthumously
awarded the Medal of Honor for actions on September 15 and 16 near Hill 749. In
the battle for Hill 570, the enemy counterattacks against the positions gained by the
2nd Battalion, 8th Cavalry, but they are unable to dislodge the UN troops. The fight
ends as the center of the battle moves south.

Sea War: An accident on USS *Essex* (CV 9)—the landing of an F2H without its tail
hook down—results in a fire and the loss of two F2Hs and two F9Fs. Three crewmen are killed, 27 are injured, and four reported missing.

September 17

Political/Administrative: Robert A. Lovett replaces George C. Marshall as secretary of defense. The Military Assistance Advisory Group (MAAG) is created in
Vietnam.

Eighth Army: Operation Clean-Up I is executed. The goal is to seize and occupy
the ridge running west of Hill 487 (just west of Chorwon) and to generally disrupt
the Chinese Communist Forces and their supply lines. The job is given to the 3rd
Infantry Division. The 7th and 15th easily take the assigned objective. The attack
resumes on Hill 980 and, catching the enemy at breakfast, the crest is taken. PFC
Herbert K. Pililaau (USA) is posthumously awarded the Medal of Honor for action
near Pia-ri.

Partisans: Officers, flying in a B-26 on a reconnaissance for Mustang II near Ha-
ri, North Korea, are shot down. Two parachutes are reported coming from the plane
but there is no report on the crew. CIA planes drop 36 replacements for White Tiger
operations. The members in place split into groups of 10 and move out in different
directions.

September 18

Eighth Army: Enemy action increases at Heartbreak Ridge as UN troops move to
take Hill 851. By the time they reach the ridge, most of their ammunition is gone.
Relying on flamethrowers and using their weapons as clubs, the UN troops reach the
top of the hill and dig in. The marines move north of the Punchbowl, with the
Soyang River in sight. Elements of the 2nd Battalion, 5th Regiment, repulse a series
of Chinese counterattacks against Hill 812. In Operation Clean Up I, units of the 3rd
Infantry Division are assigned to take Hill 487 (west of Chorwon) but fail in the
attempt. Marines on newly acquired Hills 980 and 1042 suffer counterattacks during the day, taking heavy casualties. Orders are issued to the marines that Hill 854
is also to be taken.

Sea War: HMS *Glory* (CVL) is transferred to the east coast.

September 18–19

SEA WAR: A special two-day operation conducted by Task Force 95 begins. It is a mission-coordinated attack by air, naval gun fire, and rockets on the harbor and city of Wonsan.

September 19

POLITICAL/ADMINISTRATIVE: General Robert Young is named the new 2nd Infantry Division commander. The continuing failure to take Bloody Ridge leads to a suggestion that the front needs to be broadened.

EIGHTH ARMY: Following the directive to broaden the front, General de Shazo orders the 1st Battalion of the 9th Regiment to move across the Mundung-ni Valley and seize Hills 867 and 1024, about three miles to the southwest. The attack is scheduled for September 25. The battle for Heartbreak Ridge continues with an attack on Hill 931. Eighth Army pushes north of the Punchbowl. The 1st Battalion, 5th Marines, relieves the 1st and 2nd Battalions of the 1st marines and occupies a defensive line stretching two miles to the east on a ridge that runs almost to the Soyang-gang (River). Operation Windmill II drops much needed fortification supplies on an area in the marine section called the Rock.

SEA WAR: The USS *Toledo* (CA 133), USS *Craig* (DD 885), and USS *Parks* (DD 884) engage in flak suppression bombardment that precedes air strikes by HMS *Glory*. Marine Fighter Squadron (VMF-323) departs USS *Sicily* (CVE 118) to begin land-based operations at Kangnung, Korea. In order to give the carriers of the task force more freedom for interdiction missions, it is relieved of all responsibility for front-line close air support.

AIR WAR: According to Communist sources, Lev K. Shchukin shoots down an F-86 fighter in air combat. Four F-80s are also downed by Soviet fighters. Kenneth L. Skeen of the 9th Fighter-Bomber Squadron shoots down a MiG-15.

September 20

POLITICAL/ADMINISTRATIVE: The fight for Hill 812, and the marine control of the area around it, will often be used to mark the end of the mobile war in Korea and the beginning of the war of position. It certainly marks the end of Marine Corps movement. From now on the marines will be fighting a war generally unknown to them, a defensive one.

EIGHTH ARMY: The battle for Heartbreak Ridge continues as the 23rd Infantry receives air-dropped ammunition, food, and water while holding on to the base of Hill 931. ROK troops take the crest of Hill 854 but not the ridge line to the southwest. The attack is planned but then postponed until the remains of ROK mines can be cleared from the area. At 1220, following an air strike and 10 minutes of artillery bombardment, the attack continues and How Company is able to reach the ridge and secure it by 1745. The 5th Marines hold a wide sector dominated by Hill 812. The 5th Marines try to extend their boundaries to include Hill 884 (aka Mount Helicopter). It is decided to bring in the troops by helicopter. The attack is set for September 21, 1951. Elements of the 2nd Battalion, 5th Regiment, try to hold on to Hill 812 and first lose and then retake it. The area is known at Luke the Gook's Castle.

SEA WAR: The USS *Orleck* (DD 886), using Shore Fire Control Party (SFCP) spotters, is able to hit a troop concentration, explode an ammunition dump, and register several hits on a large sampan.

AIR WAR: In the first helicopter-borne landing of combat troops in history, Operation Summit lands men from Marine Helicopter Transport Squadron HMR 161. Marine Fighter Squadron VMF-212 embarks for operations aboard USS *Rendova* (CV 114).

September 21

POLITICAL/ADMINISTRATIVE: Administrative Command, Amphibious Force, Pacific Fleet, is disestablished and its functions are transferred to Commander Amphibious Force Pacific.

EIGHTH ARMY: The marines are to extend the X Corps boundary eastward by relieving the 11th Regiment, ROK I Corps. It is decided to accomplish this by helicopter, putting the men on Hill 854. At 1000 hours, a security force is dropped, then men from the 1st Shore Party Battalion, commanded by Lieutenant Colonel Harry W. Edwards, drop, by means of knotted ropes, to clear two sites. A total of 224 men and their equipment are moved as the assignment is completed within four hours. For action on this date near Songnae-dong, Corporal Jack A. Davenport (USMC) is posthumously awarded the Medal of Honor.

SEA WAR: The USS *Perkins* (DDR 877) fires more than 500 rounds during a call-fire mission that lasts for more than 12 hours. Close air support by the Fast Carrier Task Force (77) is discontinued.

PARTISANS: Operation Mustang II, to rescue POWs, is canceled due to its possible compromise, the result of two officers being lost during a Mustang II reconnaissance flight.

September 22

EIGHTH ARMY: In the ongoing effort to take Bloody Ridge, the ROK 7th Division is ordered to take Hill 1142, about 2,000 yards north of Hill 1024. The effort is intended to lessen the enemy ability to defend either Bloody Ridge or Heartbreak Ridge. The Battle of Heartbreak Ridge continues as UN forces attack and gain Hill 931, but they are driven from the top of the hill four different times. The 1st Battalion of the Argyll and Sutherland Highlanders moves across the Naktong River.

AIR WAR: Soviet claims say two F-86s are downed by their fighters, one near Anju and one at Deeguandong.

September 23

POLITICAL/ADMINISTRATIVE: When liaison officers meet at the cease-fire site, UNC delegates propose a new truce talk meeting place and ask for a different location. At this point the Chinese are not interested in continuing the discussion.

EIGHTH ARMY: In the ongoing effort to take Bloody Ridge, the effort is focused on Heartbreak Ridge but the plan is not working. Across the Mundung-ni Valley, the diversionary attack by the 9th Regiment and the ROK 7th Division against Hill 1024 and Hill 1124 is making progress but has not yet been accomplished. The attack at

Heartbreak Ridge continues as the UN forces' fifth attempt to take Hill 931 proves successful. The Argyles achieve their objective on Hill 282 and occupy abandoned gun pits. Late in the afternoon, after resisting numerous North Korean counterattacks, the Argyles are accidentally bombed and strafed by a P-51, and then napalm is dropped on them. The cause is either a mistaken reading of the panels (identification markers) or perhaps the fact that North Korean soldiers placed decoy panels, but the attack is devastating.

SEA WAR: The USS *New Jersey* (BB 62) participates in the bombardment of the Kansong area in support of X Corps.

AIR WAR: Using SHORAN bombing techniques, eight B-29s from the 19th Bomber Group knock out the center span of the Sunchon rail bridge despite the presence of a 90 percent cloud cover over the target. USMC pilots Eugene Van Gundy and Tom Ullom, from U.S. Navy VMF-543, combine to shoot down a MiG-15.

September 24

POLITICAL/ADMINISTRATIVE: Communist negotiators at Kaesong leave the table, rejecting any plan to reopen the talks.

EIGHTH ARMY: At Heartbreak Ridge, elements of the 2nd Infantry Division briefly hold Hill 931 but are quickly forced to withdraw in the face of heavy North Korean counterattacks. The 2nd is hampered by a shortage of ammunition.

SEA WAR: Wonsan shore batteries manage to hit the ROK navy's *PF 62* three times, causing minor damage and wounding three.

September 25

POLITICAL/ADMINISTRATIVE: The cease-fire negotiations between the UN and the Communists resume, but at UN insistence, the location is moved to the village of Panmunjom.

EIGHTH ARMY: The 9th Regiment and 7th ROK Division continue to attack Hills 1024 and 1142 and late in the day are able to clear Hill 1024. The French Battalion tries to take Hill 931 but fails. In consideration of the situation, it is decided that no more uncoordinated attempts will be made.

SEA WAR: The USS *New Jersey* (BB 62) provides long-range coverage of friendly troop bunkers. ROK president Syngman Rhee presents the Unit Citation to the United Nations Blockading and Escort Force 95.

AIR WAR: More than 30 MiG-15s are met by 36 F-86s in one battle and more than 100 MiG-15s meet 37 F-86s in a separate battle; five MiGs are destroyed and one F-86 is damaged. Soviet records indicate that three F-86s are shot down, one at Hukusen, one near Kukusen that blows up in midair, and one at Kukusen. The five MiG-15s are shot down by USAF pilots Booth Holker, Charles F. Lyod, P. E. Roach, M. F. Babb, and Richard D. Creighton. Pilots Roach and Babb combine on one, and Booth T. Holker accounts for two.

September 26

EIGHTH ARMY: The ROK 7th Division, which is working with the 9th Regiment to relieve pressure on Heartbreak and Bloody Ridges, takes Hill 1142. The North Korean 6th Division's 3rd Regiment is pulled from Heartbreak Ridge to defend Hill

867, a dominant terrain feature that is now threatened. The 23rd on Bloody Ridge is still unable to take Hill 931.

AIR WAR: Nikolai V. Sutyagin and I. L. Yakovlev both claim to have downed a Meteor fighter in air combat. Sutyagin also claims shooting down an F-86A. Three F-84s and three additional F-86s and an F-80 are also claimed to have been downed on this date near Anju.

September 27

POLITICAL/ADMINISTRATIVE: General Matthew Ridgway proposes to the Chinese Communists that the cease-fire talks be shifted from Kaesong to the village of Songhyon in no-man's-land.

EIGHTH ARMY: The attack on Heartbreak Ridge has been going on for some time when a series of piecemeal frontal attacks is called off while UN forces regroup. General Byers agrees that continued effort is useless. General Young will later call the effort a "fiasco." Heavy mortar and artillery fire is directed at Hill 931.

AIR WAR: Operation Blackbird is planned with a marine unit assigned to move by helicopter from Hill 702 to the northwest rim of the Punchbowl. The movement, done at night, consists of Easy Company, 2nd Battalion, 1st Marine Regiment, under Second Lieutenant William K. Rockey. Six helicopters lift 223 men in a little more than two hours. While the movement is successful in bringing support troops in to defend the MLR, it is recommended that such night flights be limited to friendly territory. In Operation Pelican, a C-124A Globemaster being service tested flies its first payload from Japan, delivering 30,000 pounds of aircraft parts to Kimpo. Two F-86s are shot down near Jungsen and six F-84s near Anju, according to Soviet reports.

September 28

POLITICAL/ADMINISTRATIVE: Charles E. Bohlen, a State Department counselor, and General Omar N. Bradley visit Tokyo and Korea to talk with General Ridgway about returning to the negotiation table.

SEA WAR: With the Commander, United Nations Blockading and Escort Force, on board, HMAS *Murchison* (PF) moves up the Han River on an inspection trip. The ship is hit by small field gun fire, causing some minor damage and wounding one crewman.

AIR WAR: A jet aircraft, aided by in-flight refueling, is in the air for 14 hours and 15 minutes. The plane, on a combat mission, refuels multiple times from two KB-29M tankers as it completes the longest such flight to date.

September 29

EIGHTH ARMY: In Operation Clean-Up II, an effort is made to take a five-hill complex surrounding Hill 487. It is preceded by a nine-day artillery softening-up effort. The assault is made by Able, Baker, and Easy Companies, 1st Battalion, 15th Infantry, but they fail to take the area. Easy Company is able to secure its objective on the southern summit. On Hill 587, the Chinese are pushed back. The 3rd Battalion of the 65th Regiment, assigned to Twin Peaks (a part of the complex), finds the going tough until George Company joins it in the morning and they finally take the Twin Peaks. Operation Clean-Up II is only partially successful.

September 30

POLITICAL/ADMINISTRATIVE: General Joe W. Kelley assumes command of FEAF Bomber Command, replacing Brigadier General Terrill.

SEA WAR: The helicopter rescue ship, *LST 799,* rescues Captain J. W. Tuttle near Hungnam.

AIR WAR: VP Squadron 46 under Commander R. L. Donley begins its sea-based tour of duty in Korea.

October

EIGHTH ARMY: In an effort to control guerrilla activity behind the lines, the marines become involved in Operations Houseburner I and II. These are helicopter-borne activities in which Korean huts are set on fire by flame throwers and incendiary grenades to prevent them being used by the Communists.

October 1

POLITICAL/ADMINISTRATIVE: The U.S. Eighth Army officially ends segregation. All black units are replaced with integrated units.

EIGHTH ARMY: General Omar Bradley, chairman of the Joint Chiefs of Staff, visits USS *New Jersey* (BB 62). Operation Commando is launched, calling for Major General Robert H. Soule's 3rd Infantry Division to take three hills on the right flank. The first of the hills, 281, is about six miles northwest of Chorwon, and the others, Hills 373 and 324, are seven miles beyond the city.

AIR WAR: VP Squadron 28 under Lieutenant Commander E. R. Hawley begins its land-based tour of duty in Korea. According to Communist records, Dmitri A. Samoylov shoots down an American F-86 while an F-84 is downed by an unidentified pilot. Americans George L. Jones and Raymond Barton each down a MiG-15.

October 1–3

AIR WAR: The 315th AD, flying C-119s in Operation Snowball, drops 55-gallon napalm-filled drums behind enemy lines in an experiment. Six MiG-15s are downed by USAF pilots.

October 2

EIGHTH ARMY: The ROK 11th Division is created to wipe out stragglers from the North Korean People's Army and Communist guerrillas, who are becoming a problem in the rear of the advancing UN Command. As a part of Operation Touchdown, General Young is assigned the eight hills on the western side of the Mending-ni Valley, in an effort to spread out the North Koran defenders. Included in the attack are Hills 867, 1005, 980, 1040, 931, 738, 520, and 851.

SEA WAR: Spotter planes are provided for frigates bombarding at the Han.

AIR WAR: The planes of Task Element 95.11 are ordered to bomb the northern bank of the Han River, west of Yesong Gang, on a daily basis. More than 180 Communist MiG-15s are observed over Korea on this day. Grigorili L. Pulov shoots down an RF-80A, S. Moskvichev downs an F-86, and four other planes are downed by unidentified Soviet pilots. N. Volkov downs an F-84E and an F-86 is also destroyed, according to Soviet records.

PARTISANS: Operation Comeback is to clear the islands from Kunsan to the Sir James Hall Archipelago on the 38th parallel. When it finally begins, it is discovered that most of the clearing has already been accomplished as a follow-up of Operation Lee.

October 3

EIGHTH ARMY: In Operation Commando, during the following 16 days, the 1st Cavalry Division takes Hills 313, 418, 334, 287, 247, and 272. The battle for Heartbreak Ridge is still not over, and, in preparation for another attack, eight enemy bunkers are destroyed. Operation Clean-Up II, to secure the railroad running north from Uijongbu, begins.

SEA WAR: In Operation Retribution at the Han River, 13 aircraft from TE 95.11, supported by HMS *Black Swan* (PF), make a strike against enemy guns. The *Black Swan* makes a feint up the Han River to try to bring the enemy guns out in the open and then, when they are spotted, to bring in the planes to hit specific targets. The effort results in considerable damage and loss of life among enemy forces. The helicopter rescue ship, *LST 799,* saves Second Lieutenant A. M. Muller, 2nd Squadron, South African Air Force, west of Wonsan; he had flown from USS *Bon Homme Richard* (CV 31). The LST takes several hits from rifle fire on shore.

AIR WAR: Air Group 101 ends its tour of duty on USS *Bon Homme Richard* (CV 31). An F-84 is shot down near Takusen by enemy fighters.

October 3–8

EIGHTH ARMY: Operation Commando begins in an effort to secure hill positions near Yonchon and to push the UN lines forward from Line Wyoming to Line Jamestown. The assignment is given to I Corps, with the ROK I, the U.S. 1st Cavalry Division's 34th and 25th Infantry, and the newly organized British Commonwealth Division. The center of the line runs into the Chinese 47th Army where the UN left and right flanks are able to advance to the goal. It will take 16 days for the 1st Cavalry to reach Jamestown Line.

AIR WAR: Pilots Francis S. Gabreski, George J. Oka, Paul W. Bryce, George W. Dunn, and Lloyd J. Thomson each get one, and G. Dunn and C. Spath combine on one.

PARTISANS: The intelligence officer for FEAF Command decides to expand activities to include Cho-do Island in its infiltration of UN agents. The area is a prime location for interrogation of refugees.

October 3–12

EIGHTH ARMY: British and Australian troops are involved in the Battle of Kowang-san.

October 4

EIGHTH ARMY: The 25th Canadian Brigade, following up on Operation Commando, secures Kowang-san during the day. The fighting on Maryang-san grows heavier. At Heartbreak Ridge, Task Force Struman meets and engages in a firefight with the North Korean 19th Regiment. Elements of the 8th Cavalry, reinforced by the 7th, assault the ridges leading to Hill 418. This area is held by the Chinese who put up strong resistance. Colonel Mildren's 38th Regiment moves against Hill 485 as a part of Operation Touchdown. When it arrives, they discover that the enemy has left the hill. The 38th Regiment then moves on and takes Hill 728.

October 5

POLITICAL/ADMINISTRATIVE: American ambassador to the Soviet Union Allan G. Kirk meets with the Russian foreign minister Andrei Y. Vyshinsky and asks for Russia's help in restarting the cease-fire negotiations. Vyshinsky agrees to carry Ambassador Kirk's concerns to Joseph Stalin.

EIGHTH ARMY: General Robert Young launches a new operation against Heartbreak Ridge, called Operation Touchdown. Artillery fire opens up on units facing the 9th and 38th Regiments. Air strikes and napalm are sent to strike the North Korean lines before the infantry moves out late in the evening at 2100 hours and three regiments—9th, 23rd, and 38th Infantry—begin action simultaneously. On the west the 3rd Battalion, 9th Infantry Regiment, presses against Hill 867. The Commonwealth Division continues Operation Commando in heavy fighting near Maryang-san. The Ulsters, RCR, and Patricias complete their assignments in Operation Commando by taking their respective goals. The Royal Canadian Regiment, supported by elements of the Patricias, takes the area between Yongdong and Chommac near Hill 157. During the night, the Chinese withdraw from Hill 418, and the 1st Battalion, 8th Cavalry, moves on toward the hill and the accompanying ridge by afternoon. They then move on to occupy the summit of Hill 313.

SEA WAR: Shore fire from Hungnam hits USS *Firecrest* (AMS 10), resulting in light damage but no casualties. In one of the few returns since the evacuation in December 1950, an element of Task Force 77, consisting of USS *New Jersey* (BB 62), USS *Helena* (CA 75), USS *Hanson* (DD 832), and USS *Small* (DD 939), hits the Hamhung-Hungnam area with an extensive bombardment.

AIR WAR: The Communists report that two F-84s and three F-86s have been shot down by their fighters. USAF pilot Richard D. Creighton, flying with the 334th FIS, shoots down a MiG-15.

October 6

EIGHTH ARMY: In the battle for Heartbreak Ridge, Hill 728 is taken and held. Hill 931 is also taken. The Commonwealth Division continues Operation Commando as the Communists hold the ground near Maryang-san. The 1st Marine Regiment moves along the Mending-ni Valley and attacks Hill 636. The moderately defended hill manages to hold off the attack through the night.

SEA WAR: Near Pungchon on the west coast, HMS *Amethyst* (PF) dispenses fire to cover the withdrawal of friendly guerrillas. The helicopter rescue ship *LST 799* rescues Ensign W. C. Bailey from USS *Bon Homme Richard* (CV 31), northeast of Hungnam.

AIR WAR: Yevgeni G. Pepelyayev downs two F-86As while four others are destroyed by unnamed pilots, most of them over Anju and Sensen, according to Soviet records.

October 7

POLITICAL/ADMINISTRATIVE: Admiral J. J. Clark relieves Rear Admiral John Perry as Commander Fast Carrier Task Force (CTF 77).

EIGHTH ARMY: In the battle for Heartbreak Ridge, UN forces finally take Hill 967. Operation Commando continues, with the Commonwealth Division battling heavy Communist resistance near Maryang-san. UN Command attacks Hill 230, controlled by the Chinese. The enemy is able to withstand the attack but takes a large number of casualties. Attacking from both the south and southeast, the 7th Cavalry moves against Hill 418 and begins to clear it by late afternoon. By taking the hill, the 1st Cavalry Division controls the high ground that makes up the Jamestown Line in that sector. The marine attack on Hill 636, after an all-night fight, is finally successful. Air strikes by marine Corsairs lead the attack on Hill 867, and the 3rd Battalion, 9th Infantry, takes the crest after little resistance.

SEA WAR: The USS *Carmick* (DMS 33) evades six rounds that miss the ship as it sails off Songjin. While steaming off Hungnam, USS *Ernest G. Small* (DD 838) hits a mine that causes considerable damage and kills nine and wounds 18.

October 8

POLITICAL/ADMINISTRATIVE: Rear Admiral C. F. Espe aboard USS *Estes* (AGG 12) assumes command of Amphibious Group 1 and Amphibious Task Force 90, replacing Rear Admiral T. B. Hill. General Matthew Ridgway accepts the Communist proposal that the Korean cease-fire talks begin anew and be moved to Panmunjom.

EIGHTH ARMY: At Heartbreak Ridge, the North Koreans advance in a counterattack but are held off. In Operation Commando, the 28th Commonwealth Brigade begins to consolidate its forces and takes its objective, Hill 218. The ROK's 8th Division takes the crest of Hill 1005 and the Kim Il Sung Range, which runs from the hill toward the west.

AIR WAR: Soviet reports show Yevgeni G. Pepelyayev as shooting down an F-84E.

PARTISANS: The sister islands of Tan-do and Tyan-do [T'an-do] near the mouth of the Yalu River are captured by members of Donkey 15. Enlarging on their success, the partisans ask for permission, and naval support, to move on against Sinmi-do.

October 9

EIGHTH ARMY: The Commonwealth Division is able to consolidate its position upon the completion of Operation Commando. But the heavy losses (420 casualties) and wide deployment mean that the division is extended, and will soon be the target of counterattacks. For action at Mundung-ni, Sergeant First Class Tony K. Burris (USA) is posthumously awarded the Medal of Honor.

SEA WAR: The HMS *Cossack* (DD) is called on to support ROK guerrilla operations against the island of Sinmi-do.

AIR WARS: VP Squadron 28 under Commander C. S. Minter ends its land-based tour of duty in Korea.

October 10

POLITICAL/ADMINISTRATIVE: Discussions begin over reopening the truce talks. The discussions lead to the signing of the Panmunjom Security Agreement, an eight-point mutual agreement to provide security at a new location for the talks. The Department of the Army issues Field Manual 31–21: "Organization and Conduct of Guerrilla Warfare."

EIGHTH ARMY: Near the end of the fighting at Heartbreak Ridge, Hill 851 is attacked by the 23rd Infantry Regiment, supported by a tank battalion and elements of the French Battalion. By 1300 hours, after moving forward in a bayonet charge, they take the hill. It is finally secured at 1600 hours. The 2nd Infantry suffers 3,700 casualties, and the enemy losses are estimated at 25,000. The 2nd Battalion of the 9th Infantry swings down from Heartbreak Ridge and after sporadic fighting is able to take Hill 605, but the efforts to take Hill 905 are unsuccessful.

SEA WAR: Heading for Sasebo, after hitting a mine at Hungnam, USS *Small* (DD 838) loses her bow but remains watertight. Massive air and surface strikes are delivered against Kojo and vicinity by HMS *Belfast,* HMS *Concord,* and USS *Colahan* (DD 658). The carrier element consists of HMAS *Sydney,* HMCS *Cayuga,* HMS *Comus,* and USS *Shields* (DD 596).

AIR WAR: In order to harass the enemy on a significant Chinese holiday—the anniversary of the overthrow of the Manchu dynasty—FEAF pilots drop special propaganda leaflets and make a series of radio broadcasts, designed for Chinese troops in Korea. In the winning of Heartbreak Ridge, the USAF has dropped more than 250 tons of bombs. Three F-86s are destroyed by enemy fighters near the area of Yotori.

PARTISANS: Permission is given, and naval support provided, for Donkey 15 to attack Sinmi-do.

October 11

EIGHTH ARMY: In Operation Bumblebee, the 3rd Marine Battalion, 7th Marine Regiment, is sent in to relieve the 5th Marines by helicopter. Beginning at 1000 hours, 12 helicopters engage in 156 flights that take just over six hours to move 958 troops and their equipment. The landing is just behind the 7th Marines area northeast of Hill 702.

SEA WAR: During the second day of strikes against Kojo, USS *Renshaw* (DDE 499) is hit by shore batteries in the vicinity of Songjin. The attack causes only superficial damage but results in one man being wounded.

October 12

EIGHTH ARMY: After the considerable pressure maintained on the Chinese defenders of Hill 272, the Chinese abandon the hill. The 8th Cavalry takes control of the hill without firing a shot. The 1st Battalion of the 38th Infantry moves toward the Kim Il Sung Range; after launching an assault on Hill 974, it quickly takes the objective.

AIR WAR: Soviet reports say Grigorii Ohay, Dmitri A. Samoylov, Nikolai G. Dokashenko, each down an F-86 fighter, Dokashenko getting two. A B-29 is also destroyed by enemy fighters. An American pilot, Joseph R. Ellis, flying an F-86A shoots down a MiG-15.

PARTISANS: Sinmi-do, on the northwest coast of Korea, is evacuated by friendly guerrillas because of increasing pressure from enemy forces.

October 13–22

EIGHTH ARMY: UN forces advance toward Line Missouri in Operations Polar and Nomad.

October 13

EIGHTH ARMY: The last crest on Heartbreak Ridge is taken. At daybreak the French Battalion storms the peak, and after a month of hard fighting, the 23rd Infantry is in possession of Heartbreak Ridge. The casualties for the engagement are 3,700 for the 2nd Infantry, with the French Battalion and the 23rd Regiment taking half of these. The enemy losses are estimated at close to 25,000. Hill 851 in the Battle of Heartbreak Ridge is held by the 23rd Infantry Regiment and the French Battalion. Line Minnesota is operational.

SEA WAR: During the first day of Typhoon Ruth, air operations are disrupted. The storm also causes 50 percent damage to the planes of HMAS *Sydney.*

October 14

AIR WAR: The second day of Typhoon Ruth prevents any significant air operations. The Soviets report (despite the bad weather) an F-80 shot down near Anju-Jungsen, an F-86 near Anju, and two F-86s near Sensen.

PARTISANS: Donkey 15, supported by HMS *Cossack,* lands on Sinmi-do only to discover the island's garrison has recently been reinforced. Meeting heavy opposition, the landing fails and the attacking unit suffers heavy casualties.

October 15

EIGHTH ARMY: The final objective of Operation Touchdown, Hill 1220, falls to the 1st Battalion, 38th Infantry, which has attacked along the Kim Il Sung Range. Hills 346 and 230 are taken by elements of the 1st Cavalry Division.

SEA WAR: The third day of Typhoon Ruth prevents most sea, and all air, operations. The USS *Grasp* (ARS 24) receives the Presidential Unit Citation for service from February 1 to October 15, 1951. The USS *Graffias* (AF 29) is awarded the Navy Unit Citation.

AIR WAR: Air Group 15 begins its tour of duty aboard USS *Antietam* (CV 36). Operating day and night, B-29 pilots fly 31 sorties, against rail bridges, marshaling yards, and the airfield at Samchang. Leaflets are also dropped and reconnaissance missions undertaken.

October 16

EIGHTH ARMY: Elements of the 1st Battalion, 7th Marines, attack an NKPA strongpoint overlooking the village of Changhan. The enemy area is hit, the fortifications destroyed, and the units withdrawn. Operation Polecharge, to secure the dominant hills in the I Corps area, begins. The 5th Cavalry moves against the Chinese-held Hill 272 but is stopped by heavy fire from the Chinese. The 8th Cavalry moves toward the hill from the northeast in an effort to assist, but they, too, are held.

AIR WAR: Fifth Air Force Sabre fighters meet and destroy nine MiG-15s in aerial combat. Two F-86s are downed near Junsen, an F-86 and an F-84 near Kaisen. Nine enemy fighters are shot down in aerial combat. Pilots M. E. Hroch and C. F. Brossart combine on one, and Brossart gets one on his own; Franklin L. Fisher is responsible for two; Anthony Kulengosky, David B. Freeland, George W. Dunn, Benjamin S. Preston, and Orren H. Ohlinger get one each.

October 17

EIGHTH ARMY: A reinforced KMC makes a raid against enemy fortifications northwest of Hill 751 and south of Hill 1052, destroying 25 bunkers.

SEA WAR: Shore batteries near Hungnam fire on, and hit, USS *Samuel N. Moore* (DD 747), causing minor damage, killing one and wounding two.

AIR WAR: Pavel S. Milaushkin, flying a MiG-15, reports shooting down a Meteor fighter.

October 18

EIGHTH ARMY: After more than a week of fighting to take Hill 230, the Chinese defenders finally break under the pressure from 3rd Battalion, 5th Cavalry, and retreat to the north of Yokkok-chon. After two days of fighting, the 5th Cavalry, assisted by the 8th, is able to take Hill 272 with little to no opposition.

AIR WAR: Nine bombers (B-29s) of the 19th Bomber Group, escorted by 24 F-84s, bomb Samichon. They drop 306 100-pound bombs. Another nine planes of the 98th Bomber Wing fail to meet their escorts and so take on a secondary target.

October 19

POLITICAL/ADMINISTRATIVE: Congress officially ends the state of war with Germany. The U.S. Army opens up a 1,000 bed hospital at Camp Drew, north of Tachikawa Air Base in Japan.

EIGHTH ARMY: The 1st Cavalry is able to overcome the last barrier to its control of the Jamestown Line. The Chinese retreat north of Yokkok-chon to establish their next line of defense.

AIR WAR: C-54s fly medical evacuees from Korea to Tachikawa, Japan, and then C-47s shuttle them to Camp Drew. This plan reduces the transit time required to get the wounded to a hospital.

October 20

SEA WAR: The USS *Gallup* (PF 47) and USS *Glendale* (PF 36) are transferred to the government of Thailand.

October 21

POLITICAL/ADMINISTRATIVE: Chinese Communist forces invades Tibet; Beijing had earlier signed an agreement to make Tibet a "nationally autonomous region" of China. A fleet of nine 2 $1/2$ ton trucks moves out of Munsan-ni and crosses the Imjin River, loaded with supplies and heading for the village of Panmunjom. Shortly thereafter a tent city springs up to house UNC delegates and the press for the cease-fire talks.

SEA WAR: The UN Blocking and Escort Force is directed to increase its "bridge busting and roof lifting" campaign in order to keep the enemy from repairing destroyed facilities.

October 21–30

AIR WAR: In an unusual move, Chinese pilots begin a period of sorties over North Korea, often appearing in numbers in excess of 100 planes. In most cases, the MiGs outnumber the UN planes, primarily Sabres, in the air. During the following week, three F-86s are destroyed by the enemy, which, at the same time, loses five MiGs.

October 22

EIGHTH ARMY: Marine antiguerrilla raids behind the MLR are carried out using HMR-161 helicopters. In Operation Bushbeater, teams from the 1st Battalion, 1st Marine Regiment, are landed on the division's east flank and swept toward the town of Syong-gang. Teams from the Reconnaissance Company sweep in the other direction.

SEA WAR: Commander Fleet Air Japan states his intention to establish a small fleet aircraft squadron at Kangnung, Korea.

AIR WAR: Nine B-29s of the 19th Bomber Group, escorted by 24 F-84s bound for Taechon, are attacked by 40 MiGs. The 12-man crew of a downed B-29 is rescued by two SA-16s from the 3rd ARS. It is the largest group of men rescued on any day of the war. Captain Edward N. Lefarvie (USMC) is rescued by helicopter from behind enemy lines 40 miles southwest of Wonsan by Chief Aviation Pilots C. W. Buss and S. W. Manning, from the *LST 799* (a helicopter rescue ship). The rescue is hampered by small-arms fire encountered throughout the mission. Communists report that their fighters have shot down eight B-29s and nine F-84s at Taisen, Jyungsen, and Anjuy, and three F-86s at Anju and Kaisen.

October 23

POLITICAL/ADMINISTRATIVE: The Panmunjom Security Agreement is signed by Vice Admiral C. Turner Joy and then by Lieutenant General Nam Il.

EIGHTH ARMY: The enemy strikes at Hill 355 with a heavy concentration of artillery, followed up by infantry, but the units in defense are able to hold the line. Operation Pepperpot begins with a series of raids on enemy positions. The Royal Canadians hit Hills 166 and 156, reaching their objective.

SEA WAR: Four seamen on USS *Helena* (CA 75) are injured by gunfire from Hungnam; some damage is also caused by a strike on the main deck.

AIR WAR: On a day eventually to be called "Black Tuesday," a massive air battle occurs over Namsi. During a raid on Namsi Airfield, three B-29s from the 307th Bomber Wing are shot down and one F-84 and five other bombers are damaged. During the battle, UN pilots Ralph E. Banks, Farrie D. Fortner, and Richard D. Creighton each down a MiG-15, and B-29 gunners Fred R. Spivey and Jerry M. Webb each get one MiG.

October 24

POLITICAL/ADMINISTRATIVE: Final agreement is reached to begin a new phase of cease-fire discussions at Panmunjom. Major General Lee Hyung Keun (ROK) joins the UN armistice delegation as does Major General Paik Sun Yup (ROK). General Teng Hua (CPVA) and Major General Chang Pyon San (NKPA) leave the Communist delegation at the armistice talks.

AIR WAR: In the continuation of the bomber effort, eight B-29s, escorted by 16 RAAF Meteors, bomb bypass bridges at Sunchon. Ten F-84s are attacked. The massive air battle of Namsi is the largest of the war. Daylight raids against North Korean airfields at Taechon, Samichon, and Namsi cause the Chinese to send MiGs in response. An estimated 150 MiGs break through the 55 Thunderjets serving as escort and destroy four bombers over Namsi. By the end of the week, five B-29s will have been shot down and eight damaged. Alarmed over the sudden losses, Washington will temporarily suspend raids in the area and rush a second wing of Sabres to counteract the new threat.

October 25

POLITICAL/ADMINISTRATIVE: The cease-fire talks reopen at Panmunjom, a small village about six miles east of Kaesong. Talks resume on agenda item three. Winston Churchill replaces Clement Attlee as the British prime minister.

EIGHTH ARMY: The 2nd U.S. Infantry Division is replaced by the 7th Infantry Division.

AIR WAR: F-51 Mustangs flying close air support cause an estimated 200 casualties among enemy troops massed in the I Corps area. An H-5 helicopter is hit by small-arms fire while trying to rescue a downed UN pilot. The plane is forced to land in enemy territory. The following day, after the downed pilots have spent a night hiding, two other H-5s appear, hoist all four men from their predicament, and bring them to safety. An F-80 is shot down near Ryukusen and an F6F-5 near Anju.

Communists changing the guard at the armistice conference site at Panmunjom, Korea, October 27, 1951. Both sides maintained guards at the compound. *(Center for the Study of the Korean War, Graceland University)*

October 26

AIR WAR: Three Soviet pilots each report scoring a downed F-80 near Anju and one F-86 near Ryutoran. Two USAF pilots, Claude Mitson and Douglas Evans, each down a Communist MiG-15.

October 27

POLITICAL/ADMINISTRATIVE: Major General Howard M. Turner (USAF) joins the UN armistice negotiation team. General James Van Fleet sets up a plan to advance within the Iron Triangle and west beyond Kumsong, about 75 miles northeast of Seoul.

SEA WAR: USS *Toledo* (CL 133) fires 14 on-call support missions with the 1st Marine Division.

AIR WAR: In the continuing enemy air interdiction, MiGs fly an estimated 200 sorties over North Korea. Eight B-29s of the 19th Bomber

Group, 16 Meteors, and 32 F-84s are attacked by 95 MiGs. Because of this, it is decided to fly all future B-29 missions at night. B-29 gunners Leonard B. Eversol, Harry E. Ruch, Leeman Tankersley, Merle A. Goff (who gets two), and fighter pilots Harrison R. Thyng and Michael R. Martocchia each get a MiG-15. An H-5 from the 3rd ARS, with fighter escort, is able to rescue a downed UN fighter pilot despite determined fire from enemy ground forces. Two B-29s and two F-84s are shot down by enemy planes near Jyungsen, plus two F-86s and an F-84 near Anju.

October 28

POLITICAL/ADMINISTRATIVE: At the UN cease-fire negotiations, it is agreed that the cease-fire line will be the line of contact between the two armies. In order to meet the increasing need for manpower, the National Security Training Commission proposes six months compulsory military training for American youth reaching the age of 18.

EIGHTH ARMY: For actions taken near Chongdong, First Lieutenant Lloyd L. Burke is awarded the Medal of Honor.

AIR WAR: Five F-86s are shot down near Bihen according to Soviet records. Robert H. Moore of the 336th FIS shoots down a MiG-15.

October 29

SEA WAR: Communications are knocked out, the engine room is flooded, and one seaman is injured when USS *Osprey* (AMS 28) is hit by shore fire at Wonsan. The USS *Princeton* (CV 37) ends her second tour of duty in Korean waters. Admiral John Perry receives a request from Eighth Army to raid the headquarters of the Chinese Communist Party at Kapsan, North Korea. Intelligence provided by the Joint Advisory Commission, Korea (JACK) suggests that a meeting will take place there. The raid successfully destroys the compound.

October 30

EIGHTH ARMY: The attack on Hill 199 comes to an end.

SEA WAR: HMCS *Cayuga* (DD) is fired on more than 100 times from Amgak Island near Chinnampo. There is only one minor hit and no casualties. Responding to intelligence gathered by JACK guerrillas, U.S. Navy fighters attack a secret meeting of high-level Communist Party officials gathered at Kapsan, North Korea. The raid kills an estimated 144 party officials.

AIR WAR: The men who flew the mission against Communist personnel at Kapsan are labeled the "Butchers of Kapsan" by North Korean radio, and a price is put on the heads of those who participated in the strike. Lev K. Shchukin reports shooting down an RF-80A, and Sergei M. Kramarenko gets an F-84E.

October 31

EIGHTH ARMY: The marines feign an attack in order to lure North Korean troops into the open, then open fire with a heavy artillery barrage.

AIR WAR: After completing a successful service-test, the C-124A leaves Korea. The FEAF is convinced that the 315th Air Division needs a Globemaster squadron.

November 1

AIR WAR: Soviet records claim Boris S. Abakumov destroys an American F-84 on this date.

November 2

AIR WAR: N. V. Babonin shoots down a Meteor, and two additional F-84s are downed by other Soviet pilots. G. Jones and R. Pincoski combine to shoot down a MiG-15.

November 2–3

EIGHTH ARMY: The enemy attacks the entire center of the Canadian front held by Able and Charlie Companies of the Royal Canadian Regiment. The first assaults are repulsed but by early morning the Canadians are forced to withdraw.

November 3

EIGHTH ARMY: The NKPA 14th Regiment renews the fighting at Heartbreak Ridge when it launches an attack on the 160th Infantry Regiment and elements of the 40th Division. The North Korean attack is repulsed and the area remains in UN hands until the end of the war.

AIR WAR: While attempting to rescue a downed pilot, an SA-16 from the 3rd ARS is damaged by ground fire but is able to land in Korea Bay despite high seas. In the process of the flight, they rescue a second pilot. Two Meteors are shot down near Jyungsen, and five F-84s are destroyed near Anju. William F. Guss of the 336th FIS and Alfred W. Dymock of the 334th FIS each shoot down a MiG-15.

November 3–10

SEA WAR: One of the most difficult sweeps conducted during the war takes place at Chongjin on the northeast coast of North Korea, about 150 miles south of Vladivostok. The job is to clear mines from the 50th fathom curve in order to permit bombardment ships to operate at closer ranges.

November 4

EIGHTH ARMY: Elements of the 28th British Commonwealth Division take on a strong enemy force and eventually have to give up Hills 217 and 317 to Chinese forces. The enemy attacks the center of the Canadian front held by Able and Charlie Companies of the Royal Canadian Regiment. The first assault is repulsed. But, short of ammunition and greatly reduced by casualties, the Royal Canadians withdraw, and Hill 217 falls to the Chinese. The Commonwealth Division's 1st King's Own Scottish Borderers is manning Hill 355 and is under bombardment for three hours. Then, with horn and bugle, the enemy infantry storms through the wire. Attack after counterattack follow and last through the night. However, the Scottish Borderers held the position and holds Hill 355. The cost is seven killed, 87 wounded, and 44 missing. Four DSOs are awarded and one Victoria Cross.

SEA WAR: An accident onboard USS *Antietam* (CV 36) leads to the deaths of four seamen, and 10 injuries. Two of the carrier's aircraft are destroyed and six damaged.

AIR WAR: Thirty-four F-86s run into about 60 MiG-15s near Sinanju where two MiGs are destroyed and three damaged. According to Soviet records, Nikolai V.

Sutyagin, Vasili F. Shulev, and Dmitri A. Samoylov each shoot down an American F-86, and an unidentified pilot gets an F-80C. Three F-86s and two F-84s are shot down in the vicinity of Pyongyang.

November 4–6

EIGHTH ARMY: British troops are involved in the battle for Maryang-San.

November 5

EIGHTH ARMY: The defense of Hill 200 begins. The Royal Canadian Regiment, trying to hold on to an area near Hills 217 and 317, loses the second hill, 317, during the morning. The ROK 9th Division loses Hill 395 (White Horse Hill) northwest of Chorwon.

SEA WAR: Task Force 77 is assigned interdiction duties north of the immediate battlefront and east of longitude 126. All bombardment is restricted to an area at least five miles south of any part of Manchuria.

PARTISANS: The White Tiger unit is surrounded by an enemy force estimated at 1,000 men. The few operatives who survive disappear into the mountains.

November 6

EIGHTH ARMY: The ROK 9th Regiment attacks and retakes Hill 395 (White Horse Hill), which they had lost to the Chinese the day before.

AIR WAR: Eleven enemy bombers, observed to be piston-engine TU-2 light bombers, strike Taehwa-do, an island controlled by the United Nations. This is the first report of enemy air-to-ground action by a light bomber since the war began.

PARTISANS: Chinese amphibious units attack and capture the island of Tan-do and force the survivors to retreat to Tyan-do.

November 7

AIR WAR: A Meteor fighter is downed by enemy planes near Anju.

November 8

AIR WAR: More than 100 MiGs meet a smaller number of F-80s and F-86s but only a few of the planes decide to engage. One MiG is destroyed by William T. Whisner flying an F-86A and another damaged. One of the USAF F-86 planes is destroyed. Soviet reports claim that Ivan V. Suchkov and Konstantin Sheberstov each shoot down an F-84. F. M. Malshin, Boris V. Bokach, and Yevgeni G. Pepelyayev each shoot down an F-86, with Pepelyayev also getting an RF-80A.

PARTISANS: The Chinese take Tyan-do.

November 9

POLITICAL/ADMINISTRATIVE: National Security Council document 118 considers a change in U.S. policy in Korea if the cease-fire talks fail. It emphasizes the need for greater military pressure but does not recommend "hot pursuit" as a legitimate option unless the Chinese become a serious threat to U.S. forces in Korea. General Matthew Ridgway gets approval to reclassify some people, held as POWs, to civilian internees and to prepare for their release.

EIGHTH ARMY: The Chinese hit Hill 166, fighting with Charlie Company of the Royal 22nd Regiment. Two platoons reach their immediate objectives and another comes to within 100 meters of the top of the hill. By now the enemy is mounting a heavy counterattack. The 22nd holds the enemy back two times, but, on the third try, they are forced to withdraw.

AIR WAR: The 98th Bomber Wing's B-29s bomb Taechon Airfield in a night attack and fly five close-air support missions. Planes of the 19th Bomber Group attack marshaling yards at Kowon, Yangdok, and Hwang-ju. A C-47 manages to land on the beach of Paengnyong-do just off the southwest coast of North Korea, where it rescues 11 crewmen of a downed B-29. An unidentified Soviet pilot shoots down an F-80C. Three MiG-15s are shot down by USAF pilots William T. Whisner, William F. Osborne, and Joe J. Riley.

SEA WAR: A check sweep of the Mudo and Sin-do islands in Wonsan harbor is only 80 percent completed when naval craft are driven off by accurate fire from shore batteries.

November 10

EIGHTH ARMY: The defense of Hill 200 ends. In commemoration of the Marine Corps birthday, massive strikes are delivered against Hill 1052. The attack consists of 83 planes from the 1st Air Wing and USS *Los Angeles* (CA 135), as well as naval bombardment, mortar fire, and machine guns. In addition, 50,000 leaflets are dropped inviting the Chinese, who were in defense, to come to the birthday party that night. Twenty Chinese Communists surrender that night, but the cause is not clear.

AIR WAR: Two F-84s and an F-80C are shot down by unidentified Soviet pilots, according to Soviet reports.

November 11

EIGHTH ARMY: The 5th Marines relieves the 1st at Line Minnesota, occasioning the largest helicopter lifts to this date, nearly 2,000 men and their combat equipment.

SEA WAR: The USS *Gloucester* (PF 22) suffers one seaman killed and 11 wounded when a shore battery at Hungnam opens up and hits the ship.

PARTISANS: Combined Command Reconnaissance Activities, Korea (CCRAK), deploys its first Tactical Liaison Office team with the mission to dispatch and retrieve agents through frontline positions. The TLO also plans to conduct long-range missions into North Korea.

November 11–15

SEA WAR: The USS *Volador* (SS 490) conducts special ASW operations with USS *Hanson* (DD 832), USS *Mackenzie* (DD 836), and USS *Taussig* (DD 746) in the Atami area.

November 12

POLITICAL/ADMINISTRATIVE: General Matthew Ridgway, UN commander, orders General James Van Fleet, Eighth Army commander, to focus on defense and cease primary offensives. Rear Admiral H. E. Regan relieves Captain J. L. Kane as Commander Carrier Division 17, the Hunter Killer Group. General Ridgway sends orders affirming that there is to be no more aggressive ground action and that a defensive position will be assumed.

EIGHTH ARMY: At the same time, Operation Ratkiller begins, designed to wipe out a growing concern about guerrillas operating in South Korea. The operation will last until March 15, 1952.

SEA WAR: On the east coast, USS *Los Angeles* (CA 135) provides fire support to the 1st Marines and ROK troops. In the west, USS *New Jersey* (BB 62) fires at targets utilizing air spots from HMAS *Sydney* (CVL).

November 13

POLITICAL/ADMINISTRATIVE: The UN delegates at the armistice talks propose that they use the battle line as the proposed demilitarized zone, if all other issues before them can be settled within 30 days.

SEA WAR: In Operation Counter-Punch, USS *Toledo* (CA 133) directs its fire at batteries in the Kojo area where UN ships have been fired on and hit. Three direct hits are reported.

November 14

POLITICAL/ADMINISTRATIVE: In a message to Joseph Stalin, Mao Zedong (Mao Tse-tung) concludes that military operations can cease by the end of the year. "Achieving peace as a result of the negotiations is advantageous for us, but we are also not afraid of dragging out the negotiations."

EIGHTH ARMY: Intelligence reports suggest that there is a heavy buildup of artillery, automatic weapons, and troops in the Kojo area.

November 15

EIGHTH ARMY: PFC Mack A. Jordan (USA) is posthumously awarded the Medal of Honor for courageous action near Kumsong.

PARTISANS: The Chinese take the partisan-held island of Ae-do.

November 16

POLITICAL/ADMINISTRATIVE: The Communist negotiators accept the idea that the cease-fire line will be the existing battle line at the date of signing an armistice.

EIGHTH ARMY: The ROK 9th Regiment that is defending Hill 395 (White Horse Hill) loses it again to counterattacking Communists.

AIR WAR: Fighter/bombers from the Fifth Air Force make more than 100 attacks on railroad lines between Sinanju and Sukchon and between there and Kunu-ri. They also attack and damage supply buildings, fuel dumps, and enemy rail cars. A B-26 is shot down by enemy fighters near Andong.

November 17

POLITICAL/ADMINISTRATIVE: Delegates at the cease-fire meeting agree that the DMZ, once established, will be four kilometers in width.

EIGHTH ARMY: After having lost Hill 395 (White Horse Hill) the day before, the ROK 9th Regiment is able to retake it against the enemy defenders.

November 17–18

EIGHTH ARMY: The ROK 6th Division, with two tank companies of the 24th Infantry and the ROK 21st RCT, moves out about seven miles to set up a new defensive line. They move through resistance provided by elements of the Chinese 68th Army and are able to advance two miles. On November 18, they push forward, reach the new line, and dig in, after which they beat off a succession of Chinese counterattacks. British troops participate in the battle for Hill 227.

November 18

SEA WAR: The USS *Valley Forge* (CV 45) receives the Navy Unit Commendation for service from July 3, 1951, to this date.

AIR WAR: A flight of MiG-15s forces three flights of F-84 fighter/bombers to abort a mission near Sinanju. The UN planes are required to release their bombs short of the rail line they were seeking. Four F-86s hit eight MiG fighters on the ground at Uiju, destroying four and damaging four. Lev K. Shchukin shoots down two F-84s. Two others are downed by unidentified Soviet pilots. K. C. Cooley and J. M. Hewett, from the 111th Fighter-Bomber Squadron, combine to down a MiG-15.

November 20

SEA WAR: Special coordinated air and sea strikes are aimed against Hungnam by the Special Task Group (TG 95.8), including HMS *Belfast,* HMS *Tobruk,* HMNS *Van Galen,* and the carrier element HMS *Sydney,* USS *Hyman* (DD 732), HMCS *Sioux,* and HMS *Constance.* The raid consists of a total of 311 bombardments.

November 21

SEA WAR: USS *Los Angeles* (CA 135) and USS *Hammer* (DD 718) begin screening (putting fire between the bombline and the enemy) at bombline in response to an urgent request from Kirkland. The USS *Bisbee* (PF 46) is transferred to the Colombian government.

November 22

EIGHTH ARMY: First Lieutenant James L. Stone (USA) is awarded the Medal of Honor for actions near Sokkogae. Canadians complete the occupation of their assigned hill area. Americans on Hill 355 attack, but are unable to hold their ground. Hills 355 and 227 are claimed by the Chinese.

SEA WAR: LSMRs 401, 403, 404, and LSR Division 31 conduct a series of fire missions in the area of Wonsan.

November 23

POLITICAL/ADMINISTRATIVE: In armistice negotiations, a new demarcation line is proposed at the front, with a demilitarized zone that stretches out two kilometers on each side of the line.

EIGHTH ARMY: Private First Class Noah O. Knight (USA) is posthumously awarded the Medal of Honor for actions near Kowang-san. Late in the afternoon, following an artillery attack, the enemy begins to move against the Canadians of the Royal 22nd, with Hill 355 as the main focus of the assault. The permanent loss of Hill 355 would leave the Canadians in danger of being surrounded. During the night, the control of the hill passes from the Chinese to the Canadians.

SEA WAR: USS *Hyman* (DD 732) receives a hit on the main deck while turning at high speed to retire from the Kalma-Gak area. There is minor damage; other enemy batteries attempt to fire on the retreating ship but fail to connect.

AIR WAR: Lev K. Shchukin, according to Soviet sources, shoots down an F-86A.

November 24

SEA WAR: Naval gunfire supports a successful guerrilla raid on Ja-do where several enemy POWs are taken.

AIR WAR: Flying in a night operation, planes from the 98th Bomber Wing bomb Taechon Airfield and the marshaling yards at Tongchon. The unit is also involved in five close air ground support sorties. Planes from the 307th Bomber Wing bomb the marshaling yards at Munchon and Hambusong-ji. The Soviets report that two F-84s and two F-86s are shot down near Syukusen.

PARTISANS: The Chinese take Sohwa-do from the partisan defenders.

November 25

EIGHTH ARMY: In the ongoing battle for Hill 355, the Canadians hold their position while the American forces move in; the hill is left in American hands.

November 26

EIGHTH ARMY: All of the 7th Marine Regiment, minus the 2nd Battalion's Headquarters and Fox companies, collects at the road junction village of Yudam-ni where the dominant terrain feature is Hill 1167. The 1st Battalion, with Dog and Easy Companies attached, occupies Hills 1260 and 1167 north of the village.

SEA WAR: The USS *Tiru* (SS 417) ends its first tour of duty in Korean waters.

AIR WAR: An American F-86 is downed by enemy aircraft.

November 27

POLITICAL/ADMINISTRATIVE: An agreement is reached by delegates at Panmunjom on agenda item 2, the demarcation line and DMZ. The cease-fire will be coterminous with the battle line as opposed to the 38th parallel. The negotiators agree that this decision will be valid if a larger truce is reached within 30 days. Major General Laurence C. Craigie (USAF) leaves the UN armistice negotiation team. General James Van Fleet instructs his corps commanders that every UN soldier must be made aware that the war in Korea will continue until an armistice is signed.

EIGHTH ARMY: The UN summer-fall offensive campaign ends. The Canadians are instructed, as are most units, that they are not to send out any more fighting patrols and that artillery action is to be limited to defensive and counterbombardment fire. A planned attack by the Chinese against Hill 1167 is avoided when the enemy, apparently lost, ends up on Hill 1240.

SEA WAR: A flight from USS *Bon Homme Richard* (CV 31) is attacked by MiGs near Wonsan, leading to a general decision that ships will not operate without air cover.

AIR WAR: Flying with the 4th FIG, Major Richard D. Creighton shoots down a MiG. The victory makes him the fourth ace of the Korean War. George A. Davis also downs two MiG-15s on this day, and William R. Dawson gets one. Anatoly Ostapovsky downs an American F4U-4B, Alexei Kaliuzhny an AD-41, Vasili Ostapenko an F-80C, and Yevgeni G. Pepelayev an F-84E, according to Soviet records.

November 28

POLITICAL/ADMINISTRATIVE: Representatives from all the intelligence organizations operating in Korea meet to coordinate their activities. The conference results in the establishment of the Combined Command for Reconnaissance Activities in Korea. Captain Donald Nicholas represents Detachment 2 of the 6004th Air Intelligence Service Squadron.

EIGHTH ARMY: The second Korean winter campaign begins.

SEA WAR: Overnight, enemy troops in sampans attack the island of Hwangto-do in Wonsan harbor. Seven Korean marines and one civilian are killed; five civilians are captured. The raiding party escapes harm.

AIR WAR: Boris S. Abakumov downs an F-86 in aerial combat and Yevgeni G. Pepelayev destroys two F-86s. Seven additional F-86s are shot down by enemy planes near Teiju, according to claims of the Soviet command. Three MiG-15s are downed, one each by Winton W. Marshall and Dayton W. Ragland, and one by S. Groening and W. Marshall.

November 29

POLITICAL/ADMINISTRATIVE: President Harry Truman feels the need to speak out against the suggestion that Eighth Army has been halted in order to encourage the Chinese at the cease-fire talks. General Ridgway reports that 68 patrols have been sent out and 14 separate attacks against UN lines repulsed. Rear Admiral John Perry relieves Rear Admiral J. J. Clark as Commander Fast Carrier Task Force 77.

AIR WAR: An estimated 300 MiG-15s are sighted, and more than 260 of them are engaged in a series of air battles. Enemy records indicate that four F-86s and an F-84 are shot down. Vernon L. Wright shoots down a MiG-15.

November 30

EIGHTH ARMY: Communist forces begin a series of probing attacks against Hill 1182. The defenders hold on until about 0200, when they run out of grenades. The force, vastly outnumbered and out of ammunition, is ordered by the Chinese to surrender. Major McLaughlin uses the time he is given for consideration, to send out a series of men in hope they can reach a friendly line. A few of the men escape.

SEA WAR: Taehwa-do in the Yalu Gulf is invaded by Chinese Communist forces, causing a retreat; after support from the Fifth Air Force, the island is retaken.

AIR WAR: During one of the few pitched air battles of the war, 21 F-86s take on 44 enemy aircraft over the island of Taehwa-do. The pilots from the 4th FIG engage and destroy 12 and damage three of the enemy escorting 28 enemy bombers. Major George A. Davis, Jr., downs a Tu-2 and two MiG-15s to become the first ace in two wars. Major Winton W. Marshall also becomes an ace after destroying an La-0 and Tu-2 bomber. The other planes are downed by Robert W. Akin, Raymond Barton, John J. Burke, and Douglas Evans, each of whom gets a Tu-2, and Benjamin S. Preston and John W. Honaker who shoot down one La-11 each. Air Group 102 ends its tour of duty aboard USS *Boxer* (CV 21).

PARTISANS: Chinese forces attack Taehwa-do, landing in assault boats and junks. Despite the fight put up by Donkey 15, and the support provided by naval gunfire from HMS *Cossack,* they cannot be stopped.

December

AIR WAR: USAF Combat Cargo Command return to Cheju-do with Christmas items for the orphans they had transported the year before in Operation Little Orphan Annie.

December 1

POLITICAL/ADMINISTRATIVE: The ROK government declares martial law in southwestern Korea, restricting the movement of civilians, establishing a curfew, and cutting phone connnections between villages.

SEA WAR: Shore batteries hit HMS *Cockade* (DD) while they attack junks being used by forces trying to get away from Taehwa-do. One man is killed. This island, the last partisan base on the North Korean coast, falls with three British (two-man naval gunfire team and one Special Air Service [SAS]) captured.

AIR WAR: The 1st Marine Air Wing command post moves to P'ohang from Pusan. VP Squadron 22 under Commander W. Godwin begins its tour of land-based duty in Korea. Enemy records indicate that Meteor jets are shot down by Sergei F. Vishnyakov (two planes), Srafim P. Subbotin, Aleksandr F. Vasko, F. Zubakin, Pavel S. Milaushkin, A. Golovachyov, I. N. Gulyi, and an F-80C by Yevgeni G. Pepelayev, all in and around Jyungsen. Four additional F-84s are shot down near Anju. Robert E. Smith, flying an F-80C from the 36th Fighter-Bomber Squadron, shoots down a MiG-15.

PARTISANS: The Chinese take Taehwa-do, the last of the partisan bases along the southwestern North Korea coast. One U.S. officer flees and avoids capture.

December 2

EIGHTH ARMY: The 41st Independent British Royal Commandoes successfully raids facilities halfway between Songjin and Hungnam. Task Force Paik (Lieutenant General Paik Sun Yup) begins an antiguerrilla campaign called Operation Ratkiller. For 12 days, the operation tries to cut escape routes and draw a net that will enclose trapped guerrillas.

AIR WAR: Two F-86s and an F-84 are shot down by enemy planes near Anju. Five MiG-15s are shot down by USAF pilots Zane S. Amell, Nelton R. Wilson, James F. Martin, Michael J. Novak, and Paul E. Roach, each getting one.

December 2–14

EIGHTH ARMY: Operation Ratkiller begins. It is designed to locate and kill or capture guerrillas, many of whom are simply bandits, operating in South Korea. The problem became exaggerated after the victory at Inchon when there was a significant increase in guerrilla raids against supply lines. The ROK is in command of the exercise. During the first phase, until December 14, 1951, Paik Sun Yup (Task Force

Paik) establishes a perimeter around Chirisan, then flushes the area. The reported results are 1,612 dead and 1,842 captured.

December 3

POLITICAL/ADMINISTRATIVE: The Communist proposal for settling agenda item 3, the method of cease-fire inspection, is assigned to the sub-delegates for discussion. The U.S. 45th Division (National Guard) arrives in Korea.

SEA WAR: The USS *Horace A. Bass* (APD 124) transports and supports a unit of the 41st Royal Marine Commandoes in a raid on transportation facilities near Tanchon.

AIR WAR: In the first recorded Chinese air-ground attack of the war, enemy jets bomb and strafe UN ground forces near Chorwon, about 60 miles northeast of Seoul. Soviets claim two F-86s and an F-84 are shot down.

December 4

AIR WAR: Three F-86s are shot down by unidentified Soviet pilots.

December 5

AIR WAR: An estimated 300 MiG-15s are engaged or encountered by UN aircraft during the day. Reported as the largest single day total yet seen. Soviet claims include a downed F-84E, and an F-86 and an F-80 near Taisen. Four MiG-15s are shot down in aerial action by USAF pilots Winton W. Marshall, George A. Davis (credited with two). Pilots E. Neubert and G. Beck work together to get the fourth enemy fighter.

December 6

SEA WAR: The first elements of the 45th Infantry Division are shipped to Inchon from Hokkaido in an amphibious action.

AIR WAR: The Soviets claim that an F-86 and an F-84 are shot down near Taisen. Charles B. Christison, flying an F-86A from the 336th FIS, shoots down a MiG-15 fighter.

December 8

AIR WAR: Three F-86s are downed by enemy fighters.

December 9

POLITICAL/ADMINISTRATIVE: Major General Williston B. Palmer replaces Major General Clovis Byers as commander of X Corps.

SEA WAR: An anti-invasion patrol is established on the Korea's west coast.

December 10

POLITICAL/ADMINISTRATIVE: Far East Command activates a unit known as Covert, Clandestine, and Reconnaissance Activities–Korea, as the executive agency to control all military and CIA unconventional warfare activities behind enemy lines. Over bitter CIA objections, the FEC intelligence directorate appoints itself to run the new organization. Part of this shakeup includes the absorption of Army G3 Miscellaneous Group by Far East Command Liaison Detachment, Korea, 8240th Army Unit.

EIGHTH ARMY: PPCLI captures Hill 277 and RCRs take Hill 166.

December 11

POLITICAL/ADMINISTRATIVE: Debate begins at the Panmunjom concerning the exchange of prisoners of war. The American position, strongly supported by President Harry Truman, is changed from "voluntary repatriation" to "no forced repatriations." Rear Admiral Ruthven E. Libby (USN) leaves the UN armistice negotiation team and is replaced by Major General Henry I. Hodes (USA).

AIR WAR: Six F-86s are shot down by Soviet pilots, according to their reports, near Anju and Syukusen. USAF pilots Alfred C. Simmons, from the 336th FIS, and Donald Q. Griffith, from the 335th FIS, each shoot down a MiG-15 fighter.

December 12

AIR WAR: Air Task Group 1 begins its tour of duty onboard USS *Valley Forge* (CV 45).

December 13

POLITICAL/ADMINISTRATIVE: The USMC commandant announces a general policy of integration, but continues using blacks only as stewards.

SEA WAR: Air cover is increased for troop movements by sea, a joint operation for the U.S. Navy and FEAF that is focused at Inchon.

AIR WAR: In an air battle near Sinanju, 29 F-85s meet nearly 75 MiG-15s. In the battle that follows, F-86 pilots shoot down nine MiGs, giving the USAF a total of 14 aerial victories for the day. Of these victories, three are credited to George A. Davis, two to Theodore S. Coberly, and one each to Anthony Kulengosky, Alfred W. Dymock, Kenneth D. Chandler, John W. Honaker, John P. Green, Richard A. Pincoski, Benjamin S. Preston, and Claude Mitson. Soviet reports for the event indicate that seven F-86s are shot down.

December 14

EIGHTH ARMY: Operation Ratkiller ends with the death of more than 1,600 guerrillas and the taking of 1,842 prisoners.

AIR WAR: Nineteen B-29s of the 19th Bomber Group, flying at night, bomb the marshaling yards at Maengjung-dong. According to Soviet reports nine F-86s are destroyed in aerial combat near Sakusyu and Anju. Harrison R. Thyung of the 4th FIW shoots down a MiG-15.

December 15

AIR WAR: Two F-86s are shot down, according to enemy claims. Paul C. Mitchell from the 159th FIS shoots down a MiG-15.

December 16

SEA WAR: Enemy fire from the Amgak Peninsula on the west coast hits HMS *Constance* (DD), but there are no casualties.

AIR WAR: During the night, B-29s from the 19th Bomber Group cause severe damage as they raid the marshaling yards at Maengjung-dong.

December 17

POLITICAL/ADMINISTRATIVE: Major General Claude B. Ferenbaugh (USA) joins the UN armistice negotiation team. Major General Hodes (USA) is relieved.

SEA WAR: Overnight enemy troops overwhelm the islands of Ung-do and Changyang-do and all friendly resistance there ceases. USS *Bon Homme Richard* (CV 31) ends its first tour of duty in Korean waters.

December 18

POLITICAL/ADMINISTRATIVE: POW lists are exchanged between UN and Communist negotiators. The UN reports 132,000 prisoners. The Communist list contains 11,559 names.

EIGHTH ARMY: The USS *Consolation,* the American hospital ship, returns from the United States after refitting. It is the first hospital ship to receive casualties by helicopter directly from a battlefield.

AIR WAR: Three F-86s are shot down near Anju according to claims by an unidentified Soviet pilot.

December 19

EIGHTH ARMY: In Phase Two of Operation Ratkiller (until January 4, 1952), ROK units switch north to Cholla pukto Province with their focus on the mountains around Chongju. The ROK 8th and Capital Divisions move into the hills in order to trap bandits. The result is the death of about 4,000 guerrillas and the capture of about the same number. The 2nd Battalion, 5th Marines, is relieved by the 1st Battalion in Operation Farewell, the last flight for Lieutenant Colonel Herring.

December 19–20

SEA WAR: In Operation Farewell, marine helicopters relieve an infantry battalion on Hill 884 and return it to the reserve area.

December 20

POLITICAL/ADMINISTRATIVE: National Security Council document 118/2 adopts, as a minimum settlement, a position that will not jeopardize U.S.-Soviet relations, weaken Taiwan, or challenge the seating of the ROK in the United Nations. It suggests a willingness to recognize a boundary south of the 38th parallel and to support the withdrawal of U.S. troops, along with a buildup of the ROK army to the point that it can defend itself. If Soviet troops appear, the United States will withdraw from Korea and prepare to fight a general war.

SEA WAR: Anti-invasion stations are assumed in the vicinity of Cho-do and Sok-to on the Korean west coast. The primary ships involved are USS *Manchester* (CL 83), USS *Eversole* (DD 789), HMS *Tobruk,* and HMS *Alacrity.* The HMS *Tobruk,* while covering LST loadings at Cho-do and Sok-to, is hit by fire from a distant shore battery. No damage is sustained. The USS *Wisconsin* (BB 64) participates in a coordinated air and sea bombardment at Wonsan. The Hungnam Blockade and Bombardment Element, TE 95.24, is established to prevent enemy activity in the area.

December 21

EIGHTH ARMY: Task Force Paik (Lieutenant General Paik Sun Yup) conducts Operation Ratkiller in the southwest of Korea in an effort to eliminate guerrillas that are operating there.

AIR WAR: In the course of a 24-hour period, the Fifth Air Force conducts 530 sorties, cutting up more than 30 rail lines between Sinanju and Sukchon and attacking a supply depot near Kunu-ri.

December 22
SEA WAR: LST 611 (USS *Crook County*) is fired on by shore batteries from Amgak Peninsula, near Sok-to; while it is hit, there is no significant damage or casualty.
AIR WAR: Sightings confirm that the new Russian fighter, the MiG-21, is in Korea.

December 23
AIR WAR: Soviet records say that three American planes, an F-84 and two F-86s, are shot down by Communist planes.

December 24
POLITICAL/ADMINISTRATIVE: Major General Willard G. Wyman replaces Major General William F. Hodge as commander of IX Corps.
SEA WAR: The evacuation of 7,196 refugees from Cho-do, Paengnyong-do, and Taechong-do, all islands off the west coast, is completed by LSTs.
AIR WAR: The 98th Bomber Wing's B-29s hit the Taechon Airfield, as well as railroad bridges at, and near, Sinanju.

December 26
SEA WAR: Presumed to have hit a mine off To-do Island in Wonsan harbor, the ROK navy's *PC 740* sinks.

December 27
POLITICAL/ADMINISTRATIVE: The earlier agreement on the location of the demarcation line becomes invalid as the 30-day deadline passes.
AIR WAR: In a variety of missions, planes of the FEAF fly more than 900 sorties against gun positions, vehicles, locomotives, rail cars, barracks, and buildings. Three F-86s are claimed by enemy fighters. Clifford F. Brossart and Kenneth A. Shealy, both of the 25th FIS, down a MiG-15 fighter.

December 28
AIR WAR: Four UN planes are downed by enemy fighters according to Communist records. Paul E. Roach of the 25th FIS is responsible for the last MiG-15 shot down for the year.

December 29
POLITICAL/ADMINISTRATIVE: The army chief of staff orders all major commands to prepare integration programs.
SEA WAR: Patrolling south of Koto Islands, USS *Eversole* (DD 789) is strafed by an unidentified aircraft. No damage is reported.
AIR WAR: Four F-86s are shot down, according to Soviet records, with two near Hakusen and two at Anju.
PARTISANS: Sosuap-To Island, an enemy-held island off the west coast, is recaptured by friendly guerrillas.

December 31

EIGHTH ARMY: Hill 812 is the jumping-off point for a series of reconnaissance patrols and small raids designed to keep contact with the enemy.

AIR WAR: Three F-80s are downed in aerial combat, according to Soviet sources.

1952

January

At the beginning of 1952, the war in Korea is changing dramatically. Not only has the war of sweeping offensives and massive retreats come to a halt, but the resulting period seems to have more in common with the trench warfare of World War I. And it has lost its sense of momentum, a loss felt not only on the battlefield, where movement is counted in yards rather than in miles, but also in the war's ability to arouse passion or even interest. This includes the men and women on the line as well as the folks back home. The war continues but it is no longer a war of desperate losses or victory celebrations. The United States knows it will be able to hold its own against the Chinese Communists. It also knows that only a larger and more desperate war could defeat the Chinese. So, many Americans lose interest; for the man or woman in combat it is a war of days, days of "infinite boredom broken by moments of stark terror." This period will often be called a stalemate, and perhaps it is. But during 1952 there will be an estimated 140 attacks, from squad to company size, against the UN line each month. These are days when more than 130,000 rounds of fire will fall during a 24-hour period. It becomes a war of waiting, but even the waiting is deadly.

January 1

POLITICAL/ADMINISTRATIVE: The Communist delegates at the armistice talks agree in principle to the repatriation of all civilians who are being held as prisoners of war.

EIGHTH ARMY: At the beginning of the new year, the battle line is located along a front that runs from a point five miles southeast of Kosong on the east coast to a point 10 miles southeast of Kaesong on the west. Date given for the occupation of Seoul by advancing Chinese; goal failed.

SEA WAR: This date marks the 319th consecutive day of the siege and naval bombardment of the harbor at Wonsan.

AIR WAR: A massive UN air and artillery campaign commences against the Communist forces. It will last most of the month. Two bombs are dropped by an unidentified aircraft on the U.S. airfield at Kimpo, damaging 16 wingtips gas tanks and slightly damaging one F-86. Two bombs are also dropped on Inchon without damage. Two F-86s are downed by enemy fighter planes. Marine Helicopter Squadron (HMR) 161 is given a new assignment, one that will last to the end of the war. A helicopter is to be dispatched to the UN Command–Advanced, located at Munsan-ni, in order to transport UN delegates to the cease-fire talks. They fly a route between Munsan-ni and Panmunjom.

PARTISANS: The partisan unit Wolfpack is created out of the eastern part of Leopard's area of operations. Wolfpack Eight is located on the eastern half of the islands along Hwanghae Province's southern coast, from the Han River to Sunwi-do.

January 1–February 2
SEA WAR: Operation Moonlight Sonata, an effort designed to take advantage of the predawn moon for strikes against locomotives and trains, is conducted by Task Force 77. Five two-plane units fly reconnaissance flights that will be followed up later by bombing and strafing strikes.

January 2
POLITICAL/ADMINISTRATIVE: At the armistice talks, the United Nations proposes the voluntary repatriation of all POWs. The Communist delegates are unresponsive.

January 3
POLITICAL/ADMINISTRATIVE: The concept of voluntary repatriation is quickly rejected by the Communists. The establishment of a naval advisory group for the Republic of Korea is determined to be necessary, since the armistice talks are heading toward a position that would deny any augmentation of naval personnel in Korea.

January 4
EIGHTH ARMY: Phase II of Operation Ratkiller, the roundup of guerrillas, concludes with an estimated 4,000 killed and about 4,000 taken prisoner.

SEA WAR: The HMS *Belfast* (CL) anchors at the entrance to Songmo-Sudo, the first ship to reach this position in the Han River. Task Force Command instructs cruisers to be prepared to support I Corps from this position.

AIR WAR: The FEAF reports that it has identified between 100 and 150 YAK-9 fighters near the front lines. This is seen as an indication that the enemy is increasing its ability to launch night air attacks.

January 5
POLITICAL/ADMINISTRATIVE: Prime Minister Winston Churchill comes to the United States for talks with President Truman on conditions in both Europe and the Far East. The talks are to last two weeks.

SEA WAR: The USS *Swallow* (AMS 36) is fired on by enemy guns at the northern tip of the Amgak Peninsula. Fire from HRMS *Van Galen* and HMS *Alacrity* silences the guns. Seventh Fleet asks that an air and naval gunfire liaison company be provided on Kanghwa-do and Kyodong-do in the Han River entrance. The poor terrain makes direct fire from the ships very difficult.

PARTISANS: The ROK navy's *PC 704* reports that the southern half of Sonoita Island is still in friendly hands. An effort is made to evacuate all of the refugees.

January 6
SEA WAR: Blockade and Escort Force 95 is assigned responsibility for the defense of those east and west coast islands, north of the 38th parallel, that are held by UN and ROK forces. Amphibious Redeployment Group (TF 90.5), with four APAs, two LSDs, eight LSTs, and screening elements, begins the interchange of the 40th and 24th Infantry Divisions between Yokohama and Inchon. Through mistaken identity a small craft used for intelligence by X Corps is fired on and sunk by USS *Erben* (DD 631) off Kojo, Korea. The USS *Erben* grounds on an uncharted shoal and damages her screw.

AIR WAR: Two F-86s are shot down by enemy planes. Five MiG-15s are shot down, all by pilots of the 25th FIS: William T. Whisner, Van E. Chandler, John M. Heard, Donald E. Little, and Walker M. Mahurin.

January 7

EIGHTH ARMY: Hill 884 is once again the site of a historic transportation breakthrough, as the 1st Battalion, 1st Marines, is supplied by helicopters using a "flying crane" and cargo nets. One hundred and fifty thousand pounds are moved.

SEA WAR: The New Zealand destroyer *Rotoiti* begins its tour of duty in Korean waters. It will remain on station until March 19, 1953.

AIR WAR: Four F-86s are shot down near Sensen. Two MiG-15s are shot down, one each by Ralph H. Ashby and John M. Heard of the 25th FIS.

January 8

POLITICAL/ADMINISTRATIVE: Communist negotiators officially reject the UN proposal for the voluntary repatriation of all POWs. This topic will be the main stumbling block in negotiations for the next 18 months.

SEA WAR: The decision is made by Blockading and Escort Force to sweep the east coast of Korea, from Kansong to Songjin (Kimchaek), every two weeks. Captain R. L. Johnson on USS *Badoeng Strait* (CVE 116) assumes command of Tactical Control West Coast Korea.

AIR WAR: According to Soviet reports, two F-86s are shot down by Communist planes.

PARTISANS: The partisan defense area at Sunwi-do is reported to have fallen and to be in enemy hands.

January 9

SEA WAR: The West Coast Island Defense Element, TE 95.1.1, is established. U.S. Navy and Marine Corps personnel will provide a provisional landing force capable of defending any of the islands that might be threatened by the enemy. Seventh Fleet cruisers and the USS *Wisconsin* (BB 64) are made available for this effort.

January 10

POLITICAL/ADMINISTRATIVE: The UN delegates at Panmunjom reject any armistice considerations when the North Koreans refuse to ban the building of new air bases after the cease-fire is signed.

SEA WAR: The HMCS *Cayuga* (PF) and the ROK navy's *PC 702* come under fire while covering the guerrilla evacuation of Changjin. The *Cayuga* destroys three junks during the encounter. As a result of the USS *Erben* (DD 631) incident of January 6. Carrier Task Force 95 is given responsibility for the clearance of all friendly small craft operating in the area.

PARTISANS: Changjin is reported to be in enemy hands. The commander of Donkey 4, Chang Sok Lin, is assassinated by his own men who accuse him of being corrupt. He is replaced by Pak Choll.

January 11

POLITICAL/ADMINISTRATIVE: Major General Gerald C. Thomas is replaced by Major General John T. Selden as commander of the First Marine Division.

SEA WAR: Acting without cover from a support ship, USS *Redstart* (AM 378) and USS *Dextrous* (AM 341) are hit by shore fire while conducting a sweep near Hodo Pando. One crew member is killed and two are wounded aboard the *Dextrous* after it receives two hits. The USS *Gregory* (DD 802) and USS *Mackenzie* (DD 836) fight a duel at Wonsan harbor with shore batteries. No ships are struck, but three enemy locations receive hits. The HMTS *Prasae* (PF) and HMTS *Tachin* (PF) depart Sasebo with USS *Bisbee* (PF) on their first mission since being purchased by the Thailand navy. Carrier Task Force 77 outlines basic interdiction orders that are identified as Operation Package and Operation Derail. Operation Package provides for five key rail targets to be cut by air and naval bombardment. Operation Derail identifies 11 key rail targets that are to be destroyed by naval fire.

AIR WAR: Soviet reports claim six F-86s are shot down by enemy planes near Anju. Nelton R. Wilson of the 334th FIS shoots down a MiG-15. Two pilots from the 25th FIS, Thiel M. Reeves and William T. Whisner, each shoot down a MiG-15 fighter. Francis S. Gabreski of the 51st FIW and Earl S. Payne of the 16th FIS each shoot down a MiG-15 fighter.

January 12

EIGHTH ARMY: Corporal Ronald R. Rosser, Heavy Mortar Company, 38th Infantry Regiment, 2nd Infantry Division, is awarded the Medal of Honor for courage against the enemy.

AIR WAR: A flight of F-84s catches three supply trains as they rush for the tunnels near Sunchon to avoid being hit. The flight hits the tunnel mouth thereby trapping the trains in the open. After halting the trains, the F-84s destroy the boxcars and at least two engines. During the night, 10 Superfortresses based on Okinawa drop 396 500-pound bombs on the railroad bridge across the Chongchon River, east of Sinanju, and destroy the bridge. Four T-86s are downed by enemy fighters. George L. Jones of the 51st FIW, in an F-86E, downs an enemy MiG-15 fighter.

January 13

SEA WAR: The USS *Collett* (DD 730), USS *Rochester* (CA 124), and planes from USS *Badoeng Strait* (CVE 116) join together in a coordinated air-naval gunfire strike against gun batteries on Amgak Peninsula. Operation Junket is organized in an effort to encourage ships in their various operating areas to capture small enemy craft for intelligence purposes.

January 14

SEA WAR: Both USS *Mackenzie* (DD 836) and USS *Marshall* (DD 676) are taken under fire from shore batteries, but neither is hit. It is reported that Ohwa-do is now in enemy hands. Intelligence reports that an enemy battalion is planning an invasion of Walle-do and Yuk-do.

January 15

AIR WAR: VP Squadron 6 under Commander G. Howard ends its second tour of land-based service in Korea. An F-84 is shot down by enemy fighters near Syukusen. George L. Jones of the 51st FIS Headquarters, shoots down an enemy MiG-15.

January 16

SEA WAR: The city of Wonsan begins its 12th month of constant naval gunfire from Task Element 95.212 and Task Force 77.

AIR WAR: According to Soviet reports, four F-86s are shot down near Syukusen.

January 17

SEA WAR: Task Force 95 is given the responsibility for the control and clearance of small friendly craft operating in the area of Wonsan and Songjin. This assignment includes those ships on covert activity.

AIR WAR: James B. Raebel of the 25th FIS, and Frank P. Robinson and William F. Sheaffer of the 16th FIS, each down an enemy MiG-15.

January 18

SEA WAR: The USS *Halsey Powell* (DD 686), in an operation called "Chicken Stealer," sends her small boat into the waterfront area of Sam-He to direct her guns. Using this method, the *Halsey Powell* manages to damage several jetties and boats in the area. A change is made in the rail cutting effort, redirecting the attacks from widely scattered cuts to raids that focus on stretches of line from 1,500 to 4,000 yards in length. The hope is that this will lengthen the time necessary to repair the lines.

January 19

POLITICAL/ADMINISTRATIVE: The delegates at the cease-fire meetings agree to hold a conference to discuss political issues, within 90 days after the signing of an armistice.

SEA WAR: The USS *Repose* (AH 16), a navy hospital ship, departs Korean waters after a prolonged tour of duty.

AIR WAR: An F-86 is shot down after aerial combat. Iven C. Kincheloe of the 25th FIS, flying an F-86E, downs an enemy MiG-15.

January 20

POLITICAL/ADMINISTRATIVE: Rear Admiral E. E. Stone, on USS *Saint Paul* (CA 73), becomes Commander Cruiser Division One.

EIGHTH ARMY: The 40th Infantry Division (California National Guard) arrives in Korea.

SEA WAR: The USS *Halsey Powell* (DD 686) is fired on during a counter-battery engagement against guns located near Hungnam. A single gun is silenced.

AIR WAR: Lloyd D. Juhlin and Donald E. Adams, both of the 16th FIS, shoot down an enemy MiG fighter.

January 21

POLITICAL/ADMINISTRATIVE: The marines activate a Korean Island Command section, made up of east and west coast sections.

Sea War: Commander Seventh Fleet is advised that a Soviet submarine is operating in the Chongjin area of far northeastern Korea, probably on reconnaissance, but possibly also on a mine-laying mission. The Dutch destroyer *Van Galen* completes her first tour of duty in Korea.

January 22

Partisans: Mustang III is launched with 19 operators, all Korean. The mission has two purposes: sabotage and making contact with non-Korean POW camps to establish means of escape. The jump is successful but radio contact with the group is lost within a few days. The unit is assumed to have been compromised.

January 23

Sea War: Four LSTs from Task Force 90 complete the evacuation of refugees from Korean west coast islands. The USS *Philippine Sea* (CV 47) reports for duty with Seventh Fleet.

Air War: Donald E. Adams and William C. Knoy, both of the 16th FIS, 51st Wing, down a MiG-15.

January 24

Political/Administrative: General Ridgway reports to Washington that the truce talks have reached a complete state of paralysis. President Truman's anger is so great that he writes in his diary that this means an all-out war, the bombing of every major city, the destruction of every factory in China and the Soviet Union.

Eighth Army: The U.S. 24th Infantry Division begins the use of scout dogs but finds that they are not as efficient as expected.

Sea War: Operation Helicopter is completed. It has tested the possibility of evacuating patients directly from the front line to the hospital ship USS *Consolation* (AH 15) at the port of Sokcho-ri on the Sea of Japan just above the 38th parallel. At the time the *Consolation* is the only ship equipped with a helicopter platform.

Air War: Captains Harold E. Fischer, Jr., and Dolphin D. Overton III of the 51st Fighter Interceptor Wing, become aces with five kills each.

January 25

Sea War: The USS *Wantuck* (APD 125) lands ROK troops for a night demolition raid on enemy rail lines, tunnels, and bridges on the east coast.

Air War: A helicopter rescues a pilot downed in the Yellow Sea, while above F-84s strafe enemy troops in the area. Three MiG-15s are destroyed during the pickup from behind enemy lines. Also during the day, UN jets destroy six and damage four Communist planes. Of the nine, Robert H. Moore, Mose W. Gordon, and William F. Shaeffer of the 16th FIS, Anthony Kulengosky, Frank J. Gately, William C. Shoefner, and William M. Guinther of the 25th FIS, and Robert T. Latshaw and Conrad P. Nystrum of the 335th FIS, each get a plane.

January 26

Sea War: The USS *Fletcher* (DDE 445) and the tug USS *Apache* (ATF 67) are fired on by guns at the Cho-do anchorage. Return fire by HMS *Belfast,* which assists in the

Navy rescue helicopter, sometimes called a Jolly Green Giant, hovers in anticipation while planes land on an aircraft carrier. *(Center for the Study of the Korean War, Graceland University)*

bombardment, provides several direct hits on batteries. At Wonsan harbor, HMS *Constance* (DD) receives gun fire that is returned by HMS *Belfast* and HMS *Constance*. **AIR WAR:** A rescue helicopter rescues Captain A. T. Thawley, flying an F-84, from the coast line of the Yellow Sea, despite small-arms fire.

January 27
POLITICAL/ADMINISTRATIVE: Cease-fire delegates agree to defer discussion concerning the rebuilding of airfields until a later time.
SEA WAR: The HMAS *Sydney* (CVL) and HMAS *Tobruk* (D37) complete their tours of duty with the Seventh Fleet. USS *Bataan* (CVL 29) begins its second tour of duty with Task Force 77.
AIR WAR: Carrier Task Force 77 reports a record of 165 rail cuts made in a single day by its planes.

January 28
PARTISANS: The partisans report a build-up of Communist troops trying to clear the North Korean–held islands of covert activities.

January 29
SEA WAR: Two navy Corsairs and one pilot, from USS *Antietam* (CV 36), are lost to enemy action and an accident. HMS *Belfast* (CL) bombards a possible invasion

buildup west of Sok-to. Using air spotters to direct fire and report damage, the bombardment destroys or damages numerous buildings. The helicopter rescue ship *LST 799* rescues Lieutenant S. B. Murphy (USN), who crashed in Wonsan harbor.

Air War: Marine Fighter Squadron 312 moves to Itami, Japan. An F-86 is downed by enemy fighters near Hakusen.

January 30

Eighth Army: In Operation Highboy, self-propelled 155-mm howitzers attack bunkers and fortifications. The success of the operation is limited.

Sea War: HMCS *Sioux* (DDE) and USS *Apache* (ATF 67) are fired upon in the approaches to Cho-do, but there is no damage reported. Combined air and naval gun-strikes are conducted at Wonsan harbor by Task Element 77.16, accompanied by the battleship USS *Wisconsin* (BB 64).

Air War: Air Group Eleven, commanded by Commander J. W. Onstott, begins its tour of duty onboard USS *Philippine Sea* (CV 47). Freeland K. Mathews of the 336th FIS shoots down a MiG-15 fighter.

Partisans: "Big Boy" informs Kirkland Forward on Nan-do Island that it has rescued a downed U.S. Navy pilot.

January 31

Political/Administrative: Breaking a long silence, President Harry Truman denounces Senator Joseph McCarthy (R–Wisconsin) as pathological, untruthful, and a character assassin.

Sea War: The USS *Greenfish* (SS 351) arrives to begin its tour of duty in Korean waters.

February 1

Political/Administrative: Rear Admiral F. W. McMahon assumes command of Fast Carrier Task Force 77.

Sea War: The USS *Valley Forge* (CV 45) replaces USS *Essex* (CV 9) in Fast Carrier Task Force 77. Air plans are altered for Task Force 77 so that two large propeller-plane strikes are made daily, seeking better AA protection. Concern is expressed over recent infractions by U.S. aircraft of neutral areas around Panmunjom. Positive action is to be taken to avoid these infractions, which provide the Communists with significant material for propaganda. Rear Admiral John Perry relinquishes command of Task Force 77 as Rear Admiral F. W. McMahon, in USS *Valley Forge* (CV 45), assumes command.

February 2

Political/Administrative: Russian delegate to the UN, Jacob Malik, accuses the United States of using toxic gas-filled bullets.

Sea War: Task Element 95.12 reports that the enemy has evacuated Sunwi-do and Yoncho-do, leaving behind a large number of refugees. The USS *Philippine Sea* (CV 47) begins its second tour of duty in Korean waters.

February 3

Sea War: The USS *Manchester* (CL 83) and USS *Higbee* (DD 806) fire an on-call mission on enemy battalion supply dumps near Hojo. Considerable damage is done to the supply dump; an estimated 550 enemy troops are killed. The USS *Porterfield* (DD 62) is fired on and is hit by a shell from Cho-do Island. The ship suffers extensive structural damage but no casualties.

AIR WAR: A high attrition rate for spotting planes requires Fifth Air Force to discontinue daylight naval gunfire spotting missions for 10 days. Lieutenant Robert J. Geffel, of VF-653, is rescued by the helicopter rescue ship *LST 799*. An F-86 is shot down near Hakusen by enemy fighters.

February 4

SEA WAR: The USS *Philippine Sea* (CV 47) joins the Fast Carrier Task Force. The USS *Endicott* (DMS 35) is fired on near Kojo. She receives two hits that cause limited damage but no casualties.

PARTISANS: The HMS *Ceylon* (CL) and HMS *Cockade* (DD) cover a landing party of guerrillas on Mudo Island. These friendly forces use the LSTs *516* and *692* and land without opposition.

February 5

SEA WAR: HMS *Charity*, *LSMR 401*, and the ROK navy's *AMC 303* support the rescue of guerrillas from Yuk-to, Gyeonggi province.

PARTISANS: Failed attempts to rescue a navy helicopter, which has landed with the partisan unit Kirkland, cost the capture of two Americans.

February 6

POLITICAL/ADMINISTRATIVE: Two new delegates, Lieutenant General William K. Harrison, Jr., and Major General Yu Jai Hyung (ROK), are appointed as plenary members to the armistice talks. Major General Lee Hyung Keun (ROK) and Major General Claude B. Ferenbaugh (USA) are relieved.

February 7

SEA WAR: While USS *Osprey* (AMS 28) and HMS *Alacrity* (PF) are firing on shore batteries in the Songjin area, the *Alacrity* is hit five time. There are no casualties. The Naval Advisory Group to the ROK navy is established; four motor torpedo boats are turned over to the ROK navy at Pusan.

PARTISANS: The islands of Yuk-do, Mudo, Changnung-do, Ohwa-do, Sunwi-do, Yong-do, and Wi-do are evacuated by the enemy and are being occupied by friendly guerrilla forces.

February 8

EIGHTH ARMY: The enemy withdraws from the islands of Changjin, Sunwi-do, and Yongwi-do, off the west coast of Korea, because of rocket attacks launched by ROK marines.

SEA WAR: Task Force 77 suffers some high losses as helicopters from USS *Manchester* (CL 83) and USS *Rochester* (CA 124) are lost in an effort to reach a downed pilot. An AD and one F4U from USS *Valley Forge* (CV 45) are also lost. A second attempt to reach a downed pilot is executed by a helicopter from USS *Manchester* (CL 83). Lieutenant E. C. Moor and his crewman Lieutenant T. K. W. Henry crash-land. They are unable to take off because of damage to a blade that occurred during landing.

An air force helicopter based on Yo-do fails to rescue the mission because of heavy ground fire. The *Manchester* arrives in an area about 10 miles east of Wonsan to wait for the helicopter and downed pilot. Marine Fighter Squadron 212 moves from USS *Badoeng Strait* (CVE 116) to Japan. USS *Boxer* (CV 21) begins its third tour of duty with Task Force 77.

PARTISANS: Mahap-do is attacked and occupied by enemy forces. Sixty of the defending guerrillas are evacuated by HMAS *Warramunga*.

February 9

POLITICAL/ADMINISTRATIVE: The Naval Advisory Group to the ROK navy is established.

SEA WAR: The rescue attempt to reach a downed helicopter crew is terminated. Reports suggest the crew is in enemy hands. Heavy flak is received during the morning reconnaissance flight over the area. Task Force 77 planes destroy the downed helicopter.

AIR WAR: Using the radar aiming method, 10 medium bombers drop 100 tons of bombs and make the Chongju railway bridge impassable.

February 10

AIR WAR: Major George A. Davis, Jr., leading a flight of three F-86s, engages 12 MiG-15s in combat. Davis shoots down three of the enemy and disrupts their formation, but his aircraft is destroyed. His protection of the fighter-bombers he was escorting, as well as his daring actions, lead to his being awarded the Medal of Honor. An F-86 is shot down by enemy fighters near Taisen.

February 10–15

EIGHTH ARMY: Eighth Army puts into effect Operation Clam-Up, a plan designed to feign a withdrawal in the hope of luring the enemy into sending out a reconnaissance that, in turn, will result in more casualties and prisoners. In the operation, no patrols are sent out, there are no artillery missions, and no air flights are allowed to within 20,000 yards of the front lines. The 1st Marines are involved in an elaborate series of deceptions, firing massive amounts of artillery—and then, silence. Enemy patrols make probes on February 11–12, then hit the marines with a heavy bombardment on February 13. When the operation ends, there is little evidence of success. Most likely it has allowed the enemy a period for the replacement of troops and ammunition. In an incident at Sirwon-Myon, soldiers of the ROK 3rd Battalion of the 11th Division kill 719 civilians.

SEA WAR: Amphibious Task Group 90.5 completes the interchange of the 40th and 24th Infantry Divisions between Japan and Korea.

February 11

EIGHTH ARMY: Lieutenant General Maxwell Taylor replaces Lieutenant General James Van Fleet as Eighth Army commander. General Van Fleet, who is disappointed that he does not move up to command the Far East, retires from the service. General Taylor takes command with instructions from Secretary of Defense George Marshall that he should avoid casualties. He can do this by avoiding combat whenever possible. General Taylor is not happy with the restrictions, but in many of the Allied capitals, joy is expressed over the fact that the Americans seem to be taking the cease-fire seriously. Captain Margaret G. Blake, the first army nurse to earn the Bronze Star, returns to Korea for her second tour of duty.

SEA WAR: Marine Air Squadron 115's Command Post arrives at Yokosuka from the United States. Squadron 312 is moved from Itami, Japan, to USS *Bairoko* (CVE 115). Squadron 212 moves from Itami to Pusan. LST *742* loads 600 refugees and heads for Sunwi-do to load an additional 1,800.

AIR WAR: An F-86 is shot down near Deeguandong. J. E. Arnold and R. E. Stinbis, of the 16th FIS, share credit for a kill on a MiG-16.

February 12
SEA WAR: The USS *Bisbee* (PF 46) is turned over to the Colombian government and commissioned in its navy as ARC *Capital Too.* New mines begin to appear in Wonsan harbor.

February 13
POLITICAL/ADMINISTRATIVE: Rear Admiral Scott-Moncrieff (RN) assumes command of Tactical Command West Coast of Korea.

SEA WAR: The HMCS *Sioux* (DD) completes her tour of duty. The USS *Gloucester* (PF 22) arrives at Sosa Wan.

February 14
SEA WAR: There are no reported casualties when a piston-engine enemy aircraft drops two bombs on Cho-do Island.

February 15
EIGHTH ARMY: Operation Clam-Up, designed to lure enemy soldiers into showing themselves, is discontinued after it fails to achieve any significant results or its intended goals.

SEA WAR: The HMAS *Bataan* (DD) is hit, but with no casualties, near Sok-to and Cho-do. Escort Squadron Five is disestablished and the ships transferred to Escort Squadron Seven.

February 16–22
AIR WAR: MiG-15 pilots conduct an unusual number of interdiction and close air support sorties, nearly 1,400 during this week.

February 16
POLITICAL/ADMINISTRATIVE: Communist delegates to the cease-fire talks suggest that the Soviet Union be named as a member of the neutral commission in charge of supervising the cease-fire. Captain C. T. Fitzgerald relieves Captain L. T. Morse as liaison officer to Commander Seventh Fleet.

SEA WAR: The USS *Rowan* (DD 782), USS *Gregory* (DD 802), and USS *Twining* (DD 547) celebrate the first anniversary of the siege of Wonsan with an especially heavy bombardment.

AIR WAR: Soviet sources report an F-86 is shot down by enemy fighters near Hakusen.

February 17

POLITICAL/ADMINISTRATIVE: Agreement is reached at the peace talks on calling for a political conference to be held within three months after the truce is signed, to discuss the future (the potential unification) of Korea.

SEA WAR: Rounds fired at USS *Apache* (AFT 67) fail to connect. *LSMR 403,* HMAS *Bataan,* HMCS *Athabaskan* (DDE), HMS *Cardigan Bay* (PF), HMCS *Nootka* (DDE), and HMS *Ceylon* fire flak-suppression for Task Element 95.11 air strikes. Minesweeper *Murrelet* (AM 372) is in a duel with an armed sampan and nearly loses its whale boat before moving out.

AIR WAR: Fifth Air Force flies attack missions against railroads at more than 50 locations while flying more than 695 sorties. The planes destroy rail tracks, damage a locomotive and 15 rail cars at Huichon, strafe a convoy of trucks near Sinanju, and destroy supply buildings and dumps between Kumsong and Sibyon-ni. An F-86 is shot down by enemy fighters near Anju according to Soviet reports. During the day, four MiG-15 fighters are shot down by USAF pilots, Zane S. Amell and Russell H. Miller of the 335th FIS, and William M. Guinther and Walker M. Mahurin of the 25th FIS.

February 18

POLITICAL/ADMINISTRATIVE: The Soviet Union expands its charge that the United States is using biological weapons in Korea.

EIGHTH ARMY: The 1st Marine Regiment is relieved by the 5th Marine Regiment. The 1st moves into reserve near Inje. On Koje-do, Communist prisoners of war begin to riot.

AIR WAR: Enemy reports indicate that an F-86 fighter has been shot down by Chinese fighters near Sensen.

PARTISANS: The islands of Wi-do, Pa-do, Dunmad-do, and Yongho-do fall to enemy assault.

February 19

POLITICAL/ADMINISTRATIVE: It is reported that three or four ROK agents and guerrillas are surrendering each day in response to North Korea's promise to grant amnesty and full pardon to those who have committed political, military, or economic crimes. At the cease-fire talks, additional agreement is reached about dealing with the political concessions of the Korean War within three months after an armistice is signed.

AIR WAR: The Communist launch a record-high 389 MiG-15 sorties. The USAF records three victories over MiG-15 fighters. Credit is given to John C. Friend from the 16th FIS for one kill, to P. R. Henderson and A. W. Schinz of the 51st FIW who share credit for a kill.

PARTISANS: An Aviary mission is compromised and two men killed (also presumed capture of several partisans) when an agent tosses a live grenade into the C-46 as he jumps from the plane. The Chinese attack the island of Yang-do, a UN listening post in their territory, with a force of 300 men who are carried to the island in sampans. They are met by a much smaller group of Korean marines and so badly mauled that the Communists retreat, heading back to the mainland.

February 20

POLITICAL/ADMINISTRATIVE: Rear Admiral John Perry assumes command of Fast Carrier Task Force 77.

SEA WAR: The USS *Shelton* and HMNZS *Taupo* (PF), as well as USS *Endicott* (DMS 35), engage sampans trying to land troops at Yang-do. An estimated 15 sampans are sunk, causing a large loss of life among the invading force. The island resists the attack and reports that 79 enemy are killed. The island force loses eight men killed, 20 wounded, and three missing. Rear Admiral John Perry assumes command of Task Force 77. Rear Admiral F. W. McMahon aboard USS *Valley Forge* (CV-45) relinquishes command of Task Force 77.

AIR WAR: W. Whisner and F. Gabreski of the 51st FIW share credit for downing a MiG-15 fighter, and Van E. Chandler of the 25th FIS and William F. Sheaffer of the 16th FIS each get one.

February 21

POLITICAL/ADMINISTRATIVE: Brigadier Lee Il, second in command of the North Korean 24th Mechanized Artillery Division, surrenders to USMC personnel on Taedo. He brings with him a considerable number of significant papers dealing with NKPA defense plans. The commander of Naval Forces Far East recommends the use of navy women (WAVES) in several areas of the Far East.

SEA WAR: COMNAVFE acts on the recommendations of CincPacFleet to use WAVES in several areas of the Far East. The USS *Symbol* (AM 123) and USS *Murrelet* (AM 372) are fired on while doing a routine sweep. Counter-battery fire is returned by both ships.

February 22

POLITICAL/ADMINISTRATIVE: Foreign Minister Pak Hen of the DPRK charges the United States with germ warfare. The Chinese, with the Soviet Union conveying the charges to the United Nations, restate their charge that the United States is conducting germ warfare.

SEA WAR: The USS *Shelton* (DD 790) is fired on by shore batteries near Yang-do Island, and 12 seamen are wounded. The USS *Kyes* (DD 787) is hit by shore battery fire in the vicinity of Yang-do Island. There is little damage. The USS *Rowan* (DD 782) is hit by one round during a duel in which approximately 100 rounds are fired from shore. The hit on the *Rowan* does moderate damage, but no personnel are hurt.

February 23

POLITICAL/ADMINISTRATIVE: The North Korean negotiators at Panmunjom agree on the figure of 35,000 men for rotation.

SEA WAR: The USS *Henderson* (DD 785) is hit by shore batteries at Hungnam, causing minor structural damage. There are no casualties. The USS *Endicott* (DMS 35) engages in counter-battery fire with a gun position on the mainland opposite Yang-do.

AIR WAR: Major William T. Whisner, Jr., of the 25th FIS becomes an ace by shooting down a MiG-15, his fifth score.

February 23–March 5

SEA WAR: Task Force 77 launches a campaign to destroy the small boats being used by North Koreans to attack the smaller islands. During this period, 303 boats are destroyed and 537 damaged.

February 23–March 19

SEA WAR: Tour of the USS *Stickell* (DD 888).

February 24

EIGHTH ARMY: The U.S. 40th Infantry Division launches the largest tank raid (without infantry) of the war.

SEA WAR: Enemy antiaircraft batteries opposite Cho-do become increasingly active. FEAF calls on Carrier Task Group 95.1 to provide two aircraft daily in the area, running them as late into the night as it can.

February 25

POLITICAL/ADMINISTRATIVE: The Chinese denounce the American use of germ warfare, reporting the charge to the World Peace Organization in Oslo. President Syngman Rhee visits Seventh Fleet headquarters at Pusan.

SEA WAR: The HMCS *Cayuga* (DD 218) fires on enemy junks that are believed to be heading to Mudo Island (near Inchon) as an invasion force.

AIR WAR: Marine Fighter Squadron 115 Command Post moves from Yokosuka, Japan, to Pusan and is assigned to Marine Air Group 33. Marine Photo Squadron One is commissioned.

February 26

POLITICAL/ADMINISTRATIVE: The United States denies the use of biological weapons and blames the Communists for refusing an impartial investigation. Colonel Cecil H. Childre replaces General Henebry as commander of the 315th AD (Combat Cargo).

AIR WAR: Using radar aiming methods, 10 Superfortresses drop 100 tons of bombs on the Sinhung-dong Bridge near Huichon. The attack destroys two spans of the bridge.

February 27

SEA WAR: Northeast of Hungnam, USS *Henderson* (DD 785) and USS *Ptarmigan* (AM 576) are fired on by batteries on Mayang-do as they conduct minesweeping operations. The USS *Ptarmigan* (AM 576) is forced to cut her sweeping and retreat from the area.

AIR WAR: A total of 404 enemy MiG-15s are observed over northwestern Korea by 86 UN F-86 fighters. This is a high for such daily sightings. Felix Asla, Jr., of the 334th FIS brings down a MiG-15.

Tanks from a Marine company follow a streambed, Korea 1952. *(Center for the Study of the Korean War, Graceland University)*

February 28

AIR WAR: Van E. Chandler of the 25th FIS is credited with destroying an enemy MiG-15.

February 29

SEA WAR: The ROK navy's JMS 301 is hit by a shell near Sunwi-do; one seaman is killed.

March 1

SEA WAR: Patrol Squadrons VP-22 and VP-47 of Fleet Air Wing 1 investigate a 32-ship Russian convoy in the China Sea near Formosa. The USS *Endicott* (DMS 35) engages enemy batteries east of Chuuronjang and silences the guns. The USS *Greenfish* (SS 351) ends her tour of duty in Korean waters.

AIR WAR: Marine Fighter Squadron 312 is redesignated as Marine Attack Squadron 312. Three F-86s are downed by enemy fighters, as reported by enemy records.

PARTISANS: Kirkland establishes infiltration teams with a secondary role of spotting targets for naval gunfire and small coastal road interdiction. The evacuation of refugees from islands in the Raeju-Ongjin region is discontinued. Future evacuations are limited to those who have aided the UN cause in the area.

March 2

POLITICAL/ADMINISTRATIVE: Due to the threat imposed by a Japanese Communist Party demonstration planned for the Chigasaki beach area, all Naval Beach Group personnel and materiel are evacuated.

SEA WAR: The USS *Endicott* (DMS 35) is fired on by shore batteries during a bombardment mission at Kyojo-wan. *LST 561* founders off Yonpyong-do with the loss of all hands: two naval officers, two army officers, five enlisted seamen, and two Royal Marines. The New Zealand ship *Kaniere* begins its tour of duty in Korean waters. A new type of enemy anti-boat mine is discovered at Wonsan. It is designed to explode at a depth of from 18 inches to 8 feet beneath the surface. The mine contains 44 pounds of TNT. The discovery requires a new set of sweeps.

March 3

POLITICAL/ADMINISTRATIVE: Vice Admiral R. P. Briscoe assumes command of Seventh Fleet, relieving Vice Admiral H. M. Martin.

EIGHTH ARMY: Agents report that new gun positions are being constructed by the enemy on Ho-do Pan-do on the south shore of Wonsan harbor.

SEA WAR: The USS *Merganser* (AMS 26) is fired on from Yang-do and is straddled five times, but there are no casualties.

AIR WAR: Opening strikes of Operation Saturate are launched. The plan is designed to destroy transportation units in around-the-clock bombing raids. An F-86 is reported shot down by enemy fighters. Jack C. Schwab of the 335th FIS is credited with one kill on a MiG-15, and D. E. Adams and A. R. Moorman of the 16th FIS share credit for another.

March 4

POLITICAL/ADMINISTRATIVE: The House of Representatives votes in support of a universal military training bill, but it is killed in committee.

AIR WAR: An F-86 is reported downed by enemy fighters at Taisen-Teiju.

March 5

POLITICAL/ADMINISTRATIVE: Rear Admiral John Perry relinquishes command of Task Force 77. Rear Admiral F. W. McMahon on USS *Valley Forge* (CV 45) assumes command of Task Force 77.

SEA WAR: The USS *Pelican* (AMS 32) and USS *Curlew* (AMS 8) escape under oil vapor smoke while being fired on east of Kalmagak. The USS *Essex* (CV 9) departs at the end of her first tour of duty in Korean waters.

AIR WAR: Covered by fighters, a USAF helicopter lowers a hoist sling and rescues a downed USN pilot near Yongyon. Two planes are reported shot down by enemy fighters near Siojio. VP Squadron 47 under Commander W. T. Hardaker ends its second tour of sea-based duty in Korea. VP Squadron 50 under Commander W. H. Chester begins its sea-based service in Korea. Air Group Five under Commander M. U. Beebe ends its tour aboard USS *Essex* (CV 9).

AIR WAR: Robert H. Moore, Vincent J. Marzelo, and Lloyd D. Juhlin of the 16th FIS, Kenneth L. Swift of the 51st FIW, and Henry W. Frazier of the 334th FIS are each credited with the destruction of an enemy MiG-15 fighter. W. M. Mahurin and G. W. Atkinson of the 25th FIS share credit for another downed MiG-15.

March 6

POLITICAL/ADMINISTRATIVE: The Rumanian Red Cross demands immediate UN action to stop the United States from engaging in its bacteriological war of mass extermination.

SEA WAR: The HMAS *Warramunga* (DD) and USS *Moore* (DD 747) spend an hour in the inner harbor of Songjin (Kimchaek) conducting Operation Roof Lifter, during which a large number of buildings are destroyed and fires started.

AIR WAR: Enemy reports indicate that two F-86s have been shot down by fighters at Siojio.

March 6–April 1

SEA WAR: Fast Carrier Task Force 77 reports that its planes have made 2,659 rail cuts, for an average of 98 per day, and have destroyed 123 bridges.

AIR WAR: A Marine Ground Control early warning detachment, called Doodlebug Dog, moves from the Naktong River estuary to Tsushima Island, Japan, as part of an operation called Native Son Dog.

March 7

POLITICAL/ADMINISTRATIVE: In response to a request from the International Red Cross president, Paul Reugger, Secretary of State Dean Acheson once again replies that the United States is not engaged in any form of biological warfare.

EIGHTH ARMY: Enemy shore batteries fire on Sok-to. Evidence suggests the enemy may be planning an attack on Sok-to or Cho-do.

SEA WAR: Fast Carrier Task Force 77 claims that its aircraft have destroyed 211 rail cuts, a record for a day. The USS *Boyle* (DMS 34) avoids being hit by shore batteries during an engagement. There are more than 12 near-misses but no damage is incurred.

March 8

SEA WAR: Shore batteries at Wonsan harbor hit partisan-held islands for the third day.

March 9

SEA WAR: Near Songjin, HMS *Morecambe Bay* (PF) and USS *Samuel N. Moore* (DD 747) silence enemy gun positions that have fired on USS *Merganser* (AMS 26). East of Chuuronjang, HMS *Morecambe Bay* (PF) returns fire on enemy gun positions but moves on without damage.

March 10

SEA WAR: Shore fire from the Sinpo area straddles, but does not hit, USS *Boyle* (DMS 34).

AIR WAR: Air Group 2 under Commander A. L. Downing begins its tour of duty aboard USS *Boxer* (CV 21). Harrison R. Thyng of the 335th FIS destroys one MiG-15 fighter. Ralph E. Banks of the 336th FIS downs two MiG-15s. Walter M. Mahurin and Homer R. Charlton of the 25th FIS each get a MiG-15, as does Richard R. Martin of the 16th FIS.

March 11

SEA WAR: The USS *Burke* (DD 763) is fired on by batteries south of Cho-do, without inflicting any damage. Squadron Three Mine Disposal Team, assisted by Underwater Demolition Team Five, embarks from USS *Colonial* (LSD 18) and recovers the first of a new-type Russian mine. The USS *Saint Paul* (CA 73), screened by USS *Arnold J. Isbell* (DD 869), conducts strikes near Chongjin.

AIR WAR: Fighter bombers drop 150 tons of bombs, and some 33,000 gallons of napalm, on a supply-and-training area near Sinmak. During the night, 10 B-29s hit the Sinchang choke point with 91 tons of bombs, making it useless. Two Banshee jets from Marine Photo Squadron 1 suffer major damage when they are engaged by four enemy fighters. Two pilots from the 335th FIS, Billy B. Dobbs and Conrad E. Mattson, are each credited with a kill on an enemy MiG-15; from the 336th, Kenneth H. Rapp and Brooks J. Liles each down an MiG-15.

March 11–12

AIR WAR: The chokepoint at Sinchang, 10 miles east of Sunchon, is rendered impassable after 10 B-29s attack with 91 tons of high explosives.

March 12

EIGHTH ARMY: Private First Class Bryant E. Wormack, Medical Company, 14th Regiment, 25th Infantry, is awarded the Medal of Honor after giving aid to the wounded while wounded himself. Private Wormack eventually bleeds to death.

SEA WAR: The HMS *Cossack* (DD) fires in support of a successful guerrilla landing at Haeju. Naval gunfire is reported to have killed 60 percent of the enemy garrison. Later, the *Cossack* supports guerrillas who take Onchon-do. In Operation Alcatraz, a small reconnaissance landing is successfully accomplished just south of the Suwon Dam lighthouse.

AIR WAR: Enemy reports suggest a B-29 is shot down by enemy fighters near Cherenguan. An F-86 is also downed near Sensen. Conrad E. Mattson of the 335th FIS, and Charles B. Christison, Ralph E. Banks, and Felix Asla, Jr., of the 336th, each down a MiG-15 during the day.

March 13

SEA WAR: Counter-battery strikes are fired at Wonsan by USS *Manchester* (CL 83), USS *James E. Kyes* (DD 787), USS *McGinty* (DE 365), and USS *Douglas H. Fox* (DD 779). The naval fire, with help from planes of Carrier Task Force 77, eventually silences the guns. The accuracy of fire indicates the possible use of fire control equipment.

March 14

SEA WAR: USS *President Taft* runs aground at Kurobe Shire but manages to pull clear before requiring aid. A salvage vessel, USS *Greenlet* (ASR 10), is sent to assist. The USS *Toucan* (AM 387) is fired on by batteries from Mayang-do.

March 15

POLITICAL/ADMINISTRATIVE: Brigadier General Wiley D. Ganey replaces General Kelly as commander of FEAF Bomber Command. Military responsibility for Formosa, the Pescadores, and the Philippines is transferred from CINCFE to CINCPAC by order of the president of the United States.

SEA WAR: The HMS *Concord* (DD) breaks up an enemy raid on Yongmae-do. The ROK navy's *PG 22* exchanges fire with batteries along the line, which, in order to protect its own troops, limits bombing raids. There is no damage reported. The HMS *Morecambe Bay* (PF) at Songjin is fired on but escapes undamaged. The USS *Wisconsin* (BB 64), while performing suppression fire off the coast of Songjin, destroys a North Korean train. However, as the ship approaches she is taken under fire and hit by a North Korean 155-mm artillery shell. The shell tears a huge hole in the deck; three men are wounded. The *Wisconsin* manages to destroy the battery with her main guns as she moves away.

March 16

SEA WAR: The USS *Wisconsin* (BB 64) and USS *Duncan* (DDR 874) in the Songjin-Chaho area are fired on four times from shore batteries. There is one hit on the USS *Wisconsin*, but it is negligible.

AIR WAR: Enemy reports indicate six F-86s are shot down, one each at Myaogao, Tsyungdendong, Kakusan, Bihen, Deeguandong, and Ryugampo. Philip E. Colman, Zane S. Amell, and Robert W. Smith, all of the 335th FIS, each shoot down a MiG-15 fighter.

PARTISANS: Mustang IV, with the same mission as Mustangs II and III, is launched. Radio contact is lost after six days.

March 17

EIGHTH ARMY: Marines return to 8th Army, I Corps. Six weeks of amphibious familiarization training begins for the 29th Infantry Regiment on Okinawa.

March 18

SEA WAR: During the night, several small islands north of Kojo are attacked by the North Koreans. The USS *Hammer* (DD 718) bombards the island and then escorts the evacuated forces to safety. USS *Wisconsin* (BB 64) and USS *Higbee* (DD 8012) assist ground forces that are repelling the assault on those islands. Amphibious Redeployment Group composed of two AKAs, three LSDs, 10 LSTs, and two PCECs, commences an amphibious lift of 1st Marine Division, moving tanks and heavy equipment as well as troops from Sokcho-ri to Inchon.

March 19

SEA WAR: The USS *Antietam* (CV 36) completes its first Korean tour. The USS *Wisconsin* (BB 64) and USS *Higbee* (DDR 806) fire a night harassment mission for ROK's I Corps.

AIR WAR: An F-86 is shot down by an enemy fighter near Ryugampo. Robert T. Latshaw of the 335th FIS is credited with downing a MiG-15.

March 20

SEA WAR: The USS *Wiltsie* (DD 716) and USS *Brinkley Bass* (DD 887) fire on shore guns at Wonsan. The *Bass* scores 10 direct hits on one of the batteries, while collecting only minor shrapnel damage. The USS *Greenlet* (ASR 10) brings USS *Castor* (ADS 1) into port after the *Castor* is stalled in the water. The helicopter rescue ship, LST *799,* rescues Ensign E. B. Bernard (USN), who is attached to USS *Philippine Sea* (CV 47) near Wonsan.

AIR WAR: Near the Suiho Reservoir, a USAF patrol is attacked by MiG-15s. During the battle, the F-86s destroy five and damage 13 others. Robert J. Love of the 335th FIS kills a MiG-15 fighter. Donald E. Adams of the 16th FIS is credited with downing a MiG-15, and J. McCulley and R. Schoenemann also of the 16th share credit for the destruction of a MiG-15 fighter. Felix Asla, Jr., and Charles G. Carl, both of the 336th FIS, are each credited with shooting down a MiG-15 fighter. Five F-86s are reported downed by enemy fighters, two at Sensen, one at Bihen, and two at Deeguandong.

March 21

SEA WAR: The ROK navy's *AMC 309* supports a guerrilla raid on the north bank of the Han River. Twenty-five enemy soldiers are killed, and there are no UN casualties. The USS *Osprey* (AMS 28) is fired on by shore batteries while minesweeping at

Wonsan. With the aid of a spot, the *Osprey* silences the three batteries in a counter-engagement. The USS *Princeton* (CV 37) begins its third tour of duty with Task Force 77.

March 21–25

SEA WAR: The USS *Wantuck* (APD 125) begins a series of amphibious raids for intelligence and destruction, as it lands ROK troops at night against selected targets along the east coast of Korea, near Iwon.

March 22

SEA WAR: At Kalmagak, the shore batteries fire on USS *Stickell* (DD 888). She is joined by USS *Brinkley Bass* (DD 887), and they return fire. Neither ship is hit. The USS *Hammer* (DD 718), after being illuminated by enemy star shells, is fired on, but without success.

AIR WAR: Air Group Fifteen under Commander R. F. Farrington ends its tour aboard USS *Antietam* (CV 36).

March 23

EIGHTH ARMY: UN and Communist forces begin the fight for Pork Chop Hill on the western side of the Korean Peninsula near the 38th parallel.

SEA WAR: The USS *Wiltsie* (DD 716) and USS *Brinkley Bass* (DD 887) return fire from shore batteries at Wonsan. The USS *Wantuck* (APD 125) delivers a special missions group—three American officers, one army enlisted man, one civilian photographer, and 41 ROK troops—behind enemy lines near Chumunjin. Their mission is to take prisoners and destroy railroad tracks. During the raid, an enemy parol is sighted but no contact is made, and the operation, planned for the next two nights, is canceled. Marine Transport Helicopter Squadron 16 moves to a location four miles east of Munsan-ni.

March 24

SEA WAR: USS *Brinkley Bass* (DD 887) is hit amidships near Wonsan, causing some damage and wounding five enlisted men. At Ho-do Island enemy forces attack and take the island. UN losses are 31 KIA, one WIA, and one MIA.

AIR WAR: The Fifth Air Force launches 959 sorties on the rail lines near Sinanju, making more than 140 cuts in the lines. The Sunchon-Pyongyang highway is also hit 27 times. VMO 161, Marine Air Observation Squadron, moves to a new location about six miles southeast of Munsan-ni. Pilots J. McCulley and R. Schoenemann share credit for the destruction of a MiG-15 fighter, while Freeland K. Mathews, of the 336th FIS, James D. Carey of the 334th FIS, and Robert J. Love of the 335th FIS each get a MiG-15.

March 25

POLITICAL/ADMINISTRATIVE: Communist negotiators agree that each side should be able to maintain at least five points of entry into Korea after the cease-fire, but they are still unable to agree on the rebuilding of airfields.

EIGHTH ARMY: The Chinese raid Hill 132. The Canadians, despite being surrounded, manage to hold on until the Chinese withdraw.

Sea War: USS *Essex* (CV 9) ends its first tour of duty with Task Force 77.

Air War: Two F-86s are shot down, one near Hakusen and one at Bihen-Sensen.

March 26

Eighth Army: The Canadians on Hill 132 expect a counterattack but the Chinese, after a limited probe, withdraw.

March 27

Sea War: The HMS *Crane* (PF) is hit by an enemy battery located on the newly captured Ho-do Island.

Air War: A downed U.S. pilot near Pyoksong is rescued by a helicopter that is able to keep the enemy at bay with rifle fire, allowing the pilot to escape and eventually to be hoisted up.

March 28

Political/Administrative: Delay in the delivery of much-needed cement reduces repair, and thus operations, at several airfields. Rear Admiral F. X. McInerney relieves Rear Admiral C. F. Espe as Commander Amphibious Force Far East and Commander Task Force 90.

Sea War: Fire from Hodo Pando straddles USS *Burlington* (PF-51) with more than 120 rounds without scoring a hit.

March 29

Sea War: The USS *Murrelet* (AM 372) and USS *Symbol* (AM 123) are fired on near Pungho Dong.

March 30

Air War: An F-86 is lost to enemy fighter planes near Sensen.

March 31

Sea War: The aircraft carrier USS *Boxer* (CV 21) joins Fast Carrier Task Force 77 for a third tour.

Eighth Army: The Kimpo Provisional Regiment is organized by and within the 1st Marine Division sector to aid in the defense of the Kimpo Peninsula.

Air War: FEAF Bomber Command B-29s fly 29 sorties, primarily against the Sinhung-dong bridge and the Kwaksan railroad track.

April 1

Political/Administrative: Rear Admiral Apollo Soucek relieves Rear Admiral F. W. McMahon as Commander Fast Carrier Task Force 77. Shipping Control Authority for the Japanese Merchant Marine (SCAJAP) is closed down.

Eighth Army: The Chinese begin to bombard the front line held by the KMC, then follow up a half-hour later with advancing infantry. After a short battle, the Chinese withdraw, having penetrated the MLR only briefly.

Sea War: The USS *Leonard F. Mason* (DD 852) suffers an onboard explosion, but there are no casualties. The USS *Wiltsie* (DD 716) and USS *McGinty* (DE 3654) silence shore batteries that are firing on the *Wiltsie*. The USS *Condor* (AMS 5) also receives fire at Wonsan.

AIR WAR: In an aerial battle, considered one of the largest of the war, 10 MiG-15s are destroyed and more than a dozen are damaged. In the fight, only one F-86 is lost. Colonel Francis S. Gabreski, commander 51st FIW, becomes the eighth jet ace of the war. Iven C. Kincheloe of the 25th FIS is credited with downing two MiG-15s, as is William H. Westcott of the same squadron. Robert H. Moore of the 16th FIA gets a MiG-15 fighter, as do James H. Kasler, Robert W. Smith, and Robert J. Love of the 335th FIS.

April 2

POLITICAL/ADMINISTRATIVE: Questioning the idea that any North Korean or Chinese POW would want to remain in the ROK, the Communist truce talk delegation had in January 1952, agreed to the screening of all POWs concerning their repatriation in order to determine how many of the prisoners will want to avoid being returned to their original units. The Communists agreed in principle, in March 1952, to the idea of special treatment for civilians who are interned. At this point, General James Van Fleet moves the civilian internees to the mainland, but delays their release. Rear Admiral F. W. McMahon, of USS *Valley Forge* (CV 45), relinquishes command of Task Force 77. Rear Admiral A. Soucek, on USS *Philippine Sea* (CV 47), assumes command of Task Force 77.

EIGHTH ARMY: Communist prisoners once again begin to riot at the Koje-do POW camp.

SEA WAR: While providing fire support for *USS Condor* (AMS 5), USS *Symbol* (AM 123), USS *Murrelet* (AM 372), and USS *Edmonds* (DE 406) take enemy fire near Wonsan. No damage is reported.

AIR WAR: Soviet accounts report that five F-86s are down, two at Dunguan, two at Deeguandong, and one at Gisyu. Iven C. Kincheloe and Dale W. Smiley, of the 25th FIS, each shoot down a MiG-15 fighter. Robert T. Latshaw of the 335th FIS also gets a MiG-15 fighter.

April 3

POLITICAL/ADMINISTRATIVE: General Matthew Ridgway receives permission from the Joint Chiefs of Staff to go ahead with the proposed screening of POWs to determine their intended destination when released.

AIR WAR: Captain Robert H. Moore, of the 336th FIS, becomes an ace with the destruction of his fifth MiG-15. An F-86 is downed by enemy planes at Songchenni. Charles G. Carl of the 336th FIS also downs a MiG-15 fighter.

April 4

SEA WAR: The mission of Fast Carrier Task Force 77 is slightly changed to include air and gun strikes in coordination with Task Force 95 surface elements. VP Squadron 28 under Commander R. Donley ends its sea service in Korea.

AIR WAR: Rockets are sighted near Wonsan and are believed to be the first antiaircraft rockets in these naval operations. Conrad E. Mattson of the 335th FIS shoots down an enemy MiG-15 fighter.

April 5

POLITICAL/ADMINISTRATIVE: COMNAVFE reminds the fleet that the directive against the bombardment of North Korean electrical facilities is still in effect.

EIGHTH ARMY: Operation Pronto, the first major helicopter airlift in the I Corps sector, moves 670 personnel of the 2nd Battalion, 7th Marines, and their equipment, from the Munsan-ni area, across the Han River, to the Kimpo Peninsula.

SEA WAR: The USS *Ute* (ATF 76) is fired on at Cho-do. She is not hit.

AIR WAR: Marine Helicopter Squadron 161 receives a call giving it three hours to prepare to move the 2nd Battalion, 7th Marine Regiment, and 10,000 pounds of rations. It is to be a round trip of about 57 miles from the frontline area to the Kimpo Peninsula. The trip requires MHS 161 to stay clear of the demilitarized zone around Munsan-ni. Called Operation Pronto, it is the longest round-trip distance of a helicopter troop movement to that time. An F-51 is shot down at Sensen and three F-86s near Dabbong.

April 6

SEA WAR: The USS *Iowa* (BB 61) returns to active duty with Fast Carrier Task Force 77 and replaces her sister ship, USS *Wisconsin* (BB 64). The USS *Wiltsie* (DD 716) is fired on by enemy shore batteries east of Kalmagak, but there is no damage received.

AIR WAR: Captain Iven C. Kincheloe, Jr., 25th FIS, becomes the 10th ace of the Korean War as he destroys his fifth MiG-15. Billy B. Dobbs, Philip E. Coleman, and Coy L. Austin, all of the 335th FIS, are also credited with downing a MiG-15 fighter.

April 7

SEA WAR: USS *Endicott* (DMS 35) is fired on at Kyojo-wan (Chongjin) while moored. More than 75 splashes are observed during the firing, but there are no hits. After the guns are silenced by *Endicott* and USS *Chandler* (DD 717), the sweep is completed.

April 8

POLITICAL/ADMINISTRATIVE: President Harry Truman signs an executive order to seize the strike-bound U.S. steel mills. He is acting to prevent the interruption of vital war materials. Following up on the agreement at Panmunjom to screen POWs to identify their wishes concerning repatriation, Operation Scatter begins. During the count, those wishing to be repatriated are separated from those who do not. Seven POW compounds are filled with nearly 40,000 prisoners who refuse to allow themselves to be interviewed; their names are put on the list of those who do not want to return.

SEA WAR: The USS *Wiltsie* (DD 716) receives three rounds of fire from the shore but pulls out of the area unharmed.

AIR WAR: All air operations are canceled by extreme weather conditions that exist on both coasts of Korea.

April 9

AIR WAR: Air operations are limited because of extreme weather conditions.

April 10

POLITICAL/ADMINISTRATIVE: Brigadier General Chester E. McCarty assumes command of the 315th AD (Combat Cargo), a position he will hold until the end of the war.

SEA WAR: USS *Silverstein* (DE 534) is fired on near Hodo Pando. The USS *Rochester* (CA 124) reports being tracked by an unidentified aircraft. The stalking plane eventually retires to the north.

AIR WAR: Using the guns of USS *St. Paul* (CA 73) and USS *Hanson* (DD 832) in support, planes from Task Force 77 carry out a series of air strikes against enemy positions at Wonsan.

Army Deuce and a Half truck being dug out of the heavy Korean mud, 1952 *(Center for the Study of the Korean War, Graceland University)*

April 11

POLITICAL/ADMINISTRATIVE: Brigadier General Clayton C. Jerome relieves Major General Christian F. Schilt as Commanding General, First Marine Aircraft Wing.

SEA WAR: The USS *McGinty* (DE 365) and USS *Wiltsie* (DD 716) are fired on by Wonsan shore guns as they maneuver in separate areas. The USS *Silverstein* (DE 534), USS *Cabildo* (LSD 16), and USS *Apache* (ATF 67) return fire on the batteries and are able to suppress additional bombardment. At Hungnam, USS *Edmonds* (DD 534) is fired on but silences the enemy guns by return fire.

April 12

SEA WAR: The HMAS *Bataan* (DD) stops an enemy attack against Yongmae-do by illuminating the mud flats between the island and the mainland. The guns at Wonsan harbor unsuccessfully fire at USS *Wiltsie* (DD 716).

April 13

AIR WAR: Planes from USS *Philippine Sea* (CV 47) and USS *Boxer* (CV 21), supported by three destroyers, conduct a one-day strike against Chongjin. Two hundred tons of ordnance is delivered in 246 sorties. Three F-86s are downed by enemy pilots, according to Soviet sources. Seven MiG-5 fighters are shot down by pilots of the USAF. Credited are Robert L. Sands and James E. McCulley of the 16th FIS; William H. Westcott (who downs two planes), Donald J. Hemmer, and William Craig of the 25th FIS; and Francis S. Gabreski of the 51st FIS.

April 14

POLITICAL/ADMINISTRATIVE: Intelligence reports indicate that the Communists are building up defensive positions and troop strength along the entire south China coast. These appear to be anti-invasion efforts.

AIR WAR: The 403rd TCW (Medium), the first Air Force Reserve wing, arrives at Ashiya, Japan. An SA-16 Albatross with the 3rd ARS rescues a USN pilot while under small-arms fire from the shore. Air Group Nineteen under Commander William Denton, Jr., begins its tour onboard USS *Princeton* (CV 37).

April 15

POLITICAL/ADMINISTRATIVE: Operation Scatter, the screening of POWs, is completed. Of the 170,000 military and civilian personnel who respond, about 70,000 indicate an interest in returning to communist rule.

EIGHTH ARMY: Item Company, 3rd Battalion, 1st Marines, is guarding Hill 27 when it is probed by the enemy. The marines return fire and the enemy pulls back. Then the artillery opens up and is quickly followed by the next attack. The men of Item Company are overrun.

SEA WAR: The HMAS *Bataan* (DD) bombards Yukto Island. The USS *Silverstein* (DE 534) is fired on by enemy batteries in the area of Hungnam. The USS *Toucan* (AM 387) and the USS *Murrelet* (AM 387) are fired on while conducting a sweep near the Musa Dan area. There are no casualties.

April 16

POLITICAL/ADMINISTRATIVE: Rear Admiral F. W. McMahon, in the *Valley Forge,* assumes command of Task Force 77. Rear Admiral A. Soucek, on USS *Philippine Sea* (CV 47), relinquishes command of Task Force 77.

EIGHTH ARMY: A unit composed of two rifle platoons and a machine-gun section moves out in three groups toward Hill Italy. At 2100, the security group assigned to take Hill 128 moves out. Once through the wire, the unit has no trouble taking the early trenches. However, the Chinese response increases, and the Americans find it necessary to dig in. The decision is made to send out a patrol to bring the men back and to cover their withdrawal. They move back into relative safety at 0330. Corporal Duane E. Dewey, Easy Company, 2nd Battalion, 5th Marines, 1st Marine Division, survives to received the Medal of Honor for throwing his body on a grenade that landed close to other marines. Several men from the ill-fated mission of Item Company on Hill 27 drift back to the MLR to report that the remainder have been killed. A counterattack is launched, and the enemy withdraws. Item Company goes in search of five lost men, four of whom are recovered.

SEA WAR: The USS *Philippine Sea* (CV 47) is relieved by USS *Valley Forge* (CV 45).

April 17

POLITICAL/ADMINISTRATIVE: Presidential Executive Order 10345 extends enlistments involuntarily for nine months. Intelligence reports suggest a significant gathering of enemy troops across from the islands of Yongmae-do, Sogom, Porum, Kakhoe, Songmo, Kyodong-do, and Kotkpo in preparation for an attack.

SEA WAR: The USS *Thomas* (DD 833) receives bracketing fire from batteries east of Chuuronjang. HMS *Concord* (DD) returns fire as the *Thomas* sails to safety. The USS *McGinty* (DD 731) is fired on near Wonsan and returns fire, along with USS *Maddox* (DD 731). The USS *Murrelet* (AM 372) and USS *Toucan* (AM 387), while check sweeping near Song-do Gap, are fired upon by a 37-mm gun that directs 15 rounds against the ships. Undamaged, both ships return fire. Near Nan-do Island, USS *Samuel N. Moore* (DD 747) is fired on from long range, possibly by a 122-mm gun, but there is no damage.

April 18

SEA WAR: The USS *Ptarmigan* (AM 376), near Mayang-do, is unsuccessfully fired on.

AIR WAR: Marine Transport Helicopter Division 161 lifts 840 men from the 5th Korean Marine Corps, taking them from Kimpo across the Han River. VC-35 Team Able, flying a night heckler mission, destroys eight trucks, two warehouses, and an ammunition dump, and damages 12 trucks. Harrison R. Thyng of the 335th FIS downs a MiG-15 fighter.

PARTISANS: Several Leopard boats are sunk or destroyed by severe storms that lash the western Korea coast.

April 18–19

EIGHTH ARMY: In Operation Leapfrog, a battalion of the KMC is moved across the Han River and then back again by Marine Helicopter Squadron 161 to test the possibility of conducting such a move over water. Somewhat later, Operation Circus will involve the same HMR squadron moving the 1st Battalion, 7th Marine Regiment, across the Imjin River in less than 90 minutes to take up a blocking position.

April 19

POLITICAL/ADMINISTRATIVE: The Communists are upset over the figure of 70,000 seeking a return to Communist hands, and accuse UN Command of tampering with the results. Rather than helping the fight over agenda item 4, the conclusions reached seem to make it worse. The 1st Marine Division organizes a special reserve and covering force to protect the UN Truce Team at Panmunjom, if talks should break down.

EIGHTH ARMY: As a part of the plan to decentralize POW compounds, the commander of Task Group 90.3, with one APA, two LSMRs, and two AKAs, lifts interned personnel from Koje-do and take them to other locations.

SEA WAR: The USS *Endicott* (DMS 35) is hit by enemy fire in the Songjin-Chongjin area. There are no casualties. The HMCS *Nootka* (DDE) receives fire from both enemy and friendly forces near Kirin-do as she is engaged near the island and the mainland.

April 19–22

SEA WAR: A special mine sweep is conducted in the Sokcho-ri area. The sweep is repeated on April 22 with negative results.

April 20

SEA WAR: Task Force 90 lifts the 38th Infantry Regiment, 163 officers and 2,987 enlisted men, from Inchon to Koje-do.

April 21

SEA WAR: The cruiser USS *Saint Paul* (CA 73), while engaged in a gunfire support mission off Kojo, loses 30 men killed in a powder fire. The USS *Horace A. Bass* (APD 124) supports a series of raids as she lands ROK troops at night at selected targets on the northeast coast of Korea. The HMS *Concord* (DD) is fired on from Mayang-do.

AIR WAR: Marine Attack Squadron 312 is transferred from USS *Bairoko* (CVE 115) to USS *Bataan* (CVL 29). Captain Robert J. Love, 335th FIS, destroys two MiG-15s and becomes an ace. Robert L. Straub and James H. Kasler of the 335th FIS, Alvin R. Moorman of the 16th FIS, and Robert J. Liles of the 336th FIS each down a MiG-15 fighter. P. L. Saunders and D. J. Hemmer share credit for shooting down a MiG-15. Three F-86s are shot down by enemy fighters.

April 22

SEA WAR: The USS *Iowa* (BB 61) and USS *Bradford* (DD 545) are fired on at Mayang-do but escape damage. They are unable to determine the location of the fire and there is no return fire. Fast Carrier Task Force 77 supports coordinated air and gun strikes at Hungnam, involving USS *Iowa* (BB 61) and USS *Manchester* (CL 83).

AIR WAR: A shortage of fighter bombers causes Fifth Air Force to reassign the Sabres of the 4th and 5th Fighter Interceptor Wings to armed reconnaissance. Jere J. Lewis of the 334th FIS shoots down a MiG-15.

April 23

POLITICAL/ADMINISTRATIVE: Rear Admiral John Perry, on USS *Valley Forge* (CV 45), assumes command of Task Force 77. Rear Admiral F. W. McMahon, on the *Valley Forge* (CV 45), relinquishes command of Task Force 77.

EIGHTH ARMY: First Marine Division outpost line positions are withdrawn in order to strengthen the main defense line. Operation Circus provides for the air deployment of the 7th Marine Reserve Regiment less than two battalions, across the Imjin to a position on the defensive line Wyoming Forward.

SEA WAR: Two men are killed and four wounded when HMS *Concord* (DD) is hit by shore fire from the Songjin-Chongjin area. More than 30 rounds are fired by a 75-mm gun. Counter-battery fire records some hits.

April 24

POLITICAL/ADMINISTRATIVE: When the Communists are informed that 103,000 of the 173,000 prisoners held will refuse repatriation, they break off negotiations.

SEA WAR: USS *Osprey* (AMS 28) is hit, but with little damage and no casualties, while minesweeping at Songjin. The *Osprey* and USS *Doyle* (DMS 35) return fire. The USS *Brush* (DD 745) is able to destroy guns at Sokto that have been firing on UN planes. The USS *Endicott* (DMS 35) captures a sampan and kills the crew of two others near Yang-do.

AIR WAR: Richard H. Schoeneman of the 16th FIS shoots down an enemy MiG-15 fighter.

PARTISANS: Hachwira-do, Tok-to, and Yuk-do are retaken and occupied by friendly guerrillas. The enemy had withdrawn from these islands.

April 25

SEA WAR: Planes from USS *Boxer* (CV 21) report a large number of small fishing boats collected near Songgong-man Bay. The USS *Iowa* (BB 61), supported by USS *Duncan* (DD 874), USS *McCoy Reynolds* (DE 440), and HMAS *Warramunga,* is joined by 50 or so planes from Task Force 77 to destroy significant targets at Chongjin.

AIR WAR: Planes from Russian airfields, only 48 miles away, are attacked close to Chongjin, but they do not come to within 20 miles of the bombardment unit.

April 26

POLITICAL/ADMINISTRATIVE: The armistice talks resume once again. Rear Admiral Kim Won Mu (NKPN) is relieved at the armistice talks.

SEA WAR: The USS *Cabildo* (LSD 16) is fired on by shore batteries based on Hodo Pando. Several misses straddle the ship and one direct hit amidship causes some structural damage. Two persons are hurt. The USS *Silverstein* (DD 534) covers the withdrawal of two boats from Umi-do and is taken under fire. The *Silverstein* and USS *Maddox* (DD 731) provide suppression fire on the offending batteries. Aircraft from USS *Valley Forge* (CV 45) provide close air support. The *Maddox* receives two hits but there are no casualties or serious damage.

AIR WAR: Major William H. Westcott, 51st FIG, becomes an ace when he destroys his fifth MiG-15. An F-86 is shot down near Gisyu.

April 27

SEA WAR: The USS *Samuel N. Moore* (DD 748) is fired on near Kosong as more than 18 rounds of 76-mm fire is directed toward her. The battery is silenced by return fire. At Wonsan harbor, USS *Waxbill* (AMS 39) is fired on while sweeping. No damage is reported. The USS *Iowa* (BB 61) fires on coastal bridges south of Songjin. The battleship damages all the bridges and closes the tunnel entrances.

AIR WAR: An F-86 is shot down by enemy fighters near Jungen.

April 28

POLITICAL/ADMINISTRATIVE: President Harry Truman appoints General Mark W. Clark to replace General Matthew Ridgway. On orders from Washington, Admiral Joy is instructed to give in to the Communist demands that airfields can be rebuilt during the truce period. The Japanese Peace Treaty comes into effect officially, and all U.S. forces in Japan prepare to assume a new role under the Peace and Security Pact agreement. Rear Admiral Kim Won Mu (NKPN) is assigned to the armistice talks at Panmunjom. The UN delegates at the cease-fire talks offer a package proposal under which the UN would withdraw any restrictions on the rebuilding of airfields after the armistice, only POWs who wanted to be repatriated would be repatriated, and the Soviet Union would not be considered as a member of the proposed neutral nations supervisory body. The Communists reject the package without any explanation and break off the peace talks.

EIGHTH ARMY: After holding Hill 190.5 for more than two weeks, a squad from the 2nd Platoon, George Company, 3rd Battalion, 1st Marines, is ordered to come off the hill. They reach the MLR by 1600. On the way down, they discover that the Chinese are building fortifications on the forward slope.

SEA WAR: The USS *McGinty* (DE 365) fires on and damages a Soviet T-34 tank on Kalmagak. The USS *Conceiver* (ARS 39) is fired on near Yo-do. The USS *Silverstein*

(DE 534) and USS *Maddox* (DD 731) provide counterfire while the *Maddox* lays smoke through which to withdraw the ships.

AIR WAR: An H-19 helicopter of the 3rd ARS rescues a downed Hawker Seafury pilot for the second time. Three weeks earlier the pilot had been picked up by a 3rd ARS helicopter.

April 29–30

AIR WAR: Sixteen people are killed in unrelated crashes of a C-47, a C-119, and a C-46.

April 29

EIGHTH ARMY: Acting on information discovered the day before, the men of George Company return to Hill 190.5 to investigate what the Chinese are doing.

April 30

EIGHTH ARMY: The second Korean winter phase ends. On Hill 190.5, elements of George Company, 2nd Battalion, come under mortar fire. In order to retreat the men have to disarm the mines they had previously set.

SEA WAR: The USS *Princeton* (CV 37) joins the Fast Carrier Task Force for a second tour. The USS *Maddox* (DD 73) and USS *Laffey* (DD 724) damage several rail cars and shore batteries at Wonsan. The USS *Horace A. Bass* (APD 124) successfully lands troops on the north coast of Korea without opposition, and railway track and engines are destroyed. The USS *Douglas H. Fox* (DD 779) is fired on in the vicinity of Hungnam. The USS *Princeton* (CV 37) collides with USS *Cacapon* (AO 52), causing some damage to the *Cacapon*. The USS *Douglas H. Fox* (DD 779) conducts raids in Operation Fishnet, taking a small rock island in Hungnam harbor.

AIR WAR: Seven Panther jets (F9F-2) from Marine Fighter Squadron 311 encounter MiG-15s at 20,000 feet above Kunu-ri. A. P. Brietenstein and D. H. Fincher of the 16th FIS share credit for the downing of a MiG-15 fighter. Duane K. Bryant of the 335th FIS shoots down two MiG-15s, and Conrad E. Mattson and Robert T. Latshaw, also of the 335th FIS, are each credited with a kill. James B. Raebel of the 25th FIS downs a MiG-15. One F9F-2 is damaged.

May 1

EIGHTH ARMY: The Korea summer-fall phase begins. The ROK units on line are increased from six to nine.

SEA WAR: The USS *Douglas H. Fox* (DD 779) receives five rounds of fire as it patrols toward Hungnam. There are no hits reported. HMS *Whitesand Bay* (PF), near Haeju, reports receiving enemy fire but no hits. Special lifts of interned persons from Koje-do to other POW sites are completed. Since April 19, near 80,000 POWs have been relocated.

PARTISANS: Two U.S. officers and 40 members of Donkey 15 begin a junk-borne reconnaissance of the northwestern islands.

May 2

POLITICAL/ADMINISTRATIVE: Communists agree to drop the Soviet Union as a member of any cease-fire supervision in return for the United Nations agreeing to place no limit on airfield repair. The Communists still refuse to accept the UN proposal for voluntary repatriation. The delegates agree to appoint representatives from Sweden, Switzerland, Poland, and Czechoslovakia to form the Neutral Nations Supervisory Commission.

SEA WAR: After avoiding enemy fire USS *Douglas H. Fox* (DD 779) picks up six North Koreans and children who come in to surrender. The HMS *Whitesand Bay* (PF) supports a successful guerilla raid at Ponggu Myron that results in the killing of 24 enemy soldiers and the capture of communication equipment and documents. The USS *Antietam* (CV 36) concludes its tour of duty with Task Force 77.

May 3

POLITICAL/ADMINISTRATIVE: The U.S. ships LSSL *107,* LSSL *108,* PC *705,* and PC *706* are turned over to the ROK navy after a period in which they had been loaned.

SEA WAR: The USS *Douglas H. Fox* (DD 779) is fired on by shore batteries at Hungnam, then later captures several North Korean fishermen on a 40-foot sampan. The USS *Ptarmigan* (AM 376) and USS *Toucan* (AM 387) are fired on while performing mine-sweeping duties from Chaho to Mayang-do.

AIR WAR: Major Donald E. Adams of the 16th FIS, destroys two MiG-15s, and Captain Robert T. Latshaw, Jr., of the 335th FIS, destroys one, making both of them aces and helping in the total destruction of five MiG-15s in this confrontation. James B. Raebel of the 25th FIS and Robert J. Love of the 335th FIS also get a MiG-15 each. In another encounter Albert G. Tenney of the 16th FIS downs a MiG-15 fighter.

May 4

POLITICAL/ADMINISTRATIVE: General Robert Young leaves command of the 2nd Infantry Division and turns it over to Brigadier General James C. Fry, who takes command with full pomp and ceremony.

SEA WAR: The ROK navy's *PC 701,* HMS *Morecambe Bay* (PF), HMNZS *Rotoiti* (PF), HMS *Constance* (DD), and ROK navy's *AMC 301* are fired on at Upcho-ri on the west coast.

AIR WAR: Twenty-five F-86s attack the Sinuiju Airfield and destroy five YAK-9 fighters on the ground. In the air, five MiG-15s are destroyed by Richard H. Schoeneman and James A. McCulley of the 16th FIS and by Clifford D. Jolley, Philip E. Colman, and James H. Kasler of the 335th FIS

PARTISANS: A U.S. pilot who is shot down during a fight with a MiG-15, is located on Taehwa-do where he has been hiding for several weeks. He is rescued.

May 5

POLITICAL/ADMINISTRATIVE: General Mark A. Clark assumes command of the United Nations Far East Command.

SEA WAR: The USS *Douglas H. Fox* (DD 779) comes under fire near Hungnam. In counter-fire the *Douglas H. Fox* scores a direct hit on the enemy battery.

May 6

SEA WAR: The USS *Firedrake* (AE 14) and USS *Valley Forge* (CV 45) collide during a transfer of ammunition, but there are no casualties. The USS *Douglas H. Fox* (DD

779) captures three sampans with 15 North Korean personnel in the Sinchang area. Later, *Douglas H. Fox* captures 23 North Korean fishermen and a 32-foot sampan in the area of Paegan-dan. USS *Ptarmigan* (AM 376) and USS *Toucan* (AM 387) conduct night anti-sampan patrols as a part of Operation Fishnet in the area of Sinchang.

PARTISANS: Communist Chinese troops are reinforcing the peninsula opposite the island of Yongmae-do, making it difficult for friendly agents to infiltrate the area. Raiders, supported by USS *Douglas H. Fox,* suspend operations after they capture three sampans and 15 North Korean fishermen in the vicinity of Changho-ri.

May 7

POLITICAL/ADMINISTRATIVE: Negotiations continue on hold after the Communists withdraw again from the cease-fire talks due to the issue of repatriations.

SEA WAR: The USS *James C. Owens* (DD 776) is fired on by batteries near Songjin, as she conducts fire on "targets of opportunity." The *Owens* sustains six hits and several near misses that kill two and wound seven. There is damage to her four 40-mm gun mounts. The USS *Douglas H. Fox* (DD 779) is straddled by 12 76-mm, white phosphorus rounds from batteries on Mayang-do. Return fire destroys one battery. The USS *Waxbill* (AMS 39) receives 12 near-misses from a 75-mm gun, but no one is hurt. The USS *Ptarmigan* (AM 376) captures five enemy sampans.

May 7–11

EIGHTH ARMY: Riots at the POW camp on Koje-do begin with the seizure of General Francis (Frank) Dodd, the camp commander. After Brigadier General Charles Colson, acting commander, gives in to the prisoners' demands, General Dodd is released. North Korean and Chinese propaganda begins immediately. While cleared at first, both Generals Dodd and Colson are demoted to colonels.

May 8

EIGHTH ARMY: Charlie Company is assigned a diversionary attack against Hill 67, which is in a position to direct fire on the marine advance. The main drive is against peaks designated as V, X, Y, and Z. The marines are led by Item Company; after a brief strike, the marines withdraw.

SEA WAR: Raiders from USS *Douglas H. Fox* (DD 779), operating off Sinchang, destroy 6,600 feet of fish net and sink 130 floats marking harbor closure nets.

AIR WAR: Several major interdiction strikes are conducted. Over a 13-hour period, UN pilots damage or destroy more than 200 supply buildings, personnel shelters, revetments, vehicles, and gun positions. Fifty air force fighter-bombers fly 465 sorties against supply depots at Suan, 40 miles or so southeast of Pyongyang. One F-85, flying a bombing strike against the Kunu-ri marshaling yards, is shot down. James F. Low of the 336th FIS and Albert B. Smiley of the 335th FIS each down a MiG-15.

May 9

POLITICAL/ADMINISTRATIVE: General Matthew Ridgway becomes NATO commander after being replaced in Korea by General Mark Clark. Clark initiates an intensive recruiting campaign to expand the size and use of partisan units. Intelligence reports state that the enemy is building sampans on the mainland opposite Yang-do for a possible invasion.

SEA WAR: The USS *Maddox* (DD 731) and USS *Laffey* (DD 729) fire on railroad targets in the Wonsan area. They damage two buildings and destroy two railway cars. Batteries on land fire at the ships but cause no damage. While engaged in a sweep near Wonsan, USS *Merganser* (AMS 26) and USS *Redhead* (AMS 34) are fired on by gun positions at Kalmagak. No damage reported. The USS *James C. Owens* (DD 776) is hit six times by fire from Songjin. Two are killed, seven wounded, and material damage is done to the four 40-mm gun mounts. The USS *Waxbill* (AMS 39) avoids being hit when 12 rounds are fired at the ship at Wonsan. USS *Douglas H. Fox* (DD 779) is fired on by guns at Yaktaeso but escapes. Later, *Douglas H. Fox* (DD 779) launches a boat raid on the inner harbor at Hungnam and, after firing on factories in the area, returns with 12 prisoners and two junks.

May 10

POLITICAL/ADMINISTRATIVE: General Frank Dodd walks out of Compound 76 at Koje-do after his release by Communist captors. He is immediately taken to Tokyo, where he meets the anger of Army Secretary Pace. In what seems an extreme reaction, Dodd will eventually be reduced a rank and retired from the army.

SEA WAR: The USS *Douglas H. Fox* (DD 779) patrolling north of Hungnam captures four North Korean fishermen off Mayang-do. USS *Maddox* (DD 731) and USS *Laffey* (DD 729) fire on railroad targets at Wonsan. The USS *Redhead* (AMS 34) and USS *Merganser* (AMS 26) are fired on from gun positions located at Kalmagak. The USS *Murrelet* (AM 372) captures six enemy sampans.

May 11

POLITICAL/ADMINISTRATIVE: Brigadier General Haydon L. Boatner is informed that he has been selected to take command of the out-of-control POW camp at Koje-do.

SEA WAR: The USS *Evansville* (PF 70) launches a motor whaleboat with a raiding party and captures four prisoners. A navy PBM on reconnaissance over the Yellow Sea is attacked by two MiG-15s. There is no damage.

AIR WAR: Five MiG-15s are destroyed while 12 F-86s attack Sinuiju and Uiju Airfields. In the afternoon, they bomb Sinuiju with 1,000-pound bombs. One pilot is shot down and captured. A VP-42 PMB reconnaissance patrol over the Yellow Sea, near the Korean coast, is attacked by two enemy fighters. The PMB is hit with one 20-mm shell but is able to return safely to Iwakuni.

May 12

POLITICAL/ADMINISTRATIVE: General Haydon L. Boatner officially takes charge of the POW camp at Koje-do and immediately begins to make changes.

SEA WAR: In an hourlong gun duel at Wonsan, USS *Maddox* (DD 731), USS *Laffey* (DD 725), USS *Herbert J. Thomas* (DD 833), and USS *Evansville* (PF 70) and several minesweepers exchange fire with shore batteries. The duel results in the *Herbert J. Thomas* being hit once, with little damage and no casualties. At Hungnam, USS *Douglas H. Fox* (DD 779) takes 30 prisoners via an armed motor whaleboat party. The

USS *Douglas H. Fox* receives several rounds from enemy fire. The helicopter rescue ship, LST 799, rescues Lieutenant J. Newendyke (USNR) at Wonsan.

AIR WAR: The USS *Valley Forge* (CV 45) and USS *Princeton* (CV 37) each send six planes to isolate locomotives by cutting rail lines. Nine locomotives are destroyed by follow-up air groups.

May 13

EIGHTH ARMY: Chinese prisoners at the Koje-do POW compound riot once again. In response, the new camp director, Brigadier General Hayden L. Boatner, makes changes in the camp, generally creating smaller and well-separated compounds.

SEA WAR: Operation Insomnia begins. The operation is a shore-bombardment program designed to catch enemy trucks that are trying to move supplies at night.

AIR WAR: During the morning 5th Air Force Sabres destroy five MiG-15s in aerial combat. Philip E. Colman, Lewis W. Powers of the 335th FIS, Robert W. McKittrick and Herschel D. Spitzer of the 336th FIS, and Sabin L. Anderson of the 25th FIS each account for one. Twelve F-86s strike targets in extreme northwestern Korea, Sinuiju, Sinuiju Airfield, and Uiju Airfield. During the afternoon, Sabres hit the marshaling yards at Kunu-ri. In late afternoon, they bomb Sinuiju with 1,000-pound bombs. Colonel Walker M. Mahurin, commander 4th FIG, who leads the later mission, is shot down and captured.

May 14

POLITICAL/ADMINISTRATIVE: Rear Admiral John Perry, on USS *Valley Forge* (CV 45), relinquishes command of Task Force 77. Rear Admiral A. Soucek in USS *Boxer* (CV 21) assumes command of Task Force 77.

EIGHTH ARMY: Operation Timber begins as the 1st Marine Division obtains logs for bunker construction.

SEA WAR: The USS *Douglas H. Fox* (DD 779) is fired on in the vicinity of Hungnam and two men are injured. The batteries are engaged and destroyed.

PARTISANS: Mustangs V and VI are launched at different locations. These are the same intelligence and destruction missions as the other Mustang operations. No contact is established with them after they drop.

May 15

AIR WAR: Fifth Air Force fighter-bombers fly 265 sorties, destroying factories and repair facilities at Tang-dong, north of Pyongyang, as well as destroying 39 buildings and a power plant. First Lieutenant James H. Kasler of the 335th FIS becomes an ace by destroying two additional MiG-15s. Albert B. Smiley of the 335th also downs a MiG-15.

AIR WAR: Marine Fighter Squadron 312 is redesignated as Marine Attack Squadron 312. A B-26 bomber is shot down by enemy fighters near Cherenguan and an F-86 near Sakusyu.

May 16

EIGHTH ARMY: The 187th Airborne Regimental Combat Team arrives for its second tour in Korea.

Sea War: The USS *Murrelet* (AM 372) and USS *Symbol* (AM 123) are fired on without injury while sweeping in the vicinity of Songjin. Counterfire is provided by USS *Doyle* (DMS 34) and USS *Thomas* (DD 203). The ARC *304* fights an exchange of shells not far offshore at the Han River Estuary. Chinese mortars and machine guns open fire. No damage or casualties are sustained.

May 17

Eighth Army: Intelligence received from prisoners suggests that the enemy is planning an attack on Yo-do. A platoon of marines attacks Arrowhead Hill, takes it, and then withdraws on orders. The assault force is made up of the 1st Platoon of Easy Company, 2nd Battalion, 7th Marines. At 2330, they leave Outpost 2 for the attack and by 0305 ease into the first line of enemy trenches. The Chinese, caught by surprise, are cut down. The Chinese withdraw, leaving a large number of casualties. Then the marines withdraw. The 187th Airborne Regimental Combat Team arrives at the Koje-do prisoner-of-war camp to aid in the control of prisoners.

Sea War: A raiding party from USS *Buck* (DD 761) captures six prisoners and two sampans south of Kojo. The HMS *Belfast* (CL) avoids damage when fired on south of Taedong.

May 17–18

Eighth Army: The Chinese begin to assemble for an attack on the Hook near Yong Dong, but when they reach the area of the UN patrol outposts on Ronson (Green Finger Ridge), they are broken up by artillery that is called down on them.

May 18

Sea War: Two sampans and six North Korean fishermen are captured by USS *Douglas H. Fox* (DD 779).

Air War: Facing considerable small-arms fire from the shoreline, an SA-16 amphibious aircraft from the 3rd ARS, rescues a downed F-84 pilot. An F-86 is shot down near Tetsuzan.

May 19

Political/Administrative: Vice Admiral J. J. Clark assumes command of U.S. Seventh Fleet.

Sea War: The USS *Lorry* (DD 7790) is fired on by shore batteries from the mainland, southeast of Cho-do. The USS *Symbol* (AM 123), USS *Murrelet* (AM 372), USS *Doyle* (DMS 34), and HMAS *Warramunga* (DD) are fired on from batteries at Chongjin. Two of the minesweepers lose their sweeping gear, but there is no other damage. The HMS *Ocean* (CVL) and

Checking wire on the Seoul side of the Han River approach, Korea 1952 *(Center for the Study of the Korean War, Graceland University)*

HMAS *Bataan* (DD) provide support for a daring raid carried out by guerrillas on the enemy mainland at Haeju.

AIR WAR: First Marine Aircraft Wing is informed that restrictions against close air support in their area have been lifted.

PARTISANS: A highly successful raid is conducted by guerrillas on the enemy mainland in the Haeju area. It is supported by an air strike from HMS *Ocean* (CVL) and gunfire from HMAS *Bataan* (DD). Friendly forces kill or wound 150 enemy troops, destroy numerous houses, and capture a significant amount of supplies.

May 20

POLITICAL/ADMINISTRATIVE: Vice Admiral J. J. Clark replaces Vice Admiral R. P. Briscoe as Commander Seventh Fleet (TE-70).

SEA WAR: USS *Douglas H. Fox* (DD 779) receives fire near Kosong from a 122-mm gun position, but there is no damage.

AIR WAR: Colonel Harrison R. Thyng, commander of the 4th FIW, downs his fifth MiG-15, becoming the 16th jet ace of the war. Cleve P. Malone, Robert L. Straub, and Coy L. Austin of the 335th FIS each shoot down an enemy MiG-15 fighter. An F-86 is shot down near Deeguandong by enemy fighters.

May 21

SEA WAR: The USS *Mount Baker* (AE 4) and the ROK navy's *Apnok* (PF 62) collide, seriously damaging the *Apnok* while killing 25 and injuring 21.

PARTISANS: Donkey 15 returns in force to Taehwa-do and Sohwa-do with improved radio communications that allows contact with both the navy and the air force.

May 22

POLITICAL/ADMINISTRATIVE: Major General William K. Harrison succeeds Admiral C. Turner Joy as chief of the UN delegation at the peace talks; Brigadier General Frank C. McConnell joins the delegation.

SEA WAR: The USS *Bataan* (CVL 29) suffers considerable damage and four are wounded when a rocket caught in a tube explodes.

AIR WAR: Planes of the Fifth Air Force fly 472 fighter-bomber sorties against the industrial complex at Kijang-ni. During the attack, they are able to destroy about 90 percent of an area that had previously produced hand grenades, small arms, and ammunition.

PARTISANS: Guerrillas, supported by USS *Douglas H. Fox* (DD 779), land at Ch'ilbore north of Kojo.

May 23

SEA WAR: The HMCS *Athabaskan* (DD) and air patrols from USS *Bataan* (CVL 29) search the area of Taedong Man for enemy craft but none are found. The USS *Walton* (DE 361), with a raiding party, takes fire on her whaleboat but no damage is done. Shore batteries at Kosong fire on USS *Douglas H. Fox* (DD 779), but it is not hit.

AIR WAR: For the second day, planes of the Fifth Air Force fly missions against the complex at Kijang-ni, this time against the steel mills. Some 375 fighter-bombers destroy more than 80 percent of the target. A downed USMC Ad-2 pilot is rescued by an H-19 helicopter of the 3rd ARS, primarily by using instruments to fly despite the bad weather.

May 23–24

AIR WAR: B-26s return to Kijang-ni in order to seed the area with delayed-action bombs, designed to prevent the North Koreans from rebuilding.

May 24

POLITICAL/ADMINISTRATIVE: The government of the Republic of Korea declares martial law in Pusan, Korea. ROK military police arrest four members of the Korean National Assembly.

SEA WAR: USS *Douglas H. Fox* (DD 779) is fired on by 75-mm and 155-mm guns north of Kojo. The *Douglas H. Fox* silences the battery with three direct hits. Raiders and guerrillas destroy another mile of the previously damaged fish nets.

May 25

POLITICAL/ADMINISTRATIVE: President Rhee expands the declaration of martial law beyond Pusan to include 22 neighboring counties and also places Major General Won Yong duk in charge of the operation. In doing so, he bypasses the military chain of command. There is little doubt that Rhee is using martial law in order to control his political enemies; there is little that can be done about it. Rear Admiral John Perry on USS *Valley Forge* (CV 45) assumes command of Task Force 77.

EIGHTH ARMY: There is a raid on Agok. Nine tanks of the 245th Tank Battalion, 45th Infantry, retaliate for three Communist raids on the division sector.

SEA WAR: North Korean army units, using sail junks for transportation, occupy Yontgwi-do. A raiding party from USS *Douglas H. Fox* (DD 779) destroys 1,000 feet of net in an operation north of Kojo. Fast Carrier Task Force 77 launches 233 sorties in coordination with naval fire from USS *Iowa* (BB 61 and three destroyers. USS *Swallow* (AMS 36), as it conducts a sweep in Songjin harbor, is fired on by 75-mm and 40-mm shore batteries. The USS *Murrelet* (AM 372) comes to her assistance. The *Murrelet* is hit twice and the *Swallow* three times. Both ships return fire and neither is seriously damaged, nor are there any casualties.

AIR WAR: The guerrilla raid near Pongyang-ni is supported by aircraft from HMS *Belfast* (CL), HMS *Whitesand Bay* (PF), *LST 1089*, and USS *Bataan* (CVL 29). Reports indicate that 300 of the enemy are killed and four taken prisoner. James H. Kasler and John H. Moore of the 335th FIS and Frederick C. Blesse and Elbert W. Whitehurst of the 334th FIS each shoot down an enemy MiG-15.

PARTISANS: Guerrilla forces carry out a raid against the Korean west coast near Pongyang-ni.

May 26

POLITICAL/ADMINISTRATIVE: Rear Admiral A. Soucek joins USS *Boxer* (CV 21), relinquishing command of Task Force 77.

SEA WAR: The USS *Endicott* (DMS 35) on Yang-do defense patrol, raids fishing activities and captures four sampans and prisoners. The HMS *Constance* (DD) captures seven prisoners and destroys two sail-junks while on Yalu Gulf patrol.

AIR WAR: The first Globemaster arrives, as the 315th AD converts from C-54 to C-124 aircraft.

PARTISANS: Guerrillas make sampan landings near Kojo, with USS *Douglas H. Fox* (DD 779) as fire support and using *YMS 504* as a troop carrier. The unit encounters enemy opposition inland and withdraws with no casualties.

May 26–27

AIR WAR: Overnight 10 B-29s attack Sinhung-dong and destroy a part of the bridge. The planes from the 19th Bomber Group also take out one locomotive, 16 rail cars, more than 400 feet of the rail line, and 350 linear feet of the approaches.

May 27

SEA WAR: USS *Douglas H. Fox* (DD 779) trades fire with shore batteries at Suwon. There is no damage or casualties when shore batteries at Wonsan open up on USS *Cabildo* (LSD 16) and USS *Ozbourn* (DD 846).

AIR WAR: Donald E. Adams of the 16th FIS shoots down an enemy MiG-15.

May 28

POLITICAL/ADMINISTRATIVE: The UN negotiating team presents its final terms and threatens to break off discussions if they are rejected. Brigadier General Lee Han Lim (ROK) is added as a delegate to the cease-fire negotiations, and Major General Yu Jai Hyung (ROK) is relieved.

EIGHTH ARMY: A patrol from the 179th Infantry Regiment, 45th Infantry Division, is attacked by two Chinese companies. Private First Class John D. Kelly, Charlie Company, 7th Marine Regiment, 1st Marine Division, becomes the 100th Medal of Honor winner in Korea after leading his men through intense enemy fire to advance his unit. Corporal David B. Champagne, Able Company, 7th Marines, 1st Marine Division, receives the Medal of Honor for saving the lives of his companions at the cost of his own.

SEA WAR: Two North Korean army employees surrender to USS *Ozbourn* (DD 846) at Wonsan harbor. Shore batteries in the harbor fire on USS *Lofberg* (DD 759), USS *O'Bannon* (DDE 450), and USS *Condor* (AMS 5), but they escape damage or casualties. On the Yalu patrol, HMS *Constance* (DD) destroys two sail-junks and takes 11 prisoners.

AIR WAR: VP Squadron 1 under Commander W. M. Ringness enters its third tour of sea service in Korea. Robert C. Ochs of the 25th FIS shoots down an enemy fighter. Elmer W. Harris, also from the 25th FIS, destroys two MiG-15s.

May 29

EIGHTH ARMY: Private First Class Whitt L. Moreland, Charlie Company, 1st Battalion, 5th Marines, earns the Medal of Honor when he covers an exploding grenade with his body in order to save his comrades.

Sea War: One hundred and fifty North Korean army personnel, sailing in eight junks, occupy Yongwi-do. The USS *Fletcher* (DDE 445) picks up two North Koreans who are surrendering south of Hungnam. The USS *Murrelet* (AM 372) is fired on while it rescues a downed pilot. There is no damage. Sweeping the extended area between Hungnam and Mayang-do, USS *Firecrest* (AMS 18) and USS *Murrelet* (AM 372) receive fire. No damage is received. The USS *Radford* (DDE 446) returns fire and silences the guns. The USS *O'Bannon* (DD 450) silences the shore batteries that are firing on friendly islands in Wonsan harbor. Captain Warren E. Gladding takes command of the Wonsan blockade as the "mayor." The helicopter rescue ship, LST 799, rescues Ensign Glen M. Wicker (USN) of the USS *Philippine Sea* (CV 47).

May 30

Political/Administrative: Lieutenant General Glenn O. Barcus replaces General Frank Everest as commander, Fifth Air Force.

Sea War: At Wonsan harbor the USS *Ozbourn* (DD 846), USS *Radford* (DDE 446), and USS *Heron* (AMS 18) are fired on by shore batteries. The *Heron* returns fire; there are no casualties. The Colombian PF *Capital Too* silences shore guns and destroys one sampan.

Air War: VP Squadron 28 (Detachment A), under Commander C. B. McAfee, enters land-based service in Korea.

May 31

Political/Administrative: Rear Admiral John E. Gingrich relieves Rear Admiral George C. Dyer as commander, United Nations Blockading and Escort Force.

Sea War: The HMCS *Nootka* (DD), USS *John W. Thompson* (DD 760), and USS *Endicott* (DMS 35) receive fire while patrolling east of Chuuronjang but there is no damage. The HMS *Constance* (DD) captures a junk while on Yalu Gulf patrol. At Hongwan Roads, USS *Murrelet's* (AM 372) armed whaleboat captures an enemy sampan, but the enemy starts firing and throwing grenades. One man from *Murrelet* is killed and two wounded, but all 10 of the enemy are killed. The USS *Fletcher* (DDE 445) is grounded in the area of Yangdo and damages its propellers, rudder, and sonar dome.

Air War: VP Squadron 22, under Commander W. Godwin, ends its second tour of land-based service in Korea. An F-51 is shot down by enemy fighters at Kijio. Francis J. Vetort and William K. Thomas of the 335th are each credited with shooting down a MiG-15 fighter.

June 1

Political/Administrative: Commander Charles B. Langston relieves Commander Michael J. Luosey as commander of the Republic of Korea Naval Forces.

Sea War: HMS *Constance* (DD) captures her fourth enemy junk during her Yalu Gulf patrol, taking several prisoners, including some Chinese. The HMS *Amethyst* (PE) supports a guerrilla landing opposite Kyodong-do, but the operation has to be canceled because of heavy opposition. The HMCS *Nootka* (DD) receives minor damage and USS *John W. Thomason* (DD 760) escapes injury when fired on in patchy fog near the Songjin-Chongjin area. The USS *Firecrest* (AMS 18) is fired on north of Hungnam, but USS *Radford* (DDE 446) comes in and silences the battery. No damage is reported.

AIR WAR: VP Squadron 731 (Reserve) under Commander W. T. O' Dowd enters its second tour of sea-based duty in Korea.

PARTISANS: Wolfpack 8 conducts an inland reconnaissance and finds several enemy concentrations. It calls in air strikes with good results. Wolfpack is able to withdraw successfully on June 4, 1952. The island of Yongi-do will change hands several times.

June 2

POLITICAL/ADMINISTRATIVE: U.S. Supreme Court declares President Harry Truman's seizure of the steel mills is unconstitutional.

EIGHTH ARMY: A squad from Baker Company, 1st Marines, fights a 30-minute engagement against Chinese troops near Outpost Warsaw. The enemy finally withdraws, leaving behind nine dead.

AIR WAR: VP Squadron 42, under Commander J. L. Skinner, ends its second tour of sea-based duty in Korea.

June 3

SEA WAR: The USS *Redhead* (AMS 34) strikes something in the water near Yo-do and is badly damaged. The USS *Radford* (DDE 446) silences batteries firing on USS *Heron* (AMS 18) and USS *Firecrest* (AMS 10) near Hongwon.

AIR WAR: New consideration is being given to directing attacks on North Korean electric power targets.

June 4

POLITICAL/ADMINISTRATIVE: Syngman Rhee purges the South Korean Assembly. The United States and Great Britain protest the action. Vice Admiral R. P. Briscoe relieves Vice Admiral C. T. Joy as commander, Naval Forces Far East.

AIR WAR: A downed British pilot is rescued by an H-19 helicopter belonging to the 3rd ARS. The helicopter is fired on by automatic weapons during the rescue but escapes without any damage.

June 4–5

SEA WAR: In Operation Insomnia, night heckler groups fire on coastal routes from midnight to daylight. The bombardment results in the destruction of four locomotives.

June 5

SEA WAR: The ROK navy's *AMC 301* avoids damage when fired on near Wollae-do. At Wonsan, batteries firing on UN minesweepers are silenced by the guns of USS *O'Bannon* (DDE 450), USS *Lofberg* (DD 759), and USS *Radford* (DDE 446).

AIR WAR: A B-26 is shot down by enemy fighters.

June 6

Political/Administrative: Authorization is given to begin hitting power plants inside North Korea. This is a radical change in policy.

Eighth Army: As a part of an operation called Counter, several air strikes are delivered in the areas surrounding Old Baldy; after dark, the 279th Regiment under Colonel Preston J. C. Murphy and the 180th Regiment under Lieutenant Colonel Ellis B. Ritchie send out probing units that encounter little resistance other than at Outpost 10 on Hill 255 (Pork Chop Hill) and Outpost 11 on Hill 266 (Old Baldy). Hill 255 is taken after a 55-minute fight led by Item Company, 180th Infantry. On Old Baldy two squads from Able Company, 180th Infantry, exchange small-arms fire and then withdraw. In a second attack, Able Company is able to take the crest of Old Baldy.

Sea War: Eight North Korean prisoners voluntarily surrender to USS *Symbol* (AM 123).

Air War: UN Sabres from the Fifth Air Force engage and destroy eight MiG-15 fighters. Credited with the kills are James F. Low and Felix Asla, Jr., of the 336th FIS, Robert F. Fonca and John H. Moore of the 335th FIS, Paul R. Henderson and Ramon L. Koenig of the 25th FIS, Fred H. Barrett of the 16th FIS, and Jere J. Lewis of the 334th FIS.

June 6–14

Eighth Army: Operation Counter is launched by the 45th Infantry Division. This is a two-phased series of attacks to establish a set of patrol bases in the area of Old Baldy. Second and 3rd Battalions, 180th Infantry, fighting for Outpost Eerie on Hill 191, are counterattacked by two Chinese battalions.

June 7

Political/Administrative: General Mark Clark orders Major General William Harrison to break off the peace talks without advance warning. He simply tells General Nam Il, the Communist chief delegate, that they are not coming back until June 11.

Sea War: One sampan is destroyed and three fishermen are captured by HMCS *Nootka* (DD).

Air War: In Operation Hightide, 35 F-84 Thunderjets leave Japan, are refueled by KB-29Ms over Korea, and then go on to attack their assigned targets. John W. Andre (USMC) of Marine Squadron VMF (N-513) shoots down an enemy YAK-9.

June 8

Political/Administrative: Preparations are made to separate the prisoners at Koje-do into separate mini-camps of no more than 500 prisoners each. The 187th Airborne, which has come in from Japan for the purpose, will enforce the division.

Air War: An F4U engages and probably destroys a YAK-9 near Sariwon.

June 9

Political/Administrative: When word gets to the prisoners at the POW camp on Koje-do that General Boatner plans to move and separate them, the prisoners in Compound 76 set up pickets in an effort to prevent the action from being taken.

SEA WAR: The USS *Condor* (AMS 5), sweeping south of Hodo Pando and west of Suido, is fired on nine times by 76-mm artillery piece. No hits are recorded. The need for an emergency air strip on the island of Yo-do, in the Wonsan approach, leads to the transport of 78 men of Amphibious Construction Battalion One to begin construction. The unit is supported by LST *692*. The helicopter rescue ship, *LST 799*, is able to rescue Ensign F. Lofton (USN), from USS *Princeton*, at Wonsan harbor.

AIR WAR: A UN pilot is picked up by an H-19 helicopter of the 3rd ARS. The helicopter encounters small-arms fire during the rescue. Two night heckler flights destroy a locomotive and three cars south of Songjin, and a fully loaded train in the marshaling yards at Kilchu.

PARTISANS: Group Kirkland mounts a raid on railway tunnels north of Kojo. The guerrilla garrison at Mudo Island repels an attack by enemy troops who arrive on a sail junk. They report they have destroyed four of seven junks. The guerrilla unit suffers two wounded.

June 10–11

AIR WAR: The rail bridge at Kwaksan, North Korea, is attacked by eight B-29s from the 19th Bomber Group. MiG-15 fighters, apparently operating in conjunction with radar-controlled searchlights, manage to destroy two B-29s and damage a third. The action prompts FEAF to consider means to improve its electronic countermeasures (ECM) to jam enemy radar.

June 10

EIGHTH ARMY: The Eighth Army commander directs his subordinate commands to make every effort, including reconnaissance and the capture of prisoners, to identify the enemy units that are facing them, in order to strengthen Line Jamestown. At the Koje-do POW camp, General Boatner, the camp commander, and General Grapnell, the 187th Airborne Regiment commander, stand on a hill watching as, at 0615, paratroops armed with bayonets but no ammunition tear down the wire and entered Compound 76. The Koreans quickly fall back to prepared defensive positions. About 150 of them have weapons they have made, and they start to use them. Pushed, they take protection in a trench they have built. When some of the Korean soldiers try to surrender, they are killed by the men behind them. Then the engagement turns into a battle. When it is over, 43 POWs have been killed and 135 wounded (many by their own officers); 6,500 hard-core Communists are divided into groups of 500 and placed behind new wire. General Boatner controls the compound.

SEA WAR: The USS *Endicott* (DMS 35) and USS *Thomason* (DD 760) silence batteries on the eastern peninsula of Songjin (Kimchaek) harbor after they fire on USS *Evansville* (PF 70). HMS *Constance* (DD) runs aground at Yangdo, causing damage to both screws. The LST 799, a helicopter rescue ship, pulls Ensign R. N. Hensen, from USS *Princeton* (CV 37), out of the harbor at Wonsan, and also Lieutenant Commander Cook Cleland (USNR), who flies from USS *Valley Forge* (CV 45).

AIR WAR: Using radar-controlled lights, enemy MiG-15s destroy two B-29s of the eight engaged in raiding the rail bridge at Kwaksan.

June 10–12

EIGHTH ARMY: The last major riot occurs at the POW compound at Koje-do. Under Brigadier General Boatner, the new commander, crack UN paratroops, supported by six Patton tanks, bring an end to the uprising.

June 11

POLITICAL/ADMINISTRATIVE: Rear Admiral John Perry, on USS *Valley Forge* (CV 45), relinquishes command of Task Force 77. Rear Admiral A. Soucek, on USS *Boxer* (CV 21), assumes command of Task Force 77.

SEA WAR: The USS *Buck* (DD 761) embarks a reconnaissance party from a motor whale boat in the Kojo area. A sampan with six enemy sailors surrenders to the *Buck*. The USS *Duncan* (DDE 874) disembarks a reconnaissance party in a motor whale boat to inspect the shoreline. In the process, they chase three sampans and draw rifle fire. The boat returns with no damage.

AIR WAR: Albert B. Smiley of the 335th FIS shoots down a MiG-15 fighter. James F. Low of the 336th FIS is credited with downing two MiG-15s.

June 12

EIGHTH ARMY: The second phase of Operation Counter gets under way with two platoons of the 245th Tank Battalion launching a diversionary attack along the Yokkok-chon Valley westward from Chutoso to the town of Orijong. In a coordinated attack, King Company, 180th Infantry Regiment, moves north to the Pokkae area and engages the Chinese. The enemy is too well dug in, and King Company returns to the MLR. After an air strike by fighter planes from the Fifth Air Force, compounded by artillery and mortar fire, Easy and Fox Companies of the 180th attack Outpost Eerie. George Company follows as they take the objective. The Chinese respond with a series of counterattacks, but for the next two days, the men of the 180th hold on. Fox Company of the 2nd Battalion, 1st Marines, sets off to raid Ungok. The 3rd Battalion is scheduled to take the lead. After leaving the MLR a marine steps on a mine, harming himself and warning the enemy they are coming. Part of the way up the hill, they are attacked by a Chinese platoon that slows them down. Under protection of the fire base, they manage to make it to the top of the hill, take the prisoner they are after, and return to the MLR. Shortly after, a tank-infantry team sets out to find eight men who have been left behind. Three men are determined to be dead; the rest are not found.

SEA WAR: One sailor is wounded when USS *Albuquerque* (PF 7) takes fire from the southeastern shore of Wonsan harbor.

June 12–16

EIGHTH ARMY: UN forces attack Hill 190.8 with nearly seven companies, tanks, and air cover. The United Nations quickly takes the hill, but by 2200, the Chinese counterattack. In the heavy fighting that follows the Chinese retake the hill. At dawn on the 13th, the UN counterattacks and takes and holds the hill briefly. Then on the night of June 15, the Chinese take it back. By June 16, the Chinese hold it.

June 13

POLITICAL/ADMINISTRATIVE: When POW issues become bogged down again, General Mark Clark decides the time is ripe for the release of civilian internees. He receives permission from the JCS and President Truman and begins the release.

SEA WAR: Using a 50-foot motor launch, men from USS *Buck* (DD 761) and accompanying guerrillas, while still 500 yards from Kojo, are hit with heavy enemy automatic weapons fire. Two in the launch are wounded. The *Buck* delivers a counter-fire that silences the automatic weapons.

AIR WAR: Air Task Group One, commanded by Commander C. H. Crabill, Jr., ends its tour aboard USS *Valley Forge* (CV 45).

June 14

EIGHTH ARMY: The 45th Infantry Division occupies all objectives set for it in Operation Counter. Army engineers and their equipment are sent to sites selected for new POW camps in order to further separate the prisoners remaining at Koje-do. Sergeant David B. Bleak, Medical Company, 223rd Regiment, 40th Infantry Division, receives the Medal of Honor for courage in the support of his companions. Corporal Clifton T. Speicher of Fox Company, 2nd Battalion, 223rd Infantry Regiment, 40th U.S. Infantry Division, receives the Medal of Honor for giving his life in support of his companions.

SEA WAR: USS *Skagit* (AKA 105), LSMR *226,* and units of Task Force 90 transport army engineers and their equipment to sites selected for new POW compounds.

AIR WAR: Fifth Air Force fighter/bombers hit the runways at the Pyongyang Airfield with 150 sorties, making them unserviceable. The attack is ordered after reconnaissance flights indicate that the field is repaired and ready for use. There are no UN losses.

June 15

SEA WAR: One man is wounded in a guerrilla raid in the Tokhyon-san area. After landing from HMCS *Athabaskan* (DDE) and ROK navy's *AMC 301,* the group advances under aerial strafing and naval fire. Two junks loaded with fuel and secret documents are captured.

AIR WAR: Second Lieutenant James F. Low of the 336th FIS becomes an ace after downing his fifth MiG-15. Stephen A. Stone of the 334th FIS and Francis A. Williams of the 25th FIS also each get an enemy fighter.

June 16

EIGHTH ARMY: The Chinese launch a series of attacks against Outpost Snook, Pork Chop, and Old Baldy that are directed toward the 45th Division's 179th Infantry Regiment. The attacks last 10 days and cause significant casualties. The 179th Infantry Regiment relieves the 180th on the line and takes over the defense of outpost locations on Eerie, Old Baldy and Pork Chop.

SEA WAR: Fast Carrier Task Force 77 shifts from rail interdiction strikes to scheduling maximum air strikes using the entire air group to destroy key rail and transportation centers. USS *Essex* (CV 9) begins her second tour of duty with Task Force 77. AA bursts that are observed indicate the "windshield" defensive effort had been effective.

AIR WAR: Off the coast of Hungnam and with a radar countermeasure, Task Force 77's planes drop signal disrupting "Rope" at 14,000 feet with a spread of 13 miles.

June 17

SEA WAR: Planes from Task Force 77 strafe batteries that have fired on USS *Shoveler* (AS4 382) while the guns of USS *Duncan* (DD 874) also suppress fire from those batteries.

June 18

POLITICAL/ADMINISTRATIVE: All restrictions on attacking electrical power installations in North Korea are removed.

SEA WAR: Shore batteries at Mayang-do fire on USS *Firecrest* (AM 10), but the ship escapes without damage as USS *Duncan* (DD 874) silences the batteries. A helicopter rescue ship, the *LST 799*, rescues Lieutenant (j.g.) A. Zimmerly (USN), who flies off *USS Boxer* (CV 21).

June 19

SEA WAR: The HMS *Amethyst* (PF) provides fire support for a guerrilla raid near Haeju, killing 27 North Koreans in addition to 14 killed by guerrillas. Meanwhile, USS *Mockingbird* (AMS 27) and USS *Heron* (AMS 18) are fired on at Mayang-do while trying to rescue a downed pilot. Supported by USS *Rowan* (DD 782), the sweepers manage the pickup and escape. Hwangto-do is fired on by enemy shore batteries.

PARTISANS: Leopard launches an American-led reconnaissance in force across the channel from Cho-do but finds few enemy forces in the area.

June 19–20

AIR WAR: Overnight B-29s fly 35 sorties against targets in North Korea. Twenty-seven medium bombers attack the Huichon rail bridge.

June 20

POLITICAL/ADMINISTRATIVE: This is the date set by the Communist POWs to stage a massive breakout from the camps. Plans for the escape were found at Compound 76 when General Boatner had it cleared of the hard-core prisoners.

SEA WAR: The days of amphibious raids begin, designed to gain intelligence and cause destruction. Landing ROK troops at night, USS *Horace A. Bass* (APD 124) hits selected targets along the northeast coast of Korea. The operation will last until June 23. The USS *Bayonne* (PF 21) destroys 17 sampans in the area of Hungnam before taking fire from the mainland. The HMS *Cardigan Bay* (PF) returns fire from Wolsa-re directed at Sok-to. The USS *Shoveler* (AM 382) is fired on from Chojcho-do. The USS *Duncan* (DD 874) hits back with counterfire that silences the guns. *ROKN PT* reports that it received 30 rounds of gunfire from Hongwon and then from Mayang-do. No casualties are reported for either occasion.

AIR WAR: Aircraft from Task Force 77 drop 500,000 leaflets (in Korean) from Chongjin to Songjin, warning civilians that unexploded bombs are on the ground. The hope is to impede a rapid repair of the rails, which the North Koreans are capable of accomplishing. Royal N. Baker and George J. Woods, both of the 336th FIS, each are credited with shooting down a MiG-15. From the 334th FIS, Frederick C. Blesse also shoots down a MiG-15.

June 21

AIR WAR: An F-86 is shot down by enemy fighters. Asa S. Whitehead of the 25th FIS is credited with destroying a MiG-15 fighter, and D. A. McClean and W. D. Angle of the 336th FIS share credit for another.

June 22

POLITICAL/ADMINISTRATIVE: General Mark Clark issues a press release explaining the reasons for Operation Homecoming, the release of civilian internees who had been held as POWs.

EIGHTH ARMY: The 2nd Battalion of the 279th Infantry Regiment sets out to capture prisoners on the north bank of the Yokkok-chon.

SEA WAR: HMS *Amethyst* (PF), ROK *PC 701*, and ROK *AMC 310* take fire from Mundo. The *Amethyst* fires air bursts, scoring many hits. Commander of the United Nations Blockading and Escort Force orders ships into shelter as Typhoon Dinah approaches; Condition I is set at Sasebo. No damage occurs, however.

AIR WAR: Air Group Seven, under Commander G. B. Brown, begins its tour onboard USS *Bon Homme Richard* (CV 31).

June 22–24

SEA WAR: To avoid destruction from Typhoon Dinah, UN ships in Korean waters take evasive action.

June 23

POLITICAL/ADMINISTRATIVE: Brigadier General Joseph T. Morris (USAF) is added to the delegation list at Panmunjom, and Rear Admiral R. E. Libby (USN) is recalled.

SEA WAR: Four carriers, USS *Philippine Sea* (CV 47), USS *Princeton* (CV 37), USS *Boxer* (CV 21), and USS *Bon Homme Richard* (CV 31) launch a total of 290 aircraft that, united with air force planes, attack the Communist hydroelectric plant at Suiho on the Yalu River. All nine plants in the Fusen area are hit. This is the first time the enemy power plants have been targeted. Forty Skyraiders and Corsairs attack the hydroelectric plant at Chosen. Thirty-eight F9F-2s from Marine Air Group 33 hit a second plant at Chosen, destroying it.

AIR WAR: Three days of air attacks begin on the Suiho hydroelectric plant in an effort to get the Chinese to bargain at the armistice table. The plant is on the Yalu River a little more than 30 miles from Sinuiju. The dam is too strong to break, but the power plants that lie on the Korean side of the river are vulnerable to conventional bombing. The raids are successful but fail to alter the situation at Panmunjom. The British protest the bombing.

June 24

EIGHTH ARMY: The Chinese probe and cut off elements of the 5th Marines who hold Outpost Yoke. The enemy manages to overrun the position but they cannot take it. After a UN artillery bombardment, the enemy withdraws and the marines return.

SEA WAR: USS *Philippine Sea* (CV 47), USS *Boxer* (CV 21), USS *Princeton* (CV 37), and USS *Bon Homme Richard* (CV 31) send planes against the hydroelectric plants in a continued effort. All transformer stations in Hwanghae Province at the installations at Yuchon, Haeju, Chaeryong, and Kaishu are destroyed. Commander Nels C. Johnson takes over command as "mayor" of the Wonsan blockade, replacing Commander Robert M. Hinckley.

June 24–25

AIR WAR: The Samdong-ni rail complex, which is the choke point of the east-west and north-south rail lines in North Korea, is rendered unserviceable after it is hit by 26 B-26s. Night-flying B-26s will later seed the area with delayed action bombs to hamper repair efforts.

June 25

POLITICAL/ADMINISTRATIVE: A possible assassination attempt is made on Syngman Rhee, when, at a ceremony marking the second anniversary of the Korean War, a gunman fires twice at point-blank range. The gun misfires both times. Many authorities believe it is a "staged" event designed to bolster public sympathy for Rhee. The Joint Chiefs of Staff authorizes General Mark Clark to develop Operation Everready, a plan for the removal of Syngman Rhee by military force if necessary.

SEA WAR: The four carriers from Fast Carrier Task Force 77—USS *Philippine Sea* (CV 47), USS *Boxer* (CV 21), USS *Princeton* (CV 37), and USS *Bon Homme Richard* (CV 31)—continue to strike targets in the vicinity of Wonsan.

AIR WAR: Some 1,043 sorties are flown by fighter bombers of the Fifth Air Force against North Korean hydroelectric power plants. By the 27th, it is estimated that 90 percent of North Korea's power supply has been destroyed. John R. Spanding of the 25th FIS destroys an enemy MiG-15 fighter.

PARTISANS: A partisan unit establishes a base in the Diamond Mountains area south of Wonsan. Unit Kirkland lands "Daniel Boone" partisan group on the east coast.

June 26

POLITICAL/ADMINISTRATIVE: At the cease-fire talks, General Harrison suggests that the staff continue to work but calls for a recess until August 3. The Communists object, but they are informed that the UN delegates will not be back for a week.

EIGHTH ARMY: The fight for Old Baldy begins again (and will continue until March 1953). The Chinese have created a position that poses a threat to Old Baldy, and it is decided to destroy the Communist concentration. The 179th Regiment is pulled off Old Baldy to allow for air strikes and artillery barrages around the whole area. Old Baldy (Hill 266) lies west of Chorwon and was selected as one of the primary outposts in front of the U.S. 45th Division line. Earlier, the 179th Infantry Regiment relieved the 180th and took over defense of the post. Using Fox and Charlie Companies, they engage the enemy forces and, after a fight lasting about an hour, the Chinese pull back. The Chinese then counterattack but gradually the enemy forces begin to withdraw.

SEA WAR: The ROK navy's *AMS 503* provides support for a guerrilla raiding party near Sasa-ri. The reported loss is 100 North Koreans killed and five men taken prisoner. There are no friendly casualties.

June 27

EIGHTH ARMY: At 2200, the Chinese strike Love Company on Old Baldy but are repulsed, withdraw, and regroup.

SEA WAR: USS *McCoy Reynolds* (DE 440) moves in to take a sampan near Mayang-do when the ship comes under fire from machine guns located at the village of Konjap'o.

June 28

EIGHTH ARMY: The Chinese launch three more attacks on Old Baldy and each time they are held off. After suffering an estimated 320 casualties, the Chinese withdraw. Then, late in the evening, enemy artillery announces another attack. This time the enemy penetrates the perimeter.

June 29

POLITICAL/ADMINISTRATIVE: Major General Paul W. Kendall takes command of I Corps, relieving Lieutenant General O'Daniels.

EIGHTH ARMY: After fighting all night the Chinese disengage at about 0100 and move to the north.

SEA WAR: An overnight guerrilla raid, supported by HMS *Ceylon* (CL), HMS *Comus* (DD), and HMS *Amethyst* (PF), returns in the morning with two prisoners.

AIR WAR: VP Squadron 9 under Commander J. B. Filson begins its tour of land-based service in Korea.

July–August

POLITICAL/ADMINISTRATIVE: During these months, the United Nations releases approximately 27,000 civilian internees. The ROK provides transportation for a return to their homes.

July 1

POLITICAL/ADMINISTRATIVE: Operation Homecoming begins with the release of 27,000 civilian internees. The process will continue until the end of August 1952.

SEA WAR: The USS *Albuquerque* (PFT) and USS *Perkins* (DD 877) exchange fire with shore batteries in the Kojo area. More than 100 rounds are fired with no damage to either ship.

July 2

EIGHTH ARMY: The 1st Royal Australian Regiment raids Hill 227, held by the Chinese, during Operation Blaze. Elements of the 7th Marines move forward against the Chinese-held Hill 159, but after inflicting more than 200 casualties, the marines are forced to withdraw.

Sea War: USS *Perkins* (DD 887) silences shore batteries near Nan-do after receiving some 75 incoming rounds without damage.

July 2–3

Eighth Army: A George Company patrol becomes involved in one of the most violent small action engagements of the war. As it moves toward its objective at Outpost Yoke, it is hit and the patrol has to withdraw without prisoners. Able Company, 1st Battalion 5th Marines, is assigned to attack three outposts near the village of Samichon. After taking the first two objectives without firing, the unit is ordered to withdraw.

July 3

Eighth Army: Chinese forces attack the 179th Infantry Regiment on Old Baldy, but without success.

Sea War: The USS *Currier* (DE 700) silences guns that are firing at USS *Current* (ARS 22) in the headland between Wonsan and Hungnam. The USS *Symbol* (AM 123) supplies a smokescreen for the two ships. Some 350 friendly guerrillas carry out a successful raid on Mundo Island. The USS *Bausell* (DD 845) suffers boiler damage. Commander Robert M. Hinckley takes over command as "mayor" of the Wonsan blockade, replacing Commander Nels C. Johnson. USS *Valley Forge* (CV 45) ends her second tour of duty with Task Force 77. Approximately 70,000 difficult POWs are transferred from Koje-do to new prison camps on other islands. The operation is carried out by Task Force 90 amphibious vessels.

Air War: Aircraft from Task Force 77 attack the power plants at Fusen and Kuryong. In 13 sorties over enemy territory, C-47s drop more than 22,000,000 propaganda leaflets. General McCarty, 315th AD commander, flies the 374th's first C-124 Globemaster from Japan to Korea. An RB-29 is shot down by enemy fighters near Anju.

Partisans: Three hundred and fifty guerrillas carry out a successful raid north of Mundo Island, supported by HMS *Comus* (PC 703).

July 4

Eighth Army: During Operation Firecracker, a concentrated TOT (Time on Target) exercise engages the 11th Marine Battalion plus its 4.5-inch rocket battery to destroy bunkers and trenches.

Air War: Fifty-three MiG-15s attack 50 F-86s and 70 F-84s as they raid the North Korean Military Academy at Sakchu, near the Yalu. Two Sabres are lost and 13 MiG-15s. Credit for this destruction is given to Royal N. Baker and Gerald E. Lyvere of the 336th FIS; James A. Horowitz, James F. Low, Carroll B. McElroy, Lewis W. Powers, and Clifford D. Jolley from the 335th FIS; Francis A. Williams and Sabin L. Anderson of the 25th FIS; Francis A. Humpreys and Frank O. Keller of the 39th FIS; Raymond W. Staudte of the 51st FIW; and from the 16th FIS, Alvin R. Moorman. None of the bombers they were escorting were lost. It is reported that Soviet pilots were involved. VP Squadron 871 (Reserve) under Commander F. H. Holt ends its tour of land-based service in the Korean War.

July 5

Political/Administrative: Brigadier General Joseph T. Morris (USAF) is added to the armistice delegation, and Major General Howard M. Turner (USAF) is reassigned.

SEA WAR: The USS *Orleck* (DD 886) and USS *Doyle* (DMS 34) are caught turning, while firing on Chuuronjang in Korea's far northeast, and receive heavy fire from 75-mm and 155-mm guns on shore. One person is injured; counterfire silences one gun. The USS *Symbol* (AM 123) avoids damage while being fired on by shore batteries at Song-do Gap.

July 6

POLITICAL/ADMINISTRATIVE: Rear Admiral A. Soucek, on USS *Boxer* (CV 21), relinquishes command of Task Force 77. Rear Admiral H. E. Regan, onboard USS *Bon Homme Richard* (CV 31), assumes command of Task Force 77.

EIGHTH ARMY: Two companies of 7th Regiment Marines try again to take Hill 159 (Yoke) and by 0200 the following morning are successful. Then, realizing they are over-extended, they withdraw.

SEA WAR: The USS *Philippine Sea* (CVA-47) completes her second tour of duty in Korea. The USS *Zeal* (AM 131) avoids eight rounds fired by shore batteries near Mayang-do. The USS *Kimberly* (DD 52), HMS *Mounts Bay* (PF), and the ROK's *LSSL 107* support guerrillas who carry out an infiltration near Chinnampo. During the night, USS *Symbol* (AM 123), near Hungnam, is fired on; eight rounds come close, but there is no damage.

July 7

POLITICAL/ADMINISTRATIVE: The Communist delegates at the cease-fire talks once more demand the repatriation of all foreign troops in accordance with the Geneva Convention of 1949.

SEA WAR: Four men are washed overboard from USS *Arnold J. Isbell* (DD 869). Three of the men are recovered, but two of them are injured. Captain Allan A. Ovrom takes command as "mayor" of the Wonsan blockade, replacing Captain Warren E. Gladding. Limited supply reduces the allocation of smaller, general purpose bombs, causing an increased reliance on larger (500- and 2,000-pound) bombs and fragmentation ordnance.

PARTISANS: Kim Myong Ryon, who had been with the White Tiger group that was ambushed, returns with some of his men. They manage to escape and return to the base at Yong-do.

July 8

EIGHTH ARMY: In Operation Buckshot, the ROK I Corps sends a battalion into the sector west of the Nam River, looking for prisoners. During the patrol, the battalion suffers 33 killed, 157 wounded, 36 missing—and not a single prisoner taken.

Repairing a tank that has thrown a track, July 1952
(Center for the Study of the Korean War, Graceland University)

Sea War: Carrier planes report an increase in vehicle traffic moving to the north between Hungnam and Hongwon.

Air War: Air Group Eleven, under Commander J. W. Onstott, ends its tour onboard USS *Philippine Sea* (CV 47).

July 9

Sea War: While aircraft from HMS *Ocean* (CVL) hit a transformer station, HMAS *Warramunga* (DD) and USS *Kimberly* (DD 521) fire on coastal guns north of the Taedong River. The coordinated air-naval strike neutralizes many of the coastal AA positions. Captain James B. Grady takes command of the Wonsan blockade as "mayor," replacing Commander Robert M. Hinckley.

July 10

Political/Administrative: The truce talks, taking place at the village of Panmunjom, enter the second year of meetings.

Eighth Army: General Mark Clark establishes the Korean Communication Zone as a major command. In a retaliatory raid, the North Koreans attack a hill fortified by the ROK's 5th Division and hold it for more than four days, until they are forced to withdraw.

Sea War: The USS *Hollister* (DD 788) avoids being hit despite the 32 rounds fired at it from the island of Mayang-do.

Air War: Beginning on this date, and lasting for three weeks, the 315th AD airlifts the 474th FBW from Misawa Air Base in Japan to Kunsan Air Base in South Korea.

July 11

Sea War: The USS *Princeton* (CVA 37), USS *Bon Homme Richard* (CVA 31), and HMS *Ocean* (CVL) join with U.S. and Australian air forces in an attack on Pyongyang. The raid is conducted in adverse weather conditions but is deemed successful. Three North Koreans in a sampan surrender to USS *Hollister* (DD 788) near the island of Mayang-do. In the Haeju area, HMS *Comus* (DD) destroys mortar positions that had been firing on UN ships.

Air War: Massive air raids, consisting of 1,329 sorties, hit the capital city of Pyongyang as a part of Operation Pressure Pump. Nearly every active air unit in the Far East focuses on 30 targets in and around Pyongyang. Most targets sustain heavy damage. An RB-29 is shot down by enemy fighters near Finhuanchen.

July 12

Sea War: The USS *Perkins* (DD 877) is not hit despite seven rounds fired at her near Kosong. The USS *Juneau* (CLA 119) also receives seven rounds, near Sinpo. At Chaho, USS *Hollister* (DD 788) receives 104 rounds but is not hit; *Hollister* was landing a reconnaissance party near Hongwan at the time.

Air War: As a part of Operation Pressure Pump, B-29s fly 71 sorties, more than 50 against supply areas near Pyongyang. Elmer W. Harris from the 25th FIS destroys a MiG-15 fighter.

Unloading a tank from LST 883, at Wonsan, Korea, 1950
(Center for the Study of the Korean War, Graceland University)

July 13

POLITICAL/ADMINISTRATIVE: After discounting concessions by the Chinese and North Koreans, the United States makes what it claims is a final, unalterable offer. General Harrison informs the Communist delegation that revised tallies show that 76,000 Koreans and 6,400 Chinese prisoners want to be repatriated and suggests a new list be prepared.

SEA WAR: The USS *Hollister* (DD 788) while on an interdiction mission is fired at 108 times, from three guns believed to be in the vicinity of Sinchang. The *Hollister* returns fire on all three, scoring a hit on one and suppressing the others. The USS *Princeton* (CA 130) is on the receiving end of 16 rounds from an enemy shore battery as it sails in the area of Suwandan Lighthouse. There is no damage to the carrier.

AIR WAR: The Fifth Air Force begins dropping a new form of a leaflet, one that warns about attacks on specific targets. Air groups from USS *Princeton* (CVA 37) and USS *Bon Homme Richard* (CVA 31) fly Task Force 77's first close air support mission of the year. Success in earlier raids on power sources leads to an order to increase attacks on transformers and substations.

PARTISANS: Unit Donkey 4 launches a raid on an NKPA coastal gun emplacement. The raid is a success, but it costs the lives of six men and seven are wounded.

July 14

SEA WAR: The USS *Southerland* (DD 743) is hit four times, wounding eight men, when shore batteries in the Kojo area open fire. On the Korean west coast, HMS *Belfast,* HMS *Amethyst,* and USS *LST 883* support a guerrilla raid on the Changsangot peninsula. The HMS *Canadian Bay* is called to Undo when it is reported that North Korean troops are preparing to attack. She fires several air bursts but the raid, if planned, does not occur.

July 15

POLITICAL/ADMINISTRATIVE: Mao Zedong sends a telegram to Kim Il Sung, pointing out that to accept the enemy's offer, which represents no real concessions, would be very disadvantageous, politically and militarily, to the Sino-Korean position. He guarantees to provide all help possible to the continuing struggle.

SEA WAR: The first navy planes land on the new emergency landing strip on Hodo Island. The USS *Iowa* (BB 61), with the help of a helicopter spotter, destroys both batteries at Mayang-do. Earlier she had fired on USS *Hollister* (DD 788). The USS *Orleck* (DD 886) destroys 10 box cars and five flat cars caught between tunnels.

AIR WAR: The cement plant at Sungho-ri is hit by 175 sorties flown by fighter-bombers of the Fifth Air Force. The planes also hit a locomotion repair plant in the same area.

PARTISANS: Friendly guerrillas at Changnin-do are attacked by 145 North Koreans in two sail junks and wooden folding boats. Aircraft from USS *Bataan* (CV 129), and bombardment from HMAS *Amethyst*, stop the invasion. Several Leopard and Wolf-pack boats are swamped during a tropical storm that hits the west coast. Operations are discontinued while things are cleaned up.

July 16

AIR WAR: A MiG-15 attacks an RB-26 on weather reconnaissance over the Yellow Sea and is engaged by the escorts. The significance of the attack is that it indicates Communist capabilities over the Yellow Sea. A daily reconnaissance of the northern sector of the Formosa Straits begins as VP-28 starts operations from Okinawa. An F-86 is shot down by enemy fire. Arthur H. McCarthy of the 26th FIS, 51st FIW, shoots down a MiG-15 fighter.

July 17

EIGHTH ARMY: During the night, the Chinese assault Old Baldy. Easy and Fox Companies of the 23rd Infantry Regiment are defending the hill and manage to stop the

A Panther jet that failed its carrier landing burns off the side of the carrier. *(Center for the Study of the Korean War, Graceland University)*

first attack. The second attack, however, establishes a foothold and then, after the Chinese receive reinforcements, they take the crest. A counterattack by the 23rd is unable to drive them off. The 2nd Infantry Division's 23rd Infantry Regiment loses 39 killed and 84 missing.

SEA WAR: Commander Seventh Fleet announces a policy limiting the speed of advance to 18 knots during transit. Emergency and operation requirements can alter this. The HRMS *Piet Hein* (PF), USS *Endicott* (DMS 35), and USS *Orleck* (DD 886) capture two sampans and 10 prisoners. Three of the prisoners have surrender certificates with them. The island of Changjin is retaken by friendly guerrillas who are supported by HMS *Belfast,* HMS *Amethyst,* and the ROK's *PC 702.* Captain Milton T. Dayton takes over as commander of the Wonsan blockade, replacing Captain James B. Grady.

PARTISANS: Changnung-do is retaken by guerrilla units supported by HMS *Belfast,* HMS *Amethyst,* and ROK *PC 702.* Sixty North Korean soldiers are killed, 30 drown trying to escape, and 41 are taken prisoner. Friendly losses are eight killed and 12 wounded.

July 18

AIR WAR: Air Task Group Two under Commander J. G. Daniel begins its tour of duty aboard USS *Essex* (CV 9).

July 18–24

SEA WAR: The USS *Philippine Sea* (CVA 37) and USS *Essex* (CVA 9) begin a six-day sweep along the China coast to make a show of force.

July 19

POLITICAL/ADMINISTRATIVE: The *Nodong Sinumun* (a North Korean newspaper) charges the United States with planning to use political prisoners to test a new weapon.

SEA WAR: Five men are slightly wounded when USS *Orleck* (DD 886) is fired on by shore guns near Taepo. After days of silence, the batteries at Wonsan begin firing again on the islands of Hwangto-do and Yo-do and on USS *Parks* (DD 884).

July 20

EIGHTH ARMY: During the day, the 2nd Infantry Division is able to retake a portion of the east finger of Old Baldy. The beginning of torrential rains makes further efforts difficult.

SEA WAR: A collision occurs between USS *Duncan* (DD 874) and USS *Essex* (CV9) during fueling. Some damage is done to *Duncan.*

AIR WAR: Fifty-eight F-84s arrive in Japan after a transpacific flight with in-flight refueling. Ronald A. Berdoy of the 334th FIS shoots down a MiG-15 fighter.

July 20–26

EIGHTH ARMY: For six days, torrential rain turns the area into a quagmire: Streams are flooded, bridges washed away, roads destroyed, and landslides block efforts to bring in supplies. Neither side is able to move, and little is accomplished.

July 21

Sea War: The USS *Toucan* (AM 387) captures a sampan off the Ansong Gap east of Hungnam and takes five men prisoner. The USS *O'Brien* (DD 725) is damaged when hitting a net buoy.

July 22

Eighth Army: The second battle for Old Baldy ends.

Sea War: USS LSMR *536* is fired on by three guns on Amgak Island. The USS *Parks* (DD 884) catches nearly 300 enemy troops repairing a rail break south of Wonsan and fires on them, inflicting 74 casualties. Commander Robert M. Hinckley, Jr., takes command as "mayor" of the Wonsan blockade, replacing Captain Milton Dayton.

July 23

Air War: FEAF and navy planes launch a massive air strike against the North Korean hydroelectric power grid, causing a nearly complete blackout that lasts for more than two weeks. The results of the raid extend into northeast China.

July 23–30

Sea War: The HMCS *Nootka* (DDE) is fired on by shore batteries, with no hits. For a week, Underwater Demolition Team 5, supported by USS *Diachenko* (APD 123) and two ROK motor torpedo boats, carries out six successful raids against enemy fishing facilities. In addition to destroying a number of fish nets and small boats, the raiders capture five prisoners.

July 24

Sea War: The ROK navy's *PC 706* fires on a motor junk but there are no casualties reported.

July 25

Eighth Army: Intelligence reports indicate that the North Koreans are withdrawing so quickly that they are leaving portions of units behind. This is used as an explanation for an increase in raids on UN supply and rearguard groups.

July 26

Eighth Army: A large-scale exodus is reportedly taking place from Kaesong. High-ranking officials, Russian support troops, and most of the regular troops are reported as having evacuated the city.

July 27

Eighth Army: The 1st Marine Regiment is back on line and charged with the organization of a "rescue Task Force" for the UN truce team at Panmunjom. The team is ready to move in on the signal "need aid."

Sea War: A PBM is fired on by three unidentified planes over the Yellow Sea but there is no reported damage. Task Force 77 begins a new schedule of night hecklers, sending two groups, one flying from 2230 until 0200 and the other in flight from 0230 to 0530.

Air War: Planes from USS *Bon Homme Richard* (CV 31) attack a lead and zinc mine at Sindok. Eight Firefly F-51 planes from HMS *Ocean* are attacked by a MiG-15; two Fireflies are damaged.

July 27–28
Sea War: The USS *Strong* (DD 758) is fired on 12 times by a 105-mm battery but no damage is sustained. The HMCS *Nootka* (DDE) is fired on by shore batteries in the vicinity of Haeju.

July 28
Eighth Army: The 7th Marine Regiment is given the assignment of taking, or neutralizing, two Chinese positions west of Hill 104 and the Tumae-ri Ridge. Despite a heavy defense the marines take the hill.

Sea War: Thirty-eight naval aircraft (25 F4Us and 13 ADs) from USS *Princeton* (CV 37) attack a magnesite plant at Kilchu in Korea's far northeast. Damage is estimated at 60 percent of the plant facilities. The USS *Strong* (DD 758) bombards troop concentrations at Sok-to and receives return fire; there is no damage to the *Strong*. The destroyer USS *Orleck* (DD 886) is given a special classification as "DTS: Destroyer, Train Smasher," after the ship destroys a North Korean train with gunfire.

July 29
Eighth Army: Activities are delayed because of a heavy rain that drops 3.6 inches during the day.

July 30
Air War: As a result of monsoon rains, helicopters of the 3rd ARS are used to evacuate more than 650 flood-stranded U.S. military and Koreans. Flying more than 100 sorties, the five H-19s are able to transport about 600; the rest are carried by two H-5s. In the I Corps sector, two H-5s fly out more than 60 stranded Koreans and soldiers in 30 sorties. FEAF B-29s raid the Oriental Light Metal Works near the Manchurian border.

July 30–31
Air War: More than 60 B-29s focus their attack on the Oriental Light Metals Company just four miles from the Yalu River. Considerable damage is inflicted, but the B-29s are themselves the target of the largest effort yet at counter-air measures. None of the bombers are damaged.

July 31
Eighth Army: It is not until this date that the 1st Battalion, 23rd Regiment, takes Old Baldy, an area so small it could accommodate only a rifle company. Having learned their lesson, the men begin to dig deep in reinforcing the fortification. They strengthen the bunkers and place some of the areas underground.

Sea War: The ROK navy's *PC 701* goes aground east of Mundo during bad weather. She is assisted by HMCS *Nootka* (DDE) and USS *Firecrest* (AMS 10). The ship is towed to Yonpyong-do. A U.S. PBM 55 Mariner assigned to VP-731 is attacked by two Chinese MiG-15s near Formosa. The plane is on a reconnaissance mission to the west coast of Korea over the Yellow Sea. The tail gunner, Aviation Machinist's Mate H. G. Goodroad, is killed. The pilot, Lieutenant E. Bartlett, Jr., dives to 250 feet and heads to Japan. In the run back to Japan, a second man is killed, Airman Claude Playforth, and two wounded, Airman H. T. Atkins and Ordnance Man Third Class R. H. Smith. The Mariner is able to land on the island of Paengnyong-do.

August 1

POLITICAL/ADMINISTRATIVE: The army chief of staff informs army commanders they will lose half their strength through rotation during 1953. The Japanese national security law becomes effective and the Coastal Security Force is established. This force is independent of the Maritime Safety Agency and is the first step in turning over American patrol boats to Japanese operators.

EIGHTH ARMY: The third battle for Old Baldy begins. After a long delay caused by torrential rains, two companies of the 23rd Infantry Regiment, 2nd Infantry Division, take Old Baldy. General Selden assigns the reserve regiment of the 7th Marines to develop a secondary line, to be called Kansas, at the extreme right of the division sector.

SEA WAR: The USS *Essex* (CVA 9) begins her second tour of duty in Korea. HMCS *Nootka* (DDE) is fired on near Samjong with no results. The USS *Carmick* (DS 33) is bracketed by fire coming from the Songjin lighthouse and silences the enemy battery with counterfire. The ROK navy's *MTB 27* is fired on by automatic weapons from a company of troops in the Tanchon area. The USS *Porter* (DD 800) returns fire on the enemy battery and causes an estimated 75 casualties.

AIR WAR: Soviet reports claim that four F-86s are shot down by their fighters. Planes from the 334th FIS shoot down four MiG-15 fighters. The pilots are Alfred M. Miller, Gene F. Rogue, Daniel J. Denehy, and Karl K. Dittmer.

August 2

EIGHTH ARMY: During the lull in the battle on Old Baldy, the 2nd Infantry Division fortifies its position in anticipation of a Chinese counterattack.

SEA WAR: A coordinated, maximum effort, surface-air strike on Changjin is only 30 percent completed because of the increasingly bad weather, but the limited effort is successful.

August 3

SEA WAR: The HMS *Belfast* (CL) receives 20 rounds of fire from Cho-do. The rounds wound four of the crew on board. Commander Nels C. Johnson takes command of the Wonsan blockade as "mayor."

PARTISANS: A second typhoon hits the west coast of Korea, damaging more boats used by Leopard and Wolfpack. The lack of transportation brings all their operations to a halt.

August 4

POLITICAL/ADMINISTRATIVE: Rear Admiral Apollo Soucek, in USS *Boxer* (CV 21), assumes command of Task Force 77. Rear Admiral H. E. Regan, onboard USS *Bon Homme Richard* (CV 31), relinquishes command of Task Force 77.

EIGHTH ARMY: The Chinese make another attempt to take Old Baldy but the effort is broken up by well-directed artillery fire. The enemy will make no more attempts to take Old Baldy during August.

SEA WAR: Both the island of Mundo and HMCS *Nootka* (DDE) receive fire but no casualties. The ship escapes damage, but several buildings on the island are set on fire. At Yujin, USS *Carmick* (DDS 33) receives and returns fire, as does the ROK navy's *MTB 37* and USS *Porter* (DD 800) near Tanchon. The New Zealand ship *Hawea* begins a tour of duty in Korean waters.

August 4

SEA WAR: HMNZS *Hawea* is in Korean waters for its second tour.

August 5

POLITICAL/ADMINISTRATIVE: President Syngman Rhee is reelected in South Korea's second presidential election.

EIGHTH ARMY: During the night, elements of the ROK Capital Division infiltrate and capture two outposts in the area later to be known as Capitol Hill. The battle rages, with the area changing hands, for the next four days.

AIR WAR: Robinson Riser of the 336th FIS and Walter G. Savage and Charles G. Cleveland of the 39th each shoot down an enemy MiG-15. W. Cook and R. W. Hart of the 39th FIS share credit for downing a fourth.

August 6

EIGHTH ARMY: The ROK Capital Division is ordered to take Capitol Hill (Hill 297). In a direct attack it is successful, but the Chinese counterattack almost immediately. For the next four days, the Chinese continue to counterattack but with little success.

SEA WAR: A Panther jet explodes on the hangar deck of USS *Boxer* (CV 21), causing the deaths of nine persons and the destruction of 12 planes. At the time, the *Boxer* had 58 armed and fueled planes on deck waiting to take off. The explosion on the hangar deck starts a dense fire. Helicopters and destroyers of Task Force 77 rescue 63 survivors from the sea. Despite the damage, the ship remains operational. The USS *Pierce* (DD 753) is hit seven times by shore batteries firing from a position near Tanchon. The attack causes 10 casualties and does serious damage to *Pierce*'s 5-inch mount. Enemy troops in the Tanchon area fire on the ROK *MTB 27* with machine guns.

AIR WAR: More than 250 MiG-15s are reported by pilots during the day. In a major air-to-air battle, 34 F-86s destroy six out of a flight of 52 MiG-15s. Credit for these kills go to William J. Ryan of the 334th FIS, who downs two; Westwood H. Fletcher, Robert Barnes, and Frederick Blesse of the 334th each get one, and S. T. Rohrer and W. S. Borders share credit for one kill. Considerable effort is being made by Detachment 3, 6004th Air Intelligence Service Squadron, to increase the evasion-and-escape techniques understood by pilots. An F-86 is shot down by fighters near Sensen.

August 6–October 14

EIGHTH ARMY: The Cavalry Regiment of the ROK Capital Division is overrun at a long, finger-shaped ridge called Finger Ridge. The give-and-take battle for the ridge will continue until mid-October, when the ROK division will be in full control.

August 7

POLITICAL/ADMINISTRATIVE: A Court of Inquiry is appointed to investigate the explosion on USS *Boxer* (CV 21).

EIGHTH ARMY: After a successful attack on Hill 123, elements of the 5th Marines are returned to Outpost Elko. When the marines move out to occupy Outposts Elmer and Felix, they are fired on by Communist troops on Hill 123. Artillery fire and a reinforcement squad come to their aid and together they make a frontal assault on Hill 123. They receive heavy fire but are able to engage the enemy near the top; after a brief fight the Chinese withdraw. The marines return to outpost Felix.

SEA WAR: A U.S. Navy Mariner PBM crashes near Bataan Mountain (Manila Bay), killing 13. There are no survivors.

AIR WAR: John A. Inferrera of the 39th FIS shoots down an enemy MiG-15. Clifford D. Jolley from the 334th FIS shoots down two MiG-15s. Charles D. Owens of the 336th FIS brings down one enemy MiG-15.

August 8

SEA WAR: A U.S. Navy Mariner PBM crashes on a night ASW flight. It comes down on the main island of Shikoku, Japan, killing all the passengers and crew, as well as nine enlisted men and five officers. The USS *Philippine Sea* (CV 47) ends its first tour of duty with Task Force 77.

AIR WAR: Captain Clifford D. Jolley of the 335th FIS destroys three MiG-15s in two days. He becomes the 18th ace of the war. In addition, Philip H. Van Sickly of the 335th FIS and James E. Tilton and Heber M. Butler of the 16th FIA shoot down 2 MiG-15s. Fifth Air Force fighters fly 285 close air support sorties.

August 9

EIGHTH ARMY: The 1st Marine Division defends itself against a Chinese attack in the area of Bunker Hill. In an effort to bring pressure on the negotiators at Panmunjom, there are several attacks on UN positions, including a significant one by the Chinese on Hill 58 (Siberia). It is defended by elements of Company Easy, 2nd Battalion, 1st Marines, who, after defending the hill against large odds for 20 minutes, are forced to withdraw. The marines try a counterattack at about 0400, but it fails. Finally, after bringing in air support, the men of Easy Company take the top of the hill and drive the enemy back. Within 20 minutes, the Chinese have returned and the marines, now exhausted, are finally forced to move back to the MLR. A brief return to the hill is accomplished by Charlie Company, but they, too, are forced to withdraw.

SEA WAR: The USS *Kimberly* (DD 521) is called on to suppress fire from Ongjin that has been directed toward the mainland.

AIR WAR: Eight MiG-15s, north of Chinnampo, attack four piston-engine Sea Furies from a British carrier. One MiG-15 is destroyed; no British planes are damaged.

August 10

EIGHTH ARMY: Canadian units return to the line, taking responsibility for Paujol-gol and Kojanharisaemal. The Chinese, who have counterattacked Capitol Hill four times, finally pull back. The cost of the hill for the 26th ROK Regiment is 48 killed and 150 wounded.

SEA WAR: The USS *Barton* (DD 722) and USS *Jarvis* (DD 799) are fired on from Hodo Pando (Wonsan area). The *Barton* suffers some damage and one killed and one wounded. The *Jarvis* is undamaged. Enemy shore installations near Songjin fire at HMS *Mounts Bay* (PF), killing one seaman and wounding four. The counterbattery fire, more than 130 rounds of four-inch shells, scores a hit on one gun. The USS *Van Valkenburgh* (DD 656) escapes damage at Kangson-ni, as does HMS *Concord* (DD) near Ponghwang-ni.

August 11

POLITICAL/ADMINISTRATIVE: Rear Admiral Kim Won Mu (NKPN) is replaced at the armistice talks by Major General So Hui (NKPA).

EIGHTH ARMY: The marines feint an attack on Outpost Siberia to confuse the enemy about their change of plans—to attack Bunker Hill rather than returning to Siberia. After light resistance, the marines capture Hill 102 at about 1700 hours. As night approaches, the Chinese make another effort, but three American tanks fight off the T-34s sent by the enemy. Despite a heavy counterattack, the marines hold the hill. The marines extend their defensive line over to Hill 108. Baker Company, 1st Battalion, 1st Marines, assaults Bunker Hill and by 2200 reaches the crest and starts pushing the Chinese away from the slopes. The Chinese, surprised and defeated, form pockets of resistance but are unable to halt the assault. The marines take the forward slope. After repulsing an enemy counterattack, the defenders hold the hill during the night.

SEA WAR: The ROK navy's *Duman* (PF) and USS *Soley* (DD 707) escape damage when they are fired on by antiaircraft artillery positions south of Wonsan. The USS *Kearsarge* begins its tour of duty with Task Force 77.

August 11–17

EIGHTH ARMY: Period of the Battle of Bunker Hill (Hill 122), the first major ground action for the marines in the western part of Korea. While the hill is taken on August 11, the defenders are subject to a series of counterattacks. The Chinese attack again on August 13 and the position is in question, but the marines manage to hold on. The Chinese try again on August 14. On August 16, they are able to penetrate the crest of the hill but are pushed back and also on August 17. After several more attempts, the enemy withdraws.

August 12

EIGHTH ARMY: The marines wait on Bunker Hill for the anticipated Chinese counterattack. It comes at about 1500 when an artillery bombardment starts. An hour later, more than 350 Chinese come out of the low ground around Hill 125.

SEA WAR: In the Wonsan area, the battle of the shore batteries continues as USS *Grapple* (ARS 7) is hit by a round that causes some damage below the water line. The USS *Barton* (DD 722) avoids damage as it also receives fire. Off Yo-do Island the ROK navy's *FS 906,* loaded with gasoline and ammunition, is hit but escapes injury. On the Ongjin Peninsula HMS *Concord* (DD) prevents a group of North Koreans, estimated at 100, from invading Cho-do. Captain Richard B. Levin takes command of the Wonsan blockade as "mayor," replacing Commander Nels C. Johnson.

AIR WAR: An RB-29 that is conducting routine shipping surveillance over the Sea of Japan is intercepted for more than five hours, by flights of from one to 20 unidentified enemy jets. The enemy jets do not use running lights and are, at all times, above the RB-29.

August 12–14

EIGHTH ARMY: Marines are able to catch the Chinese unaware on Hill 122 (Bunker Hill) and take the post. The marines withstand several counterattacks.

August 13

EIGHTH ARMY: In the morning, mortar fire begins to fall on Bunker Hill and near 0100 the Chinese are heading toward the area defended by Item Company. The battle continues for more than four hours. The enemy artillery increases, suggesting a withdrawal, and this occurs soon afterward. Baker Company, 3rd Royal Australian Regiment, attacks Hill 75 in Operation Buffalo, but the attack is repulsed after a period of hand-to-hand fighting. Navy Hospital Corpsman John E. Kilmer, attached to the 1st Marine Division, is awarded the Medal of Honor for heroic action in aiding and evacuating the wounded.

August 14

EIGHTH ARMY: Corporal Lester Hammond, Jr., Able Company, 1st Battalion, 187th Airborne Regimental Combat Team, is awarded the Medal of Honor for heroic action that enables his platoon to rescue a cut-off patrol.

SEA WAR: The USS *Porter* (DD 600) and USS *Jarvis* (DD 799) conduct night anti-train patrols near Songjin. Motor whaleboats operating close to shore relay news of an approaching train, which is then fired on by the ships. In the action, two trains are damaged. The *Porter* takes several rounds from shore batteries but escapes any damage. HMS *Mounts Bay* (PF) is also fired on, but there are no hits.

August 15

EIGHTH ARMY: What appeared at first to be a minor engagement turns into a major one when Chinese troops move aggressively along the Hills 122–124 ridge. The light from a hit burning tank marks the position and discloses the advancing Chinese.

SEA WAR: After a mistaken identity check, USS *Chief* (AM 315) on "Flycatcher Patrol" (anti-sampan) fires on USS *Grapple* (ARS 7) in the darkness, hitting it with two rounds that kill two and wound nine. In the Yujin area, USS *Redhead* (AMS 34) and USS *Heron* (AMS 18) are fired on. The *Heron* is straddled by five near-misses but no damage occurs. The HMCS *Crusader* (DDE) and HMNZS *Rotoiti* (PF) fire in support of a guerrilla raid on the mainland opposite Kirin-do. The USS *Segundo* (SS 398) arrives to begin her tour of duty in Korean waters.

AIR WAR: The 315th AD transports 300 medical evacuees.

August 16

EIGHTH ARMY: The marines successfully defend Hill 122 (Bunker Hill) against a determined Chinese attack. The enemy casualties are high.

SEA WAR: The island of Hwangto-do (in Wonsan harbor) receives heavy fire from four 155-mm guns on Kalmagak. The island is also hit by machine-gun fire. No damage is reported.

August 17

EIGHTH ARMY: Private First Class Robert E. Simanek, Able Company, 2nd Battalion, 5th Marine Regiment, 1st Division, is awarded the Medal of Honor for throwing his body on a grenade and saving the lives of his companions. The Chinese attack and take Outpost Irene (Rome).

SEA WAR: At Chaho, ROK motor torpedo boats are fired on while they are on spotting duty. All shots go wild.

August 18

EIGHTH ARMY: Fighting begins for the fourth time on Old Baldy.

SEA WAR: Typhoon Karen passes just south of Wonsan, creating considerable damage. One of the major problems is that the typhoon blows free more than 40 mines that break their moorings and drift out to sea. During the typhoon, the siege ships temporarily leave the harbor—the only break in the long blockade.

August 19

EIGHTH ARMY: In the early morning hours, Dog Company, 2nd Battalion, 1st Marine Regiment, takes over the responsibility for Hill 124 and almost immediately comes under heavy fire.

AIR WAR: During the night, FEAF aircraft drop leaflets over Pyongyang warning of the coming night attack. HMR 161 takes part in Operation Ripple, designed to test the ability of helicopters to move rocket launchers and personnel from one firing position to another. Because of the heavy smoke the rockets give off, they are quickly located by enemy artillery and need to be moved to a new location.

August 20

POLITICAL/ADMINISTRATIVE: Joseph Stalin and Zhou Enlai meet to discuss the progress at the cease-fire negotiations. Neither Stalin nor Mao Zedong seem anxious to bring the war to an end, believing the commitment in Korea is keeping the United States from preparing for a larger war.

SEA WAR: The USS *Waxbill* (AMS 39), momentarily grounded while rescuing a badly wounded Korean from Taesupto, receives some damage. The USS *Thompson* (DMS 38), in a near repeat of its June 14, 1951, action, is hit by 155-mm guns while off Songjin. The enemy fire strikes the flying bridge; three men are killed and 10 injured. The *Thompson* replies with counterfire as she starts moving out. Late in the evening, USS *Iowa* (BB 61) bombards the enemy position. Six MiG-15s clash with 12 F9Fs from USS *Princeton* (CV 37). The F9Fs easily counter all passes and receive no damage. Commander Task Force 77 orders aircraft operations south of Wonsan to be conducted at a minimum pullout altitude of 3,000 feet to avoid heavy concentrations of enemy fire.

AIR WAR: Thirty-eight B-29s hit the supply areas around the enemy's capital at Pyongyang. Navy, marine, and air force planes team together on a massive attack on the supply area at Chongpyong-ni. These raids result in an estimated damage of 80 percent. Frederick C. Blesse and Edward P. Ballinger of the 334th FIS each shoot down an enemy MiG-15. William A. Korbel of the 39th FIS also gets credit for shooting down a MiG-15.

August 21

POLITICAL/ADMINISTRATIVE: General Mark W. Clark establishes the Korean Communication Zone with responsibility for all activities south of a line roughly along the 37th parallel.

EIGHTH ARMY: At 0345, four enemy groups are converging on Hill 124. The main assault is made up of about 20 Chinese and lasts only a few minutes. During the attack, nearly all the men of the marine defense are wounded, but they hold. Chinese POWs attack the compound commander at Cheju-do, injuring him and two of his assistants. The administrators had entered the compound to determine the extent of the damage caused by a recent typhoon.

SEA WAR: The USS *Boyd* (DD 544) is fired on at a range of 21,000 yards. The two 155-mm shells cause no damage.

August 22

SEA WAR: The ROK navy's *MTB 26* is fired on from shore near Yangdo, at some 800 yards, by enemy mortars. There is no damage. The USS *Strong* (DD 758) has the same adventure near the western shore of the Haeju approaches.

PARTISANS: Leopard's Donkey 2 undertakes a raid near Chinnampo.

August 22–23

AIR WAR: For three nights during 60-minute sorties, three C-47s broadcast as a part of the UN Command emphasis on psychological war.

August 23

SEA WAR: Captain Selby K. Santmyers takes command of the Wonsan blockade as "mayor," replacing Captain Richard B. Levin.

August 25

POLITICAL/ADMINISTRATIVE: Secretary of the Navy Francis P. Matthews announces in a speech that the price of peace may include instituting a war in order to compel nations to cooperate. The State Department disavows the remarks and President Truman personally chastises Matthews.

EIGHTH ARMY: The marines are able to withstand yet another Chinese counterattack on Hill 122 (Bunker Hill).

SEA WAR: Commander Frederick M. Stiesberg take command of the Wonsan blockade as "mayor," replacing Captain Selby K. Santmyers.

August 26

SEA WAR: The USS *Bataan* (CVL 29) ends her second tour of duty with Task Force 77.

August 27

SEA WAR: In a case of mistaken identity, USS *Tingey* (DD 539) fires at a shore battery on the island of Songdo. Before the firing is stopped, four men are wounded. Later in the same day, enemy mortars hit the same area, killing one and wounding another. At Chaho, shore batteries fire more than a hundred rounds at USS *Competent* (AM 336), causing no damage to the ship but wrecking all her sweep gear. She and her companion, USS *McDermott* (DD 677), escape damage.

August 28

SEA WAR: The USS *Sarsi* (ATF 11) strikes a mine while on the Hungnam patrol and sinks within 21 minutes. Ninety-two of the 97 men on board are rescued by USS *Zeal* (AM 131), USS *Competent* (AM 316), and USS *Boyd* (DD 554). Since command cannot verify the destruction of the operation plans that are in a locked safe aboard *Sarsi,* ships remain in the area to prevent possible enemy salvage. At Wonsan harbor, USS *McDermott* (DD 677) receives minor damage from enemy shore fire, but there are no casualties. The ROK navy's MTB 23 receives small-arms fire in the vicinity of Songjin but no casualties are reported.

AIR WAR: Guided Missile Unit 90, while operating from USS *Boxer* (CVA 21), launches six radio-controlled F6F drones equipped with a television guidance system, loaded with high explosives, and directed toward selected targets. Results are of limited value: one hit, four misses, and one abort.

August 29

POLITICAL/ADMINISTRATIVE: The U.S. Department of State requests that Far East Command launch an attack to coincide with a visit by Zhou Enlai to the Soviet Union, in the hope that it might encourage the Soviets to bring pressure in support of accepting an armistice.

SEA WAR: Carrier planes from Task Force 77 join in a major attack against Pyongyang. Three planes are lost to ground fire. Enemy mortars on the mainland fire on friendly forces on the island of Songdo. Counterbattery fire by USS *Tingey* (DD 535) silences the mortars.

AIR WAR: FEAF conducts a massive raid against Pyongyang at the request of the U.S. State Department. They fly about 1,400 air-to-ground sorties, causing considerable damage at the cost of losing three planes. Charles A. Gabriel of the 16th FIS shoots down a MiG-15.

August 30

Sea War: There is return fire on HMAS *Bataan* (DD) from Ongjin after *Bataan* tries to silence enemy guns at Mundo. Four Americans and four others are killed when USS *Sarsi* (AFT 111) hits a mine around Hungnam. It is the last American vessel to be lost in the war. USS *LSSL 108* is fired on by a gun of unreported caliber located on the mainland east of Cho-do. Counterbattery fire from HMS *Newcastle* (CL) silences the gun.

Air War: Francis A. Williams and Paul R. Henderson of the 25th FIS each get credit for shooting down an enemy MiG-15 fighter. From the 334th FIS, Leonard W. Lilley gets credit for one kill while L. R. Blakeney and R. A. Berdoy share credit for one kill. Robert L. Sands of the 16th FIS shoots down a MiG-15.

August 31

Eighth Army: Corporal William F. Lyell, Fox Company, 2nd Battalion, 17th Infantry Regiment, 7th Infantry Division, receives the Medal of Honor for his heroic leadership after the death of his commanding officer.

Sea War: Attempts are made to salvage USS *Sarsi* (AFT 111), but, after USS *Boyd* (DD 544) is fired on during the operations, it is decided that salvage is impossible and demolition is ordered.

September 1

Eighth Army: General Mark Clark determines that the shortage of artillery ammunition is getting serious and acknowledges that stocks have been reduced to a 60-day supply contrary to the policy requirement of 90 days.

Sea War: USS *Lewis* (DD 535) is fired on by shore batteries at Wonsan, but there are no hits. One man is slightly wounded when shore batteries in the Kansong area hit USS *Agerholm* (DD 826). The first guided missile fired from a carrier hits more than 150 miles inside North Korea. Three carriers, USS *Essex* (CV 9), *Princeton* (CV 37), and *Boxer* (CV 21), launch 143 planes to smash the Aoji oil refinery.

Air War: Planes from Task Force 77 hit the synthetic oil-producing center at Aoji, only four miles from the Manchurian border and eight miles from Russia. Two F-86s are shot down by enemy fighter planes, one at Deeguandong and one at Andong.

September 2

Sea War: Ships of the UN protective fleets are warned of a major storm approaching. Most naval and air activity is limited.

September 3

Sea War: A tropical storm hits Task Force 77 while at sea. Winds up to 60 knots sweep the force. DESDIV 132 (Destroyer Division) suffers minor damage to topside gear.

Air War: Fifty-two sorties are flown against the Changjin (Chosin) hydroelectric power plant complex, by B-19s. VP Squadron 40, under Commander M. S. Whitener, begins its second tour of sea-based duty in Korea.

Partisans: Wolfpack reports losing three motorized and 10 sail junks to the winds of the typhoon.

September 4

Political/Administrative: Rear Admiral A. Soucek, onboard USS *Boxer* (CV 21), relinquishes command of Task Force 77. Rear Admiral H. E. Regan, onboard USS *Bon Homme Richard* (CV 31), assumes command of Task Force 77.

Eighth Army: The Chinese attack Outpost Bruce (Reno) with two companies, but the men of the 5th Marines are able to repulse three attacks and hold the outpost.

Air War: Seventy-five fighter-bombers attack targets well north of the Chongchon River, where they seek to flush out an estimated 89 MiG-15s from bases in Manchuria. The 39 UN fighters screening the F-84s engage a flight of MiG-15s, destroying 13, with four F-86s falling to Chinese pilots. Four F-86s are destroyed. Major Frederick C. Blesse, 334th FIS, destroys his fifth aircraft to become an ace. Others engaged in aerial combat include Norman Box, Laverne G. Strange, Arthur H. McCarthy, and Garry A. Willard, of the 25th FIS; Ira M. Porter (who gets two), Justin W. Livingston, and Martin J. Bambrick from the 335th FIS; Leonard W. Lilley of the 334th FIS; and Robert L. Sands of the 16th FIS. An H-19 from the 3rd ARS rescues a downed fighter pilot, and then goes on to rescue the two crewmen of an SSN helicopter that lost power and crashed in the water while itself attempting the rescue.

September 5

Eighth Army: Chinese forces again attack in the area of Outpost Agnes but are halted by Able Company of the Wolfhound Regiment. The outpost is finally lost to the Chinese. The Chinese make a half-hearted attack on Bunker Hill but are repulsed. Private First Class Alford L. McLaughlin, Love Company, 3rd Battalion, 5th Marines, 1st Marine Division, receives the Medal of Honor for his stand that accounts for an estimated 150 enemy casualties. Hospital Corpsman Third Class Edward C. Benford, attached to the 1st Marine Division, is awarded the Medal of Honor for his heroic actions against the enemy. Private First Class Fernando Luis Garcia, Item Company, 3rd Battalion, 5th Marines, 1st Marine Division, receives the Medal of Honor for heroic action in which he gives his own life to save another.

Sea War: The island of Sosa-ri is fired on by enemy guns located at Cho-do. The USS *Cardigan Bay* (PF), HMS *Morecambe Bay* (FF), USS LSMR *412*, and USS *Bradford* (DD 545) return fire and silence the guns. The USS *Blue* (DD 744) and USS *Swallow* (AMS 36) are fired on at the Hungnam approaches; both ships escape damage. On the other hand, one death and two injuries occur on the island of Hwangto-do as a result of enemy fire. The HMTS *Tachin* (PF) is fired on by guns at Pipa-Got and USS *Lewis* (DE 535) fires on batteries at Kalmagak that have been firing on the islands in Wonsan harbor.

Air War: In two strikes, the FEAF fly 200 sorties, attacking a processing plant northeast of Sinanju. Seventy buildings are destroyed in the raid. An F-86 is shot down near Sensen. Richard L. Ayersman of the 334th FIS and Aubrey C. Moulton of the 25th FIS each get a MiG-15, and P. A. Kauttu and W. E. Powers share credit for one.

September 6

EIGHTH ARMY: Corporal Benito Martinez, Able Company, 1st Battalion, 27th Infantry Regiment, 25th Infantry Division, is awarded the Medal of Honor for heroic action in a stand against heavy enemy forces. Capitol Hill on Finger Ridge is over-run by Chinese troops. The ridge and the hill will change hands several times but will eventually remain under control of the ROK.

AIR WAR: Air Group Two, under Commander A. L. Downing, ends its tour aboard USS *Boxer* (CV 21). An F-86 is shot down by enemy fighters at Sakusyu.

September 6–8

EIGHTH ARMY: The battle for Outpost Bruce (Hill 148) begins. During a 58-hour siege the marines will sustain 19 KIA and 38 WIA.

September 7

EIGHTH ARMY: Commanders are warned that the Chinese are about to try and seize key terrain features over which there has been dispute at the armistice table. Among these are two areas that General Pollock determines must be held: Bunker Hill and Outpost Bruce. Outpost Kelly, held by the 65th Infantry Regiment, is hit by Chinese troops.

SEA WAR: No damage results from shore fire at Haeju directed at the ROK navy's *PC 702*.

AIR WAR: P. A. Kauttu and W. E. Powers from the 16th FIS share credit for destroying an enemy MiG-15. E. N. Powell and J. E. Taylor of the 335th FIS also share credit for downing one MiG-15. Cecil G. Foster, from the 16th FIS, shoots down a MiG-15.

September 8

AIR WAR: The USS *Evans* (DD 754) suffers slight damage after being fired on at a range of 12,500 yards from the vicinity of Tanchon. Frederick C. Blesse of the 334th FIS shoots down two MiG-15s. Richard L. Ayersman and William Craig, also of the 334th FIS, each shoot down a MiG-15. The carrier USS *Antietam* (CV 36) enters New York Naval Shipyard at Brooklyn for the experimental installation of a deck angled to port at 10.5 degrees.

September 9

EIGHTH ARMY: The 65th Infantry is assigned to the task of defending Outpost Bubble on the Jamestown Line. Among the key terrain features that General Pollock says must be preserved, eight new spots are identified: Hills 86, 38, 56, and 48A and Outposts Allen, Clarence, Felix, and Jill. The Chinese once again try to take Capitol Hill and manage to gain the crest temporarily. The ROK's 26th Regiment and the 1st Regiment join up to retake the hill.

AIR WAR: When a flight of 45 F-84s attacks the military academy at Sakchu, it is hit by 64 MiG-15s. The MiG-15s attack the F-84s as the F-86 escort planes prepare to defend the fleet. The MiG-15s are able to shoot one or two down, and the Thunderjets are forced to jettison their bombs. Five MiG-15s are destroyed by fire from the F-86s. The five pilots who are credited with kills are Francis A. Humpreys and Theon E. Markham from the 39th FIS, Walter R. Copeland and Simon K. Anderson from the 16th FIS, and Thomas L. Moore of the 25th FIS.

September 10

AIR WAR: USMC pilot Jesse G. Folmar from VMA-312, and flying an F4U-4B, shoots down an enemy MiG-15.

September 11

SEA WAR: Six F9F-4s from VMF-115 crash into a mountain during an instrument failure. They are all killed. Batteries at Umi-do fire at USS *Lewis* (DE 535) without success. The USS *Curlew* (AMS 8), USS *Osprey* (AMS 28), and the ROK navy's AMS *513* escape damage when fired on in the Napchin-ni area.

September 12

POLITICAL/ADMINISTRATIVE: Mexican ambassador to the United Nations, Luis Padilla Nervo, proposes a means of breaking the deadlock over the repatriation of POWs. The proposal calls for those resisting repatriation to be sent to one of the UN nations and granted immigration status. If they change their mind during this temporary period, they can request repatriation under UN guidelines.

AIR WAR: Two F-96s and a B-29 are shot down in action with enemy fighters. Joe A. Caple from the 39th FIS shoots down an enemy MiG-15 fighter.

September 12–13

AIR WAR: In a night flight, 25 B-29 bombers attack the generator building at the Suiho power plant. In anticipation of the attack, several B-26s and USN aircraft drop low-level fragmentation bombs to suppress enemy searchlights. In the same operation, four B-29s orbit the east in an effort to jam enemy radar. The B-29s drop their bombs on target, but one is shot down in the attack, and several others are damaged by flak. The plant is rendered unserviceable.

September 13

SEA WAR: The USS *Devastator* (AM 318), USS *Lewis* (DE 535), and USS *Evansville* (PF 70) are fired on by shore batteries but avoid damage.

AIR WAR: Planes from USS *Bon Homme Richard* (CVA) catch an enemy naval vessel near Wonsan and sink it by rocket fire.

September 14

AIR WAR: Air Group 101, redesignated Air Group 14, begins its tour of duty on board USS *Kearsarge* (CV 33). Leonard W. Lilley of the 334th FIS, Norman L. Box from the 25th FIS, and John J. Hockery from the 39th FIS all shoot down enemy MiG-15 fighters.

September 15

SEA WAR: The USS *Walke* (DD 723), while patrolling independently near Chaho, is fired on by approximately 450 rounds but avoids any hits. The USS *Barton* (DD 722) strikes a floating mine about 100 miles east of Wonsan harbor. Five enlisted men are missing and six injured. The *Barton* returns to Sasebo on its own power. USS *Oriskany* (CV 34) begins its tour of duty with Task Force 77.

AIR WAR: General Glenn Barcus begins sending pilots to the front lines, in groups of 15, to improve understanding between the services and for them to see the results of air-ground sorties. Herman W. Visscher and Calvin G. Davis from the 25th FIS, Alexander J. Gillis, Clifford Jolley, Carroll B. McElroy of the 335th FIS, Frederick C. Blesse and Charles G. Cleveland of the 334th FIS, and Robinson Riser from the 336th FIS each shoot down a MiG-15 fighter.

September 16

EIGHTH ARMY: The CCF tries again on Old Baldy. A 1,000-round artillery bombardment falls on the small hill for about 10 minutes. Then a battalion of the Chinese Communist Forces moves out, surrounds the hill, and assaults from all sides. Within a few minutes they have taken Old Baldy and King Company, 38th Infantry Regiment, with it. A diversionary CCF raid launched against Pork Chop Hill is also successful.

SEA WAR: The USS *Bradford* (DD 545) silences batteries that have wounded three guerrillas on Hachwirado. The USS *Barton* (DD 722) strikes a mine about 90 miles east of Wonsan, while serving as a plane guard for Task Force 77. The mine is believed to have broken lose from the Wonsan minefield during the recent typhoon.

AIR WAR: Fifth Air Force flies 110 night armed reconnaissance and interdiction missions with B-29s. The raids destroy more than a hundred Communist vehicles. R. J. Condrick and W. G. Savage of the 39th FIS share credit for downing a MiG-15. William L. Craig from the 39th FIS and Alphonse R. Pena from the 335th each bring down a MiG-15.

September 17

EIGHTH ARMY: The battle for Outpost Kelly begins. The 65th Infantry Regiment, 3rd Infantry Division, is attacked by elements of the Chinese Communist Forces. The defense of Outpost Kelly is in the hands of Charlie Company (under operational control) of the 2nd Battalion, 65th Infantry Regiment, when it is probed by a company-sized unit from the 2nd Battalion, 345th Regiment (NK). The North Koreans sweep over the hill and take the Baker Company position. Communications are lost and UN prisoners are seen being taken down the slope. An attempt to approach the hill for reconnaissance ends in a fire fight.

SEA WAR: The USS *Bradford* (DD 545) is fired on by a flight of eight MiG-15s in the area of Cho-do, but no hits are recorded. The planes do not attack the *Bradford*. The USS *O'Brien* (DD 725) avoids damage when fired on by guns at Chung-dong. Captain Raymond D. Fusselman takes command of the Wonsan blockade as "mayor."

AIR WAR: Frederick C. Blesse of the 334th FIS shoots down a MiG-15 fighter.

September 17–24

EIGHTH ARMY: Battle for Outpost Kelley begins as the 65th Infantry Regiment, 3rd Division, is besieged by CCF. The regiment takes 350 casualties.

September 18

EIGHTH ARMY: Infiltrating groups of Chinese soldiers break through the 2nd Infantry Division position on Old Baldy. At first the defenders pull back, giving about 400 yards.

SEA WAR: The ROK navy's MTB *26* suffers an engine room explosion and sinks. The USS *Heron* (AMS 18) is fired on by guns located in the Wonsan area, but escapes damage.

AIR WAR: An F-84 with standard U.S. markings attacks a friendly aircraft without damage. It is believed that the Chinese have been able to construct a plane from the parts of those shot down.

September 18–21

EIGHTH ARMY: Chinese and UN forces continue to fight for Hill 226.

September 19

POLITICAL/ADMINISTRATIVE: Chinese premier Zhou Enlai and Soviet leader Joseph Stalin discuss the prisoner exchange issue that is holding up armistice talks.

SEA WAR: Eight persons are wounded when USS *Cunningham* (DD 752) is fired on at Wonsan.

AIR WAR: After a suspension of the daylight raids that have lasted nearly 11 months, 32 B-29s, escorted by F-86s, attack enemy barracks and supply areas southwest of Hamhung. An RB-45 precedes the raid and orbits the area, providing updated weather information.

September 19–25

EIGHTH ARMY: There is a lull at the Panmunjom conference table but at Outpost Kelley a platoon from Fox Company of the 65th Infantry Regiment runs into deadly fire from the Chinese. The members of Fox Company are forced to withdraw. For two days, companies are sent against the hill only to receive heavy casualties. On the 24th, a barrage is laid down on Kelley, and King Company leads the assault with Love Company in support. The fire is so heavy the battalion commander asks for permission to withdraw, but it is denied. When, late in the day, he reports having lost 141 men, he is ordered back.

September 20

POLITICAL/ADMINISTRATIVE: Waiting until the day's talks are over, General Mark Clark announces that the first of 11,000 North Korean prisoners who have been reclassified from POW to civilian status will be released on October 1. The State Department denies charges that it has been working behind the scenes to have Syngman Rhee defeated in the presidential elections. The charge is that the State Department has been trying to elect a Communist.

EIGHTH ARMY: After the U.S. 2nd Infantry Division soldiers are driven off Old Baldy, they pull back to regroup and prepare for a counterattack. Elements of the 38th Infantry Regiment try to surround the Chinese but fail. As the marines prepare to assault Yongdungpo, it is determined that Hills 80 and 85 need to be taken first. Assigned to take the hills, Charlie Company manages to take Hill 80 with very little opposition. From there they surround the base of Hill 85, planning to attack in the morning. Two platoons from Easy Company attempt to retake Outpost Kelley but they are met with strong Chinese opposition and forced to withdraw to the MLR. As night approaches, Able and Charlie Companies advance to the base of the hill where Kelley is located. They take heavy casualties from mortar and small-arms fire.

AIR WAR: Near Shanghai, a VP-28 P4Y is attacked by two MiGs. Five passes are made, but there is no damage.

September 21

POLITICAL/ADMINISTRATIVE: Rear Admiral H. E. Regan, on USS *Bon Homme Richard* (CV 31) relinquishes command of Task Force 77. Rear Admiral R. F. Hickey, onboard USS *Kearsarge* (CV 33), assumes command of Task Force 77.

EIGHTH ARMY: A platoon of tanks moves up to support the 38th Infantry Regiment and they are able to force the Chinese off Old Baldy. After a night of fighting, UN forces once more control Old Baldy. There is no counterattack. At Outpost Kelley, a concentrated artillery barrage pounds the Chinese positions before the survivors from Able and Charlie Companies try to take the crest. A Chinese counterattack drives the men off, and Able, Baker, and Charlie Companies return to their staging areas. The 1st Battalion relieves the 3rd after the latter receives more than 70 casualties.

SEA WAR: The USS *Taylor* (DDE 468), USS *Jenkins* (DDE 447), and HMS *Charity* (DD) come under fire from shore batteries, but all avoid damage.

AIR WAR: During a bombing raid by 41 F-84s on a Pukchong munitions plant, Captain Robinson Riser, flying a Sabre of the 336th FIS, destroys two MiGs and becomes an ace. Other pilots credited with downing a MiG-15 are Joseph E. Fields and Richard B. Moyle of the 336th FIS and Simon K. Anderson of the 25th FIS.

September 22

POLITICAL/ADMINISTRATIVE: General Mark Clark establishes a sea defense zone, reportedly to prevent enemy agents from landing, but primarily to keep Korean and Japanese fishermen separated after a squabble in which the ROK navy drove off several Japanese fishermen.

EIGHTH ARMY: The 245th Tank Battalion, 45th Infantry Division, launches an attack on the Chinese forces. North Korean troops attack and take Cradle Hill, which overlooks the Punchbowl.

SEA WAR: Batteries off Wonsan fire on the friendly island of Yo-do. On the west coast HMS *Cardigan Bay* (PF) and USS *Bradford* (DD 545) come under fire. The USS *Carp* (SS 338) arrives to begin its tour of duty in Korean waters. The Canadian destroyer *Nootka* captures a North Korean minelayer south of Cho-do. The ship has been laying magnetic mines.

September 23

POLITICAL/ADMINISTRATIVE: The Communists denounce the release of civilian prisoners, stating that the release makes the whole armistice effort null and void. The United Nations announces that 49 POWs have been injured at the camp on Cheju

Island. General Omar Bradley, chairman of the JCS, says in Washington that nuclear secrets should be shared with Western European countries on a limited basis. He says that it will change their minds about not needing standing armies in the belief that they are protected by the American nuclear umbrella. Captain Gilbert R. Hershey (USMC) is wounded. He is the son of Major General Lewis B. Hershey, director of the Selective Service System.

EIGHTH ARMY: ROK forces, after more than 15 hours of fighting, retake Cradle Hill from the Chinese. The 1st KMC Battalion hits Hill 56 and, after dealing with stiff resistance from the North Koreans, is able to take the hill.

SEA WAR: The battleship USS *Iowa* (BB 61) is fired on by shore batteries at Kalma Gak, but its returning fire silences the guns. The USS *Walker* (DD 517) and USS *Cunningham* (DD 752) are also fired on near Songjin, but both ships escape damage.

September 23–30

EIGHTH ARMY: After dark on the 24th, George Company, 65th Infantry Regiment, 3rd Infantry Division, relieves the South Koreans on Hill 391. The hill will soon become known as Jackson Heights for Captain George D. Jackson, the company commander.

September 24

POLITICAL/ADMINISTRATIVE: A large demonstration is held in Seoul demanding that Japanese fishing boats be denied the right to fish in Korean waters. The Japanese are accused of an act of aggression when they send armed ships to escort Japanese boats out of Korean waters.

EIGHTH ARMY: The United Nations renews its efforts at Outpost Kelley. It begins with a 30-minute barrage of 105-mm howitzers from the 58th Field Artillery Battalion. Then a platoon of tanks from the 64th Tank Battalion comes into position. At 0610, King and Love Companies launch the assault. The Chinese defense is strong, however, and Captain English of Love Company asks for permission to withdraw and regroup. It is denied. Afterward, communications with King Company are lost. One squad of Love Company, however, is able to reach the crest and then call in tank support. Item Company is ordered up to take over King Company duties. Then, following a heavy Chinese mortar attack, the surviving elements of Item and King Companies begin to drift into the MLR. Love Company, down to a few men, is ordered to remain on the hill no matter what the cost. Nevertheless, as casualties continue to mount, the survivors

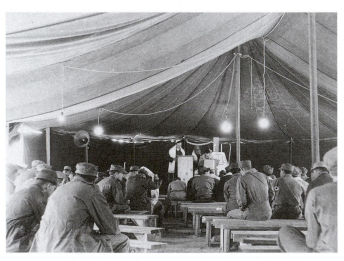

Off-duty soldiers attending Rosh Hashanah service in Seoul, fall 1952 *(Center for the Study of the Korean War, Graceland University)*

of Love Company are ordered off. It is decided not to attempt to retake Outpost Kelley.

Sea War: The ROK navy's AMS *506* runs aground near Yo-do Island but is refloated. The HMNZS *Rotoiti* (FF) is called on to silence fire from Wollae-do.

September 25

Sea War: The USS *Taylor* (DDE 468) is fired on by batteries at Wonsan but escapes. The *Taylor*'s return fire silences the batteries.

September 26

Sea War: The USS *Kimberly* (DD 521) is damaged during a storm. The USS *Boxer* (CV 21) ends its third tour of duty with Task Force 77.

Air War: G. A. Carus and T. E. Markham of the 39th FIS share credit for downing a MiG-15 fighter. Cecil G. Foster from the 16th FIS records credit for two MiG-15s, and Charles G. Cleveland of the 334th FIS gets credit for one.

September 27

Air War: Three B-26s fly for more than three hours over the central section of Korea, making loudspeaker announcements that urge the enemy troops to surrender. VP Squadron 29, under Commander L. B. Smith, begins its tour of land-based service in Korea.

Partisans: Orders are received to expand the UNPFK to a total of 20,000 by March 15, 1953. Kirkland group becomes the Kirkland Regiment. Task Force Scannon is formed on the east coast.

September 28

Political/Administrative: The United Nations proposes three alternatives in an effort to solve the stalemate over voluntary prisoner repatriation. The Communists reject all three. UN delegates present yet another proposal designed to settle the POW repatriation issue. The UN asks for a 10-day recess.

Air War: Seven F-86s are shot down by enemy fighters, according to Soviet reports. Tom P. Garvin of the 334th FIS, Alexander J. Gillis of the 335th FIS, Albert S. Kelly of the 25th FIS, and Joseph R. Butler of the 39th FIS each shoot down a MiG-15.

Partisans: Wolfpack puts together a reconnaissance-in-force party, consisting of four Americans and 475 partisans. The success of the unit is limited by the sheer size of the group.

September 29

Air War: Bombers from Fifth 5th Air Force fly 207 sorties providing close air support for ground troops and hitting bunkers and gun positions. Two F-86 fighters are shot down in aerial combat near Gisyu.

September 30

Air War: Forty-eight B-29 bombers, from the 19th, 98th, and 307th Bomber Groups, preceded by ECM flack-suppression aircraft, bomb and destroy the Namsan-ni chemical plant near the Suiho dam. The area is only 1,300 feet from the Yalu River. It is considered to be the last strategic target of the Korean War.

PARTISANS: Wolfpack's September 28 raid concludes and the party is withdrawn under fire. There are considerable casualties.

EIGHTH ARMY: The defense of Outpost Kelley ends.

SEA WAR: The USS *Thompson* (DMS 38) avoids three rounds that are fired at her from Chaho.

October

SEA WAR: During the month, in Operation Decoy, UN naval forces strike targets near Kojo, North Korea, and Force 90, with the 1st Cavalry, simulates a Regimental Combat Team landing. The result, as anticipated, is that the CCF will move in reinforcements thus weakening their hold on other locations.

October–November

POLITICAL/ADMINISTRATIVE: After rescreening POWs and identifying an additional 11,000 people who qualify as civilians, the UNC begins the gradual release of civilian internees.

October 1

POLITICAL/ADMINISTRATIVE: The Chinese broadcast a warning to the South Koreans that if they do not surrender the outposts they are holding, Allen, Clarence, Felix, and Jill, they will be overrun and killed.

EIGHTH ARMY: Just two days after Colonel Richard D. Boerem is placed in charge, Chinese prisoners at Cheju-do demonstrate in celebration of the formation of the People's Republic of China. Trouble focuses on Compound 7, where about 5,000 hard-core Communists are being held. The prisoners finally attack the guards with stones and sharpened tent-poles. When the rioters refuse to stop, Colonel Boerem sends in troops: two platoons of the 1st Battalion, 35th Infantry Regiment, and 15 members of the Military Police Service Company. After tear gas proves ineffective, the troops use rifle butts. By the time order is restored, 56 prisoners have been killed and 120 injured. Nine UN personnel are hurt.

AIR WAR: VP Squadron 1 under the command of Commander J. D. Quillin ends its third tour of land-based service in Korea.

October 2

EIGHTH ARMY: The Communists follow up a bombardment with an assault against Outposts Seattle and Warsaw. The defense is in the hands of Item Company, 3rd Battalion, 7th Marines. The Chinese are successful, and at 1945, the survivors, 13 men, return to the MLR to report that the enemy is in control of Outpost Warsaw. In this action, Private First Class Jack William Kelso, 1st Marine Division, earns the Medal of Honor for heroic action in the battle for Bunker Hill. At 1925, the Chinese unleash an attack against Hills 37, 36, and 86, all close to the Sachon River. Hill 86 is the strongest fortified. In the attack, the Chinese are able to drive the ROK back just before midnight.

SEA WAR: The USS *Marsh* (DE 699) and HMCS *Iroquois* (DE 217) are fired on near Songjin. The *Marsh* escapes without being hit, but the *Iroquois* receives a direct hit and is hurt by an air burst that kills three and wounds seven.

AIR WAR: A Meteor jet and an F-86 are shot down by enemy fighters. Francis A. Humphreys of the 39th FIS shoots down an enemy MiG-15.

October 3

POLITICAL/ADMINISTRATIVE: Great Britain explodes its first atomic bomb at Monte Bello Island, 50 miles northwest of Australia. This makes Great Britain the third member of the atomic club.

EIGHTH ARMY: Charlie Company joins Item Company in a counterattack against Outpost Warsaw. When they arrive on the crest, they discover that the Chinese have withdrawn. Six wounded marines are discovered. Reacting to their own withdrawal from Hills 36, 27, and 86 the night before, the Korean marines counterattack and by noon retake the areas. Information taken from prisoners indicates that the Chinese are planning to attack Hill 395 (White Horse Hill). The hill is in the ROK 9th Division sector. The hill, really more of a ridge, is the top of a tree-covered area that extends in a northwest to southwest direction overlooking the Yokkok-chon Valley.

SEA WAR: The ROK navy's MTB 25 and MTB 27 are hit when two aircraft from Task Force 77 strafe Yang-do. Both the USS *Marsh* and USS *Taylor* (DD 551) are fired on but avoid hits.

AIR WAR: An F-86 is shot down near Gisyu by enemy fighters. Three MiG-15s are shot down, one each by Jesse L. Saunders of the 39th FIS, Frederick C. Blesse of the 334th FIS, and one for which credit is shared between C. Canady and A. Whitehead of the 25th FIS.

October 4

EIGHTH ARMY: Reenforcements are sent to the ROK 9th Infantry Division defending White Horse Hill. The marines attack Outpost White, believed to be unoccupied, but as they approached, they are hit with rocket fire. They hold on to the hill for some time and then are forced to withdraw.

SEA WAR: Near Chaho, the ROK navy's *MTB 25* is hit by machine-gun fire but there are no casualties. ROK AMS 515 is grounded southeast of Wollae-do. USS *Heron* (AMS 18) is fired at but avoids damage.

AIR WAR: Task Force 77 planes hit the 67th Chinese Communist Army at Hoery-ong in a 263-plane raid, one of the largest navy air efforts of the war. Pilots from Task Force 77 encounter enemy jets when seven Corsairs from the USS *Kearsarge* (CVA 33) are attacked by seven MiG-15s. One Corsair is shot down. Manuel J. Fernandez of the 334th FIS and Ralph E. Keyes of the 336th FIS each shoot down a MiG-15.

October 5

POLITICAL/ADMINISTRATIVE: Brigadier General William P. Fisher succeeds General Ganey as commander, FEAF Bomber Command.

AIR WAR: Fifth Air Force fighters and USN aviators attack the Chinese Communist 67th Army at Hoeryong.

PARTISANS: CCRAK (Reconnaissance Activities Korea) is redesignated as the 8242nd AU and assumes operational control of Far East Command Liaison Detachment in Korea. This includes all the partisan units.

October 6

POLITICAL/ADMINISTRATIVE: Warren R. Austin, U.S. ambassador to the United Nations, cautiously welcomes the Mexican POW settlement plan offered by Luis Padilla Nervo. The Soviet delegate makes it clear, in private meetings, that the Russian government does not trust the Mexicans.

EIGHTH ARMY: Communists send a battalion-size unit against Arrowhead Hill near White Horse to pin down the French Battalion on the ridge and to keep the 2nd Infantry Division occupied. Communists suffer heavy casualties during the battle, which includes 36 attacks and counterattacks. The Communist troops that had been driven off Hills 36, 37, and 86 on the night of September 3, regroup and again attack the area. This time they manage to push the Korean marines off the hills. The anticipated Chinese attack on White Horse Ridge is precluded by an opening of the floodgates of the Pongnae-Ho Reservoir, about seven miles to the north of the target, in hope of flooding the area and preventing the U.S. 2nd Infantry Division from providing reinforcements. Two battalions of the 340th Regiment, 114th Division, 38th CCF Army, move up the north end of the White Horse area complex. The Chinese try three times to penetrate the ROK perimeter and fail.

SEA WAR: The USS *Sicily* (CVE 118) provides close air support and naval gunfire for the mock invasion of Kojo. They remain on line until October 16. Commander Frederick M. Stiesberg takes command of the Wonsan blockade as "mayor."

AIR WAR: Two F-86s are destroyed in aerial combat, according to Soviet records.

October 6–12

EIGHTH ARMY: During this time, the Chinese make a series of probes against Hill 391, about seven miles northeast of White Horse Mountain. The ROK eventually pulls back.

October 6–15

EIGHTH ARMY: Battle of White Horse Hill begins, signaling that the Chinese are accelerating the ground war. The Chinese, who were repulsed the day before, hit again. During the next several days the hill changes hands four times. On October 10, the ROK is driven off only to take it again later in the evening and to lose it again on October 11. The battle is fought again on October 13–14, and on October 15, the Communist forces decide to withdraw. During the numerous assaults, the Communists have suffered an estimated 9,500 casualties.

October 7

POLITICAL/ADMINISTRATIVE: When the enemy fails to respond to UN efforts to settle the question of POWs, an indefinite recess is called, leaving both military and political prospects stalled.

EIGHTH ARMY: In a series of assaults against White Horse Ridge, the Chinese force elements of the ROK 30th Regiment to withdraw from the crest. But a counterattack less than two hours later allows two battalions of the ROK 28th Regiment to drive the Communists out of their defensive positions. In the seesaw battle that has been going on over Hill 86, the Korean marines counterattack once again and are successful, but after a heavy bombardment they are once again forced to withdraw. This time the enemy is able to hold on. The men of Item Company, 3rd Battalion, 7th Marines, try to set up an ambush in front of Outpost Warsaw but quickly find themselves under attack from Chinese troops on the lower level. The men move forward in an assault and finally manage to take the hill. There are two Chinese counterattacks but by night the outpost is in UN hands.

SEA WAR: During call-fire missions, USS *Iowa* (BB 61) fires its 4,000th round of 16-inch shells during the Korean War. Task Force 77 is attacked three times by MiG-15s in the area between Hungnam and Wonsan.

AIR WAR: Fifth Air Force pilots and USN aviators strike against troop compounds and supply stocks of the Chinese Communist 26th Army at Yongpyongni. A U.S. Air Force RB29A disappears from a routine flight off the coast of Japan. Eight crew members are lost.

October 8

POLITICAL/ADMINISTRATIVE: The United Nations takes up the question of the Mexican POW settlement proposal but no action is taken. President Truman wants the cease-fire talks suspended because he believes the Communists are showing no sign of a willingness to discuss the issues involved in the repatriation of POWs. The Communist delegation at the cease-fire talks says it is willing to accept the UN repatriation concept for the Korean POWs, but the delegation still demands the return of all Chinese prisoners. UN peace talks delegate William Harrison, now a lieutenant general, informs the Communist delegation that the United States is not interested in continuing the talks unless some progress is made.

EIGHTH ARMY: Relieving its forces on White Horse, the Chinese 342nd Regiment, 114th Division, fights its way to the crest during the afternoon but loses it again during a counterattack that night. Operation Showdown is approved.

AIR WAR: Ten B-29s of the 98th Bomber Wing conduct a daylight air raid near Kowon in coordination with a feint of an amphibious attack. A joint navy-air force mission, Operation Red Cow, is conducted with navy Banshees and air force B-29s attacking positions near Kaesong. It is the first such cooperation since August 1951. Twelve F2H2 Banshees from USS *Kearsarge* rendezvous with 10 B-29 Superforts over South Korea. Three F-86s are downed by enemy fighters.

October 9

EIGHTH ARMY: Determined Chinese forces attack White Horse again. Once more the battle goes back-and-forth, with one side and then the other claiming to hold the hill. The Chinese diversionary attack against the French on Hill 282 (Arrowhead) fails.

SEA WAR: More than a dozen North Korean PT boats are sighted in Unggi Bay. The USS *Carmick* (DMS 33) is fired on near Songjin without any damage being caused. In support of X Corps, Task Force 77 flies 91 missions against troop concentrations. Seventh Fleet begins its bombardment of enemy supply lines and facilities at the beginning of the "Cherokee" strikes.

AIR WARS: Fighter-bombers attack Communist communication centers from Hui-chon in North Korea to the bombline (the point where friendly troops are in danger). Heavy casualties are caused among Communist regiments. Karl K. Dittmer of the 335th FIS shoots down two enemy MiG-15s.

October 10

AIR WAR: Robinson Risner of the 336th FIS, 4th FIW, shoots down an enemy MiG-15 fighter.

October 11

SEA WAR: In an accident aboard the USS *Kearsarge* (CVA 33), a helicopter overturns and the blades kill four and injure five.

AIR WAR: Three F-86s are downed by enemy fighters, according to Soviet reports. Jesse L. Saunders and Robert W. McBride of the 39th FIS and Clifford D. Jolley, William B. Hoelscher, and Clyde A. Curtin of the 335th FIS each get an enemy fighter.

October 12

POLITICAL/ADMINISTRATIVE: Mickey Rooney and members of his USO show perform for UN troops as part of the ongoing presence of American entertainers.

EIGHTH ARMY: The ROK launches a counterattack against the Chinese who are massing firepower at White Horse Hill. There is a break in the struggle as the ROK's 30th Regiment passes through the 29th Regiment, which has dug in, and the 28th Regiment passes through the 30th to counterattack. The second Chinese diversionary attack against the French on Hill 282 (Arrowhead) fails. The Chinese begin to send probes against Hill 355. Private First Class Ernest E. West, Love Company, 14th Infantry Regiment, 24th Infantry Division, is awarded the Medal of Honor for heroic action against the enemy.

SEA WAR: In offering protection for minesweepers, USS *Toledo* (CA 133) receives half-a-dozen rounds, apparently from tanks. She returns fire and drives the tanks away. The Kojo Amphibious Feint is carried out from October 12 to 16. More than 100 ships are involved.

AIR WAR: Overnight, 26 B-29s representing all of the medium bombardment units hit nine separate troop concentrations on the Haeju Peninsula. Five F-86s are shot down by enemy fighters. Paul A. Kauttu, Charles A. Gabriel, Cecil G. Foster, and Charles A. Gabriel of the 16th FIS, and Vernon J. Lyle of the 25th FIS, each shoot down an enemy MiG-15.

October 12–14

AIR WAR: Pre-assault exercises are conducted by the 315th AD and the 187th Regiment Combat Team, as a part of the Kojo deception.

October 13

EIGHTH ARMY: After more than 30 days of fighting, Heartbreak Ridge is in the possession of the 23rd Infantry Regiment.

SEA WAR: The USS *John R. Craig* (DD 885) near Kijin-ni and USS *Toledo* (CA 113) at Kojo receive fire but there is no damage. In the same area, USS *Osprey* (AMS 28) receives minor damage, with four men and the executive officer wounded, as *Osprey* guards minesweeping efforts. The USS *Perkins* (DD 877) is also damaged by a near-miss that results in the death of one man and the wounding of 17. Naval units shell the beach area at Kojo as a part of the demonstration there.

AIR WAR: In preparation for the Kojo amphibious demonstrations, aircraft of the FEAF and USN hit enemy positions around Kojo. Bedcheck Charlie shows up again to harass Cho-do and Seoul, after more than a year's absence. An F-86 is shot down by enemy fighters.

October 14

EIGHTH ARMY: Beginning of a six-week battle near Kumhwa for Triangle Hill and Sniper Hill. The object of this effort, known as Operation Showdown, is Hill 598 (Triangle Hill). To its left is Pike's Peak and on the right are two hills called Jane Russell and Sandy Ridge. The name Triangle is given to the battle for these areas. The complex is the goal of the U.S. IX Corps. The complex is defended by the 135th Regiment, 45th Division, 15th CCF Army. The mission is assigned to the 31st Regiment, 7th Infantry Division. The 3rd Battalion, with Love Company in the lead, is sent in as a column to take the apex of the hills complex. The operation quickly comes to a halt due to strong Chinese opposition, and the survivors are held to a small depression near the Chinese stronghold. Seen at first as a fairly routine mission to improve the XI Corps defensive line, the Chinese are determined to stay. King Company joins Love Company and takes Sandy Ridge, then moves along the ridge to Hill 598. By early afternoon Baker and Charlie Companies have taken the crest of Jane Russell. The Chinese counterattack four times before retaking the hills. First Lieutenant Edward R. Schowalter, Able Company, 1st Battalion, 31st Infantry Regiment, 7th Infantry Division, is awarded the Medal of Honor for leadership and courage against the enemy.

SEA WAR: The USS *O'Brien* (DD 725) is fired on by shore batteries near Kojo but escapes undamaged.

October 14–25

EIGHTH ARMY: Operation Showdown is primarily the battle for Hill 598. The 7th Infantry Division battles the Chinese near Kumhwa on the right leg of the Iron Triangle.

October 15

EIGHTH ARMY: In the Battle of Triangle Hill, two fresh battalions are committed to the battle. Troops, supported by artillery and mortar fire, take the hill. The Communists halt their attacks on White Horse Hill after a loss estimated at 10,000 men. Private First Class Ralph E. Pomeroy, Easy Company, 2nd Battalion, 31st Infantry Regiment, 7th Infantry Division, is awarded the Medal of Honor for heroic action against the enemy. The battle for White Horse Ridge is finally over. During the battle, there had been nine ROK attacks and 28 Communist attacks. Operation Feint is launched. It is called the greatest hoax of the war.

SEA WAR: The USS *Diachenko* (APD 123) is fired on near Kojo. Counterfire is offered by USS *Perkins* (DD 877), USS *O'Brien* (DD 725), and USS *Evans* (DD 754) as a part of

Operation Decoy, a feint-invasion against Kojo designed to keep the enemy off-guard. Captain Walter E. Linaweaver takes command of the Wonsan blockade as "mayor."

AIR WAR: As a part of the amphibious hoax at Kojo, 32 C-119s of the 403rd TCW fly over the area, drop down to an approach altitude, and then return to Taegu Air Base.

October 16

EIGHTH ARMY: The Battle of Triangle Hill continues. Jane Russell Hill, part of the Triangle Hill complex, is taken against strong Chinese resistance. The Chinese, who launch a major attack against Outposts Seattle and Warsaw, move against Outpost Ronson as well. The Chinese take more than 20 marines prisoner. The ROK 9th Division sends a battalion from the 28th Regiment to clear Hill 391. Able and Charlie Companies meet little resistance but, as they near the crest, elements of the 135th Regiment (Communist) sweep down on them and counterattack. Heavy artillery continues to be poured on the UN troops during the night.

October 17

EIGHTH ARMY: The Chinese who have taken most of Outpost Ronson are driven off in a counterattack launched in deep fog. Troops at the Triangle Hill complex are rotated, with two battalions of the 17th Regiment, 7th Infantry Division, taking responsibility.

SEA WAR: The USS *Toledo* (CA 133) is fired on, but all the rounds fall more than 1,000 yards short.

AIR WAR: An F-86 is shot down by enemy fighters.

October 17–23

EIGHTH ARMY: Hill 355, known as Little Gibraltar, is the scene of bitter fighting. Canadian troops successfully hold the hill despite heavy bombardment.

October 18

POLITICAL/ADMINISTRATIVE: Rear Admiral H. E. Regan, onboard USS *Bon Homme Richard* (CV 31), assumes command of Task Force 77. Rear Admiral R. F. Hickey, on USS *Kearsarge* (CV 33) relinquishes command of Task Force 77.

EIGHTH ARMY: The 3rd battalion, 17th Regiment, fights its way to the top of Pike's Peak against heavy Chinese resistance. It is able to hold on during the long day.

SEA WAR: The *Daishin Maru* sinks after a collision with USS *Chourre* (ARV 1) near the Shimonoseki Straits (Japan). The USS *Craig* (DD 885) avoids damage when 16 rounds are fired at her from Kosong. Near Sondok, USS *Impeccable* (AM 320) and USS *Chief* (AM 315) are fired on. Their sweep gear is cut but later recovered. The USS *Yarnall* (DD 541) avoids 38 rounds of fire from Songjin.

AIR WAR: Air Group 19, under Commander William Denton, Jr., ends its tour of duty aboard USS *Princeton* (CV 37). Soviet sources report that four F-86s are shot down in aerial combat. Paul A. Kauttu of the 16th FIS and Kirk Vandeventer of the 39th FIS both shoot down a MiG-15.

October 19

EIGHTH ARMY: The day is spent fighting off repeated attacks by the Chinese at Pike's Peak. Heavy artillery and intense small-arms fire finally stop the enemy.

SEA WAR: The HMS *Morecambe Bay* (PF) fires in response to batteries shooting from Haeju at friendly junks in the area. The USS *Parks* (DD 884) avoids damage near Yusong. Captain Milton T. Dayton takes over command of the Wonsan blockade as "mayor."

October 20

EIGHTH ARMY: Heavy artillery and mortar fire are directed at enemy units to slow their attacks on UN troops on both Triangle and Jane Russell. The Chinese are able to counterattack on Hill 391, which has been held by the ROK 9th Division. They are able to maintain control of the hill for two days. In the Pike's Peak area, it is reported that some of the Chinese appear to be "bugging out" and fire is directed on the retreating troops.

October 20–July 27

EIGHTH ARMY: The Hook (called Bloody Hook by the British) is located on the western portion of the Korean peninsula, south of the 38th parallel and north of the capital city of Seoul. It dominates the Samichon Valley. It becomes the scene of one of the longest series of battles in the war.

October 21

SEA WAR: The USS *Lewis* (DE 535), arriving in the area of Hapchinni to silence batteries firing at the ROK navy's AMS *501* and AMS *503,* is itself hit twice. Seven are killed and one wounded in the exchange. The New Zealand frigate *Taupo* ends its duty in Korean waters.

October 22

EIGHTH ARMY: The Chinese launch a heavy bombardment against Hill 355. It is devastating to the men in the poorly constructed bunkers.

AIR WAR: An F-86 is shot down by an enemy fighter somewhere near Siojio. The pilot is captured by the Chinese. Robinson Risner of the 336th FIS shoots down an enemy MiG-15.

October 23

EIGHTH ARMY: Chinese troops move against the Triangle Hill complex. In the Pike's Peak area the Chinese attack again but run into strong defensive fire and a reinforced element from George Company that finally cause the Chinese attack to end. On Jane Russell the same pattern develops and the area is quickly restored to UN hands. The Chinese focus their artillery on Outposts Hook, Warsaw, and Ronson. At 1850, Warsaw is hit by a large enemy force and, despite calling in box-me-in fire, the marines are overrun. The ROK 51st Regiment drives the Chinese off Hill 391, repulses a massive counterattack, and then withdraws.

AIR WAR: An F-86 is shot down at Taisen and crashes near Gisan. The pilot is missing in action. Murray A. Winslow of the 335th FIS and Houston N. Tuel of the 336th FIS each shoot down a MiG-15.

October 24

POLITICAL/ADMINISTRATIVE: A 21-power UN resolution calls for the People's Republic of China to agree to an armistice on terms that include the voluntary repatriation of POWs. The Republican Party's presidential nominee, Dwight D. Eisenhower, promises to "go to Korea" if elected. The secretary of defense informs the United Nations that the Russians signed 17 different treaties at the end of World War II, none of which required forcible repatriation of prisoners.

EIGHTH ARMY: Battle of Triangle Hill (598) comes to an end, as the defense of Hill 301 begins.

SEA WAR: Enemy guns at Kanghwa-do fire more than 60 rounds at the ROK navy's PCS *201* without a hit.

AIR WAR: The important rail and supply center at Hyesanjin is hit by aircraft from Task Force 77.

PARTISANS: Mustangs VII and VIII, with the same mission as the others, are dropped near POW camps. The landings are successful but, as in earlier cases, radio contact is lost after just a few days.

October 24–25

EIGHTH ARMY: George Company takes over the defense of the ground immediately south of Hill 391. It will soon be called Jackson Heights. Early in the afternoon of October 25 artillery in support of the 87th Regiment (NK) begins to fire on Jackson Heights from Camel Back, the adjacent hill controlled by the Communists.

October 24–30

EIGHTH ARMY: The Battle of Jackson Heights sees the 65th Infantry Regiment, 3rd Infantry Division, retreat from the fight without orders. After withdrawing and retaking the hill twice, the men of the 65th "bugged out" on October 29 and more than 50 of them refuse to obey orders to return.

October 25

POLITICAL/ADMINISTRATIVE: It is recommended that the ROK army be expanded to a force of 463,000 men. Five days later President Harry Truman approves the recommendation.

EIGHTH ARMY: The ROK's 2nd Infantry Division is relieved by the U.S. 7th Infantry Division. The 7th Infantry battles the Chinese near Kumhwa and suffers nearly 2,000 casualties. The Chinese return to hit Outpost Warsaw. The marines hold for several hours and then call in VT (time-fuse) fire on their position. Communication with the outpost ends as the Chinese take control. The ROK 2nd Infantry Division is relieved by the 7th Infantry Division as the Chinese hold on to Pike's Peak. The Chinese Communists strike east of Old Baldy against Arrowhead and White Horse during an immense artillery bombardment.

AIR WAR: Fifth Air Force B-26s and fighter-bombers attack the political school at Kumgang, nearly destroying the institution. Royal N. Baker of the 336th gets credit for shooting down a MiG-15, and J. Fields and G. Hulse of the same fighter interceptor squadron share the credit for a kill.

October 26

EIGHTH ARMY: The Battle of the Hook begins and will last, on and off, until July 25, 1953. The Hook is a ridgeline four miles northwest of the point where the

Samichon and Imjin Rivers form to dominate the Samichon Valley. The Chinese attack the Hook but the attack is resisted by the U.S. 7th Marine Regiment. The battle continues during the night, with the 7th Marines fighting a successful defense. Later, when Commonwealth forces take over, they are attacked and lose a significant number of men in the defense. Second Lieutenant Sherrod E. Skinner, Jr., Fox Battery, 2nd Battalion, 11th Marines, 1st Marine Division, receives the Medal of Honor for his heroic action as a forward observer. At the Koje-do prisoner-of-war camp, guards enter the compound and use bayonets and rifle butts to stop a riot. One prisoner is killed and 74 wounded. The Chinese on Camel Back Hill fire on Jackson Heights, and several probes are sent against the UN positions at Jackson Heights.

Soldiers from Headquarters Company moving along a ridgeline *(Center for the Study of the Korean War, Graceland University)*

Sea War: The ROK navy's PC *705* and USS *Chief* (AM 315) collide off the east coast of Korea with little or no damage to either ship.

Air War: Two F-86s are shot down by enemy fighters. E. Hatzenbuehler and E. Webster share the credit for downing a MiG-15, and John E. Taylor of the 335th FIS takes one out himself.

October 27

Political/Administrative: President Syngman Rhee announces that all Japanese technicians and engineers employed in Korea by the United Nations will be replaced by South Koreans.

Eighth Army: The attack against the Hook by the CCF is so strong it drives the marines off the crest. The Chinese are unable to hold it long, however. After being run off major portions of the Hook, the 1st Battalion, 7th Marines, counterattacks and retakes the hill. George Company manages to beat off another attack by the Chinese against Jackson Heights. A second attack further reduces the number of men in defense and the available ammunition. Second Lieutenant George H. O'Brien, How Company, 3rd Battalion, 7th Marines, 1st Marine Division, is awarded the Medal of Honor for heroic action in covering the withdrawal of his men.

Sea War: The USS *Orleck* (DD 886) locates an enemy boat near the bombline that is trying to land troops behind UN lines. She chases the boat but the enemy makes it back to Communist territory.

Air War: Aviation engineers of the Fifth Air Force complete a heavy-duty runway for combat cargo operations at the Seoul Municipal Airport.

October 28

EIGHTH ARMY: Fox Company finally is able to take Jackson Heights from the Communists. Then an enemy shell puts most of the officers out of commission and a large number of men begin to bug out. By nightfall the few remaining officers and men are ordered down and the Communists are once more in control.

SEA WAR: Near Kojo, USS *Orleck* (DD 885) returns fire on a battery that has fired on the ROK navy's YMS *518*. The shore battery is silenced. Near Songjin, USS *DeHaven* (DD 727) is fired on, and at Wonsan USS *Mansfield* (DD 728) avoids 40 rounds sent toward her. The USS *Oriskany* (CVA 34) joins Task Force 77, bringing the first combat employment of the F9F-5 Panther.

AIR WAR: Air Group 102, redesignated 12, begins its tour of duty onboard USS *Oriskany* (CVA 34). The first all-ROK close air support mission is flown to protect ROK troops on the MLR.

October 29

POLITICAL/ADMINISTRATIVE: Soviet foreign minister Andrei Y. Vyshinsky requests that the General Assembly of the United Nations set up a commission of concerned, but not involved, parties to take measures to end the war. The British, French, and Colombian delegates respond that any committee on the war is useless if the Communists do not give up their position on repatriation.

EIGHTH ARMY: The 65th Regiment makes one more effort to take control of Jackson Heights. Charlie Company moves up and takes control of the crest without any serious resistance. The artillery barrage has stopped, and there is no small-arms fire, when, for some reason, the men on the hill panic and start to run. Efforts to get them back fail as more than 50 men refuse orders to return. It is the last effort to take Jackson Heights.

SEA WAR: USS *Bataan* (CVL 29) begins its third tour with Task Force 77.

October 29–30

POLITICAL/ADMINISTRATIVE: Soviet foreign minister Andrei Y. Vyshinsky tells the UN Political and Security Committee that the United States forced South Korea to attack the north in 1950 because the American capitalists needed a war to maintain their economy.

October 30

EIGHTH ARMY: Three Chinese battalions sweep forward and knock the ROK defenders off the crest of Hill 598 (Triangle). The Chinese then beat off three counterattacks.

October 31

EIGHTH ARMY: The Chinese attempt to take four outposts that screen Hill 167, the most prominent terrain feature in the KMC sector. The Korean marines manage to repel the assault and hold the hill. The Chinese attack Outposts 22 and 31 but the ROK army prevents their loss.

PARTISANS: Mustang VII, with five men, and Mustang VIII, with six men, are dropped in the vicinity of POW camps in the far north. Some initial success is reported, but once again radio contact fails and within a few days the units are out of touch.

November 1

POLITICAL/ADMINISTRATIVE: The United States successfully detonates a hydrogen bomb at Eniwetok in the South Pacific. It is deemed 700 times more powerful than Little Boy. Two new elements are discovered in the fallout. The United Nations takes up the Mexican POW settlement proposal but by this time the United States has cooled on the idea. Rear Admiral H. E. Regan on USS *Bon Homme Richard* (CV 31) relinquishes command of Task Force 77. Rear Admiral R. F. Hickey, on USS *Kearsarge* (CV 33), assumes command of Task Force 77.

EIGHTH ARMY: The Chinese launch an attack against Pork Chop Hill, which is being guarded at the time by the Thailand Battalion, assigned to the 2nd Infantry Division. Finally, after three attacks the Chinese withdraw. The Chinese take Jane Russell after a heavy force assaults the hill. The Chinese are still there after they repulse a series of ROK counterattacks.

SEA WAR: The USS *Oriskany* (CVA 34) and USS *Bon Homme Richard* (CVA 31) launch aircraft that attack targets in the capital city of Pyongyang.

AIR WAR: Fighter-bombers attack Yongmi, hitting three railway bridges. Three F-86s and an F-84 are shot down by enemy fighters. Robert A. Windoffer of the 336th FIS, Royal N. Baker of the 335th, and Thomas R. White of the 16th FIS each get an enemy MiG-15.

November 2

POLITICAL/ADMINISTRATIVE: After rejection by the Soviet Union and a cool reception by the United States, nothing more comes of the POW initiative.

SEA WAR: Commander Antoine W. Venne, Jr., takes command of the Wonsan blockade as "mayor."

AIR WAR: The first night air battle between opposing jet aircraft occurs when one USMC F3D-2 shoots down a MiG-15. Soviet reports say six F-80s are shot down by their fighters during the day.

November 3

POLITICAL/ADMINISTRATIVE: Peru submits a resolution to the United Nations designed to break the deadlock over the repatriation of prisoners. It calls for the creation of a commission of five members who will ensure that all prisoners are immediately repatriated according to their wishes. It is rejected by the Soviets as "unworkable."

EIGHTH ARMY: Hill 841 (Heartbreak Ridge) is held by the 2nd Battalion, 160th Infantry Regiment, 40th Infantry Division. Coming from the north a North Korean battalion attacks Hill 930 about dusk. The attack fails, as the four companies on the line are able to drive them back.

SEA WAR: A Marine F3D shoots down a YAK-15. The USS *Princeton* (CV 37) concludes its third tour of duty with Task Force 77.

AIR WAR: William Stratton and Hans Hoglind share the credit for downing a MiG-15.

November 4

POLITICAL/ADMINISTRATIVE: Dwight D. Eisenhower is elected president of the United States.

Eighth Army: The mounting casualties in the Triangle Hill area lead General Jenkins to suspend any further attacks on the complex.

Sea War: The USS *Uhlmann* (DD 687) receives three hits while conducting interdiction fire near Chaho. Three men on board are wounded.

Air War: Reconnaissance shows that enemy repairs have been completed and the bridges at Yongmi are again serviceable.

November 5

Eighth Army: Because of growing casualties, the ROK suspends attacks on the Triangle Hill complex. Estimates are that the Chinese lost 19,000 men defending these positions.

Air War: All air activity is canceled on Okinawa as typhoon conditions prevail.

November 6

Sea War: Intelligence reports the presence of 15 twin-engine, Il-28 light jet bombers in Manchuria, suggesting that the Communists have the ability to bomb any target in Korea.

Air War: Returning to attack the Yongmi railway bridges, 100 night fighter-bombers discover the enemy has moved its antiaircraft artillery and has begun to build a fifth bypass bridge. Kirk Vandeventer from the 39th FIS shoots down a MiG-15 fighter. A. Kelly and J. Kumpf of the 25th FIS share credit for downing a MiG-15.

November 7

Eighth Army: The Chinese renew their attack on Pork Chop Hill. It is preceded by a heavy mortar barrage. After 45 minutes, the Chinese come forward in a wave formation. They move in as far as the first line of trenches, but then the defenders hold and the trenches remain in UN hands. During the night, three additional attacks are staged, but each one is repulsed. Toward dawn the Chinese withdraw.

Air War: In a battle between an American and Soviet pilot Lieutenant I. P. Kovalev, the latter is guided by ground-based radar to a single F-94B. In the fight, the American pilot is reported shot down.

November 8

Eighth Army: The end of Operation Showdown. The UN Command achieves minor gains and suffers 9,000 casualties among ROK and UN personnel. The operation stresses the difficulty of direct ground assaults on enemy positions and encourages General Mark W. Clark to revive the strategy of using air assaults to break the deadlock at the armistice talks.

Air War: Oliver R. Davis and F. D. Fessler (USMC), flying for VMF(N)-513, share credit for downing a MiG-15.

November 9

Eighth Army: The ROK defenders on Anchor Hill are under observation by Chinese forces that want Hills 268 and 345, less than two miles away. Then, a North Korean force attacks Hill 268 (Triangulation Hill), briefly taking the hill. The 1st Battalion, 7th Cavalry, mounts an unsuccessful counterattack and the North Koreans are able to hold it overnight. A North Korean unit attacks Hill 345, but the assault force is dispersed by artillery fire before they get started.

November 10

POLITICAL/ADMINISTRATIVE: Soviet foreign minister Andrei Y. Vyshinsky in a speech to the United Nations rejects the Mexican POW settlement proposal. It is not discussed again.

EIGHTH ARMY: On Hill 268, the 1st Battalion of the 7th Cavalry again attacks; this time they are able to drive the North Korean defenders off the hill.

AIR WAR: The 315th AD air evacuates a significant number of patients from Korea to Japan.

November 11

SEA WAR: Commander Colin J. MacKenzie takes command of the Wonsan blockade as "mayor."

PARTISANS: Partisans are redesignated as United Nations Partisan Infantry, Korea, 8240th AU. Operations Leopard, Wolfpack, and Task Force Scannon are redefined as Partisan Infantry Regiments. Baker Section is now the 1st Partisan Airborne Infantry Regiment (1st PAIR).

November 12

AIR WAR: During the night, six B-29s blow out four spans of the restored bridge at Yongmi.

November 13

PARTISANS: Leopard partisans use silent British sten guns on a raid for the first time.

AIR WAR: In an experimental attack, five B-29s from the 307th BW try to knock out supply areas near Sopo with incendiary clusters. The results are much less than expected.

November 14

POLITICAL/ADMINISTRATIVE: The Communists propose a demarcation line that will maintain the integrity of Line Kansas and the protection of Line Wyoming. UN delegates agree.

November 15

POLITICAL/ADMINISTRATIVE: Ellis O. Briggs replaces John J. Muccio as ambassador to the ROK.

AIR WAR: A 403rd TCW C-119, returning to Korea with 40 men who have finished their R&R, crashes in Japan, killing all onboard.

November 16

EIGHTH ARMY: The Chinese launch themselves against the Black Watch at nightfall. The British have used what time they had to build up fortifications and are able to put up a strong defense. Though they hold it during the night, it costs them more than a hundred casualties.

SEA WAR: Both USS *Swenson* (DD 729) and HMAS *Anzac* (DD) are fired on by enemy guns near Cho-ao. There is no damage to either ship.

AIR WAR: USMC planes, attached to the Fifth Air Force, attack hydroelectric facilities at Kongosan. An F-86 jet is shot down by enemy fighters.

November 17

SEA WAR: The USS *Missouri* (BB 63) and USS *Helena* (CA 75) coordinate with three carriers to support a massive strike on Chongjin, Kilchu, and Hoeryong in the far northeast.

AIR WAR: Fifth Air Force planes attack hydroelectric facilities at Kongosan. Colonel Royal N. Baker, commander, 4th FIG, flying in MiG Alley with the 335th FIS, scores his fifth MiG-15 kill and becomes an ace. Chester Van Etten of the 335th FIS, William L. Cosby of the 336th FIS, Stuart L. Brown and George I. Ruddell of the 39th FIS, and Edwin L. Heller of the 16th FIS each score a MiG-15 kill.

November 18

POLITICAL/ADMINISTRATIVE: A Soviet L-11 flies over Japanese air space and is escorted out of the area by UN fighters.

EIGHTH ARMY: The Communists attack the Hook again, this time under the cover of darkness and with an estimated 500 soldiers. The group manages to infiltrate several marine positions and fighting breaks out in scattered areas. The Black Watch is finally able to get control of the hill but it does so with the loss of 16 killed. The battle for Sniper Ridge comes to a close when ROK units take a part of the ridge for the 14th time since the beginning of Operation Showdown. During the morning, two companies of Chinese infantry leave the assault on Finger Ridge and redirect themselves to an assault against Green Finger Ridge. UN artillery that is called in manages to break up the attack.

SEA WAR: In a four-plane engagement, Task Force 77 pilots score their first kill of an enemy MiG-16. Eighty-six offensive sorties are launched from two carriers in support of air force photo-missions against Hoeryong on the Tumen River. Commander Robert J. Ovrom takes command of the Wonsan blockade as "mayor."

AIR WAR: When USN Task Force 77 fighter-bombers hit the border town of Hoery-ong, unmarked but reportedly Russian MiG-15s flying from Vladivostok attempt to attack the fleet. Carrier-based F9F planes engage the MiG-15s and destroy one. In MiG Alley, Captain Leonard W. Lilley, 334th FIS, scores his fifth victory and becomes an ace. Other pilots downing MiG-15 fighters during the day are Royce Williams, J. Middleton, and Rowlands (USN), from VF-782; and Albert S. Kelly of the 25th FIS. Air Group Seven, commanded by Commander G. B. Brown, ends its tour of duty aboard USS *Bon Homme Richard* (CV 31). The Sonchon supply center, only 35 miles from the Manchurian border, is attacked by six B-29s from the 98th Bomber Wing. In the clear evening, the Communists use new techniques and manage to shoot down one of the bombers.

November 19

Sea War: Guns from Kalmagak fire nearly 50 rounds against USS *Kite* (AMS 22) and USS *Heron* (AMS 18). *Kite*'s float is hit and destroyed and the explosion causes injuries to one officer and four enlisted men.

Air War: Two separate groups, the 49th and 56th Fighter/Bomber Wings, with a total of 179 planes, attack concentrated troops at Kanggye.

Eighth Army: Communist pressure continues against the Hook, but there are no significant efforts to retake the hill during this period.

November 20

Sea War: The USS *Thompson* (DMS 38) is hit by one round, but USS *Kite* (AMS 22) escapes injury when guns from Wonsan are fired at her. One minor casualty is suffered on the *Thompson*. The USS *Valley Forge* (CV 45) begins its third tour of duty with Task Force 77.

Air War: Three F-86s are shot down by enemy planes. Glenn A. Carus and David P. Copeland of the 335th FIS each gets a MiG-15 fighter. Paul E. Jones of the 39th FIS and Manuel J. Fernandez of the 334th FIS each get a MiG-15.

November 21

Sea War: Two ships are hit by shore batteries during the day: USS *Miller* (DD 535) at Sin-po and USS *Kite* (AMS 22) at Wonsan. The USS *Pelican* (AMS 32) collides with USS *Hanna* (DE 449) in the Youngdong defense area.

Air War: James P. Hagerstrom of the 334th FIS, Vernon J. Lyle of the 25th FIS, and Richard B. Smith of the 39th FIS are each credited with downing a MiG-15 fighter.

November 22

Air War: Two F-80s, from the 8th FBW, are lost to ground fire while flying a support mission in IX Corps territory. One of the pilots, Major Charles J. Loring, Jr., is posthumously awarded the Medal of Honor for diving his damaged plane into an enemy gun emplacement. First Lieutenant Cecil G. Foster, flying in MiG Alley for the 16th FIS, scores his fifth kill and becomes a Korean War ace. Other pilots shooting down a MiG-15 during the day are Howard P. Mann of the 39th FIS and Louis A. Green of the 336th FIS. A Chinese MiG-15 makes eight firing passes on a VP-28 P4Y at sea near Shanghai. The P4Y fires back, and after several runs, the Chinese plane flies off. Soviet sources say seven more F-86s are destroyed during the day than UN sources say.

November 23

Sea War: The USS *Wiseman* (DE 667) hits a submerged rock and damages her sonar dome.

Air War: An F-86 is shot down near Kijio.

November 24

Eighth Army: A Royal Fusiliers patrol is ambushed inside its own wire and virtually wiped out, losing 14 dead, 20 wounded, and eight missing.

SEA WAR: One man is killed and the evaporator damaged when USS *Hanna* (DE 449) is hit by guns in the Songjin area.

PARTISANS: Wolfpack partisans are issued and use flamethrowers for the first time.

November 25

POLITICAL/ADMINISTRATIVE: Rear Admiral R. F. Hickey, onboard USS *Kearsarge* (CV 33), relinquishes command of Task Force 77. Rear Admiral W. D. Johnson, onboard USS *Bon Homme Richard* (CV 31), assumes command of Task Force 77.

SEA WAR: The USS *Thompson* (DMS 38) is in the Wonsan area when it hears six to eight explosions. The closest is more than 300 yards away. It is believed to have been an attack by enemy jets but there is no damage sustained.

November 26

SEA WAR: The ROK navy's *PC 315* is fired on by shore batteries from Hungnam but there are no casualties or damage to the ship.

AIR WAR: Six F4Us from VMA-312 on board USS *Badoeng Strait* (CVE 116) are attacked by MiG-15s over Chaeryong with no results. Six enemy single-engine piston aircraft drop five bombs on the friendly island of Cho-do on the Korean west coast.

November 27

AIR WAR: Harold E. Fisher of the 335th FIS shoots down a MiG-15.

November 28

AIR WAR: The 3rd Air Rescue Squadron (USAF) is redesignated the 3rd Air Rescue Group. The group consists of four squadrons and a detachment. An F-86 is shot down near Kijio.

November 28–29

AIR WAR: Three medium bomber units hit Sinuiju and Uiju targets at 45-minute intervals. They fly against an estimated 116 heavy guns, 94 of which are controlled by radar, 40 searchlights, and enemy interceptors. Five B-26s lead the mission, performing flak suppression. Fourteen of the bombers hit the Sinuiju Airfield, six hit the Sinuiju locomotive repair plant, four attack the Uiju communication center, and 10 strike the Uiju Airfield. The B-29s escape with no losses.

November 29

POLITICAL/ADMINISTRATIVE: Two CIA agents (John Downey and Richard Fecteau) are captured by the Communists after their plane is shot down in Manchuria. During the night, an "all-American" operation attempts an extraction.

EIGHTH ARMY: Able Company of the 15th Infantry is ambushed by a unit of North Koreans as it moves toward Majon-ni. The area has suffered so many such incidents that it is known as "Ambush Alley."

AIR WAR: VP Squadron 47, under Commander H. E. Thayer, begins its third tour of sea-based duty in Korea.

PARTISANS: The first extraction using the "Hook" is attempted at Kirin, Manchuria. In this effort a rope is strung between two trees, it is then wrapped around a person's waist, When the aircraft snatches the loop with a hook, it then reels the person in. This attempt fails when the Chinese show up and fire on the airplane.

November 30

POLITICAL/ADMINISTRATIVE: Those responsible for Joint Advisory Commission, Korea (JACK) decide that the operation has been so penetrated by Communists that its effectiveness has been compromised and so the project is abandoned.

EIGHTH ARMY: Private First Class Charles George, Charlie Company, 1st Battalion, 179th Infantry Regiment, 45th Infantry Division is awarded the Medal of Honor after he is killed in an effort to save his companions. The Korean summer-fall phase ends.

SEA WAR: A gasoline explosion while in port results in the loss of one man and three injuries aboard USS *Ashtabula* (AO 51). The explosion does considerable material damage to the ship.

AIR WAR: VP Squadron 28 (Detachment A) under Commander C. B. McAfee ends its land service in Korea. VP Squadron 22 under Commander W. P. Tanner begins its third tour of land-based duty in Korea.

December

POLITICAL/ADMINISTRATIVE: At a meeting in Geneva of the executive committee of the League of Red Cross Societies, by a vote of 15-2 (Soviet Union and Red China opposed) the committee urges that both sides in the Korean War repatriate sick and wounded prisoners as a gesture of goodwill.

December 1

EIGHTH ARMY: The third Korean winter phase begins. It is discovered that the Chinese are improving the fortifications on Hill 134, in the valley of Three Fingers Ridge. A fire mission lobs mortar shells into the area, and it is decided to go out and see what is happening.

AIR WAR: A Patrol Squadron 22 aircraft, flying a routine patrol in the East China Sea, is tracked by four unidentified planes. Only radar contact is made, and the planes move on without firing a shot.

December 1–5

AIR WAR: Marine Helicopter Squadron 161 moves several prefabricated bunkers into rugged hill country, where even the tough Korean Service Corps is unable to carry supplies.

December 2

EIGHTH ARMY: The beginning of Operation Ratkiller, an effort to clean out guerrilla fighters who have been harassing behind the lines. Placed under control of the ROK, the operation is executed in four phases. An element of the ROK 9th Division is on Sniper Ridge. After an all-night battle, the enemy takes the hill. At about 2100, a reinforced squad from Dog Company, 2nd Battalion, 5th Marines, departs from Outpost 2 to check out Hill 134. The Chinese, occupying the hill, wait until the marines are closing in and then open fire. Finding the hill occupied, the mission is changed from a probe to a withdrawal. A relief team brings back the wounded.

AIR WAR: James F. Low of the 335th FIS brings down a MiG-15.

President-elect Dwight D. Eisenhower fulfills his promise to "visit Korea," with a December 1952 trip. General Van Fleet is behind him. *(Center for the Study of the Korean War, Graceland University)*

December 2–5

POLITICAL/ADMINISTRATIVE: Dwight D. Eisenhower fulfills his campaign pledge and visits Korea for three days.

December 2–7

AIR WAR: The number of B-29s allocated for radar-direction bombing in front of IX Corps during the battle for Sniper Ridge, is increased from one to three.

December 3

POLITICAL/ADMINISTRATIVE: The UN General Assembly adopts the Indian resolution 54 to 5. At the armistice talks an effort is made to conduct some discussion that does not impinge on the question of repatriation of prisoners. This is the second day of president-elect Eisenhower's visit to Korea. He is accompanied by General Omar Bradley, chairman of the Joint Chiefs of Staff; General Mark W. Clark, Commander Far East; General James Van Fleet, Commander Eighth Army; Lieutenant General Paul W. Kendall, commander of I Corps; Mr. Charles E. Wilson, secretary of defense-designate; Major General Parson (ret.), special assistant to the president-elect; and Mr. James J. Haggerty, Jr., the presidential press secretary-designate.

EIGHTH ARMY: Heartbreak Ridge, held by elements of the 160th Infantry Regiment, 40th Infantry Division, is again attacked, this time by the NKPA 14th Regiment. The assault is repulsed and the ridge remains in UN hands until the end of the war. ROK units take back Sniper Hill from the Chinese and hold it during numerous counterattacks made by the enemy on the area.

AIR WAR: Over the Pyongyang area, F-86 pilots engage enemy swept-wing jets in strength. Clyde R. Gilber of the 39th FIS downs an enemy MiG-15, and R. Hodge and E. Webster from the same squadron split the credit for a second MiG-15.

December 4

POLITICAL/ADMINISTRATIVE: Prisoners at the Pongam-do POW camp refuse to prepare their clothing and articles for a required inspection. While not of major significance, it is the opening of a period of discontent that will lead to an uprising later in the month.

AIR WAR: Robinson Risner of the 336th FIS brings down an enemy MiG-15.

December 5

POLITICAL/ADMINISTRATIVE: General Douglas MacArthur tells an industrial conference that he has a plan to bring victory in Korea.

AIR WAR: Planes from a U.S. carrier bomb the port city of Rashin to destroy rail facilities. Several enemy aircraft drop three bombs on Cho-do at about 2100 hours. No damage is done. Two F-86s are shot down by enemy planes.

December 6

POLITICAL/ADMINISTRATIVE: Authorities at the Pongam-do POW camp uncover evidence of an escape plan to be attempted at all the POW camps.

SEA WAR: No damage occurs when USS *Moore* (DE 442) and HMCS *Haida* (DD) are fired on near Songjin, receiving more than 15 rounds. Counterbattery fire silences the enemy guns before there are any casualties on board.

AIR WAR: A new flak suppression technique is being tried across the Eighth Army front. It is found to be effective in close air support missions.

December 7

EIGHTH ARMY: Prisoners at the Pongam-do POW camp conduct military drills in defiance of camp authorities.

SEA WAR: More than 30 rounds are fired at USS *Merganser* (AMS 26) by shore installations near Kalmagak. There are no damages or casualties.

AIR WAR: Royal N. Baker and John M. Nichols from the 335th FIS each get a MiG-15 in aerial combat, and R. Baker and J. Ludwig from the same squadron share the credit for another. Cecil G. Foster and Edmund G. Hepner from the 16th FIS each shoot down a MiG-15 fighter, and squadron mates E. Heller and G. Woodworth share credit for another. Louis A. Green and Huston N. Tuel from the 336th FIS each are credited with shooting down a MiG-15 fighter.

December 8

SEA WAR: Aircraft from USS *Essex* (CVA 9) raid railroad facilities near Hunyung. TE 95.11 attacks on the North Korean rice supply culminate in a successful attack on Ongjin that destroys nearly 80 percent of the rice bag supply.

AIR WAR: VP Squadron 731 (Reserve) under Commander W. T. O'Dowd ends its second tour of sea-based duty in Korea.

December 9

SEA WAR: Planes from Task Force 77, in a maximum effort, strike an ammunition factory and rail facilities near Rashin. Observers note that 12 buildings are destroyed and five damaged.

AIR WAR: A B-29 is shot down by enemy fighters near Teiju.

December 10

EIGHTH ARMY: A small group of prisoners at the Pongam-do POW camp assault an administrator at the camp dispensary.

SEA WAR: An all-navy attack by Task Force 77 hits Rashin's munition factories for the third time. It includes planes from the *USS Bon Homme Richard* (CV 31) and USS *Oriskany* (CV 34).

AIR WAR: James F. Low of the 335th FIS downs an enemy MiG-15. Joseph Corvi and Dan George share credit for two Po-2s.

Partisans: The 3rd PIR, formerly known as Task Force Scannon, is assigned a larger operational area. Three battalions, Storm, Avonlee, and Torchlight, join the Kirkland Regiment (battalion) as a part of the 3rd PIR.

December 11

Eighth Army: The 1st Royal Australian Regiment launches Operation Fauna to capture prisoners and destroy enemy emplacements.

Sea War: A marine F3D night interceptor destroys a Russian-built Po-2, a biplane that is being used to drop leaflets. The USS *Waxbill* (AMS 39) is struck by USS *Marshall* (DD 676) causing minor damage. The USS *Shields* (DD 596), USS *Seiverling* (DE 441), and minesweepers avoid damage when fired on at Wonsan harbor.

Air War: Three B-26s are destroyed and six F-84s damaged at Kunsan when a fully loaded B-26, from the 47th FBW, explodes.

December 12

Political/Administrative: Rear Admiral John C. Daniel succeeds Rear Admiral W. F. Paterson as commander of the area minesweeping (COMSTSWEST-PACAREA).

Sea War: The USS *Marshall* (DD 676), USS *Grasp* (ARS 24), and USS *Seiverling* (DE 441) are all fired on by shore batteries from the area around Wonsan harbor. None of the ships are damaged.

Air War: Two F-86s are shot down by enemy planes and a B-29 is taken out near Sakchu.

December 13

Sea War: The USS *Waxbill* (AMS 39) and USS *Marshall* (DD 676) receive more than 40 rounds of fire at Wonsan harbor, some shells coming as close as 10 feet, but no hits or casualties. Twelve rounds of counterbattery fire are returned.

December 14

Political/Administrative: President-elect Eisenhower announces a new policy of firmness in dealing with the Communists.

Eighth Army: There is a prisoner uprising in the small island camp on Pongam-do, where more than 9,000 Communists were sent after the Koje-do uprising. South Korean soldiers are sent in to restore order. In doing so, they kill 85 internees and wound 113 others. This leads to charges of brutality from the Chinese and criticism from the International Committee of the Red Cross. Task Force Paik competes phase one of Operation Ratkiller, killing 1,612 and capturing 1,842 insurgents.

Sea War: The USS *Rochester* (CA 124) delivers return fire, silencing a shore battery at Chongjin that has fired more than 50 rounds at the ROK navy's *YMS 504*. No damage or casualties are reported among UN personnel.

December 15

Air War: Two F-86s are shot down by enemy fighters.

Partisans: Reports from the 3rd PIR suggest that morale is low. There have been several desertions, and the size of the group has dropped from August to December.

Investigations suggest that many UNPIL members joined the group to avoid service in the Korean army. Guerrillas who are holding Mundo receive 30 rounds of fire from Haeju but suffer no casualties.

AIR WAR: An AF-86 is shot down by an enemy fighter near Oksan and another near Fynhuanchen.

December 16

SEA WAR: Previously spared, the railroad facilities and factories in the city of Yusong are hit by a maximum strike from the carriers of Task Force 77. Captain Alvert L. Shepherd takes command of the Wonsan blockade as "mayor."

AIR WAR: Five F-86s are shot down by enemy fighters as reported in Soviet records. Clyde A. Curtin and Ira M. Porter of the 335th FIS each get credit for downing a MiG-15, and squadron mates R. Baker and J. Mass share credit for one downed MiG-15. Leonard W. Lilley and Manuel J. Fernandez from the 334th FIS are credited with a victory over a MiG-15.

December 17

POLITICAL/ADMINISTRATIVE: President-elect Eisenhower meets with General MacArthur, who presents a plan for victory in Korea. The plan calls for an ultimatum to Joseph Stalin to unify Korea and, if that fails, to clear North Korea of military forces by the use of the atomic bomb and by sowing the land with suitably radioactive materials.

EIGHTH ARMY: The 179th Regiment of the 45th National Guard Division arrives at Inchon. It is the first contingent in the transfer by which the 45th Division will replace the 1st Cavalry Division.

SEA WAR: Photo interpretation reveals a drastic increase in the number of antiaircraft guns in the areas for which the navy is responsible. Sixty-one heavy guns and 632 automatic weapons are identified.

AIR WAR: The new Communist Il-28 twin-jet bomber is spotted, having crossed the Yalu River south of the Suiho Reservoir. Three F-86s are shot down by enemy fighters.

December 18

POLITICAL/ADMINISTRATIVE: Rear Admiral W. D. Johnson, onboard USS *Bon Homme Richard* (CV 31), relinquishes command of Task Force 77. Rear Admiral R. F. Hickey, onboard USS *Kearsarge* (CV 33), assumes command of Task Force 77.

EIGHTH ARMY: The 7th Cavalry Regiment of the 1st Cavalry Division sets sail for Japan in the first stage of its replacement by of the 45th National Guard Division.

SEA WAR: At Sasebo, stocks of aviation gasoline are exhausted until the arrival of a USNA tanker.

AIR WAR: James F. Low of the 335th FIS gets credit for the downing of an enemy MiG-15 fighter.

December 19

EIGHTH ARMY: Phase II of Operation Ratkiller begins around the area of Chonju. The operation lasts until January 4, 1953. During this time, the ROK collects nearly 8,000 guerrillas and kills about half of them.

SEA WAR: Guns at Wonsan harbor fire on USS *Waxbill* (AMS 39), but there are no hits to the ship.

AIR WAR: Three aircraft are spotted on the airfield at Pyongyang by reconnaissance planes. It is the first aircraft seen there since October 1952.

December 20

EIGHTH ARMY: The transfer of the 45th National Guard Division for the 1st Cavalry Division is completed.

PARTISANS: Operation Jesse James I (consisting of 10 men) is dropped north of Kaesong, but they are immediately captured upon landing.

December 21

SEA WAR: An accidental bomb drop kills one soldier and wounds three from X Corps. It was dropped by a flight of seven planes from USS *Essex* (CVA 9) flying close air support.

AIR WAR: The new landing strip at Pusan-east is completed by the 366th Aviation Battalion.

December 22

SEA WAR: Three carriers from Task Force 77 send a maximum strike against the billeting areas at Kwangsuwon Airfield.

AIR WAR: A Seafury pilot from HMS *Glory* is rescued near Haeju, on the Yellow Sea north of the 38th parallel, by the crew of an SA-16. The only fatal accident during the aeromedical evacuation occurs when a Royal Hellenic Air Force C-47 hits an F-80 jet while it is transporting patients. Herbert Weber of the 334th FIS and Stuart L. Brown and Harold E. Fisher of the 39th FIS are each credited with the downing of a MiG-15.

December 23

EIGHTH ARMY: At Outpost Arsenal elements of the 38th Regiment are hit by Chinese from the 113th Division. The area is attacked several times, but the regiment holds on at the cost of 47 casualties.

SEA WAR: At Wonsan harbor several ships are fired on with no serious results: USS *Marshall* (DD 676), USS *McGowan* (DD 678), USS *Toledo* (CA 133), and the ROK navy's *AMS 512* and AMS 503. There is no damage or casualties. At Ongjin, the ROK navy's *MTB 23* and *MTB 25*, after firing 32 rockets at a village west of the peninsula, are fired on by machine guns and mortars. The eastern side of Sok-to Island catches 200 rounds of enemy fire. Sosari, on the friendly island of Cho-do, is hit by about 125 rounds. The ROK navy's *AMS 503* and *AMS 512*, are fired on by enemy batteries at Wonsan harbor. The ships are in the vicinity of an estimated 20 rounds of 105-mm fire. No casualties are reported.

December 24

AIR WAR: Four F-86s are reported as being shot down by enemy fighters

December 25

EIGHTH ARMY: The 38th Infantry Regiment, 2nd Infantry Division, repels Chinese forces during an intense battle on T-Bone Hill. Elements of the 179th Infantry Regiment, 45th Infantry Division, hold on to Hill 812 despite an attack by North Koreans.

SEA WAR: The USS *McGowan* (DD 678) is fired on by 105/15-mm enemy shore fire in the Wonsan area. The USS *The Sullivans* (DD 537) receives 50 rounds at Songjin. A plane from the South African Air Force is shot down due to mistaken identity, by a flight of ADs from VMA 121.

AIR WAR: Two F-86s are shot down by enemy fighters near Sensen. William S. Borders of the 16th FIS and James P. Hagerstrom of the 335th FIS are each credited with a MiG-15 kill.

PARTISANS: The island of Mudo on the Korean west coast is hit by more than 130 rounds of unknown caliber. Two guerrillas are wounded. Ten rounds of 76-mm enemy shells fall on Hwangto-do without damage.

December 26

SEA WAR: A PBM-5 crashes at sea while conducting antisubmarine patrol, killing 10 members of the crew of 14. The cause of the crash is undetermined.

AIR WAR: An F-86 is shot down by enemy fighters.

December 27

EIGHTH ARMY: At 0300 hours, a three-company attack group moves out against Harlow Hill and takes it within four hours. Defensive positions are established along the slopes, but the unit finds that it needs to return to locate several missing men. Several efforts to find the men fail.

AIR WAR: Task Force 77's planes fly an all-out raid on rail and highway bridges in their area of responsibility.

December 27–31

AIR WAR: The 581st ARCW sends a flight of four H-19 helicopters from Seoul on an experimental agent-insertion sortie into enemy territory. The raid is designed for covert and clandestine intelligence activities.

December 28

AIR WAR: A downed pilot in the Yellow Sea, north of Cho-do, is picked up by an SA-16 crew from 3rd ARS. Biffle O. Pittman and Harold E. Fisher of the 39th FIS each shoot down a MiG-15.

PARTISANS: Operations Jesse James II and III, composed of 10 men each, are dropped north of Kaesong. No radio contact is established after the drop.

December 29

PARTISANS: Sunwi-do, a friendly island, is hit by 240 rounds of enemy mortar fire from the Changyonsan Peninsula. There is no damage reported and no casualties.

December 29–30

AIR WAR: The 407th BW sends eleven B-29s to attack the Taegam-ni headquarters area. The raid destroys 146 buildings. VP Squadron 17 under Commander R. L. Dahlof begins its tour of land-based duty in Korea.

December 30

AIR WAR: Acting in Operation Spotlight, an RB-26 locates five locomotives in one marshaling yard, and two B-26 light bombers destroy four of the five, damaging the fifth. Air Group Five, under Commander C. V. Johnson, begins its tour of duty onboard USS *Valley Forge* (CV 45). The 19th Bomber Group bombs the ore processing plant at Choak-tong near the Yalu River. Enemy interceptors down one B-29 and manage to damage two others that are forced to land at Suwon Air Base. Soviet records report five B-29s shot down by fighter planes.

December 31

POLITICAL/ADMINISTRATIVE: As the year comes to an end, the strength and security of the UN forces in Korea has brought the cease-fire negotiators to a point where they are no longer willing to meet without any signs of progress. At this point, while they are still willing to make some concessions, the UN position is to take a harder line. Yet each day is costing more and more lives.

1953

January 1

POLITICAL/ADMINISTRATIVE: President Harry S. Truman signs an executive order that expands loyalty screening to include those Americans who are working with the United Nations.

PARTISANS: Far East Command authorizes an increase in the strength of the partisan force to a total of 40,000. The men and women are to be recruited by July 15, 1953.

January 2

POLITICAL/ADMINISTRATIVE: The militant senator Joseph P. McCarthy (R–Wisconsin) is investigated by the Senate Privileges and Election Committee. While his power base in Washington has been in decline, this marks the beginning of the end for the anticommunist crusader.

EIGHTH ARMY: A company of the 1st ROK Infantry Division makes a daylight raid against the Chinese-held outpost Big Nori. The 1st is supported by the 2nd Infantry Division artillery and tanks. The unit takes and then holds the position long enough for it to destroy the emplacements and fortifications and then to make an orderly withdrawal.

SEA WAR: Enemy artillery at Wonsan fire seven rounds on Hungto-do Island, with no casualties.

AIR WAR: An F-86 is shot down by enemy fighters. Captain Charles C. Carr of the 39th FIS and Second Lieutenant William R. Bowman of the 25th FIS are each credited with shooting down an enemy MiG-15 fighter.

January 3

EIGHTH ARMY: First Lieutenant Richard T. Shea, Jr. (USA), is posthumously awarded the Medal of Honor for action near Sokkogae.

AIR WAR: VP-9 Squadron under the command of Commander B. J. Filson ends its land-based service in Korea.

January 4

EIGHTH ARMY: Phase three of Operation Ratkiller begins. This time it is under the command of the ROK's Capital Division working in the area of Chirisan. By the end of January, the operation has killed or captured another 18,000 guerrillas.

SEA WAR: The USS *McGowan* (DD 678) provides counterbattery fire for partisan forces at Hwangto-do.

AIR WAR: The Fifth Air Force sends 124 planes on a strike against the Huichon supply center. During the night, 12 B-29s of the 307th Bomber Wing bomb the Huichon supply area and railway bridge.

PARTISANS: Enemy batteries fire 13 rounds on Hwangto-do Island. There is no damage or casualties.

January 5

SEA WAR: Heavy snow and low clouds prevent the normal operation of planes from Task Force 77.

January 7

EIGHTH ARMY: During the night, engineers sweep the area in front of Hill 134 for mines, in preparation for a planned attack the next day.

January 8

EIGHTH ARMY: With its primary objective to kill or capture enemy soldiers and to destroy fortifications, Item Company, 2nd Battalion, 7th Marines, raids Hill 134 located near Outpost 2. The attack force, with tanks, artillery, aircraft and the men of Item Company, moves forward. Each tank comes forward to make range cards (identifying distance to pre-selected targets) so it can continue to fire even after the smoke of the attack begins. Hit-and-run shock troops reach the objective and deploy flamethrowers and satchel charges. The main force advances, charging in a skirmish. The force manages to take the trenches but the enemy is deeply dug in; with grenades and automatic fire, the enemy stops the advance. A platoon from the 7th Marine Regiment assaults and takes Hill 67 just a mile or so east of Panmunjom. They used seven flame-throwing tanks in the attack. After clearing the crest, the marines withdraw.

January 9

POLITICAL/ADMINISTRATIVE: UN Command launches a last-ditch attempt to force the Chinese Communists to come to an agreement at the negotiation table before President Truman leaves office.

AIR WAR: In an air campaign against the Sinanju communications complex, 17 B-29 bombers launch an attack. Planes from the 307th BW bomb rail bridges at Yongmi-dong, antiaircraft gun positions near Sinanju, and marshaling yards at Yongmi-dong and Maejung-dong.

January 10

EIGHTH ARMY: United Nations Command goes on full alert as North Korea threatens to interfere with the release of 22,500 anticommunist POWs taken by the United Nations during the war. The UN insists that the prisoners are civilians and must be set free. North Korea wants them to remain in captivity pending further discussion. General Maxwell Taylor warns that any attempt by the North Koreans to interfere with the transfer will "most likely start the Korean War over again."

SEA WAR: The USS *Merganser* (AMS 26) and USS *Firecrest* (AMS 10) are on the receiving end of more than 40 rounds of 105-mm enemy fire, from guns located in the vicinity of Ponggang-nio. There is no damage. Captain Carl E. Bull takes command as "mayor" of the Wonsan blockade.

AIR WAR: After B-29s bomb the area near Sinanju at night, fighter-bombers follow up with a 158-aircraft daylight raid against bridges, rail lines, and gun positions. Two B-29s are shot down by enemy fighters and crash northeast of Anju.

January 10–11

AIR WAR: In a night raid, B-29s from the 307th BW bomb the Sonchon and Anju marshaling yards. One B-29 is shot down after searchlights illuminate it, allowing a fighter to attack.

January 11

EIGHTH ARMY: The ROK's 5th Infantry Division waits until a unit of North Korean soldiers enters a tunnel near Arrowhead Hill, and then seals them in with explosives. Earlier the ROK had discovered this tunnel where the enemy was attempting to dig its way close to the Arrowhead defenders. Within a few days, the North Koreans will have opened the tunnel again and then artillery will be called in to close it more permanently.

AIR WAR: Reconnaissance and analysis determine that, as a result of bombing raids, all the railway yards in the Yongmi-dong area have been rendered unusable.

January 12

POLITICAL/ADMINISTRATIVE: Four days of testing begin on USS *Antietam* (CV 36), which has been fitted with a canted (angled) flight deck The effectiveness of this British innovation will determine if the new USS *Forrestal* (CVA 59) will be completed with canted decks.

EIGHTH ARMY: The 1st Marine Division's Reconnaissance Company is sent out on patrol to Hill 266 (known as Old Baldy) to capture a prisoner but ends by losing two men instead. After working through two artillery attacks, the men from Able Company are able to take Hill 266 and to hold the crest against several counterattacks.

SEA WAR: UN-held islands Wollae-do and Yukto are hit by enemy shore fire. No casualties reported.

AIR WAR: The crew of a B-29 bomber and the commander of air force special operations, who is onboard, are shot down by a combination of air-ground tactics that has rarely been used by the Communists. The odd circumstances of the action suggest a major security leak within the American command. An RB-29 is destroyed by enemy fighters.

January 12–15

AIR WAR: Bad weather prevents normal bombing raids, which do not start up again until late on January 15, when fighter-bombers restart the around-the-clock attacks on the Sinanju area.

January 13

EIGHTH ARMY: Two platoons from George Company, 3rd Battalion, 7th Marines, move forward to conduct a raid on the enemy-held positions in the vicinity of Outpost Hilda, lost on August 11, 1952. The unit arrives at the MLR at 0100. The weather is cold and clear when the unit suddenly is engaged by an estimated 25 enemy soldiers that have dug in. Both the officer and the sergeant are wounded and squad leader Howard C. Hensley, Jr., continues the attack. The hard-hit unit moves forward, achieves its objective on Hilda, and then executes an organized withdrawal that takes them more than an hour and a half to travel the 750 yards to the MLR.

SEA WAR: Air Task Group 2, under Commander J. G. Daniel, ends its tour of duty aboard USS *Essex* (CVA 9).

AIR WAR: Twelve enemy fighters shoot down a B-29 flying a psychological warfare leaflet drop over North Korea. Among those lost is Colonel John K. Arnold, commander of the 51st ARCW. The 307th BW and the 19th BG combine forces to launch attacks on the Sinanju and Kunu-ri marshaling yards. Colonel Royal N. Baker of the 336th FIS shoots down a MiG-15, and Colonel James K. Johnson and Lieutenant Colonel George I. Jones, both of the 335th FIS, share a kill.

January 14

AIR WAR: Fighter-bombers hit gun positions and railroad bridges near Sinanju as a follow-up to the previous day's bomber raids. Three F-86s are shot down by enemy fighters and crash in the sea. Eight MiG-15s are shot down: Captain Charles C. Carr and First Lieutenant Fred W. Gray of the 25th FIS share a kill; Captain V. C. Eisenhut, Captain Jack E. Mass, and Captain Murray A. Winslow, all of the 335th FIS, each get one; Captain Manuel J. Fernandez and Captain Leonard W. Lilley of the 334th FIS are each credited with a kill; as are First Lieutenant Joseph McConnell and Second Lieutenant Robert G. Cooke of the 39th FIS.

January 15

SEA WAR: Six PF and four LSSL are formally transferred to the Japanese government. The ships are destined for the coastal Security Force. HMS *Sparrow* is hit by enemy shore fire from the area of Huryomdong. One hit causes splinter damage. During minesweeping operations near Haeju, USS *Pelican* (AMS 32) is the object of 10 rounds of enemy shore fire. There are no casualties reported.

AIR WAR: Reconnaissance photography indicates that the Sui-ho hydroelectric dam and two of the four generators located there are still able to operate. Two F-84s and an F-86 are downed by enemy fighters near Anju. One pilot is captured by the Chinese. Captain David T. Davidson of the 334th FIS gets a MiG-15.

January 16

SEA WAR: Two F9Fs from Task Force 77 are responsible for mistakenly attacking a friendly vehicle from an air control party; one man is killed and three wounded.

AIR WAR: An F-86 is shot down by enemy fighters near Sinijiu and crashes at the gulf near Unden. First Lieutenant Peter J. Frederick of the 336th FIS shoots down a MiG-15 fighter plane.

January 17

AIR WAR: The 98th BW attacks the Pyongyang radio installation, which is located 42 feet underground and only 1,000 feet or so from a suspected POW camp. The 11

B-29s successfully hit the target with eight of their 10 2,000-pound general purpose bombs. However, the bombs cannot penetrate deeply enough to silence the station. Captain Vincent E. Stacy of the 335th FIS brings downs a MiG-15 fighter.

January 18

EIGHTH ARMY: An A-42 dozer tank from Able Company rolls up to Outpost Hedy in order to begin work on a road. It quickly comes under fire. They continue to work to smoothe the area, stopping every once in a while to return small-arms fire.

SEA WAR: USS *Colahan* (DD 650) receives three rounds of fire from Yujin Point, but there is no damage or casualties. The ROK navy's *YMS 514* is bracketed by nine rounds of enemy fire from a shore battery near Haeju, but there is no damage. The UN-held island of Cho-do receives seven rounds of enemy fire from the mainland but there is no damage or casualties. The USS *Waxwing* (AM 389) and USS *Merganser* (AMNS 26) are fired on by shore batteries on the mainland near Onjuin that send in nine rounds of fire with no reported damage. The destroyer HRMS *Piet Hein* leaves Korean waters after a long tour.

AIR WAR: An enemy prop aircraft drops two bombs on frontline troops, resulting in three killed and eight wounded. A navy Neptune patrol plane of VP-22, on a routine reconnaissance patrol near the southern Formosa Straits, crashes after being fired on by Communist gunners on the island of Swatow. Salvage operations begin immediately. A Coast Guard PBM Mariner picks up 11 of the crewmen but crashes on takeoff, burns, and sinks. Efforts by U.S. and Royal Navy surface units, and the U.S. Navy and Coast Guard, are hampered by gunfire from the shore.

January 20

POLITICAL/ADMINISTRATIVE: General Dwight D. Eisenhower is sworn in as president of the United States. John Foster Dulles is named secretary of state, and Charles Wilson is appointed to the job of secretary of defense.

AIR WAR: Engaging several MiG-15s, Captain Richard J. Condrick of the 39th FIS and Captain Robert Wade (USMC) of the 16th FIS each take on an enemy fighter and shoot down their opponents.

January 21

AIR WAR: Three F-86s are downed by enemy fighters near the area of Siojio. Two pilots from the 336th FIS, First Lieutenant Frank H. Arbuckle and Major Robinson Risner, each shoot down an enemy MiG-15. First Lieutenant Joseph M. McConnell and Colonel John Mitchell from the 39th FIS each down a MiG-15 fighter. In addition, Colonel Royal N. Baker of the 335th FIS gets a MiG-15 and Captain Dolphin D. Overton III of the 16th FIS is credited with two.

January 22

POLITICAL/ADMINISTRATIVE: Special Forces units at Fort Bragg, North Carolina, are ordered to send 60 officers and 15 enlisted men to Korea.

EIGHTH ARMY: The U.S. 40th Infantry Division replaces the 24th Infantry Division on line.

AIR WAR: The use of single-engine propeller-driven aircraft in combat ends in Korea with the transfer of the 18th Fighter-Bomber Wing's F-51 Mustangs. The Mustangs are replaced by F-86 Sabres. The capture of Colonel Arnold and three of his crew, shot down earlier, is announced by the North Koreans. An F-86 is downed by enemy aircraft near Siojio. Second Lieutenant William R. Bowman of the 39th FIS is credited with the kill of one MiG-15 jet, Captain Cecil G. Foster, and Captain Dolphin D. Overton, III, of the 16th FIS each get one, and Lieutenant Colonel Edwin I. Heller of the 16th FIS is credited with two MiGs.

January 23

EIGHTH ARMY: After a period of inactivity in reserve, the 5th Marine Regiment returns to positions on the Jamestown Line. After two months on the line, and with 24 men killed, 19 missing, and 366 wounded, the 1st Marine Regiment is relieved and replaced by the 5th Marine Regiment.

SEA WAR: Commander Robert J. Ovrom takes command as "mayor" of the Wonsan blockade, replacing Captain Carl Bull.

AIR WAR: Soviet reports claim an F-86 is shot down by fighters during the day. First Lieutenant Harold E. Fischer of the 39th FIS and Major Harold J. Herrick of the 16th FIS are each credited with downing an enemy MiG-15 fighter.

January 24

EIGHTH ARMY: Two platoons of the Ethiopian Battalion, attached to the 7th Infantry Division, take portions of Old Baldy in a battle that lasts 45 minutes, and then set up for a counterattack. The anticipated attack comes but is repulsed, after which the Ethiopians withdraw.

AIR WAR: Captain Dolphin D. Overton III of the 16th FIS and Lieutenant Harold E. Fischer of the 39th FIS become aces. In Captain Overton's case, it takes only four days. Captain Cecil G. Foster of the 16th FIS also downs a MiG fighter at this time.

PARTISANS: In Operation Green Dragon, a unit of 97 Korean partisans is parachuted into North Korea in the largest clandestine operation of the war. The group is reinforced on May 15 with an additional 57 partisans. During the next few months, the entire group is killed or captured.

January 25

POLITICAL/ADMINISTRATIVE: UN Command restricts immunity to only one Communist convoy per week that makes the supply run from Pyongyang to the Panmunjom area. Evidence suggests that the Communists are using the immunity as cover for the movement of supplies and reenforcements to frontline troops without the threat of air attack.

EIGHTH ARMY: Operation SMACK consists of a failed assault on Spud Hill by elements of the 31st Infantry Regiment, 7th Infantry Division. The operation is an experiment in air-tank-artillery offensive coordination, and because it is an experiment it is attended by a large number of officers. Those witnessing the event are provided with a brochure to explain the exercise. Unfortunately, the word *scenario* is used to describe the action, and in the reporting of the event an enterprising but

misinformed reporter causes such an uproar that the accusation arises that troops have been used for a "demonstration." The failure of the effort adds fuel to this fire.
AIR WAR: An F-86 is shot down by enemy fighters.
PARTISANS: Additional supplies are dropped to the men of Green Dragon, who are in the DMZ to set up a stay-behind mission designed to foment a popular uprising against the North Korean dictator, Kim Il Sung. Two months later, Green Dragon reports that it is down to 31 men as a result of desertion and enemy action.

January 26
AIR WAR: Three F-86s are downed by enemy aircraft near the area of Siojio.

January 27
SEA WAR: CTU 95.2.2 tracks a small radar contact for an hour or more, at speeds up to 25 knots, in the vicinity of Kalmagak, on the northeast coast of Korea. It is assumed to be a PT boat. If so, it confirms intelligence reports that the North Koreans are building PT boats.
AIR WAR: Enemy fighters shoot down an F-86.

January 28
SEA WAR: The USS *Kidd* (DD 661), operating off Kojo, is bracketed by 18 rounds of enemy shore fire but with no casualties.
AIR WAR: Fighter-bombers, taking a break from their focus on enemy transportation targets, attack a troop concentration near Pyongyang. COMAIRPAC declares that the rotation of squadron personnel has to be as a unit fully trained. A B-29 is shot down by enemy aircraft near Pyongyang.

January 28–29
AIR WAR: A B-29 from the 19th Bomber Group explodes over the target during a raid on Sariwon. A 319th FIS pilot in an F-94 uses radar to track down and destroy an La-9 aircraft, marking the first Starfire kill in Korea. For the first time, USMC fighters destroy an enemy interceptor plane at night—guided by radar.

January 29
AIR WAR: Fighter-bombers again attack a troop buildup near Pyongyang. Air Group Nine under Commander T. D. Harris begins its tour of duty aboard USS *Philippine Sea* (CVA 47).

January 30
SEA WAR: The island of Mundo, a UN-held area near the Haeju approach, is hit by 120 rounds of enemy fire from batteries on the mainland. There are no casualties reported.
AIR WAR: An F-86 fighter of the 4th FIW shoots down a Russian-built TU-2 twin-engine bomber over the Yellow Sea. A B-29 from the 307th BW is so badly damaged, after being pounced on by an estimated 10 enemy fighters, that it has to make an emergency landing. Three F-86s are downed by enemy fighters, one each at Siojio, Kijio, and Deeguandong. First Lieutenant Raymond A. Kinsey of the 335th FIS and First Lieutenant Joseph M. McConnell of the 39th FIS each shot down a MiG-15 fighter.

January 31

AIR WAR: Two F-86s and a B-26 are shot up by enemy fighters. One of the downed fighters crashes at Yan-ria and one at Sakchu. First Lieutenant Joseph M. McConnell of the 39th FIS gets his second MiG-15 in two days.

February 1

EIGHTH ARMY: The addition of a Chinese division brings CCF forces facing the UN Command to an estimated all-time high of 841,000 troops. The Chinese send two platoons against Outpost Betty and Hill 105. The ROK withdraws from the two hills and allows artillery to zero in; after about an hour, Hill 105 is retaken.
AIR WAR: USAF F-86s are committed to fighter-bomber missions.

February 2

POLITICAL/ADMINISTRATIVE: President Dwight Eisenhower, in his State of the Union speech, unleashes the Nationalist China president, Chiang Kai-shek (Jiang Jieshi). The U.S. president orders Task Force 72 to cease the blockade of Formosa. This is more political than strategic, with little or no effect on the Formosa Patrol. It is, however, designed to send a serious message to the Chinese Communists about UN intentions.
EIGHTH ARMY: During the night, the North Koreans return to Hill 812 where they face the 37th Regiment of the ROK 12th Division. Artillery fire is called in on the assembling North Koreans but it is not enough to put off the assault. As they get to within 50 yards, a savage exchange of hand grenades occurs and the outcome is in the balance until a reinforcing ROK company comes forward and the combined force is able to push the North Koreans off the hill.
SEA WAR: Two F4Us from USS *Kearsarge* (CVA 33) find it necessary to jettison six bombs. The bombs are probably responsible for three UN soldiers killed and five wounded. Four rounds from the shore batteries at Hungnam are fired on USS *Halsey Powell* (DD 686) but no damage or casualties result.
AIR WAR: Ninety-six fighter-bombers from the Fifth Air Force strike troop billeting areas six miles south of Kyomipo. The raid destroys an estimated 107 buildings. An F-86 fighter is shot down by enemy aircraft. Colonel James K. Johnson of the 335th FIS and Major Foster I. Smith of the 334th FIS each bring down an enemy MiG-15 fighter.

February 3

EIGHTH ARMY: Elements of the 5th Marines conduct a raid on Hill 101 (Ungok), sustaining heavy losses of 15 KIA and 55 WIA. Second Lieutenant Raymond G. Murphy, 5th Marines, is awarded the Medal of Honor for bravery in protecting his wounded men near Ungok Hill. A feint tank attack is launched on the Kumgok Hills west of Ungok. The assault is made with snow on the ground and an air temperature of 2°F. The marines attack is successful on the third try; after capturing the hills and accomplishing the mission, the marines are ordered to withdraw.
SEA WAR: With USS *Badoeng Strait* (CVE 116), Task Unit 95.1.1 launches 66 sorties in a test of the ship's capability to mount an offensive.

February 4

POLITICAL/ADMINISTRATIVE: Zhou Enlai announces that China is ready for an immediate cease-fire on the basis of the agreement already reached at Panmunjom. Of course, this would mean that the United States would yield on the issue of voluntary repatriation.

EIGHTH ARMY: Master Sergeant Stanley T. Adams, 19th Infantry Regiment, 24th Infantry Division, is awarded the Medal of Honor for courage in protecting his comrades and preventing a potential disaster for the battalion.

SEA WAR: Enemy shore batteries at Wonsan fire on a friendly island in their vicinity. The USS *Halley* (DD 556) silences the guns with return fire.

AIR WAR: Two F-86s are shot down by enemy fighters in the area of Gisyu.

February 5

PARTISANS: The friendly island of Hwangto-do, in Wonsan harbor, is fired on seven times by a 105-mm gun that is in a cave.

February 6

SEA WAR: While conducting a whaleboat raid on Hwa-do Island, USS *Halsey Powell* (DD 686) is fired on by four 75/76-mm guns and small-arms fire. Two crewmen are wounded. Off the coast of Chinnampo, four Sea Fury planes are attacked by two MiG-15s, but no casualties are sustained. COMNAVFE issues a directive for the protection of friendly troops by reestablishing control over naval activities south of the bombline.

February 7

EIGHTH ARMY: Outpost Corinne, located about 500 yards ahead of the MLR, is finally in the hands of the 3rd Battalion, 7th Marine Regiment.

AIR WAR: Captain R. T. Dewey of the 334th FIS and First Lieutenant Merton E. Ricker of the 335th FIS each is credited with downing a MiG-15.

PARTISANS: Operations Boxer I and II drop agents on the east coast of Korea, north of Hungnam. The unit is commanded by the CIA; no results of the effort are known.

February 8

SEA WAR: The ROK navy's *MTB 23* and *MTB 25* attack enemy positions on the mainland near Paengnyong-do with 5-inch rockets. A shore gun in the Kojo area fires 10 rounds at an ROK motor sampan but does not hit the small ship. The USS *Swenson* (DD 729) silences the shore gun with counterfire.

February 9

SEA WAR: Several friendly islands in Wonsan harbor are fired on by shore batteries. The island of Yo-do is hit eight times, Sin-do receives 14 rounds, and Hwangto-do receives 19 rounds of mortar and 195-mm fire. The HMNZS *Hawea* (FF) reports contact with a submarine. The contact is held for 18 minutes and missile is fired but there are no observable results. During the night, aircraft from USS *Philippine Sea* (CVA 47), USS *Oriskany* (CVA 34), and USS *Kearsarge* (CVA 33) attack supply concentrations from Wonsan to Songjin, Chongjin, and Hoeryong.

AIR WAR: The Suiho hydroelectric power plant is struck by 22 F-84 Thunderjets of the 47th FBW, which drop 1,000-pound bombs. F-86 Sabres manage to challenge the 30 MiGs that rise to engage them; all the fighter-bombers return.

PARTISANS: Members of Operation Boxer III are dropped, but the makeup of the unit, and the results of the operation, as with Boxers I and II, remain unknown.

February 10

SEA WAR: Several ships—HMS *Crane* (PF), HMNZS *Hawea* (PF), and HMS *Opossum* (PF)—spend several hours investigating a possible submarine contact. At Wonsan harbor friendly islands come under fire. Both Tae-do and Yo-do are hit, but there are no casualties.

February 11

EIGHTH ARMY: Lieutenant General Maxwell Davenport Taylor replaces General James Van Fleet as commander of Eighth Army in Korea.

SEA WAR: Islands in Wonsan harbor are hit for the third day in a row. Yo-do, Hwangto-do, and Tae-do receive hits but there are no casualties.

PARTISANS: The partisan unit Boxer IV drops into enemy territory, with the same results as Boxers I, II, and III.

February 12

EIGHTH ARMY: During the night a CCF platoon, supported by mortar and artillery fire, probes Outpost Hedy, but it is repulsed.

SEA WAR: Attacks on islands in Wonsan harbor continue as Hwangto-do, Sin-do, No-do, and Tae-do are all hit by artillery fire.

February 13

POLITICAL/ADMINISTRATIVE: The first test flight of the Sparrow air-to-air missile is executed, using full radar guidance.

SEA WAR: Hwangto-do receives four hits from shore batteries at Wonsan harbor as the CCF extends the week of sustained bombardment.

February 14

SEA WAR: Shore batteries at Wonsan harbor continue to fire at the friendly islands of Hwangto-do and Yo-do. During the attack on Yo-do, two are killed and nine wounded. A DUKW is destroyed and two others are damaged on Yo-do. The USS *DeHaven* (DD 727) and USS *Moore* (DE 442) provide counterbattery fire, but they, in turn, are fired on. No damage is reported.

AIR WAR: Colonel Royal N. Baker of the 335th FIS shoots down an enemy MiG.

February 15

SEA WAR: The bombardment of the Wonsan islands continues for an eighth consecutive day. The USS *DeHaven* (DD 727) returns fire on the shore batteries.

AIR WAR: Twenty-two F-84 Thunderjets from the 474th FBW hit the Suiho hydroelectric power plant, halting power production for several months. During the night, an attack by B-29s is launched against the Pingjang-ni communications center, causing Radio Pyongyang to go off the air. During the attacks, 82 escorting fighters draw off an estimated 300 MiGs so that the raid can continue. First Lieutenant Lester A. Erickson of the 16th FIS gets a MiG-15, as does Colonel James K. Johnson of the 335th FIS. First Lieutenant Harold E. Fisher and Captain Howard P. Mann of the 39th FIS each are credited with one kill.

February 16

POLITICAL/ADMINISTRATIVE: Two Soviet La-11 fighters fly over the northern Japanese island of Hokkaido. Two USAF F-84 jets are sent up and fire on the Soviet planes. One is apparently hit but both manage to get back into Soviet airspace. Neither the United States nor the Soviet Union make anything of the incident.

SEA WAR: The USS *Segundo* (SS 398) ends its tour of duty patrolling Korean waters.

AIR WAR: Captain Joseph C. McConnell, Jr., 39th FIS, becomes an ace. A second MiG-15 is destroyed on this date, credited to First Lieutenant Harold E. Fisher of the 39th FIS. The 45th TRS transfers all remaining RF-51s to Japan, making the unit an all-jet (RF-80) outfit. Marine and Fifth Air Force planes lead a 178 aircraft formation, including some FEAF fighter-bombers, against troop concentrations and supply storage areas in the Haeju-Sariwon region.

February 16–17

EIGHTH ARMY: The Chinese set up a heavy artillery barrage against friendly positions south of Hill 317. Friendly forces withdrew to the MLR. Counter-artillery fire scatters the Chinese on the hill, and they quickly withdraw.

February 17

AIR WAR: Five F4U aircraft run into six MiG-15s in the air west of Pyongyang. The MiGs make four firing runs and the F4Us three. No damage is incurred by either group. In a separate incident, Second Lieutenant John L. McKee of the 335th FIS scores a kill on a MiG-15 fighter.

PARTISANS: In Wonsan harbor, the friendly island of Yo-do is hit by three rounds of 155-mm fire. The shore guns had been hit the day before by three eight-inch shells from USS *Toledo* (CA 133).

February 18

SEA WAR: The USS *Wiseman* (DE 667) captures a sampan 25 miles south of Chongjin, removes the prisoners, and destroys the boat.

AIR WAR: Four F-86s meet a formation of 48 MiG-14s south of Suiho and shoot down two aircraft. Two other MiGs, trying to follow, are also hit and destroyed. During the battle Captain Manuel J. Fernandez, 334th FIS, downs two MiGs, his fifth and sixth planes, to become an ace. Other MiGs shot down on this date include one by First Lieutenant Ivan J. Ely and First Lieutenant Donald H. Hooten of the 334th FIS; one by First Lieutenant Peter J. Frederick of the 336th FIS; and one each by First Lieutenant Robert Strozier, Colonel James Johnson, and Second Lieutenant John L. McKee of the 335th FIS. During the night, 511 fighter-bombers drop explosives on the tank and infantry school at Kangso, southwest of Pyongyang. The attack destroys an estimated 243 buildings. Two F-86s are shot down by enemy fighters.

February 19

EIGHTH ARMY: Two platoons of the CCF engage KMC defenders in combat at Outpost 33. Artillery, firing in support of the outpost, break off the Chinese attack.

SEA WAR: The USS *Prichett* (DD 561) and USS *Gushing* (DD 796) collide while operating with Task Force 77. There are no casualties, but both ships require dry docking.

AIR WAR: Enemy fighters report shooting down four F-86s, three near Siojio and one at Teiju. Colonel Royal N. Baker and Colonel James K. Johnson, both of the 335th FIS, are each credited with shooting down a MiG-15.

February 20

EIGHTH ARMY: In order to attack Outpost Eerie, the Chinese send two companies along the far ridge of T-Bone Hill, but run into a patrol from the 7th Infantry Division. In the fight that develops, the 17th Regiment is sent to aid the patrol. All members of the patrol are killed or wounded, but their actions have prevented attacks on both Arsenal and Eerie.

AIR WAR: Ted Williams, well-known baseball star, crash-lands his crippled jet after completing a successful mission. He is not hurt.

February 21

POLITICAL/ADMINISTRATIVE: Internecine warfare breaks out between ROK authorities and all partisan commands. The difficulty results from a fear that the expansion of partisan forces might create a group capable of turning on the ROK government. UNC takes steps to deal with the difficulty.

EIGHTH ARMY: An off-and-on battle at T-Bone Hill, which lasts more than nine hours, finally forces the UN troops to withdraw from the outpost.

AIR WAR: Two F-86s are downed by enemy fighters near Gisyu. First Lieutenant Robert D. Carter, Captain Vincent E. Stacy, and Major Vermont Garrison, all of the 335th FIS, are credited with two kills, Carter and Stacy sharing one.

February 22

POLITICAL/ADMINISTRATIVE: In a letter to Kim Il Sung and General Peng Dehuai, CCF commander, the United Nations indicates a willingness to exchange wounded and ill POWs who are fit to travel. The letter asks if the North Koreans and Chinese will consider doing the same. The North Koreans renew their charge of germ warfare against UNC.

EIGHTH ARMY: Twenty-eight marines from Item Company, 2nd Platoon, 3rd Battalion, 7th Marines, commanded by Second Lieutenant James Severn, depart Outpost Dagmar on an ill-fated raid on Hill 144. They never get to the hill. Several marines are killed in an ambush set up by the Chinese, with mortar fire that wounds five men. They return to the MLR. During the morning How Company, 3rd Battalion, 5th Regiment, armed with four flamethrowers, raids Kungok, hitting the hill at daybreak. The battle is indecisive and the marines finally withdraw after suffering 14 casualties.

SEA WAR: The USS *Moore* (DE 442) and USS *Chauncey* (DD 367) trade fire with the shore batteries at Wonsan.

Air War: Air Group 101 (redesignated as Air Group 14) ends its tour of duty aboard USS *Kearsarge* (CVA 33).

February 23

Political/Administrative: After letting the idea sit for two months, the State Department finally approves General Mark Clark's suggestion that the United Nations follow up on the Red Cross idea about the exchange of sick and wounded prisoners. It looks as if they are acting at this time because there are rumors that the Red Cross is going to bring its proposal to the United Nations, which is scheduled to meet later in the month.

Eighth Army: Elements of the 7th Marines attempt to raid Outpost Yoke, a few miles north of Freedom Bridge, but are ambushed and forced to withdraw. The raid is called off. At 2020, a Baker Company platoon and four tanks from Charlie Company leave for an attack on Hill 90. The hill is blocking the way for a desired attack on the Boot. The Chinese launch a counterattack but finally decide they will not be able to take it, and withdraw. At 2400, the Chinese come back and get to within 20 yards of the tanks, but are fought off. After destroying the fortification on Hill 90, the marines withdraw.

Sea War: Captain Lester C. Conwell takes over command as "mayor" of the Wonsan blockade, replacing Commander Robert J. Ovrom.

February 24

Eighth Army: A mile or more from Outpost Eerie, at an area known as Alligator's Jaw, a Chinese company catches a patrol from the 7th Infantry Division and brings considerable fire to bear. Every member of the patrol is either killed or captured.

Sea War: VF Squadron 46 under Commander R. S. Dail begins service at sea. VP-40 Squadron under Commander M. S. Whitener ends its sea-based Korean service.

February 25

Eighth Army: Sent on a mission to capture prisoners and destroy fortifications on Hill Detroit, a marine patrol runs into a reinforced Chinese company hunkered down in fortified bunkers and caves. After a 45-minute fight, using flamethrowers, the marines disengage.

Air War: First Lieutenant Harold E. Fisher of the 39th FIS and Major James P. Hagerstrom of the 67th FBS each down an enemy MiG-15 fighter.

February 26

Eighth Army: During the night, a reinforced Chinese company probes positions held by the 5th ROK Regiment. After more than an hour and an intense fight, it is driven back. Two probes are made by Chinese units but they are beaten back by units of the 2nd Infantry Division. A patrol is sent to investigate the area north of Outpost Carson. The men make no contact but hear noises like men digging on Ungok. On the return, the patrol receives some isolated mortar fire.

Air War: In response to an increase in enemy truck movements, the Fifth Air Force institutes a daily daylight reconnaissance over northwestern Korea.

February 27

EIGHTH ARMY: Lieutenant Livingston and 30 men from the 1st Platoon of the 1st Marine Reconnaissance Company proceed down a finger of land that extends from COP 2, known as Gray Rock Ridge. The group runs into a Chinese ambush. Discovering that they have not recovered all of their platoon, Able Company is ordered to cover an evacuation. Receiving incoming fire, they return unsuccessfully to base, having suffered an additional six casualties. The 26th Infantry Scout Dog Platoon is cited in General Orders, Department of the Army, No. 21, for exceptionally meritorious conduct in direct support of combat operations in Korea. The Reconnaissance Company, 1st Marine Division, fights a battle for control of Gray Rock Ridge, after the failure of an attack that produces numerous casualties.

February 28

EIGHTH ARMY: The Reconnaissance Company is notified that the four men listed as missing from the 3rd Platoon patrol, have been found and rescued by marines from Able Company, 1st Battalion, 7th Regiment, during its sweep of Gray Rock. The commander of the Reconnaissance Company calls in an artillery strike on a group of 15 Chinese soldiers who have been seen in the moonlight near Hill 134. The fire that is delivered kills all of the enemy soldiers.

AIR WAR: Two new and much-larger H-19 helicopters are crated and flown in to the Third Air Rescue Squadron. Aircraft from Task Force 77 bomb and strafe Communist power plants.

March 1

EIGHTH ARMY: Pork Chop Hill comes under an 8,000-round artillery barrage from the CCF, but the anticipated ground attack never comes. A patrol from George Company, 3rd Battalion, 7th Marines, beats off a small probe against Bunker Hill. An enemy company attacks the French-held positions along the 2nd Infantry Division front. At 0030, a patrol from George Company, 3rd Battalion, 7th Regiment, engages five soldiers it finds digging a trench near Bunker Hill. The patrol advances, kills the men, and blows up the trench. A Communist company attacks the French Battalion on line and puts them under heavy artillery bombardment. The French are able to meet the assault and repulse it.

PARTISANS: After a brief pause, the enemy shore guns at Wonsan harbor fire on the partisans on Yo-do Island.

March 2

AIR WAR: An F-86 jet is shot down by enemy fighters near Anju.

SEA WAR: The New Zealand ship HMNZS *Kaniere* joins UN Command in Korean waters.

March 3

EIGHTH ARMY: The Chinese launch another attack, first on the Hook, which they are able to overrun, and then they turn their mortars, and send their troops, against Pork Chop Hill. The hill is being held by elements of the 31st Infantry

Regiment, 7th Infantry Division. The 31st manages to hold on through the night, though the battle will continue for more than 20 days. Easy Company, 2nd Battalion, 5th Marines, engages the enemy at Hill 98 near Outpost Frisco. After a three-minute fight, the marines, one killed, one missing, and 17 wounded, return to the MLR.

AIR WAR: Three F-86s and an F-94 are shot down near Teiju by enemy fighter planes.

March 4

POLITICAL/ADMINISTRATIVE: A Polish air force pilot defects to the West, bringing with him his MiG-15 fighter. Leaving from his base in the Baltic, he flies to the Danish island of Bornholm where he delivers the first complete MiG-15 in exchange for asylum.

SEA WAR: The ROK navy's *LSSL 110*, in attempting to go alongside USS *Laws* (DD 558), anchored off Nan-do Island, collides with the *Laws* and causes slight damage to the destroyer's starboard side.

March 5

POLITICAL/ADMINISTRATIVE: Soviet dictator Joseph Stalin dies following a stroke. He has been chairman of the CPSU since 1922. Leadership is temporarily invested in a troika composed of Georgi Malenkov, Nikolai Bulganin, and Nikita Khrushchev. The role of general secretary of the Communist Party of the Soviet Union fell to Malenkov. The change of leadership brings a new tone to the Korean armistice talks.

SEA WAR: At Wonsan harbor, USS *Missouri* (BB 63) trades fire with shore batteries, but the battleship is not hit.

AIR WAR: Planes flying off USS *Valley Forge* (CVA 46) hit and destroy the hydroelectric station at Chosan. After a period of bad weather Fifth Air Force is able to complete 700 sorties, as F-84 Thunderjets strike industrial targets near Chongjin, less than 65 miles south of the Siberian border. The planes destroy several buildings, two roads, and two rail bridges. In ground-support missions, several bunkers and gun positions are hit. During the night, two medium bombers fly close air support missions for the U.S. I and X Corps. Seventeen B-29s of the 98th BG strike near Onjong, North Korea, a major supply area. Two B-29s hit the east coast marshaling yards at Naewan-ni.

PARTISANS: Yo-do Island, in Wonsan harbor, receives eight rounds of unreported-caliber enemy fire. No damage occurs.

March 6

EIGHTH ARMY: During the early morning, several large Chinese units attack the ROK's 1st Division in the area of Kelly Hill. Fighting hand-to-hand, the enemy is driven back several times only to counterattack and take back some of the area they have lost. Eventually, after control of the hill changes hands several times, the enemy pulls back and withdraws. A combat patrol from the 31st Infantry Regiment, 7th Infantry Division, ambushes a Chinese battalion en route to attack Pork Chop Hill. The Chinese artillery bombardment in preparation for the attack on Pork Chop had already begun, but the enemy's plan to attack is interrupted.

Skyraiders prepared for takeoff from USS *Valley Forge (Center for the Study of the Korean War, Graceland University)*

SEA WAR: A Corsair lands aboard USS *Oriskany* (CVA 34) with an unexploded, 200-pound general purpose bomb. The bomb explodes when it hits the deck, destroys the number three elevator platform, kills two, and wounds 13 others.

AIR WAR: Aircraft from USS *Laws* (DD 558), in coordination with planes from Task Force 77, hit Hungnam, destroying several rail cars. A new type of MiG is sighted over Korea. The new plane has swept-back wings, a flow-fence (for better control) on each wing, and appears to be painted silver.

March 7

EIGHTH ARMY: Communist prisoners of war on the island of Yoncho-do revolt and stage an attack on the compound commander. The riot is put down at the cost of 27 POWs killed and 60 wounded. A combat patrol from Able Company, 1st Battalion, 5th Marines, is confronted by two enemy squads near Outpost Stromboli (Corinne). The unit withdraws to the MLR with three casualties, only to discover that it is missing a man. A rescue squad goes back to look for the man at 0330. It returns empty-handed after suffering four casualties from mortar fire.

SEA WAR: The USS *Black* (DD 666) collides with and sinks a South Korean intelligence boat near Nan-do. Six men aboard the ROK vessel are lost.

March 8

AIR WAR: Marine jets planes conduct a night radar bombing mission. Colonel Royal N. Baker of the 335th FIS, Major Harold J. Herrick and First Lieutenant Leon B.

Perkins of the 16th FIS, and First Lieutenant Joseph M. McConnell of the 39th FIS are each credited with downing an enemy MiG-15 fighter.

March 9

POLITICAL/ADMINISTRATIVE: Charges are made that UNC planes are following MiGs into Manchuria and attacking the planes while they are in Chinese territory. The FEAF admits that some crossings have been made in the heat of battle, but instructs all pilots to be sure that no more such incidents occur. This ensures a safe sanctuary for retreating enemy fighters.

EIGHTH ARMY: A 34-man patrol of the 7th Infantry Division falls into an ambush. Surrounded by an estimated 60 Chinese soldiers, the patrol is decimated, with 20 killed, two missing, and 12 wounded. A patrol of the 2nd Infantry Division is also ambushed and loses 12 killed, five missing, and 43 wounded. A body is discovered in the vicinity of the March 7 firefight, but it is not the missing man.

SEA WAR: Near Anbyon, three enemy guns fire on the ROK navy's *AMS 506* and *AMS 510*. Both ships are hit, but there are no casualties. The USS *Graffias* (AF 29) receives the Presidential Unit Citation.

AIR WAR: Enemy fighter planes shoot down two F-86s in the area of Teiju. Captain Manuel J. Fernandez of the 334th FIS, First Lieutenant John W. Goodwill of the 16th FIS, and Colonel John W. Mitchell of the 39th FIS are each credited with a downed MiG-15.

PARTISANS: Islands in Wonsan harbor are fired on by shore batteries in a series of isolated incidents.

March 10

SEA WAR: Wonsan harbor islands are hit once again by fire from shore batteries. The USS *Missouri* (BB 63) is fired on during a gun strike in the harbor. There are no hits. USS *Merganser* (AMS 26) is also fired on by shore batteries, with no hits.

AIR WAR: An observation plane is hit by gunfire near the MLR. The plane catches fire and two men bail out. Efforts by a fire team from Outpost Reno to rescue the men fail, and the men are captured.

March 11

SEA WAR: Friendly islands in Wonsan harbor continue to receive incoming fire from shore batteries.

AIR WAR: The South African squadron arrives in Korea flying Mustangs that are replaced as quickly as possible. On this date, they fly their first operational mission with new Sabre jets.

March 13

AIR WAR: Colonel Royal N. Baker, with the 4th Fighter-Interceptor Wing, becomes the fifth-ranking ace of the Korean War. Air Group 5 under Commander John E. Parks begins its tour of duty aboard USS *Princeton* (CVA 37). Aircraft of Task Force 77 devastate Chonjin, North Korea. During the night, 12 B-29s, from the 307th BW, strike the cantonment near Choak-tong's ore processing plant, located near the Yalu River. Two F-86s are shot down by enemy fighters. Colonel Royal N. Baker of the

335th FIS is credited with downing a MiG-15. Captain Elmer N. Dunlap and Major James P. Hagerstrom of the 67th FBS divide two credits, with Hagerstrom downing one-and-a-half. Major Raymond E. Evans and Captain Lonnie R. Moore of the 335th FIS share one credit. Squadron Leader Graham S. Hulse (RAF) and Major Eugene M. Sommerich of the 336th FIS divide a credit. Colonel Maurice L. Martin of the 67th FIS and First Lieutenant William F. Loyd of the 336th FIS each get a MiG-15.

PARTISANS: The shore batteries at Wonsan continue to fire on friendly islands in the harbor region.

March 14

EIGHTH ARMY: With the end of Operation Ratkiller, the effort to clean out guerrillas and insurgents operating behind UN lines comes to a close. The success of the operation is doubtful, not because the operation was unable to kill or capture a significant number of insurgents, but because it uncovered evidence that there was still large-scale support for the Communist movement in South Korea.

AIR WAR: In an effort to provoke aerial engagements with Communist fighter planes, Fifth Air Force combat crews drop leaflets asking "Where is the Communist Air Force?" USS *Oriskany* (CVA 34) flies 104 sorties against complexes northwest of Songjin. Colonel Robert P. Baldwin and First Lieutenant Joseph M. McConnell of the 39th FIS each are credited with downing a MiG-15 fighter. First Lieutenant Walter W. Fellman of the 336th FIS and Captain Manuel J. Fernandez of the 334th FIS are also each credited with one downed MiG. Major Raymond E. Evans and Second Lieutenant Joe B. Farris, Lieutenant Colonel George L. Jones, and Major Jack E. Mass of the 335th FIS each are credited with half a kill. Captain Manuel J. Fernandez of the 334th FIS is credited with two kills. Captain Harold E. Fisher of the 39th FIS, Second Lieutenant Richard P. Guidroz, and Captain Murray A. Winslow of the 335th FIS, and Captain Houston N. Tuel of the 336th FIS are each credited with a kill.

March 15

POLITICAL/ADMINISTRATIVE: The Soviet Union merges the Military Ministry and the Ministry of the Navy to form the Ministry of Defense, ending the independent status of the Soviet navy.

EIGHTH ARMY: Vehicle sightings indicate a significant decrease in enemy activity from that in January and February. The assumption is that muddy and slippery road conditions, created by the spring thaws, already hamper Communist movement.

AIR WAR: On one of the few good flying days, pilots of VMA-312, flying from USS *Bataan* (CVL 29), destroy eight rail cars, a power transformer, and numerous other assorted targets.

March 16

POLITICAL/ADMINISTRATIVE: The Soviet Union gives the peace talks a boost when Georgi Malenkov speaks in support of a cease-fire in Korea and suggests that the differences between the United States and the Soviet Union are such that they can be solved by peaceful means.

SEA WAR: The USS *James E. Kyes* (DD 787) is fired on by shore batteries at Songjin (Kimchaek). Ten rounds of mixed 82-mm mortar and 120-mm fire come close to the ship but do not cause any damage. The USS *Gull* (AMS 15) is fired on by shore batteries, taking one minor hit. The hit, one out of more than 60 enemy rounds, causes minor damage and wounds two persons.

PARTISANS: Hwangto-do Island is again bombarded by enemy guns at Wonsan. There is no significant damage to the encampments or the inhabitants.

March 17

EIGHTH ARMY: Little Gibraltar (Hill 355), held by the 9th Infantry Regiment, 2nd Infantry Division, is assaulted by a Chinese unit. The enemy is able to push through the wire and into some of the advanced trenches. One platoon position is overrun, but the second platoon held as reinforcements were sent in. The Chinese began to disengage as 2nd Infantry Division artillery begins to zero in. The cost of the defense is more than 100 casualties, but the enemy loss is estimated at 4,000.

SEA WAR: Shore batteries at Songjin fire on USS *Taussig* (DD 746) and USS *James E. Kyes* (DD 787). The *Taussig* is hit with one shell, and one seaman is wounded.

AIR WAR: During the night, medium bombers from the 307th WB and the 19th BG drop bombs on troop concentrations near Punghwa-dong. This serves notice, as well, that UN planes will continue to strike the area known as MiG Alley. The bombers suffer a good deal of flak but no planes are destroyed.

March 18

EIGHTH ARMY: On a cold evening, a George Company patrol departs the MLR at 2000 and makes contact at 2100 near Outpost Ginger. They observe eight Chinese soldiers in the process of setting up an ambush. The marines move unseen to a high bluff overlooking them, call in 60-mm mortar fire, and then attack with grenades and small-arms fire. Surprised that they are able to kill or wound all the Chinese and with no casualties, they withdraw to the MLR. An outpost held by ROK marines is overrun by two enemy platoons as preparation for an attack against the 5th Marine Regiment sector the following day.

SEA WAR: USNS *LST 623* suffers minor damage when she runs aground near Sokch'o-ri.

March 18–29

EIGHTH ARMY: The 1st Marines launch a series of harassing attacks on Outposts Hedy, Bunker Hill, Esther, Dagmar, and Kate, but attacks are repulsed.

March 19

POLITICAL/ADMINISTRATIVE: The Council of Ministers of the Soviet Union approves a letter addressed to Kim Il Sung and Chairman Mao Zedong, stating that an exit from the Korean War must be achieved. The letter instructs the two leaders on how an end to the war can be accomplished. The Soviets send a message to the West when Radio Moscow concedes, for the first time, that the United States and Great Britain made a significant contribution to the defeat of Germany in 1945.

EIGHTH ARMY: At 0518, two reinforced platoons of more than 111 men from Baker Company, 1st Battalion, 5th Marines, leave the MLR supported by artillery fire on nearby hills. When the artillery fire is moved to Hill Ungok, one 90-mm round is placed on target every 30 seconds. Heavy return fire coming from caves holds the 3rd Platoon just after they get to the advance trenches. When they got there, the Chinese retreat into a feeder trench and leave only a small guard. After making contact, the involved platoons receive word to disengage. At 0005, a George Company patrol leaves the MLR to cover an area west of Outpost Esther. After an hour, they run into elements of a Chinese company on its way to the outpost. They immediately open fire and surprise the enemy enough for the marines to withdraw to Outpost Esther. The Chinese follow with an attack on the outpost. The battle is fierce but short, and the defenders are able to fight off the attack and eventually drive the enemy away.

SEA WAR: Enemy shore batteries at Wonsan fire on Yo-do and Hwangto-do. The USS *Los Angeles* (CA 135), sailing in the area of Wonsan harbor, is also fired on, also with no damage.

AIR WAR: Task Force 77 launches a three-carrier strike against Chongjin.

March 20

POLITICAL/ADMINISTRATIVE: Operation Moolah is established to encourage a Chinese or North Korean defector to bring a MiG to the West. The plan offers $100,000 and political asylum to the first North Korean or Chinese pilot to deliver a MiG-15 to Kimpo Airfield. Two million leaflets announcing the operation are dropped over enemy territory, and the message is broadcast in three languages.

EIGHTH ARMY: A 21-man patrol from Fox Company, 2nd Battalion, 1st Regiment, leaves the MLR for Hill 64, a Chinese position opposing Outpost Ingrid. At 2115, the patrol locates and engages a Chinese platoon west of Ingrid. After an exchange of small-arms fire and hand grenades, Fox Company loses radio contact. Fearing the worst, reinforcements are dispatched to Ingrid. At 2200, three men from the patrol return to Fox Company and report the unit to be pinned down behind Outpost Ingrid. A platoon leaves the MLR with stretchers to locate the men. By 2320, four of the men are still unaccounted for. At 0255, two more of the missing are located, both dead. The remaining bodies will be found on April 7.

SEA WAR: The heaviest naval bombardment of the war is directed on Communist lines at Kosong, just north of the future cease-fire line on the east coast.

March 21

POLITICAL/ADMINISTRATIVE: North Korean truce delegates, acknowledging they are willing to accept the provisions of the Geneva Convention, agree to an exchange of sick and wounded POWs.

EIGHTH ARMY: The battle for the Hook continues with a Chinese attempt at the ridge line. The defense is conducted by the U.S. 2nd Infantry Division, which had relieved the Commonwealth Division in February. The Americans repulse attacks by several companies of Chinese soldiers.

Sea War: Captain Lester C. Conwell takes command as "mayor" of the Wonsan blockade.

Air War: U.S. Air Force captains Manuel J. Fernandez, Jr., of the 4th Fighter Wing and Harold Fischer of the 51st Fighter Wing qualify as double aces in the war. During the night, 28 medium bombers conduct Operation Spring Thaw, during which they knock out spans of two major bridges in the Yongmi-dong area and damage a third, making the bridges useless.

March 22

Eighth Army: The Chinese send two companies, preceded by heavy mortar and artillery fire, against the 1st Marine Regiment's outposts at Bunker Hill and Outpost Hedy. In hand-to-hand combat, with the enemy under the light of a UNC flare plane, the marines are able to force the enemy to pull back.

Sea War: Shore batteries at Wonsan harbor fire on USS *Missouri* (BB 63) but there are no hits. The USS *Prichett* (DD 561) and USS *Waxbill* (AMS 39) are also fired on with no reported damage.

Air War: During the night, eight B-29s of the 19th once again attack the Yongmi-dong bridges. The enemy has managed to repair one of the bridges damaged the night before. A third attack is canceled after reports of increasing flak.

March 23

Political/Administrative: ROK president Rhee threatens to remove the ROK army from United Nations Command in protest over what he perceives as vastly weakened armistice terms.

Eighth Army: A regiment-size force consisting of elements of the CCF 67th Division, 23rd Army, and the 141st Division of the 47th Army, assaults both Hill 266 (Old Baldy) and Hill 255 (Pork Chop). The fighting is intense and made even more so by the political pressure being brought to bear. Defended by the U.S. 31st Infantry Regiment, 7th Infantry Division, and its attached Colombian Battalion, Hill 266 is the focus. When their ammunition is gone and promised reenforcements are slow to arrive, the defenders are forced to pull back. The attack on Pork Chop forces the defenders off Pork Chop, but a counterattack recaptures the hill. On April 6, the Chinese try again and the fight continues through April 18, when the Chinese withdraw. They continue to bombard the hill, however, and on July 6 are back. As the battle escalates, General Maxwell Taylor determines that the area is becoming more costly than the potential political gains warrant, and on July 11, 1953, he orders a withdrawal.

Sea War: At Songjin, USS *Owen* (DD 536) is fired on by shore batteries but not hit. The friendly island of Yo-do in Wonsan harbor is fired on, but the hits do no damage. At Wonsan harbor, USS *Eversole* (DD 789) and the ROK navy's *AMS 502* and *AMS 515* are fired on, with no damage.

Air War: The waterpower site below the Fusen Reservoir is hit by aircraft from USS *Oriskany* (CVA 34).

March 24

Eighth Army: After retreating during the night, a reinforced 7th Infantry Division, lead by Easy and Able Companies of the 31st Regiment, retakes Pork Chop

Hill against light resistance. They find Pork Chop nearly destroyed. The 2nd Infantry Division artillery, in support of the 7th, fires more than 15,000 rounds in a week.

March 25

EIGHTH ARMY: Chinese Communist Forces attack and take Hill 266. A series of minor battles breaks out in the 1st Marine sector as units of one or two platoons probe in the area of Outpost Dagmar. These are part of a regiment-sized raid against Outposts Vegas, Carson, and Reno.

March 26

EIGHTH ARMY: The fifth battle for Old Baldy ends. The third battle for Pork Chop ends. At 1900, breaking the calm on a warm evening, the Chinese attack with small-arms fire, coming from the enemy at Hills 40, 44, 35, and 33. Attacks expand against outposts in the Nevada Complex (Reno, Vegas, Carson) of the area held by the 5th Marine Regiment. The areas come under heavy assault. The Chinese launch a significant attack against Outpost Dagmar where the marine unit is able to hold the hill. The Chinese launch an attack against Outposts Berlin and East Berlin in the 3rd Battalion, 5th Marine, sector. Both outposts remain in marine hands. As many as 3,500 Chinese from the 358th Regiment, 120th Infantry Division, swarm down from their positions on Hill 190 and begin a move toward Outpost Vegas. Before nightfall they have overrun Vegas and Reno.

AIR WAR: Reports from Fifth Air Force acknowledge seeing more than 289 MiG-15 fighters during the day, the highest number of enemy fighters recorded in several months. Major Vermont Garrison of the 335th FIS is credited with downing an enemy MiG-15.

March 26–March 30

EIGHTH ARMY: The dates given for the Battle of the Nevada cities. The Chinese launch a massive attack against marine positions south of Hill 167. The Chinese continue to hold positions on the reverse slope of the hill. Believing that the hill will be in the UN area after the armistice, efforts are made to fortify it.

March 27

POLITICAL/ADMINISTRATIVE: The Joint Chiefs of Staff recommends the use of tactical nuclear weapons in Korea, suggesting they will provide greater efficiency. They suggest that the potential use be a part of any consideration of further military plans that involve the Chinese Communists.

EIGHTH ARMY: In a fierce battle, the 5th Marine Regiment takes back Outpost Vegas, which had been taken the day before by a significant unit of Chinese troops. Chinese units probe at Outpost Kate but are driven off by marine defenders after a 15-minute fight. Hospital Corpsman Francis C. Hammond, 1st Marine Division, is awarded the Medal of Honor for staying with his wounded comrades near Sanac-dong. At about 1800 hours, planes from VMA-323 provide a two-hour bombardment and smoke attack against enemy emplacements located on Hill 139. The Communists are using it for observation. Hospital Corpsman Third Class William

R. Charette, 1st Marine Division, receives the Medal of Honor for his aid in protecting the wounded under his charge near the Panmunjom Corridor. At 1900, the Chinese launch a direct attack on Outpost Reno, and by evening, the enemy takes control of the lower trenches. Efforts to dislodge them fail.

Sea War: At Wonsan harbor, USS *Los Angeles* (CA 135) is hit by incoming fire, causing minor damage but no casualties.

Air War: During the night, Task Force 77 launches saturating attacks on a supply area 10 miles north of the main line of resistance, flying 216 sorties from USS *Princeton* (CVA 37), USS *Philippine Sea* (CVA 47), and USS *Oriskany* (CVA 34). Two MiG-15s attack two RF-80s and two RAAF Meteors between Sariwon and Sinmak. The MiGs are equipped with external fuel tanks. This is one of several such attacks near the front lines, apparently a response to the provocations issued by UN fighters. Major James P. Hagerstrom, 67th FBS, destroys his fifth MiG-15 to become the 28th ace of the Korean War. First Lieutenant John I. Metten, also of the 67th, is credited with a MiG-15 kill. An F-86 is shot down by an enemy aircraft near Teiju. Pilots of Colonel Bowman's MAG-12 sweep the enemy outposts, including Hill 190, in an effort to aid in the defense of Outpost Vegas. Even after the attack, Hill 190 remains in Communist hands.

March 28

Political/Administrative: Premier Kim Il Sung and North Korea's General Peng Dehuai, commander of the CPV, accept General Mark Clark's offer to exchange sick and wounded prisoners. Indicating that this might set the tone for a settlement of the POW question, the Communists suggest a resumption of the peace talks.

Eighth Army: The defense of the Nevada Complex outposts (Vegas, Reno, Carson) continues by the 85 marines in the area, with Panther jets from VMF-115 and VMF-311 dropping several tons of bombs and thousands of rounds of ammunition on the enemy strongpoints at Vegas, Reno, and Hill 25A. Chinese probes against Outpost Hedy are driven off after a brief fight. A second Chinese attack on Outpost Dagmar drives the defenders to the rear slope, but they return after VT fire breaks up the enemy assault. Sergeant Daniel P. Matthews, 7th Marines, is awarded the Medal of Honor for courage in enabling the evacuation of the wounded.

Sea War: The shore batteries at Wonsan harbor, after firing on USS *Prichett* (DD 561) with no hits, begin to fire on the island of Hwangto-do. The island is hit by 24 rounds, but there are no casualties. Also fired on is USS *James E. Kyes* (DD 787) and USS *Waxbill* (AMS 39) but, again, there is no damage.

Air War: From the 4th FIW, pilot Colonel James K. Johnson downs his fifth MiG-15 to become an ace. An F-86 is shot down near Kijio by enemy planes.

March 29

Eighth Army: After falling back, the enemy reorganizes and tries once again to drive the marines from Outpost Vegas. At 0033, two companies attack but the marines drive them off with heavy casualties. Afterward the Chinese troops come under mortar and artillery fire as they try to police up their dead. During the remainder of the night, the marines consolidate and improve the defenses, and the Korean Service Corps supply trains replenish everything that is needed. After a full day of fighting, the enemy is able to hold Outpost Reno and Hill 25A but is unable to retake Outpost Vegas in the face of stiff marine resistance.

SEA WAR: Enemy shore batteries at Wonsan harbor fire on Yo-do without success.

AIR WAR: Lieutenant Colonel George L. Jones, 4th FIW, becomes the 30th jet ace of the Korean War. VP-57 Squadron under Commander V. J. Coley begins land-based service in Korea. An F-84 is shot down near Pyongyang and an F-86 near Kijio. Captain Maynard E. Stogdill of the 334th FIS and Captain Murray A. Winslow of the 335th FIS are both credited with shooting down one enemy MiG-15.

March 30

POLITICAL/ADMINISTRATIVE: Premier Zhou Enlai indicates that the Communists will accept India's proposal on the repatriation of prisoners, that is, that prisoners of war who refuse repatriation will be turned over to a neutral nation. The plan has been endorsed by the new Soviet foreign minister, Vyacheslav Molotov. The cease-fire talks resume.

EIGHTH ARMY: The defense of the Nevada Complex outposts ends. General Maxwell Taylor determines that possession of Old Baldy is not worth what it is costing in lives. The Chinese, it has become obvious, are willing to expend any amount of manpower to take the objective. Orders to take the hill are canceled. The ROK 15th Division's 13th Regiment engages the enemy in two raids on their positions west of the Nam River. The ROK takes the crest of Hill 350, which is located just south of Sindae-ri.

SEA WAR: The USS *Prichett* (DD 561) and USS *Shelton* (DD 790) are fired on by shore batteries at Wonsan harbor. Neither of the ships is hit. Friendly islands in Wonsan harbor receive harassing fire from the shore batteries. No significant damage is reported.

March 31

POLITICAL/ADMINISTRATIVE: Korean leader Kim Il Sung accepts the Chinese POW repatriation proposal.

EIGHTH ARMY: After heavy fighting, the marines still hold, and send relief units to, Outposts Vegas, Corinne, Hedy, Dagmar, and Bunker Hill in the 1st Marine sector.

SEA WAR: The USS *Prichett* (DD 561) is fired on by enemy guns at Wonsan harbor, with no hits or casualties recorded. Captain Dale Mayberry takes over command as "mayor" of the Wonsan blockade, replacing Captain Lester C. Conwell.

PARTISANS: The radio team for Donkey (code-named Hurricane) is dropped behind the lines. The first of the Special Forces units arrives for duty.

April 1

POLITICAL/ADMINISTRATIVE: The Soviet foreign minister endorses Zhou Enlai's POW suggestion on the prisoner repatriation.

EIGHTH ARMY: During a lull in the battle for the Nevada cities, the day is spent in replacing Reno. In the first battalion sector, gangs of KSC laborers bring the materials for, and establish, Outpost Elko, another of the Nevada cities. As night falls, the Chinese make a token probe against Outpost Vegas. Easy Company, 2nd Battalion, 5th Regiment (under operational control of 3rd Battalion, 5th Regiment), fights off enemy soldiers on the forward slope. Following a mortar barrage, the Chinese charge the outpost. In a 55-minute fight, the Chinese are repulsed.

SEA WAR: A downed pilot is rescued at sea by a helicopter from USS *Valley Forge* (CVA 45).

AIR WAR: A B-29 bomber from the 307th BW is unable to reach its primary target because of weather and instead raids a truck convoy. It reports excellent results.

PARTISANS: The 5th PIR was created from the western section of the 2nd PIR, code-named Wolfpack, and becomes independent. Rabbit I, a sleeper mission, drops 50 members.

April 2

POLITICAL/ADMINISTRATIVE: National Security Council Document 147, "Analysis of Possible Courses of Action in Korea," is released. It considers the combined use of air and naval operations against the Chinese Communists but suggests, in a seeming change of heart, that the use of nuclear weapons would be less efficient, considering the nature of the target.

SEA WAR: The USS *Prichett* (DD 561) is fired on by enemy shore batteries at Wonsan but it is not hit. Not as lucky, USS *Los Angeles* (CA 135) sustains one hit that destroys part of the mast and causes the wounding of 13 crewmen. Captain Harold G. Bowen, Jr., takes over command as "mayor" of the Wonsan blockade, replacing Captain Dale Mayberry.

April 3

EIGHTH ARMY: The 3rd Kagnew Battalion (Ethiopia) arrives in Korea and relieves the 2nd Battalion (Ethiopia). The second Australian Battalion arrives for service in Korea.

SEA WAR: USS *Prichett* (DD 561) is again fired on by Wonsan shore batteries. No damage is sustained.

April 4

SEA WAR: Friendly islands, located in Wonsan harbor, are hit by gun fire from shore batteries. The island of Yongwi-do is invaded by about 90 North Korean troops supported by gunfire from nearby Ongjin.

AIR WAR: Aircraft from Task Unit 95.1.1 return fire on the Yongwi-do attackers; after about 10 hours, the invaders are forced to return to the mainland. An F-86 is downed by an enemy pilot near Andong.

April 5

POLITICAL/ADMINISTRATIVE: New commanders are assigned to CCRK Liaison Detachment and United Nations Partisans in Korea (UNPIK). Some are considered to be unqualified. The Munsan-ni Provisional Command is established to prepare for the housekeeping details involved in the processing of UN prisoners in the anticipated Operation Little Switch. The exchange is directed by one marine and two army officers, as well as an ROK army representative under Colonel Raymond Beggs in overall command. Operation Rainbow, the building of facilities for the exchange of prisoners of war, begins.

EIGHTH ARMY: At 2100 Dog Company, 2nd Battalion, 1st Marine Regiment, dispatches a reinforced platoon of 60 men to setup an ambush in the vicinity of Hill 90. At five minutes before midnight, while en route, the platoon itself is ambushed by an enemy company. The lead fire team is overwhelmed, and the Chinese move on to attack the main body. A reinforced platoon of marines is dispatched from nearby Star Hill; as they reach the platoon that is pinned down, the Chinese break contact and withdraw.

SEA WAR: One man is killed and 10 are wounded when Wonsan harbor shore batteries fire on the island of Sosa-ri. The USS *Maddox* (DD 731) is hit by fire with no casualties, while the ROK's *AMS 515* avoids more than 50 rounds fired at her, and the USS *Kyes* (DD 787) escapes injury.

AIR WAR: VP-29 Squadron ends its land-based service in Korea.

Communist liaison officers arriving at Panmunjom, Korea, on April 6, 1953, to begin talks on the exchange, known as "Operation Little Switch," of sick and wounded prisoners. *(Center for the Study of the Korean War, Graceland University)*

April 6

POLITICAL/ADMINISTRATIVE: National Security Council Document 148, "United States Policy in Far East," is an effort to create a single policy to cover conditions in various Asian nations. President Dwight Eisenhower does not endorse it, however, and it fades from view. Negotiators return to the talks at Panmunjom after nearly six months of stalemate.

EIGHTH ARMY: Following the ambush at Hill 90, the survivors begin to return to the MLR by 0218. During the short fight, the marines have lost one killed, 23 wounded, and five missing. Later the area is swept for the missing men but none are found.

SEA WAR: The USS *Maddox* (DD 731) and USS *Redhead* (AMS 14) avoid fire from Wonsan shore batteries. Yo-do and Tae-do islands are hit, but there are no casualties. Vice Admiral Joseph H. Clark, Commander Seventh Fleet, raises his flag on USS *New Jersey* (BB 62).

AIR WAR: Bomber Command B-29s bomb the railroad bridges spanning the Chongchon River at Sinanju. Following the raid, in the early morning, fighters hit the backed up traffic on the approaches to the damaged bridge.

PARTISANS: The sixth PIR unit is created from the northern area of 1st PIR, code-named Leopard, and becomes operational.

April 7

POLITICAL/ADMINISTRATIVE: The UN General Assembly elects Dag Hammarskjold of Sweden to be secretary-general.

EIGHTH ARMY: One of the missing men from the ambush patrol is returned by the Chinese, wounded and with his pockets full of propaganda leaflets urging peace. Patrol 99, made up of 39 men, leaves Nan in the KMC sector near Panmunjom. An hour and 45 minutes later it is fired on by the Chinese, who have attacked from an area between the patrol and the neutral corridor in order to force the patrol to fire into the forbidden zone.

SEA WAR: The USS *Los Angeles* (CA 135) and USS *McDord* (DD 534) avoid fire from shore batteries at Wonsan harbor.

AIR WAR: A plane from VP-47 avoids fire from *Chung 104,* a Chinese Communist LST. For the second night in a row Bomber Command B-29s hit the railroad bridges spanning the Chongchon River at Sinanju. Once again, following the raid, fighters hit the backed up traffic on the approaches to the damaged bridge. Two F86s are shot down by enemy planes near Sensen. Colonel Robert P. Baldwin and Major Roy I. Reed (USMC) of the 39th FIS, and Lieutenant Colonel George I. Jones of the 335th FIS are all credited with each downing an enemy MiG.

PARTISANS: Yo-do Island receives 57 rounds of 122-mm fire, Tae-do Island receives either 122-mm shells or 82-mm mortar fire. No friendly casualties are reported.

April 8

EIGHTH ARMY: The Chinese begin a slow but consistent preparatory bombardment of Outpost Carson and the MLR and then bring in troops for an assault. The assault begins against Outposts Elko and Carson at 0315. The British Commonwealth Division returns to the line. At 0315, movement is reported across the front and 15 minutes later Outpost Elko reports movement. Fire increases, and the assault begins. The defenders are led by First Lieutenant George Yates who is wounded. The defenders hold on. A platoon from Dog Company is dispatched to reinforce Outpost Carson, but it is so badly mauled in the approach that it is of little help. Easy Company, 2nd Battalion, 7th Regiment, tries to help but suffers 11 killed, 64 wounded, and three missing. **Sea War:** Shore batteries at Wonsan continue to fire at U.S. vessels and on the UN-held island of Sok-to, with no success. The USS *Carp* (SS 338) ends its tour of duty in Korean waters.

April 9

Political/Administrative: In an official letter to General Mark W. Clark, Chinese and North Korean negotiators at the peace talks express their willingness to accept a repatriation system that operates through a neutral nation.

Eighth Army: Following a heavy bombardment, about 300 Chinese soldiers launch an attack against Outpost Carson and for nearly two hours the outcome is in question. The Chinese attacks come in two formations, one from Reno and one from Arrowhead. After finally being reinforced, the enemy is driven back. Coming to the aid of Outpost Carson, Easy Company, 2nd Battalion, 7th Regiment, finally reaches the defenders at about 0800 and is able to maintain a successful defense. Chinese attempts to take Outpost Carson will last three more days.

April 10

Sea War: The islands of Yo-do and Cho-do are hit by Communist fire without casualties. In the Cho-do area, *LSSL 107* avoids more than 20 rounds of fire by shore batteries.

April 11

Political/Administrative: Negotiators from both sides sign the final agreement for the exchange of all sick and wounded prisoners of war, to begin on April 20, 1953. Within 10 days, the operation that the United Nations calls "Operation Little Switch" (code-named Little Swap) is to begin. Major General Bruce C. Clarke takes command of I Corps.

Eighth Army: A Chinese unit, estimated at about 300, attacks Outpost Elko but is driven back after a 15-minute exchange.

Sea War: The USS *Eversole* (DD 789) avoids more than 50 rounds of fire from mainland batteries.

Air War: For the third time, Bomber Command B-29s hit the railroad bridges spanning the Chongchon River at Sinanju. Developing a pattern, fighters follow the raid and strike the backed-up traffic at the approaches to the damaged bridge. First Lieutenant Thomas F. Kozak, Colonel John W. Mitchell, and Lieutenant Colonel George I. Ruddell, all of the 39th FIS, each down a MiG-15 fighter.

April 12

Eighth Army: Leaving Outpost Nan at 2005, 39 marines are ambushed by 20 Chinese lying in wait. In a 15-minute fight, five marines are wounded. A later search locates two of the missing men, one dead and the other wounded.

SEA WAR: The USS *New Jersey* (BB 62) begins her second tour of duty on the firing line with the bombardment of Chongjin. In the bombardment, she scores seven direct hits and blows away half of the main communication building.

AIR WAR: Captain Joseph C. McConnell, Jr., flying an F-86 and with eight air victories to his credit, is rescued by an H-19 helicopter, from the 581st ARCW, after he ejects from his damaged aircraft over the Yellow Sea. The 1st Marine Air Wing flies its first night combat mission using intersecting searchlight beams to locate enemy targets. Four F-86s are shot down by enemy pilots near Hekido, as is one F-84. Major William I. Cosby and Second Lieutenant Len C. Russell, both of the 334th FIS, are each credited with downing an enemy MiG-15. Captain Joseph H. McConnell of the 39th FIS, First Lieutenant George D. Matthews of the 25th FIS, Captain Roy L. Reed (USMC) and Lieutenant Colonel George I. Ruddell of the 39th FIS, and Captain Lonnie R. Moore of the 335th FIS each shoot down an enemy MiG fighter.

April 13

SEA WAR: Enemy shore batteries fire on friendly islands in Wonsan harbor and on USS *Los Angeles* (CA 135) without success.

AIR WAR: Chongjin is hit by 119 sorties from Task Force 77. A pilot from the 8th FBW flies the new F-86F Sabre on its first air-to-ground combat mission. Major James P. Hagerstrom of the 67th FBS gets another MiG-15 fighter.

April 14

SEA WAR: Tae-do in Wonsan harbor is fired on but sustains no casualties.

AIR WAR: First Lieutenant Robert D. Carter and Second Lieutenant Harry A. Jones, both of the 335th FIS, are each credited with downing a MiG-15.

April 15

SEA WAR: The HMCS *Crusader* (DDE) stops three trains in the area of Tanchon. Cho-do Island is bombed by unidentified enemy aircraft that are able to kill two and wound 22. The USS *Mispillion* (AO 105) rescues 14 survivors and locates 27 bodies from the Chinese Nationalist steamer *Menten,* which sank while sailing for Sencho.

AIR WAR: Reconnaissance reports that the Communists have completed nearly 75 miles of railroad track that provides a link among Kusong, Kunu-ri, and Sinpyong-ni. The job is completed

North Korean prisoners of war released under Operation Little Switch march into Compound #13 for processing and repatriation. *(Center for the Study of the Korean War, Graceland University)*

in less than 70 days and manages to bypass most of the destruction caused by FEAF bombing raids. First Lieutenant Robert D. Carter and Second Lieutenant Harry A. Jones of the 335th FIS share credit for a kill.

April 16

POLITICAL/ADMINISTRATIVE: Orders are cut to reduce partisan strength to 20,000 no later than July.

EIGHTH ARMY: All battalions of the 31st Regiment, 7th Infantry Division, are alerted to expect an immediate attack. Outer guards are put in position, and at about 2205, an Easy Company ambush patrol reports contact. A few minutes later Easy Company is under fire. Easy Company realizes the immensity of the attack and calls for reinforcement, reporting that it is under heavy fire. Love Company and a platoon from Fox Company head out, but both are halted by enemy fire. They are ordered to withdraw.

SEA WAR: The USS *Maddox* (DD 731) is hit in Wonsan harbor by shore fire that causes the deaths of three sailors. Supported by USS *Owen* (DD 536) a marine attack party destroys rail lines on the east coast of Korea. The USS *New Jersey* (BB 62) strikes at Kojo. Commander Stephen W. Carpenter takes over as "mayor" of the Wonsan blockade, replacing Captain Harold G. Bowen, Jr.

AIR WAR: Colonel James K. Johnson of the 335th FIS and Captain Joseph H. McConnell of the 39th FIS are each credited with a MiG-15 kill.

April 17

POLITICAL/ADMINISTRATIVE: Henry J. Tasca is sent (Tasca Mission) to survey the economic needs of South Korea following a cease-fire agreement. The report becomes the basis of NSC document 156/1.

EIGHTH ARMY: Enemy artillery begins to fall on Pork Chop Hill, rising to a level of 30 rounds a minute. By 0310, the enemy holds portions of the hill. King and Love Companies are ordered to attack, but they both run into intense fire and are halted. By 0600, however, they are able to reach the top and join the survivors from Easy Company. The first elements of George Company reach the crest. By noon all units except King and Love Companies are withdrawn, and the 1st Battalion, 17th Regiment, takes over. At 2040, Fox Company, 2nd Battalion, 17th Regiment, departs for Pork Chop, and by 2235, King and Easy Companies are withdrawn. George Company, 3rd Battalion, 1st Regiment, sets out on an ambush patrol, leaving the MLR on a moonless night, only to run into a Chinese ambush in which several of the marines are killed or wounded.

AIR WAR: Marine Air Groups 33 and 12 fly a 24-hour-record number of sorties, totaling 262 among them. First Lieutenant Philip C. Davis and First Lieutenant John W. Goodwill of the 16th FIS get credit for a kill on a MiG-15 fighter. First Lieutenant Frederick E. Mamerow and Captain Floyd W. Salze of the 25th FIS, Captain Manuel J. Fernandez of the 334th FIS, and Lieutenant Colonel George I. Ruddell of the 39th FIS are all credited with downing a MiG-15 fighter.

April 18

POLITICAL/ADMINISTRATIVE: The General Assembly of the United Nations passes Resolution 705 VII, calling for a resumption of consideration of the Korean question as soon as the armistice is signed.

EIGHTH ARMY: The Chinese move against Pork Chop Hill at 0055 and reach friendly trenches despite counterfire from Fox Company, 17th Regiment. The outpost is surrounded and the hill is under illumination. Easy Company of the 17th Regiment moves forward, advancing on the north side of adjacent Hill 200 in order to avoid the crossfire. As it does so, the Chinese are moving more troops to the hill. Friendly fire is called in on one finger of the hill where the UN position is secure, but the Chinese are massing for another attack. At 1000, the enemy breaks off contact. Easy and Fox Companies withdraw under a smoke screen.

SEA WAR: In Wonsan harbor, USS *Eversole* (DD 789) is fired on but no damage results. The USS *James E. Kyes* (DD 787) is fired on by enemy shore batteries after she destroys three railway trains. The USS *New Jersey* (BB 62) is at Wonsan harbor.

AIR WAR: An F-86 is shot down by enemy aircraft.

April 19

SEA WAR: One serious injury and several minor ones occur aboard USS *Kyes* (DD 787) when she is hit by enemy shells in Wonsan harbor. The USS *Shelton* (DD 790) is also fired on but with no casualties. Shells are directed against USS *Curlew* (AMS 8) with no effect, as with shelling of the USS *New Jersey* (BB 62) and USS *Renshaw* (DDE 499).

April 20

POLITICAL/ADMINISTRATIVE: Operation Little Switch, the exchange of ill and wounded POWs, begins at 0815 with the first group of 50 men reaching freedom at 0825. One group of North Korean prisoners en route from Pusan to Panmunjom dumps their breakfast on the ground, complaining about the poor food. UN prisoners are taken to Freedom Village. Those needing immediate medical treatment are sent on the *Haven* and *Consolation,* anchored at Inchon.

SEA WAR: Communist shore batteries continue to fire on the friendly islands in Wonsan harbor. Captain John C. Woelfel takes command as "mayor" of the Wonsan blockade, replacing Commander Stephen W. Carpenter.

PARTISANS: Twenty partisans in Operation Seadragon, led by two Americans, make a survey of the Yalu River estuary islands, by junk.

April 20–May 3

POLITICAL/ADMINISTRATIVE: During this time, seriously ill Communist and UN POWs are exchanged in Operation Little Switch.

April 21

SEA WAR: Hwangto-do, Yo-do, and Tae-do Islands in Wonsan harbor are hit by shore batteries. The USS *Henderson* (DD 785) is fired on in this area, with no damage. Commander Edward J. Foote takes command as "mayor" of the Wonsan blockade, replacing Captain John C. Woelfel. Navy jet pilots are given the chance to select their own targets. The team from the USS *Oriskany* (CVA 34) selects the bridge on the Hamhung highway in northeast Korea and manages, in three attacks, to destroy two spans.

AIR WAR: The Soviets report that an F-84 is shot down near Sensen by its aircraft.

April 22

POLITICAL/ADMINISTRATIVE: President Dwight Eisenhower approves the arms and equipment necessary for the creation of two new ROK army divisions.

EIGHTH ARMY: In a firefight at Kalmagak, five UN personnel are wounded.

SEA WAR: The USS *Manchester* (CL 83) suffers light damage from shore batteries in Wonsan harbor. The USS *Henderson* (DD 785) and USS *Owen* (DD 536) are sent to cover rescue operations. Aircraft from Task Force strafe Kalmagak, and the rescue is completed. Intense fire is leveled on the islands in the harbor by shore batteries. Four Royal Navy Sea Furies are attacked by unidentified aircraft, with one of the Furies damaged. Commander Donald F. Quigley takes command as "mayor" of the Wonsan blockade, replacing Commander Edward J. Foote.

AIR WAR: Near Kaisen, an enemy aircraft shoots down an F-84. First Lieutenant Walter W. Fellman of the 336th FIS shoots down an enemy MiG-15 fighter.

April 23

POLITICAL/ADMINISTRATIVE: The UN General Assembly names a five-power commission to investigate Communist charges that the United States is engaged in germ warfare. Later, when the cease-fire is signed, the Communists will quickly lose interest in the inquiry.

EIGHTH ARMY: In Operation Left Hook, South Korean soldiers, supported by 2nd Division artillery, attack the Chinese-held Hill 153 and take it. They hold the hill long enough to destroy the fortifications there and then withdraw.

SEA WAR: Shore batteries, firing at targets in Wonsan harbor, are unable to hit either USS *James C. Owens* (776) or USS *Henderson* (DD 785). The USS *New Jersey* (BB 62) scores six direct hits on a railroad tunnel as she destroys two railroad bridges at Songjin (Kimchaek).

April 24

SEA WAR: The UN-held islands in Wonsan harbor continue to receive heavy bombardment from shore batteries.

AIR WAR: Captain Joseph H. McConnell of the 39th FIS shoots down another MiG-15.

April 25

POLITICAL/ADMINISTRATIVE: ROK president Syngman Rhee informs Washington, D.C., that he will pull ROK troops out of General Clark's command if the armistice agreement allows Chinese troops to remain south of the Yalu River. Brigadier General Edgar E. Glenn (USAF) joins the UN delegation at the armistice talks.

SEA WAR: The USS *Saint Paul* (CA 73) exchanges fire with Wonsan shore batteries; there are no hits on the U.S. ship. The USS *James C. Owens* (DD 776) is also fired on with no results.

ROK president Syngman Rhee with members of his staff at a military review in Seoul, Korea, 1953 *(Center for the Study of the Korean War, Graceland University)*

April 26

POLITICAL/ADMINISTRATIVE: Cease-fire talks resume at Panmunjom after a six-month suspension, still facing the question of naming a neutral state to oversee the repatriation of prisoners of war. Georgi Malenkov, the new Communist Party secretary, has announced that the issues between the warring parties can be settled. The Communists want prisoners taken out of Korea before the decision on repatriation is made. The Communists deliver the last of the sick or wounded men as their part of Operation Little Switch. Brigadier General Frank C. McConnell (USA), Brigadier General Lee Han Lim (ROK), and Brigadier General Joseph T. Morris are relieved of responsibilities as UN armistice delegates, and Brigadier General Choi Duk Shin (ROK) is appointed. Major General Xie Feng (Hsieh Fang) (CPVA) and Major General So Hui (NKPA) are relieved from the Communist delegation at Panmunjom. General Ding Guoyu Ting Kuo-yu (CPVA), Major General Zhang Zhunsan (Chang Chun San) (NKPA), and Major General Zai Zhengwen (Tsai Cheng-wen) (CPVA) join the delegation.

AIR WAR: During the night, a B-29 bomber drops leaflets over North Korea in the continuation of Operation Moolah, the effort to get a Communist pilot to deliver a complete MiG-15 to UN forces.

April 27

POLITICAL/ADMINISTRATIVE: General Mark Clark flies to Seoul to meet with President Rhee and try to talk him into accepting a compromise armistice. They meet for two days. Rhee is unresponsive.

SEA WAR: Communist shore batteries at Wonsan continue to fire on friendly islands and on UN ships. The USS *Gurke* (DD 783), USS *Owen* (DD 536), and USS *Maddox* (DD 731) are all targets but there is no damage reported.

April 28

POLITICAL/ADMINISTRATIVE: Eighth United States Army in Korea is redesignated as simply Eighth U.S. Army. In addition, the many lines of defense that have been given names will from now on be referred to simply as the main line of resistance. This change of instruction has little effect in the nomenclature used by the men in the field.

SEA WAR: USS *Owen* (DD 536) is taken under fire but with no success. The islands of Hwangto-do, Tae-do, and Yo-do are also targets of the Wonsan shore batteries.

April 29

SEA WAR: Hwangto-do, Yo-do, Tae-do all receive enemy fire in Wonsan harbor, as does USS *Gurke* (DD 783). All avoid casualties.

April 30

POLITICAL/ADMINISTRATIVE: President Dwight Eisenhower issues his plans for an "Efficient and Prepared Defense Establishment" that will place more control in the hands of the civilians of the Department of Defense and limit the activities in which military leaders can be engaged. He insists that the professional military has to stay clear of politics, and acknowledges that the Joint Chiefs of Staff may have gone beyond its bounds as military advisers.

EIGHTH ARMY: The third Korean winter phase ends.

SEA WAR: Wonsan guns continue to fire on friendly islands in the harbor and on USS *Owen* (DD 536), with no significant damage. The USS *Gull* (AMS 16) fouls her gear on friendly fishing nets.

AIR WAR: The USAF retires the F-80 fighter from combat operations. Captain George P. Kelley and Major Clyde I. Wade of the 39th FIS are each credited with downing a MiG-15.

May 1

EIGHTH ARMY: The Korean summer-fall phase begins. It will continue until July 27, 1953.

SEA WAR: The USS *Ruddy* (AMN 380) loses her magnetic tail after she and USS *Dextrous* (AM 341) are fired on at Hungnam. The USS *New Jersey* (BB 62) conducts a major surface strike at Wonsan.

AIR WAR: Planes of the Fifth Air Force strike Radio Pyongyang, putting it off the air for broadcasting "filthy lies" about the Fifth Air Force and also to spoil any proposed May Day celebrations. The bombers are heavily screened by planes from the 4th and 57th FIW and the 18th FBW. The USMC retires the F7F-3N from combat service. The F-80 Shooting Star is withdrawn from Korean service. It is replaced by the more reliable F-86.

May 2

POLITICAL/ADMINISTRATIVE: The United States declares "Korea Day," as citizens are encouraged to give money to aid the Republic of Korea.

EIGHTH ARMY: After a Canadian unit spends nearly a month trying to gain control of the area around Hill 187, the Chinese attack during the night and take the position. When the Canadians began to counterattack, they discover that the Chinese are already pulling back, and the advancing unit is able to take the hill.

SEA WAR: At Hodo Pando, USS *Maddox* (DD 731) and USS *Owen* (DD 536) are both hit when fired at with nearly 200 rounds. The damage to the ships is minor.

May 3

POLITICAL/ADMINISTRATIVE: The United Nations delivers the last of the ill or wounded Communist troops to be released under Operation Little Switch.

SEA WAR: A guerrilla landing in the Haeju area is supported by HMS *St. Bride's Bay* and the ROK navy's *PCS 201*. At Wonsan harbor, USS *Gurke* (DD 783) is fired on by shore batteries, with no hits.

AIR WAR: Air Group 102 (redesignated Air Group 12) completes its tour of duty aboard USS *Oriskany* (CVA 34). Two planes are shot down by enemy aircraft near Kaisen.

May 4

SEA WAR: The USS *Maddox* (DD 731) avoids being hit near Hamhung as 18 rounds are fired at her.

May 5

EIGHTH ARMY: The 2nd Battalion, Australian Regiment, enters the line and assumes command of Hill 159, with Charlie Company on the left knoll and Baker Company on the right. They oppose the enemy at four main terrain features.

SEA WAR: In separate events, USS *New Jersey* (BB 62), the cruiser USS *Bremerton* (CA 130), and the destroyers USS *Twining* (D 540) and *Colahan* (DD 658) destroy shelters, caves, concrete ammunition bunkers, and an observation post. Two enlisted men are hurt by near-misses when USS *Bremerton* is fired on in Wonsan harbor. The USS *New Jersey* is on a firing mission at Kodo Pando. Commander Albert L. Gebelin takes command as "mayor" of the Wonsan blockade, replacing Commander Donald F. Quigley.

EIGHTH ARMY: The 1st Marine Division is relieved by the 25th Infantry Division. The marines are placed in I Corps Reserves. The Australian battalion enters the line and assumes responsibility for Hill 159.

May 6

POLITICAL/ADMINISTRATIVE: The National Security Council meets with President Eisenhower to discuss the use of atomic weapons in Korea. The primary targets they consider are Korean and Chinese airfields.

AIR WAR: Carrier planes from USS *Princeton* (CV 37) and *Valley Forge* (CV 45) destroy a mining area northwest of Songjin. The USS *Saint Paul* (CA 73) and *Nicholas* (DD 449) fire on coastal supplies.

May 7

POLITICAL/ADMINISTRATIVE: The Communist leader, Lieutenant General Nam Il, advances an eight-point settlement proposal that is not unlike the Indian proposal rejected earlier. It accepts the idea that prisoners can be screened in Korea rather than being sent to a neutral nation. The proposal accepts the establishment of a Neutral Nations Repatriation Commission and agrees to India, Sweden, Switzerland, Poland, and Czechoslovakia. It requires each nation to furnish troops to guard its own non-repatriated prisoners and to establish such areas in South Korea. The proposal is void of any statements that oppose the idea of voluntary repatriation taking place at the location of the individual's area of detention. Non-repatriated prisoners are to be kept in the custody of a neutral nation. They accept the idea that screening can be done in South Korea. In a speech at a Republican dinner in New York, John Foster Dulles states that, while America wants peace, the United States will not tolerate a delay of the armistice negotiations in Korea.

EIGHTH ARMY: A small Chinese Communist unit probes against the Hook, apparently to test its defenses. The British Black Watch hands over defense of the Hook to the 1st Battalion, Duke of Wellington's Regiment.

SEA WAR: More than 40 rounds are fired at HMS *Cockade* (DD) near Songjin but fail to cause any damage. The USS *New Jersey* (BB 62) is on a fire mission at Kalmagak.

May 8

SEA WAR: Enemy shore guns in the Wonsan area fire, and score a hit, on USS *Samuel N. Moore* (DD 747) with a 90-mm shell. More than 60 rounds are fired at *Samuel N. Moore* in order to get one hit. There is no significant damage. The same enemy guns fire two rounds at USS *Brush* (DD 745) but cannot hit the ship. In the Haeju area, enemy guns on the mainland fire 130 rounds of 76-mm shells at HMNZS *Hawea* (DDE) and 15 rounds at the ROK navy's *YMS 514*. There is no damage reported.

Repatriated UN prisoners of war at Panmunjom, Korea *(NARA Still Photos Division)*

AIR WAR: Captain Manuel J. Fernandez of the 334th FIS shoots down an enemy MiG-15 fighter.

May 9

SEA WAR: After firing at USS *Brush* (DD 745) and missing, the shore guns at Wonsan turn on USS *Samuel N. Moore* (DD 747). They do little damage. The same story is true for HMNZS *Hawea* (DDE) and the ROK navy's *YMS 514* at Haeju.

AIR WAR: Colonel James K. Johnson and Second Lieutenant Samuel J. Reeder of the 335th FIS each are credited with a downed MiG-15.

May 10

SEA WAR: The ROK navy's *AMS 503* is fired on at Kojo and USS *Maddox* (DD 731) is the target of fire from Yang-do. Neither ship is hit or damaged.

AIR WAR: Eight Thunderjets from the 58th FBW, under Colonel Victor E. Walford, attack the hydroelectric generating plant at Suiho near the Yalu River. During the night, 39 Superfortresses raid a massive troop concentration southeast of the city of Sinuiju. Reports indicate a 63 percent destruction of this 375-acre troop assembly point. Captain Manuel J. Fernandez of the 334th FIS is credited with one-and-a-half MiG-15s, and Major Foster L. Smith of the 335th FIS is credited with half a kill.

May 11

SEA WAR: U.S. destroyers surprise and damage four enemy railroad trains near Tanchon as the "package destruction" program continues unabated.

PARTISANS: The HMS *St. Bride's Bay* (DE) supports a partisan raid on the west coast of Haeju-man. The raid fails to reach its objective, however, and the raiders withdraw.

May 12

POLITICAL/ADMINISTRATIVE: President Rhee informs General Clark's headquarters that he is still opposed to the armistice agreement at it is being presented. Rhee states that he will not allow North Korean non-repatriated prisoners to be released to neutral nations and, moreover, that he does not consider India to be a neutral nation. He says he will not allow Indian troops to enter South Korea. General Clark tries to respond and suggests to the cease-fire delegates the possibility that North Korean troops who do not want repatriation can be released immediately after the signing of the armistice.

EIGHTH ARMY: The U.S. 1st Marine Division is pulled off-line after 33 months of combat. It is relieved by the U.S. 25th Infantry Division.

SEA WAR: The USS *Philip* (DDE 498) is fired on at Soho-ri but sustains no damage.

AIR WAR: Air Task Group One under Commander A. L. Whitney begins its tour of duty aboard USS *Boxer* (CVA 21).

May 13

POLITICAL/ADMINISTRATIVE: General Harrison offers a return proposal in response to the eight-point Chinese proposal. He urges agreement to the idea that only Indian troops will be used as guards for prisoners being screened and rejects the idea that a political conference will be the final arbiter of a prisoner's destiny. After China responds with anger, the talks are suspended until May 20, 1953, when another five-day extension will be sought while the United States works out its continuing position. General Mark Clark approves the arming and equipping of four additional South Korean divisions, bringing the total to 20 divisions. Meeting with the National Security Council, President Eisenhower discusses the fact that the use of atomic weapons in Korea would be far less expensive that a continuation of the conventional war.

EIGHTH ARMY: Occupying the Hook, the Duke of Wellington's Regiment begins to repair the defenses in anticipation of continuing Chinese attacks.

AIR WAR: A raid is executed on Toksan Dam. The 58th Fighter-Bomber Wing conducts a massive raid by 59 Thunderjets and destroys a major irrigation system. This is the first of a series of raids designed to bring the enemy to terms by the use of air power. Water escaping from the dam washes out six miles of embankment and five bridges, destroys several miles of the major north-south highway, ruins several square miles of rice crops, and makes the Sunan Airfield unusable. Captain Manuel J. Fernandez of the 334th FIS and Major John C. Giraudo of the 25th FIS each get a MiG-15 fighter.

SEA WAR: The USS *Boxer* (CVA 21) launches its first combat sorties as she begins her fourth tour of duty in Korea.

May 13–16

AIR WAR: UN bombers attack two of North Korea's 20 major irrigation dams, the first being 20 miles north of Pyongyang.

May 14

POLITICAL/ADMINISTRATIVE: Communist and UN truce negotiators split over details concerning POWs who refuse repatriation; they recess the truce talks indefinitely.

SEA WAR: An estimated 25 rounds are fired on the ROK navy's *AMS 503* from shore batteries, with no damage.

AIR WAR: Second Lieutenant Edwin E. Aldrin of the 16th FIS, Second Lieutenant Al B. Cox of the 335th FIS, and Major John C. Giraudo of the 25th FIS each are credited with downing an enemy MiG-15 fighter.

May 15

EIGHTH ARMY: CCF sends a two-battalion probe against Outposts Vegas, Carson, and Elko, recently defended by the Turkish Battalion. They also hit Outposts Berlin and East Berlin, held by the marines, but are thrown back after the heavy use of supporting artillery fire.

SEA WAR: Five men are injured when the ROK navy's *AMS 506* is hit by enemy gun fire in the Haeju area. Nine are injured when shore batteries fire on and hit USS *Brush* (DD 745) on duty at Wonsan. The USS *Princeton* (CVA 37) receives its third Presidential Unit Citation.

AIR WAR: An F-86 is shot down during contact with an enemy plane. Major Lowell K. Brueland, Captain Joseph H. McConnell, and Colonel John W. Mitchell, all of the 39th FIS, are each credited with a MiG fighter. Following up the raid on the

Toksan Dam, the Fifth Air Force hits, and finally breaches, a dam north of Pyongyang at Chosan on the Yalu. The rushing waters destroy a railroad line and several bridges.

PARTISANS: All partisans are ordered evacuated from, and all activities are ordered to cease, north of the 38th parallel. This is done as a concession to the talks taking place at Panmunjom.

May 16

POLITICAL/ADMINISTRATIVE: Brigadier General Choi Duk Shin (ROK) is released from responsibilities as a UN delegate at the armistice talks.

EIGHTH ARMY: As relative quiet is enjoyed, the Chinese III and IX Army Groups, comprising the 12th, 15th, 60th, 20th, and 27th Armies, move an estimated 137,000 Chinese and 38,000 North Koreans south in a new offensive. They are faced by the ROK and the U.S. 2nd Infantry Division.

AIR WAR: Ninety sorties by 58th FBW planes hit the Chasan irrigation dams, releasing water that destroys three railroad bridges and several rice fields. Aircraft from Task Force 77 catch and damage an 18-car railway train along the east coast. Captain Manuel J. Fernandez, Jr., 4th Fighter-Interceptor Wing, becomes the third-ranking ace, with 14 $\frac{1}{2}$ kills. Eleven MiG-15 fighters are shot down, one each by First Lieutenant Forist G. Dupree, First Lieutenant Walter W. Fellman, and Captain Peter J. Frederick of the 336th FIS; Captain Manuel J. Fernandez, First Lieutenant Bruno A. Giordano, Major James Jabara, and Major David T. Davidson of the 334th FIS; Major James P. Hagerstrom of the 67th FIS; Captain Joseph M. McConnell and Major John F. Bolt (USMC) of the 39th FIS; Second Lieutenant Philip A. Redpath and First Lieutenant Merton E. Ricker of the 335th FIS also down MiG-15s.

May 17

EIGHTH ARMY: The Second Infantry Division is exposed at Kunu-ri as the Chinese move out.

SEA WAR: The USS *Brush* (DD 745) and USS *James E. Kyse* (DD 787) support a raid on Kojo. The USS *Maddox* (DD 731) destroys a train near Songjin. The USS *Bairoko* (CVE 115) provides close support for an amphibious raid on the west coast, about 50 miles north from Seoul.

AIR WAR: Major David T. Davidson of the 334th FIS is credited with downing a MiG fighter. From the 335th FIS, Major Vermont Garrison is credited for one, while Colonel James K. Johnson and Captain Dewey F. Durnford (USMC) receive credit for half a kill. Major John H. Jones of the 16th FIS and First Lieutenant Cleve B. Watson of the 39th are each credited with one kill.

PARTISANS: The 2nd PIR, code name Wolfpack East, lands a partisan force of 450 men, with three Americans in the lead.

May 18

AIR WAR: An H-19 helicopter rescues two crew members of a downed B-26 some 20 miles inside enemy lines after fighters clear a path to the downed man. During the night, Superfortresses return to Yangsi to destroy a troop concentration area. Lieutenant Colonel George I. Ruddell becomes the 31st jet ace, while Captain McConnell downs three more, for a total of 16, and becomes the Korean War's first triple ace. McConnell completes his tour with 106 missions and 16 kills. Lieutenant Colonel Louis A. Green of the 336th FIS is given credit for two MiG-15s, and First Lieutenant Robert E. Perdue, also from the 336th FIS, gets credit for one, while First Lieutenant Harold B. Schmidt gets credit for half a kill. Second Lieutenant James L. Thompson and First Lieutenant Walter G. Zisette of the 39th FIS each get one, as does Captain Harvey I. Jensen (USMC) of the 25th FIS. During a return mission, 18 Superfortresses complete the destruction of the Yangsi troop concentration. Three F-86s are downed by enemy planes, one near Bugdin, one at Siogyao that blows up in midair, and one at Sakusyu.

May 19

EIGHTH ARMY: General Almond orders the 3rd Battalion, 38th Regiment, to move out just ahead of the Chinese advance.

SEA WAR: A locomotive is destroyed, along with six cars, near Chaho by USS *James E. Kyse* (DD 787) and USS *Eversole* (DD 789).

AIR WAR: B-29s from the 19th BG hit the supply complex at Unsan and destroy more than 400 buildings. The area, eight miles west of Sinanju, is a sheltering point for troops moving south.

May 20

POLITICAL/ADMINISTRATIVE: The National Security Council agrees to extend ground and air operations into Communist China if "conditions arise."

EIGHTH ARMY: Some 4,000 shells and mortar rounds fall on the Hook in a little more than two hours. Then the probing attacks begin. But the anticipated attack does not come.

SEA WAR: After an identification failure, USS *Bradford* (DD 545) destroys a friendly boat, killing 19.

May 21

EIGHTH ARMY: At this point, the CCF thrust against Ruffner's Division has been contained. Realizing that the Communists may be in retreat, X Corps is ordered to counterattack. In support, General James Van Fleet gives him the use of the 187th Airborne with tanks from the 72nd Tank Battalion. They form Task Force Gerhaerdt to advance against Soyang.

SEA WAR: Based on the success of USS *Antietam* (CV 36) trials, the navy announces a revision in the design of the carrier USS *Forrestal* to include an angled deck. Captain Richard E. Myers takes command as "mayor" of the Wonsan blockade, replacing Commander Albert Gebelin.

AIR WAR: B-29s score seven direct hits on the Kuwonga Dam, but it does not burst. The failure is probably due to the fact that the North Koreans lowered the level of the water nearly 12 feet and thereby reduced the pressure against the dam. However, the reserve water supply is gone. Using SHORAN, a B-29 secures seven hits on the Kuwonga Dam, but it does not break.

May 22

POLITICAL/ADMINISTRATIVE: General Clark sends Operation Everready (a plan to remove President Rhee from office if it becomes necessary in the armistice effort) proposal to Washington, D.C., for final approval. Secretary of State Dulles warns the Chinese, through India, that the United States might use atomic weapons if the UNC prisoner-of-war settlement plan is rejected.

PARTISANS: Partisan forces now stand at 22,000 men.

May 23

POLITICAL/ADMINISTRATIVE: The USS *New Jersey* (BB 62) celebrates her 10th anniversary with Korean president and Madame Rhee and Lieutenant General Maxwell D. Taylor onboard. The French government requests the loan of a second carrier for use in its war in Indochina. The USS *Langley* (CVL 27) has been on loan to the French since 1951.

EIGHTH ARMY: A three-pronged patrol from Baker Company attacks Pheasant Ridge. The patrol runs into a minefield and six of the 10 men in the patrol are wounded. The attack is called off.

AIR WAR: An F-86 is shot down by enemy fighters. Major Vermont Garrison of the 335th FIS and First Lieutenant Samuel R. Johnson of the 16th FIS each shoot down an enemy MiG-15.

May 24

SEA WAR: While USS *Bremerton* (CA 139) executes firing missions at Wonsan harbor, she experiences return fire but is not hit.

May 25

POLITICAL/ADMINISTRATIVE: When the peace talks begin again, the United Nations has dropped the Rhee appeasement demand concerning the release of South Korean prisoners. The UN makes a proposal to the negotiation talks, suggesting that non-repatriated prisoners of war remain in neutral custody for up to 120 days after the armistice, until their governments can confirm their attitude toward repatriation. An exchange will then be made in Korea under the control of India, a neutral nation. Major General Chang Chun San (NKPA) is relieved as a Communist delegate at the armistice talks and is replaced by Admiral Kim Won Mu (NKPN).

EIGHTH ARMY: The Chinese artillery opens up on the Turkish positions at Outposts East Berlin and Berlin. Counterfire is supplied by batteries from the 25th Infantry Division and the marines. Elements of the Chinese 120th Division launch simultaneous attacks all along the I Corps front, including COP 2. An artillery attack is directed to the area, and by midnight, the men of the 35th Infantry have driven them back.

SEA WAR: There is a collision between USS *Mispillion* (AO-105, an oiler) and USS *Boxer* (CVA 21) that causes minor damage to both ships.

May 26

SEA WAR: Shore batteries at Wonsan fire on USS *Duncan* (DDR 874) without result. Rounds also fall close to an ROK freighter.

AIR WAR: An F-86 and an F-84 are destroyed by enemy fighters. Major James Jabara of the 334th FIS gets two MiGs while his companions—First Lieutenant Richard W. Frailey, First Lieutenant William P. Mailoux, First Lieutenant Robert H. McIntosh, First Lieutenant Merton E. Ricker, and First Lieutenant George J. Spataro of the 334th FIS—are each credited with downing an enemy MiG-15. Major Jack Mass of the 335th FIS is credited with two kills. First Lieutenant Thomas H. McQuade of the 336th FIS and Lieutenant Colonel George I. Ruddell of the 39th FIS each get a MiG-15.

May 27

POLITICAL/ADMINISTRATIVE: Major General Tsai Cheng-wen (CPVA) is relieved from his duties as a Communist representative to the armistice talks.

SEA WAR: At Chinnampo, HMS *Newcastle* (CL) is fired on without causing any damage.

AIR WAR: Fifth Air Force aerial reconnaissance uncovers evidence that the Communists are preparing for a significant ground offensive. Some 123 sorties are flown by the Marine Air Wing in support of the British Commonwealth Division at the Hook.

May 28

POLITICAL/ADMINISTRATIVE: The UN team presents its final terms and threatens to break off talks if they are rejected. The Communists announce that the May 25, 1953, proposal by UN Command is unacceptable and that, on instructions from their government, they are boycotting future negotiations.

EIGHTH ARMY: Major elements of the Chinese 120th Division move against the 17,500-yard-long front of I Corps, from Outpost 2 eastward to the Hook. After six hours of fighting, the enemy advance is halted. In an attempt to improve their situation at the peace talks, the Chinese attack the Hook again. The Duke of Wellington's Regiment holds against an attack that is preceded by heavy Chinese artillery fire. The Commonwealth unit losses are 23 KIA, 105 WIA, and 20 MIA. More than 170 Chinese dead are counted. Company Baker, 1st Battalion, 14th Infantry Regiment, takes Outpost Elko. The first attack against the Turkish positions occurs at Outposts East Berlin and Berlin. There are 16 men on the defense at East Berlin, 20 at Berlin, 33 at Elko, and 41 at Carson. The Chinese manage to take a piece of Vegas but are driven off. Then the Chinese cross over to Carson and Elko, hitting them six times. Through all this the Turks hold on. Elements of the 1st Battalion, 1st Regiment, 1st Marine Division, are sent to occupy Outpost 1 (aka Nan). Once again it is considered too costly to try and hold the area if the Chinese intend the same and the attacks are called off.

SEA WAR: The USS *New Jersey* (BB 62) joins with aircraft of Task Force 77 to silence several Wonsan coastal defense guns.

May 28–29

EIGHTH ARMY: CCF units hit the 35th Regiment during the night at Outpost 2, held by Company George. Concluding that the war is about over and that possession of the Nevada cities outposts is not worth the loss of more men, General Bruce C. Clarke, I Corps commander, orders the defending units to pull off. The outposts are abandoned. Following three days of increasingly harsh artillery attacks, the CPVA launches a three-battalion attack against the 1st Battalion, Duke of Wellington's Regiment, on the Hook. Despite the desperation of the attacking force, and the loss of nearly 1,000 men, the Chinese are unable to shake the British hold on the position. The cost to the Commonwealth is 148 casualties.

AIR WAR: B-29s hit the Kuwonga Dam again, managing to get five direct hits with 2,000-pound bombs. The dam still does not burst, but it does require the emptying of the reservoir and thus exhausts the water available for irrigation.

May 29

POLITICAL/ADMINISTRATIVE: General Mark Clark warns the Joint Chiefs of Staff that ROK president Syngman Rhee might release POWs unilaterally. Secretary of State John F. Dulles and Secretary of Defense Charles E. Wilson agree that General Clark can offer President Rhee a bilateral security agreement if the general thinks it might save the situation.

EIGHTH ARMY: Outpost Vegas changes hands several times as the staunch Turkish defenders hold against repeated Chinese attacks. Supported by the 11th Marine Battalion and firing more than 41,000 rounds, they hold off the enemy for most of the night. However, the Chinese are able to take Vegas on the following morning. The decision is made to pull out from the Nevada Complex.

SEA WAR: While at anchor in the lee of Yang-do Island, USS *Swift* (AM 122) and USS *Redstart* (AMS 378) are fired on by an estimated 25 rounds of 76-mm shells. One shell hits the *Swift*'s acoustic boom and results in minor damage and one casualty. West of Chinnampo, HMS *Newcastle* (CL) and HMS *St. Bride's Bay* (PF) are harassed by enemy fire from a 105-mm gun. Six shells fall about 20 yards from the *Newcastle,* but no damage or casualties occur.

AIR WAR: During the battle for Outposts Vegas, Elko, and Carson, VMF-311 and VMF-115 fly 119 sorties against the enemy. Three F-86s are shot down by enemy fighters, all crashing in the gulf. Second Lieutenant Robert H. Erdmann of the 16th FIS and Lieutenant Colonel George I. Ruddell of the 39th FIS each get a kill on a MiG-15.

May 29–July 27

EIGHTH ARMY: During this period, the Communists continue to shell the Hook and to launch an occasional probe right up to the moments just prior to the cease-fire.

May 30

AIR WAR: VP 1 Squadron under Commander J. D. Quillin begins land service. VP 22 Squadron under Commander W. P. Tanner ends its land-based service in Korea.

May 31

POLITICAL/ADMINISTRATIVE: President Syngman Rhee explains that he will continue to fight for reunification even if the ROK must stand alone. Lieutenant General Samuel E. Anderson assumes command of Fifth Air Force, replacing General Barcus. The U.S. secretary of state, John Foster Dulles, says that if the Vietnamese defeat the French the countries of Asia will fall like dominoes under Soviet control—the first use of "dominoes" to explain the U.S. stand against the expansion of communism.

PARTISANS: Forty enemy artillery shells fall on Yo-do and Hwangto-do Islands in Wonsan harbor, but the friendly installations are not hit.

June

AIR WAR: Air support for the ground troops, as well as bombing missions, is greatly curtailed during the month of June because of weather. During the month, there are 23 days of marginal to nonoperational weather.

June 1

EIGHTH ARMY: Chinese forces seize Hill 812 just four miles northeast of the Punchbowl, defeating elements of the ROK 12th Division.

AIR WAR: Captain Lonnie R. Moore of the 335th FIS brings down a MiG-15 fighter.

June 2

POLITICAL/ADMINISTRATIVE: The coronation of Queen Elizabeth II is marked by a massive display of shells over Chinese positions. The crowning will bring no changes in English policy toward the war in Korea.

SEA WAR: The USS *Saint Paul* (CA 73) and USS *Manchester* (CL 83) exchange fire with enemy batteries at Wonsan, but neither ship is hit. The same is the case near Chaho with USS *Wiltsie* (DD 716) and USS *James F. Kyse* (DD 787).

AIR WAR: B-29s begin a series of night missions against targets where Communist troops are gathered for training.

June 3

POLITICAL/ADMINISTRATIVE: The prisoner of war question at Panmunjom is finally resolved, with the Chinese accepting the principle of voluntary repatriation.

SEA WAR: The HMS *Morecambe Bay* is fired on at Wonsan, as is USS *Lofberg* (DD 759) and USS *Bole* (DD 755). The USS *Wiltsie* (DD 716) hits a locomotive near Tanchon, and aircraft from USS *Boxer* (CVA 21) finish the destruction of the train.

June 4

EIGHTH ARMY: The Communists launch nine counterattacks in order to halt the UN forces advancing in the Chorwon-Kumhwa-Pyonggang triangle. The Chinese seize Anchor Hill from the ROK I Corps. Private First Class Charles H. Barker, 7th Infantry Division, is awarded the Medal of Honor for his courage in allowing the men of his unit to escape while he provided cover.

SEA WAR: The USS *LSMR 409* suffers damage, and five men are wounded, when it is hit by fire from the mainland at Wonsan.

June 5

EIGHTH ARMY: Given the political situation and the high casualties already taken, the decision is made not to try and retake Outposts Carson, Elko, and Vegas.

SEA WAR: The USS *Valley Forge* (CV 45) receives its third Presidential Unit Citation.

AIR WAR: Lieutenant Colonel Vermont Garrison, 335th FIS, becomes the Korean War's 32nd jet ace. VP Squadron 50 under Lieutenant Commander N. D. McClure begins its sea-based tour of duty in Korea. A B-26 is downed, as are four F86s, due to enemy aircraft. Captain Floyd W. Salze and First Lieutenant Thomas W. Seuffert of the 25th FIS each down a MiG-15 fighter. Major Stephen L. Bettinger, First Lieutenant Frank D. Frazier, and Lieutenant Colonel Julian A. Harvey, all of the 336th FIS, are each credited for downing MiG-15 fighters. Bettinger gets one and Frazier and Harvey share the credit for the other. First Lieutenant Harry A. Jones, Second Lieutenant William E. Schrimsher, and Captain Lonnie R. Moore of the 335th FIS are involved in downing MiG-15 fighters; Schrimsher gets a half-credit and Moore a credit-and-a-half.

June 6

POLITICAL/ADMINISTRATIVE: The ROK National Assembly demands freedom for anticommunist, North Korean prisoners of war presently being held in South Korea. President Dwight Eisenhower informs President Syngman Rhee of the impending armistice and that the United States supports its signing. In protest, civilian demonstrations break out in various locations within the I Corps area.

EIGHTH ARMY: Following a heavy artillery barrage, the Chinese again attack Pork Chop Hill. The battle escalates as each side throws in more and more men.

SEA WAR: Orders are received from Commander Seventh Fleet to put the entire piston-engine plane inventory into the support of ground troops, while the jets are to be occupied in interdiction raids against supply lines.

June 7

POLITICAL/ADMINISTRATIVE: All ROK army officers on duty in the United States are ordered home, and extraordinary security precautions are imposed on all of South Korea by President Rhee.

SEA WAR: The wind and rain of Typhoon Judy delay operations of Task Force 77. The USS *New Jersey* (BB 62) is at Kosong, participating in shore bombardment.

AIR WAR: First Lieutenant Walter W. Fellman and Second Lieutenant James H. Howerton of the 336th each bring down a MiG-15 fighter. First Lieutenant Edwin E. Aldrin of the 16th FIS downs one MiG-15, and Captain Ralph S. Parr of the 335th FIS is credited with two.

June 7–19

SEA WAR: The major effort of naval air is directed against the Communists at the front lines and is designed to slow the Chinese efforts to gain last-minute ground before the signing of the armistice. Flight operations are carried out on a 24-hour basis—not suspended even for fueling operations. Replenishment ships are retained with the task force. As a further deterrent to Communist forces along the lines, USS *New Jersey* (BB 62) is employed against frontline positions near the eastern coast.

AIR WAR: Two F-86s are shot down by enemy pilots.

June 8

POLITICAL/ADMINISTRATIVE: Both sides agree on the voluntary repatriation of all prisoners of war, using India as the neutral nation to conduct the exchange. The solution is made more difficult by Syngman Rhee, who will not allow Indian forces to enter Korea. He threatens to shoot them if they land. Finally, the Indian forces are flown in through the Han River estuary.

SEA WAR: The USS *Lofberg* (DD 759) and USS *Bole* (DD 755) are fired on at Wonsan, but there is no damage.

June 9

POLITICAL/ADMINISTRATIVE: The ROK National Assembly unanimously rejects the truce terms as they are presented. Sweden announces that it is willing to serve on the Neutral Nations Repatriation Commission and on the Neutral Nations Supervisory Commission. Switzerland, however, does not want to send its citizens unless all the forces involved have agreed to observe the terms of the armistice.

AIR WAR: The USS *Bole* (DD 755) is shelled unsuccessfully. Massive efforts are carried out by aircraft from USS *Princeton* (CVA 37), USS *Philippine Sea* (CVA 47), and USS *Lake Champlain* (CVA 39) in support of ground efforts. All this is accomplished despite bad weather that limits the ceiling around the task force to 300 feet.

June 10

EIGHTH ARMY: Communists open the heaviest offensive in two years against South Korean troops. Two companies from the CCF 33rd Division capture Hill 1220 in the Christmas Hill area. The ROK 61st Regiment counterattacks several times but is unable to retake the hill. The Chinese open a series of assaults against Outpost Harry, about two miles south of Jackson Heights, taking it only to lose it again on the following morning. Chinese Communist Forces begin an intense artillery bombardment as elements of the 58th and 60th armies move forward. They manage to smash through outposts on Hill 973 and Hill 882 northeast of Heartbreak Ridge. Two battalions of the ROK 22nd Regiment attempt to regain the hill and get near the crest, but there they have to dig in. The battle for the Kumsong bulge begins as the CCF penetrates UN lines.

SEA WAR: The USS *Wiltsie* (DD 716) is hit, but no casualties are reported from this incident near Wonsan.

AIR WAR: Fifth Air Force focuses its strikes on the few remaining serviceable airfields in North Korea. Sixteen B-29s strike the fields at Sinuiju and Uiju, where they run into heavy flak and fighters but escape with no losses. Aircraft from Task Force 77 hit troop concentrations and billeting near Chaeryong. Thirty-one F-84s strike the airfield at Kanggye. Captain James Jabara of the 4th Fighter-

Interceptor Wing becomes a double ace. Captain Ralph S. Parr of the 335th FIS is credited with downing a MiG-15. Air Group 4 under Commander John Sweeney arrives for duty in Korea onboard USS *Lake Champlain* (CVA 39). Air Group 5 under Commander C. V. Johnson completes its tour of duty aboard USS *Valley Forge* (CVA 45). One B-29 and five F-86s are downed by enemy planes.

June 10–17
EIGHTH ARMY: In the Battle of Outpost Harry, the UN defenders hold the hill but take 186 fatalities, as the U.S. 3rd Infantry Division and the 5th Regimental Combat Team withstand an assault by elements of the CCF 74th Division.

June 11
EIGHTH ARMY: On Pork Chop Hill, five U.S. battalions are trying to hold a small area from nearly an entire Chinese division. Forced to decide between sending even more troops or withdrawing in hope that the armistice talks will conclude, General Maxwell Taylor orders the withdrawal of troops and leaves Pork Chop

Korean demonstrators in Pusan protest any armistice agreement that does not include the unification of Korea, June 11, 1953. *(Center for the Study of the Korean War, Graceland University)*

in the hands of the Chinese. The Chinese hit Arrowhead Hill (281) with a company-size unit but are unable to take the area from the ROK 2nd Infantry Division. Master Sergeant Ola L. Mize, 3rd Infantry Division, is awarded the Medal of Honor for courage and leadership at Outpost Harry. Elements of the ROK 35th Infantry Regiment counterattack on Hill 973 but are only partially successful. The enemy moves quickly to answer the drive, and in the face of the attack, the ROK troops pull back. Assuming containment will be less costly, Lieutenant General Isaac D. White calls off the attack and moves the ROK 7th into a supporting defensive position.

SEA WAR: The USS *Wiltsie* (DD 716) receives minor damage but no casualties when it is hit by guns in the Wonsan harbor area.

AIR WAR: Fighter-bombers penetrate deep into North Korea, attacking the Chunggangjin airfield located near the Manchurian border. Combat reports state that the field is made unusable.

PARTISANS: Orders are given to evacuate civilians, supplies, and equipment beyond immediate needs. This will also be a preparation for the evacuation of partisans, particularly at Yo-do and Yang-do, as armistice talks near an end.

June 12

EIGHTH ARMY: A regiment of Chinese troops moves through its own lines and friendly artillery and gains the trenches at Outpost Harry. At 0032, the CCF is in control of the northern outpost but the UN still holds on to the southern end. At 0545, the enemy withdraws and the action ceases. During the night, however, the bombardment continues. The Chinese put pressure on the ROK II Corps as they attack elements of the ROK 8th Division. In the Capitol Hill sector northwest of Hill 973, the Communists send two companies to penetrate the outposts and then the line of the ROK 21st Regiment.

SEA WAR: Nearly 16 rounds are fired at USS *Carpenter* (DDE 825) and USS *Manchester* (CL 83) at Hungnam harbor, but there is no damage. Task Force 90 is put on alert and sent to Pusan to outfit with wood and wire cribbing as cages for the transportation of prisoners of war.

AIR WAR: Due to the deteriorating situation in the ROK II Corps area, the 3,000-foot minimum-altitude restriction is lifted by the Fifth Air Force commander, Lieutenant General Samuel E. Anderson.

PARTISANS: All American and partisan forces complete the withdrawal from islands north of the 38th parallel. Units of "stay behinds" are left to provide small reconnaissance patrols to keep track of enemy movements. CincFE directs the outloading of all civilians and supplies and the evacuation of partisans and their dependents from the Wonsan islands and from Yang-do.

June 13

POLITICAL/ADMINISTRATIVE: Switzerland agrees to serve on the Neutral Nations Repatriation Commission.

EIGHTH ARMY: Three Chinese battalions of the 70th Division, hit outposts in the Boomerang area, but make no attempt to hold or occupy the territory taken. The three-day assault on Outpost Boomerang proves to be very costly to the Chinese and they withdraw. Two battalions of the ROK 10th Regiment move against the Chinese but are unable to regain the lost positions. A second Chinese attack forces the ROK to move back farther.

SEA WAR: Two planes are destroyed aboard USS *Lake Champlain* (CVA 39) as the result of an accident.

AIR WAR: An F-86 is shot down by enemy fighters near the Supun Dam. First Lieutenant Don R. Forbes of the 12th FBS shoots downs a MiG-15 fighter.

June 13–18

AIR WAR: The Fifth Air Force, flying F-84s and B-29s, and the marines in F4U Corsair fighter-bombers hit irrigations dams at Toksan and Kusong, in hope of flooding the airfields at Namsi and Taechon. The attack fails to breech the dams.

June 14

EIGHTH ARMY: The CCF 33rd Division renews its offensive against the ROK 5th and 20th Divisions and forces them to fall back south of the Pukhan River. The withdrawal exposes the flank of the ROK's 7th Division, but the Chinese fail to follow up. The Chinese launch their second major assault against Outpost Harry in the Jackson Heights area but fail to regain the position. The battle for Boomerang Hill begins. At the time, the hill complex is held by the United Nations. The attack focuses on Triangle Hill, Sniper Ridge, and Boomerang, where the ROA's 9th Division is located. In intense fighting that goes on for several days, the ROK holds the hill.

SEA WAR: In response to the Communist offensives, Task Force 77 strikes the Hasepori marshaling yards. At Wonsan USS *Lofberg* (DD 759) and USS *Bole* (DD 755) are fired on several times but avoid damage.

AIR WAR: Task Force 77 launches more than 500 sorties in support of troops facing ground offensives. Six F-86s are downed by enemy fighters.

June 15

POLITICAL/ADMINISTRATIVE: Brigadier General Richard H. Carmichael replaces General William P. Fisher as commander FEAF Bomber Command. The Tasca Mission, the presidential survey being conducted on the economic needs of South Korea following the war, is concluded.

EIGHTH ARMY: Chinese forces attack the line in the U.S. I Corps sector. Communist forces attack the ROK in east-central Korea.

SEA WAR: More than 100 rounds are fired by enemy batteries near Wonsan at USS *Lofberg* (DD 759), USS *Bole* (DD 755), and USS *Current* (ARS 22), but there are no hits. The USS *Princeton* launches 184 sorties against enemy ground targets along the front line.

AIR WAR: The USS *Princeton* (CV 37), in launching 184 sorties, establishes a single-day record for offensive sorties flown from a carrier. Navy and Marine Corps aircraft fly 910 sorties, the highest combined numbers for a single day. An F-86 is shot down by enemy aircraft near Dapu.

June 16

EIGHTH ARMY: The Chinese overrun the ROK 10th Regiment at an outpost on Finger Ridge, but the Chinese withdraw after taking the area.

SEA WAR: Captain Jack Maginnis takes command as "mayor" of the Wonsan blockade, replacing Captain Richard E. Myers.

AIR WAR: Fifth Air Force flies 1,834 sorties against troop concentrations and supplies in the Pukhan Valley. Two unidentified enemy planes drop five bombs on a fuel dump at Inchon, causing considerable damage. Six F-86s are shot down by enemy planes. Captain Robert P. Baldwin and Major George W. Howell of the 25th FIS, Major Stephen L. Betinger of the 336th FIS, and First Lieutenant James L. Thompson of the 39th FIS each are credited with downing a MiG-15 fighter.

June 17

POLITICAL/ADMINISTRATIVE: Both sides at the cease-fire negotiations agree to a revision of the truce line designed to incorporate the more current battle lines.

EIGHTH ARMY: After two quiet nights at Outpost Harry, the Chinese return at about 0052, coming from the northeast and the northwest. The Chinese gain control of some trenches just after 0300. Helped by reenforcements, the defenders are able to drive the Chinese out of the trenches, and by 0400, the badly mauled enemy withdraws. An estimated 22,000 rounds are fired by the Chinese in support of the attack.

SEA WAR: The USS *Comstock* (LSD 19) is struck by a significant number of diarrhea cases, probably caused by fresh provisions taken on board from Korean sources. Enemy guns at Wonsan fire on, but do not hit, USS *Irwin* (DD 794), USS *Rowan* (DD 782), and USS *Henderson* (DD 785) sailing in the area.

AIR WAR: Near Myaogao, an F-86 is shot down by Communist fighters.

June 17–18

POLITICAL/ADMINISTRATIVE: ROK president Rhee announces that he has, on his own authority, released more than 20,000 anticommunist prisoners from POW camps under his jurisdiction. He does not give any explanation other than to draw attention to the way in which the cease-fire talks are going. General Clark has considered the chance that Rhee would do this and has discussed the possibility of replacing ROK prison guards with UN troops but decides against it because he knows that Rhee is already irritated.

June 18

POLITICAL/ADMINISTRATIVE: General Mark Clark informs the Chinese cease-fire negotiators of the release of POWs, claiming no prior knowledge. The Chinese accuse UN Command of being a partner in the action, but they appear far less shocked about what happened. They want General Clark to capture and return the prisoners.

EIGHTH ARMY: In a third attempt in two weeks, the Chinese launch a two-battalion assault against Outpost Harry, only to be pushed back. At the same time, outbursts of Chinese activity began to slow down. The UN forces reestablish themselves about

3,000 meters south of their earlier line. The Chinese gains have cost them about 7,000 men.

SEA WAR: The USS *Irwin* (DD 794) is hit and has five casualties. The USS *Rowan* (DD 782) suffers 10 casualties caused by shore battery fire at Wonsan. The batteries also fire at USS *Saint Paul* (CA 73) but do not hit the ship.

AIR WAR: Captain Lonnie R. Moore and Captain Ralph S. Parr, Jr., both of the 335th FIS, become the 33rd and 34th jet aces. Colonel Robert P. Baldwin of the 25th FIS and Major James Jabara of the 334th FIS also down a MiG-15 each. Flight Leader R. T. Dickinson (RAF) is credited with the destruction of a MiG-15. An F-86 is shot down by enemy fighters near Kijio.

June 19

EIGHTH ARMY: Sergeant Gilbert G. Collier (USA) is posthumously awarded the Medal of Honor for services near Tutayon. Communist forces attack and overrun outposts Berlin and East Berlin.

SEA WAR: On the Yang-do patrol, enemy guns fire more than 125 rounds at USS *Rowan* (DD 782) without scoring a hit. The USS *Bremerton* (CA 130) is fired on at Wonsan, but there are no hits.

AIR WAR: Two F-86s are shot down by enemy fighters, one near Sinuiju and one at Kijio. Second Lieutenant Alvin R. Bouchard of the 16th FIS, First Lieutenant Henry Buttelmann of the 25th FIS, and Captain Ralph S. Parr and First Lieutenant Lawrence Roesler of the 335th FIS also down MiG-15 fighters, as does Lieutenant Colonel George I. Ruddell of the 39th FIS.

June 20

POLITICAL/ADMINISTRATIVE: Following Rhee's release of prisoners of war under his control, the Communists break off the armistice talks. Assistant Secretary of State Walter S. Robertson goes to Korea to convince Rhee to agree to the armistice conditions. In return, Rhee makes several demands that are acceptable to President Dwight Eisenhower, with only one exception. Yet when Rhee is told of the agreement he increases his demands. Rhee's actions anger the Communists who demand the return of all POWs and remain away from the peace talks. Brigadier General Edgar E. Glenn (USAF) is released as a UN delegate at the armistice talks.

EIGHTH ARMY: The infantry holds on to a series of outposts in the central sector despite heavy artillery bombardments and battalion-sized assaults. The United Nations establishes a new MLR on the south bank of the Kumsong River.

AIR WAR: Two people are killed and eight wounded when nine enemy propeller aircraft drop bombs on Seoul.

SEA WAR: The USS *Current* (ARS 22) collides with USS *LST 855* while transferring cargo, but the damage is slight.

June 21

EIGHTH ARMY: The 187th Airborne Regimental Combat Team arrives in Korea for its third tour of duty.

June 22

POLITICAL/ADMINISTRATIVE: Assistant Secretary of State Walter S. Robertson continues his mission to bring Syngman Rhee around to accepting the armistice agreement. The mission will last until July 22.

SEA WAR: The HMAS *Culoga* evacuates friendly forces after Chinese Communist troops from Haeju invade Yongmae-do.

AIR WAR: Colonel Robert P. Baldwin of the 25th FIS becomes a jet ace. In flying the 187th Airborne Regimental Combat Team—about 3,252 men and 1,771 tons of cargo—to reinforce Eighth Army reserves, the 315th AD uses 27 C-46s and 61 C-119s in a total of 284 sorties. Four F-86s are shot down by enemy fighters. Colonel Robert P. Baldwin and First Lieutenant Henry Buttlemann of the 25th FIS, Second Lieutenant Alvin R. Bouchard and Captain Philip C. Davis of the 16th FIS, First Lieutenant Homer J. Carlile of the 39th FIS, and Captain James G. Nichols of the 335th FIS are each credited with downing an enemy MiG-15.

June 23

POLITICAL/ADMINISTRATIVE: Lieutenant General Maxwell D. Taylor is promoted to the rank of full general.

EIGHTH ARMY: A second major attack is launched by the Chinese against the complex called Boomerang Hill, now held by the 2nd Infantry Division. The attacks continue for several days and are still underway when the armistice agreement is signed. The area will become a part of the demilitarized zone.

AIR WAR: General Weyland advises the air force that it should limit its attacks on airfields for fear of destroying them completely. The hope is that the United States will be able to use the fields after the cease-fire.

June 24

EIGHTH ARMY: The U.S. 40th and 45th Divisions and the 5th RCT are redeployed along the front lines to bolster the ROK army during a renewed CCF offensive. The Chinese make their final attack on the Hook, after a barrage estimated at 4,000 shells. The defending force, the 2nd Battalion, Royal Australian Regiment, supported by American and Commonwealth artillery, holds. The Australians suffer 30 casualties and the Chinese an estimated 2,000 to 3,000 casualties. The foci of the renewed Chinese attacks are against the ROK 9th Division in the IX Corps sector.

AIR WAR: An F-86 is shot down by enemy planes near Gisyu. Major Foster I. Smith of the 335th FIS is credited with downing two MiG-15s. First Lieutenant Roscoe E. Anderson of the 25th FIS, Major Vermont Garrison, Captain James G. Nichols, and First Lieutenant George W. Ober of the 335th FIS, Major John F. Bolt (USMC) of the 39th FIS, and Captain Dean A. Pogreba of the 336th FIS are each credited with downing a MiG-15.

SEA WAR: The USS *Irwin* (DD 794) is fired on by shore batteries at Wonsan without damage.

June 25

EIGHTH ARMY: Elements of two regiments of the 7th Infantry Division, CCF, strike at Hannah, Bak, and Hill 179. Despite orders for UN forces to hang on at all costs, the Chinese are able to advance into the trenches and bunkers. The 1st ROK Infantry Division on the eastern flank of I Corps is pounded by another Chinese infantry division. The ROK holds on for most of the night.

SEA WAR: Task Force 77 transfers four F4U-5N aircraft to the control of Fifth Air Force in order to provide Seoul protection. The air force no longer has any propeller-driven night fighters, and its jets are too fast to catch propeller planes that have been dropping bombs on the capital city. Guns at Tanchon fire on USS *Gurke* (DD 783), which receives two direct hits, wounding three crewmen and creating a hole in the radio room.

June 26

EIGHTH ARMY: By morning the two outposts of Bak and Hannah, as well as Hill 179, are overrun. Several unsuccessful counterattacks are attempted. During the night the CCF 179th Division sends one regiment against the 5th ROK position east of the Pukhan River and a second against the 7th ROK Division along the main ridge leading to Hill 1220. Both units pull back to maintain a defensive line. During the night, the Chinese hit elements of the ROK 7th Division on Hill 938, and take the hill. The ROK counterattacks but to no avail. The continuing probes against the ROK 1st have taken several of the forward outposts but are held from advancing too far by 4.5-inch rocket fire directed from the 1st Marine 4.5-inch rocket battery.

AIR WAR: First Lieutenant Thomas H. McQuade of the 335th FIS and First Lieutenant Henry Buttlemann of the 336th FIA are each credited with downing a MiG-15.

June 27

SEA WAR: The HMNZS *Kaniere,* on patrol near Chinnampo, is fired on by enemy batteries that unleash 55 rounds without scoring a hit.

AIR WAR: Three F-86s are shot down by enemy aircraft. Flight Leader John H. J. Lovell (RAF) and First Lieutenant Henry Buttlemann of the 25th FIS each shoot down an enemy MiG-15.

June 28

EIGHTH ARMY: The ROK, still trying to retake Outposts Bak and Hannan, as well as Hill 179, again tries a counterattack. Finally, after several failed attempts, General Mark Clark of I Corps determines that the hill is not worth the cost. Chinese forces take Queen Hill from the ROK and several attempts to retake the hill fail.

June 28–July 2

AIR WAR: In transporting the 19th and 34th Regimental Combat Teams—3,937 troopers and 1,227 tons of cargo—from Japan to Korea, the 315th AD uses C-46s and C-119s.

June 29

POLITICAL/ADMINISTRATIVE: General Mark Clark proposes that the peace talks be continued.

EIGHTH ARMY: General Clarke, I Corps commander, says the outposts at Bak and Hannah and Hill 179 are becoming too costly and decides against any further attacks.

SEA WAR: At Wonsan, Communist gunners fire on USS *Irwin* (DD 794) but do not hit the ship.

AIR WAR: An F-86 is shot down by an enemy fighter near Andong. Flight Leader John H. Granville-White of the 39th FIS, First Lieutenant Henry Buttelmann and First Lieutenant Kenneth I. Palmer of the 25th FIS, and First Lieutenant Roland B. Howell, First Lieutenant Thomas E. Nott, and First Lieutenant George W. Jensen of the 16th FIS are each credited with downing an enemy MiG-15.

June 30

POLITICAL/ADMINISTRATIVE: General Hoyt Vandenberg is replaced by General Nathan Twining as Air Force chief of staff.

SEA WAR: There are neither wounded personnel nor serious damage caused to USS *Manchester* (CL 83) when the shore batteries at Wonsan fire on the ship. VP Squadron Seven, under Lieutenant Commander R. L. Mildner, begins its land-based tour of duty in Korea.

AIR WAR: Sabres set a record by destroying 16 MiGs in one day. First Lieutenant Henry Buttelmann, of the 25th FIS, becomes the Korean War's 36th ace. Lieutenant Colonel William L. Cosby of the 334th FIS and Lieutenant Colonel Vermont Garrison of the 335th FIS; Major James Jabara of the 334th FIS; Colonel James K. Johnson of the 335th FIS; Second Lieutenant Cecil E. Lefevers (half a credit), and Captain George W. Love of the 336th FIS (half a credit); Lieutenant Colonel Earle P. Maxwell of the 16th FIS; Captain Lonnie R. Moore of the 335th FIS; First Lieutenant Waymond C. Nutt, First Lieutenant Jimmie Pierce, and First Lieutenant George J. Spataro of the 334th FIS; Captain Ralph S. Parr of the 335th FIS (credited with two); and Major John F. Bolt (USMC) and Squadron Leader John McKay (RCAF) of the 39th FIS, are each responsible for downing enemy MiG-15s. Marine Air Group 12 flies a record 217 combat sorties.

July 1

EIGHTH ARMY: The First Marine Division returns to the line at its former sector in relief of the 25th Infantry Division.

SEA WAR: Nearly 20 boxcars are destroyed when HMCA *Athabaskan* (DDE) fires on a southbound train on North Korea's east coast. Seventeen of the cars are destroyed by fire from USS *Wiltsie* (DD 716) and planes from Task Force 77. Task Force 77 is equipped with weapons of nuclear capability. Captain Richard E. Myers takes command as "mayor" of the Wonsan blockade, replacing Captain Jack Maginnis.

July 2–12

EIGHTH ARMY: The 24th Infantry Division is transferred from Japan to help with POW camp security in anticipation of the cease-fire.

July 3

EIGHTH ARMY: General Mark Clark seeks to reinforce his line. Lieutenant General Isaac D. White shifts to a policy of containment and moves to create a strengthened line rather than trying to retake outposts lost in the Chinese offensive. After three days trying to take Hill 938, the ROK 7th Division is called off.

July 3–8

POLITICAL/ADMINISTRATIVE: Walter S. Robertson, assistant secretary of state, continues his mission for President Dwight Eisenhower to work out some arrangement to prevent President Syngman Rhee from opposing a cease-fire with the Chinese Communist Forces.

July 4

POLITICAL/ADMINISTRATIVE: President Rhee sends a message to Washington, D.C., asking the United States to continue the war according to the original objectives of their common cause.

AIR WAR: During the night, 24 B-29s hit airfields at Taechon, Namsi, and Pyongyang.

July 5

EIGHTH ARMY: The approximate date on which U.S. Navy Task Force 77 is equipped with operational nuclear weapons.

SEA WAR: USNS *LST 578* runs aground near Cheju-do. The SS *Cornhusker Mariner* runs aground in rough seas off the entrance of Port Pusan.

July 6

EIGHTH ARMY: The battle for Pork Chop Hill (Hill 255) begins again as the Communists attack the 7th Infantry Division position and take the hill. Elements of the CCF 73rd Division attack through the 69th and strike against two ROK outposts in the area of Arrowhead. The area will hold through six days of attacks.

July 6–10

EIGHTH ARMY: Members of the 7th Infantry Division on Pork Chop Hill are attacked by elements of the CCF 7th Division. During the first wave, the Chinese are able to take the hill. During the conflict, the 7th Infantry Division suffers 232 fatalities. The 7th is ordered to evacuate its defensive positions on Pork Chop Hill. On July 9, the duel begins again as each side takes and then loses the crest. Finally, it is decided by Generals Taylor, Trudeau, and Clarke, after several days of fierce fighting, that UN forces shall withdraw.

July 7

POLITICAL/ADMINISTRATIVE: National Security Council Document 154.1 is directed toward "United States Tactics Immediately Following an Armistice in Korea." It acknowledges that even if there is peace in Korea the Chinese will continue their aggression elsewhere in Asia, and it recommends a trade embargo and a multinational statement against further aggression. President Eisenhower considers the idea of a blockade too broad. He believes that he could not get the allies to agree. National Security Council Document 157.1, "United States Objectives with Respect to Korea Following an Armistice," suggests that the Soviet Union might accept a neutralized Korea in return for the removal of all troops from Korea. President Eisenhower favors the idea, believing that it is not necessary to have troops in Korea. Neither Kim Il Sung nor Syngman Rhee is open to this suggestion.

EIGHTH ARMY: During the night, the enemy opens up a limited offensive against the ROK II Corps in central Korea. The 7th Infantry Division attempts to retake Pork Chop Hill, but after a prolonged fight, it fails to dislodge the enemy. At 2100, several companies of Chinese attack Outposts East Berlin and Berlin. This comes as UN units are involved in a relief operation; each unit is about company-size. At first the area is subjected to heavy artillery fire in an effort to isolate the posts. There is heavy resistance, partly from the Turks who have remained in defense and partly from the survivors of Fox Company, 2nd Battalion, 7th Regiment, ambushes, who have taken shelter there. Berlin falls quickly, and by midnight it is overrun and communications lost. East Berlin holds on a little longer but by 0031 communications are cut off. The fighting continues all night. The 3rd Battalion, 7th Marines, moves in to supply reinforcements on the MLR. The fighting continues until the survivors are ordered to withdraw. Of the original platoon on East Berlin nothing is known. It seems to have vanished. Spoonbill Bridge is submerged under more than 11 feet of water due to heavy rains and is finally destroyed by the water pressure.

SEA WAR: Both USS *Symbol* (AM 123) and USS *Wiltsie* (DD 716) are fired on by batteries from Yang-do, but there is no damage. At Hodo Pando, Communist gunners fire over 300 rounds at ships in the harbor—USS *Lofberg* (DD 759), USS *Thomason* (DD 760), and USS *Hammer* (DD 718)—only one of which, the *Thomason,* is damaged. The destroyers fire more than 800 rounds in counter-battery fire before the Communist guns are silent.

AIR WAR: Sixteen medium bombers raid a supply area and marshaling yard at Namsi.

July 8

POLITICAL/ADMINISTRATIVE: The Communists agree to return to the armistice talks recessed since President Rhee released the POWs. They indicate, however, that they will not sign an agreement until they are sure that Washington can control Rhee's behavior. A State Department spokesman announces the American dead in Korea at 24,685 and casualties at 137,914.

EIGHTH ARMY: By dawn the Chinese are in full control of East Berlin. On Berlin, 18 marines and some Turks still hold on. An attempt is made by 1st Platoon of How Company, 3rd Battalion, 7th Regiment, to reinforce, but in the charge the company strength is cut down, leaving only 20 effective men. The remainder move through the earlier lines and reached the trenches, killing all the Chinese and taking the outpost. The 7th Infantry Division attempts to take Pork Chop Hill from the Communists but cannot dislodge them. First Lieutenant Richard T. Shea, 7th Infantry Division, earns the Medal of Honor for courage and leadership in a counterattack against enemy forces. The Chinese on East Berlin fire on the marines as they attempt to take the outpost.

Sea War: The USS *Wiltsie* (DD 715) is hit near Chaho by fire from shore batteries that causes five casualties. South of Songjin, USS *Irwin* (DD 794) is hit, and the DesRon 25 squadron commander is hit along with four other men.

July 9

Eighth Army: The Chinese continue to probe the outposts around Berlin. Each assault is preceded by artillery and mortar fire. Each time the attack is beaten off as the casualties mount on both sides. The last attack on Berlin breaks off at 0130. East Berlin, during this time, suffers five more attacks. But, it was over for a time. The outpost remained in marine hands at a cost of nine killed, 140 wounded, and 12 missing. After several days of fighting on Pork Chop Hill, control of the crest comes to a stalemate. The army corps and division commanders, in a conference, decide that the cost of holding the Chinese, who seem willing to pay almost any price, is just too much. The hill is given up. Hill 126 is a major marine observation post, located in the western sector of the 3rd Regiment area. A platoon of the 3rd Battalion, along with five tanks, is sent to fortify the hill.

July 9–18

Eighth Army: Massive rainstorms and a continuing ground fog nearly stop the activity of air observers and encourage the Chinese to dig in.

July 10

Political/Administrative: Talks resume at Panmunjom after the United Nations assures Communist China that the ROK will accept a cease-fire.

Eighth Army: General Maxwell Taylor decides that Pork Chop Hill is not worth the casualties being taken and decides to evacuate the 7th Infantry Division. The ROK's 20th Division relieves the U.S. 40th Infantry Division in the Heartbreak area. Corporal Dan D. Schoonover, 7th Infantry Division, is awarded the Medal of Honor for his courage against an enemy attack.

Air War: Fifth Air Force fighter-bombers begin raids directed toward bridges in the Sinanju and Yongmi-dong areas, designed to delay the buildup of Communist troops. During the night, 98th Bomber Wing B-29s attack the bridges at Sinanju, and the 307th Bomber Wing's B-29s bomb rail bridges at Yongmi-dong.

July 11

Political/Administrative: With promises of enormous economic aid, and the continued presence of U.S. troops in the Republic of Korea, President Rhee agrees not to further obstruct the armistice. The release of the Rhee-Robertson Communique suggests the two officials have arrived at a mutual understanding of the troublesome issues between them.

Eighth Army: The U.S. 7th Infantry Division withdraws from Pork Chop Hill on orders from the Eighth Army commander.

SEA WAR: The American cruiser USS *Saint Paul* (CA 75) is hit at Wonsan, damaging two guns. The HMCS *Huron* (DE) runs aground at the western tip of Yang-do.

AIR WAR: Major John F. Bolt becomes the first jet ace in Marine Corps history when he shoots down his fifth and sixth MiG-15s east of Sinuiju.

July 12

POLITICAL/ADMINISTRATIVE: Assistant Secretary of State Walter S. Robertson leaves Korea after completing his mission to convince President Rhee to accept the armistice agreement.

EIGHTH ARMY: Using armored personnel carriers, the 7th Infantry Division is withdrawn from Pork Chop Hill and the much-disputed hill is abandoned to the Communists. Marines from a squad of Baker Company, 1st Battalion, 7th Regiment, are wounded when they detonate newly laid mines. Later, a two-squad patrol from Baker Company comes within 15 yards of the trenches on Outpost Elko when it is attacked by machine-gun fire from Outpost Carson. The attack is followed by a barrage of grenades from Elko. After a half-hour, the marines withdraw under mortar fire, having taken only one casualty.

SEA WAR: The USS *New Jersey* (BB 62) fires 168 rounds of 16-inch projectiles during a heavy strike near the Kojo area, destroying a radar tower, two bridges, and a control bunker.

AIR WAR: RF-80 reconnaissance aircraft photograph large concentrations of antiaircraft artillery facilities facing the front held by the U.S. IX Corps and the ROK II Corps, suggesting an enemy offensive. An F-86 is shot down by enemy fighters. Major Stephen L. Bettinger of the 336th FIS, Major John J. Glenn (USMC) and First Lieutenant John D. Winters of the 25th FIS, Captain Lonnie R. Moore (who is credited with two), Captain Ralph S. Parr, Captain Clyde A. Curtin, and First Lieutenant Curtis N. Carley of the 335th FIS, are all credited with downing MiG-15s.

July 12–20

EIGHTH ARMY: The CCF launches a large offensive along the central Korean front. U.S. IX Corps and ROK II Corps establish their MLR south of the Kumsong River.

AIR WAR: FEAF aircraft provide close air support by flying nearly 100 sorties against the Communists attacking ROK II Corps troops.

July 13

EIGHTH ARMY: Elements of five Chinese divisions—nearly 80,000 strong—attack in central Korea in a final push that causes heavy casualties among South Korean forces near Kumsong. They face the ROK 9th and Capital Divisions, all of the U.S. IX Corps, and four divisions of the ROK II Corps. The attacks make serious inroads against the ROK positions. The ROK is able to fight back, however, inflicting heavy losses on the Chinese. The CCF nevertheless gains a few miles that will change the cease-fire line in case of an armistice. It is estimated that the Chinese casualties are as high as 28,000. Outpost Ingrid, in the center of the 5th Marine Regiment line, comes under fire from Chinese artillery and small-arms fire.

Sea War: The USS *New Jersey* (BB 62) is pounding coastal guns at Hungnam, her last mission of the war.

July 13–20

Eighth Army: One of the deadliest battles of the Korean War is fought at the Kumsong River salient. The Chinese, in their last major offensive, attack with six divisions focused on the sections occupied by the U.S. IX Corps.

Air War: B-29 medium bombers launch nearly 100 ground-support flights, dropping air-burst and delayed-action antipersonnel bombs.

July 14

Eighth Army: The Imjin crests at 26 feet at Libby Bridge, cutting the supply route to a single crossing at Freedom Bridge. The U.S. 555th Field Artillery Battalion is overrun at the loss of 300 killed and missing. Units of the ROK II Corps are ordered to pull back to the southern side of the Kumsong River to straighten out the defensive line. To bolster the defenses, the 187th Airborne Regimental Combat Team is rushed from Japan and is attached to the 2nd Division.

Air War: VMF-311 and VMF-115 unleash 25 tons of explosives near marine trouble spots.

July 15

Sea War: Near Songjin, HMAS *Tobruk* (D 37) sinks a large enemy motor sampan.

Air War: Major James Jabara scores his 15th kill to become the Korean War's second triple jet ace. Captain Clyde A. Curtin of the 335th FIS is also credited with a kill. Two F-86s are shot down by enemy fighters.

July 16

Political/Administrative: Communist delegates request a two-day recess, then later ask that it be extended to July 19. During this period, the Chinese halt the UN counterattack along the Kumsong River.

Eighth Army: The limited Communist offensive drags to a halt. The negotiators at Panmunjom reconfigure the lines. A 15-man reconnaissance patrol from 2nd Battalion, 5th Marines, is ambushed by a group of 30 to 40 Chinese near Hill 90, two miles east of the Neutral Corridor. The marines are surrounded but manage to beat back the assault. An incoming relief squad is intercepted by concentrated mortar fire and every man in the patrol is wounded. Before breaking off, the Chinese make several attempts to capture prisoners. After the withdrawal, the marines find seven of the missing men. A search the following night (July 17) finds an additional six bodies.

Sea War: An unusually large number of sorties, 111, are flown off USS *Boxer* (CV 21), all directed to the bulge area on the front near Kumhwa.

Air War: Commander Guy Bordelon, flying with Fifth Air Force, becomes the 38th ace and the only navy pilot to qualify. Two F-86s are shot down by enemy fighters. Major Stephen L. Bettinger of the 336th FIS, Major Lowell K. Brueland and Lieutenant Colonel Harold C. Gibson of the 39th FIS, and First Lieutenant Lawrence Roesler of the 335th FIS are all credited with downing a MiG-15.

July 16–20

EIGHTH ARMY: The ROK's army is given instructions to engage in a counterattack designed to retake any land south of the Kumsong River that has been lost. As a result of heavy fighting, the 3rd, 6th, and 7th ROK Divisions press forward and by July 20 are able to retake the ground.

AIR WAR: Fighter-bombers continue a series of attacks against the bridges at Chong-chon, making them unpassable.

July 17

POLITICAL/ADMINISTRATIVE: National Security Council Document 156.1, "Strengthening the Korean Economy," reflects the agreement reached with Syngman Rhee and is based on the idea that a stronger economy is needed to counteract the appeal of communism. Accepted by the president, it will become the economic lifeline for the ROK.

EIGHTH ARMY: At 0100, a two-squad patrol from Able Company, 1st Battalion, 7th Marines, encounters an enemy patrol twice its size. After a brief fight, the marines break off and return to Outpost Ava. Corporal Charles A. Pendleton, 3rd Infantry Division, is awarded the Medal of Honor for his courage against the enemy near Chou Gun Dong.

AIR WAR: An F-86 is shot down by enemy fighters near Deeguandong.

July 18

AIR WAR: Captain Lonnie R. Moore and Major Foster L. Smith of the 335th FIS each down an enemy MiG-15 fighter.

July 19

POLITICAL/ADMINISTRATIVE: The final session of the armistice negotiation meetings at Panmunjom convenes. Apparently both sides are ready to come to an agreement. They agree to let their staffs work out the details for the final approval document. UN Command directs its forces that they are to make no more efforts to retake lost ground.

EIGHTH ARMY: Chinese Communist Forces overrun Outposts Berlin and East Berlin. The Chinese move off their positions at Outpost Jersey to hit Bunker Hill and Outpost Detroit. Following the information that the negotiators are reaching the final stages, no effort is made to recapture the lost posts. The attack comes on the same day as the negotiators at Panmunjom agree on a final settlement.

AIR WAR: Planes from MAG-12 fly 162 combat sorties in support of UNC action. Captain Ronnie L. Moore and Lieutenant Colonel Vermont Garrison of the 4th Fighter-Interceptor Wing become the ninth and 10th double aces of the Korean War. Captain Clyde A. Curtin of the 335th FIS shoots down two MiGs to become the 39th ace. An F-86 is shot down by enemy fighters. First Lieutenant Henry Buttelmann, First Lieutenant Jerald D. Parker and Major John H. Glenn (USMC) of the 25th FIS, Lieutenant Colonel Jack R. Best of the 336th FIS, First Lieutenant Frank D. Frazier of the 335th FIS, and First Lieutenant Robert Strozier of the 35th FIS are all credited with downing MiG-15 fighters.

July 20

POLITICAL/ADMINISTRATIVE: As a result of the heaviest rains in 19 years in the Wakayana Prefecture of Honshu, Japan, the Arita River overflows and causes a flood described officially as the worst in Japanese history.

EIGHTH ARMY: ROK II Corps and U.S. IX Corps establish the MLR along the Kumsong River, where they halt the Communist advance. In the face of heavy Chinese attacks, the 1st Marine commander calls for immediate reorganization and to employ defense in depth. Sergeant George D. Libby, 24th Infantry Division, earns the Medal of Honor for courage during the battle around Taejon. Sergeant Gilbert G. Collier, 40th Infantry, earns the Medal of Honor for courage shown in trying to save his endangered leader. Red gunners fire 60 rounds of antitank shells at the Wonsan islands but cause no damage. Two additional companies of the 5th Marine Regiment are sent to increase the defenses at Hill 126. It is determined that Hill 126 and Outpost Boulder City have to be kept.

AIR WAR: Bomber Command attacks the runways at Uiju, Sinuiju, Namsi, Taechon, Pyong-ni, Pyongyang, and Saamcham. The 336th FIS's Major Stephen L. Bettinger becomes the 40th ace of the Korean War with his fifth MiG kill. Four F-86s are shot down by enemy fighters. Major Thomas M. Sellers (USMC) of the 336th FIS is credited with downing two enemy MiG-15 fighters.

July 21

SEA WAR: The HMNZS *Hawea* arrives shortly after North Korean troops attack the island of Ohwa-do, and she evacuates surviving friendly guerrillas and refugees. The *Hawea* destroys a large number of enemy junks.

AIR WAR: Eighteen B-29s from Bomber Command blanket the Uiju dispersal area with incendiary and fragmentation bombs. Despite heavy rains, more than 15 radar missions are flown by three squadrons as they hit CCF mortar and 76-mm gun positions, bunkers, and supply areas.

PARTISANS: Approximately 150 NKPA troops attack the friendly held island of Ohwa-do. Using eight large junks for transportation, the enemy swarms ashore and succeeds in killing seven officers and wounding 20 men. HMNZS *Hawea* arrives about four hours after the landing and is able to fire on the gathered troops, causing a large number of enemy dead and wounded.

July 22

SEA WAR: Captain Carl M. Dalton takes command as "mayor" of the Wonsan blockade, replacing Captain Richard Myers. Captain Dalton will hold the position until the end of hostilities.

AIR WAR: An air battle between three 51st FIW Sabres and four Communist jets ends with the downing of one MiG-15. Major John H. Glenn, Second Lieutenant Sam P. Young, and First Lieutenant Henry Buttelmann of the 25th FIS each shoot down a MiG-15.

July 22–23

EIGHTH ARMY: The Chinese attack the 7th Marine Regiment defense along the MLR and manage to gain control of Hill 139, which they quickly use as an observation post.

July 23

POLITICAL/ADMINISTRATIVE: President Dwight Eisenhower approved the recommendations of the Tasca Mission on economic aid to South Korea.

EIGHTH ARMY: UN forces begin the defense of Outposts Dale and Westview.

SEA WAR: The USS *Saint Paul* (CA 73) draws 12 rounds of 155-mm shells from enemy gun complexes along the Wonsan perimeter. The enemy shells splash 10 to 15 yards from the ship and do not damage the cruiser.

July 24

EIGHTH ARMY: The Chinese attack the marines on the flank of the Commonwealth Division. They hit at a series of hills that serve as boundaries between the two divisions. The defensive fortifications of Outpost Dale and Westview are complete. Chinese mortar and artillery rounds begin to fall on Outpost Boulder City. Soon the first waves of Chinese infantrymen are seen moving into assault positions. For the next 36 hours two Chinese battalions claw at the hill. By 2400, George Company, now reduced to 25 percent strength, is reenforced and starts pushing the Chinese away from the recently taken ground. Following a period of bombardment, Chinese infantry begin to probe the MLR at Hill 119 in the Marine battalion sector. After a heavy fight, the Communists are able to penetrate Hill 111, but at about 2120, they begin to withdraw. The attack has apparently been a diversion to ease pressure on Outpost Boulder City. During the night, more than 4,000 artillery and mortar shells hit in the vicinity of the outpost.

AIR WAR: Flying off USS *Boxer* (CV 21) 598 sorties are flown against bridges and enemy forces to slow down the Chinese forces.

July 25

POLITICAL/ADMINISTRATIVE: The UN Command staff completes work on the details on a cease-fire agreement at Panmunjom and interpreters begin putting it into final shape.

EIGHTH ARMY: At 0820, the Chinese again assault Hill 119 in company strength. The attack is repulsed by heavy marine mortar and artillery fire. The battle continues most of the day with one side, and then the other, making limited gains. But elements of the 7th Marines hold on, gradually forcing the Chinese from the forward slope of Boulder City by 1335. Staff Sergeant Ambrosio Guillen, 7th Marines, earns the Medal of Honor for courage shown in the direction of his men during heavy fire.

AIR WAR: Task Force 77 flies 608 offensive and defensive sorties, a record number for a single day. Flying 32 F9Fs from VMF-115 and VMF-311 and working in tandem over the battlefield, the two squadrons bombard the enemy with more than 30 tons of high explosives.

July 26

EIGHTH ARMY: With the armistice near and the opportunity passing, the Chinese launch another attack, at 2130, on Outpost Boulder City. The area is under Captain Esmond E. Harper of Easy Company, 2nd Battalion, 1st Marines, who is able

Sitting, left to right: General Otto P. Weyland, General Mark Clark, Admiral Robert Briscoe, Admiral Joseph Clark, and General Samuel Anderson at the armistice signing in Munsan-Ni, July 27, 1953 *(Center for the Study of the Korean War, Graceland University)*

to fight off the Chinese effort. If they had taken Boulder City, they would have a high ground allowing them direct observation of the marine rear and supply areas.

SEA WAR: The USS *Swift* (AM 122) escapes damage and silences enemy artillery fire at Hungnam harbor. The USS *New Jersey* (BB 62), on her last mission in Korea, strikes at Wonsan, where she destroys large-caliber guns, bunkers, caves, and trenches.

AIR WAR: Planes from Task Force 77 fly 649 sorties against bridge targets and enemy formations in an effort to slow down the Chinese offensive.

July 27

POLITICAL/ADMINISTRATIVE: As provided in the cease-fire agreement, the overt combat of the Korean War ends at 2200 hours. The agreement is signed by Lieutenant General William Harrison and Lieutenant General Nam Il. It takes the two men 11 minutes to conclude the agreement, available in English, Chinese, and Korean. After two years and 17 days, the talks have led to an armistice. The division of Korea is to remain much as it had been on June 25, 1950. A Joint Policy Statement is issued by United Nations (Greater Sanctions Statement) members who have contributed military forces to the war in Korea. It pledges to uphold the armistice agreement and claims that any violation will result in a wider war. Neither General Mark Clark nor Kim Il Sung appear at the signing.

EIGHTH ARMY: Early in the morning, the enemy advances from Berlin to the wire of Hill 119 and noses around Hill 111 for an hour or so. These last enemy efforts are halted by small-arms fire, and their probes seem to just peter out. The Korea summer-fall phase ends. Sergeant Harold R. Cross, Jr., of the 5th Regimental Combat Team, is the last man killed in action, hit by mortar fire just before 2000 on the day of the armistice. Battle of Boulder City ends with the marines still in possession. Throughout the combat zone the war continues all day with units fighting, artillery firing, planes strafing, and units engaging—up to the arrival of the armistice hour At 2200 a silence covers the nation.

SEA WAR: Task Force 77 is busy all day, destroying 23 railway cars, 11 rail bridges, one tunnel, 69 buildings, and 40 rail cuts. The USS *Philippine Sea* (CV 47) receives its third Presidential Unit Citation. The USS *Princeton* (CV 37) receives its fourth Presidential Unit Citation.

AIR WAR: Captain Ralph S. Parr, Jr., becomes a double ace, shooting down an Il-12 transport near the Manchurian border. A B-26 of the 8th Bomber Squadron drops the last bombs of the Korean War at night, in a radar-directed close air support mission. Helicopter Squadron One and Marine Observation Squadron Six receive the Presidential Unit Citation.

The Korean War ends, but the fighting will continue indefinitely.

★ POSTWAR EVENTS ★

Ever since the signing of the cease-fire agreement, there has been a continual stream of violations. None of these appear to have threatened the armistice, although both sides have often suggested the possibility. Most of the violations will seem to be unprovoked and often arbitrary. Some will have the appearance of deliberate and well-planned operations. It is estimated that between July 27, 1953, and December 31, 2003, there have been more than 40,000 breaches of the armistice (Preliminary Post Korean War Death Statistics, Washington, D.C.: GPO, 2003). The two sides meet constantly to discuss these violations, but little is done other than to record the events. At first the United States will treat these as cold war events rather than Korean War events and between 1956 and 1978 will not record them as a part of the official story of the war. However, on one occasion the danger involved led the United States to begin to reissue the Combat Infantryman Badge and recording battle deaths. In the main, the violations seem to be consistent with, and most likely reflect, the political situation at the time.

Korean students protesting the arrival of troops from India to conduct the POW exchange during the summer of 1953. The sign reads: UN Have to Censure the violent Conduet (sic) of Indian Force. *(Center for the Study of the Korean War, Graceland University)*

1953

July 28

POLITICAL/ADMINISTRATIVE: The first meeting of the Korean Military Armistice Commission, as required by the terms of the armistice, is held.

MILITARY: The last official U.S. casualties of the Korean War are reported as five men from Companies Baker and Charlie, 23rd Infantry Regiment, are killed in an explosion near Ansan, North Korea.

July 31

MILITARY: On this day, U.S. ground forces in Korea reach a peak strength of 302,483 men. Following this date, there will be a steady decline in the number of troops in Korea.

August 3

POLITICAL/ADMINISTRATIVE: Secretary of State Dulles and Korean president Rhee agree to the terms of the U.S.-Korean Mutual Defense Treaty. The treaty has continued in some form ever since this date.

August 5

POLITICAL/ADMINISTRATIVE: The final exchange of prisoners of war, which the United Nations calls "Operation Big Switch," begins after several false starts on both sides. The exchange runs until December 23, 1953. The United Nations returns 75,823 prisoners and the Communists 12,773.

August 17

POLITICAL/ADMINISTRATIVE: The Soviet Union conducts a test of a (hydrogen) thermonuclear device successfully, thus ending the U.S. monopoly.

August 28

POLITICAL/ADMINISTRATIVE: The UN General Assembly approves the Korean War armistice agreement.

September 4

POLITICAL/ADMINISTRATIVE: The screening and repatriation of POWs, under the auspices of the government of India, begins at Freedom Village, Panmunjom. Among the prisoners who are released is General William F. Dean. Dean is the highest-ranking officer held as a prisoner and was awarded the Medal of Honor shortly after he was considered missing and presumed dead.

AIR WAR: The Soviets shoot down a P2V5 over the Sea of Japan.

September 21

AIR WAR: Lieutenant No Kom-sok, North Korean Air Force, lands his MiG-15 at Kimpo Airfield as a defector. He claims no knowledge of the large reward being offered. It is the first combat model of this plane available for testing.

September 23

POLITICAL/ADMINISTRATIVE: The UN Command releases, to the Neutral Nations Repatriation Commission, more than 22,600 prisoners of war who refused repatriation. These men and women will be held until they can work out a location for release.

December 13

PARTISANS: The *Shark,* one of the CIA's boats, braves a heavy snow and picks up two CIA agents who have been operating behind enemy lines. The mother ship is shelled by the North Koreans but is finally able to bring the men out.

1954

February 20–21

PARTISANS: Two 50-foot patrol boats slip across the mud flats of the Han River estuary and come to a halt about 200 yards off the beach at Hasenam-ni, North Korea. They quickly load up 32 survivors from the ill-fated Beehive stay-behind mission. In what is called "Operation Haul Ass," the last mission by the United Nations Partisan Infantry, Korea, 8204th Army Unit, comes to an end.

February 22

PARTISANS: The survivors of those stay-behind missions identified as "Camel" and "Beehive" are lifted from the southern Hwanghae Province on the Yellow Sea coast.

March 16

POLITICAL/ADMINISTRATIVE: In a news conference, President Eisenhower comments on Secretary of State Dulles's remarks that in any future war in Asia we "would probably make use of small tactical atomic weapons." Eisenhower says that the weapons would be used by the military as it would use a bullet.

Marilyn Monroe's arrival in Korea as part of a USO tour, February 1954 *(Center for the Study of the Korean War, Graceland University)*

April 26

POLITICAL/ADMINISTRATIVE: The Geneva Conference, arranged during the armistice talks to resolve the question of Korean reunification, opens to deal with Korea and other Asian matters.

July 25

AIR WAR: Two F9F Panther fighters from USS *Hornet* (CVA 12) are attacked by Chinese fighters. Both of the Communist planes are shot down.

July 26

AIR WAR: Two AD Skyraiders from USS *Philippine Sea* (CVA 47) are attacked off Hainan Island (almost 2,000 miles south of Korea) by two Chinese La-7 fighters. Both Communist fighters are destroyed.

July 28, 1954–September 30, 1968

POLITICAL/ADMINISTRATIVE: The UNC determines that medals will be awarded to UN troops in Korea during this period.

1955

January 19

AIR WAR: The North Koreans shoot at and hit an army L-20 Beaver on reconnaissance. The two-man crew is killed.

February 5

AIR WAR: A UN RB-45 plane is attacked by four Chinese MiG-15s over the Yellow Sea. In the engagement that follows, between eight U.S. F-86s and 12 MiG-15s, one MiG-15 is shot down.

March 1

POLITICAL/ADMINISTRATIVE: The CIA concludes that the vast majority of the intelligence collected during the period between 1952 and 1953 was fabricated, or otherwise compromised, and often controlled by Chinese and North Korean security agents.

March 17–18

EIGHTH ARMY: The 1st Marine Division leaves Korea and is relieved by the U.S. 24th Infantry Division.

August 18

AIR WAR: An unarmed U.S. T-6 trainer plane is shot down by NKPA ground fire near Panmunjom. The pilot, Captain Charles Brown, is killed and one crewman is listed as missing in action.

October 27

EIGHTH ARMY: X Corps is deactivated at Fort Riley, Kansas.

1957

POLITICAL/ADMINISTRATIVE: During early 1957, several significant weapons are brought into South Korea. They include Nike Hercules surface-to-air missiles, Davy Crockett nuclear bazookas, and 155-mm nuclear artillery shells; the nuclear arsenal in South Korea is at its largest point, with approximately 950 nuclear warheads of eight types in country.

March 27
EIGHTH ARMY: A 12-man U.S. patrol is fired on south of the DMZ, but there are no reported casualties.

July 1
POLITICAL/ADMINISTRATIVE: The UN Far East Command officially comes to an end.

1958

February 2
POLITICAL/ADMINISTRATIVE: A group of North Korean agents hijacks a South Korean airliner on its way from Pusan to Seoul. The hijackers take the captured plane to Pyongyang. Eventually, all but eight of the 28 passengers on board are released.

March 6
AIR WAR: A U.S. F-86 is shot down by North Korean ground fire over the DMZ. North Korea claims it was in North Korean air space.

October
POLITICAL/ADMINISTRATIVE: As per the armistice agreement, Chinese Communist Forces withdraw from North Korea.

1959

January 29
POLITICAL/ADMINISTRATIVE: United Nations Command in Seoul reveals that the United States has stationed nuclear weapons in South Korea.

September 7
POLITICAL/ADMINISTRATIVE: North Korea and the USSR conclude an agreement on the peaceful use of nuclear energy.

1960

POLITICAL/ADMINISTRATIVE: Civil disorders in the Republic of Korea grow as a result of increased dissatisfaction with corruption in the government of President Syngman Rhee. At the age of 85, President Rhee is forced to resign from office; he flees to Hawaii.

April 20

Air War: A U.S. pilot is fired on by a North Korean plane, and the American pilot is killed during an emergency landing attempt.

1961

July 6

Political/Administrative: Nikita Khrushchev and Kim Il Sung sign the "Treaty of Friendship, Cooperation and Mutual Assistance" in Moscow. The agreement includes a military assistance provision.

July 11

Political/Administrative: Zhou Enlai and Kim Il Sung sign the "Treaty of Friendship, Cooperation and Mutual Assistance" in Beijing. Article Two of the treaty provides for mutual military assistance.

1962

October 1

Eighth Army: A U.S. soldier is killed while on duty in the DMZ, the first such event since the end of the war.

October 3

Eighth Army: A U.S. soldier, PFC Richard Rimer, is killed while on guard duty at the DMZ.

November 23

North Korean soldiers kill an American soldier and wound another with grenades in an attack launched on Outpost Susan.

December

Political/Administrative: The Soviet Union suspends aid to the DPRK because it feels that the North Koreans are moving too far in the direction of China.

December 4

Political/Administrative: Kim Il Sung announces that the whole nation will need to be turned into a fortress to guarantee survival in case of a nuclear attack.

December 10

Political/Administrative: In a speech delivered to the Fifth Plenum of the Korean Workers Party Central Committee, Kim Il Sung announces his support for the Maoist approach to guerrilla fighting.

1963

May 17

Eighth Army: An Eighth Army OH-23 helicopter is shot down in Communist territory, and two crewmen are captured. They are not returned for a year.

July 29

EIGHTH ARMY: Two U.S. soldiers are killed and one is wounded when North Korean troops ambush an American jeep.

August 4

EIGHTH ARMY: North Korean soldiers assault a 13-man UNC guardpost held by the 1st Reconnaissance Squadron, 9th Cavalry Regiment, 1st Cavalry Division. The probe, which turns into a two-hour firefight, produces no casualties.

1964

POLITICAL/ADMINISTRATIVE: With Chinese assistance, North Korea conducts a uranium mining survey that reveals large deposits of commercial-grade uranium ore near Unggi-kun. The same year, the North Koreans construct and open the Nuclear Physics Research Institute in Yongbyon-kun, North Korea.

November 14

AIR WAR: A U.S. Air Force plane is attacked in the area of the DMZ.

1965

April 27

AIR WAR: Two North Korean MiG-17s fire on and damage a U.S. RB-47 reconnaissance plane flying over the Sea of Japan. The incident is estimated to have occurred about 50 miles east of North Korea.

May–June

POLITICAL/ADMINISTRATIVE: North Korea completes the installation of a Soviet-supplied, IRT-2000 nuclear pool-type research reactor at Yongbyon-kun.

May 18

EIGHTH ARMY: An army light aircraft on a reconnaissance mission is shot down by North Korean ground fire.

July 1

EIGHTH ARMY: The 2nd Infantry Division returns to Korea to replace the 1st Cavalry Division.

July 19

POLITICAL/ADMINISTRATIVE: Syngman Rhee, longtime advocate for Korean independence and a much-disputed president of the Republic of Korea, dies in exile.

November 18

EIGHTH ARMY: An American soldier is wounded in a clash with a North Korean patrol.

1966

September 1

At the beginning of what called in response to the heating up of the military situation, the Second Korean War, General Charles H. Bonesteel III assumes duties as

Commander in Chief, United Nations Command; Commander, U.S. Forces, Korea; and Commanding General, U.S. Eighth Army.

October 5

POLITICAL/ADMINISTRATIVE: Kim Il Sung addresses the Second Korean Workers Party Conference; he renews his vows to pursue immediately and with vigorous effort the subversion of the ROK and a fight with the United States. A set of hard-line Communists is assigned the task of prosecuting the policy.

November 2

EIGHTH ARMY: The official start of the Second Korean War comes on the heels of an ambush. During the early morning hours, an eight-man patrol from the U.S. 1st Battalion, 23rd Regiment, 2nd Infantry Division, is ambushed about a half-mile south of the DMZ. Six Americans and one Korean of the 1st Battalion, 23rd Infantry Regiment, 2nd Division, are killed. The event, which signals a harder line by the North Koreans, is considered by some as the beginning of the "Second Korean Conflict." The period of unrest will last through 1969. Private First Class Ernest D. Reynolds (who has been in Korea only 17 days) is posthumously nominated for the Medal of Honor for his courage and actions during this time.

November 6

POLITICAL/ADMINISTRATIVE: Commander U.S. Eighth Army forms a Special Working Group to address the growing threat from North Korea.

1967

January 10

North Korean shore batteries fire on ROK *PCE 56* and sink it just off the northeast coast of Korea. Thirty-nine ROK navy men are killed and 15 wounded.

February 9

POLITICAL/ADMINISTRATIVE: The Special Working Group, Eighth Army, recommendations are implemented, thus forming a UNC plan to meet the new Communist challenge.

February 12

EIGHTH ARMY: An American soldier of the 1st Battalion, 23rd Infantry Regiment, 2nd Division, is killed in an ambush by North Korean soldiers. ROK troops bring in artillery to drive off a company of Korean People's Army soldiers. It is the first use of artillery since the armistice and reflects the new discretionary powers and rules of engagement for Eighth Army.

April 5

EIGHTH ARMY: A U.S. 2nd Infantry Division guardpost engages KPA infiltrators south of the DMZ. Five KPA soldiers are killed.

April 26
EIGHTH ARMY: The 3rd Battalion, 23rd Regiment, 2nd Infantry Division, ambushes a group of KPA infiltrators who are south of the DMZ. One KPA soldier is killed, one wounded, and one taken prisoner.

May 22
EIGHTH ARMY: North Korean intruders explode a demolition charge in the barracks of the 2nd Infantry Division not far off the DMZ. Two U.S. soldiers are killed and 17 wounded, two ROK soldiers are wounded.

July 16
EIGHTH ARMY: Three U.S. soldiers are killed by North Koreans in a short skirmish after KPA infiltrators attack a guard post.

July 28
POLITICAL/ADMINISTRATIVE: Construction begins on a defensive barrier fence in the U.S. sector of the DMZ.

August 10
EIGHTH ARMY: Three soldiers of the 13th Engineers, a 7th Infantry Division construction team, are ambushed and killed. There are also 16 wounded in this daylight ambush of a truck near Freedom Village.

August 22
EIGHTH ARMY: One soldier from the 2nd Infantry Division is killed and one is wounded when their jeep hits an enemy mine. Following the explosion, the driver is fired on by North Korean soldiers.

August 28
EIGHTH ARMY: Two U.S. soldiers from the 76th Engineers, Eighth Army, are killed and 14 wounded in a North Korean attack, as more than 3,000 rounds are fired at the location of Charlie Company. Nine KATUSA and three civilians are killed.

August 29
EIGHTH ARMY: Three soldiers from the 2nd Infantry Division are killed and five wounded when their vehicle is destroyed by an enemy mine. The men were south of the DMZ.

September 13
EIGHTH ARMY: North Korean agents blow up two trains near Seoul, destroying seven carloads of army supplies. There are no casualties.

September 28
POLITICAL/ADMINISTRATIVE: The United States completes the anti-infiltration fence in its sector. A battalion of the 7th Infantry Division joins the 2nd Infantry Division in a new rotation system that places four battalions on the DMZ and a fifth battalion in quick reserve.

October 3
POLITICAL/ADMINISTRATIVE: The commanding general, U.S. Eighth Army, releases his proposals for the Counterinfiltration-Guerrilla Concepts Requirement.

October 7
SEA WAR: A 2nd Infantry Division patrol boat is ambushed on the Imjin River south of the DMZ.

December 15
POLITICAL/ADMINISTRATIVE: ROK Presidential Instruction Number Eighteen delineates South Korea's counterinsurgency plans.

1968

January 17
EIGHTH ARMY: A platoon from the 124th Army Unit of the KPA infiltrates through the U.S. sector of the DMZ and makes an assassination attempt on ROK president Park Chung Hee.

January 21
EIGHTH ARMY: Disguised as South Korean soldiers, 31 members of a North Korean commando unit try to assassinate President Park Chung Hee at his official residence, the Blue House. The assassins are intercepted by South Korean police and all but one of the enemy are killed.

January 22
EIGHTH ARMY: A 2nd Infantry Division guard post is damaged by KPA infiltrators.
AIR WAR: A B-52 crashes off Greenland, spilling four nuclear weapons into the ocean.

January 23
SEA WAR: The first U.S. ship to be captured in 161 years, the USS *Pueblo,* is taken not far off the port of Wonsan by North Korean naval units. One American dies and 82 are captured. Under North Korean pressure, the commander, Captain Lloyd Bucher, signs a confession. In response, USS *Enterprise* and USS *Ticonderoga* deploy with a 32-ship task force to the Sea of Japan. However, no military action is taken. The crew of the USS *Pueblo* is finally released in December 1968.

January 24
EIGHTH ARMY: An American soldier of the 1st Battalion, 23rd Infantry Regiment, 2nd Infantry Division, is killed by gunfire.

January 26
EIGHTH ARMY: An American soldier of the 2nd Battalion, 72nd Armored Regiment, 2nd Infantry Division, is killed south of the DMZ by members of the KPA's 124th Army Unit.

January 29
EIGHTH ARMY: Members of the 2nd Infantry Division are able to repel four North Korean infiltration teams, without casualties.

January 31
POLITICAL/ADMINISTRATIVE: The Tet Offensive sweeps across South Vietnam, and the Korean War becomes a sideshow.

February 6
EIGHTH ARMY: A 2nd Infantry Division guard post is attack by North Koreans but there are no casualties.

February 15
POLITICAL/ADMINISTRATIVE: President Park Chung Hee orders the establishment of a Home Land Defense Reserve Force. He also takes steps to strengthen the ROK intelligence gathering agencies.

March 21
EIGHTH ARMY: A brigade headquarters of the 7th Infantry Division is deployed north to assist the U.S. forces along the DMZ.

March 27
EIGHTH ARMY: The 2nd Infantry Division Reaction Force and the ROK 25th Infantry ambush a team of KPA infiltrators. There are no U.S. or ROK losses.

April 1
POLITICAL/ADMINISTRATIVE: The Defense Department authorizes hostile fire pay for those U.S. soldiers serving north of the Imjin River. There is so much activity in the area that it is considered a combat zone. As of this date, the United States has sustained 31 killed and 71 wounded.

April 14
EIGHTH ARMY: North Korean soldiers ambush a UN Command security guard truck that is in the Joint Security Area on the way to its assignment. In the ensuing fight, two American soldiers are killed and two ROK soldiers are wounded.

April 17
POLITICAL/ADMINISTRATIVE: President Park of Korea and President Johnson of the United States meet in Honolulu to coordinate allied strategy.

April 21
EIGHTH ARMY: A patrol from the 2nd Battalion, 31st Regiment, 7th Infantry Division, engages KPA infiltrators in the DMZ. One U.S. soldier is killed and three wounded.

April 27
EIGHTH ARMY: Two soldiers from the 2nd Battalion, 31st Regiment, 7th Infantry Division, are wounded when their patrol is ambushed by North Koreans near the village of Panmunjom.

June 1
POLITICAL/ADMINISTRATIVE: The U.S. Congress approves an emergency $100 million Military Assistance Program Grant for the ROK.

July 3

Eighth Army: A 2nd Infantry Division patrol is ambushed in the DMZ. One American is wounded.

July 20

Eighth Army: A 2nd Infantry Division patrol is ambushed in the DMZ; one American is killed. One American is also killed when a patrol from the 1st Battalion, 7th Infantry Division, is ambushed.

July 21

Eighth Army: A 2nd Infantry Division patrol from the 2nd Battalion, 38th Regiment, is ambushed in the DMZ, and one American is killed.

July 30

Political/Administrative: The ROK First Army completes its portion of the DMZ anti-infiltration fence that links up with the American fence built the year before. The fence now runs the entire width of the DMZ.

August 5

Eighth Army: North Korean soldiers ambush a patrol from the 1st Battalion, 38th Regiment, during the day. The attack is south of the DMZ, and one U.S. soldier is killed and four others wounded.

August 18

Eighth Army: Two NCOs of the 1st Battalion, 32nd Regiment, 7th Infantry Division, are killed when their patrol clashes with North Koreans who are south of the DMZ.

August 19

Eighth Army: Soldiers from a combined unit isolated and destroyed a squad of infiltrating KPA troops. Eight casualties are taken by the American forces. The UN units involved are: the 2nd Battalion, 38th Regiment, 2nd Infantry Division; the Quick Reaction Force (4th Battalion, 7th Cavalry), the 2nd Battalion, 9th Infantry Regiment [motorized]; and the 2nd Counter Agent Company.

August 21

Sea War: A boat being used by North Korean agents is intercepted off Cheju Island; 12 NKPA soldiers are killed and two captured.

August 30

Political/Administrative: The first two of 20 planned ROK Reconstruction villages open just south of the DMZ.

September 2

Eighth Army: Three U.S. officers are assaulted at Panmunjom by 15 to 20 North Korean soldiers. There are no casualties.

September 19

Eighth Army: Four North Koreans are killed in a firefight within the zone occupied by the 2nd Infantry Division.

September 24
EIGHTH ARMY: ROK army units battle a small battalion of KPA troops south of the DMZ.

September 27
EIGHTH ARMY: Two members of the 2nd Infantry Division are killed when their jeep is ambushed south of the main line of defense.

October 3
EIGHTH ARMY: A 7th Division squad, 1st Battalion, 31st Regiment, engages KPA infiltrators south of the DMZ. There are no losses.

October 5
EIGHTH ARMY: One American soldier of the 2nd Infantry Division is killed and two others are wounded in a North Korean ambush in the DMZ.

October 10
EIGHTH ARMY: A 2nd Infantry Division boat patrol engages infiltrators crossing the Imjin River.

October 11
EIGHTH ARMY: The 2nd Infantry Division ambushes a unit of the KPA that has infiltrated into the DMZ.

October 15
POLITICAL/ADMINISTRATIVE: The ROK-U.S. Operational Planning Staff is formed. Until this point, the ROK has no voice in UN planning.

October 23
EIGHTH ARMY: One American soldier from the 2nd Infantry Division is killed and five others wounded during a firefight with the North Koreans.

October 24
EIGHTH ARMY: The Samchok areas, on the east coast of South Korea are invaded by a large group of seaborne North Korean commandoes from the 124th Army Unit. Of the 131 invaders, 110 are killed and the ROK has 63 dead. The effort had been to establish a guerilla movement.

December 23
POLITICAL/ADMINISTRATIVE: The crew of the USS *Pueblo* is released.

December 26
POLITICAL/ADMINISTRATIVE: The Army Department authorizes the Combat Infantryman Badge and Combat Medic Badge for select troops serving in Korea.

1969

January 23
EIGHTH ARMY: A U.S. 2nd Infantry Division guard post is attacked by troops of the KPA. The attack is repulsed with no loss of life.

February 4

EIGHTH ARMY: During the late evening on an extremely cold night, a U.S. 2nd Infantry Division guard post is attacked by a group of KPA infiltrators who cause some damage but take no casualties.

March 7

POLITICAL/ADMINISTRATIVE: The ROK army forms two antiguerrilla units from its special forces element.

March 13

EIGHTH ARMY: A 2nd Infantry Division fence repair patrol (2nd Battalion, 38th Infantry Regiment) engages KPA troops in the DMZ.

March 15

EIGHTH ARMY: A North Korean guard post opens fire on a 10-man working party that is replacing markers. One soldier is killed and two wounded in a four-hour fire fight.
AIR WAR: A helicopter crashes as it attempts to evacuate the wounded from the clash at the North Korean guardpost. The crash kills seven.

March 16

EIGHTH ARMY: A 2nd Division patrol engages KPA infiltrators.

March 20

EIGHTH ARMY: A routine patrol from the U.S. 2nd Infantry Division is operating in the DMZ when it runs into a patrol of KPA troops. There is a brief engagement but no casualties.

March 29

EIGHTH ARMY: A 2nd Infantry Division patrol is ambushed and one soldier killed.

April 10

POLITICAL/ADMINISTRATIVE: UN delegates at Panmunjom propose a meeting of the Military Armistice Commission in an effort to reduce tension. The proposal is met with four-and-a-half hours of silence.

April 15

SEA WAR: Task Force 71, composed of 29 ships, is formed to protect future reconnaissance flights.
AIR WAR: Two North Korean MiG-17s intercept and shoot down an unarmed U.S. Navy EC 121 reconnaissance plane with 31 men onboard. They are flying over the Sea of Japan about 90 miles off the North Korean coast.

April 18

POLITICAL/ADMINISTRATIVE: The president announces that all U.S. reconnaissance flights over Korea will be accompanied by armed escorts.

April 23

North Korean troops open fire on a UNC guard post in the southern half of the DMZ.

May 8
AIR WAR: It has taken a month to locate fighters that can accompany air reconnaissance flights over Korea.

May 15
EIGHTH ARMY: A patrol from the 2nd Infantry Division is ambushed in the DMZ and one soldier is killed.

May 20
EIGHTH ARMY: A 2nd Infantry Division guard post is hit but the KPA is repulsed without casualties.

June 5
POLITICAL/ADMINISTRATIVE: The last U.S. reservist departs Korea. They had been called up in response to the USS *Pueblo* incident.

July 21
EIGHTH ARMY: A probe by North Korean troops is repulsed by Americans from the 2nd Infantry Division after a 35-minute firefight. There are no casualties.

July 29
POLITICAL/ADMINISTRATIVE: Richard Nixon announces the Guam Doctrine. The doctrine promises American advice and equipment for America's allies, but warns them not to expect the commitment of ground troops. U.S. overseas commitments, including Korea, will be reduced.

July 30
EIGHTH ARMY: Forty-five North Korean soldiers fire on a patrol consisting of 15 Americans.
POLITICAL/ADMINISTRATIVE: North Korea announces the establishment of the Party for Unification and Revolution, with the aim of overthrowing the South Korean government and replacing it with people more in favor of cooperation with North Korea.

August 17
AIR WAR: A U.S. helicopter with a three-man crew strays over North Korean territory and is shot down there. The crewmen, who are wounded, are not released until December 3, 1969.

August 25
POLITICAL/ADMINISTRATIVE: President Park and President Nixon meet in San Francisco to discuss the implementation of the Guam Doctrine for Korea.

August 29
POLITICAL/ADMINISTRATION: Six American 4DF Phantom II fighter jets are turned over to the ROK air force.

October 1

POLITICAL/ADMINISTRATIVE: General John H. Michaelis succeeds General Bonesteel as the commander of U.S. troops in Korea.

October 18

EIGHTH ARMY: Four soldiers of the U.S. 7th Infantry Division are killed in a daylight ambush executed by North Korean troops near the southern boundary of the DMZ. Each man is shot through the head. The truck they were in was flying a white flag.

December

POLITICAL/ADMINISTRATIVE: North Korean agents hijack a South Korean airliner en route from Kangnung to Seoul. Of the 51 persons on board, 39 of the crew and passengers are later released.

December 3

POLITICAL/ADMINISTRATIVE: After holding them for a few weeks, the DPRK returns three captured American helicopter crewmen.

1970

April

EIGHTH ARMY: South of the DMZ, near Kumchon, three North Korean infiltrators who had come across the DMZ are killed.

June 5

SEA WAR: A ship of the ROK navy is fired on and sunk by North Korean vessels in the Sea of Japan. The attack costs the lives of 20 ROK navy personnel.

June 14

EIGHTH ARMY: Soldiers of the 2nd Infantry Division fire on and kill an NKPA soldier near Panmunjom.

SEA WAR: A South Korean fishing vessel with 20 people onboard is seized by a North Korean vessel off the west coast of Korea.

August 31

EIGHTH ARMY: On three separate occasions, U.S. troops intercept and fire on North Korean patrols in unauthorized areas.

October 1

EIGHTH ARMY: A U.S. Army helicopter is fired on by North Korean gunners, but the aircraft is not hit.

October 12

EIGHTH ARMY: Seven UN Command security personnel are injured as the result of an attack by club-wielding North Korean guards and people dressed as civilians.

1971

January
POLITICAL/ADMINISTRATIVE: After more than 20 years of discussion, the People's Republic of China is formally admitted to the United Nations, replacing the Nationalist Chinese delegation.

EIGHTH ARMY: Soldiers of the 2nd Infantry Division fire on and kill an NKPA soldier near Panmunjom. The North Koreans try to hijack a Korean airliner that is on its way to Sokcho from Seoul, but the effort is unsuccessful.

March 12
POLITICAL/ADMINISTRATIVE: Responsibility for the U.S.-patrolled 18.5-mile sector of the DMZ is officially transferred from the U.S. 2nd Infantry Division to the ROK 1st Division.

April 1
POLITICAL/ADMINISTRATIVE: The 7th Infantry Division rotates out of Korea after nearly 24 years of service in the country.

July 4
POLITICAL/ADMINISTRATIVE: North and South Korea sign a joint communique that defines the three principles that are required for Korean unification. It is determined that unification must be achieved without foreign interference, it must be accomplished by peaceful means, and it must happen in such a way that it confirms the racial unity of the Korean people as one people.

1973

March 7
EIGHTH ARMY: A North Korean artillery piece opens up on a work party replacing MDL markers. Two ROK soldiers are killed and one is wounded.

September 1
POLITICAL/ADMINISTRATIVE: Hostile fire pay is again terminated for American troops stationed in Korea.

1974

January 23
POLITICAL/ADMINISTRATIVE: North Korea's Atomic Energy Act is passed. It is considered a first step in the north's drive to produce its own atomic weapons.

February 15
SEA WAR: A North Korean patrol boat sinks two South Korean fishing boats, killing 12 and capturing 30 fishermen.

March 3
EIGHTH ARMY: One-hundred-and-twenty North Korean guards attack a unit of about 30 U.S. soldiers in the Joint Security Area.

May 9

EIGHTH ARMY: Two U.S. helicopters are fired on by North Korean batteries along the Imjin River. There is no damage reported.

June 28

SEA WAR: Three North Korean gunboats attack and sink an ROK Maritime Police craft in the East Sea (Sea of Japan) near the MDL extension. In the attack, 26 ROK constabulary are killed and two captured.

July 1

POLITICAL/ADMINISTRATIVE: The Department of the Army determines that no medals will be awarded to American troops in Korea during the period of July 1, 1974, to October 4, 1991.

August

POLITICAL/ADMINISTRATIVE: The wife of South Korean president Park Chung Hee is killed during an attempt on the president's life. North Korean agents are blamed for the assassination attempt.

September 16

POLITICAL/ADMINISTRATIVE: North Korea agrees to the International Atomic Energy Agreement.

November 15

EIGHTH ARMY: Intelligence sources in the ROK army uncover a North Korean-built, underground tunnel that extends more than 1,000 yards into the UNC side of the armistice zone. This is the first of several tunnels that will be discovered.

November 20

EIGHTH ARMY: An enemy device, probably a land mine, explodes in the tunnel complex that was discovered the previous day. The explosion kills a navy officer and wounds four U.S. servicemen.

1975

June 30

EIGHTH ARMY: Major Henderson, the acting commander of the UNC Joint Security Force, is attacked and captured by 10 North Korean guards near Panmunjom.

1976

June

EIGHTH ARMY: Two North Korean infiltrators are caught in Kochang. One of the North Koreans is shot in the event.

August 18

EIGHTH ARMY: North Korean soldiers, with axes and metal pikes, attack a U.S.–South Korean tree-trimming team inside the DMZ. In the attack, two U.S. Army officers and four enlisted men are wounded. Five South Korean soldiers are killed in the attack.

August 21–September 8

Eighth Army: In Operation Paul Bunyan, 26 gun ships and a 300-man backup force cut down the tree involved in the August 18 incident. Naval Task Force 77.4 (USS *Midway*) is dispatched to the Korean coast.

November 24

Political/Administrative: North Korea and Pakistan sign a protocol on technical cooperation.

1977

May 3

Eighth Army: North Korean intruders attack a group of ROK army personnel in the central section of the DMZ. One ROK soldier is killed and one is wounded.

July 14

Air War: A U.S. Army CH-47 is shot down on the east coast of Korea after the craft accidentally crosses over into North Korean territory near the MDL. Three U.S. personnel are killed and one wounded. The North Koreans return the casualties after several days by way of Panmunjom.

July 20

Political/Administrative: North Korea signs an INFCIRC/66 trilateral safeguard agreement with the International Atomic Energy Agency.

1978

June 2

Political/Administrative: South Korean actress Choi Eun-hee and her film director husband, Shin Sang-ok, are kidnapped in Hong Kong and taken to Pyongyang in order to work on propaganda films. The films will reportedly glorify Kim Il Sung and his son, Kim Jong Il. They will escape in 1986 while filming in Vienna.

July 16

Political/Administrative: North Korea releases a captured helicopter pilot after 57 hours of captivity.

April 28

Eighth Army: One ROK soldier is killed and four wounded when North Korean agents attack an ROK National Police patrol boat. Six North Koreans are killed in the exchange.

October

Eighth Army: A second North Korean tunnel is discovered under the DMZ. Well constructed and quite large, it extends 400 meters south of the DMZ. The tunnel is designed so that an estimated 30,000 armed men can move through the tunnel in an hour.

1979

October
EIGHTH ARMY: Three North Korean agents are caught as they try to enter the eastern sector of the DMZ. In the capture, one of the agents is killed.

December 7
EIGHTH ARMY: An American patrol accidentally crosses over the MDL and while there sets off several North Korean mines. One man is killed and two wounded. The body of the dead soldier is returned by the North Koreans at the Military Armistice Commission meeting. The wounded man is returned safely after the incident.

1980

March 23
EIGHTH ARMY: Three North Korean soldiers are killed across the estuary of the Han River when they are discovered by ROK defenders.

March 27
EIGHTH ARMY: North Korean intruders fire on members of an ROK army patrol in the central section of Korea, resulting in the deaths of one South Korean and one North Korean. One soldier from each side is also wounded.

June 21
EIGHTH ARMY: North Korean agents in a boat attack an ROK navy patrol boat. The attack results in the wounding of two ROK soldiers and one North Korean agent.

November 3–6
EIGHTH ARMY: Three North Korean agents are killed after they land on Hoenggan Island. During the landing the North Korean soldiers kill one civilian and wound four others.

December 1–6
EIGHTH ARMY: Three North Korean agents are killed off the southern coast of Kyongsong Namdo.

1981

June
EIGHTH ARMY: Off the coast of Sosan, a North Korean spy boat is sunk. Members of the crew are either killed or captured.

July 4
EIGHTH ARMY: Three ROK soldiers are killed and three wounded when North Korean agents infiltrate through the DMZ. Three of the North Korean infiltrators are killed.

1982

August

POLITICAL/ADMINISTRATIVE: Canadian police uncover a plot by North Korean agents to assassinate South Korean president Chun Do Hwan when he visits their nation.

1983

May 15

EIGHTH ARMY: North Korean agents land on the east coast of South Korea, where they are discovered and one is killed.

June 19

EIGHTH ARMY: North Korean agents are discovered near Munsan-ni in the western corridor. Three of the enemy agents are killed.

August 5

EIGHTH ARMY: North Korean agents attempt to land near Kampo on the southeast coast. Five of the group are killed after they are discovered by ROK soldiers.

August 13

EIGHTH ARMY: A boat carrying North Korean agents is sunk east of Ullung Island in the Sea of Japan (East Sea), killing five North Koreans.

October 9

POLITICAL/ADMINISTRATIVE: An explosion goes off just a few minutes before President Chun Do Hwan is to lay a wreath at the Martyr's Mausoleum in Rangoon, Burma. The explosion fails to harm the president, but it kills 17 senior South Korean officials. As a result of the terrorist attack, Myanmar (Burma) severs relations with North Korea (November 4, 1983) and a North Korean terrorist will be sentenced to death (December 9, 1983).

October 10

POLITICAL/ADMINISTRATIVE: After the explosion of a powerful bomb among South Korean officials, killing 17 and wounding 14, President Chun Do Hwan states that if such an action occurs again, a retaliation in kind will follow.

December 3

EIGHTH ARMY: North Korean agents land at Tadaepo beach near Pusan. Once the group is discovered, three of the agents are killed and two captured.

1984

February

POLITICAL/ADMINISTRATIVE: Charles Yanover and Alexander Gerol, both Canadians, testify in a Canadian court that they were hired by North Korean agents to assassinate South Korean president Chun Do Hwan.

November 23

EIGHTH ARMY: A U.S. soldier is shot and wounded, and an ROK soldier killed, by North Korean troops who are firing on a Soviet defector. Shots hit UNC Joint Security Area guards at Panmunjom. In the exchange, three North Korea soldiers are killed and one wounded.

1985

August 14

POLITICAL/ADMINISTRATIVE: The 5-Mwe reactor at Yongbyong goes critical. It will become operational in January 1986.

October 20

EIGHTH ARMY: Two North Korean agents, attempting to land from a boat near Pusan, are caught and killed by ROK soldiers.

December 12

POLITICAL/ADMINISTRATIVE: North Korea signs the Nuclear Non-proliferation Treaty.

1986

April 24

EIGHTH ARMY: An armed North Korean vessel is sunk in an exchange of gunfire, when the North Korean boat refuses to stop after crossing the MDL extension line in the Sea of Japan (East Sea).

September

EIGHTH ARMY: Five persons are killed and 30 wounded when a bomb goes off at the Kimpo International Airport near Seoul.

December 30

POLITICAL/ADMINISTRATIVE: Kim Il Sung is reelected president of North Korea's Supreme People's Assembly. He uses the occasion to call for high-level political and military talks between the two Koreas.

1987

November

POLITICAL/ADMINISTRATIVE: A Korean Airlines Boeing 707, with a crew of 20 and 95 passengers, explodes in midair over the Andaman Sea in the eastern waters of the Bay of Bengal. It is reported to be a warning against those who plan to attend the 1988 Olympics in Seoul.

November 21

EIGHTH ARMY: North Korean guards fire on an ROK army outpost in the central section, wounding one ROK soldier.

1990

March

EIGHTH ARMY: A fourth North Korean infiltration tunnel is discovered, extending some distance under the DMZ.

1991

POLITICAL/ADMINISTRATIVE: With very little public acknowledgment, President George H. W. Bush orders the removal of all remaining nuclear weapons from South Korea. The removal will be completed in early 1992.

October 4

POLITICAL/ADMINISTRATIVE: The last American soldiers are withdrawn from the one-mile, U.S. sector of the DMZ. Only 150 remain on duty with the ROK army.

December 13

POLITICAL/ADMINISTRATIVE: North and South Korea both sign an accord calling for reconciliation.

1992

May 22

EIGHTH ARMY: North Korean armed intruders are intercepted in the central section of the DMZ. In order to protest the intrusion, UN Command calls for the 460th meeting of the MAC, but the North Koreans reject the request.

October

POLITICAL/ADMINISTRATIVE: A Communist spy ring, composed of nearly 400 members, is uncovered in South Korea. The group is directed by the North Korean Communist Party and led by Lee Son-sil.

1993

December

POLITICAL/ADMINISTRATIVE: The chief of the General Staff of North Korea announces that the military has the responsibility to reunite the two factors of Korea, and that it will do so in the nineties.

1994

October 21

POLITICAL/ADMINISTRATIVE: North Korea and the United States sign an "Agreed Framework" to defuse a serious crisis. In violation of the nonproliferation agreement, North Korea has not declared all of the spent nuclear fuel it reprocessed. The agreement was that North Korea would freeze and eventually dismantle its nuclear program, to be verified by the International Atomic Energy Agency (IAEA). In return North Korea would receive heavy fuel oil for heating and electricity production.

December 17

EIGHTH ARMY: One crewman is killed and the other wounded after a U.S. Army OH 58A helicopter accidentally crosses the MDL and flies nearly 10 miles into North Korean airspace. The helicopter is shot down by North Korean forces. The wounded man is returned after 13 days.

1995

October 17

EIGHTH ARMY: Several NKPA soldiers try to infiltrate near the Imjin River. One is killed and the others escape.

1996

April

Over a period of many weeks, several hundred armed North Koreans cross through the DMZ, following the Pyongyang announcement that it will no longer abide by the armistice provision concerning the integrity of the DMZ. The military forces of both the ROK and the NKPA are put on a high state of alert (Watchcon 2).

May

EIGHTH ARMY: Five North Korean vessels cross into South Korean waters on the west coast. The ships withdraw after a standoff of about four hours.

July 27

POLITICAL/ADMINISTRATIVE: The Korean War Memorial is opened in Washington, D.C., on the 42nd anniversary of the signing of the armistice. President Bill Clinton and President Kim Young Sam of the ROK both speak at the occasion.

September

EIGHTH ARMY: A disabled North Korean submarine is spotted near Kangnung. Twenty-six soldiers land on the east coast, apparently on an espionage-and-reconnaissance mission. They are quickly rounded up.

October

POLITICAL/ADMINISTRATIVE: A South Korean diplomat, Choi Duk Keun, is murdered in Vladivostok, Russia. The murder occurs shortly after North Korea had threatened to retaliate for the submarine "incident" of September.

1997

July 16

EIGHTH ARMY: Fourteen North Korean soldiers penetrate the DMZ to a distance of about 75 yards, leading to an exchange of gunfire. There are no casualties.

POLITICAL/ADMINISTRATIVE: Russia finally acknowledges the fact that, during the Korean War, the USSR maintained more than 26,000 military personnel in the area.

September 9
EIGHTH ARMY: North Korean intruders, moving south into ROK territory, threaten an ROK guard who shoots and kills one of the North Koreans.

1998

POLITICAL/ADMINISTRATIVE: Documents released through the Freedom of Information Act indicate that the U.S. Air Force carried out simulated nuclear strikes against North Korean targets.

February 3
POLITICAL/ADMINISTRATIVE: A NKPA captain crosses the MDL and surrenders to UNC personnel there. He says that he wishes to defect to South Korea. He remains in South Korea despite NKPA claims that he has been abducted.

June 11
EIGHTH ARMY: The NKPA fires several rounds at UNC Guardpost #247. One round strikes the hut but there are no casualties reported.

June 22
EIGHTH ARMY: A North Korean midget submarine is discovered entangled in fishing nets near the South Korean town of Sokcho-ri, south of the DMZ. When it is brought ashore, nine dead crewmen are found on board, apparently from suicide.

July 12
EIGHTH ARMY: The body of a dead North Korean frogman is discovered on a beach south of the DMZ. His equipment suggests he was on an infiltration mission.

August
POLITICAL/ADMINISTRATIVE: U.S. intelligence agencies report finding a huge and secret underground area where the North Koreans are reported to be working on a nuclear weapons program.

August 31
POLITICAL/ADMINISTRATIVE: North Korea fires a three-stage Taepodong-1 missile, capable of carrying a DPRK satellite into orbit. It is launched from a facility at Musundan-ri. The missile flies over Japan, causing a great deal of political fallout.

December 18
EIGHTH ARMY: The ROK navy sinks a North Korean semi-submersible landing craft about 120 miles southwest of Pusan. The body of a North Korean frogman is discovered on a beach nearby.

1999

June 4–15
SEA WAR: A short naval battle occurs in disputed waters in the Yellow Sea. It is fought over the disputed border known as the Northern Limit Line. During the

battle, each side loses a torpedo boat. In addition, the ROK navy has five other vessels damaged.

July 1

POLITICAL/ADMINISTRATIVE: North and South Korea resume talks in Beijing to discuss the question of reuniting families separated by the war. As the meeting starts, the North Koreans demand an apology for the sinking of a North Korean gunboat in disputed waters on June 15, 1999. Both sides leave with no plans to return. Seoul suspends fertilizer shipments to the North.

July 4

POLITICAL/ADMINISTRATIVE: Canada's Prime Minister Jean Chretien calls on North Korea to stop exporting weapons. The *Hindustan Times* reports that Indian authorities have discovered missile parts on a North Korean freighter detained on suspicion.

July 7

POLITICAL/ADMINISTRATIVE: North Korea says that testing a ballistic missiles is a "sovereign right" and that it will continue to do so.

August 11

POLITICAL/ADMINISTRATIVE: The South Korean National Intelligence Service confirms that North Korea has purchased 30 MiG-21 fighters from Kazakhstan.

August 30

POLITICAL/ADMINISTRATIVE: North Korea announces that it will establish a new sea border in the Yellow Sea unless UN Command agrees to a rewriting of the armistice agreement that specifically designates the line.

2000

March 9

POLITICAL/ADMINISTRATIVE: North Korea rejects a U.S. request that it stop providing shelter to members of the Japanese Communist League-Red Army faction. The members were responsible for hijacking a Japanese airliner to Pyongyang in 1970.

March 23

POLITICAL/ADMINISTRATIVE: North Korea declares new navigation zones and waterways in the disputed waters of the Yellow Sea. This is in violation of the limits, established by United Nations Command, of the sea border between North Korea and South Korea. North Korea threatens that it will take military action, without warning, against any ships found in the area without permission.

April 10

POLITICAL/ADMINISTRATIVE: North Korea and South Korea agree to a date for the first summit to discuss unification. It will be the first discussion on unification since the peninsula was divided in 1945.

July
POLITICAL/ADMINISTRATIVE: Radio Pyongyang threatens to blow up the conservative daily newspaper, *Choson Ilbo,* for slandering the Democratic People's Republic of North Korea.

October 6
POLITICAL/ADMINISTRATIVE: The United States and North Korea issue a joint statement agreeing to oppose all forms of terrorism and to try to resolve all issues regarding terrorism between the two nations.

2001

March 7
POLITICAL/ADMINISTRATIVE: President George W. Bush meets with South Korean president Kim Dae-jung and tells him that the United States considers North Korea a threat. He announces that the United States will not, in the near future, resume negotiations with the Communist regime.

June 2–4
SEA WAR: Three North Korean merchant ships cross the Cheju Strait. The ROK navy issues verbal warnings to the ships, telling them not to attempt to pass without approval, but the captains ignore the warnings.

June 8
SEA WAR: A North Korean merchant ship crosses the Northern Limit Line and enters the contiguous waters of the ROK, passing north to the port of Nampo. They are warned but enter anyway.

September 4
SEA WAR: North Korean patrol boats begin challenging the Northern Limit Line in the Yellow Sea that has been the de facto border between the North and the South. Within the next several months, there will be more than a dozen intrusions. In each case, the North Korean boats return to international waters after being challenged.

September 19
EIGHTH ARMY: An exchange of fire occurs along the fence line near a UNC guard post. Twenty to twenty-five shots are fired, but there are no casualties.

October 26
AIR WAR: Two U.S. aircraft accidentally fly over the DMZ while taking part in an exercise with the ROK.

November 27
EIGHTH ARMY: There is an exchange of small-arms fire at a South Korean guardpost. The North Koreans fire three rounds toward a UNC guard post; the ROK returns fire. A window is broken, but there are no casualties.

2002

June 29

Sea War: In the Yellow Sea, South Korean and North Korean naval ships exchange fire in a gun battle, during which several seamen are killed.

December 11

Political/Administrative: A North Korean ship heading for Yemen is stopped in the Persian Gulf and some Scud missiles are found hidden under bags of cement.

December 26

Political/Administrative: North Korea moves some 1,000 nuclear fuel rods from storage to the Yongyon nuclear power plant.

2003

January 2

Political/Administrative: North Korea threatens to withdraw from the armistice agreement that is keeping the peace between it and South Korea. Acknowledging that relations on the Korean peninsula have become very tense because of "U.S. nuclear racket," North Korea says that it will be left "with no option but to take a decisive step to abandon its commitment to implement the armistice agreement."

January 10

Political/Administrative: North Korea withdraws from the Nuclear Non-proliferation Treaty.

February 24

North Korea fires a short-range antiship missile into the Sea of Japan.

March 10

Political/Administrative: For the second time in two weeks, North Korea fires a Silkworm ground-to-ship nonballistic missile into the Sea of Japan (East Sea).

July 17

Eighth Army: Thirty-five miles north of Seoul, North and South Korean soldiers exchange fire. The NKPA fires four artillery rounds at ROK soldiers, who return 17 shots. Warning announcements are made on an ROK loudspeaker and the soldiers put on alert. There is no further action or casualties.

July 25

Political/Administrative: On the 50th anniversary of the armistice, the North Korean government celebrates the "victory" in the Fatherland Liberation War, which, it claims, was forced on them by the United States and its allied nations.

2004

November 1

Political/Administrative: After 50 years of an American presence at Panmunjom in Korea's demilitarized zone, the United States is withdrawing its troops 50 miles south of the ROK capital. The zone, which has been guarded by 225 Americans and 225 ROK soldiers, will now be guarded only by South Koreans.

2005

November 18

POLITICAL/ADMINISTRATIVE: President George W. Bush announces that the United States will start to withdraw troops from South Korea, pointing out that the South Korean military is now able to take over, thereby the United States can redeploy these troops to combat terrorism in other parts of the world.

BIOGRAPHIES

Short biographies have been provided for most of those leaders who were involved in, or had a primary influence on, the war in Korea. Somewhat more information is provided for those playing expanded roles. The biographies focus on an individual's role in the Korean War, and the length of the biography should not be seen as an indication of anyone's overall importance in world history. For sake of easy identification, Korean and Chinese names are listed as they are spoken.

Acheson, Dean G. (1893–1971)
Secretary of state

Dean Acheson was one of the most significant figures in the Korean War. A lawyer, statesman, and secretary of state, he was born in Middletown, Connecticut, on April 11, 1893. He attended Yale and Harvard Law Schools. From 1941 he held lower posts in the State Department and in 1949 became secretary of state under President Harry Truman. He served in that position until January 1953.

Dean Acheson was a man of strong opinions on how and when to make use of the armed forces in international affairs. After World War II, he helped work out an agreement with the Soviet Union on the control of nuclear arms. However, when the Soviet Union exploded a nuclear weapon, Acheson began to push for a stronger NATO and a significant increase in the armed forces of the United States. The possibility of an East-West war caused him to push for creation of a military force capable of stopping Communist aggression. He had little respect for the United Nations and felt it was incapable of dealing with

the difficulties of the Korean War. He favored the U.S. position on nuclear weapons and urged President Harry Truman to build the hydrogen bomb.

As secretary of state, Dean Acheson urged U.S. involvement in the Korean War while, at the same time, he pushed for maintaining a stronger force in NATO. In January 1950, he delivered a much-quoted talk to the National Press Club, during which he excluded Korea from the U.S. defense perimeter. While the speech is often listed as a reason for North Korea's decision to go to war, he disclosed nothing that was not already a part of Joint Chiefs of Staff policy. After first excluding South Korea from the U.S. military commitment, and working for the withdrawal of American troops, he became a staunch supporter of the war after the North Korean invasion. He urged the United Nations to cross the 38th parallel, thus taking the war to the enemy. And yet, he worked to avoid any escalation to a wider conflict.

After leaving the State Department, Dean Acheson became a defense adviser to Presidents Kennedy, Johnson, and Nixon. In 1958, he came to believe that the war in Vietnam was harming America and afterward was an advocate for withdrawal from the war. He wrote *Present at the Creation*, which won a Pulitzer Prize in 1970. He died on October 13, 1971.

Allison, John M. (1905–1978)
State Department official

Allison served as chief, State Department Division of Northeast Asian Affairs, as special assistant to John Foster Dulles, and as assistant secretary of state for Far Eastern affairs. Born in Holton, Kansas, he spent considerable time in the Orient. He was the one who suggested turning the Korean question over to the United Nations when the trustees issue reached an impasse. He supported the use of arms in the defense of South Korea and the UN's crossing of the 38th parallel, believing that no peace could be achieved as long as Korea was divided. From 1953 to 1957, he served as ambassador to Japan. He retired in 1960 and taught at the University of Hawaii.

Almond, Edward Mallory (1892–1979)
Commander, X Corps
General Edward Almond was born December 12, 1892, in Luray, Virginia. Almond (called Ned) graduated from Virginia Military Institute in 1915. He attended the Army Command and General Staff College, the Army War College, the Air Corps Tactical School, and the Naval War College.

Almond served in World War I as the commander of a machine-gun battalion and in Europe during World War II. In the European theater, he was given the task of reorganizing the 92nd Infantry, an all-black unit, in Europe. The poor performance of this command was damaging to his military career. He then joined General Douglas MacArthur's command in the Pacific. As chief of staff, he ran the headquarters as MacArthur wanted it, doing the things that MacArthur hated to do himself. In 1950, General MacArthur named him commander of the new X Corps, then being formed for the invasion at Inchon. At the same time, Almond continued to hold his job with MacArthur's command. He held this position as chief of staff until General MacArthur was relieved in April 1951.

A highly controversial figure, General Almond was not an easy man to get along with. He had numerous run-ins with the Eighth Army commander, General Walton Walker, the marines, and a good number of ROK army officers who served under his command. He was, nevertheless, an effective and aggressive combat commander. General Almond received his third star in February 1951, partly for his skillful withdrawal of X Corps from Hungnam by sea. He was an early proponent of the use of helicopters for combat mobilization. He

retired from the army in January 1953 after a period as commander of the Army War College, then worked for a while in Alabama. From 1961 to 1968, he was president of the Board of Visitors of the Virginia Military Institute. He died June 11, 1979.

Andrewes, William G. (1899–1974)
Commander, British Naval Forces
Admiral William Andrewes entered the Royal Naval College at the age of 13. He served at sea during World War I and was promoted to lieutenant by the end of the war. During World War II, he commanded the seaplane carrier HMS *Albatross* and a cruiser. He took part in the invasion of Italy and served in the Pacific Theater. He commanded the aircraft carrier HMS *Indomitable* after the war. When the Korean War broke out, he was a rear admiral assigned to the Far East and then for a time served as the commander of British Commonwealth Forces. When England decided to commit to the war in Korea, he served briefly as commander of the UN's Blockading and Escort Force. After the war, he commanded the Royal Navy's Atlantic-West Indies Station and was deputy supreme allied commander at NATO. He died in Winchester, Hampshire, England, on November 22, 1974.

Attlee, Clement R. (1883–1967)
Prime minister of Great Britain
Clement Attlee was prime minister of Great Britain from 1945 to 1951. In this position, he played a major role in the formation of British policy toward the Korean War. Born in London on January 3, 1883, he was educated at Haileybury College and University College, Oxford. Deeply involved in the growing labor movement, he led the Labour Party to its landslide postwar victory. He was deeply committed to resisting any effort by the Soviet Union to expand its influence. Attlee had some significant differences of opinion with the United States, and he walked the difficult line between supporting the U.S. program and serving as the spokesperson for British policy. He supported the call for a UN response to events in Korea, believing that it was a Soviet test of the U.S.

and UN commitment to restrict communism. He believed that the British needed to be involved in the war, if only for loyalty's sake, and in July 1950, he overrode the objections of the British military and sent troops to aid the United States in Korea.

However, Attlee was afraid that U.S. leaders might push the Korean War into a major conflict with China and the Soviet Union. He dissociated Britain from the U.S. decision to neutralize Taiwan, fearing that the Chinese would respond, but he also was supportive of the UN decision to cross the 38th parallel. Nevertheless, his Labour Party suffered a split over the Chinese military intervention. He supported the general UN policy that the war in Korea should be ended by armistice rather than pushing for a total victory. Clement Attlee left office in 1951 and died in London on October 8, 1967.

Austin, Warren R. (1877–1962)
U.S. ambassador to United Nations

As the United States representative to the United Nations from 1946 to 1953, Warren Austin played a major role in the policies that dominated the Korean War. He was a tireless defender of the U.S. position on UN action in Korea. Warren Austin was born in Highgate Center, Vermont, on November 12, 1877, and graduated from the University of Vermont. While practicing law, he became involved in Republican Party politics. In 1931, he won a seat in the United States Senate where he served for 15 years. He was one of the small group of men during those lean years that advocated an increase in military spending. At General Dwight Eisenhower's request, he joined a group of eight called the Foreign Policy Group. The group was to play a major role in encouraging Republicans to support the formation of the United Nations in 1944.

In 1946, President Harry Truman appointed Austin as the first U.S. ambassador to the United Nations. When the Korean War broke out, he supported a unified command in Korea under American leadership. He saw the war in Korea as a moral crusade and believed that the ultimate outcome of UN involvement had to be the unification of Korea. There is some indication that Austin saw

the effort in Korea as a moral endeavor, a view that often disturbed the allies in the war.

In 1951, Austin argued against the proposals of Arab/Asian powers to end the war by making concessions to the People's Republic of China. He took a strong position against any action that might endanger the independence of the Nationalist government on Taiwan. He opposed any Chinese Communist representation in the United Nations. He was influential in the UN resolution of February 1, 1951, identifying China as the aggressor in Korea. He was supportive of President Harry Truman's decision to release General Douglas MacArthur.

In 1952, problems with his health limited his activities, and in 1953, Austin retired from his role at the United Nations. His vocal opposition to Communism was rewarded by his being named honorary chairman of the Committee of One in a Million whose job was to exclude the People's Republic of China from the United Nations. He died December 25, 1962, in Burlington, Vermont.

Baille, Hugh (1890–1966)
War correspondent

Born in Brooklyn, New York, Baille graduated from the University of Southern California in 1910. In 1915, he joined the United Press (UP) and became its president in 1935. He had the ability to gain interviews with some of the most powerful people in the world, including Adolf Hitler, Benito Mussolini, Chiang Kai-shek, Emperor Hirohito, Joseph Stalin, Douglas MacArthur, Syngman Rhee, and Presidents Truman and Eisenhower. It was his interview, in which General MacArthur suggested that the United States should bomb Manchuria, that led to the early attempts to muzzle the general. Always a supporter of the United Nations, he called for international action to guarantee the freedom of news dissemination. In 1955, he retired as president of UP but continued reporting and writing until his death in 1966.

Bajpai, Girja S. (1891–1954)
Indian minister of external affairs

Girja Bajpai was India's minister of external affairs from 1947 to 1952. He was a central character in the important role played by India during, and after, the Korean War. Born in Lucknow on April 3, 1891, he entered the Indian Civil Service in 1914. He was regarded as brilliant, dependable, and loyal. In 1941, he was sent to Washington where he served as India's first agent general. He stayed in the United States for six years, during which time he established many good relations with members of the U.S. Congress, as well as Presidents Roosevelt and Truman.

In 1947, he was appointed secretary-general. He believed that India needed to keep good ties with the British Commonwealth and supported the British position during the cold war. However, he was a strong advocate of normalizing relations with Communist China. In the fall of 1950, he became involved in the diplomacy of the Korean War. K. M. Panikkar, the Indian ambassador to the People's Republic of China, reported to Bajpai about conversations with several Chinese officials. He was the one who was given the message to convey that, if the forces of the United Nations Command crossed the 38th parallel, the People's Republic of China would be forced to enter the war. Bajpai passed this on to British officials because he believed China was not bluffing. He was not listened to, or perhaps not believed, because the U.S. leadership—Truman, Acheson, and MacArthur—was afraid that any restraint at this point would be seen as a sign of weakness.

During his last year in office, he encouraged negotiations that he believed would lead to a peace settlement. In 1952, Bajpai left office because of poor health but he continued to work with the Office of External Affairs. He died on December 5, 1954, in Bombay.

Barr, David G. (1895–1970)

Commander, 7th Infantry Division

General David Barr, who commanded the 7th Infantry Division during the early period of the Korean War, was born June 16, 1895, in Alabama. He attended Alabama Presbyterian College. In November 1917, he was commissioned as a second lieutenant of infantry in the Reserve Officer Corps. He then served with the 1st Division in France and with occupation forces in Germany until September 1919. In 1920, he was promoted to first lieutenant.

In the years between the wars, Barr was at Camp McClellan, Alabama, as an instructor and then served with the New York National Guard and at Camp Meade, Pennsylvania. He attended the Versailles French Tank School and was assigned as U.S. military attache in Paris. In 1936, he attended the Army Command School at Fort Leavenworth, Kansas. He became Corps G-4 and in June 1942 advanced to brigadier general. Later he was assigned as chief of staff of the U.S. Sixth Army Group in France. In 1948, he commanded the Sixth Army Group, a 1,000-man unit of advisers assigned to the Republic of China (Nationalist). His reports on events there were highly critical of the Nationalist Chinese military and political leadership, suggesting Chiang Kai-shek (Jiang Jieshi) played to the elite class. He recommended an end to U.S. military aid, stressing that Chiang's government had little support from the people.

He assumed command of the 7th Infantry Division on occupation duty in Japan. The division moved into the war in Korea in September 1950, and it was involved in the amphibious landings at Inchon and later at Wonsan and in the march toward the Yalu River with X Corps.

General Barr had little battle experience and was considered a liability by General Almond, with whom he argued tactics. Nevertheless, he remained in command of the 7th Infantry until his rotation in 1951, after which he was assigned to training commands. He was opposed to General MacArthur's plan for victory, and was one of the officers who testified against MacArthur at the Senate hearing. He retired in 1952 and died in 1970 in Falls Church, Virginia.

Bebler, Ales (1907–1981)

Yugoslavian delegate to United Nations

In 1929, Alex Bebler joined the Communist Party, served with the International Brigade in the Spanish Civil War, and was a member of the assembly that formed the Federated People's Republic of Yugoslavia. Bebler was a firm believer in the Soviet Union's program for economic development. He was also a worker for national self-interests. A veteran of the International Brigade and a Yugoslav partisan during World War II, he served as Yugoslavia's permanent delegate to the United Nations and as a member of the Security Council at the beginning of the Korean War. Trying to maintain some neutral ground between his nation's Eastern and Western concerns, and unable to prevent the June 25, 1950, vote, Yugoslavia abstained, and then was the only negative vote against the Security Council resolution of June 27, 1950. Following the vote, Tito announced that Bebler did not represent Yugoslavia correctly and that the nation would no longer block UN actions relating to the defense of South Korea. In November 1950, he served as president of the UN Security Council and in that position pushed for bilateral talks between the PRC and the United States. Bebler continued to work for some sort of compromise that would prevent the war in Korea from expanding. He later served as ambassador to Indonesia and France. He died in 1981.

Berendsen, Sir Carl A. (1890–1973)
New Zealand ambassador to United Nations

Carl Berendsen was head of the New Zealand delegation to the United Nations when the North Koreans invaded the Republic of Korea. In this position and in line with his highly anticommunist attitude, he supported the U.S. and UN action in Korea. He believed that the DPRK was under Soviet control and that appeasement would lead to ever-widening war. He tended to link New Zealand's participation in the Korean War with his nation's effort to become a member of the U.S.-directed Pacific Pact. While his government often required him to vote in favor of some of the peace proposals that came before the United Nations, he personally believed that any kind of cease-fire short of victory was appeasement. He was in favor of bombing Chinese troop concentrations in Manchuria.

Bevin, Aneurin (1897–1990)
Prime minister of Great Britain

An early supporter of involvement in Korea, he quickly became disillusioned with developments there. Extremely nationalistic, he was concerned over the cost of the Korean involvement and the effect it was having on British affairs. A supporter of maintaining good relations with the Chinese Communists, he opposed all UN efforts to attach labels to or resist China. After internal posturing split the Labour Party, he resigned on April 22, 1952.

Bevin, Ernest (1881–1951)
British foreign secretary

Ernest Bevin came into political office by way of the labor unions. He won office in the government when the Labour Party was in power, and he supported the British involvement in World War I. In 1940, he regained his seat in the Commons and held it the rest of his life. In 1945, he was appointed foreign secretary, a position from which he expressed his anticommunist feelings and distrust of the Soviet Union. His commitment to an Anglo-American stand against Communism caused him to support the intervention in Korea. However, in trying to maintain good relations with both China and India, and to protect British interests in Hong Kong, he often felt the need to dissociate Great Britain from U.S. policies. He was unwilling to support the U.S. policy regarding Taiwan and proposed that the cease-fire talks over Korea should include American concessions in its policy toward Taiwan, and a UN seat for the Communist Chinese. Nevertheless, he supported the UN decision to cross the 38th parallel and push for the unification of Korea. He proposed several peace initiatives both to the United States and through the UN but received little support for them. He resigned in 1951 due to poor health and died in London in April 1951.

Boatner, Haydon Lemaire (1900–1977)
Commander, Koje Island POW camp

Haydon L. Boatner was the commandant of the Koje Island POW camp during the Korean War. Called "Bull," he was born in New Orleans on October 8, 1900. In 1918, he enlisted in the Marine Corps. After World War I, he attended the U.S. Military Academy and in 1924 was commissioned as a second lieutenant of infantry. He was assigned to the 15th Infantry in Tientsin, China. After his

China assignment, he attended the Army Command School, Fort Leavenworth, Kansas.

In 1941, he was assigned to the War Department's General Staff, where he organized the U.S. Military Mission to China. Boatner was appointed as chief of staff of the Chinese Army in India in November 1942, at which time he was promoted to brigadier general. In 1944, he took command of the Northern Combat Area Command. He represented the United States in the negotiations surrounding the Japanese surrender of their forces in China.

In 1948, he was named as a professor of military science and tactics at Texas A & M University and in August 1951 was appointed assistant commander of the 2nd Infantry Division in Korea. In May 1952, he was given command of the Koje-do POW camp. Famous for his position that "prisoners do not negotiate," he acted with swift efficiency. The previous camp commander, General Dodd, had been captured during a prisoner rebellion. Boatner's assignment was to bring in UN troops to put down the rebellion. In August 1952, he was named commander of the Pusan POW Complex and became responsible for all POWs held by UN Command. He was promoted to major general and returned to the United States in September 1952.

He was named deputy commander of Fourth Army and then commanded the 3rd Infantry Division. He later served in the Joint U.S. Military Air Group in Greece (1955–57) and retired from active duty in October 1960. During these years, he was openly critical of U.S. policy toward prisoners of war. He died on May 27, 1977, in San Antonio, Texas.

Bohlen, Charles E. (1904–1974)
Soviet expert
Charles "Chip" Bohlen was a Harvard-educated Soviet expert who entered foreign service in 1929. He served as an interpreter/adviser to Presidents Franklin D. Roosevelt and Harry S. Truman. When North Korea invaded the south, he tried to reassure the administration that it was not a prelude to Soviet action elsewhere. He supported the use of military forces in South Korea but was strongly opposed to crossing the 38th parallel into North

Korea. After a visit with General Omar N. Bradley to Korea, he determined that the conflict could not be solved by military action.

Bolte, Charles L. (1895–1989)
Deputy chief of staff for planning
After serving in France as a commissioned officer, Charles Bolte worked with the historical branch of the War Department, attended the major military schools, and in 1940 was a member of the War Planning Group at the Army War College. During World War II, he was chief of staff of U.S. forces in the United Kingdom and, after promotion to brigadier general, chief of staff of the European theater (ETO). After service with the 91st Division and the 69th Division, he returned to Europe as commander of the 34th Infantry. In 1948, he became director of the Special Joint Planning Group. In February 1951, as a lieutenant general, he became the army's chief planner. He was concerned that putting too much effort into the war in Korea would weaken the United States, which he expected would be called on to meet other global problems. He objected to the Joint Chiefs of Staff fulfilling General MacArthur's request for more troops to Korea. He recommended the evacuation of U.S. forces after the Chinese intervention in 1950, for he was convinced that this was but the first step in a global war. Both of his sons were wounded while on active duty in Korea. He was named commander of Seventh Army in Germany and in July 1953, as general, became vice chief of staff. He retired in April 1955.

Bradley, Omar N. (1893–1981)
U.S. Army chief of staff
A U.S. Army general and first chairman of the Joint Chiefs of Staff (1949–53), Bradley was born February 12, 1893, in Clark, Missouri. He graduated from West Point in 1915 and was commissioned as a second lieutenant. In 1918, he was promoted to major. He taught at West Point. In 1925, he graduated from the Infantry School at Fort Benning, Georgia. Later he attended the Command and General Staff School at Fort Leavenworth, Kansas, and

the Army War College. He served on the Army General Staff from 1938 to 1941.

In February 1941, he was promoted to brigadier general and took command of the 82nd Infantry. He served briefly as an aide to General Dwight Eisenhower and then was given command of First Army during the invasion of France. In August 1944, he was in command of the Twelfth Army Group, which included 1.2 million men. Bradley was known as a "Soldier's General" for he was low-key and modest about his rank and concerned about the welfare of his men. In March 1945, he was promoted to general and three years later to Army Chief of Staff. Then, in August 1949, he became chairman of the newly formed Joint Chiefs of Staff.

During the Korean War, Bradley supported and participated in Truman's decision to commit U.S. forces to Korea. It was his job to keep President Harry Truman briefed during the war and to advise him on the conduct of the war. He found himself in the midst of the Truman-MacArthur confrontation. He visited the battlefields twice during the three-year conflict. At an April 6, 1951, meeting he recommended that MacArthur be fired for insubordination. He testified against General MacArthur at the Joint Hearings and was the author of the often misdirected remark that a war with China would "involve us in the wrong war, at the wrong place, at the wrong time, and with the wrong enemy."

He continued as chairman of the Joint Chiefs of Staff until August 1953, when he retired from the army. In 1968, he advised President Johnson against a U.S. withdrawal from Vietnam. He died in Washington, D.C., on April 8, 1981.

Bridgeford, Sir William (1894–1971)
Commander, British Commonwealth Forces
From 1951 to 1953, William Bridgeford was Commander in Chief, British Commonwealth Forces in Korea. Born on July 28, 1894, in Ballarat, Australia, he attended the Royal Military College at Duntroon in 1915. During World War I, he received the Military Cross for Valor. Remaining in the peacetime army, he rose slowly in rank and then served in World War II.

During the summer of 1950, he was named quartermaster-general of Australian Military Forces

and headed a mission to Malaya to push for Australian support of the British anti-insurgency campaign. However, the start of the Korean War changed his plans, as Australia supported the UN decision and agreed to send troops to aid Douglas MacArthur. In November 1951, he was assigned to Korea as a replacement for Sir Horace Robertson as commander in chief of Commonwealth Forces. In May 1952, General Mark Clark requested troops to guard Chinese and North Korean prisoner-of-war camps. Bridgeford approved the transfer of British and Canadian troops to Koje-do for this purpose, thereby causing disquiet in Commonwealth relations. The Canadian government tried to have him removed from his assignment. Bridgeford remained in his position until February 1953 and retired from the army that same year. In 1956, he was the chief executive officer of the Melbourne Olympic Games. He died in Brisbane on September 21, 1971.

Briggs, Ellis O. (1899–1976)
U.S. ambassador to Republic of Korea
When the relationship between U.S. ambassador John J. Muccio and President Rhee began to sour, Ellis Briggs took over the American embassy. His role was complicated by the fact that Rhee considered himself free to deal directly with the U.S. president and secretary of state and often left Briggs out of the picture. Nevertheless, he played a significant role as a watchdog and adviser on the numerous policies on which Rhee and the United States disagreed. Briggs, who had been a foreign service officer since 1925, was strongly anti-Communist. After he retired in 1959, he worked as a freelance author. He died in 1976.

Briscoe, Robert Pierce (1897–1968)
Commander, Naval Forces Far East
Born in Centerville, Missouri, in 1897, Robert Briscoe graduated from the U.S. Naval Academy in 1918. He served in a series of assignments with the Atlantic Fleet, including a tour aboard the battleship USS *Alabama*. He served for at time with the Yangtze River Patrol in China. A pioneer of modern naval electronics, he was assistant director of the U.S. Naval Research Laboratory when World War II

began. During World War II, he joined the Third Fleet in the Pacific and served in a variety of command assignments, including, in 1943, the USS *Denver* where he won the Navy Cross. He took command of the Seventh Fleet in 1952; in June of that year, when Admiral Joy, commander of NAVFE, became the U.S. negotiator at Panmunjom, Vice Admiral Brisco replaced him. After the war he served as deputy chief of naval operations. He retired in 1959 and died on October 14, 1968.

Burke, Arleigh A. (1901–1996)

Commander, Seventh Fleet

"Thirty-one Knot Burke" was a highly respected naval officer. He was born October 19, 1901, in Boulder, Colorado, and is the namesake for the Arleigh Burke Class of destroyers. He received his nickname for the speed at which his destroyer groups would operate in the Pacific during World War II. Burke attended the Naval Academy from 1919 to 1923, after which he joined the battleship USS *Arizona*. He served as commander of Destroy Division, and chief of staff, First Carrier Task Force, during the Pacific War.

During the Korean War, he served as deputy chief of staff and commander, U.S. Naval Forces Far East. He was called to join the U.S. negotiation team at the armistice talks and served as delegate from 1951 to 1952. He was three times chief of naval operations, refusing a fourth term when he retired in 1961. During his tenure, the navy was modernized from coal and oil and then to nuclear power. He died in 1996.

Cassels, Sir Archibald James H. (1907–1996)

Commander, Commonwealth Division

British army officer and commander of the 1st Commonwealth Division during the Korean War, Archibald Cassels was born in Guetta, India, on February 28, 1907, and attended the Royal Military Academy at Sandhurst. He was commissioned into the Seaforth Highlanders in 1926. He rose quickly through the ranks and in World War II was one of the youngest major generals in the British army. He commanded the 51st Highland Division at the

crossing of the Rhine. In 1946, he commanded the 6th Airborne Division in Palestine.

In 1951, he took command of the British Commonwealth Division in Korea. Nicknamed "Gentleman Jim" his division was made up of brigades representing five different Commonwealth governments. Pulling on both his sound operational knowledge as well as his political and diplomatic skills, his ability to unify the command was one of the major achievements of his service. In August 1952, he was promoted to lieutenant general and left Korea.

He later commanded troops in Europe, directed operations against the Malayan insurgency, was commander of the NATO Northern Army Group (1960–63), and served as chief of the British General Staff (1965–68). In 1968, he was promoted to field marshal and retired from active duty. He died at Suffolk on December 13, 1996.

Cates, Clifton Bledsoe (1893–1970)

Commandant, U.S. Marine Corps

Born August 31, 1893, in Tiptonville, Tennessee, he graduated from the University of Tennessee with a law degree. In June 1917, he was a lieutenant in the Marine Reserves. Called to active duty in 1918, he served in France with the 6th Marine Regiment (assigned to 2nd Army Infantry Division) and was wounded in action. Cates fought at the Meuse-Argonne offensive and was decorated.

When he returned from the war, he was assigned as an aide to President Woodrow Wilson and commander of the Marine Corps detachment on board USS *California*. He attended the Army Industrial College, Marine Corps School, and the Army War College.

In World War II, Cates commanded the 1st Marine Regiment during the landing at Guadalcanal. He was promoted to brigadier general and commandant of the Marine Corps School at Quantico, Virginia. In January 1948, he made general. During the Korean War, he was the commandant of the Marine Corps. He struggled to maintain the Marine Corps's air divisions while overseeing the expansion of the Corps as required by the war. In January 1952, he was replaced by General Lemuel C. Shepherd.

Due to a legality, he was unable to retire and so was demoted to lieutenant general and made commandment of the Corps School. In June 1954, he was restored to rank and allowed to retire. He died in Annapolis, Maryland, on June 4, 1970.

Chang, John M. (Chang Myon) (1899–1966)
Korean ambassador to Washington

As the South Korean ambassador to the United States, it was Chang who brought Syngman Rhee's urgent appeal for help to President Harry S. Truman. He believed that the United States had not fulfilled its obligations to aid the ROK and, after Secretary of State Dean G. Acheson's National Press Club speech, he demanded an explanation. He served for a time as the delegate to the United Nations in Paris and returned to Korea during the political crisis of 1952. Later he split with Rhee and formed an opposition party. He became prime minister in the 1960s but was quickly overthrown by a coup led by Park Chung Hee.

Chae Byung Dok (1914–1950)
Chief of staff, Republic of Korea

Republic of Korea chief of staff when the war in Korea began, the heavy, outgoing general, known to UN personnel as "Fat Chae," became commander of the South Korean Interim Armed Forces. Born in Pyongyang he attended the Japanese Military Academy. After World War II, he joined the Korean National Guard and became commander of the 4th Brigade in April of 1948. Faced with the invasion, he launched a brave but poorly planned counterattack on the morning of June 26, 1950, and was pushed back and lost the capital of Seoul. Following this failure to stop the enemy he was relieved of command on June 30. He remained involved, however, when he was named commander of the Interim Armed Forces, and quickly attached himself to South Korean troops as an adviser and interpreter. He was caught in a firefight and killed on July 27, 1950. He was promoted to lieutenant general posthumously.

Chiang Kai-shek (Jiang Jieshi) (1887–1975)
Generalissimo/president, Republic of (Nationalist) China

Chinese statesman and military leader Chiang Kai-shek was a pivotal figure in the history of modern China. He was born in Fenghua, Zhejiang (Chechiang) province. While studying in Japan, he joined Sun Yat-sen's United Revolutionary League, the forerunner of the Kuomintang (KMT) Party, which was in opposition to the reigning Qing (Ching) dynasty. When an uprising broke out in 1911, he joined. In 1927, he ended the KMT's alliance with the Communists and tried to unite China under his own leadership. Working with the Allies against the Japanese, in 1942 Chiang Kai-shek became supreme commander of Allied Forces in the China theater. In 1943, he signed the Cairo Declaration that, among other things, promised the eventual independence of Korea.

Following the end of World War II, Chiang Kai-shek tried to regain the leadership of China, but the Red Chinese launched an attack. When the commander of the Beijing-Tianjin (Peking-Tientsin) area surrendered to the Communists, Kuomintang forces collapsed and the Communists rapidly took control of the mainland. Chiang removed his government to the island of Taiwan (Formosa), which became the home of the Nationalists. Under his leadership, the island became competitive in foreign trade and, with U.S. help, moved toward becoming a modern nation-state. Actually, the outbreak of war in Korea was a gift to the Nationalist leader. At the time, the U.S. policy was to accept the anticipated Chinese Communist takeover of Taiwan. The North Korean attack reversed this policy and led Chiang to believe that the United States would support a Nationalist attack on the mainland. Chiang Kai-shek died in 1975 while in his fifth term of office as president.

Chin Chi-Wei (Qin Ji-Wei) (1911–1978?)
Commander, Chinese People's Army

A longtime Communist soldier, he began the Korean War as the commander of the Fifteenth Army, Chinese People's Volunteers. He led the Fifteenth Army in the Chinese spring offensive of

1951. After failing to stop the United Nations on two significant occasions, he was relieved from his assignment and was sent to undergo "training." In October 1952, he returned to the field, where he managed to defend against the U.S. 7th Infantry Division and the ROK 2nd and 7th Divisions. After the war, he rose to the rank of general; following a brief period of disgrace during the Great Proletarian Cultural Revolution, he served as minister of defense. He is believed to have died in 1978.

Choi Duk Shin (Choe Tok Sin) (1914–1989)

General, Republic of Korea Army

Born in North Korea, he moved to China in 1921. After serving with the Nationalist Army, he joined the Korean Restoration Army that fought the Japanese. He returned to Korea in 1946 and at the outbreak of the war was chief of staff, and then commander, of the ROK I Corps. He was assigned to the truce talks at Panmunjom in April 1953 where he was a determined voice for national unification. When the cease-fire talks reached a compromise on the question of POWs, he boycotted the meetings and criticized the action. He retired in 1956 and served as ROK minister to the Republic of Vietnam. After moving to Canada in the 1970s, he became outspoken in his criticism of the government of South Korea and, in 1987, moved to North Korea. He served, until his death in 1989, on the Committee for the Peaceful Reunification of the Fatherland.

Choi Yong-Kon (Choe Yong Gon) (1900–1976)

Commander, North Korean People's Army

Choi Yong-Kon was an avid anti-Japanese nationalist who graduated from Wunnan Military Academy. Born in North Pyongan Province he was a member of the March First Movement. He became friendly with Kim Il Sung and in 1939 fled with him to the Soviet Union. He returned with Kim in 1945 and joined with revolutionary leaders in the creation of the Kapsan (Soviet exile) faction. He played a significant role in the establishment of the Democratic People's Republic of Korea. Having risen to the second position in North Korea, he was influential in planning the attack on South Korea. In December 1955, he was presiding judge of the military court of the Supreme Court and was responsible for imposing the death penalty on political rival Pak Hon-yong. He was finally to serve as chairman of the Presidium of the Supreme People's Congress, a post he held until he was released by Kim Il Sung in 1972.

Chung Il Kwon (Chong Il-Gwon) (1917–1994)

Chief of staff, Republic of Korea Army

In 1956, Chung Il Kwon was appointed the Republic of Korea army's chief of staff. The next year, he retired to become the ambassador to the United States, France, and Turkey. Much of his military training was in the United States; he attended the infantry school at Fort Benning and later the Command and Staff College.

On June 30, 1950, he was promoted to major general and named commander of the Republic of Korea's army. He left Korea to attend school in the States, and on his return in July 1952, he was demoted and given a division primarily, it later became evident, to gain experience. After that he became deputy commanding officer of the IX Corps. He was then assigned as commander of the ROK III Corps. He remained in this position until the end of the war. He died in 1994.

Church, John H. (1892–1953)

Commander, 24th Infantry Division

General Church headed the first investigation unit dispatched to Korea after war broke out. Born in Glen Iron, Pennsylvania, on June 28, 1892, he attended New York University. He entered the army during World War I and was commissioned a second lieutenant. During the Great War, he was wounded twice (and wounded three times in World War II) and earned a Distinguished Service Medal and two Silver Stars for heroism. In later assignments, he served as assistant commander of the 45th and then the 84th Infantry Divisions, returning to the 45th Division as chief of staff. In September 1944, he became assistant division commander of the 84th, one of the first divisions to reach the Elbe River.

When war broke out in Korea, John Church, now a brigadier general and terribly disabled by arthritis, was in Tokyo. General Douglas MacArthur sent Church to head a survey team to South Korea to assess the situation. There he tried to create a defensive line at the Han River but that failed. He advised MacArthur that only U.S. troops could stop the invasion. Receiving elements of the 24th Infantry Division, he made an effort to halt the drive of the North Korean People's Army at the Naktong River.

Church was given command of the 24th Division after the capture of General William Dean and was involved in the Pusan Perimeter breakout. In January 1951, he was relieved of his command in General Matthew Ridgway's housecleaning, and left Korea to assume command of the Army Infantry School at Fort Benning, Georgia. He retired from there in 1952 and died in November 1953 in Washington, D.C.

Churchill, Winston S. (1874–1965)
Prime minister of Great Britain

Winston Churchill was prime minister of Great Britain during a portion of the Korean War. Born at Blenheim Palace in Oxfordshire, England, on November 30, 1874, he entered politics to become a Conservative member of Parliament in 1900. He was named prime minister in 1940. He lost his seat in the 1945 elections but continued to speak out against Soviet expansion. In 1946, he made his famous "Iron Curtain" speech in Fulton, Missouri. During 1946–49, he was the leader of the opposition and also completed his six-volume history of World War II.

He was returned as prime minister in the general election of October 1951. He wanted a swift and decisive end to the war in Korea and was supportive of UN policies as long as they kept the war within Korean territory. He considered it a part of his role to keep a lid on the U.S. tendency to seek quick and often violent solutions to its problems. Always a strong anticommunist, Churchill was nevertheless worried about the consequences of an expanded war. And he was well aware of England's long history with China and knew the concerns of many members of the Commonwealth. He supported voluntary repatriation of POWs and sought India's help in working out the problem. While a staunch supporter of the United States, he nevertheless pushed British interests, seeking a peace that would not expand the war. He lost the election in 1955 but remained in Parliament. Bad health forced his retirement, and he died in London, January 4, 1965, as the result of a stroke.

Clark, Joseph J. (1893–1971)
Commander, Seventh Fleet

The initiator of the "Cherokee Strikes," Admiral Joseph "Jacko" Clark was determined to make the naval war in Korea as effective as possible. He felt it was necessary to take the initiative rather than just respond to close air support requests and advocated a series of preplanned missions designed to hit stocks of supplies and, if possible, the source of the supplies. Serving as commander of Task Force 77, then as commander Seventh Fleet, he pushed for air strikes against Communist refineries and hydroelectric plants.

Admiral Clark graduated from the U.S. Naval Academy, served in a wide variety of air-operation assignments, and led aircraft carrier formations during World War II. During the later years of the Korean War, Clark advocated the use of atomic weapons in Korea to force the Chinese Communists to negotiate. He published the book *Carrier Admiral* in 1967 and died in 1971.

Clark, Mark (1896–1984)
Commander, Eighth Army

Clark was the supreme commander UN Forces in Korea from May 12, 1952, to October 10, 1953. Born in Watertown, New York, in May 1896, Clark graduated from West Point in 1917. He was wounded as an infantry officer during World War I, he was promoted to captain in 1919, and went on to graduate from the Infantry School at Fort Benning, Georgia. He also attended the Command and General Staff College at Fort Leavenworth, Kansas, and the Army War College. He was promoted to major in 1933. He received his first star in August of 1941 and became a major general and then lieutenant general, in November 1942.

General Clark commanded land forces in North Africa, led the U.S. Fifth Army during the invasion of the Italian peninsula, and commanded the Fifteenth Army Group. In June 1950, he became responsible for the training of U.S. forces as head of the U.S. Army Field Force. In 1952, he traveled to Korea to inspect conditions and consider tactics for training. He replaced General Matthew Ridgway in May 1952 as Commander, Eighth Army. During his tenure he handled the prison riot at Koje-do and supervised "Operation Everready" (the outline of a plan to replace Rhee if the Korean president did not cooperate with the peace talks). In operations he preferred to use aircraft rather than risking ground troops. During his tenure he had difficulty working with President Rhee. While he supported Rhee's anticommunist position, he was angered by the ROK president's arbitrary and often unreasonable behavior. He disagreed with the Truman policy that avoided attacks on Manchuria and hoped that the election of President Eisenhower would give him a free hand to end the war in Korea with a victory. But that was not to be the case, and he signed the armistice agreement in July 1953 with "a heavy heart," believing that he was the only American officer to end a war without a victory.

Clark retired from the army in 1954. He expressed his belief that the later war in Vietnam was the result of not having reached a final solution to the question in Korea. Appeasement was the cause for this extended war, he wrote in his two books about his military service. He died on April 17, 1984, in Charleston, South Carolina.

Collins, J. Lawton (1896–1987)
U.S. Army chief of staff
A U.S. Army general and chief of staff of the Army from 1949 to 1953, Lawton Collins was born in New Orleans on May 1, 1896, and graduated from West Point in 1917. After that he served as a second lieutenant with the U.S. occupation forces in Europe, and was assigned to the Philippines from 1933 to 1936. He was a graduate of the Industrial War College and the Army War College. He spent a

ROK president Rhee and General Mark Clark at Base Camp, near Seoul (*Center for the Study of the Korean War, Graceland University*)

period as chief of staff for VII Corps. During World War II, he earned the name "Lightning Joe" for defeating the Japanese forces at Guadalcanal. He commanded VII Corps during the invasion of Normandy and served as deputy chief of staff under Eisenhower. In 1948 he was promoted to general.

He agreed with General Douglas MacArthur about the deployment of troops in Korea but was against the Inchon landing. His was the difficult job of coordinating the wishes of the Joint Chiefs of Staff with the desires and actions of General MacArthur. When it came time, he supported Truman's decision to fire MacArthur and gave key testimony against the general during the Senate hearings. Himself frustrated with the war, and how it was being fought, he resigned from the Joint Chiefs right after the armistice was signed. He worked with NATO for a brief time and then was sent to Vietnam by President Eisenhower to assess the situation. He recommended that the United States not support the Diem government. He returned in March 1956 and died on September 12, 1987, in Washington, D.C.

Connally, Tom (1877–1963)
Senate Foreign Relations Committee member
A powerful Democrat and believer in the United Nations, he was at first convinced that the fall of the Republic of Korea was inevitable and that, because it

had no military or political value to the United States, it should be abandoned. He considered the North Korean invasion to be Soviet backed and supported Truman's immediate response. He recommended that the president not ask Congress for a declaration of war, in order to avoid a disastrous Republican delaying action. Not a fan of General MacArthur, Connally urged the president to relieve the general for overstepping his authority. He was instrumental in seeing that the MacArthur hearings were held in closed session so as to avoid giving the general a platform. He did not run for reelection in 1952 and died in 1963.

Coulter, John B. (1891–1983)
Commander of occupation troops

Born in San Antonio, Texas, on April 27, 1891, John Coulter graduated from the West Texas Military Academy in 1911 and served with the 14th Cavalry on the Mexican border. During World War I, he was an aide to the commander of the 42nd "Rainbow" Division and a battalion commander during the St. Mihiel offensive. During the years between the wars, he served in the personnel branch of the War Department General Staff, commanded 2nd Squadron of the 14th Cavalry, and graduated from the Cavalry School and the Command and General Staff. He was squadron commander for the 8th Cavalry and the 4th Cavalry Regiments, and was promoted to brigadier general in 1941.

During World War II, he commanded the 3rd Cavalry Brigade and then became division commander of the 85th Infantry Division in North Africa. In January 1948, he was commander of the 7th Infantry Division in Korea. By August 1948, he was commander of USAFIK.

When war broke out in Korea he was in command of I Corps (April 18, 1950). General Walker did not totally concur with this decision and transferred Coulter to IX Corps and then shortly back again. At the Battle of Chongchon River, his IX Corps and the ROK II Corps did not fare well, and many felt that Coulter had underestimated the Chinese. Some believed that, when the U.S. 2nd Infantry Division was forced to abandon its position, he failed to send the necessary assistance. Nevertheless, in February 1951, Coulter was promoted to lieu-

tenant general and assumed duties as deputy commander of Eighth Army. He was assigned as liaison officer to the UN Commission for the Unification and Rehabilitation of Korea. He had good relations with President Rhee and was responsible for much of the economic growth of Korea after the war. The Republic of Korean erected a statue of him in 1959. He died in Washington, D.C., on March 6, 1983.

Dean, William F. (1899–1981)
Commander, 24th Infantry Division

William Dean was the commanding officer of the 24th Infantry Division during the most difficult days of the Korean War. Born in Carlyle, Illinois, on August 1, 1899, he graduated from the University of California at Berkeley. He served with the 38th Infantry Regiment and was assigned to the 30th Infantry Regiment. He attended Army Command and General Staff School, Army War College, and served in the operations and training division of the War Department during World War II. He was promoted to brigadier general and assigned as assistant commander of the 44th Infantry Division in France. Promoted to major general in 1945, he joined the staff of the Army Command and General Staff

Major General William F. Dean, commander of the 24th Division during the Korean War. Dean won the Medal of Honor and was the highest-ranking officer to be held prisoner during the war. (Center for the Study of the Korean War, Graceland University)

School. In 1949, he assumed the assignment as military governor of South Korea. When war broke out in 1950, he was also named to the 24th Infantry Division and was with the first ground troops to move into Korea when the war broke out. In July 1950, he took command of all U.S. forces in Korea.

Leading his division in the defense of Taejon, July 19–20, 1950, he became separated from his command after the North Koreans pushed their way into Taejon and, after avoiding capture for nearly a month, was finally caught. During his confinement, while he was still considered to be dead, Dean was awarded the Congressional Medal of Honor by President Harry Truman. He was kept in solitary confinement a good deal of the time he was a prisoner. Released by the Communists on September 3, 1953, Dean was assigned as deputy commander of Sixth Army at the Presidio of San Francisco. Held in high esteem by both officers and enlisted men, General Maxwell D. Taylor awarded Dean the Combat Infantryman's Badge, one of the very few officers ever to receive the honor. He retired from the army and died in Berkeley, California, on August 26, 1981.

Deng Hua (Teng Hua) (1910–1980)
Vice commander, Chinese People's Army
The author of China's "night-fight, near-fight" strategy designed to defeat General Douglas MacArthur's UN aggression. Hitting at night and from all sides, the Chinese were very successful. When the UNC counterattack threatened his army, Deng Hua, the vice commander of the Chinese People's Volunteer Army, organized the "underground China wall," a new tactic in tunnel warfare that helped decrease the number of Chinese casualties. In 1954 he was appointed vice-commander of the Northeast Military Zone. In 1959, after some political involvement, he was purged and exiled to Szechwan province.

Doyle, James H. (1897–1981)
Commander, U.S. Amphibious Forces Far East
Admiral Doyle was an experienced and highly capable amphibious commander and was in command of the amphibious forces that first took men and materiel to Korea. During the invasion of

Inchon, he served as commander of the attack force from aboard the USS *Mount McKinley*. He was then responsible for moving the 1st Marine Division to Wonsan, on the east coast, in October of 1950 and was the prime agent in the cautious withdrawal of so many troops and refugees, as well as equipment, from Hungnam, some 50 miles to the north. Known as a "can-do" officer, he had commanded amphibious forces in the Pacific during World War II. A lawyer, he also served in the Judge Advocate General's office, and, after retiring from the navy, returned to the practice of law.

Born in Jamaica, New York, on August 29, 1897, he graduated from the U.S. Naval Academy in 1920. During World War II, he was operations officer and staff commander of Amphibious Forces South Pacific. Leaving Korea, he became president of the Navy Board of Inspection and Survey in Washington and then chairman of the Joint Amphibious Board at Norfolk, Virginia. He retired in 1953 and died on February 9, 1981.

Drumright, Everett F. (1906–1993)
Counselor, U.S. embassy in Seoul
A U.S. diplomat and embassy counselor in Seoul when the Korean War broke out, Everett Drumright was born in Oklahoma on September 15, 1906. He attended Oklahoma Agricultural and Mechanical College for two years and received his B.A. from the University of Oklahoma in 1929. He entered the U.S. Foreign Service in 1931 and then was posted to Hankow, China; he also served as a language officer in Beijing and as vice-consul at Shanghai. He was a secretary at the U.S. Embassy in Nanking (Nanjing) from 1938 to 1941. Thereafter he held various diplomatic posts in Chungking (Chongqing), Washington, D.C., London, and Tokyo.

When John J. Muccio came from the United States, Drumright was in charge of the embassy and was primarily concerned with the administrative aspects of the work in the Republic of Korea. He wrote most of the cables between Seoul and Washington, so was aware of what was going on. He did not anticipate a full-scale invasion, however, and took the position that considerable progress had been made in the relationships between the opposing forces. However, when he was informed of the invasion, he ordered the embassy evacuated. He had high praise for the ROK army but little respect for the ROK president, Syngman Rhee. In 1951, he left Korea and was assigned to India; then he worked for several years at Hong Kong, and was U.S. ambassador to the Republic of China (Taiwan). He received the Cordon of Brilliant Star from the Republic of China (Taiwan) for his services.

Dulles, John Foster (1888–1959)
U.S. secretary of state

Secretary of state under President Dwight D. Eisenhower during the last year of the war, Dulles's primary job was to find a way to end the war. He did so by pushing the Chinese Communists to make the choice between an all-out invasion (with a hint at atomic weapons) or a peace treaty. He was concerned about the possibility that the Soviet Union might make a miscalculation and lead the world into a larger conflict. And he was less than enthusiastic about the role, or the ability, of the United Nations to control the situation. He supported the idea that was later defined as the domino theory. Severely critical of the Korean War, he suggested that with more forethought the war might not have been necessary. He believed it was a mistake for President Truman to have removed General Douglas MacArthur before a peace treaty could be signed. During the war, his support of Truman's policies diminished as did his belief in the role of the United Nations. He was the author of the ideas expressed in the concepts of "deterrence" and the "domino theory."

Born into politics, both a grandfather (John W. Foster) and an uncle (Robert Lansing) had been secretary of state, he became prominent in Republican Party politics, briefly representing the United States at the United Nations. He was influential in the passage of the United Nations' December 13, 1948, resolution on Korea. He died in 1959.

Du Ping (Tu P'ing) (1908–1989)
General of Thirteenth Army Group

General Du Ping joined the Chinese Red Army in 1930, and during the Chinese Civil War, he was director of the Northeastern Field Army. After the founding of the Peoples' Republic of China, he was named political director in the Thirteenth Army Group and later as vice political commissar of the Shenyang Regional Command. He spent three and a half years in Korea as a successful field commander and rose to the rank of lieutenant general in 1955. He served as the party committee chairman of the Chinese delegation to the Korean Armistice Negotiations. Retiring at 80, he published his recollections of the Korean War in a book entitled *Memoirs of Du Ping*.

Eden, Anthony (1897–1977)
British foreign secretary

A scholar in oriental languages, Eden served as a Conservative member of Parliament. Independently wealthy, he traveled for several years after which he became undersecretary for foreign affairs. He was appointed as the British representative to the League of Nations. He served as secretary of state for foreign affairs but resigned in February 1938 in protest of Prime Minister Chamberlain's apparent appeasement. Under Winston Churchill he became foreign secretary and was a key figure in the essential diplomatic negotiations of that difficult period. He supported British participation in the Truman Doctrine, the Marshall Plan, NATO, and the intervention in Korea in 1950. In this latter case, however, he disagreed with the American interpretation of the event, believing that China's involvement was a matter of national interest rather than international Communism. He was worried by the American "exaggerations" about the war and attempted to find compromise on the POW issues. He was critical of President Eisenhower's threats of the use of atomic weapons. In 1955, he succeeded Churchill as prime minister but resigned in 1957 following the Suez Canal fiasco.

Eisenhower, Dwight D. (1890–1969)
President of the United States

Dwight D. Eisenhower was born in Denison, Texas, in 1890. He attended West Point, graduated in 1915, and spent most of World War I in training duties. In 1922, as a major, he served in the Panama Canal Zone and at the War Plans Division, reaching the rank of lieutenant colonel. A brigadier general at the time of Pearl Harbor, he was promoted again in 1942 and placed in charge of the Operations Division. Promoted to four-star general, he was first the commanding general of Allied Forces and then the Supreme Allied Commander in Europe during World War II. From 1945 to 1948, he served as army chief of staff. In 1950, he was named to command NATO.

In 1952, he ran for president and, as part of his campaign, promised to go to Korea to see what could be done to end the war. After the election, in December 1952, he visited Korea. As president he pushed for an armistice, even to the point of considering attacks on China itself. He apparently had reached the conclusion that, if a cease-fire could not be arranged quickly, it would be necessary to bomb Chinese bases. He also took seriously the possible use of nuclear weapons. He served two terms in office, after which he retired to his farm in Pennsylvania. He died at the Walter Reed Army Hospital in 1969.

Fechteler, William M. (1896–1967)
U.S. Navy chief of staff
In 1950, William Fechteler was promoted to full admiral and assumed command of the Atlantic Fleet. In August 1951, President Harry Truman named him as naval chief of staff, following the death of Forrest P. Sherman. His primary job was to maintain U.S. naval strength and to oversee the blockade of North Korea and Communist China.

Born on April 6, 1896, in San Rafael, California, the son of Admiral F. Fechteler, he was a graduate of the U.S. Naval Academy. During World War I, he served as an aide to the Atlantic Fleet commander on board the USS *Pennsylvania*. He commanded USS Perry in 1935. During World War II, he was operations officer for the Destroyer Command, assistant director of the Naval Personnel Bureau, and commander of Amphibious Group I of the Seventh Fleet Amphibious Force. From 1953 to

1956, Fechteler commanded the NATO Forces in southern Europe. He was critical of the concessions given to the Communists at the Panmunjom peace talks. He retired from the navy in 1956 and died July 4, 1967, at Bethesda Naval Hospital.

Finletter, Thomas K. (1893–1980)
Secretary of the air force
Thomas Finletter was born on November 11, 1893, did undergraduate work at the University of Pennsylvania and, following law school, served in France during World War I. In 1941, he was appointed special assistant to the secretary of state, then director of the Office of Foreign Economic Coordination. In 1945, he was a consultant to the U.S. delegation to the United Nations. President Harry Truman named him chairman of the Air Policy Commission in 1947 to investigate military and civil aviation under the cloud of the cold war. In May 1948, he became head of the Economic Cooperation Commission in Great Britain. In 1950, he was appointed secretary of the air force, taking office following the aggressive Stuart Symington.

Finletter had a limited influence on the war in Korea, but was responsible for accomplishing many of the adjustments necessary to build up the newly formed, independent U.S. Air Force. He attended the first Blair House meetings and counseled against involving ground troops. He negotiated the Finletter-Pace agreement concerning "organic aviation" that allowed the army to acquire its own helicopters. He would later serve as U.S. ambassador to the North Atlantic Treaty Organization, where he played an important role in the Cuban Missile Crisis. He died in New York on April 24, 1980.

Gay, Hobart R. (1894–1983)
Commander, First Cavalry Division
Born in Rockport, Illinois, on May 16, 1894, General Gay graduated from Knox College and, in 1917, was commissioned a second lieutenant of cavalry. During World War I, he served with the 7th and 12th Cavalry Regiments on the Mexican border. From 1941 to 1942, he served as commander of the 2nd Armored Division. From 1942 to

1943, Gay was chief of staff, I Armored Corps, in North Africa where he was promoted to brigadier general. From 1949 to 1951, he was commanding general, 1st Cavalry Division, entering action in Korea in July 1951. He was involved in the defense of the Pusan perimeter and the breakout, and of Eighth Army's drive north. In 1952, he served as commanding general, VI Corps, and in 1954 as commander, III Corps. He retired in 1955. He later served as superintendent of the New Mexico Military Institute. He died on August 19, 1983.

Gromyko, Andrei R. (1909–1989)
Soviet ambassador to United Nations
A leading Soviet diplomat and the ambassador to the United Nations during a significant period, Andrei Gromyko was born on July 18, 1909. He received a Ph.D. in economics at Moscow University. During World War II, he was a diplomat, serving for a time in the United States, and from 1946 to 1952, he represented the Soviets at the United Nations. He would later claim that he opposed the decision to absent the Soviet delegation from the UN discussions of the Korean War. He played a significant role in keeping peace with the Chinese. He encouraged the Chinese to cross the 38th parallel in pursuit of retreating UNC forces; yet it was his suggestion that the Soviet Union and India desired a peace settlement that led to initial peace talks. Gromyko was to become the Soviet's primary foreign minister from 1957 to 1985 and in 1985 served as nominal president. He retired in September 1988 and died in Moscow the next year.

Hammarskjold, Dag (1905–1961)
Secretary-general of United Nations
Dag Hammarskjold was secretary-general of the United Nations from 1953 to 1961, replacing Trygve Lie. Born in Jonkoping, Sweden, on July 19, 1905, he received his doctorate in political economy at Uppsala University. He was appointed secretary of the Swedish government's committee on unemployment in 1933, secretary of the Bank of Sweden in 1935, and undersecretary for finance for the Swedish government, 1936–45. In 1946, he entered the diplomatic service and served as Sweden's delegate for the Mar-

shall Plan. In 1951, he became the minister of state while also serving as vice chairman of the Swedish delegation to the United Nations. Finally, with agreement by the Soviets, he was elected secretary-general.

During the armistice talks and the trials afterward, Hammarskjold was responsible for working out several problems, including the release of airmen being held by the Chinese. In the midst of his work, he died in a plane crash on September 19, 1961, in northern Rhodesia. He was posthumously awarded the Nobel Peace Prize in October 1961.

Harriman, W. Averell (1891–1986)
Special assistant for national affairs
Averell Harriman was chairman of the board of Union Pacific Company in 1942. He became the U.S. ambassador to the Soviet Union as President Roosevelt's appointee in 1943. In 1946, Harry Truman appointed him secretary of commerce, where he worked on the implementation of the Marshall Plan. After a visit to Korea in 1946, Harriman recommended a firm policy toward the Soviet Union and provided a favorable impression of the occupation commander, Lieutenant General John Hodge. He served as President Truman's national security adviser during the Korean War. In August 1950, he visited General MacArthur to persuade him to cooperate with Truman's China policy; it soon became obvious that he had been unsuccessful. Harriman was influential in the formation of the Truman Doctrine and supported President Harry Truman's decision to fire General Douglas MacArthur. Harriman ran for the Democratic presidential nomination in 1952 and 1956 and also served in several posts under Presidents Kennedy and Johnson. He was the U.S. negotiator during the preliminary peace talks in France in 1968 between the United States and Vietnam. In 1979, he was appointed as senior member of the U.S. delegation to the UN General Assembly's Special Session on Disarmament.

Harrison, William K., Jr. (1895–1987)
UN Command delegate to armistice talks
William Harrison graduated from the U.S. Military Academy on April 20, 1917, and began his career as

an officer in the horse cavalry. During World War I, he served in France with the 1st Cavalry. He returned to West Point in 1922 as an instructor. He served with the 7th Cavalry and at the 26th Cavalry School in the Philippines. In 1944, Harrison was assistant division commander of the 30th Infantry Division. He was wounded in France. Between 1946 and 1949 he served on the staff of General Douglas MacArthur during the occupation of Japan.

In December 1951, he was named deputy commander of Eighth Army in Korea and in January 1952 was picked to serve on the U.S. armistice delegation. On May 19, 1952, Major General Harrison replaced Admiral C. Turner Joy as the chief negotiator at the truce talks. He regarded the Communists with considerable contempt. He was a tough, unruffled negotiator and maintained his calm during the worst of the Chinese provocations. He concluded this assignment in July 1953 with the signing of the armistice. He retired from the army in 1957, accepting the executive directorship of the Evangelical (Child) Welfare Agency. He died May 25, 1987.

Hickey, Doyle O. (1892–1961)
Deputy chief of staff under General Matthew Ridgway

Born in Rector, Arkansas, in 1892, Major General Hickey graduated from Hendrix College and served in France at the close of World War I. He was then assigned to a series of field artillery assignments. In 1936, after graduating from the Command and General Staff College, he was assigned to the Philippines. In 1944, as brigadier general, he commanded the 3rd Armored Division in France. The division played a key role in halting the enemy advance at the Battle of the Bulge. After the war, in 1949, he was assigned as acting chief of staff under General Douglas MacArthur. After the release of General MacArthur in April 1951, he served briefly as temporary commander, United Nations Command, until the arrival of General Matthew Ridgway. General Hickey then became Ridgway's chief of staff and served until he retired from the army in 1953. He died in Pass Christian, Mississippi, on October 20, 1961.

Major General William K. Harrison attends the daily briefing at the UN Base Camp in Munsan-Ni, Korea, March 15, 1952. *(Center for the Study of the Korean War, Graceland University)*

Higgins, Marguerite "Maggie" (1920–1966)
War correspondent

Maggie Higgins worked for the New York *Herald Tribune* as a city reporter but she wanted to go overseas during World War II. She was eventually assigned to Seventh Army in Germany (1944) and covered it in the field. In 1945, she was named chief of the Berlin bureau, and covered the final victory and reported on the liberation of the death camps. In 1950, she went to Tokyo. At the outbreak of war, she was the first of many reporters to travel to Seoul only to be caught in the retreat. She fled from the city with the rest, crossing the Han River on a raft.

Born in Hong Kong on September 3, 1920, she was educated in France and Britain and at the University of California at Berkeley, and graduated from the Columbia University School of Journalism with an M.A. in 1942. She was one of the first persons to report from Seoul after the war in Korea began. She was in Suwon when General MacArthur visited the field. She was the only woman correspondent in Korea at the time, and many did not like her being there. General Walker banned women from the front line, but MacArthur approved her continued stay.

She was with the marines as they invaded Inchon and was with them during the evacuation from Hungnam. She won the Pulitzer Prize in 1951 for her war reporting. She remained in Asia after the war, then served as a journalist in Washington for a while. She died on January 3, 1966, of a rare tropical disease. She is buried at Arlington National Cemetery.

Hodge, John R. (1893–1963)
Commander, Occupation forces

Lieutenant General John R. Hodge was born on June 12, 1893, at Golconda, Illinois. After receiving officer training at Fort Sheridan, he was commissioned a second lieutenant and served with the 61st Infantry in France. During the 1920s, he served in a variety of military assignments and from 1932 to 1936 attended the Army Command and Staff College at Leavenworth, Kansas, the Army War College in Washington, and the Air Corps Tactical School at Maxwell Field. He was appointed assistant divisional commander of the 25th Division and assumed temporary command of the 43rd Division in 1943. He was wounded while on New Georgia Island. In 1944, he was commander of XXVII Corps. General Douglas MacArthur chose Lieutenant General Hodge to command U.S. Army forces in Korea. More a combat commander than a civil administrator, he was often at odds with Korean president Rhee. An avid anticommunist, he worried about the threat the Soviets presented to his command. He quarreled with President Rhee, a situation that led to Hodge's recall. In 1948, when the South Koreans elected their first assembly and chose Rhee as president, Hodge transferred control of the national security forces to the new government on August 24. In 1952, President Harry Truman appointed General Hodge as Chief of Army Field Forces. On November 12, 1963, he died in Washington, D.C.

Hoge, William M. (1894–1979)
Commander, IX Corps

William Hoge was born in Booneville, Missouri, where his father was principal of Kemper Military School. He moved with the family when his father assumed responsibility for Wentworth Military Academy in Lexington, Missouri. He graduated from West Point in 1916. During World War I, he rose to the rank of major and commanded a battalion in France. He received the Distinguished Service Cross and the Silver Star. After a stint in the Philippines, he was called back by General Douglas MacArthur and served as chief of engineers for the Philippine army. During World War II, he was responsible for the building of the Alaska-Canada highway. By the end of the war, he was a major general and in command of the 4th Armored Division. He was called to Korea by General Matthew Ridgway and assigned the command of IX Corps. He led his command through several major battles in central Korea and displayed the aggressiveness for which he was known. He retired a four-star general in 1955 and died in 1979.

Hull, John E. (1895–1975)
Commander, United Nations Command

Hull became UNC commander on October 7, 1953, replacing General Mark W. Clark, and assumed responsibility for the difficult implication of the armistice agreement. He served during World War I and was disappointed with his "desk" job on the War Department General Staff during World War II. When he took command, he was labeled by one reporter as "the general that nobody knows," but he managed to administer the armistice and the repositioning of UN forces with a great deal of ability. Quiet and unassuming, he had an impressive record both in military command and diplomatic skills. In his responsibility for execution of the cease-fire agreement, he had to work with the Neutral Nations Repatriation Commission, with which he took a hard line. He insisted that POW repatriations be completed on January 22, 1954. He retired from the army in 1955 and became president of the Manufacturing Chemists Association.

Jamieson, Arthur (1910–1991)
Australian representative, UN Commission on Korea

A longtime critic of ROK president Syngman Rhee, Jamieson believed that Rhee had used brutal methods to consolidate his position of leadership. Unhappy with what was happening, and on instructions from the Australian government, he was absent from the August 1948 inauguration. In June 1950, he was with the UN Commission on Korea and was sent there to determine who was the aggressor in the outbreak of war. The commission reported that there was sufficient reason to declare North Korea as the aggressor. Jamieson continued to emphasize the importance of the role of the United Nations and stressed the point that Australia was involved in Korea as a gesture of collective security as embodied by the United Nations, and not to offer support for the government of Syngman Rhee.

Jessup, Philip C. (1897–1986)
U.S. ambassador to United Nations

Philip Jessup played a significant role as U.S. representative to the UN General Assembly (1948–52) during the difficult years of the Korean War. Born in New York City, he attended Hamilton College and Yale and Columbia Universities. He became an expert on international law and during the 1920s and 1930s taught at Columbia. During the 1940s, he accepted several positions and, in 1948, was named as deputy ambassador to UN representative, Warren R. Austin. In 1949, Truman appointed him an ambassador at large, during which time he wrote the famous "white paper" that was supportive of the Chinese Communist effort, gaining himself a place on Senator McCarthy's list of Communists. Charged with disloyalty, he was investigated but was cleared of all implications.

Jessup was in the Blair House meetings during the first days of the war and traveled with President Harry Truman on his Wake Island visit with General Douglas MacArthur. He felt he was becoming an embarrassment to the Truman administration and resigned in 1952. He returned to teaching international law. From 1961 to 1979, he served as a judge on the International Court of Justice in Geneva. He died January 31, 1986, in Norfolk, Connecticut.

Johnson, Louis A. (1891–1966)
Secretary of defense

Born in Roanoke, Virginia, in 1891, Johnson earned a law degree from the University of Vir-

ginia. He served in the West Virginia House of Delegates in 1916 and saw action as a captain in the army during World War I in France. He returned to help establish the American Legion, serving as its commander from 1932 to 1933. A strong supporter and fund-raiser for President Harry Truman, Johnson was named secretary of defense on March 28, 1949. His aggressive budget cutting and the cancellation of the navy's planned supercarrier created a bitter rivalry between the services and led to the "revolt of the admirals." In 1949, the House Committee on the Armed Services investigated questions concerning aircraft procurement relating to Johnson and Secretary of the Air Force Stuart Symington, but nothing was ever determined.

He took part in the Blair House meetings during the early days of the war and advocated the acceptance of Chiang Kai-shek's (Jiang Jieshi) offer of troops. He disagreed with both the president and Secretary of State Dean Acheson concerning the role of the State Department. This added to his already weakened position with the military, all of which led President Harry Truman to request his resignation on September 19, 1950. He was replaced by General George C. Marshall. Johnson was bitter over the removal but returned to his law practice in Washington until he died on April 24, 1966.

Joy, C. Turner (1895–1956)
Commander, Naval Forces Far East

Born in St. Louis, Missouri, on February 17, 1895, Joy was commissioned an ensign on graduation from the Naval Academy. He served on the USS *Pennsylvania* during World War I and later as aide and flag lieutenant to the commander of the Yangtze River Patrol. He commanded destroyers, served as an instructor at the Naval Academy, and then became executive officer of the heavy cruiser USS *Indianapolis*. He commanded the heavy cruiser USS *Louisville* from September 1942 to June 1943.

He was sent to the Western Pacific where he served as Commander, Naval Forces Far East, a post he held until mid-1952. Vice Admiral C.

Turner Joy was also the first UN delegate to the armistice talks. He was critical, but not openly, of U.S. policy in dealing with the Chinese. He requested his release in May 1952. His final assignment was as superintendent of the U.S. Naval Academy. A posthumous publication, *How Communists Negotiate,* was highly critical of President Eisenhower's policies concerning the negotiations and approach to an armistice. He retired in 1954 and died on June 13, 1956 in California.

Kang Kon (1918–1950)
Chief of staff, North Korean People's Army
Lieutenant General Kang Kon began his career when he joined the East Manchurian Communist Youth League in 1932. Born in Sangju, North Kyongsang province, he became a follower of Kim Il Sung and gained a position of some significance after the close of World War II. In February 1946, he was involved in the creation of the North Korean People's Army. He assumed the position of chief of staff in December 1947. In this position, he was heavily involved in the decision and in the preparations to attack South Korea. Kang was killed in action by a land mine in September 1950.

Kean, W. B. (1897–1981)
Commander, 25th Infantry Division
Born in Buffalo, New York, on July 9, 1897, Kean was an early graduate at West Point due to the American entry into World War I. At the outbreak of World War II, he went with General Bradley as chief of staff for the 28th Infantry Division, rising to this position with II Corps and then First Army. After World War II, he commanded the 5th Division and in 1948 the 25th Division in Japan. In July 1950, his division deployed to Korea, and he led it through the withdrawal and then the breakout at Pusan and acted brilliantly during the "Great Naktong Offensive." He was relieved by General Matthew Ridgway as a part of the shakeup of frontline generals. After his return, he assumed command of III Corps at Camp Roberts. He retired from the army as a lieutenant general in September 1954. He died on March 10, 1981.

Kennan, George F. (1904–2005)
State Department Soviet expert, diplomat, adviser, political analyst, historian
Born in Milwaukee, Wisconsin, on February 16, 1904, Kennan attended St. John's Military Academy and Princeton University, where he graduated in 1927. Joining the foreign service, he was assigned to Geneva, Tallinn, and, in 1933, to the U.S. Embassy in Moscow. He served as the first secretary to Sumner Wells and was in Berlin when the United States declared war on Nazi Germany. During the war, he was in Portugal and in 1944 returned to Moscow.

In 1947, George C. Marshall put Kennan in charge of policy planning at the State Department, where Kennan advocated the "containment" of the Soviet Union. However, he supported the withdrawal of U.S. troops from Korea. Many consider him to be the architect of the cold war. In his famous "X" article in *Foreign Affairs,* he argued against seeking an armistice while on the defensive. As a consultant to President Harry Truman he pushed the view that Communist conquest of South Korea would be harmful, and he had some disagreement with Truman about the use of the United Nations in Korea. Yet during the Korean War, it was Kennan who was able to speak to the Soviets and bring about the talks that eventually led to a cease-fire. His short tenure as ambassador to the Soviet Union ended when he compared it and Nazi Germany. He retired from the foreign service in 1953 and joined the Institute for Advanced Studies at Princeton. He died on March 17, 2005.

Kim Chaek (1903–1951)
Commander, North Korean People's Army
Born in the northernmost part of Korea, he joined the Chinese Communist Party in 1925 and thereafter developed the guerrilla background that was common to the DPRK leadership. He returned to Korea with the Russian army in 1945 and supported Kim Il Sung and grew in power with him. He was named to the North Korean Worker's Party presidium and held key cabinet positions once the new government was established. During the war, he held several significant positions and, in 1950, organized the retreating North Korean troops into a powerful guerrilla unit. He was killed in a bombing raid in January 1951.

Kim Chong-Won (1922–1964)
Military leader, Republic of Korea

Born in North Korea, Kim Chong-Won, known as "Tiger," rose through the ranks to become a battalion commander in the Yosu-Sunchon rebellion. There is a long-standing tradition, unsubstantiated, that it was his 17th Regiment that actually started the Korean War by attacking North Korea on the morning of June 25, 1950. As commander of the 23rd Regiment he was relieved after executing two men for losing ground near Yongkok. Later he was blamed for having more than 50 North Korean POWs beheaded. He was given command of the military police during the brief occupation of Pyongyang. He was sentenced to three years in prison for firing on members of an investigation team looking into the massacre of several hundred suspected Communist sympathizers. After three months he was pardoned by Syngman Rhee. In July 1961, he was sentenced to 15 years in prison for the assassination attempt on the life of John M. Chang, the vice president who belonged to Rhee's opposition party. He died in 1964.

Kim Il Sung (1912–1994)
Premier, Democratic People's Republic of Korea

Kim Il Sung was premier of the Democratic People's Republic of Korea and supreme commander of the Democratic People's Republic of Korea Army. Originally named Kim Song Ju, he was born on a farm near Pyongyang, Korea. He migrated with his family to Manchuria in 1926 and there, in 1931, he joined the Korean Communist Party. Following World War II, Kim returned to Korea with the Soviet occupation forces. In 1948, he became premier of North Korea—the Democratic People's Republic of Korea.

After three years of bitter fighting, Kim finally signed an armistice agreement and turned his attention to domestic matters. He eliminated his last rivals and set out to improve the nation's economy. He began to relinquish control of the Korean Communist Party to his son, Kim Jong II, but remained in ultimate control until his death. He died of a heart attack in 1994. He was honored with the title Eternal President.

Kim Paek-il (1917–1951)
Commander, Republic of Korea I Corps

Kim Paek-il was serving as the deputy chief of staff for the ROK army when the Korean War broke out. While under attack he proposed a new line of defense on the south bank of the Han River, but his plans were ended with the premature blowing of the Han River bridge. Promoted to brigadier general he was assigned to command I Corps. On October 1, 1950, he led his troops across the 38th parallel and was with them when they took the east coast port city of Wonsan. He was promoted to major general in October 1950. His unit was extracted at Hungnam following the Chinese intervention. He was killed in a helicopter crash in 1951.

Kim Ung (1928–?)
Commander, North Korean I Corps

Trained at Whampoa Military Academy in China, Kim Ung joined the Chinese Communists in the 1930s. He was the commander of the Eighth Route Army during the civil war. When the Korean War broke out, Kim Ung was involved at the highest levels of command. When Lieutenant General Kang Kon died in September 1950, Kim Ung was appointed chief of staff. After the war he served as vice minister of defense until he was purged by Kim Il Sung in 1958. Twenty years later he appeared on the scene again as the ambassador to South Yemen, a position he held until 1978.

Kirk, Alan G. (1888–1963)
Ambassador to the Soviet Union

During the first year of the war, Alan Kirk served as the U.S. ambassador to the Soviet Union. Prior to this time he had been a career naval officer with a wide variety of interesting and significant assignments—executive officer on the presidential yacht, gunboat captain, and chief of staff for the commander of the European Fleet. He then served as commanding officer for the U.S. Atlantic Fleet, Amphibious forces. After having risen to the rank of admiral (1946), he retired from the navy and became the diplomatic representative to several countries. In 1949, President Harry Truman selected him as ambassador to the Soviet Union. He was strongly supportive of UN involvement in the fighting in Korea and was determined that the United States not permit Soviet-inspired aggression. In 1951, he became the chair of the American Committee for Liberation of the Russian People, just one of his many anticommunist activities. In 1962, he replaced Everett F. Drumright as ambassador to the Nationalist government on Taiwan. He died in 1963.

Knowland, William F. (1908–1974)
U.S. senator

U.S. senator and right-wing Republican, Knowland was an outspoken hawk and China lobbyist who accused the Truman administration of appeasement in Korea. He referred to the cease-fire talks as "surrender on the installment plan." He was a supporter of Senator Joseph R. McCarthy's effort to "weed out" Communists in the State Department and a vicious opponent of Truman's recall of General Douglas MacArthur. His foreign policy seemed to center around the preservation of the Republic of China. He campaigned for the governorship of California in 1958 but lost. In 1974, he took his own life.

Lee Chong Chan (Yi Chong-chon) (1916–1983)
Chief of staff, Republic of Korea

A graduate of the Japanese Military Academy in 1937, he was appointed commander of the ROK 3rd Division as a brigadier general. Following the Inchon landing, he led his troops across the 38th parallel on September 30, 1950, the first ROK unit across. He became the ROK army's chief of staff, but he was released when he refused to deploy his divisions to Seoul during the political crisis of 1952. He was sent to the United States for military training and became president of the ROK Army College. Following the war, he was involved in a variety of political roles and served under South Korean president Park Chung Hee.

Lee Hak-Ku (1920–1953)
North Korean prisoner of war

He was the second-ranking (colonel) North Korean officer held as a POW during the war. As a prisoner, he was cooperative and helpful, providing detailed information on his division and on North Korean military deployments. When captured, he was chief of staff of the 13th Division. He was assigned to the POW camp at Koje-do and became a leader there, playing a major role in the prison riots. He was returned to North Korea after the armistice agreement and was caught up in a purge there.

Lee Kwon Mu (Yi Kwon-Mu) (1910–1986?)
Major general, North Korean People's Army

In 1948, he was appointed chief of staff in the newly created Democratic People's Republic of Korea army. Prior to that he had served with China's Red Army against Japan, then defeated Chiang Kai-shek's (Jiang Jieshi) Nationalist army in China's civil war, and underwent military training in the Soviet Union. While commander of the NKPA's 4th Division, he first entered Seoul on June 28, 1950. Later he assumed command of the NKPA II Corps. After the war, and Kim Il Sung's purge of his political opposition, Lee Kwon Mu was named chief of staff for the NKPA. He served there until his retirement in 1960.

Lemnitzer, Lyman L. (1899–1988)
Commander, 7th Infantry Division

During the Korean War, Major General Lyman Lemnitzer was commander of the 11th Airborne Division in 1950, where he made his first jump at the age of 51. He then commanded the 7th Infantry Division. A graduate of West Point in 1919, he was born in Honesdale, Pennsylvania, on August 29, 1899. During World War II, he was assigned to Field Marshal Alexander's Allied Headquarters and helped form the plans for the invasions of North Africa and Sicily. In August 1952, he was promoted to lieutenant general. From 1955 to 1957, he was commander in chief of Far Eastern Command and UNC. In July 1957, he became chief of staff and, in

1960, chairman of the Joint Chiefs of Staff. He served as the supreme allied commander of NATO until he retired in 1969. In 1975, President Ford appointed Lemnitzer to the Commission on CIA activities. He died on November 12, 1988.

Lie, Trygve (1896–1968)
Secretary-general of the United Nations
During the debates over Korea, Trygve Lie tried to be non-aligned. When the North Koreans invaded the Republic of Korea, however, he began to take an active role in identifying the aggressor and in calling for a UN response, including the creation of United Nations Command. He was sharply criticized by the Soviet delegate but continued to support UN involvement, calling for a peaceful solution as quickly as possible.

Born in Oslo, Norway, he graduated from Oslo University Law School. He worked within the Norwegian Labor Party and was appointed the minister of justice in a coalition government. He was forced to flee Norway after the Nazi occupation. Having been associated with the United Nations from the beginning in January 1946 Lie represented his nation at the first UN meeting. He disagreed with the United States on the decision to cross the 38th parallel. He supported the Uniting for Peace resolution of November 3, 1950. During the three years of war, he made numerous efforts to bring about some sort of peace in Korea. Feeling the pressure of the Soviet Union against his taking a second term, he resigned in 1952. After returning to Norway, he assumed several diplomatic posts and died in 1968.

Li Kenong (Li K'o-nung) (1898–1962)
Chief, Chinese People's Volunteer Army
He joined the Chinese Communist Party in 1926 and was chief of security of the First Front Army during the Long March. In 1949, he was named deputy chief of staff of the Chinese People's Liberation Army and was commissioned a full general in 1955. As the armistice talks began, he was chief of the CPVA Negotiations Delegation Party Committee. While the North Koreans were to be the major negotiators for the Communists, it was Li Kenong and his staff who called

most of the shots. In 1956, he became a member of the Chinese Communist Party Central Committee.

Lovett, Robert Abercrombie (1895–1986)
Secretary of defense
Robert Lovett served as undersecretary of state and secretary of defense during the period of the Korean War. Born in Huntsville, Texas, he attended Yale University and entered the Naval Reserve. During World War I, he commanded the first U.S. naval air squadron. In December 1940, he was appointed assistant secretary of war in charge of the production and procurement of aircraft. In 1947, General Marshall appointed Lovett as undersecretary, and he worked on the industrial mobilization of the nation. After General Marshall resigned, he served as secretary of defense until January 1953. He was a member of President Kennedy's adviser circle during the Cuban Missile Crisis.

Lowe, Frank E. (1885–1968)
Truman's military observer
Lowe served in France during World War I. During World War II, he was an assistant to General George Marshall, specializing in Reserve affairs. After the war, he returned to civilian life (as a major general in the Reserves). When the Korean War broke out, Truman called him to active duty (at the age of 65) and asked him to go to Korea and to report on what he saw. During his reports, he praised the work of the marines but was somewhat critical of the efforts of the U.S. Army. Nevertheless, he received the Distinguished Service Medal in 1951 for his service. He failed in his efforts to support MacArthur during the conflict between the general and the president. After leaving the army, he contributed to a series of exposes in which he charged the Army General Staff with misleading the president. He died in 1968.

MacArthur, Douglas (1880–1964)
Commander, United Nations Command
One of the most controversial military leaders in American history, MacArthur was born in Little Rock, Arkansas, and graduated with honors from

General Douglas MacArthur greets John Foster Dulles at Haneda Air Force Base, Tokyo, Japan. Mr. Dulles had visited Syngman Rhee in Korea and then conferred with General MacArthur. *(Harry S. Truman Library)*

West Point in 1903. He served in the Philippines, in Mexico, and with the expeditionary forces at Veracruz, Mexico. During World War I, MacArthur helped organize the 42nd (Rainbow) Division and went with it to France as a brigade commander. On his return, he was named superintendent of the U.S. Military Academy. In 1930, President Herbert Hoover named him chief of staff of the army. He held the post until 1935, when he was reappointed by President F. D. Roosevelt and went to the Philippines as a military adviser to develop the Filipino defense force. He was there when World War II broke out. He was restored as a lieutenant general on July 17, 1941, and became a full general on December 18, 1941. He directed the defense of the Philippines until February 22, 1942, when he was ordered to proceed to Australia and take command of the Southwest Pacific area. He was promoted to general of the army in 1944.

When the Korean War broke out and the United Nations asked the United States to name a commander for UN forces, President Harry Truman named MacArthur. He managed the massive retreat to the Pusan Perimeter, then the risky Inchon landing and the return of South Korea to President Rhee. Following this success, he crossed the 38th parallel in an effort to bring all of Korea under UN control. MacArthur disagreed with the manner in which the war was being fought and was quite vocal about his criticism of the Truman administration. This finally came to a head when MacArthur disobeyed his orders to remain quiet on matters of foreign affairs, and he was relieved by President Harry Truman in April 1951. Arriving home a hero, he addressed the U.S. Congress, during which he was able to express many of his concerns. There was a brief joint committee of the House and Senate to investigate the conditions of his release, but little came of it. He returned to the Philippines briefly, held a series of significant civilian positions, but his political aspirations, if they were in fact real, came to naught. He died April 6, 1964.

Malenkov, Georgi Maximilianovich (1902–1988)
Soviet premier

Born in Orenburg, Russia, Malenkov was a Red Army political commissar and became one of Joseph Stalin's confidants. Working his way in and out of power, he became a member of the Communist Party Secretariat in 1952. The death of Stalin in 1953 brought Malenkov to power briefly. During this time, he launched a "peace offensive" that led to the 1953 armistice agreement. He became chairman of the Council of Ministers (premier) and first secretary of the party. He was forced to resign as secretary in 1954 when the post was taken over by Nikita Khrushchev. During his two years as premier, he was vocal about his opposition to nuclear armaments and, in February 1955, was forced to resign. In 1961, he was expelled from the Communist Party and sent into exile within the Soviet Union. He died in Moscow January 14, 1988.

Malik, Jacob A. (1906–1980)
Soviet representative to United Nations
It was Jacob Malik who stomped out of the Security Council to protest the refusal to grant Red China the seat at the United Nations held by the Republic of China. During his time at the United Nations he was an outspoken advocate for the policies of the Soviet Union and argued on numerous occasions with representatives from the United States and Great Britain over policies related to China and Korea. A graduate of the University of Moscow Institute of Foreign Affairs, he served as ambassador to Japan in 1942. Late in 1946, he assumed the duties of deputy foreign minister for the Soviet Union, and in May 1948, he replaced Andrei A. Gromyko as permanent Soviet representative to the United Nations.

After a series of private conversations with U.S. diplomats, Malik addressed the world on June 23, 1951, suggesting that an armistice in Korea was possible. This led, eventually, to the peace talks. He remained at his post until October 1952, when he became first deputy foreign minister. He was appointed the ambassador to the United Kingdom and remained there until 1960. In 1968, he returned to the United Nations as the Soviet representative and stayed there until 1976.

Mao Zedong (Mao Tse-tung) (1893–1976)
Chairman, Chinese Communist Party
Born on December 26, 1893, in Hunan, Mao Zedong joined the revolution led by Dr. Sun Yat-sen to overthrow the imperial government. In 1921, he was one of 21 delegates to the First Congress of the Communist Party (international). A revolutionary leader, he fought the five "Encirclement Campaigns" against the Kuomintang after Chiang Kai-shek (Jiang Jieshi) abandoned his coalition with the Chinese Communist Party in 1927 and was the leader in the "Long March" of 1934–35. A full-scale civil war broke out in 1946 and in 1949 Beijing fell, forcing the Nationalists to withdraw to Taiwan. At first, Mao seemed very reluctant to become involved in the war in Korea, but once he became alarmed by the UN advance, he was a predominant force in the decision to join the Korean War.

In 1953, he launched his Five Year Plan, as the economic growth of China was promoted by the development of hundreds of communes. While hostile to the Western powers, he nevertheless moved further away from the Soviet Union. Following an attempted coup by Lin Piao in 1971, Mao moved to restore order, including better relations with the West. In 1972, with President Nixon's visit to China, relations between the two nations improved. Mao Zedong died on September 9, 1976.

Marshall, George C. (1880–1959)
Secretary of state
In January 1947, President Harry Truman appointed Marshall as secretary of state. Up to that time, he had served in a variety of major commands. Born in Uniontown, Pennsylvania, on December 31, 1880, he was a graduate of the Virginia Military Institute. He served in the Philippines, on the Western Front during World War I, and for four years as an aide to General John Pershing, with duty in China. In June 1933, he was in charge of the Civilian Conservation Corps operating in the southern states. In October 1936, he was promoted to brigadier general, then chief of the War Plans Division and deputy chief of staff. During World War II, he commanded the U.S. Armed Forces as the U.S. Army grew to a force of nearly eight and a half million. In 1944, he received his fifth star. In 1946, Marshall resigned from the army and became the U.S. ambassador to China.

Secretary of State Marshall was the chief architect of the economic recovery plan that bears his name. He saw an economically strong Europe as the best defense against the growing threat of communism. In 1949, he resigned as secretary of state, but in the following year he accepted the position as secretary of defense, following the resignation of Louis A. Johnson. He was a powerful force in the organization of U.S. forces in the Korean War. In December 1950, he argued that the Republic of Korea should not be abandoned and that any cease-fire at that time would be seen as a sign of weakness. Nevertheless, he worked carefully to avoid any expansion of the war. Attacked by Senator McCarthy for being soft on communism and frustrated by the continuing struggle, Marshall again retired. In 1953, he was awarded the Nobel Peace Prize for his efforts in the recovery of Europe. He died in Washington on October 16, 1959.

Martin, Joseph W. (1884–1968)
Speaker of the U.S. House of Representatives
An old friend of General Douglas MacArthur, Martin was instrumental in the general's demise when he publicized a letter from MacArthur that was highly critical of President Harry S. Truman and his policies in Korea. As the Republican (Massachusetts) minority leader, he was close to both Presidents Calvin Coolidge and Franklin D. Roosevelt. However, he clashed with President Harry Truman and was a strong supporter of Chiang Kaishek (Jiang Jieshi), criticizing Truman's refusal to use Nationalist troops in Korea. He was opposed to the firing of General MacArthur and was instrumental in arranging for MacArthur to address Congress. He was replaced in his position as minority leader in 1959, lost his seat in the primary of 1966 and retired from politics.

Matthews, Francis P. (1887–1952)
Secretary of the navy
Matthews was secretary of the navy at a most difficult time, when internal feuding in the armed services, primarily as a result of defense funding and controversial priorities, was almost uncontrollable. He served during the first year of the Korean War but resigned in July 1951 to become the U.S. ambassador to Ireland.

Born in Albion, Nebraska, on March 15, 1887, he practiced law in Omaha, serving as the director and vice president of the United Service Organizations (USO) during World War II. Appointed by President Harry Truman in 1949, he was known as the "rowboat secretary" because of his lack of any experience for the job. He was present at the Blair House meetings at the beginning of the war but had little to offer and provided little to the waging of the war. Having come into office at a time of extreme cuts, he suddenly found himself in charge of a rapid expansion. On August 25, 1950, he caused considerable embarrassment for the Truman administration when he announced that he was willing to fight a "preventive war" against the Soviet Union. He died on October 18, 1952, at Omaha, Nebraska.

McCarthy, Joseph (1908–1957)
Senator
A key figure in the Red Scare that gripped the United States during the 1940s and 1950s. As a senator (R-Wisconsin) he led paranoid anti-Soviet and anti-Communist campaigns, accusing numerous Americans, from all walks of life, of being Communists. His accusations were shown to be false, and he was censured by the U.S. Senate in 1954. He left office and died in 1957.

Menon, V. K. Krishna (1896–1974)
Indian special representative to United Nations
Though he was known for his abrasive manner, and sometimes accused of being pro-Soviet because of his attacks on U.S. foreign policy, it was Menon who was greatly responsible for the compromise settlement at the cease-fire talks. The Menon POW settlement proposal was the basis for the June 8, 1953, agreement between the warring parties. Educated in London and deeply involved in the Labour Party, he was a determined nationalist, a fighter for Indian independence, and, as a close friend of Indian prime minister Jawaharlal Nehru, he represented India's position of non-alignment.

Milburn, Frank W. (1892–1962)
Commander, I Corps
Born in Jasper, Indiana, on January 11, 1892, Milburn graduated from West Point. Nicknamed "Shrimp" because of his stature, he held a series of responsible positions. During World War II, he commanded XXI Corps when in France and Germany. In August 1945 Milburn was deputy commander of American forces in Germany.

In June 1950, Milburn was sent to Korea to command I Corps. On his arrival he was given the responsibility of the breakout from the Pusan perimeter. During the last two weeks of September, he led the Eighth Army drive to link up with X Corps and then the push into North Korea. After the Chinese entered the war, General Milburn, whom Ridgway felt lacked the needed spark, was promoted to lieutenant general. But then Ridgway established his command post with Milburn. Following his term in Korea, Milburn returned to serve as inspector of the infantry and then retired in May 1952. In 1955, he served on the committee that wrote a new code of conduct for captured American military personnel. He died in Montana on October 25, 1962.

Molotov, Vyacheslav M. (Scriabine) (1890–1987)
Soviet foreign minister
He did not appear on the scene, in relation to the Korean War, until he assumed the role of foreign minister after the death of Joseph Stalin. In this position, he was a powerful voice during the final stages of the cease-fire negotiations. He had been Stalin's personal representative to the Chinese Communist conference in August 1950, to discuss what should be done if UN forces crossed the 38th parallel. He believed that it was necessary to end the war in Korea, primarily because of Soviet difficulties at home. In 1957, he participated in a failed attempt to overthrow Nikita Khrushchev and was punished by assignment as the Soviet ambassador to Outer Mongolia.

Muccio, John J. (1900–1989)
Ambassador to the Republic of Korea
Born in Naples, Italy, John Muccio came with his parents to the United States and settled in Rhode Island. He served in the U.S. Army in 1918 and received his M.A. from George Washington University. In 1924, he began a series of diplomatic appointments, a good portion of them in the Orient. In August 1948, when the United States recognized the Republic of Korea, President Harry Truman appointed him to replace General Hodge as head of the diplomatic mission in Korea. His primary job was to deal with President Syngman Rhee and to prepare for the withdrawal of American troops. He was the one who notified the State Department of the North Korean invasion and supervised the evacuation of American dependents. As the war began, he provided invaluable service as a liaison between the Korean government and the U.S. military, but he

was unable to convince President Rhee that dictatorial rule was a threat to the security of the republic. Following his service in Korea, he left in 1952 to accept appointments in Guatemala and Iceland.

Mu Cong (Kim Mu Chong) (1905–1951)
Commander, North Korea
From the Yanan faction of the North Korean Communist Party, he was one of those early leaders, and the only Korean, to survive the Long March. In the early 1940s, the North Korean Volunteer Corps was reorganized into the North China Korean Independence League under Kim Tu-bo, and Mu Cong was named commander. At the beginning of the Korean War, he commanded the North Korean II Corps. In December 1950, he was held responsible for the fall of Pyongyang and was purged from office. He reportedly died in China in 1951.

Murray, Charles S. (1909–1983)
Special counsel to President Harry S. Truman
Murray was one of the behind-the-scenes workers who had a great deal of influence on presidential decisions. A friend of President Harry Truman and a member of the "little cabinet" as well as the president's speech writer, Murphy was instrumental in establishing both domestic and foreign policy. He served as undersecretary of agriculture and supervised the transition following the election of Richard M. Nixon. He died in 1983.

Murray, Raymond L. (1894–1978)
Commander, Fifth Marine Regiment
A highly decorated marine lieutenant colonel and World War II veteran, Murray was ordered to Korea in 1950 to command the 5th Marine Regiment. He was in command of his regiment when it landed at Inchon and advanced to take the capital city of Seoul. He was awarded the Army Distinguished Service Cross for extraordinary heroism during the marine breakout from the Chosin (Changjin) Reservoir. He advanced to the rank of colonel as his regiment fought on the central Korean front. After leaving Korea, he held several

positions with the Marine Corps and was promoted to brigadier general in June 1959.

Nixon, Richard M. (1913–1994)
California congressman

A critic of U.S. policies in the Far East, Nixon claimed that the truce in Korea had deprived the United Nations of a victory. He had, however, voted in support of President Harry Truman's action against the North Koreans. He was a supporter of General Douglas MacArthur and called on Truman to reinstate him to command. During the presidential race of 1952, Nixon, the vice presidential candidate, played the role of "bad guy" on the war, leaving General Eisenhower to play the "good guy" role. Nixon visited Korea in 1953, where he talked with Syngman Rhee, extracting from him a promise not to take any unilateral action without first checking with President Eisenhower. Nixon went on to become president of the United States, and the first president to resign.

O'Donnell, Emmett "Rosy" (1906–1971)
Commander, Far East Air Force

Major General O'Donnell commanded the Far East Air Force from July 1950 to January 1951. A graduate of West Point, he was commissioned in the infantry. Transferring to the Air Corps, he had achieved the rank of major when World War II broke out. In 1944, he led the first major air raid on Tokyo. On July 13, 1950, he was ordered to Korea and took the 22nd and 92nd Bombardment Groups with him. While his planes were used for this purpose, he was very critical of the use of bombers for close air support. He also supported the idea of bombing supply areas in China and believed that the Chinese phase of the war could have been prevented by such action. After leaving Korea, and while testifying at the MacArthur hearings, he challenged General Douglas MacArthur's plan for victory but complained that during the war bombers were reduced to "blowing up haystacks." He was promoted to four-star general and commanded the U.S. Pacific Air Force. He retired in 1963 and died in 1971.

Pace, Frank, Jr. (1912–1988)
Secretary of the army

After successful participation in World War II, Frank Pace joined the staff of Attorney General Tom Clark. In 1949, President Harry Truman appointed him director of the Bureau of the Budget and, when Gordon Gray resigned as secretary of the army in April 1950, Truman appointed Frank Pace. During the prewar sessions he was heavily involved in, and supportive of, the commitment of U.S. forces. He had reservations about the Inchon landing, the pursuit of the Chinese Communists north of the 38th parallel, and the rotation of troops. He was scheduled to inform General Douglas MacArthur that he had been dismissed, when a press leak came out, making it unnecessary. He resigned in January 1953 and served as chairman of the board at General Dynamics Corporation. He died January 8, 1988.

Paik Sun Yup (1920–?)
Chief of staff, Republic of Korea

Paik Sun Yup was born near Pyongyang and graduated from Manchuria's Mukden Military Academy in 1942. Recognizing the growing influence of the Communists, he fled to the south and joined the South Korean Constabulary. On June 25, 1950, then a colonel, he commanded the ROK 1st Infantry Division. General Paik led the 1st Division drive north and was the first to enter Pyongyang in October 1950. In 1951, he was promoted to major general and assigned to the ROK I Corps. In July 1952, he was named the ROK army's chief of staff. Again promoted, he was placed in command of the ROK III Corps. In January 1953, he was the first Korean officer to attain four-star rank. In 1969, he retired from the army and served as ambassador to Taiwan, France, and Canada.

Panikkar, Sardar K. M. (1893–1963)
Indian ambassador to the People's Republic of China

When Panikkar was named the representative to the newly formed People's Republic of China, it emphasized India's interest in the PRC's independence from Moscow, and Prime Minister Jawaharlal Nehru's desire to maintain India's nonaligned foreign policy. An Asian scholar by training, and friendly with Communist diplomats, he served as a conduit between the Chinese government and the governments at London and Washington. Unfortunately, many in the United States considered him pro-Communist, and so he was not listened to as carefully as might have been profitable. It was through Panikkar that China issued its warning against the UN crossing of the 38th parallel. In 1952, he was assigned to head the Indian embassy in Cairo.

Partridge, Earle E. (1900–1990)
Commander, U.S. Fifth Air Force
Born in Winchendon, Massachusetts, Earle Partridge served in the army during World War I, then attended West Point. He attended several military schools; when World War II broke out, he commanded the 3rd Bombardment Division in Britain and then Fifth Air Force in Japan. In 1950, he was responsible for the evacuation of dependents from South Korea. He took the Fifth Air Force from Japan to Korea and commanded it until June 1951. During this time, his unit supported the ground war and maintained a heavy schedule of bombardment against enemy targets. In the summer of 1951, he directed the Research and Development Command and then, in 1954 and 1955, was back in Japan in command of the Far East Air Force. In 1960, he became a trustee of Aerospace Corporation. He died on September 7, 1990.

Pearson, Lester (1897–1972)
Canadian secretary of state
Pearson was the Canadian secretary of state for external affairs during the period of the Korean War. While he supported the U.S. foreign policy, he was concerned about the implications of that policy when it came to dealing with China. He was highly critical of General Douglas MacArthur who, he believed, was arrogant and belligerent. He was in favor of a negotiated settlement of the war,

and worked with Great Britain and India to break the deadlock on the cease-fire issue of prisoner repatriation. He was alarmed by the growing possibility that the war would expand and worked with British foreign minister Anthony Eden and India's V. K. Krishna Menon to support the peace talks. He was considered as a replacement for UN secretary-general but his nomination was blocked by the Soviet Union. He later became chancellor of Carleton University.

Peng Dehuai (P'eng Te-huai) (1898–1974)
Commander, Chinese People's Volunteers
Born in Hunan province, China, on October 24, 1898, Peng Dehuai was involved early on in revolutionary activities, having joined a warlord in 1916 and taking a significant role in the Pingchiang Uprising. He fought in the defense of the Red Army on its Long March. In the war with the Chinese Nationalists, he commanded the People's Liberation Army in the northwest. In October 1950, he was appointed commander of the People's Volunteer Army that was to fight in Korea. He launched three major offensives that drove the United Nations back across the 38th parallel and, after the UN advance, conducted an active defense. He was one of the signers of the armistice agreement. In 1955, he was awarded the title of marshal, but in 1959, he spoke out against Mao Zedong's radical economic efforts and was arrested and given a partial rehabilitation. He was arrested again at the beginning of the Cultural Revolution. He died in a prison hospital on November 29, 1974.

Pyun Yung Tai (Pyon Yong-Tae) (1892–1969)
Minister of foreign affairs, Republic of Korea
As minister of foreign affairs for the Republic of Korea (1951–55), this scholar was an advocate of President Syngman Rhee's policies, taking a hard anti-Communist, anti-Japanese, and unification stance during the discussions at Panmunjom. He was an able spokesperson in exchanges with repre-

sentatives of other nations. He advocated "moral totalitarianism" as a response to Communism.

Qin Jiwen (Chin Chi-wen) (1914–1997)
Minister of defense, People's Republic of China
During his long career, Qin Jiwen advanced from private soldier in a revolutionary army to minister of defense for the People's Republic of China. His 15th Army entered Korea in 1951, and his unit saw some of the most difficult fighting of the war. After the war, he served as deputy commander of the Yenan (Yunnan) Military District and then as political commissar of the Second Field Army. In 1988, he was named the minister of defense, a position he held until 1993.

Radford, Arthur W. (1896–1973)
Commander in chief, Pacific Fleet
Born in Chicago, Illinois, on February 27, 1896, he graduated from the Naval Academy in 1916. He served in World War I aboard the USS *South Carolina*. During the 1920s and 1930s, he served with a variety of aviation assignments. During World War II, he was executive officer on the carrier USS *Yorktown*. From 1941 to 1943, as captain, he headed aviation training for the Bureau of Aeronautics. From 1943 to 1944, he commanded the Northern Carrier Group, and in 1944 was named assistant deputy chief of naval operations. In April 1949, Vice Admiral Radford became commander of the Pacific Fleet. A leading figure in the "revolt of the admirals," he was a strong proponent of naval air power. In 1953, he succeeded General of the Army Omar Bradley as chairman of the Joint Chiefs of Staff and held the post until his retirement in August 1957. He died in Bethesda, Maryland, on August 17, 1973.

Ridgway, Matthew B. (1895–1993)
Commander, Eighth Army
Matthew Ridgway was commander of the Eighth United States Army in Korea (EUSAK) from December 23, 1950, to April 11, 1951, at which time he became supreme commander, UNC. He held this position until May 11, 1952. Ridgway, born in

Fort Monroe, Virginia, graduated from West Point in 1917. After a year as an infantry officer, he returned to West Point as an instructor. In 1925, he commanded an infantry company in China and in 1927 was sent on several diplomatic missions to Nicaragua, the Panama Canal Zone, the Philippines, and Brazil. During World War II, he served with the Department of War's planning division. In August 1942, Ridgway was given command of the newly formed 82nd Airborne Division and jumped with his troops into battle during the invasion of Normandy. In August 1944, he commanded the new 18th Airborne Corps and operated in the Netherlands, Belgium, and Germany. In 1946, he was a military adviser to the U.S. delegation to the United Nations General Assembly in London.

He assumed command of Eighth Army in Korea in December 1950 and was able to reverse the low morale among the military and to halt and then throw back the massive Chinese offensive. When MacArthur was relieved in April 1951, Ridgway succeeded him as commander in chief in the Far East. In May 1952, Ridgway succeeded General Dwight D. Eisenhower as supreme commander, NATO. Ridgway became army chief of staff in 1953. He clashed with his superiors, however, over the question of downgrading the role of ground forces and, frustrated, he retired in 1955. His memoir, *Soldier,* was published in 1956.

Roberts, William L. (1891–1969)
Commander, Korean Military Advisory Group
On June 30, 1949, the United States established the Korean Military Advisory Group, designed to prepare the South Korean army to defend its country. Before this, Brigadier General William Roberts had been head of the Provisional Korean Military Advisory Group. When the United States pulled out its troops, Roberts took command of the remaining troops (the 5th Regimental Combat Team). Determined to complete his task, he engaged in a public relations campaign to portray the ROK as being far stronger than it was—on June 5, 1950, he told *Time* magazine that the ROK army was "best doggone shooting army outside

the United States"—leading to a great deal of bad information about ROK capabilities to stop a North Korean invasion. He left Korea for retirement only a week before the invasion.

Rusk, Dean (1909–1994)
Assistant secretary of state
Born in Cherokee County, Georgia, Rusk entered World War II as a captain. In April 1945, he was asked to go to Washington to aid in planning for the postwar world, then held several posts with the Department of State and the Department of Defense. In 1950, he became assistant secretary of state for Far Eastern affairs. He was heavily involved with the decision to go to war and with the negotiations with the United Nations. In 1952, he became president of the Rockefeller Foundation and continued to be a spokesman for foreign affairs. President John F. Kennedy called on him to serve as secretary of state in 1961. He died on December 20, 1994, in Athens, Georgia.

Shepherd, Lemuel C., Jr. (1896–1990)
Commander, Fleet Marine Force
Born in Norfolk, Virginia, in 1896, he served in France in World War I. Taking a commission in the marines, he was wounded three times. After the war, he became an aide to General John Lejeune and served in a variety of military posts and attended the primary military schools. In 1940, he commanded the 9th Marine Regiment. Promoted to brigadier general in 1943 and then major general, he commanded marine units in the Pacific. He took command of Fleet Marine Forces in the Pacific in 1950. He was with MacArthur at Inchon as a personal adviser. He was promoted to general in 1952 and became the commandant of the Marine Corps. He retired in 1956.

Sherman, Forrest P. (1896–1951)
Chief of naval operations
Sherman was chief of naval operations when the Korean War broke out and was at the Blair House meetings during the early days of the war. But perhaps his most important contribution to the war came in the preceding years when he successfully fought for a balanced military that could meet the Soviet threat wherever it might appear. The availability of adequate naval forces to meet the needs in Korea was a direct result of his ability to deal with both the Congress and representatives of the other services. He came to this position after a long and successful career as a naval officer, rising to vice admiral at the close of World War II. He served as deputy chief for operations, during which time he was a significant player in the development of the U.S. strategic position. In July 1951, on his way to negotiations over U.S. bases in France and Spain, he suffered a series of heart attacks and died.

Smith, Oliver P. (1893–1997)
Commander, First Marine Division
Oliver Smith was born in Menard, Texas, on October 26, 1893, and graduated from the University of California at Berkeley in 1916. In World War I, he was commissioned a lieutenant in the Marine Reserves. While stationed at Guam he transferred to the regular Marine Corps. Between the wars, he held a variety of assignments and attended military schools. During World War II, he served for nearly two years as executive officer of the Division of Plans and Policies at Marine Corps headquarters. In March 1944, Smith assumed command of the 5th Marine Regiment and saw service in the South Pacific. Later that year, he received his first star and became assistant commander of the 1st Marine Division.

Assigned to Korea, Major General Smith, commanding the 1st Marine Division, was given the job of the amphibious landing at Inchon. After the invasion and the drive along the east coast toward Chosin, he led the retreat, claiming he "was attacking in another direction." His unit then took part in the Eighth Army counteroffensive in February 1951. On April 24, 1951, he relinquished command and returned to direct operations at Camp Pendleton. In 1953, he was promoted to lieutenant general and given command of the Fleet Marine Force, Atlantic. He retired in 1955 as a general. He died in Los Altos, California, on Christmas Day, 1997.

Song-Shinlun (1907–1991)
Commander, CPV 9th Army Group

Song-Shinlun was a graduate of Whampoa Military Academy and a participant in the Long March. He commanded the People's Liberation Army, Ninth Army Group, during the Korean War. A successful battlefield commander, he was appointed director of the PLA Academy of Military Science. He died in 1991.

Stalin, Joseph (1879–1953)
General secretary, Communist Party (Soviet Union)

Born in 1879 as Iosif Vissarionovich Dzhugashvili in the town of Gori, Georgia, Stalin attended the Gori Church School. He was general secretary of the Communist Party of the Union of Soviet Socialist Republics from 1922 to 1953. More than any other person, he dominated, and molded, the features of the Soviet Union. He led the army in its counterattack against Nazi forces during World War II. By 1950, Stalin's health had begun to deteriorate. He feared the consequences of an attack on Korea by the north but finally allowed it when he became convinced the United States was not going to enter any conflict. In 1950, he gave Kim Il Sung his cautious endorsement. A political aggressor, he already controlled many subject states and saw the events in Korea as another opportunity to expand the influence of international communism.

In January 1953, Stalin ordered the arrest of a group of Kremlin doctors on the grounds that they were plotting the medical murder of high-ranking officials. Just as it appeared there would be another purge, Stalin died of a stroke in March 1953. After his death, negotiations over the Korean War took on a more serious tone.

Stratemeyer, George Edward (1890–1969)
Commander, Far East Air Force

USAF general and commander of the Far East Air Force, George Stratemeyer was born in Cincinnati, Ohio, on November 24, 1890. He attended the U.S. Military Academy at West Point and completed flight training in 1917. From 1920 to the beginning of World War II, he held several assignments, primarily related to the air arm, and rose through the ranks. In 1938, he was promoted to lieutenant colonel and commanded the 7th Bombardment Group. During World War II, he was chief of the Army Air Corps in Washington, then, as major general, commander of the Army Air Corps in the China theater. In 1945, he was promoted to lieutenant general. He moved to Tokyo as commanding general of the Far East Air Force in 1949 and took command in 1950 of the war effort in Korea. He supported President Harry Truman's decision to dismiss General Douglas MacArthur. He had a heart attack in May 1951 and retired from active duty January 31, 1952. He died in Orlando, Florida, on August 9, 1969.

Struble, Arthur D. (1894–1983)
Commander, Seventh Fleet

In May 1950, Arthur Struble was given command of the Seventh Fleet and in June was ordered to prevent the Chinese Communists from attacking the island of Taiwan. He commanded Task Force Seven, which was assigned to land X Corps at Inchon, Korea. He remained there to oversee the east coast evacuation of X Corps from Hungnam after the retreat from the Chosin Reservoir.

Born in Portland, Oregon, in 1894, he attended the Naval Academy and rose in rank through a variety of sea and shore assignments. In November 1943, he was appointed to the planning of the D-day landings at Omaha and Utah beaches and helped oversee those landings. In August 1944, he commanded Group Two, Seventh Amphibious Force, in the Pacific. In 1946, he was given command of Amphibious Forces Pacific Fleet.

He retired from the navy as a full admiral in July 1956, after which he chaired the United States Military Staff Mission to the United Nations.

Syngman Rhee (1875–1965)
President, Republic of Korea

Born in Hwanghae province, Korea, on April 26, 1875, Syngman Rhee was a dedicated nationalist and an ambitious leader from his early years. He led a demonstration against the Japanese in 1897 and was condemned to life imprisonment but was released in 1904 during an amnesty. He went to the United States and studied at Harvard and Princeton Universities where, at the latter, he received his Ph.D. After a brief return to Korea he went to Hawaii. In 1919, he was named president of the Korean government in exile. After the end of World War II, he became the leader, then president, of South Korea and began his efforts at unification. A determined nationalist and individualist, he was a source of constant difficulty for the Americans. He maintained strict control over his nation. He did everything he could to prevent the signing of an armistice; in fact, South Korea never did sign it. Reelected to his fourth term in 1960, he was accused of rigging the election. Student demonstrations protesting corruption in government led to riots that forced him out of office in May 1960. At that time, he went into exile in Hawaii. He died on July 19, 1965.

Taft, Robert A. (1889–1953)
U.S. senator

An outspoken critic of the Truman administration, Senator Taft (R-Ohio) supported the original decision to send troops to Korea. But, after the war started, he attacked Truman for not seeking a declaration of war, and for his bungling and inconsistent foreign affairs. As the war went on, he increased his criticism of the failure to win a victory, and supported numerous positions contrary to the administration's policies; defended General Douglas MacArthur; and supported the use of Nationalist troops offered by Chiang Kai-shek (Jiang Jieshi) and the bombing of Chinese supply lines in Manchuria. He sought the nomination for his party in the presidential election of 1952 but lost out to Dwight D. Eisenhower.

Taylor, Maxwell D. (1901–1987)
Commander, Eighth Army

As the commander of Eighth Army in Korea, beginning in February 1953, Maxwell Taylor took on one of the most difficult tasks given to a field

commander: attack and negotiate. President Eisenhower, determined to end the war, had expressed a willingness to use atomic weapons if necessary. In March 1953, the Chinese launched a massive series of attacks near Old Baldy and Pork Chop Hill, which Taylor defended and then withdrew from because of the disproportionate number of casualties. Yet he supported the ROK units that were focused in the attack. He had to deal with President Rhee's release of POWs, which was designed to disrupt the armistice talks, but also caused the Chinese to intensify their attacks on ROK units.

A successful career officer, he had served in World War II, led the predawn assault at Normandy as commanding general of the 101st Airborne Division, and after the war served as superintendent of West Point. Before being assigned to Korea, he was deputy army chief of staff for operations. Following the war, he worked at rebuilding the South Korean army, became U.S. Army chief of staff in 1955, and retired in 1959. Called back into the service after the failure of the Bay of Pigs invasion of Cuba, he was chairman of the JCS and ambassador to Saigon.

Truman, Harry S. (1884–1972)
President of the United States

From the beginning, President Harry Truman considered the invasion of South Korea to be a part of a larger, cold-war threat, possibly a diversion for an attack in Europe. He appears to have been genuinely surprised at the outbreak of violence. He entered the discussions at Blair House pretty well determined to take some action and, after serious discussion, agreed to the commitment of American forces. He was concerned about a larger war in the Orient, but also believed that action was required to maintain the credibility of the United States and the United Nations. His decision to act without congressional approval was legal, but questionable, and would haunt him and his other decisions about the war for the rest of his life. He never liked General Douglas MacArthur; the decision to relieve him came fairly easily and he had considerable support in his decision from the Joint Chiefs of Staff. As a result, however, his popularity rate dropped to a low of 23 percent. While he was interpreted on one occasion as considering the use of atomic weapons, there is no serious evidence that he ever had any intention of doing so. Certainly his insistence on the voluntary repatriation of POWs prolonged the peace talks for more than a year. His popularity had fallen so low by the election year of 1952 that he did not consider the option of running for a third term in office (the last president to have such an option), and he was replaced by General Eisenhower, who promised to end the war. He maintained, throughout the rest of his life, that his toughest decision as president was taking the United States into war in Korea.

Vandenberg, Hoyt Sanford (1899–1954)
U.S. Air Force chief of staff

Air Force chief of staff Hoyt Vandenberg was born in Milwaukee, Wisconsin, on January 24, 1899. He graduated from the Military Academy at West Point in 1923 and was commissioned a second lieutenant in the air service. During World War II, he was a top planner and, at the end of the war, became director of military intelligence (G-2) of the army general staff. President Harry Truman, in 1946, appointed him director of the newly created Central Intelligence Agency and, the following year, vice chief of staff for the newly formed air force. In 1948, Truman appointed him chief of staff, U.S. Air Force.

President Harry S. Truman and General Douglas MacArthur meeting for the first time, on Wake Island, at a conference on Communist aggression in the Far East, the Korean War, and world peace, October 14, 1950 *(Harry S. Truman Library)*

He supported the U.S. involvement in Korea, though he was not enthusiastic about it and was cautious in the matter of the Chinese and Soviet borders. He considered the advisability of a U.S. withdrawal from the conflict in 1952. In March 1953, he was one of the officers who urged President Dwight D. Eisenhower to use strategic and tactical nuclear weapons to end the war. He retired on June 30, 1953, and died on April 4, 1954, in Washington.

Van Fleet, James (1892–1992)
Commander, Eighth Army

Born in Coytesville, New Jersey, on March 19, 1892, Van Fleet graduated from the U.S. Military Academy in 1915 as a second lieutenant of infantry. He participated in the Mexican border campaign (1916–17) and in World War I. In February 1941, as a colonel, he commanded the 8th Infantry Regiment. Promoted to brigadier general, Van Fleet was assistant commander of the 2nd Infantry Division, then was placed in command of the 4th Infantry Division. In 1945, as a major general, he commanded III Corps.

General James Van Fleet was assigned to Korea in April 1951 and given command of Eighth Army. He arrived just as the Chinese Communists and North Koreans were preparing to launch their greatest military effort. He led a major offensive against the Chinese Communist forces after the truce talks stalled. In November 1951, Van Fleet was ordered to cease offensive action. An aggressive leader, he chafed under the restrictions imposed on his leadership. He relinquished his command in February 1953 and two months later retired from the army.

During the Eisenhower administration, he served as special ambassador to the Far East and from 1961 to 1962 served as a consultant on guerrilla warfare for the Office of the Secretary of the Army.

Walker, Walton H. (1899–1950)
Commander, 8th Army

Lieutenant General Walker was commander of the U.S. Eighth Army in Korea from July 17, 1950, until his death on December 23, 1950. Born in Belton, Texas, he entered Virginia Military Institute in

The commanding general of the Armed Forces in Korea, Lieutenant General Walton Walker, with Colonel Alford G. Katzin, a personal representative of the United Nations, July 24, 1950 *(Harry S. Truman Library)*

1907. During World War I, he saw action and received the Silver Star for bravery. In 1942, he assumed command of 3rd Armored Division. One of General Patton's "generals," he adopted many of the senior officer's characteristics. After World War II, he filled a variety of assignments before being given command of all U.S. ground troops in Korea. He was commander during the trying days of the initial retreat and in the defense of Pusan. Pressing the attack toward the Yalu River, he managed the withdrawal that followed the Chinese intervention. He directed the retreat and by early December had moved his Eighth Army south of the 38th parallel.

Walker was killed in December 1950 in a road accident while passing a stalled South Korean convoy; he was replaced by General Matthew B. Ridgway. He is buried at Arlington National Cemetery.

West, Sir Michael M. A. A. (1905–1978)
Commander, Commonwealth Division

During World War II, Michael West was a regimental and brigade commander of British troops in Europe; in 1950, he was appointed as commander of British occupation troops in Austria. In 1952, he assumed command of the Commonwealth Division in Korea. His division was on the line during most of the period when the fighting and the negotiations were carried on in concert. While a tough fighter and determined leader, with a long list of military successes, he clashed with U.S. authorities on the need for offensive pressure during the negotiations. His contributions to the war included his ability to deal with the manpower problem caused by limited replacements and the continued diplomacy necessary to maintain a working relationship between the various nations represented in the Commonwealth Division. After the war, he served as chairman of the British Defense Staff in Washington. He retired in 1965.

Weyland, Otto P. (1902–1979)
Commander, Far East Air Force

Born in Riverside, California, Otto Weyland received his commission in the Air Corps Reserve in 1923. During World War II, he commanded the 19th Tactical Air Command. In 1945, he served as commander of the Ninth Air Force and then was assigned to lead the Command and General Staff School. He also served as assistant chief of staff for planning and then as deputy commander of the National War College. In 1950, he was assigned as Far East Air Force's vice commander and later took command, replacing General Stratemeyer. He was an advocate for the power of interdiction and used the air force to bring pressure on the Communists to respond at the Panmunjom cease-fire talks. On his return to the United States, he served as commander of the Tactical Air Command until he retired in 1959.

Whitney, Courtney (1897–1969)
Aide to General Douglas MacArthur

Beginning his military career in 1917 as a private in the National Guard, Courtney Whitney went on to assume assignments in the areas of legal concerns and military publications, which included a stint as adjutant for the 66th Service Squadron in the Philippines. After an assignment in Washington, he resigned from the army to return to the Philippines. There he practiced law and became a friend of General Douglas MacArthur. He returned to active duty as a major and, in 1944, went to the Philippines to organize MacArthur's secret service. After World War II, General Whitney followed MacArthur to Japan and served with him during the occupation. When the Korean War broke out, he was a significant adviser to General MacArthur and was his primary defender. After MacArthur's dismissal in April 1951, General Whitney served as his press secretary during the Joint Congressional Committee hearings called to investigate the war in Asia. He promoted the view that the Chinese Communists would not have entered the war if the United States had followed MacArthur's wishes and threatened to bomb Manchuria. Loyal to the end, he wrote one of the most defensive of the many books written on his commander, MacArthur: His Rendezvous with History.

Willoughby, Charles A. (1892–1972)
Intelligence officer to General Douglas MacArthur

Born in Heidelberg, Germany, Charles Willoughby came to America in 1910 and enlisted in the army. In 1916, he reentered the army and, as a second lieutenant, served on the Mexican border and later in France, where he flew as a pursuit pilot. Willoughby was a captain teaching at the Command and Staff College at Fort Leavenworth, Kansas, when he met General Douglas MacArthur. In 1940, MacArthur sent for Willoughby and there followed a long period of dedicated and loyal service. He began his duties as a supply officer but soon assumed the duties of G-2 (Intelligence). He predicted that there would be no civil war in Korea and, when the war broke out, he continued to paint a picture of an orderly retreat, with the South Korean government still in control. He considered the Chinese buildup prior to their invasion as "diplomatic blackmail," and right up to the Chinese intervention he continued to express the view that neither the Chinese nor Soviets would become involved. When the Chinese entered the war, he identified them as a poorly trained unit, most likely only isolated volunteers with no combat experience against a major power. He seemed unwilling to acknowledge the extent of the Chinese intervention. Even after UN Command forces began a massive retreat, he viewed the Chinese attack as "a minor one" and his estimates of the number of Chinese troops involved were always low.

After the war, Willoughby was often blamed for providing General MacArthur with poor intelligence; it is also generally agreed that he provided MacArthur with what the general wanted to hear. When MacArthur was released by President Harry Truman in April 1951, General Willoughby voluntarily resigned. After retiring from the U.S. Army he became the editor of *Foreign Intelligence Digest*. He used this position to continue the defense of his service and that of General Douglas MacArthur. He died in 1972.

Xie Feng (Hsieh Fang) (1904–1983?)
Chief of staff, Chinese People's Volunteer Army
During the Korean War, Xie Feng was chief of staff of the Chinese People's Volunteer Army. He had served as a staff officer in the Kuomintang (Guomindang) Northeast Army, which fought the Chinese Communists in 1935. During the Sino-Japanese war, he commanded a brigade and in 1939 joined the Communist Party, taking many of his troops with him. He went to the Soviet Union to study modern warfare. In June 1950, he was appointed chief of the Thirteenth Group Army. He was involved in the planning of all five major Chinese campaigns, but perhaps made his greatest contribution by maintaining an acceptable relationship between the Chinese Communist and North Korean leadership.

Zhou Enlai (Chou En-lai) (1898–1976)
Premier/foreign minister, People's Republic of China
Premier and foreign minister of the People's Republic of China during the Korean War, Chou was a significant figure in the decision to invade the Republic of Korea. He was totally against the U.S. policy concerning Taiwan and opposed the American reaction to the invasion. He saw this as a violation of previously understood U.S. policy. He worked tirelessly to avoid a direct confrontation between the United States and China. He was the one who issued the statement, sent through K. M. Panikkar of India, warning the United States that it must not cross the 38th parallel.

He became involved in the Communist movement when, as a student in France during World War I, he joined the Chinese Communist Youth League. He managed to delay the civil war in China (1936) long enough for the Chinese factions to unite against the Japanese invasion. He was a participant in the U.S. attempts—General Marshall's efforts at negotiations—to end the civil war and then was involved in the formation of the People's Republic of China. Following the death of Joseph Stalin in 1953, he led China in its difficult agreement to agenda item four (repatriation of POWs) and the eventual armistice. He died in 1976.

WEAPONS

The nations that participated in the Korean War used a wide variety of weapons. Most of the weapons that were available were those left over from World War II, and there are far too many of them to all be listed here. The Communist nations, in particular, put into use weapons confiscated from previous actions, including a good many American weapons taken from the Nationalist Chinese at the end of the Chinese Civil War, as well as those left behind by troops cut off in the opening days of the Korean War. As well, the various nations that made up United Nations Command, though armed primarily by the United States, brought with them weapons of all kinds. The following list describes only those weapons that were fairly standard or were, at least, in wide use.

UNITED STATES AND ITS ALLIES, INFANTRY WEAPONS

A note about nomenclature: During the Korean War, the U.S. Army Ordnance Department continued the nomenclature system used during World War II. These are:

T—indicates an experimental item (e.g., T-26 heavy tank)

E—indicates a major change that affects a weapon's operational characteristics

M—is used to indicate that a piece of equipment has been adopted as standard

A1—is used to indicate that a piece of standard equipment has been modified

B—suggests a change in components used in the production of the item, usually caused by a shortage of parts.

WEAPONS USED BY UNITED NATIONS TROOPS

U.S. Rifle, Caliber .30 (M-1) (Garand)

The Garand was the primary weapon used by American and Republic of Korea troops as well as by many of the UN regiments. First introduced by John C. Garand in 1920, it became the standard weapon of the infantry in 1936 and was a mainstay during World War II. It was equally popular in Korea. The rifle was a gas-operated, semiautomatic weapon with an eight-round internal clip. It weighed 9.5 pounds (10.5 with bayonet) and had an effective range of about 550 meters. The M-1 could fire at a rate of about 30 rounds per minute. Two versions were used (with telescopic sights) as sniper weapons.

U.S. Carbine, Caliber .30 (M-1)

The carbine was designed to be an intermediary between the weight and velocity of a rifle and the lightweight but unreliable pistol. The carbine was considered underpowered by many of the men who carried it because its shorter barrel and lighter ammunition restricted both its range and hitting power. Considered as a replacement for the pistol, it was carried primarily by officers, non-commissioned officers, and support troops, including artillerymen, who needed less fire power. The carbine was gas-operated and could fire both semiautomatically and fully automatically. It accepted a 15- to 30-round detachable box magazine and weighed 6.5 pounds. It had an effective range of about 300 meters and a cyclical rate of fire of 750 rounds per minute. The M-1A1 had a folding stock and was used by airborne troops.

Pistol, Caliber .45 M-1911 (A-1)

The .45 pistol was the standard sidearm for U.S. States troops. With minor changes, it was basically the same weapon that was developed before World War I. It served through both World Wars and Korea with distinction and was carried by field-grade officers, gun crews, tankers, and others whose duties made carrying a rifle difficult. It was a large semiautomatic pistol with an effective range of 25 yards. The U.S. government also made some commercially available weapons, all of which used the .38 caliber Police Special cartridge.

Sniper Rifle (M-1903A1)

Using an M-82 Marine Corps contract eight-power scope, this World War I bolt-action weapon was effective up to 1,000 yards.

Browning Automatic Rifle (BAR), Caliber .30 M-1918 (A-2)

Considered by many as the most effective infantry weapon, the BAR was the basic automatic support weapon and the mainstay of the squad during both World War II and Korea. One or more were issued to each squad. The BAR used the same ammunition as the M-1 Garand and could be fired either semiautomatically or fully automatically. It took a 20-round detachable box magazine. It weighed about 16 pounds and had a rate of fire

between 300 and 600 rounds per minute. Its effective range was about 800 meters. It could be fired either as a shoulder weapon or supported by an integral bipod.

Submachine Gun M-1938 (A-1)

Made by Browning, this was an open-bolt, blow-back, selective-fire weapon. It weighed about 10 pounds and was used during World War II. One version, known as the "grease gun," was equipped with a retractable wire stock and made out of stamped steel.

Submachine Gun, Sten Mark

This 9-mm selective fire gun was used primarily by Australian troops and was similar to the Austin Mark I, the Mark II, and the 9-mm Owen Mark I. These weapons were manufactured in Great Britain and used a .303 caliber round. They were gas-operated and carried a 30-round magazine.

U.S. Machine Gun, Caliber .30 M-1919 (A-3) (Light)

The M-1919A3 was developed during World War II, and it was basically the same weapon as the M-1917A except that the 1919A3 was air-cooled. This distinction makes it much lighter but also reduces the range, accuracy, and rate of fire. Each rifle platoon had one or more of these weapons assigned to it.

U.S. Machine Gun, Caliber .30 M-1917 (A-1) (Heavy)

Developed during World War I and used extensively in World War II, this gun fired the same ammunition as the M-1 rifle and BAR. It was issued to weapons companies, and an infantry division would have nearly 500 of these weapons. Fed by a belt, it could fire more than 500 rounds per minute. A heavy, water-cooled gun, it was mounted on a tripod.

U.S. Machine Gun, Caliber .50 (Browning)
Primarily a mounted weapon, it was used on trucks, tanks, and other tracked vehicles as an infantry support weapon. Air-cooled it had a heavy barrel and could fire about 575 rounds per minute.

Rocket Launcher, 2.36 inch (Bazooka)
This rocket launcher fired a hollow-shaped charge that could penetrate tank armor. It was not very effective, however, against powerful tanks like the Russian T-34s that were used by the North Koreans. It also may have been less efficient because of poor training with the weapon and the fact that, during the early period of the Korean War, so much of the old ammunition was duds. The UN divisions in Korea were given about 600 of these weapons. It weighed about 15 pounds and consisted primarily of an aluminum tube. It was effective up to about 65 meters against medium tank armor.

Rocket Launcher, 3.5 inch (Bazooka)
This larger rocket launcher was issued as a long-awaited replacement for the 2.35 inch during the early days of the Korean War. Firing an 8.5-pound projectile, it could stop a T-34 if done perfectly. As replacements occurred, each division would have about 600 of these weapons available.

Recoilless Rifles, 57 mm, 75 mm, 106 mm
These weapons fired a traditional artillery shell along a flat trajectory. The high blast from escaping gases prevented recoil, and they were effective against both troops and fortifications. The 57 mm could be manned by a two-man crew as a shoulder weapon with a maximum range of about 4,300 yards. The larger calibers required a crew and were mounted, but they also had longer ranges. The 75 mm had a range of about 6,000 yards and was sometimes mounted on a machine-gun carriage. The 57 mm was the most available, but the 106 mm, developed during the Korean War, was much more effective.

Grenades
Each of the basic types can be converted to be launched as a rifle grenade.

Offensive: The Mark IIIA-1 held about eight ounces of flaked TNT and was designed to cause demolition and to stun the enemy. By 1953, most of the concussion grenades were half-pound blocks of C-3 packed in a cardboard case and set off by the standard fragmentation timed fuse. Despite its distinction, they were most widely used from defensive positions.

Fragmentation: Contains an explosive charge in a metal body designed to break into fragments. It had a killing radius of from five to 10 yards and was dangerous up to 50 yards. These grenades came with a time-delay safety pin of about four seconds. The Mark IIA-1 was the most common. It weighed about 21 ounces and was made of cast iron that broke into about 1,000 fragments. There were also a good number of the British "Mills Bomb" (36 M), which was larger, weighing about two pounds and using a seven-second fuse. It had a pattern of about 80 yards.

Chemical: These grenades produced casualties by unleashing a toxic or irritating effect. The category also included grenades used for signal smoke or as incendiaries. Baseball-size tear gas grenades were special issue for riot control. The most common was the M-15 White Phosphorous that weighed about 32 ounces with a four-second time delay. It had a burst radius of about 25 yards and burned for almost a minute. Also in use was the M-6 irritant gas and the M-7A1 tear gas.

Bangalore Torpedo: Usually identified with the grenade, this was simply a three-foot length of pipe filled with flaked TNT or C-3 and capped at both ends. The fuse was screwed into one end of the pipe. Several pipes could be screwed together. It was designed to blow a hole in barbed wire or other obstacles.

UNITED NATIONS ARTILLERY AND MORTARS

In many respects, Korea was an artillery war. Massive numbers of artillery pieces were in use, both among UN troops and Communist forces. The development of the proximity fuse during World War II meant that artillery could be directed toward targets and timed to explode near or above those targets, rather than on them, thus causing a larger number of casualties.

Recoilless Rifle, 106-mm M-40

Designed primarily as an antitank weapon, it required a two-man crew. It had a range of up to 1,100 yards and a rate of four rounds per minute. It weighed 250 pounds and was 11 feet long, without tripod.

Infantry Mortar, 60 mm (M-224), 81 mm (M-29A1, M-252), 4.2 inch

These mortars were primarily infantry anti-personnel weapons. As indirect fire weapons, they were used to attack unseen targets located in dead spaces, trenches, or valleys. The mortars were sealed-breech tubes, mounted on a heavy baseplate and supported by a bipod, that fired high projectiles toward targets in an arc. The 60 mm was carried by rifle companies and had a range of 1,800 yards. The 81 mm weighed more than 100 pounds but had an effective range of 4,000 yards and was assigned to a weapons company. The 4.2 inch was manned by a special mortar company with the regiment. While carried by infantry units it was almost an artillery weapon and was usually mounted on a vehicle of some kind. The 4.2 inch was probably the most used UN mortar during the Korean War.

Multiple Gun Motor Carriage, Quad .50 (M-16)

A carryover from World War II, this was a 10-ton half-track vehicle (wheels in front and tracks in back) with four .50-caliber machine guns capable of being fired as a unit. Originally designed as an antiaircraft weapon, it found considerable use as an antipersonnel weapon. It could throw as many as 100,000 rounds per day into an area or against an advancing enemy.

Multiple Gun Motor Carriage, Dual 40 mm (M-19)

Designed as an antiaircraft weapon, it was a fully tracked vehicle with a tanklike silhouette. It mounted two Bofors 40-mm antiaircraft cannons. Outdated by the faster moving aircraft, it was put to a new use in the same manner as the Quad .50, as an infantry support weapon.

Howitzer, 105 mm (M-101A1)

Production of this gun began in 1920, and by the time manufacturing stopped at the end of the Korean War, more than 10,200 weapons had been produced. It had a range of about 12,000 yards (nearly seven miles) and a rate of fire of 100 rounds per hour. It was mounted on a two-wheeled carriage and on a tracked vehicle as a self-propelled artillery piece. The backbone of the artillery in Korea, it could fire up to 20,000 rounds before a barrel had to be replaced. Some were fixed on a chassis as a self-propelled piece identified as the M-7.

Gun (Long Tom), 155 mm (M-1A1)

An innovation based on the 1930 French 155 gun, it used the same carriage as the M-1 8-inch howitzer and was pulled by a utility vehicle or a 10-ton truck. It had a range of about 25,000 yards (14 miles) and could fire up to 60 rounds per hour. It took a full crew of 14. It was sometimes identified as the M-59 and, when mounted on a self-propelled tracked chassis, as the M-40.

Howitzer, 203.2 mm (8 inch) (M-1)

A massive weapon developed during World War II, it weighed about 15 tons and was mounted on a four-wheeled carriage. It was about 36 feet in length. The weapon was towed by either a 10-ton truck or a tracked utility vehicle and required a full crew of 14 about 20 minutes to set up. It had a range of 18,000 yards (about 10 miles) and could be fired at a rate of 30 rounds per hour.

"Atomic Cannon," 280 mm

Powerful enough to destroy an entire hill, a few of these massive weapons were deployed, but there is no documented case in which they were used.

United Nations and Its Allies: Tanks and Armored Vehicles

Centurion Cruiser, MK II (U.K.)

This British-built heavy tank weighed 58 tons, carried a 120-pound (83.4-mm) gun and two or three machine guns. It could reach a speed of 21.5 mph and a range of 60 miles. It was too heavy and often too wide for most Korean bridges. Carried a crew of four.

Churchill VIII (U.K.)

Operated with a crew of five. It carried a 75-mm gun and two machine guns. It was powered by a Bedford twin-6 engine, weighed 44.9 tons, and could travel at a rate of 15.9 mph for a range of 90 miles.

Heavy Cruiser, Comet (A-34)

The Comet was armed with a 76.2-mm gun (called 77-mm), two machine guns, and was crewed by five men. The 33-ton tank was powered by a 600-hp engine and could reach a speed of 29 mph.

Reconnaissance, Cromwell (A27-M)

Powered by a Rolls-Royce V-12 Meteor engine, this 28-ton tank could travel 40 mph. Armed with a 75-mm gun and two machine guns, it was manned by a crew of five.

Medium Tank, Sherman (M-4A3E8)

This World War II, 35-ton medium tank became the primary tank of the Korean War. It was armed with a high-velocity 76-mm main gun and an M2 .50-caliber heavy machine gun mounted on the turret, plus a .30-caliber medium machine gun mounted in the hull. It was protected by 63-mm-thick armor in front and 38-mm-thick on the sides. Its wide track and mechanical system made it well suited for the terrain in Korea, and it could move at speeds up to 26 mph and with a range of 100 miles. The power pack was a Ford V-8 gasoline-fueled engine capable of 500 hp. It fired a 22-pound M-42A1 high-explosive round and the T-4HVAP-t, a tungsten-cored "hyper-shot" antitank round, as well as the M-62 APC-T, which could penetrate 90 mm of armor at 1,000 meters. It was crewed by five men.

Chaffee, M-24

Introduced in 1943 as a light tank, but employed periodically as a reconnaissance unit, it had a squat hull and turret with relatively thin armor. It was armed with a 75-mm medium-velocity cannon and two .30-caliber and one .50-caliber machine guns. It weighed about 18 tons and, powered by two Cadillac V-8 gas engines, was capable of speeds up to 35 mph an hour. It had a range limitation of about 110 miles and was operated by a crew of five.

Pershing (Heavy), M-26

Introduced in 1945, this 46-ton tank was operated by a crew of five. It could reach speeds of 25 mph with a range of 100 miles. It was armed with a 90-mm main gun, a .50-caliber machine gun on the turret, and a .30-caliber machine gun mounted in the hull. It was powered by a Ford 500-hp gas engine. Larger than the Sherman, it had, nevertheless, a lower silhouette and was just slightly slower.

Patton, M-46 (M-47)

In 1948, pending the release of a totally new tank design, the M-46 Patton was provided as a utility tank. Nearly 2,000 of these had been in storage since the end of World War II, and they were rebuilt, giving them newly developed engines and transmissions. When the Korean War broke out, the T-42 was still in development, but its turret and range finder were mounted on the M-46 and thus the M-47 was created. It weighed 48.5 tons and was armed with a 90-mm gun and two .30-caliber and one .50-caliber machine guns. It carried a crew of five. In 1952, the M-48 was released, much the same as the M-47 but with a one-piece, cast ellipsoidal hull and rounded turret. It was this tank that became the standard U.S. Army medium tank. It carried a 90-mm and three machine guns. It ran at 30 mph with a range of 80 miles.

Armored Car, M-8

The M-8 was the heaviest armored vehicle in the ROK army. With a crew of four and powered by two Hercules six-cylinder engines, it could reach 56 mph and travel for 350 miles. It was armed with a 37-mm gun, one .30-caliber mounted coaxially, and one .50-caliber antiaircraft machine gun mounted atop the turret.

Armored Personnel Carrier, M-59

Similar to the M-75, this 18.7-ton personnel carrier was introduced near the end of the Korean War. It utilized civilian components, thus keeping the costs down. Its relative bulk gave it limited amphibious capabilities, but it could operate in fairly calm water. With the same mechanical design as the M-75, the M-59 could accompany tanks over most terrain and thus was able to provide support for infantry moments.

Armored Personnel Carrier, M-75

The 18.8-ton M-75 could carry about a dozen troops, including the driver. It was developed to replace the World War II open-topped M-39 and the M-44, which could carry 27 passengers. It was a tracked vehicle chassis on which was mounted a boxlike compartment that provided all-around protection for the traveling troops. Only a small number of these vehicles were used during the Korean War, and then only toward the end.

Landing Vehicles

Landing vehicles were fully tracked personnel carriers that were used for ship-to-shore amphibious assaults. These vehicles, known as amphibians, were used during the Korean War. Several types were available when the Korean War broke out: the LVT1 and LVT3, the LVTA-4 and the LVTA-5. The LVT3 was used in Korea at the Inchon Landing and on the drive on Seoul and the crossing of the Han River. It had a ramp at the rear that could be used to load or unload vehicles. The LVTA, also used, was basically the same vehicle but had an open top. The LVTA-4 was altered, with a closed top and a turret, and armed with a short-barreled 75-mm howitzer. The LVTA-5 was redesigned with a ramp in the front. A demonstrated need called for continued development. These machines were much larger and heavier than their predecessors.

COMMUNIST WEAPONS, INFANTRY

It is significant to note that during the Korean War the Communists were very good at capturing and adapting U.S. weapons and equipment. During the early months of the war, some Communist divisions were almost totally equipped with American arms that had been intended for friendly forces. Some of the Chinese troops were initially armed with the M-1, thousands of which had been sent to support the Chinese Nationalist government during World War II and afterward. They also had a large number of surrendered Japanese arms and ammunition. The Soviet arms, which were used in Korea and adopted by both the North Korean and Chinese troops, had two essential characteristics: They were extremely rugged and of the simplest design possible. The tendency of Communist armies was to discard rifles and issue submachine guns that were better suited for unskilled personnel. As with the United States, the vast majority of equipment provided was of World War II vintage.

Parabellum, 9-mm Mauser C-96

There were three varieties in use during the Korean War. The 1915 model was 9 mm, with a 10-round box; the 1932 version fired a 7.63-mm round with a 10 to 20 staggered-row box; and the 1936 fired a 7.63-mm round. Most of the changes made in the various models were slight. They weighed from 2.7 to 2.9 pounds, getting heavier as the magazine size increased.

Carbine, 7.62-mm Russian (M-1944)

This Soviet-made bolt-action carbine of 1944 vintage could hold five rounds in an internal clip. It weighed 8.9 pounds and had a permanently fixed bayonet that folded down along the right side of the stock when not being used.

"Long Rifle," 7.7-mm Japanese Type 99 WWII Model

This Arisaka type was a Japanese weapon built for the Imperial Army during World War II. A bolt-action rifle, it fired five rounds from a nondetachable box magazine designed to chamber a 7.7 mm round. It weighed 9.1 pounds and was 50 inches in length. It had very light recoil and little muzzle flash. An accurate weapon, it had several variants, including a sniper rifle with a four-power scope and a shorter version that was only 44 inches long.

Semi-Automatic, 7.62-mm Russian Ruchnoy Pulemyot

This extremely simple, yet remarkably efficient, weapon was the primary rifle supplied to North Korean troops during the Korean War. More than 50 inches in length, it weighed something more than 20 pounds. It had a magazine of 47 rounds and an effective range of about 1,000 meters.

Semiautomatic Rifle, 7.62-mm Tokarev (SVT-40)

It used Russian light ball ammunition, weighed 8.9 pounds, and carried a 10-round detachable box magazine. The Tokarev weapons were gas-operated and cooled by air circulation holes drilled in the guard. Some SVT-40s were equipped with telescopic sights and used by snipers.

Submachine Gun (Burp Gun), 7.62-mm Shpagin (PPSh-41)

This weapon was the most widespread among the communist troops. Created and used during

World War II, the Russian-made weapon was the key to the Soviet concept that ground troops required a high rate of fire, rather than accuracy, from their weapons. Called a "burp gun" by UN forces because of its characteristic sound, it became the principal weapon used by attacking Chinese forces during the final stages of the Korean War. It was cheap to produce and rugged and dependable under battlefield conditions. It could be fired either fully or semiautomatically, operated off a 35-round box or 72-round drum magazine. It weighed about 8.5 pounds and had an effective range of about 150 meters. It fired the Soviet 7.62-mm pistol ammunition at a cyclic rate of fire of 700 to 900 rounds per minute.

Semiautomatic Rifle, 7.62-mm Tokarev (SVT-38)

This Soviet-made weapon used a detachable 10-round box magazine. Fulfilling the same role as the BAR for Communist forces, it weighed 8.7 pounds (10.8 with magazine and bayonet) and had a rate of fire of 25 rounds per minute. It was fitted with a flash hider.

Medium Machine Gun, Goryunov (SG-43)

The SG-43 fired 250 rounds from a metallic link ammunition belt, weighed 30.4 pounds, and had a maximum effective range of nearly 1,500 meters. Gas-operated and bolt-action, it was mounted on a wheeled carriage and had a cyclic rate of 600 to 700 rounds per minute.

Heavy Machine Gun, 7.92-mm Sokolov Pulemyot Maxima Type 24

This Chinese heavy machine gun was produced in large numbers and used by North Korean and Chinese troops in Korea. Recoil-operated and water-cooled, it fired a heavy ball from a 250-round fabric belt. It had a rate of fire of about 530 rounds

per minute. The Soviet version had a wheeled carriage but the more common version was set on a tripod. It had a range of about 1,100 yards. It was sometimes fitted with protective shields and could be equipped with sled fittings and drag ropes to be moved during the winter.

Grenades

The Soviet F-1 was similar to the U.S. pineapple. The newer (Chinese version) L/2PRC was a stick grenade. Some antitank grenades were also used. These TNT-filled grenades, with a shaped charge, had limited range but was effective against light armor.

Antitank Rifle, 14.5-mm Degtyarev (PTRD-1941)

Designed for use against armor during World War II, this ungainly weapon became an anti-vehicle rifle and was used for long-range sniping against personnel. Called the "elephant" or "buffalo" gun by UN forces, each NKPA division carried 36 of these antitank rifles.

Heavy Machine Gun, 7.62-mm Goryunov

Used by both the North Korean People's Army and the Chinese Communist Forces, this heavy machine gun was wheel-mounted and fired the 7.62-mm cartridge.

COMMUNIST ARTILLERY AND MORTARS

Mortars, 61 mm, 81 mm, 120 mm

The Communist forces used a variety of mortars, from the 61, which had the advantage of being able to fire U.S. 61-mm ammunition, to the 81-mm mortar, which could also use American ammunition. Each company would have a few 61-mm mortars assigned, and a battalion would have 81 mms. They were usually assigned six of the 120-

mm mortars. The 120 mm had a barrel length of about three feet and was the heaviest mortar used by the Chinese in their attack on X Corps during the Chosin withdrawal. The 120 mm was simple and reliable and was the weapon given to Soviet satellite countries.

Field Guns

A division would be equipped with 12 122-mm howitzers. Each took a crew of eight and had a range of about 20,000 meters. A division would also have 24 76-mm field guns, and each of the three regiments was assigned four. The guns took a crew of seven and had a range of about 14,000 meters. In addition, each division would have 12 Du 76-mm self-propelled guns on a T-34 chassis. The average division would be assigned 12 of the 45-mm antitank guns. The largest of the long-range artillery pieces, the 152 mm, was used only occasionally.

COMMUNIST TANKS AND PERSONNEL CARRIERS

Tank (Medium), Russian T-34/76/85

The main battle tank of World War II weighed 35 short tons and could reach 34 mph, with a range of 86 miles. It had excellent traction and was perfectly suited for the terrain in Korea. During the early phases of the war, the UN forces had little that could stop this tank. The invasion, on June 25, 1950, was launched with T-34s in the lead. Each mounted an 85-mm gun and two 7.62-mm machine guns. They were powered by a 12-cylinder 439-hp diesel engine and operated with a crew of five. The heavier Josef Stalin III was never furnished to satellite armies.

Self-Propelled Gun, North Korean SU-76

The GAZ self-propelled gun weighed 12.35 tons and carried two 7.62-mm guns. The 2X GAZ-202

gas-fueled engine carrier was capable of traveling at a speed of 28 mph for approximately 166 miles. It carried a crew of four.

UNITED NATIONS AIRCRAFT

For the sake of easy identification, aircraft are listed by their popular names rather than by the code of the manufacturer.

Albatross (Grumman) SA-16

First flown in 1947, the Albatross was powered by two 1,425-hp Wright R-1820 engines and used by the air force, navy, and coast guard for air rescue and reconnaissance. It had a range of 3,274 miles and could fly at 172 mph. Last used in 1963 by the coast guard.

Auster A.O.P.6

A lightweight observation plane powered by a 145-hp 130 Lycoming 290 3 flat four-piston engine (de Havilland Gypsy Major) engines. It had limited use in Korea, but did see service as a liaison plane. It could travel at a speed of 190 mph. It carried a crew of four.

Avenger (General Motors) TBM-3E

Made by General Motors, the Avenger was a mid-wing, single-engine torpedo bomber built for World War II. It had a large fuselage and was powered by an R-2600 8 engine with 1,500 hp and a top speed of 250 mph. Two Avengers were used as flying ambulances to evacuate the wounded during the retreat from the Chosin Reservoir, during which time 103 seriously wounded marines were flown out. Generally, however, the Avengers served as utility planes.

Banshee (McDonnell) F2H-2

This fighter was powered by two Westinghouse J-34-We-34 jets with 3,150 pounds thrust each.

It had a top speed of 582 mph and a range of 1,278 miles. It had a crew of one. The plane was first flown on January 26, 1945. It was developed from the Phantom but was larger and more powerful. It was equipped with four 20-mm cannons at the bottom of the nose. It served as a fighter-bomber and reconnaissance aircraft and saw service off the carrier USS Essex (CV 9) and later from the field in Korea. It was slower than the MiG and so was used predominantly as a ground attack aircraft.

Beaver (de Havilland) L-20

A small but useful plane, its strong, wide landing gear made it available for use on non-improved areas. It served in Korea, and later in Vietnam, as a liaison plane.

Bird Dog (Cessna) L-19

The Cessna L-9 observation and forward air control aircraft, based on the civilian 170, was designated the L-19 and given the nickname "Bird Dog." The passenger capacity was reduced to two, with two transparent panels installed on the wings above the pilot. The access door was made wider in order to accommodate a standard military stretcher. They were used in small numbers during the Korean War for observation and forward air control. The L-19 also served as a general purpose plane for the transportation of officers. The L-19 was powered by one 213-hp Continental O-470-11 flat six-piston engine. It had a wingspan of 36 feet and a length of 25 feet nine inches. The maximum speed was 151 mph, with a range 530 miles. Though rarely armed, they had four underwing pylons for smoke and white phosphorus rockets to identify targets. The plane was used primarily as an army aircraft.

Chickasaw (Sikorsky) H-19

The Chickasaw was used in the Korean War for rescue and medical evacuation. On occasion, it served for observation and liaison. It was first flown in 1949. It flew the first combat airlift mission while serving with the U.S. Marines in Korea, providing short hauls for men and their equipment and then bringing back wounded on the return. Big enough to carry medical personnel as well as a crew, the wounded could get medical attention while en route. The engine was mounted in the nose, leaving the main cabin free. It could be equipped with a sling with a 400-pound-capacity hoist. It was powered by a Wright R-1300-3 engine that made 700 hp. The maximum speed was 112 mph, with a range of 330 miles and a ceiling of 15,000 feet. It carried no armament and was primarily an air force plane.

Commando (Curtis) C-46

Modeled after the commercial transport, it is best known for its flights over the "Hump" in the CBI theater during World War II. It was powered by two Pratt and Whitney R-2800 2,000-hp engines and was operated by both USAF and civil operators in the Korean War. Weight was 56,000 pounds, speed 269 mph, range 1,200 miles, and ceiling 27,600 feet. This plane was an incredible workhorse.

Corsairs (Chance Vought) F4U/AU1

The U.S. Navy and Marine Corps flew these planes in Korea. They were a leftover from World War II, with one Pratt and Whitney R-2800 at 2,100 hp, and a cre w of one; it could fly at 445 mph for 1,005 miles. It was armed with four 20-mm cannon.

Firefly (Fairey) Mk 1

A British-made carrier-borne fighter, it was powered by a 1,735-hp Rolls-Royce Griffon 74 at 2,245 hp, with a liquid-cooled engine. It had a speed of 386 mph and a range of 1,300 miles. Armed by four forward 20-mm Hispano-Suiza cannon, it took a crew of two and flew off the carrier HMS Theseus.

Flying Boxcar (Fairchild) C-119

A significant development from the C-82, it was officially the C-119 packet. It first flew in November 1947. It was used extensively during the Korean War for everything from massive troop movements to dropping "safe conduct passes" over enemy lines. Powered by two Wright R-3350-85 Duplex Cyclones, it was designated R4Q when used by the Marine Corps for transportation. The plane had a speed of 281 mph, could fly 1,630 miles, and had a ceiling of 21,500 feet. Identified by its twin-boom fuselage, this hardworking cargo plane saw extensive service in Korea.

Flying Fortress (Boeing) RB-17

A major weapon during World War II, the B-17 was adapted for photographic mapping, reconnaissance, and rescue work. Powered by four Wright Cyclone R-1820 1,200-hp engines, its weight was 55,500 pounds, speed 287 mph, range 2,000 miles, and a ceiling of 36,600 feet. It was replaced after about three months' service in Korea. The SB-17 was used for rescue work.

Globemaster (Douglas) C-124A

The Globemaster II, also known as "Old Shakey" was used extensively in the Korean War. It was a remake of the C-74 Globemaster developed at the end of World War II. Powered by two troublesome Pratt & Whitney R-4360 engines, it nevertheless did well in dropping supplies, paratroopers, and outsized equipment. It weighed 72,700 pounds, speed 281 mph, range 1,630 miles, ceiling 21,580 feet. It was the mainstay of heavy transport. It could carry 200 fully equipped troops, or 123 litter patients and their attendants.

It featured a "clamshell" loading door that facilitated outsized cargo and had a hydraulic ramp. During the Korean War, it was one of the few planes that was capable of carrying many of the army's vehicles. It remained in service until 1970.

Grasshopper (Piper Cub) L-4A

Used by both American and South Korean air forces in the 1950s. During the Korean War, the L-4 was reborn and served in many of the same roles it had fulfilled during World War II. Later models were fitted with the capacity to carry a stretcher. These were light, high-wing, two-seaters, powered by one Continental A65 flat four-piston engine, with a maximum speed of 92 mph, a range of 250 miles, and a ceiling of 12,000 feet. It carried no armament but could be adapted to carry a stretcher.

Guardian (Grumman) AF S-2

The Guardian is said to have been the largest single-engine piston aircraft ever flown by the U.S. Navy. It was originally designed for carrier-based antisubmarine warfare. It was driven by a Pratt and Whitney R-2800-48W Double Wasp radial engine that provided 2,400 hp to the four-bladed propeller. It could reach a speed of 315 mph, with a range of 1,500 miles and a ceiling of 32,500 feet. It carried a crew of three and could lift a 4,000-pound bomb-load. While the Guardian conducted war patrols in Korean waters from March 1951 to May 1953, it did not remain in service much longer.

Hastings (Handley Page)

This British transportation and medical evacuation plane was powered by four 1,675-hp Bristol Hercules radial engines and was used primarily by the Royal Air Force.

Sea Fury (Hawker) FB Mk. 11

A British-built carrier-borne interdiction and ground attack aircraft. Powered by a Bristol Centaurus 18 radial engine at 2,480 hp, it could reach a speed of 460 mph and had a range of 700 miles. Armed with four 20-mm cannon plus ordnance, the Hawker Sea Fury was the direct result of a Focke-Wulf Fw-190A-3 fighter captured from the Luftwaffe on a channel coast airfield.

Hellcat (Grumman) F7F

A carrier-based fighter, it was powered by one 2,000-hp Pratt and Whitney R-2800-19W Double Wasp 18-cylinder double-row radial engine. It could reach a maximum speed of 380 mph, with a range of 945 miles and a ceiling of 37,300 feet. With a crew of one, it had six .05-inch Browning machine guns. The Hellcat, which made its reputation against the Japanese in World War II, was used in Korea as a pilotless drone, guided to its target with a 2,000 pound bomb by radio control.

Raven Helicopter (Hiller) UH-12/OH-23

This helicopter, sometimes called the Raven, was powered by a variety of engines, including the 323-hp AVCO Lycoming VO-540 AIB flat six-piston, but the 178-hp Franklin was the most popular. Used for training (as the HTE) and reconnaissance, it was easily identified by its bubble canopy and a canted tail boom. More than 2,000 were built before production ended in 1965.

Invader (Douglas) A-26

This Douglas-built bomber appeared in the Korean War as the B-26.

Invader (Douglas) B-26

Originally the A-26 Invader (Douglas Aircraft), it was designated as the B-26 in 1948. Based in Japan, it proved to be very successful in a night interdiction role. During World War II, the B-26 was identified as the Martin Marauder, but during the Korean War, this medium bomber was designated as the Invader. Powered by Pratt and Whitney R-2800 engines, the Invaders were credited with flying nearly 60,000 sorties and were credited with the destruction of 38,500 vehicles, 3,700 railway cars, and 406 locomotives. Weight was 35,000 pounds, speed 355 mph, range 1,499 miles, ceiling 22,100 feet.

L-17 Ryan (North American) 9 Navion

U.S. Army aircraft used primarily for VIP transport and aeromedical evacuation. Most were powered by a 205- or 260-hp Continental engine. Later redesignated U-18, they even did some ground spotting. It could carry four persons with a range of 700 miles, a ceiling of 17,000 feet, and a speed of 163 mph.

Mercator (Martin) P4M

The Mercator combined two 3,000-hp Pratt and Whitney R-4360 piston engines and two Allison J33, 4,600-pound jet engines. It was used primarily for highly classified intelligence missions.

Mariner (Martin/162) PBM-5

This long-range flying boat first flew in 1943 and was updated with increased fuel capacity; an amphibian with a tricycle undercarriage, it was heavily used in both World War II and Korea. Powered by two Pratt and Whitney R-2800 2,100-hp engines, the range of 2,700 miles made it ideal for rescue and maritime patrol. More than 500 were in service during the Korean War.

Meteor (Gloster) F. Mk 8

A British ground attack fighter, the Meteor was the first Allied jet fighter to see service in World War II. In Korea, they operated as fighter-bombers. The

RAAF 77th Squadron traded its F-51 Mustangs for the Meteor-8 in 1951. It was generally outclassed by the MiG-15. It was powered by two 3,600-pound static-thrust Rolls-Royce Derwent 8 Centrifugal Turbojet engines. It had a speed of 580 mph and a range of 965 km, with a 44,000-foot ceiling. Armed with four 20-mm Hispanic nose cannon plus underwing weapons and a load capability of two bombs or eight rockets, it operated with a crew of one.

Mustang (North American) F-6/RF-51D, P-51, F-51D

Known as the P-51, this North American single-seat fighter was first flown in 1940 and became one of the primary piston-engine planes of World War II. Designed for ground support, it was especially adapted to the rough Korean landing fields that were available. Powered by a 1,695-hp liquid-cooled Packard engine built by Rolls-Royce-Merlin, it was highly valued as a ground support fighter. It weighed 11,600 pounds, had a speed of 450 mph, a range of 950 miles, a ceiling of 41,900 feet, and was armed with six .50-caliber machine guns.

Neptune (Lockheed) P2V4

Two Wright B-3350 engines powered the aircraft, which had a crew of nine. With a maximum speed of 352 mph and a range of 4,200 miles, its remarkable range made it perfect for search missions. It carried a wide variety of ordnance.

Panther (Grumman) F-9F-2/5

The Panther was the first jet fighter to see widespread service with the U.S. Navy and Marine Corps. It entered service in May 1949. It flew off USS Valley Forge (CV 45). It was originally designed to be a four-engine night fighter, but in 1946, it was redesigned as a single-engine day fighter. It was powered by a single Pratt and Whit-

ney J42-P-8 with 5,570 pounds of thrust. A later model modified the air frame and added an engine capable of 6,250 pounds of thrust. It carried four 20-mm cannon and could carry a 2,800-pound ordnance load. Later it was armed with high-velocity aircraft rockets. It could reach a maximum speed of 575 mph, with a range of 1,353 miles and a ceiling of 44,600 feet. The first U.S. Marine Corps Panthers (F9F-2B) appeared in combat in December of 1950, just in time to support the withdrawal of troops from the Chosin Reservoir. The F9F-5 appeared in October 1952. During the Korean War, Panthers supported UN Command by flying close air support missions and brought down five MiGs.

Peacemaker (Convair) RB-36-H

A reconnaissance-bomber, the Convair Peacemaker was first flown on August 8, 1946. It had a top speed of about 415 mph, with a range of 10,000 miles. The wingspan was 230 feet in length. Powered by six Pratt and Whitney R-4360 engines, it served for strategic reconnaissance. It featured a new An/APG-41A radar system that aimed the two 20-mm cannon in the tail turret. It appeared in Korea for the first time on April 5, 1952.

A Navy Panther jet getting ready for takeoff (*Center for the Study of the Korean War, Graceland University*)

Rescuer (Piasecki) HRP-1

A navy and marine helicopter, it was designed as a troop transporter. It was powered by one Pratt and Whitney R-1340-An-1 600-hp engine that could move it at 104 mph.

Vertol (Piasecki) HRP-17

Called the "flying banana," it had twin tandem rotors and was first used by the navy and marines. It could carry 10 troopers. Using a 600-hp Pratt and Whitney R-1340-AN-1, a Wright R-975, or a Continental 525-hp engine, it had a crew of two sitting side by side. At the time, it was the world's largest helicopter.

Retriever (Piasecki) HUP-18 Army Mule

First used in Korea in 1953, the Retriever was a utility helicopter that used a Continental R-975-46A delivering 550 hp, a range of 357 miles, and a speed of 120 mph. Its ceiling was limited to 12,467 feet. It had a crew of one. Used primarily by the navy and marines.

Privateer (Consolidated) PB4-Y

This plane was used primarily as a flare ship, illuminating targets for marine Intruder night aircraft. They carried up to 250 high-intensity parachute flares. Initially called the Sea Liberator, it was powered by four Pratt and Whitney R-1830-94 14-cylinder air-cooled radial engines each rated at 1,350 hp. The maximum speed was 248 mph at 12,000 feet. The ceiling was 18,300 feet with a 4,000-pound payload. Range was 2,900 miles. It had a crew of 11 to 13. Armament consisted of 12 .50-inch machine guns. When on flare missions, they carried up to 250 high-intensity parachute flares. The "Privateer" entered navy service in 1943 and was used exclusively in the Pacific theater during World War II. It flew numerous missions in Korea in search of North Korean or Chinese infiltrators. There were numerous conversions for special purposes: The

PB4Y-2M was a meteorological research version created by taking off the turrets and installing a nose transparency. The PB4Y-2P was a photographic reconnaissance version. The PB4Y-2S was an antisubmarine version that carried additional radar, and the PB4Y-2K was a target drone. The last PB4-Y left service during 1954. In 1950, 22 were provided to France's Aéronautique Navale for service in Indochina.

Sea Fury (Hawker) FB Mk 11

Descending from the famous Hawker Hurricane, it ranked at the top of the prop-driven fighters developed and was capable of speeds up to 460 mph. Powered by the Bristol Centares 18 radial engine, it could deliver 2,555 hp. The maximum speed was 460 mph and it had a range of 1,126 miles. It mounted four 20-mm cannon, plus a bomb load of up to 2,000 pounds. It was employed in Korea as a fighter-bomber, able to carry up to one ton of underwing ordnance. It was flown by the British off the carrier HMS Glory in 1951 and also by the Royal Australian Navy from HMAS Sydney.

Sabre (North American) F-86

The design incorporated a good deal of German research and used a 35-degree swept wing. It became the premier USAF fighter of the Korean War. More than 792 MiGs were shot down by the Sabre. The early models used a 5,270-pound static thrust General Electric J47 engine, but later models were more powerful. Weight was 16,357 pounds, speed 600 mph, range 785 miles, and ceiling 48,300 feet, and the swept-wing fighter reflected the latest technology of the time. It was equipped with air brakes and a transonic tail, which made it very maneuverable.

Savage (North American) AJ-1

The marines kept in reserve, from 1952 on, a squadron of North American Savage bombers, armed with nuclear warheads in case it was necessary to attack China. Designed as the first American atomic bomber, it was powered by two Wright R-2800 44W piston engines of about 2,300 hp each (as well as a J-33-A10 thrust jet of 4,600 pounds), the Savage was able to reach a top speed of only 392 mph. It was 63 feet long, with a wingspan of 71 feet.

Seafire (Supermarine) 47s

The Seafire was powered by one Rolls Royce-Griffon 87 engine with 2,350 hp. It could fly at 451 mph, with a range of 940 miles. With a crew of one it was primarily a naval fighter. It was equipped with four 20 mm guns and eight 60-pound air-to-ground rockets. The Supermarine Seafire flew off HMS *Triumph.*

Sentinel (Stinson) L-5

Larger than the more popular L-4, it was powered by a 185-hp Lycoming engine. One of these planes was used by South Korean president Syngman Rhee. It could be equipped with a stretcher. The Stinson Sentinel was derived from the prewar Stinson Model 105 Voyager. First flown in 1941, it has a short takeoff and landing requirement, as well as the ability to operate off unimproved airstrips. They proved to be invaluable. The L-5, with a crew of two, was used during the Korean War for reconnaissance, the transportation of key personnel, rescue work, delivering supplies, and occasionally carrying wounded. Nicknamed "the flying jeep," the small plane was very versatile. Used first in World War II, it served with distinction during the Korean War, and some were still on active duty as late as 1962. It was powered by one 185-hp Lycoming O-435-1 flat six-piston engine, with a maximum speed of 130 mph and a ceiling of 15,800 feet. The range of the L-5 was 360 miles.

Shooting Star (Lockheed) F-80

The Shooting Star made its first flight on January 8, 1944. It was the first operational jet available to the USAF, and it was used in Korea extensively as a ground attack plane, primarily for low-level, rocket, and napalm attacks. It was a Shooting Star that Lieutenant Russell J. Brown was flying when he met a MiG-15 in the first jet-to-jet air battle on November 8, 1950. Weighing 16,856 pounds, it was powered by a 4,600-pound static-thrust Allison 133 engine with a speed of 580 mph and a range of 1,380 miles, ceiling 42,750 feet. In its RF-80 identification it served as a reconnaissance plane. Designed as a high-altitude interceptor, it had a massive fuel consumption and was so fragile it could not use unimproved airfields.

Short (Sunderland) GR.5

A general-purpose maritime reconnaissance-bomber, called the Porcupine during World War II. It was powered by four Pratt & Whitney R-1830-90B radial piston engines. It could fly at 300 mph, with a range of 3,600 miles. Armed with 10 .303-machine guns with four fixed forward, two in the bow turret, and four in a tail turret, it had a crew of 10 and was used primarily for rescue work.

Dragonfly (Sikorsky) H-5

Known in the U.S. Navy and Marine Corps as the HO3S-1 and then later as the HO5S1, the H-5 was powered by one Pratt and Whitney R-985An-5 radial piston engine with 450 hp. A tandem two-seater, it could carry one passenger inside and two on litters on the outside. The range was 85 miles. Used by both the army and navy, this helicopter saw extensive action in Korea in its role of rescuing UN pilots from behind enemy lines.

Helicopter (Sikorsky) H-19

Built in large numbers, this S-55 helicopter was used by the USAR and the U.S. Army as the H-19, by the navy as the HO4S-1, and by the Marines as

A Bell observation helicopter at Munsan, Korea *(Center for the Study of the Korean War, Graceland University)*

HRS-2. Powered by a 600-hp Pratt and Whitney R-1340 engine, the helicopter was used for troop transports, cargo, and on occasion for clandestine operations.

Helicopter (Sikorsky) HO4S-1

Weighing 7,200 pounds, it was powered by one Pratt and Whitney R-1340-57 with 500 hp, a speed of 85 mph, and a range of 405 miles. Designed as an ASW observation and rescue plane, it had a crew of two and could carry six passengers.

Helicopter (Sikorsky) HO5S-1

It had a 245-hp Franklin 0-425-1 engine, could reach a speed of 110 mph, and had a tactical range of 212 miles. It had room for three or four. The navy procured them to replace the HO3S.

It was used as a scout and observation helicopter. It also worked for day and night evacuation of personnel. Under the designation HO5S-1, it served with the Coast Guard, and under the designation YH-18, it was employed by the air force. Pilots often referred to its "tinker toy" landing gear.

Sioux Helicopter (Bell) 47H-13G

This was the military model of the 47G2 and was provided with an increased fuel capacity and external stretcher fittings; about 265 were built. With a possible crew of two and powered by one Lycoming VO-435A engine with 260 hp, it could reach a ceiling of 12,300 feet and fly at 105 mph, with a maximum range of 323 nautical miles. Primarily used for communication and ambulance service, it is best remembered as a medical evacuation helicopter. It was used by VMU-6 in Korea and flown by the navy and marines.

Skymaster (Douglas) C-54

Built in the 1930s as the DC-4A passenger transport, it was quickly adopted in World War II and during the Berlin Airlift. A C-54 was the first aircraft destroyed during the Korean War. Powered by four 1,290-hp Pratt and Whitney R02000 engines, it was a workhorse for the Military Air Transport Service. With a weight of 62,000 pounds, speed of 270 mph, range of 3,900 miles, and ceiling of 22,000 feet, the navy used this aircraft under the designation R5D.

Skynight (Douglas) F3D2

The F3D had a straight flying surface, with hydraulically folding wings, nose radar, pressurized accommodations, and a tricycle landing gear. It started out in naval service but was phased out and then used by the marines as a land-based plane. It was powered by two Westinghouse J34-WE-36/36Axial-flow turbojets with 3,400 pounds thrust. The Skynight, often called the Blue Whale by its crews, had a maximum speed of 493 mph and a ceiling of 38,200 feet. It was armed with four 20-mm cannon of 800 rounds each and up to 4,000 pounds of ordnance. Basically a carrier-borne all-weather fighter, it was as a land-based plane with the U.S. Marine Corps that it scored the majority of the naval air victories in Korea.

Skyraider (Douglas) AD-2/ADY

The Douglas AD-2 Skyraider, also known as "Able Dog" and "Spad," was an enormous, low-wing, piston-driven, single-seat, carrier-based bomber with a large bomb-carrying capacity. Designed in World War II, it was produced too late in the hostilities for much use. It was powered by a Wright R-3350 25W engine that made 2,700 hp and 365 mph. The Skyraider was aboard every fleet carrier

when the Korean War broke out and became the backbone of the naval attack forces in Korea. Its ability to employ a large variety of weapons made it serviceable against nearly all Korean targets. Many believe that the Skyraider was the most effective close air support aircraft in the world at the time. It was used primarily for ground support and night interdiction.

Skytrain (Douglas) C-47

This Douglas-built plane, sometimes known as the "Gooney Bird," served as well in Korea as it had during World War II. Known as the DC-3 in civilian life and the "Dakota" in the RAF, it was powered by two 1,200-hp Pratt and Whitney R-1830 engines; it did everything from carrying paratroopers to dropping flares. Weight was 26,000 pounds, speed 240 mph, range 1,600 miles, ceiling 24,000 feet, and it could carry 28 passengers. The navy operated this plane as the R4D.

Starfire (Lockheed) F-94A/B

The Starfire was a development of the F-80. The F-94 was a two-seater, all-weather night interceptor. Powered by an Allison J33 with 6,000 pounds of thrust in an afterburner, it was the first U.S. jet to have afterburners. It carried four 12.7-mm machine guns in its nose; it also carried a highly secret airborne radar system. The F-94C, which was not flown in Korea, was called the Starfire, and the name eventually was applied to all F-94s. Weight was 16,844 pounds, speed 600 mph, range 805 miles, service ceiling 51,000 feet, and it was armed with 24 2.75-inch Mighty Mouse FFARs (rockets) in the nose, plus 12 FFARs in each of two wing pods. It was used to provide an escort for bombers and to protect Korean airfields. The F-94B served with the 319th Fighter Interceptor Squadron from which Pilot Ben Fithian and Radar Observer Sam Lyons shot down a Communist Lavochkin La-9 on the night of January 31, 1953. The F-94C did not serve in Korea but was nonetheless called Starfire; eventually, all F94s were referred to by that name.

Stratofreighter (Boeing) C-97

Used to evacuate casualties and as tankers (KC-97), the Stratofreighter was equipped with a flying boom. First flown on November 9, 1944, it could reach 375 mph, had a range of 4,300 miles, and a ceiling of 35,000 feet.

Superfortress (Boeing) B-29, RB-50

The B-29 (Boeing) first flew on September 21, 1942, was successful during World War II, and was called into service in Korea. Powered by four Wright Cyclone R-3350 engines, it was capable of carrying a 10-ton bomb load. Superforts were effective as day and night bombers until the arrival of the MiG-15; after that they flew primarily against night targets. In about 21,000 sorties, they dropped 167,000 tons of bombs and claimed 16 MiGs and 17 other fighters shot down. They flew in all but 21 days of the 37-month war. Sixteen B-29s were shot down by enemy fighters and 48 crash-landed. Their weight was 137,500 pounds, speed 364 mph, range 4,200 miles, and ceiling 31,800 feet. Two of these planes were used to drop atomic bombs on Japan.

The Superfortress RB-50 was an updated version of the B-29 and was first flown in January 1949. It was used for strategic reconnaissance during the Korean War. It operated out of Yokuta AB, Japan. It had a speed of 385 mph, a range of 4,650 miles, and a ceiling of 37,000 feet.

Texan (North American) AT-6

This trainer took on a new dimension in Korea as it became the prime aircraft of the forward air controller. The Texans flew "mosquito" missions to locate targets and mark them with smoke bombs. With a weight of 5,155 pounds, speed 210 mph, range 630 miles, ceiling 24,200 feet, the Texan, as it was sometimes called, was also used by the South Korean air force. Unarmored, unarmed, and powered with a Pratt and Whitney 1340 piston engine with 600 hp, it could fly at 215 mph. It was developed as a trainer for the U.S. Air Force Army in World War II and was used for liaison and training.

Thunderjet (Republic) F-84

Initially assigned to escort duty with B-29s, it soon became useful in ground attack operations. First flown on February 28, 1946, it arrived in Korea in December 1950. Powered by a 5,000-pound static-thrust Allison J35 engine, it often had to be aided in its takeoffs from Korean airfields by jet thrusters (JATO). Thunderjets provided daily attacks with bombs, rockets, and napalm on enemy concentrations. They were not well matched to the MiG-15 at high altitude but were more effective at medium and low altitudes. Built by Republic, with a weight of 23,525 pounds, speed of 540 mph, range of 1,500 miles, it had a ceiling of 40,500 feet. A later model, the RF-86, was used for reconnaissance.

Tigercat (Grumman) F7F-3N

Flown primarily by the U.S. Navy and Marine Corps, it was a World War II airplane that appeared too late to see much combat. It was a swift, mid-wing fighter-bomber with a crew of two and was armed with four .50-caliber machine guns, four 20-mm cannon, and two 2,000-pound bombs. Powered by two Pratt and Whitney R-2800 34W engines of 2,100 hp, it had a top speed of about 425 mph and a range of 1,595 miles. It was used primarily in support of ground troops and on night intruder missions against convoys and troops.

Tornado (North American) B-46

First flown in 1950, it was powered by four General Electric J47 jet engines. It was the first American four-jet bomber. The Tornados took on risky night reconnaissance missions over North Korea, but only a small number were available. Weight was 110,721 pounds, speed 570 mph, range 2,530 miles, ceiling 40,250 feet; the reconnaissance version was the RB-45.

Twin Mustang (North American) F-82

Among the first aircraft to operate over Korea and gainly in appearance, it looked like two F-51s joined together, with a wing center section and a horizontal stabilizer. Designed as an ultra-long-range escort fighter and night fighter, it was powered by two 1,600-hp Allison V-1710 engines. Late in the war it was used primarily as a night fighter until a shortage of parts made it necessary to retire them from combat. With a weight of 25,891 pounds, speed of 461 mph, range of 2,250 miles, and ceiling of 38,900 feet, this plane was involved in the first air clash of the Korean War.

PRIMARY COMMUNIST PLANES

Shturmovik (Ilyushin) IL-2

A Soviet plane designed for close air support, this was one of the best low-level bombers to come out of World War II. These planes were used in the initial attack on South Korea but proved to be vulnerable to most of the UN aircraft. Despite this, the Shturmovik remained in service not only in North Korea but also in China and with the Soviet Union. It was retired in 1956. It was powered by one 1,750 M-38 vee-12 liquid-cooled piston engine. It could reach a speed of 329 mph and had a range of 500 miles. Armed with two 20-mm ShVak and two 7.62-mm ShKas fixed in the wing, it also carried eight RS 82 rockets.

LA-9 (Lavochkin)

In 1947, the improved version was tested after conversions to make it more aerodynamic; one of the four cannons was removed, and the engine cooler was moved to the engine cowling. They were used by the Soviet air force and in North Korea and China. Used primarily as fighter-bombers, they were fighting in the initial combats of the Korean War. A single-seat fighter, they were powered with a 1,870-hp Shvetsov 2FNV and could reach a speed of 500 mph with a range of 570 miles. They were armed with four 20-mm ShVak. The last piston airplane made of an S. A. Lavochkin design, it had straight "cut off" wings.

MiG-15 (Mikoyan & Gurevich Fagot)

Originally designed as an interceptor, it was the first operational Soviet jet fighter to see combat. The clandestine deployment of Soviet fighter regiments to China and North Korea presented United Nations Command with experienced adversaries. First Lieutenant Russell Brown, flying an F-80, is reported to have been the first to destroy a jet when he shot down a MiG-15 in the first all-jet dogfight, on November 8, 1950. Despite this, it was apparent to most that the MiG-15 was superior to any aircraft the United States had in Korea. The USAF rushed the swept-wing Sabre to Japan in an effort to match the MiGs. The MiG-15 was developed as an interceptor. Originally powered by an RA-45 engine with hydraulic ailerons, it was updated to a VK-1, 6,000-pound-thrust engine (a copy of the British Rolls-Royce "Nene"). It could travel 670 mph, with a range of 500 miles. It was armed with one 37-mm N-37 cannon, two 23-mm NS-23 cannon, and rockets or bombs up to 2,000 pounds. It had a speed advantage over the F-86 and a slight edge in its ceiling. At the end of the war, a North Korean pilot defected to UN Command and brought his MiG with him.

PO-2 (Polikarpow)

This fabric-covered biplane was often used by "bed check Charlie." The light construction made them nearly impossible to track on radar, and they were difficult to track with antiaircraft batteries. This slow plane, called the "corn cutter" by the Soviets, caused considerable damage, as it destroyed more F-86s on the ground at Pyongyang (UN-held at the time) than had been lost in the air to that date.

Tu-2 (Tupelov)

Twin-engine bomber powered by two 1,850-hp A SH-82 radial engines. It was supplied to many Soviet satellite states and was effective but not too successful in Korea.

YAK-3/7/9 (Yakovlev)

First flown in 1942, several versions of this plane appeared in Korea. Based on the YAK-9, it was powered by a 1,750-hp M-38 V-12 liquid-cooled engine and could reach a speed of 530 mph and a range of 780 miles. It was armed with one 20-mm ShVak and two 12.7-mm BS. The North Koreans opened the war with attacks by YAK-3, YAK-7, and YAK-9 fighters.

YAK-15/18 (Yakoulev)

The jet fighter that grew from developments of the YAK-3 piston-powered plane, it was powered by an RD-10 engine with 1,980 pounds of thrust. The Yak-18 was heavier, with a tricycle landing gear. Never that effective, only a few were used in Korea.

PARTICIPATION:
UNITED NATIONS /
COMMUNIST NATIONS

When the United Nations passed the resolution (June 25, 1950) calling on member nations to furnish assistance to the Republic of Korea, many nations responded by providing military and economic aid. Several European nations were still reeling from the effects of World War II and were simply unable to provide much help. Other nations were involved in conflicts of their own, fighting guerrilla actions either in their homelands or in their colonies. Several nations, such as Great Britain, were still involved in occupation duties in Germany and Austria. Most of those already aligned with the West had commitments to the North Atlantic Treaty Organization and shared a common fear of Soviet intentions in Europe. Nevertheless, many nations responded with the intention of carrying a portion of the load imposed by the UN call for collective security. This account of the nations that participated is divided into four sections; (1) allied nations who sent nonmilitary aid, (2) nations that offered aid but whose participation was not accepted for some reason, (3) those nations that had troops in-country, including medical units and, (4) Communist nations that participated in the war.

NONMILITARY AID

Argentina
This South American state provided canned goods and frozen meat that was delivered to the troops stationed in Korea.

Australia
In addition to its considerable military force, the people of Australia provided penicillin and 116,000 pounds of laundry soap.

Brazil
The nation of Brazil was unable to send troops but did provide financial aid in support of the war.

Chile
Chile provided a small amount of strategic material, the nature of which is unknown.

Cuba
In addition to an offer of troops, the island nation provided supplies of sugar, alcohol, and blood.

Ecuador

Ecuador provided small amounts of medical supplies and a significant amount of rice for feeding the troops. This was particularly helpful as the United States was feeding troops from several nations, many of whom were used to a basic rice diet.

Greece

In addition to sending troops to fight in Korea, Greece provided medical supplies and several loads of soap. It also made available the use of eight Dakota transport planes.

Iceland

Unable to send troops, Iceland provided 125 tons of cod liver oil.

Israel

The new state of Israel, fighting its own war of national survival, provided medical supplies to the UN contingent.

Lebanon

The government of Lebanon sent financial aid.

Liberia

This small African nation provided raw rubber.

Mexico

The government of Mexico, not wanting to send troops, did provide significant amounts of beans.

New Zealand

In addition to the troops sent to fight in the war, the government of New Zealand sent peas, milk, and 200 tons of soap.

Nicaragua

This Latin American nation sent shipments of rice and alcohol.

Pakistan

The new nation of Pakistan sent wheat in support of UN troops in Korea.

Panama

Panama provided the use of merchant marine vessels for shipments to Korea.

Paraguay

Paraguay provided medical supplies.

Peru

Peru provided the UN effort with 1 million shoe soles.

Uruguay

The government of Uruguay provided money and supplies of blood.

Venezuela

This nation sent medical supplies, blankets, and supplies of blood.

CONTRIBUTIONS REFUSED/ ACCEPTANCE DEFERRED BY THE UNITED NATIONS

The Republic of (Nationalist) China

Nationalist leader Chiang Kai-shek (Jiang Jieshi) offered three infantry divisions and 20 C-47s to support the UN effort in Korea. General Douglas MacArthur, and many members of the China Lobby, favored their use, but President Truman, on the advice of his staff, rejected the offer on the grounds that it would antagonize the Chinese Communists and provoke their entry into the war.

Bolivia

This nation offered the participation of 30 officers to be a part of a Latin American unit. The offer was never accepted because it was deemed too difficult to train and integrate such a unit.

Costa Rica

Costa Rica offered to provide a small contingent of volunteers to fight in a South American unit, but the difficulties of putting such a unit together, training it, and getting it to Korea appeared too large and the offer was not accepted.

Cuba

The Cuban government offered to send a rifle company as its contribution to the UN effort in Korea, but it was never trained or deployed. Consideration was given to forming a Latin American battalion, but this was deemed impractical.

El Salvador

El Salvador offered a small contingent of volunteers to fight with a UN unit, but they were basically untrained and not accepted.

Panama

Panama was willing to send a small contingent of volunteers to Korea, but these were untrained and integration into units appeared too difficult. They were not accepted.

ALLIED NATIONS PROVIDING TROOPS

Australia

Australia had been involved with the problems of Korea long before the Korean War began. It was represented on both the United Nations Temporary Commission on Korea (UNCOK) and its successor, the UN Commission on Korea (UNCOK). During this time Australia was often critical of the government formed around Syngman Rhee and of the U.S. policy that supported him. Australian leaders were quick to condemn the invasion by the Democratic People's Republic of Korea and saw it as a major challenge to peace. While they were quick to respond to the UN appeal for help in the fight in Korea, Australia continued to be committed to the idea of collective security rather than any particular support for the government led by Rhee.

The Australian government provided significant military support to the UN effort, although Australia's diplomatic and policy leadership may well have been its greatest role. However, it quickly committed army, naval, and air units. These included the 77th Squadron of the Royal Australian Air Force (RAAF) and the 3rd Battalion, Royal Australian Regiment, both of which were stationed in Japan at the outbreak of the Korean War. Australia also sent a second battalion, the 1st Battalion, Royal Australian Regiment, that arrived and joined the Commonwealth Division on June 1, 1952.

Australia also contributed naval forces. On June 29, 1950, the frigate HMAS *Shoalhaven* and the destroyer HMAS *Bataan,* still in Japanese waters, joined the UN forces at sea. Later, HMAS *Warramunga* relieved *Shoalhaven*. In October 1951, Australia augmented its naval force with the aircraft carrier HMAS *Sydney* and its complement of two squadrons of Sea Furies and one of Fireflies (piston engines) organized as the 29th Carrier Air Group.

During the war, Australian casualties amounted to 339 killed in action and 1,161 wounded in action.

Belgium

On August 25, 1950, the government of Belgium decided to send an expeditionary force to Korea in response to the UN request for aid. Belgium was motivated both by a concern for European security and a desire to be seen as a reliable ally. Under Belgian law, only volunteers could be sent to Korea, but these were quick in coming. The Belgian United Nations Command (BUNC) included a platoon of volunteers from the Grand Duchy of Luxembourg. Belgium's Korea Volunteer Corps (Corps Volontaires Corea) was composed of 900 infantry troops in the 1st Belgian Battalion, commanded by Lieutenant Colonel Albert Crahay. Because Belgium is a bilingual nation, the battalion was divided into separate French- and Flemish-speaking infantry companies. It sailed from Antwerp on board the *Kamina* and was put into the fight near Seoul on March 7, 1951, under the command of the U.S. 3rd Infantry Division. The 2nd Battalion, which replaced the 1st, was to remain in Korea until June 1955. More than 100 ROK personnel from the Korean Service Corps were assigned to the Belgian Battalion. During the war, 97 members of the BUNC were killed and 350 wounded or missing in action. In addition, Belgium provided DC-4s, and two nurses who were stationed in Japan.

Canada

Canada provided significant military support for the UN forces fighting in the Korean War. At first the Canadian government, though it agreed with the need to stop the expansion of communism, was not immediately ready to send its forces to Korea. Canada had been involved in Korean affairs before; in 1947, it had a representative on the United Nations Temporary Commission on Korea. After the conclusion of World War II, it had reduced its armed forces, as had the United States, to peacetime strength. These men and women were trained for the defense of Canada and not the kind of war that was being fought in Korea. Besides, Canada had never had any significant interest in Asia. However, the Canadians decided to help. The first units that were sent were from the Royal Canadian Navy. On July 12, 1950, three Canadian destroyers, HMCS *Cayuga, Athabaskan,* and *Sioux,* were deployed to Korea to serve under UN Command in the U.S. Naval Forces Far East, Task Force 95, which was the blocking and escort unit. Several other destroyers were later sent: the HMCS *Crusader, Haida, Huron, Iroquois,* and *Nootka.* The HMCS *Nootka* had the

distinction of securing the only enemy warship captured during the war, a North Korean minelayer.

At the same time, a Royal Canadian Air Force (RCAF) squadron, the 426th Transport Squadron (Thunderbird), was assigned to help in the Pacific airlift. By early 1951, the 426th flew regular flights between airfields in Tokyo and air force bases in Washington. Twenty-two pilots also came and were attached to the U.S. Fifth Air Force. During the war, the RCAF claimed 20 kills against jet fighters.

On August 7, 1950, the Canadian government finally authorized the recruitment of the Canadian Army Special Force. The original units were the 2nd Battalion of the Royal Canadian Regiment (RCR), the 2nd Battalion of the Princess Patricia's Canadian Light Infantry (PPCLI), and the 2nd Battalion of the Royal 22nd Regiment (R22eR). Also, to come were C Squadron of Lord Strathcona's Horse, Royal Canadians; 2nd Field Regiment, Royal Canadian Horse Artillery (RCHA); 25th Canadian Infantry Brigade Signal Squadron; No. 54 Canadian Transport Company, Royal Canadian Army Service Corps (RCAMC); and No. 25 Field Ambulance of the RCAMC.

Later expansion included the 1st and 3rd Battalions of the Princess Patricia's Canadian Light Infantry; the 1st and 3rd Battalions of the Royal Canadian Regiment; and the 1st and 3rd Battalions of the French-speaking Royal 22nd Regiment, the Royal Canadian Engineers; the 2nd Field Regiment, Royal Canadian Horse Artillery; the 81st Field Regiment of the Royal Canadian Artillery; and a significant number of support units.

For some time, the Canadians resisted the effort to group them with the Commonwealth forces. Not only did they prefer to remain independent, but there was also the very practical reason that the Canadian army was much closer in formation and equipment to the United States than it was to the British. But in the end Canada agreed and on July 28, 1951, became operational within the Commonwealth Division. Canada began the withdrawal of its forces shortly after the armistice, the last troops departing in April 1955. A medical detachment remained for another two years, leaving in June 1957.

All in all, 26,791 Canadians served in Korea. Of this number, Canada suffered 516 KIA and 1,202 wounded in action. Forty-two prisoners of war were repatriated at the end of the war.

Colombia

The Colombian government had been a strong advocate for the United Nations from the beginning and supported the decision to enter the war against the North Korean invaders. It was the only Central American country to do so. His country torn by civil unrest, the right-wing dictator Laureano Gomez most likely sent troops to gain U.S. and UN favor. Colombia was to provide four 1,000-man battalions during the Korean War. The first, the 1st Battalion Colombia, arrived in June 1951 and remained until replaced by the 2nd Battalion Colombia in July 1952. It, in turn, was replaced by the 3rd Battalion Colombia in November 1952, and the 4th Battalion that arrived in June 1953 remained until October 1954. Each of the battalions had a strength of 1,000 men. The 1st Battalion was assigned to the U.S. 24th Infantry Division but transferred to the 7th Infantry Division on January 23, 1952. The 2nd and 3rd also fought with the 7th U.S. Infantry Division. The 3rd Battalion was badly mauled in March 1953 when it was overwhelmed by a full division of Chinese troops at Old Baldy.

The Colombian government also committed naval forces to the effort. These included the frigate *Almirante Padilla* and the *Capitan Tono,* and then later the frigate *Almirante Brion.* Of those Colombian soldiers who fought in Korea, 146 were killed, 448 wounded, and 69 missing in action.

Denmark

Declaring its neutrality, Denmark would not send combat troops. Nevertheless, at the outbreak of hostilities the Danish government sent a fully equipped and staffed hospital ship. To provide this aid, the 8,500-ton motor vessel *Jutlandia* was converted to meet the need. When it was completed, the ship provided 300 beds, three operating rooms, a dental clinic, and X-ray facilities. It arrived at Pusan in October 1950, where it served primarily as an evacuation hospital. When it returned to Korea after its first tour, a helicopter deck had been installed. When on her second term of duty in Korea, the *Jutlandia* was anchored at Inchon or Pusan harbor, where the wounded could be evacuated directly from battalion and regimental aid stations. The *Jutlandia* returned to Denmark on October 16, 1953.

Ethiopia

The infantry battalion sent to Korea was recruited from Emperor Haile Selassie's bodyguard. It was called the Kagnew Infantry Battalion (named for the war horse of King Menelik in the first Ethiopian-Italian War). They were the only ground force sent to Korea from Africa, and it was the first time the African nation had fought outside its own country since the 13th century. Having suffered the consequences of the League of Nations' inability to halt fascist aggression in 1935, Emperor Haile Selassie was a strong supporter of the UN effort and saw his nation's involvement as a significant gesture to the Western alliance. The first contingent of troops, the 1st Kagnew Battalion, a 931-man unit under Lieutenant Colonel Teshome Irgetu, sailed on the American transport *General MacRae,* arriving at Pusan on May 7, 1951. There they were given American equipment and trained in the use of the weapons. The Ethiopian troops entered combat in Korea in August 1951 after being attached to the U.S. 32nd Regiment, 7th Infantry Division, in June 1951. They fought along the Kansas Line, at Sam-Hyon and Tokan-ni, and were on Pork Chop Hill during the final days before the armistice. It was a fierce, highly motivated, and excellent fighting force. It boasted of the fact that it never lost a prisoner, nor did it leave any of its dead behind.

There were some difficulties, however, mostly with officers. They did not like being classified as *Negro*—the term connoting slavery—and many of the elite Ethiopian forces found it difficult to work with UN Command. With time, offending officers were replaced while the enlisted men never made any trouble. Linguistic problems existed because of the limited number of other nations with Amharic speakers, and this often led to difficulties, especially with the medical evacuation system. Units that served in Korea were: 1st Kagnew Battalion, 2nd Kagnew Battalion, and the 3rd Kagnew Battalion. A number of Ethiopian nurses also served with the Red Cross in Japan.

Using a unit, rather than an individual, rotation system, the units were replaced in March 1952 and again in the spring of 1953. At its peak, some 1,600 Ethiopians were serving in Korea. Of the total 3,158 who served in Korea, there were 122 KIA and 566 missing in action.

France

At the time of the Korean War, the French government and the United States maintained cordial but strained relations. France's military was already deeply involved, in 1950, in a fierce struggle in its Indochina colonies with the Communist leader Ho Chi Minh. Nevertheless, the French sent a contribution to the war in Korea.

At sea, France sent the frigate RFS *La Grendiere,* committed on June 22, 1950, which operated with other UN blockade and escort forces patrolling the coast near Wonsan. The ground forces consisted of the French infantry battalion, the Battalion de Coree. The battalion was assigned to the U.S. 23rd Infantry Regiment, 2nd Infantry Division. During its period of service, the unit won three U.S. Presidential Unit Citations. At its peak, the French had 1,185 soldiers in Korea. The battalion rotated in the winter of 1951 and was replaced with a new unit from France. When the armistice was signed, the Battalion de Coree was transferred to Indochina. The French, who advocated the value of the bayonet charge, established a strong military presence.

Of the 3,421 Frenchmen who served, 271 were killed, 1,008 wounded in action, seven missing in action, and 12 became prisoners of war. Following their service in the Korean War (the French pulled out on October 22, 1953), the French troops were sent to Indochina, where they were known as the "Korean Regiment." Many people, even then, saw a strong connection between Korea and Indochina; in fact, it was as early as June 27, 1950, when President Harry Truman announced an increase in military assistance to Indochina. Nevertheless, the French were somewhat angry when the United States pushed for an armistice in Korea and yet encouraged the French not to conclude such an arrangement with the Viet Minh guerrillas in Indochina.

Greece

In October 1950, Greece authorized the sending of an infantry battalion to Korea. The 840 infantrymen of the Royal Hellenic Battalion, drawn from the regular army, arrived on December 9, 1950. The unit, commanded by Dionyssios G. Arbouzis, was composed primarily of well trained and experienced veterans who had served in the Greek Civil War. The Greeks arrived on December 9, 1950, and by December 19 were attached to the U.S. 7th Cavalry Regiment, 1st Cavalry Division. In May 1952, a company of the Hellenic Battalion was sent to Koje-do to quell the POW riots. The Greek unit was augmented by a second battalion shortly after the Korean War ended. At its peak in 1951, 1,263 Greeks were in Korea.

Greece also sent Flight 13 of the Royal Hellenic Air Force, which arrived on November 26, 1950. It was composed of 397 men, flying C-47 Skytrains, and was attached to the U.S. Air Force 21st Troop Carrier Squadron. It flew its first missions in December 1950 and helped evacuate 1,000 wounded marines from the Chosin Reservoir area. At their peak strength, there were 1,200 Greek soldiers serving with the UNC. During the war, the Greeks had 10,184 servicemen in Korea; their losses were 199 killed and 610 wounded.

India

The 60th Parachute Field Ambulance Platoon, which the Indian government offered, was more realistically a mobile army surgical hospital. It was commanded by Lieutenant Colonel A. G. Rangaraj. The 346-member contingent included a number of Sikhs. A smaller unit under Major N. B. Fanerjee was stationed in Taegu where it provided medical support. The Field Ambulance Platoon joined the UN forces at Pyongyang on December 4, 1950, and took part in the Eighth Army withdrawal. On December 14, 1950, it became the medical evacuation unit for the 27th British Commonwealth Brigade (later designated the 28th Commonwealth Division) and supported this unit throughout the war. Nearly all Commonwealth troops that were evacuated from the front lines would pass though the 60th PFAP before moving on to long-term care. The unit dropped with the U.S. 187th Regimental Combat Team at Munsan-ni on March 22, 1951.

In August 1953, the unit withdrew from the Commonwealth Division to serve in support of the Indian Custodial Force responsible for screening North Korean and Chinese POWs unwilling to return to their nation of origin. It returned, however, in February 1955 after the repatriation exchanges were completed.

Italy

Italy did not become a member of the United Nations until 1955; however, in 1950, when the appeal for support for Korea went out, the Italian government sent the Croce Rossa Italiana Ospedale 68 (Italian Red Cross Hospital 68), which arrived in Korea in November 1951. It served both military and civilians there until January 1955.

Japan

When the Korean War broke out, Japan was still occupied by the U.S. Eighth Army. The 24th Infantry Division was on the island of Kyushu, the 25th Division in the south, on Honshu, the 1st Cavalry Division in Tokyo, and the 7th Infantry Division on the northern island of Hokkaido. Australia, the only other allied power with forces in Korea, maintained a fighter squadron.

Because it was still an occupied country, General Douglas MacArthur was able to use Japanese bases without the permission of the Japanese government, and did so. This changed, on April 28, 1952, when the Japanese Peace Treaty returned Japanese sovereignty. Nevertheless, there was little change in the use of air bases.

The primary port in Korea, Pusan, was only 175 miles from Sasebo on the main island of Kyushu, Japan, making Japanese facilities high priority: This meant not only Japanese supply depots but also a number of hospitals and the development of manufactured goods. On August 24, 1950, the Japanese Logistical Command (JLC) was established to process supply needs from Eighth Army. On October 1, 1952, a new unit, the U.S. Army Forces Far East, was established as the principal army administrative headquarters in Japan and JLC was disbanded.

After World War II, several landing craft and minesweepers had been given to the Japanese; when the United Nations faced a critical need for these types of vessels, Japanese boats—sometimes with Japanese crews—were sent into action. One Japanese sailor was killed during the war.

Throughout the war there was concern about the security of Japan, especially since Japan had become a kind of sanctuary for UN forces. Because of this, the availability of troops and equipment for Korea, was always tempered by the needs—and often by fears based on the proximity of Japan to China, North Korea, and the Soviet Union—and assumed needs of securing Japan.

Luxembourg

The Luxembourg military was very small, but it still managed to send a 44-man volunteer infantry platoon in November 1950. It served with the French-speaking company of the Belgian Battalions that were, in turn, assigned to the 3rd U.S. Infantry Division. The platoon returned home in 1953. The combined unit was known as the BELUX Battalion. Out of a total of 89 who served in Korea, seven were killed in action and 21 wounded.

Netherlands

The Netherlands unit (commonly called the Dutch Battalion) was the quick response offered by the Dutch. At first they sent the destroyer HRMS Evertsen; it arrived in Korea on July 19, 1950. All during the war, the Netherlands navy was represented by a rotation of warships in Korean waters. Transferring from the fighting in the Dutch East Studies, the first contingent of the Dutch arrived in Korea on October 24, 1950, the remainder arriving in December of that year. The contingent was made up of volunteers. The Netherlands had fought a guerrilla insurgency in what had become the nation of Indonesia and many of the men had considerable combat experience. The battalion was divided into four groups, and each was composed of two companies. They were first dispatched to the 38th Infantry Regiment (later to be the 38th Regimental Combat Team). In most cases, the Netherlands Battalion was assigned to the 38th U.S. Infantry Regiment, the "Rock of the Main," 2nd Division.

The Royal Netherlands Navy provided three destroyers and three frigates and a total of 1,360 naval officers and enlisted men. The ships were the destroyers HRMS *Evertsen, Van Galen* (April 1951–January 1952), and *Piet Hein* (January 1952–January 1953), and the frigates were HRMS *Johan Maurits van Nassau* (January 1953–May 1953), *Dubois* (May 1953–October 1953), and *Van Zijll* (October 1954–January 1955). During the course of the war, four of the ships were awarded the ROK Presidential Unit Citation. The *Piet Hein* was cited for destroying an enemy train with its guns.

Ground forces consisted of 26 detachments amounting to 3,972 men. They served in Korea on different dates. The Netherlands unit was usually below official battalion strength and was often assigned KATUSA. The unit consisted of a staff company, two rifle companies, and an auxiliary company. In May 1951, a third company was added. At this point, the Netherlands was still a colonial power, and 73 of those who served were from the colony of New Guinea and 115 from Dutch Guiana. During the war, the Netherlands detachments fought at Hoengsong, Wonju, Hill 325, Taeusan, Mundung-ni, Silver Star Hill, Sagimak, Chungmoksil, Old Baldy, and at the Iron Triangle on three separate occasions.

Of those who served—158 officers and 3,192 enlisted men—120 were killed in action, 381 men wounded, three were missing, and at least one died while a POW. Adding those Dutch troops that served with other units, it was a total of 163 KIA.

This unit, the first of a new regiment that was formed on June 1, 1950, was named the Van Heutsz Regiment and was kept alive by that name. The colors of the regiment carry the words: Korea 1950–1954. The color guard of this regiment wears the U.S. 2nd Infantry Division "Indianhead" patch on its right sleeve.

New Zealand

There was some debate in New Zealand about the decision to send armed forces to fight in Korea. The debate was not over participation but whether the unit should be deployed as a joint force with Australia. On July 26, 1950, however, the country decided to send naval and ground forces on its own. In the end, a force of 1,044 men, known as Kayforce, was selected from among volunteers. Kayforce sailed for Korea on December 10, 1950, aboard the *Ormande* and arrived at Pusan on December 31, 1950. It was initially attached to the 27th Commonwealth Brigade and went into action on July 29, 1951. Later, Kayforce became a section of the newly formed 27th Commonwealth Division. In 1951, the United States asked New Zealand to send another contingent, but at the time they represented about 5 percent of the UN force and the decision was made not to send additional troops. After the war, there was a gradual reduction of New Zealand troops, but units stayed there until the 10th Transport Company returned home in 1957. At their peak in 1953, there were 1,389 New Zealanders serving.

Even before Kayforce was committed, New Zealand provided six RN Loch-class frigates. At sea New Zealand furnished the frigates HMNZS *Pukaki, Tutira, Rotoiti, Hawea, Taupo,* and *Kaniere*. They sailed for Korea on July 3, 1950. The frigates served with the U.S. Naval Command Far East's

Blocking and Escort Force. Two frigates, HMNZS *Pukaki* and *Tutira* were a part of the screening force for the Inchon landing. One sailor was killed during these shore raids. On July 26, they decided to train and provide a transportation platoon and the 16th Field Artillery Regiment.

At the outbreak of the Korean War, New Zealand's army consisted of only 3,000 men. It was required to initiate a special recruiting program in order to meet its commitment of ground forces. The military ground units that served in Korea were: New Base Headquarters, Base Signal Troop, Base Transport Section, Base Ordnance Section, Base Workshops Section, Base Dental Section, Base Provost Section, Base Detachment (Administrative), Reinforcement Training Unit, 28th Field Engineer Light Aid Detachment, 16th NZ Field Regiment, 16th NZ Field Regiment Light Aid Detachment, 10th NZ Transport Company, 1st Commonwealth Division Transport Platoon, C Troop, No. 1 Squadron; D Troop, No. 1 Squadron; G Troop, No. 2 Squadron; H Troop, No. 2 Squadron.

Thirty-one New Zealanders were killed and 79 wounded or missing in action. One New Zealander was repatriated during Operation Big Switch.

Norway

When war broke out in Korea, Trygve Lie, a Norwegian, was secretary-general of the United Nations, and Norway was willing to help. They sent a 105-man mobile surgical unit, the 1st Norwegian Army Surgical Hospital, which was known as NOR-MASH. The unit arrived in June 1951 and was first stationed at Uijongbu, where it opened to receive wounded on July 19, 1951. It later moved to Tonduchon and finally to Habongam-ri. The hospital had a staff of 59 and support personnel of 47. It was administered by the Norwegian Red Cross until November 1951, after which the unit received logistical support from the United States. The members of the staff rotated every two months, so about 623 served during the war. During its tenure, they performed surgery on more than 9,000 wounded and treated about 90,000 people. The unit remained in Korea until November 1954.

Philippines

When the Korean War broke out, the Philippines government was in the middle of an insurrection by Huk guerrillas and had its hands full. Nevertheless, it sent an expeditionary force to Korea in response to the UN call for troops. It provided four motorized battalion combat teams, one at a time, and a fifth after the signing of the armistice. The 1,496-man 14th Infantry Battalion Combat Team (BCT), called the Avengers (from the anti-Huk campaign), was composed of three infantry companies, an M-4A3ES Sherman tank company, a Reconnaissance Company, and a 105-mm howitzer battalion. The unit was supplied with trucks for transportation. It was under the direction of Colonel Nicanor Jimenez. It was collectively known as the Philippine Expeditionary Force to Korea, or PEFTOK, and it served in Korea from the time it went on line on September 5, 1951, until May 1955.

These BCTs were reinforced infantry battalions with three rifle companies and an artillery battery. The 10th BCT was a reconnaissance company and was equipped with M-24 Chaffee light tanks. The units that fought in Korea included the 10th (Fighting Tenth), 20th (The Leaders), 19th (Bloodhounds), 14th (Avengers), and the 2nd Battalion combat team (Black Lions or Bulldogs). The 10th Battalion Combat Team was motorized. During a large part of their time in Korea, they were assigned to the 3rd Infantry's 65th (Puerto Rican) Infantry Regiment, primarily because of the mistaken belief that they spoke Spanish (they spoke Tagalog). They were also assigned to the U.S. 25th Infantry, the 45th Infantry, and the 1st Cavalry. The units fought in numerous battles: Sandbag Castle, Heartbreak Ridge, and Christmas Hill. Of those who served in Korea, 92 were killed and 356 wounded or identified as missing in action.

Republic of Korea

The early U.S. claim that the Republic of Korea army was prepared to defend itself was to prove disastrously untrue. When called on to face the disciplined and professional army of North Korea, the ROK was simply not prepared. The first steps toward building an army for South Korea were made before the new nation was established. From September 8, 1945, the United States began to train South Koreans as security police, using the model of the U.S. regiment. The 1st Battalion, 1st Regiment Korean Constabulary was activated on January 14, 1946. By April of the same year, constabulary regiments of the same kind were established at Pusan, Kwangju, Taegu, Iri, Taejon, Chongju, and Chunchon. However, they were regiments on paper, for there were only about 2,000 men involved. Within two years, however, the constabulary had been increased to about 26,000 men.

Following the official birth of the Democratic People's Republic of Korea Army, on February 8, 1948, Lieutenant General John R. Hodge, the commanding general of U.S. Forces, announced on March 1, 1948, that the Korean Constabulary was to be increased to 50,000 men, with U.S. weapons including artillery.

In late November, the new National Assembly passed the Republic of Korea Armed Forces Organization Act and on December 15, 1948, the ROK army and navy became official. At this time, the constabulary units were renamed and reorganized as divisions: 1st to 7th. In February 1949, the Capital ROK Infantry Division was formed from the Capital Security Command. The new division was equipped with 24 M-8 and M-20 armored cars and 12 M-3 halftracks. The two remaining constabulary regiments became the 8th and 11th Divisions.

By June 1950, the strength of the army had risen to about 65,000 men, but only about half were equipped with U.S. arms, the rest using World War II Japanese weapons. None of the tanks, or more than 25 percent of what the artillery called for, were available and only about half of the divisions were at the three-regiment strength required by their table of organization.

The early losses of the war meant that the divisions had to be reorganized. During the fight for the Pusan Perimeter, the 2nd, 5th, and 7th Infantry Divisions were disbanded and the men moved into the 1st, 3rd, 6th, 8th, and Capital Divisions. From this point forward, the size of the ROK army expanded so that by the end of the war the following units were active: I, II, and III Corps; 1st Division, with the 11th, 12th, and 15th Infantry Regiments; 2nd Division, with the 17th, 31st, and 32nd Infantry Regiments; 3rd Division, with the 22nd, 23rd, and 26th (later the 18th) Infantry Regiments; 5th Division, with the 27th, 35th, and 36th Infantry Regiments; 6th Division, with the 2nd, 7th, and 19th Infantry Regiments; 7th Division, with the 3rd, 5th, and 8th Infantry Regiments; 8th Division, with the 10th, 16th, and 21st Infantry Regiments; 9th Division with the 28th, 29th, and 30th Infantry Regiment; the Capital Division, with the 1st Cavalry, 17th, and 18th Infantry Regiments (later 1st Cavalry and 26th Infantry Regiments; 11th Division, with the 9th, 13th, and 20th Infantry Regiments; 12th Division, with the 37th, 51st, and 52nd Infantry Regiments; 15th Division, with the 38th, 39th, and 50th Infantry Regiments; 20th Division, with the 60th, 61st, and 62nd Infantry Regiments; 21st Division, with the 63rd, 65th, and 66th Infantry Regiments; 22nd Division, with the 67th, 68th, and 69th Infantry Regiments; 25th Division, with the 70th, 71st, and 72nd Infantry Regiments; 26th Division, with the 73rd, 75th, and 76th Infantry Regiments; 27th Division, with the 77th, 78th, and 79th Infantry Regiments; 53rd and 55th Independent Infantry Regiments; 1st Anti-Guerrilla Group, with the 1st, 3rd, 5th, 13th, and 15th Security Battalions; 31st, 33rd, 35th, and 36th Security Guard Battalions (POW guards); 1st, 3rd, 8th, and 11th Field Artillery Groups, with two battalions of 105-mm howitzers; 88th, 93rd, 95th, and 99th Independent Field Artillery, with 105-mm howitzers; the 51st, 53rd, 55th, 59th Tank Companies with M-41 tanks; 1st and 2nd Army Replacement Centers; and the Ground General School.

The Korean Marine Corps was organized in April 1949 with volunteers from the ROK navy and coast guard. While never intended to be a large unit, the Marine Corps grew quickly to include two battalions by the end of 1949 and when the war broke out it was enlarged to a third battalion. The three regiments were organized as the 1st Korean Marine Corps Regiment and were, for most of the war, attached to the U.S. 1st Marine Division. A second marine unit was organized to provide island security.

In February 1951, groups of partisans were consolidated under the control of Eighth Army as Korea's Eighth Army G-3 Miscellaneous Group, 8086th Army Unit. On December 10, 1951, the personnel were absorbed by Far East Command's 8240th Army Unit and renamed the United Nations Partisan Forces, Korea.

When war broke out, the South Korean air force was barely more than a name. It consisted of L-4 and L-5 single-engine liaison planes with a crew of two, and two C-47s. Volunteers for flight training were sent to the United States and returned late in 1951, qualified to fly the F-51 fighter. Eventually three squadrons were formed.

The South Korean navy was small and made up of a few American-made 105 patrol craft and several landing ships, tanks (LST). The ROK navy's −703 fired the first shots of the war when it sank an old Japanese transport as it approached Pusan with the 3rd Battalion, 766th Independent Regiment of the North Korean People's Army.

During the war, the Republic of Korea suffered an estimated 416,004 killed and 428,568 missing or wounded.

Sweden

Sweden responded to the UN request for help by dispatching a field hospital, organized and staffed by the Swedish Red Cross. King Gustav V told the Red Cross that the Swedish state would cover all the expenses for a field hospital. It was a 200-bed mobile field hospital with 174 doctors, nurses, and medical support personnel, all volunteers. As the tactical situation became unstable, it was decided that the Swedish hospital could be of more use as a 400-bed base hospital. It later was expanded to 600 beds. It opened in Pusan on September 23, 1950, and continued to operate there until 1956. During this period of service, it treated 19,100 UN personnel and 2,400 Koreans. During the war, 1,124 Swedish men and women served at the hospital at Pusan.

Though the Swedish government had avoided taking sides in the war, it did participate in the Neutral Nations Supervisory Commission founded in 1953.

Thailand

The small nation of Thailand was one of the first nations to send units to fight in Korea. It contributed air, naval, and ground forces to the United Nations effort. The Royal Thai Air Force air transport detachment arrived on June 24, 1951, and was assigned to the U.S. Air Force 21st Troop Carrier Squadron.

The advance element of the 2,100-man 21st Royal Thailand Regiment consisted of three infantry battalions. It arrived in Korea between August and October 1950. At the peak of their service in 1952, 2,174 Thai soldiers were serving in Korea. The Thai battalion was attached to the 2nd U.S. Infantry Division.

The Thai nation also provided two Royal Thai Navy frigates, the HMTS *Bangpakon* and the HMTS *Prasae,* both of which served with U.S. Naval Command Far East's Blockade and Escort Force. During the war, Thailand lost 136 killed and 469 wounded.

Turkey

Turkey was a major contributor to the combat strength of UN forces in Korea. At the height of their involvement, 5,455 men served with the Turkish Brigade (officially the Turkish Army Command Force), which included its own artillery regiment. The brigade was commanded by Brigadier General Tahzin Yazici. When they arrived near Taegu for training, they received U.S. Army equipment. Then the brigade joined Eighth Army in November 1950 as a part of the U.S. 25th Infantry Division. They moved into the area north of Kaesong to join the division. At Kunu-re, the Turkish Brigade lost one-fifth of its personnel. Fierce fighters, they launched one of the few bayonet charges of the war.

During the course of the war, the following Turkish units were in Korea; a brigade headquarters, motorized howitzer battalion, motorized anti-aircraft battery, motorized engineer company, support units, and the 1st, 2nd, 3rd, and 4th Turkish Brigades. Turkey lost 717 killed and 2,413 wounded or missing in action. There were 243 Turks repatriated at the prisoner of war exchange in August 1953.

The Union of South Africa

The Union of South Africa sent to Korea an all-white South African Air Force Squadron Number 2, called the Flying Cheetahs. It was attached to the Fifth U.S. Air Force, 18th Fighter-Bomber Wing. It refused to become a part of the still projected Commonwealth Wing. On September 26, 1950, 49 officers and 157 enlisted men, all volunteers, left South Africa for deployment in Korea. The first flight of four F-51D Mustangs departed for Korea on November 16 and was operational three days later. They flew an early-model P-51 Mustang that was slower than those flown by the Americans, and they concentrated on ground-strafing missions. The South Africans blew klaxon horns at they dove on the attack. In 1952 they were equipped with the American F-86 Sabre jet and took part in the bombing raids on Pyongyang.

Their assignments, mostly ground attack and interdiction missions, took them to K-24 (Pyong-yang East), K-13 (Suwon), K-10 (Chinhae Airbase), and finally K-55 (Osan). During the Korean War, the squadron flew 12,067 sorties, with a loss of 34 pilots killed in action. Two other ranks were killed, and nine were taken prisoner and later repatriated. The aircraft losses were 74 out of 97 Mustangs and four out of 22 Sabres. The Union of South Africa lost 20 killed and 16 wounded or missing in action; eight were held as prisoners of war. These figures include civilians working with the military.

United Kingdom

Great Britain was the first member of the United Nations, after the United States, to send support to Korea. First to arrive was a contingent of the Royal Navy that included the aircraft carrier HMS *Triumph,* the cruisers HMS *Belfast* and *Jamaica,* the destroyers HMS *Cossack* and *Consort,* and the frigates HMS *Black Swan, Alacrity,* and *Heart.*

During the course of the war, they would also send the aircraft carriers HMS *Glory, Ocean,* and *Theseus;* the cruisers HMS *Birmingham, Kenya,* and *Newcastle;* the destroyers HMS *Cockade, Comus,* and *Charity;* the frigates HMS *Morecombe Bay, Mounts Bay,* and *Whitesand Bay;* and the hospital ship HMS *Maine.*

British ground troops began to arrive on August 29, 1950. The British 27th Brigade, composed of the First Battalion of the Middlesex Regiment and the First Battalion of the Argyll and Sutherland Highlanders Regiment, disembarked at Pusan and moved into the Naktong Perimeter of defense. Next came the King's Royal Irish Hussars, with Cromwell and Centurion tanks. On October 24, 1950, the command was expanded by three infantry battalions—50th Northumberland Fusiliers, the First Battalion of the Gloucestershire Regiment and a battalion of the Royal Ulster Rifles, and the 45th Royal Artillery—of the 29th Brigade. In July 1951, the British forces were combined into the First British Commonwealth Division. All in all, nine British regiments served in Korea. At the peak, there were 14,198 British ground forces in Korea. The costs to the Commonwealth Division were 1,263 KIA, 4,817 WIA, and 977 repatriated. One British soldier chose to remain with his Communist captors after the war.

United States

When the North Koreans crossed the 38th parallel, the United States was quick to act. Before combat troops were assigned, permission was given to provide air cover for evacuees and then for fighter bombers to hit ground troops in South Korea.

The first significant troop movement was Task Force Smith, which arrived in July 1950. Soon the U.S. contribution grew to a significant number. It consisted of the following major (down to battalion-level unless specialized) units: I Corps (command entity for the Eighth Army); IX Corps; XVI Corps, established as a headquarters in Japan but did not see action; X Corps; 2nd Infantry Division, with the 9th, 23rd, and 38th Infantry Regiments; the 502nd (later 12th), 15th, 37th and 38th Artillery Battalions; the 72nd Medium Tank Battalion; the 2nd Engineering Battalion; the 82nd Antiaircraft Artillery Battalion; 3rd Infantry Division, with the 7th, 15th, and 30th (later replaced by the 65th Puerto Rico) Infantry Regiments; the 9th, 10th, 39th, and 58th Artillery Battalions; the 64th Tank Battalion; 10th Engineering Battalion; the 3rd AA Battalion; 7th Infantry Division, with the 17th, 31st, and 32nd Infantry Regiments; the 31st, 48th, 9th, and 57th Artillery Battalions; the 73rd Tank Battalion, 13th Combat Engineering Battalion; 15th AA Battalion; 24th Infantry Division, with the 19th, 21st, and 34th Infantry Regiments; the 11th, 13th, 52nd, and 63rd Artillery Battalions; the 78th Tank Battalion; 3rd Engineering Battalion; 26th AA Battalion; the 25th Infantry Division, with the 24th (later the 14th, 27th, and 35th Infantry Regiments); the 8th, 64th, 69th, and 90th Artillery Battalions; the 79th Tank Battalion, the 65th Engineering Battalion; the 21st AA Battalion; the 40th Infantry Division (National Guard), with the 160th, 223rd, and 224th Infantry Regiments; the 143rd, 625th, 980th, and 981st Field Artillery Battalions, the 14th Tank Battalion; the 578th Engineering Battalion; the 45th Infantry Division, with the 179th, 180th, and 279th Infantry Regiments; the 158th, 171st, and 189th Artillery Battalions; the 245th Tank Battalion, the 14th Antiaircraft Artillery Battalion, and the 120th Engineering Battalion; 1st Cavalry Division, with the 5th, 7th, and 8th Cavalry Regiments; the 61st, 77th, 82nd, and 99th Artillery Battalions; and a company of the 71st Tank Battalion, the 8th Engineering Battalion, and the 92nd AA Battalion; the 5th Regimental Combat Team, with two battalions that would be integrated into the 25th Infantry Division; 187th Airborne Regimental Combat Team, supported by the 674th Field Artillery Battalion; and the Korean Military Advisory Group.

The U.S. Air Force had been established in 1947 after it separated from the U.S. Army, and Korea was to be its first action as an independent command. The Fifth Air Force in Korea was organized as a component of General MacArthur's command. It consisted of the Fifth Air Force as the primary unit and the Thirteenth Air Force and Twentieth Air Force as tactical wings. The units were as follows: the 374th Troop Carrier Wing (C-54), the 21st Troop Carrier Wing (C-47), and the 314th Troop Carrier Wing.

The United States Navy was far more involved in the Korean War than most people realize. It made up a good portion of United Nations Command. The first ship to deliver the war to the enemy was USS *Juneau,* when it fired on positions near Samchok on June 28, 1950. Command was exercised by Naval Forces Far East (NAVFE), which provided headquarters services and had operational command over the Seventh Fleet and the British Commonwealth Navy. The NAVFE consisted of several task forces: TF 77, the fast carrier force; TF 90, the amphibious force, and TF 95, the blocking, logistics, and escort force. It was first led by Vice Admiral C. Turner Joy and then Vice Admiral Robert P. Briscoe.

The primary ships of the fleet were the **Flagships:** USS *Eldorado,* USS *Estes,* USS *Mt. McKinley, and* USS *Taconic.* The **Aircraft Carriers** were: USS *Valley Forge,* USS *Bon Homme Richard,* USS *Antietam,* USS *Boxer,* USS *Lake Champlain,* USS *Kearsarge,* USS *Philippine Sea,* USS *Oriskany,* USS *Leyte,* USS *Essex,* USS *Princeton,* USS *Bataan,* USS *Badoeng Strait,* USS *Bairoko,* USS *Rendova,* and USS *Sicily.* **Battleships** were: USS *Iowa,* USS *Missouri,* USS *New Jersey,* and USS *Wisconsin.* **Cruisers** were: USS *Bremerton,* USS *Canberra,* USS *Columbus,* USS *Helena,* USS *Juneau,* USS *Los Angeles,* USS *Manchester,* USS *Pittsburgh,* USS *Quincy,* USS *Rochester,* USS *Saint Paul,* USS *Toledo,* and USS *Worcester.* **Destroyers** were: USS *Agerholm,* USS *Allen M. Summer,* USS *R. B. Anderson,* USS *Arnold J. Isbell,* USS *Barton,* USS *Bausell,* USS *Black,* USS *Boyd,* USS *Brush,* USS *Buck,* USS *Carpenter,* USS *Champlain,* USS *Charles S. Sperry,* USS *Chevalier,* USS *Clarence K. Bronson,* USS *Colahan,* USS *Collett,* USS *Cony,* USS *Corry,* USS *Cotten,* USS *Dashiell,* USS *DeHaven,* USS *Douglas H. Fox,* USS *Duncan,* USS *English,* USS *Ernest G. Small,* USS *Epperson,* USS *Erben,* USS *Fechteler,* USS *Fiske,* USS *Fletcher,* USS *Floyd B. Parks,* USS *Forest B. Royal,* USS *Frank E. Evans,* USS *Frank Knox,* USS *Fred T. Berry,* USS *Gregory,* USS *Gurke,* USS *Hailey,* USS *Hale,* USS *Halsey Powell,*

USS *Hammer,* USS *Hancock,* USS *Hank,* USS *Hanson,* USS *Harry E. Hubbard,* USS *Hawkins,* USS *Healy,* USS *Henderson,* USS *Henley,* USS *Henry W. Tucker,* USS *Hickox,* USS *Higbee,* USS *Hopewell,* USS *Ingraham,* USS *James C. Owens,* USS *Joseph P. Kennedy, Jr.,* USS *John R. Pierce,* USS *Keppler,* USS *Laffey,* USS *Laws,* USS *Leonard F. Mason,* USS *Lyman K. Swenson,* USS *MacKenzie,* USS *Maddox,* USS *Mansfield,* USS *Marshall,* USS *McDermott,* USS *McGowan,* USS *McKean,* USS *McNair,* USS *Miller,* USS *Moale,* USS *New Jersey,* USS *Nicholas,* USS *Norris,* USS *O'Bannon,* USS *O'Brien,* USS *Orleck,* USS *Ozbourn,* USS *Perkins,* USS *Philip,* USS *Picking,* USS *Porter,* USS *Radford,* USS *Renshaw,* USS *Robinson,* USS *Rogers,* USS *Rooks,* USS *Rowan,* USS *Rupertus,* USS *Samuel N. Moore,* USS *Soley,* USS *Southerland,* USS *Stembel,* USS *Stockham,* USS *Storms,* USS *Strong,* USS *Taussig,* USS *Theodore E. Chandler,* USS *The Sullivans,* USS *Tingey,* USS *Trathen,* USS *Twining,* USS *Uhlmann,* USS *Walke,* USS *Walker,* USS *Wallace L. Lind,* USS *Watts,* USS *Wedderburn,* USS *Wilkinson,* USS *Wiltsie,* USS *William R. Rush,* USS *Yarnall, and the* USS *Zellars.* The **Destroyer Escorts** were: USS *Blair,* USS *Charles Berry,* USS *Cowell,* USS *Currier,* USS *Darby,* USS *Foss,* USS *Howard,* USS *Lewis,* USS *McCoy Reynolds,* USS *McMorris,* USS *Whitehurst,* and USS *Wiseman.* The **Frigates** were: USS *Albuquerque,* USS *Bayonne,* USS *Burlington,* USS *Everett,* USS *Glendale,* USS *Glouschester,* USS *Hoquiam* (Patrol Frigate), and the USS *Tacoma.* The **Submarines** were: USS *Besuga,* USS *Blackfin,* USS *Bowfin,* USS *Bream,* USS *Catfish,* USS *Greenfish,* USS *Hammerhead,* USS *Perch* (Special Operations), USS *Pickeral,* USS *Queenfish,* USS *Sea Fox,* USS *Segundo,* USS *Sword Fish,* and USS *Tang.*

The United States Marine Corps in Korea consisted of the 1st Marine Division and the 1st Marine Aircraft Wing. During the period between the wars, the Marine Corps had fallen to only 73,279 men and women and, when called on by General MacArthur for the landing at Inchon, it had to rebuild. As the 1st Division was building, the 1st Brigade was established under Brigadier General Edward A. Craig and landed at Pusan to join up with the 25th Infantry Division.

The 1st Marine Division consisted of the 1st, 5th, and 7th Marine Regiments; the 1st, 2nd, 3rd, 4th, and 11th Artillery Regiment; and the 1st Tank Battalion, and 1st Engineer Battalion, and 1st Amphibious Battalion. The 7th Marine Regiment joined the division after the landing at Inchon.

The 1st Marine Aircraft Wing arrived in Korea in September 1950, with Corsairs and Tigercats flown from shore stations. Later it added Skyraiders, Panther Jets, Banshees, and the F-3D Skynight fighter.

U.S. losses during the war were 147 aircraft, including 78 F-86 Sabrejets.

West Germany

At the time of the war, the Federal Republic of Germany was not a member of the United Nations, but it sent a German Red Cross Hospital (Deutschen Rotkreuz Lazarett) to Pusan after the war, in support of the remaining UN troops.

COMMUNIST NATIONS PARTICIPATING

China

The Chinese Communist Party (CCP) had fought a long and hard war against the Kuomintang (Guomindang, Nationalist) before finally overthrowing it. On December 9, 1949, the last of the Nationalist forces withdrew to the island of Taiwan (Formosa), 90 miles from the mainland. The leadership of the new Communist nation consisted of Premier Zhou Enlai and Chairman Mao Zedong.

The history of the Chinese decision to become involved in the Korean War is long and more complex than can be told here. But when the United Nations ignored Premier Zhou's explicit warning on October 3, 1950, the Chinese Politburo, on the next day, decided to enter the war in defense of North Korea. On October 13–14, 1950, corps-sized Chinese Communist Forces (CCF) crossed the Yalu River.

The ground forces that operated in Korea were the Chinese People's Liberation Army—identified as the Chinese People's Volunteers and often referred to in texts as the People's Liberation Army (PLA). There continues to be some disagreement about who commanded the Chinese forces during the war, but a high possibility is that it was General (Marshal Dehuai) Peng (P'eng Te-huai). He had under his command about 380,000 men, divided into the IX and XIII Army Groups, each of which was composed of nine field armies about the size of a U.S. corps. The units involved were: IX Army Group, which contained the Twentieth Army, with the 58th, 59th, 60th, and 89th Infantry Divisions; the Twenty-sixth Army with, the 76th, 77th, 78th, and 88th Infantry Divisions; the Twenty-seventh Army that included the 79th, 80th, 81st, and 90th Infantry Divisions. The XIII Army Group included the Thirty-eight Army, with the 112th, 113th, and 114th Infantry Divisions; the Thirty-ninth Army, with the 115th, 116th, and 117th Infantry Divisions; the Fortieth Army, with the 118th, 119th, 120th Infantry Divisions; the Fiftieth Army, with the 148th, 149th, and 150th Infantry Divisions; the Sixty-sixth Army, with the 196th, 197th, and 198th Infantry Divisions; the Forty-second Army, with the 124th, 125th, and 126th Infantry Divisions; the 1st Motorized Artillery Division; the 2nd Motorized Artillery Division; 8th Motorized Artillery Division; one or more U/I cavalry divisions; 5th and 42nd Truck Regiments; and several independent antiaircraft battalions.

During the war, the Chinese used a number of deceptive designations that, at first, successfully hid the size and disposition of the force that was sent against the UN troops.

The Chinese Communist Air Force (CCAF), in November of 1950, had an estimated strength of 650 aircraft. Most of these were MiG-15 Fagot fighters. By June 1951, the size of the force had increased to 1,050 planes, including 445 newer MiG-15s. By June 1952, the air force reached its peak of 22 air divisions and 1,830 aircraft, including 1,000 jet fighters. Commanded by Lieutenant General Liu Ya-lou, the CCAF operated with the short range of the MiG-15 and focused on defense against UN bombers. There was only a limited close air support or interdiction. The CCAF committed to action in

Korea included 10 to 14 aviation corps, 21 fighter aviation divisions, and two bomber regiments. These included the 3rd, 4th, 6th, 12th, 13th, and 15th Aviation Corps. The fighter divisions included the 6th, 7th, 9th, 12th, 15th, 16th, 24th, 34th, 36th, 43rd, 48th, 49th, and 52nd. A number of these units were identified as "Guards."

Most of the planes of the CCAF flew from bases located in Manchuria. Since Manchuria was off-limit to UN fighters for political reasons, the area provided sanctuaries that gave the CCAF a distinct advantage. The estimate of CCAF losses includes those of the very small North Korean Air Force and stands at 960 aircraft.

The navy was small indeed compared to other nations. The People's Liberation Army Navy was established on November 11, 1949, adopting Nationalist vessels that had been captured. It had available a few small craft provided by the Soviet Union, some landing craft, and a number of former Japanese river gunboats. There were no large combat ships available. Most of PLAN's limited force was based on the southeast coast of China, across from Taiwan, or was engaged in patrolling the extensive Chinese river ways.

The Democratic People's Republic of China was one of the signers of the Korean Armistice Agreement and it withdrew its troops shortly after the cease-fire was signed in July 1953. It was 20 years later, when President Richard Nixon made a trip to China, that relations began to normalize between China and the United States.

Democratic People's Republic of Korea (North Korea)

While the North Korean People's Army (NKPA) was a totally separate force, about one-third of the units had fought with the Communists against the Japanese invaders and then with the Chinese Communist Forces against the Nationalists during the Chinese Civil War. Known as the "In Min Gun," the army consisted of 135,000 men. When China entered the war, it bolstered the NKPA and the army grew until, sometime in July 1953, it was reconstituted to about 211,100 troops in seven corps. During the war, the NKPA was under the command of Marshal (premier) Kim Il Sung, but it is assumed that during most of the war many of the orders came from the Chinese commanders. The North Korean units were as follows: 1st Infantry Division, 2nd Infantry Division, 3rd Infantry Division, 4th Infantry Division, 5th Infantry Division, 6th Infantry Division, 7th Infantry Division, 8th Infantry Division, 9th Infantry Division, 10th Infantry Division, 12th Infantry Division, 13th Infantry Division, 15th Infantry Division, 27th Infantry Division, 37th Infantry Division, 45th Infantry Division, 46th Infantry Division, 47th Infantry Division, and 10th Tank Division.

What was identified as the North Korean navy was extremely limited. It began as the Korean coast guard during 1946 and became the Korean People's Navy in 1948. In 1950, it was organized into three naval squadrons: 1st Squadron at Changjin, 2nd Squadron at Wonsan, and 3rd Squadron at Chinnampo. When the war began North Korea had about 45 small boats, including a few aluminum-hulled Russian torpedo boats. Nevertheless, on July 2, 1950—just south of the 38th parallel—the first and only surface naval engagement occurred when two cruisers, HMS *Jamaica* and USS *Juneau,* and a frigate, HMS *Black Swan,* engaged the North Korean navy and sank three torpedo boats and two motor gunboats. Throughout the war the major naval contribution was the sowing of minefields outside the major port cities.

The North Korean air force was not large. It had its origins in a group called the Korean Aviation Society. In 1946, it assumed military status and was moved to Pyongyang where it became the aviation section of the newly formed Korean People's Army. In 1948, it was designated as the Korean Air Regiment and was elevated in status to that of the army and navy under the Ministry of National Defense. It was expanded to an air division in January of 1950, with the 1st Battalion becoming a fighter regiment composed of three battalions.

By April 1950, it consisted of 1,675 officers and 76 pilots, 365 non-rated officers, and 875 enlisted men. It had available about 178 planes, most of which were Russian-built. Forty of them were the propeller-driven Yakovlev (YAK), plus 60 YAK trainers. They also had 70 IL-10 and 10 reconnaissance aircraft, including 25-year-old Polikarpov PO-2 biplanes. Small as it was, this force, commanded by Major General Wang Yong, was superior to that of the Republic of Korea.

United Nations attacks on North Korean air fields, and the efficiency of U.S. coordination in fighter-inception, meant that the North Korean air force was not to play a major role in the fighting— some say it was nearly destroyed by July 10, 1950— but there were occasions when North Korean planes appeared in air-to-air combat and against ground targets.

Soviet Union

The Soviet Union maintained a shadowy participation in the Korean War. Recent documents leave no room for doubt that the Russian government was involved, but the degree of involvement is open to question. Despite what persons felt at the time, there was most likely no Communist "monolith," nor was there unity in the Communist block. The pressure to begin the war must, realistically, be attributed to North Korea and to Kim Il Sung. Joseph Stalin supported the decision and, at some point, sent his countrymen to fight. How many, what kind, and to what purpose, are all questions still seeking answers.

Modern scholarship provides excellent evidence that the Soviet Union, even some pilots and ground personnel, were involved in the Korean War. It is known, of course, that the Soviet Union provided a good deal of help in terms of arms, equipment, and ammunition.

As far as can be determined, the Soviet Union had the following units in Korea during the war. The Soviet Order of Battle consisted primarily of the 64th Fighter Aviation Corps and supporting units. They were the 32nd Fighter Aviation Division (September 1952–July 1953); 37th Fighter Aviation Division (July 1953); 97th Fighter Aviation Division (January 1952–July 1953); 100th Fighter Aviation

Division (July 1953); 133rd PVO Fighter Aviation Division (May 1952–July 1953); 190th Fighter Aviation Division (February 1952–July 1953); 216th PVO Fighter Aviation Division (February 1952–July 1953); 303rd Fighter Aviation Division (August to December 1951); 324th Fighter Aviation Division (April 1951–February 1952); 28th Fighter Aviation Division (November 1950–February 1951); 153rd Fighter Aviation Division (June 1951); 149th Fighter Aviation Division; 50th Fighter Aviation Division (November 1950–February 1951); 351st Independent Fighter Aviation Regiment (July 1951–February 1953); 298th Independent Fighter Aviation Regiment (February to July 1953); 28th Antiaircraft Artillery Division (January to July 1953); 35th Antiaircraft Artillery Division (January to July 1953); 87th Antiaircraft Artillery Division (March 1951–January 1953); 92nd Antiaircraft Artillery Division (March 1951–January 1953); 16th Aviation Technical Services Division (July 1953); 18th Aviation Technical Services Division (June 1951–July 1953); 10th Independent Searchlight Artillery Regiment (March 1951–January 1953); 20th Independent Searchlight Artillery Regiment (January to July 1953); 1406th Hospital for Infectious Diseases; 8th Mobile Field Hospital; 81st Independent Communications Company (November 1950–April 1953); 727th Independent Communications Battalion (April to July 1953); 133rd Independent Radio Technical Battalion (April to July 1953); 61st Independent Radio Technical Company, Radio Navigation (April to July 1953); 114th Radio Technical Regiment (OSNAZ) Special Task Force; 55th Independent Fighter Aviation Corps (PVO); and 151st Guards Fighter Aviation Division (November 1950–February 1951).

The Soviet Union did poise a serious threat. Without sending a single individual or piece of equipment, it tied up a significant proportion of UN forces—submarines to patrol, destroyer screens, air reconnaissance—in fear of momentary Soviet intervention.

East Germany

During the war, the communist government of the Democratic People's Republic of Germany sent volunteer hospital units to Manchuria and to North Korea in support of the Communist troops fighting there.

Hungary

The Communist-bloc People's Republic of Hungary provided volunteer hospital units in both Manchuria and North Korea in support of the Chinese and North Korean forces fighting in the Korean War.

Manchuria

Inclusion of Manchuria is arbitrary because it is officially a part of Communist China, but it was such an integral part of the Korean War equation, it is worth mentioning. When China decided to enter the war, Manchuria became the staging area for Communist troops, much as Japan did for the United Nations. It was, as well, the site of numerous airfields from which not only Chinese and North Korean, but also Soviet pilots few against UN Command. It was estimated that at the three major fields in Manchuria—Changchun, Mukden, and Antung—more than 1,115 aircraft were stationed.

GLOSSARY, ABBREVIATIONS, DESIGNATIONS, AND TERMS

AAA   antiaircraft

A-Frame   back carrier used by Korean porters

ace   fighter pilot who has downed five enemy aircraft

AGC   amphibious command ship

AH   hospital ship

aircraft designations   Aircraft in the United States are designated by a first letter, indicative of functional category.

    A   attack

    F   fighter

    H   helicopter

    U   utility

    P   patrol

    PB   patrol bomber

    R   transport

aircraft manufacturer designations

    D   Douglas

    F   Grumman

    H   McDonnell

    M   Martin

    O   Lockheed (former)

    S   Sikorsky

    U   Chance Vought

    V   Lockheed (current)

    Y   Consolidated

AKA   attack cargo ship

AM   fleet minesweeper

AMS   motor minesweeper

AP   transport

AT   antitank

battle fatigue   nervous condition resulting from too much fear and stress; called "shell shock" during World War I

BAR   Browning Automatic Rifle

BB   battleship

BCT   battalion combat team (Filipino)

Bedcheck Charlie   small plane that would fly over allied positions and drop grenades or small bombs to harass troops; were usually Soviet-built Yakovlev YAK training planes or Polikar-pow PO-2, a wood and fabric plane, which both had a cruising speed of 100 knots

Benjo   slang term meaning outhouse

Big Switch   the main POW exchange that followed the armistice

Bn   battalion

Bomber Command   a major subordinate of Far East Air Force

box-me-in fire   a call for artillery and mortar fire to surround an area and prevent enemy movement

Boysan   slang for male youth

brigade   a headquarters and two or more battalions, generally used by Commonwealth forces, but identifying the first marine troops sent to Korea

bugout running from forward areas to return to safer lines

CA heavy cruiser

casualties encompassing killed, wounded, and POWs

CAS close air support missions

CCF Chinese Communist Forces/ sometimes Communist Chinese Forces

China Lobby those, primarily in the U.S. Congress, who supported the Nationalist China of Chiang Kai-shek (Jiang Jieshi)

Chinks racist term used by Americans for the Chinese

CIA Central Intelligence Agency

CIC Counter Intelligence Corps

CINCE Commander in Chief, Far East

CINCUNC Commander in Chief, United Nations Command

CinCPacFlt Commander in Chief, Pacific Fleet

Changjin Reservoir Korean name for the Chosin Reservoir

CL light cruiser

close air support use of fighters, fighter-bombers, and sometimes bombers to hit the front lines

Corps army tactical unit larger than a division

CP command post

CPV (A) Chinese People's Volunteer (Army)

CV aircraft carrier, changed to CVA in October 1952

CVA aircraft carrier attack

CVE aircraft carrier escort

CVL aircraft carrier small

DE destroyer escort

DMS fast minesweeper

DMZ two-kilometer-wide demilitarized zone set up by the 1953 armistice

DOW died of wounds

DUKW amphibious truck (manufacturer's designation)

DWC died while captured

EUSAK Eighth United States Army in Korea

FA field artillery

FAFIK Fifth Air Force in Korea

FEAF Far East Air Force

FECOM Far East Command

FF frigate

FO forward observer

givupitis attitude that was every man for himself; sometimes called bugouts

Gook racist term for Asian, usually referring to Chinese soldiers

Great Debate the May 1951 MacArthur Hearings before congressional committee

HMAS His/Her Majesty's Australian Ship

HMCS His/Her Majesty's Canadian Ship

HMNZS His/Her Majesty's New Zealand Ship

HNLMS *Harr Nederlands Majesteit Schip* (Her Netherlands Majesty's Ship)

HTMS His Thai Majesty's Ship

hostilities only men signed up for the duration of the war; used first in World War II and then in Korea

HUAC House Un-American Activities Committee, a response to America's fear of communism, in operation from 1938 to 1975

hubba hubba used by both Koreans and Americans to mean "hurry up"

HVAR high velocity aircraft rockets

Ichi bahn Japanese term meaning top-rated; used by Americans

infiltration when enemy soldiers pose as refugees in order to cross a battle line

Japanese air bases

Ashiya

Bofu

Brady

Chitose

Itami (Osaka)

Itazuki

Iwakuni

Johnson

Komaki

Matsushima

Miho

Misawa

Tachikawa

Tsuiku

Yokota

JATO jet assisted take off

JCS Joint Chiefs of Staff (U.S.)—military body composed of army, navy and air force representatives (the marines were added later) who advise the president and direct military field operations

JMS Japanese minesweeper

JTF joint task force

Juche form of nationalism that expresses adulation of the leader; formulated under Kim Il Sung to stress Korea's right to determine its own foreign policy, independent from either Communist or Western influences; became popular in the 1950s

K air bases, airfield, and emergency landing strips in Korea

K1 Pusan West Air Base
K2 Taegu East Air Base (Taegu 1)
K3 Pohang Air Base
K4 Sachon Airfield
K5 Taejon Airfield
K6 Pyongtaek Airfield
K7 Kwangju Air Base
K8 Kunsan Air Base
K9 Pusan East Air Base
K10 Chinhae Air Base
K11 Urusan Airfield
K12 Mangun Airfield
K13 Suwon Air Base
K14 Kimpo Airfield
K15 Molpo Airfield
K16 Seoul Municipal Airport
K17 Ongjin Airfield Oshin NK
K18 Kangnung Airfield Koryo
K19 Haeju Airfield Kaishu NK
K20 Sinmak Airfield NK
K21 Pyongyang Airfield NK
K22 Onjong-ni Airfield NK
K23 Pyongyang West Airfield NK
K24 Pyongyang East Airfield NK
K25 Wonsan NK
K26 Sondok A. NK
K27 Yonpo A. NK
K28 Hamhung West Airfield NK
K29 Sinanju A. NK
K30 Sinuiju A. NK
K31 Kilchu A. NK
K32 Oesichon-dong A. NK
K33 Hoemun Airfield, Kaibun, NK
K34 Chongjin A. Seishin, NK
K35 Hoeryong A. Kainsei NK
K36 Kanggye A. NK
K37 Taegu West Air Base (Taegu 2)
K38 Wonju A.
K39 Cheju-do 1
K40 Cheju-do 2
K41 Chungju A.
K42 Andong A.

K43 Kyongju A.
K44 Changhowon-ni
K45 Yoju A. Yoido
K46 Hoengsong A.
K47 Chunchon A.
K48 Iri A.
K49 Seoul East A.
K50 Sokcho-ri A. Seoul East
K51 Inje A.
K52 Yanggu A.
K53 Paengnyong-do A.
K54 Konsong A. Cho-do
K55 Osan-ni Air Base
K56 Yangyang Emergency Strip
K57 Kwangju A.
K58 planned but not built

KAS Korean Army Service Corps; a bearer corps used to resupply army units in the field

KATCOM Korean Augmentation Troops, Commonwealth; Korean soldiers used as replacements with Commonwealth units

KATUSA Korean Augmentation Troops, United States Army; Korean soldiers used as replacements with U.S. Army units

KCOMZ Korean Communication Zone; a communication zone being an area behind the front lines where supply and administrative facilities can be established

KIA killed in action

KLO Korean Labor Union

KMAG Korean Military Advisory Group (USA); 500-man group with responsibility for training the ROK army, remained as advisers during the war

KMC Korean Marine Corps

LPA amphibious transport

LSD landing ship, dock

LSMR landing ship medium, rocket

LST landing ship, tank

LSV landing ship, vehicle cargo

leaflets in context, psychological warfare efforts: safe conduct, warnings, other

Little Switch exchange of sick and wounded POWs on April 20–26, 1953

MAG marine air group

MAW marine air wing

MASH mobile army surgical hospital

MATS Military Air Transport Service

MDR   military demarcation line

MIA   missing in action

MLR   main line of resistance

MP   military police

mop-up   clearing of an area after primary enemy resistance has stopped

mortars   high-angle fire weapons particularly suitable for Korea's mountainous terrain

MSR   main supply route

MSTS   Military Sea Transport Service: most men and supplies came by ship

Mustang   F-51 fighter; also a term for an officer who had risen from the enlisted ranks

NATO   North Atlantic Treaty Organization

napalm   naphthenic and palmitic acids, whose salts are used in the manufacture of a jellied gasoline used in flame throwers and aerial bombs

NAVFE   Naval Forces Far East

NCO   noncommissioned officer

NDVN   *Nederlands Detachement Verenigde Naties* (Netherlands Detachment United Nations)

"Niupitang"   Chinese strategy for the war

NK   North Korea

NKPA   North Korean People's Army

no man's land   area between the main resistance lines of the opposing forces

PG   patrol gunboat

PLA   People's Liberation Army (Chinese)

POW   prisoner(s) of war

PT   patrol torpedo boat

PVA   People's Volunteer Army, used to describe the Chinese Communist Forces

OPLR   outpost line of resistance—outposts that sat in front of the MLR

R&R   rest and recuperation—brief rest period provided individual soldiers, usually in Japan

RAAF   Royal Australian Air Force

RAF   Royal Air Force (British)

RAN   Royal Australian Navy

RCN   Royal Canadian Navy

RCAF   Royal Canadian Air Force

RCT   Regimental Combat Team

RN   Royal Navy (United Kingdom)

RNZN   Royal New Zealand Navy

ROK   Republic of Korea

ROKA   Republic of Korea Army

ROKN   Republic of Korea Navy

SCAP   Supreme Commander, Allied Powers

Social Affairs Organ   Chinese spy organization

sortie   one flight by one airplane

squadron   basic unit in the air force, navy and marine air wings

SS   submarine

strategy   use of various means to accomplish ends, primarily to achieve a goal

TAC   tactical air controller

TF   task force, a group of units assembled temporarily for a specific mission

TF-90   Amphibious Force Far East

TF-95   Blockage and Escort Force

TO&E   table of organization and equipment, basic number of men and equipment assigned to a unit

UDT   underwater demolition team

UN   United Nations

UNC   United Nations Command

UNSC   United Nations Security Council

USA   United States Army

USAF   United States Air Force

USAFR   United States Air Force Reserve

USAR   United States Army Reserve

USMC   United States Marine Corps

USMCR   United States Marine Corps Reserve

USN   United States Navy

USNR   United States Navy Reserve

USS   United States Ship

VMF   marine fighter squadron

VMO   marine observation squadron

VMR   marine transport squadron

VT   variable time fuse, a fuse setting that allows artillery to explode over, rather than on, the target

wing   major organizational element of the air force, navy, and Marine Corps

WP   white phosphorus

yard bird   derogatory term for "less-than-bright" common soldier

Yuk Gun   name for the army of the Republic of South Korea

ZI   zone of interior, term used to designate the United States during the Korean War

(−)   less (indicates missing elements detached from parent unit)

(+)   more (indicates the addition of elements attached from other units)

APPENDIX I

Medal of Honor Winners in Korea

Corporal Charles G. Alrell	Terre Haute, Indiana	USMC
Sergeant Stanley T. Adams*	Olathe, Kansas	USA
Captain William E. Barber*	West Liberty, Kentucky	USMC
Private Charles H. Barker*	Pickens, South Carolina	USA
Private First Class William Baugh	Harrison, Ohio	USMC
HM3 Edward C. Benfold	Philadelphia, Pennsylvania	USN
Private First Class Emory L. Bennett	Cocoa, Florida	USA
Sergeant David B. Bleak*	Shelly, Idaho	USA
Sergeant First Class Nelson V. Britin	Audubon, New Jersey	USA
Private First Class Melvin L. Brown	Mahaffey, Pennsylvania	USA
First Lieutenant Lloyd L. Burke*	Stuttgart, Arkansas	USA
Sergeant First Class Tony K. Burris	Blanchard, Oklahoma	USA
Private Hector A. Cafferata, Jr.	Montville, New Jersey	USMC
Corporal David B. Champagne	Wakefield, Rhode Island	USMC
HM3 William R. Charette*	Ludington, Michigan	USN
Sergeant Cornelius H. Charlton	New York, New York	USA
Private First Class Stanley R. Christianson	Mindoro, Wisconsin	USMC
Corporal Gilbert G. Collier	Tichnor, Arkansas	USA
Corporal John W. Collier	Worthington, Kentucky	USA
Second Lieutenant Henry A. Commiskey	Hattiesburg, Mississippi	USMC
First Lieutenant Samuel S. Coursen	Madison, New Jersey	USA
Corporal Gordon M. Craig	Elmwood, Massachusetts	USA
Corporal Jerry K. Crump*	Forest City, North Carolina	USA
Corporal Jack A. Davenport	Mission, Kansas	USMC

* indicates a living award

Lieutenant Colonel George A. Davis	Lubbock, Texas	USAF
Lieutenant Colonel Raymond G. Davis*	Goggins, Georgia	USMC
Major General William F. Dean*	Berkeley, California	USA
Captain Reginald B. Desiderio	El Monte, California	USA
HM Richard D. DeWert	Taunton, Massachusetts	USN
Corporal Duane E. Dewey*	South Haven, Michigan	USMC
Second Lieutenant Carl H. Dodd*	Kenvir, Kentucky	USA
Sergeant First Class Ray E. Duke	Whitewell, Tennessee	USA
Sergeant First Class Junior D. Edwards	Indianola, Iowa	USA
Corporal John Essebagger, Jr.	Holland, Michigan	USA
Lieutenant Colonel Don C. Faith, Jr.	Washington, D.C.	USA
Private First Class Fernando L. Garcia	Utado, P. R.	USMC
Private First Class Charles George	Whittier, North Carolina	USA
Corporal Charles Gilliland	Yellville, Arkansas	USA
Private First Class Edward Gomez	Omaha, Nebraska	USMC
Corporal Clair Goodblood	Burnham, Maine	USA
Staff Sergeant Ambrosio Gullen	El Paso, Texas	USMC
HM Francis C. Hammond	Alexandria, Virginia	USN
Corporal Lester Hammond, Jr.	Quincy, Illinois	USA
Master Sergeant Melvin O. Handrich	Manawa, Wisconsin	USA
Private First Class Jack G. Hanson	Escatawpa, Mississippi	USA
First Lieutenant Lee R. Hartell	Danbury, Connecticut	USA
Captain Raymond Harvey*	Pasadena, California	USA
First Lieutenant Frederick F. Henry	Clinton, Oklahoma	USA
Corporal Rodolfo P. Hernandez	Fowler, California	USN
Lieutenant (j.g.) Thomas J. Hudner, Jr.*	Fall River, Massachusetts	USN
Corporal Einar H. Ingman*	Tomahawk, Wisconsin	USA
Sergeant William R. Jecelin	Baltimore, Maryland	USA
Sergeant James E. Johnson	Pocatello, Idaho	USA
Private First Class Mack A. Jordan	Collins, Massachusetts	USA
Private Billie G. Kanell	Poplar Bluff, Missouri	USA
Sergeant First Class Loren R. Kaufman	The Dalles, Oregon	USA
Private First Class John D. Kelly	Homestead, Pennsylvania	USMC
Private Jack W. Kelso	Fresno, California	USMC
Staff Sergeant Robert S. Kennemore*	Greenville, South Carolina	USMC
HM John Edward Kilmer	San Antonio, Texas	USN
Private First Class Noah O. Knight	Jefferson, South Carolina	USA
Lieutenant (j.g.) John K. Koelsch	Scarborough, New York	USN

Master Sergeant Ernest R. Kouma*	Dwight, Nebraska	USA
Captain Edward C. Krzyzowski	Cicero, Illinois	USA
Second Lieutenant Darwin K. Kyle	Charleston, West Virginia	USA
Master Sergeant Hubert L. Lee*	Leland, Mississippi	USA
Sergeant George Libby	Casco, Maine	USA
Private First Class Herbert A. Littleton	Nampa, Idaho	USMC
Sergeant Charles B. Long	Kansas City, Missouri	USA
First Lieutenant Baldomero Lopez	Tampa, Florida	USMC
Major Charles J. Loring, Jr.	Portland, Maine	USAF
Corporal William F. Lyell	Old Hickory, Tennessee	USA
First Lieutenant Robert McGovern	Washington, D.C.	USA
Private First Class Alford L. McLaughlin	Leeds, Alabama	USMC
Corporal Benito Martinez	Fort Hancock, Texas	USA
Sergeant Daniel P. Matthews	Van Nuys, California	USMC
Sergeant Frederick W. Mausert, III	Dresher, Pennsylvania	USMC
Sergeant Leroy A. Mendonca	Honolulu, Terr. of Hawaii	USA
Captain Lewis L. Millett*	South Dartmouth, Massachusetts	USA
First Lieutenant Frank N. Mitchell	Roaring Springs, Texas	USMC
First Lieutenant Hiroshi H. Miyamura*	Gallup, New Mexico	USA
Master Sergeant Ola L. Mize*	Gadsden, Alabama	USMC
Private First Class Walter C. Monegan, Jr.	Seattle, Washington	USMC
Private First Class Whitt L. Moreland	Austin, Texas	USMC
Sergeant First Class Donald R. Moyer	Keego Harbor, Michigan	USA
Lieutenant Colonel Raymond G. Murphy*	Pueblo, Colorado	USA
Major Reginald R. Myers*	Boise, Idaho	USMC
Private First Class Eugene A. Obregon	Los Angeles, California	USMC
Second Lieutenant George H. O'Brian, Jr.	Big Springs, Texas	USMC
Private First Class Joseph R. Ouellette	Lowell, Massachusetts	USA
Lieutenant Colonel John U. D. Page	St. Paul, Minnesota	USA
Corporal Charles F. Pendleton	Fort Worth, Texas	USA
Corporal Lee H. Phillips	Ben Hill, Georgia	USMC
Private First Class Herbert K. Pililaau	Waianae, Terr. of Hawaii	USA
Sergeant John A. Pittman*	Tallula, Mississippi	USA
Private First Class Ralph E. Pomeroy	Quinwood, West Virginia	USA

Sergeant Donn F. Porter	Ruxton, Maryland	USA
Sergeant James I. Poyner	Downey, California	USMC
Second Lieutenant George H. Ramer	Lewisburg, Pennsylvania	USMC
Corporal Mitchell Red Cloud, Jr.	Friendship, Wisconsin	USA
Second Lieutenant Robert D. Reem	Elizabethtown, Pennsylvania	USMC
Private First Class Joseph C. Rodriguez	San Bernardino, California	USA
Corporal Ronald E. Rosser*	Crooksville, Ohio	USA
Corporal Dan D. Schoonover	Boise, Idaho	USA
First Lieutenant Edward R. Showalter, Jr.	Metairie, Louisiana	USA
Major Louis J. Sebille	Harbor Beach, Michigan	USAF
First Lieutenant Richard I. Shea, Jr.	Portsmouth, Virginia	USA
Staff Sergeant William E. Shuck, Jr.	Ridgeley, West Virginia	USMC
Private First Class Robert E. Simanek	Detroit, Michigan	USMC
Sergeant William S. Sitman	Bedford, Pennsylvania	USA
Captain Carl L. Sitter*	Pueblo, Colorado	USMC
First Lieutenant Sherrod E. Skinner, Jr.	East Lansing, Michigan	USMC
Private First Class David M. Smith	Livingston, Kentucky	USA
Corporal Clifton T. Speicher	Gray, Pennsylvania	USA
First Lieutenant James L. Stone*	Pine Bluff, Arkansas	USA
Private First Class Luther H. Story	Americus, Georgia	USA
Second Lieutenant Jerome A. Sudut	Wausau, Wisconsin	USA
Private First Class William Thompson	New York, New York	USA
Sergeant First Class Charles W. Turner	Boston, Massachusetts	USA
Staff Sergeant Archie Van Winkle	Everett, Washington	USMC
Corporal Joseph Vittori	Beverly, Massachusetts	USMC
Captain John S. Walmsley, Jr.	Silver Spring, Maryland	USAF
Staff Sergeant Lewis G. Watkins	Seneca, South Carolina	USMC
Master Sergeant Travis E. Watkins	Gladewater, Texas	USA
Private First Class Ernest E. West*	Wurtland, Kentucky	USA
First Lieutenant Benjamin F. Wilson*	Vashon, Washington	USA
Technical Sergeant Harold E. Wilson*	Birmingham, Alabama	USMC
Private First Class Richard G. Wilson	Cape Girardeau, Missouri	USA
Staff Sergeant William G. Windrich	East Chicago, Indiana	USMC
Private First Class Bryant H. Womack	Rutherfordton, North Carolina	USA
Private First Class Robert H. Young	Vallejo, California	USA

≈ APPENDIX II

United Nations Senior Military Commanders[1]

COMMANDER IN CHIEF, UNITED NATIONS COMMAND (CINCUNC)

General of the Army Douglas MacArthur	July 8, 1950
Lieutenant General Matthew B. Ridgway	April 11, 1951[2]
Lieutenant General Mark W. Clark	May 12, 1952

COMMANDING GENERAL, EIGHTH U.S. ARMY IN KOREA (EUSAK)

Lieutenant General Walton H. Walker	July 13, 1950
Lieutenant General Matthew B. Ridgway	December 26, 1950
Lieutenant General James A. Van Fleet	April 14, 1951[3]
Lieutenant General Maxwell D. Taylor	February 11, 1953[4]

COMMANDING GENERAL, U.S. I CORPS

Major General John B. Coulter	August 2, 1950
Major General Frank W. Milburn	December 23–26, 1950
Major General William B. Kean	December 27, 1950
Major General John W. O'Daniel	July 19, 1951
Major General Paul W. Kendall	June 29, 1952[5]
Major General Bruce C. Clarke	April 11, 1953

COMMANDING GENERAL, IX CORPS

Major General Frank W. Milburn	August 10, 1950
Major General John B. Coulter	September 12, 1950

[1] James I. Matray, *Historical Dictionary of the Korean War*. Westport, Conn.: Greenwood Press, 1991; p. 556.
[2] Promoted to general on May 11, 1951
[3] Promoted to general on August 1, 1951
[4] Promoted to general on June 23, 1953
[5] Promoted to lieutenant general on September 16, 1952

COMMANDING GENERAL, IX CORPS, CONTINUED

Major General Bryant E. Moore	January 31, 1951
Major General Oliver P. Smith (USMC)	February 24, 1951
Major General William F. Hoge	March 5, 1951[6]
Major General Willard G. Wyman	December 24, 1951
Major General Joseph P. Cleland	July 31, 1952
Major General Ruben E. Jenkins	August 9, 1952

COMMANDING GENERAL, X CORPS

Major General Edward M. Almond	August 26, 1950
Major General Clovis E. Byers	July 15, 1951
Major General Williston B. Palmer	December 5, 1951
Major General I. D. White	August 15, 1952[7]

COMMANDING GENERAL, FAR EAST AIR FORCES (FEAF)

Lieutenant General George E. Stratemeyer	April 26, 1949
Lieutenant General Earle E. Partridge (acting)	May 21, 1951
Major General O. P. Weyland	June 1, 1951[8]

COMMANDING GENERAL, FIFTH AIR FORCE

Lieutenant General Earle E. Partridge	October 6, 1948
Major General Edward J. Timberlake	May 21, 1951
Major General Frank F. Everest	June 1, 1951
Lieutenant General Glenn O. Barcus	May 30, 1952
Lieutenant General Samuel E. Anderson	May 31, 1953

COMMANDER, NAVAL FORCES FAR EAST (COMNAVFE)

Vice Admiral C. Turner Joy	August 26, 1949
Vice Admiral R. P. Briscoe	June 4, 1952

COMMANDER, SEVENTH FLEET, TASK FORCE 70

Vice Admiral A. D. Struble	May 6, 1950
Vice Admiral H. H. Martin	March 28, 1951
Vice Admiral R. P. Briscoe	March 3, 1952
Vice Admiral J. J. Clark	May 20, 1953

[6] Promoted to lieutenant general on June 3, 1951
[7] Promoted to lieutenant general on November 7, 1952
[8] Promoted to lieutenant general on July 28, 1951, and to general on July 5, 1952

CHIEF OF STAFF, ROK ARMY

Major General Chae Byung Dok	April 11, 1950
Lieutenant General Chung Il Kwon	June 30, 1950
Major General Lee Chong Chan	June 23, 1951
Lieutenant General Paik Son-yup	July 23, 1952

APPENDIX III

SHIP	DATE	CAUSE
	U.S. Ships Sunk or Damaged	
USS *A.A.Cunningham*	September 19,1952	shore battery, major damage
USS *Agerholm* (DD 826)	September 1, 1952	shore battery, minor damage
USS *Barton* (DD 722)	August 10, 1952	shore battery, minor damage
	September 16, 1952	mines, major damage
USS *Bremerton* (CA 130)	May 5, 1953	shore battery, minor damage
USS *Brinkley Bass* (DD 887)	May 22, 1951	shore battery, minor damage
	March 24, 1952	shore battery, minor damage
USS *Brush* (DD 745)	September 26, 1950	mines, minor damage
	May 15, 1953	shore battery, major damage
USS *Buck* (DD 761)	June 13, 1952	shore battery, launch damaged
USS *C. S. Sperry* (DD 697)	December 23, 1950	shore battery, minor damage
USS *Cabildo* (LSD 16)	April 26, 1952	shore battery, minor damage
	May 25, 1952	shore battery, minor damage
USS *Competent* (AM 316)	August 27, 1952	shore battery, minor damage
USS *Dextrous* (AM 341)	August 11, 1951	shore battery, major damage
	January 11, 1952	shore battery, minor damage
USS *D. H. Fox* (DD 779)	May 14, 1952	shore battery, minor damage
USS *Firecrest* (AMS 10)	October 5, 1951	shore battery, minor damage
	May 30, 1952	machine-gunned, no damage
USS *Frank E. Evans* (DD 754)	June 18, 1951	shore battery, minor damage
	September 8, 1952	shore battery, minor damage
USS *Endicott* (DMS 35)	February 4, 1952	shore battery, minor damage
	April 7, 1952	shore battery, minor damage
	April 19, 1952	shore battery, minor damage
USS *Ernest G. Small* (DDR 838)	October 7, 1951	mines, extensive damage

USS *Everett* (PF 8)	July 3, 1951	shore battery, minor damage
USS *Gloucester* (PF 22)	November 11, 1951	shore battery, minor damage
USS *Grapple* (ARS 7)	August 12, 1952	shore battery, major damage
USS *Gull* (AMS 16)	March 16, 1953	shore battery, major damage
USS *Gurke* (DD 783)	June 25, 1953	shore battery, minor damage
USS *Hanna* (DD 449)	November 24, 1952	shore battery, major damage
USS *Halsey Powell* (DD 686)	February 6, 1953	shore battery, minor damage
USS *Helena* (CA 75)	July 31, 1951	shore battery, minor damage
	October 23, 1951	shore battery, minor damage
USS *Henderson* (DD 785)	February 23, 1952	shore battery, minor damage
	June 17, 1953	shore battery, minor damage
USS *Heron* (AMS 18)	September 10, 1951	shore battery, minor damage
USS *H. J. Thomas* (DDR 833)	May 12, 1952	shore battery, minor damage
USS *Hoquiam* (PF 5)	May 7, 1951	shore battery, minor damage
USS *Hyman* (DD 732)	November 23, 1951	shore battery, minor damage
USS *Irwin* (DD 794)	June 18, 1953	shore battery, major damage
	July 8, 1953	shore battery, minor damage
USS *James C. Owens* (DD 776)	May 7, 1942	shore battery, major damage
USS *John R. Pierce* (DD 753)	August 6, 1952	shore battery, minor damage
USS *John W. Thomason* (DD 760)	July 7, 1953	shore battery, minor damage
USS *James E. Kyes* (DD 787)	April 19, 1953	shore battery, minor damage
USS *Kite* (AMS 22)	November 19, 1952	shore battery, minor damage
USS *Laffey* (DD 724)	April 30, 1952	shore battery, minor damage
USS *Leonard F. Mason* (DD 852)	May 2, 1952	shore battery, minor damage
USS *Lewis* (DD 535)	October 21, 1952	shore battery, major damage
LSMR *409*	June 4, 1953	shore battery, major damage
LST *611*	December 22, 1951	shore battery, minor damage
USS *Los Angeles* (CA 135)	April 2, 1953	shore battery, minor damage
USS *Maddox* (DD 731)	April 30, 1952	shore battery, minor damage
	April 16, 1953	shore battery, minor damage
	May 2, 1953	shore battery, major damage
USS *Magpie* (AM 25)	September 29, 1950	mines, blew up
USS *Manchester* (CL 83)	June 30, 1953	shore battery, minor damage
USS *Mansfield* (DD 728)	September 30, 1950	mines, minor damage
	October 28, 1952	shore battery, minor damage
USS *McDermott* (DD 677)	August 27, 1952	shore battery, minor damage
USS *Murrelet* (AMS 36)	May 26, 1952	shore battery, minor damage
USS *New Jersey* (BB 62)	May 20, 1951	shore battery, minor damage
USS *Orleck* (DD 886)	July 19, 1952	shore battery, minor damage

USS *Osprey* (AMS 28)	October 29, 1951	shore battery, major damage
	April 24, 1952	shore battery, minor damage
	October 14, 1952	shore battery, minor damage
USS *Owen* (DD 536)	May 2, 1953	shore battery, minor damage
USS *Ozborn* (DD 846)	December 23, 1950	shore battery, minor damage
USS *Partridge* (AM 31)	February 2, 1951	mines, sunk
USS *Perkins* (DDR 887)	October 13, 1952	shore battery, minor damage
USS *Pirate* (AM 275)	October 12, 1950	mines, sunk
USS *Pledge* (AM 277)	October 12, 1950	mines, sunk
USS *Porterfield* (DD 682)	February 3, 1952	shore battery, minor damage
USS *Redstart* (AM 378)	September 10, 1951	shore battery, minor damage
USS *Renshaw* (DDE 499)	October 11, 1951	shore battery, minor damage
USS *Rowan* (DD 782)	February 22, 1952	shore battery, minor damage
	June 18, 1953	shore battery, major damage
USS *Saint Paul* (CA 73)	July 11, 1953	shore battery, extreme damage
USS *Samuel N. Moore* (DD 747)	October 17, 1951	shore battery, minor damage
	May 8, 1953	shore battery, minor damage
USS *Sarsi* (ATF 111)	August 27, 1952	mines, sunk
USS *Shelton* (DD 790)	February 22, 1952	shore battery, minor damage
USS *Swallow* (AMS 36)	May 25, 1952	shore battery, minor damage
USS *Swift* (AM 122)	May 29, 1953	shore battery, minor damage
USS *Taussig* (DD 746)	March 17, 1953	shore battery, minor damage
USS *Tucker* (DDR 875)	June 28, 1951	shore battery, minor damage
USS *Thompson* (DMS 38)	June 14, 1951	shore battery, extensive damage
	August 20, 1952	shore battery, minor damage
	November 20, 1952	shore battery, minor damage
USS *Uhlmann* (DD 678)	November 3, 1952	shore battery, major damage
USS *Walke* (DD 723)	June 12, 1951	mines, extensive damage
USS *William Seiverling* (DD 441)	September 8, 1951	shore battery, minor damage
USS *Wiltsie* (DD 716)	June 11, 1953	shore battery, minor damage
USS *Wisconsin* (BB 64)	March 16, 1952	shore battery, minor damage

APPENDIX IV

Ground Troop Commitment by Nation			
IN MIDYEAR OF	1951	1952	1953
UN Ground Forces	554,577	678,051	932,539
Australia	912	1,844	2,282
Belgium	588	579	900
Denmark (medical personnel)	100	100	100
Luxembourg	44	44	44
Canada	5,403	5,155	6,146
Colombia	1,050	1,007	1,068
Ethiopia	1,153	1,094	1,217
France	738	1,185	1,119
Great Britain	8,278	13,043	14,198
Greece	1,027	899	1,263
India (medical personnel)	333	276	70
Italy (medical personnel)		64	72
Netherlands	725	565	819
New Zealand	797	1,111	1,389
Norway (medical personnel)	79	109	105
Philippines	1,143	1,494	1,496
Republic of Korea	273,266	376,418	590,911
Sweden (medical personnel)	162	148	154
Thailand	1,057	2,274	1,294
Turkey	4,602	4,878	5,455
United States	253,250	265,864	302,483

APPENDIX V

Combat Sorties by Mission[1]		
MISSION	USN/USMC	USAF
Interdiction	126,874	192,581
Air superiority	44,607	79,928
Close air support	65,748	57,665
Reconnaissance	26,757	60,971
Antisubmarine patrol	11,856	n/a
Strategic bombing	n/a	994
Total missions flown	275,842	392,139

[1] R. P. Hallion, *The Naval War in Korea.* Baltimore, Md.: Nautical and Aviation Publishing Company of America, 1986.

═ Appendix VI

Aces of the Korean War

To qualify as an ace, a pilot must shoot down at least five enemy aircraft in air-to-air combat. In the qualification process, the terms "half" and "third" are used to indicate that a kill is credited to more than one pilot. No pilots from allied nations reached ace status, but several claimed two or three kills. The figures here are as accurate as current records indicate, but keep in mind that both the United States and the Soviet Union exaggerated their claims so that the combined figures do not match.

United States Aces	
PILOT	KILLS
Captain Joseph C. McConnell, Jr.	16 kills
Major James Jabarra	15 kills
Captain Manuel J. Fernandez	14 $^1/_2$ kills
Major George A. Davis, Jr.	14 kills
Colonel Royal N. Baker	13 kills
Major Frederick C. Blesse	10 kills
Lieutenant Harold E. Fischer	10 kills
Lieutenant Colonel Vermont Garrison	10 kills
Colonel James K. Johnson	10 kills
Captain Lonnie R. Moore	10 kills
Captain Ralph S. Parr, Jr.	10 kills
Lieutenant James F. Low	9 kills
Robinson Risner	8 kills
Clifford Jolley	7 kills
Leonard Lilley	7 kills
Lieutenant Henry Buttelman	7 kills
Major Donald Adams	6 $^1/_2$ kills
Colonel Francis S. Gabreski	6 $^1/_2$ kills

United States Aces, continued

PILOT	KILLS
Major James P. Hagerstrom	6 $\frac{1}{2}$ kills
George Jones	6 $\frac{1}{2}$ kills
Winton Marshall	6 $\frac{1}{2}$ kills
Robert Love	6 kills
Major John F. Bolt	6 kills
James Kasler	6 kills
Major William T. Whisner	5 $\frac{1}{2}$ kills
Robert Baldwin	5 kills
Captain Richard S. Becker	5 kills
Major Stephen L. Bettinger	5 kills
Lieutenant Guy B. Bordelon	5 kills
Richard Creighton	5 kills
Clyde Curtin	5 kills
Cecil Foster	5 kills
Ralph Gibson	5 kills
Captain Robert Latshaw	5 kills
Robert Moore	5 kills
Dolphin Overton	5 kills
George Ruddell	5 kills
Colonel Harrison Thyng	5 kills
William Westcott	5 kills

Chinese Aces

Chao Bao Tun	9 kills
Kim Tsi Oc	9 kills
Fan Van Chou	8 kills

Russian Aces

Yevgeni Pepelyaev	32 kills
Nikolai Sutyagin	21 kills
Dimitri Oskin	15 kills
Lev Schukin	15 kills
Aleksandr Smurchkov	15 kills

Russian Aces, continued

PILOT	KILLS
Serafim Subbutin	15 kills
Mikhail Ponomarev	14 kills
A. Sherberstov	14 kills
Sergei Kramarenko	13 kills
Stepan Bakhaev	11 kills
Nikolai Dokaschenko	11 kills
Mikhail Mihin	11 kills
Grigory Okhay	11 kills
Dmitri Samoylov	10 kills
Arkady Boytsov	10 kills
Grigory Ges	9 kills
Vladimir I. Alfeyev	8 kills
Nikolai I. Inanov	8 kills
Grigory Pulov	8 kills
B. Bokach	7 kills
Muraviev	7 kills
Fedor Shebanov	6 kills
Nikolai Zameskin	6 kills
I. Zaplavnev	6 kills
Boris Abakumov	5 kills
Anatoliy Karelin	5 kills

MAPS

Northwest Pacific, 1950

USSR

MONGOLIA

CHINA

NORTH KOREA

Sea of Japan

SOUTH KOREA

JAPAN

Yellow Sea

PACIFIC OCEAN

East China Sea

TAIWAN

THAI-LAND

FRENCH INDOCHINA

South China Sea

PHILIPPINES

0   500 miles

0   500 km

© Facts On File, Inc.

Korean Peninsula

CHINA

Najin

NORTH KOREA

Sinuiju   Hamhung

Sunchon   Wonsan

Chinnampo   Pyongyang

Kaesong

Inchon   Seoul   SOUTH KOREA

Suwon   Wonju

Chongju

Yellow Sea

Kunsan   Taejon   Pohang

Chonju   Taegu

Kwangju   Chinju   Masan

Pusan

Cheju

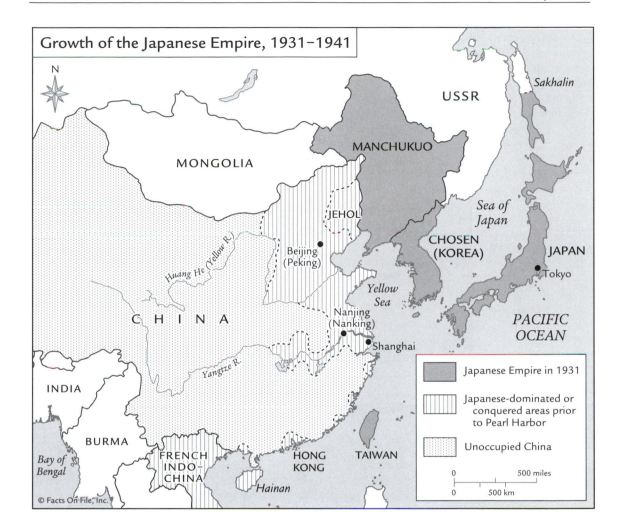

Growth of the Japanese Empire, 1931–1941

N

USSR

Sakhalin

MONGOLIA

MANCHUKUO

JEHOL

Sea of
Japan

CHOSEN
(KOREA)

JAPAN

Beijing
(Peking)

Huang He (Yellow R.)

Tokyo

Yellow
Sea

C H I N A

Nanjing
(Nanking)

PACIFIC
OCEAN

Yangtze R.

Shanghai

INDIA

■ Japanese Empire in 1931

BURMA

▨ Japanese-dominated or
conquered areas prior
to Pearl Harbor

Bay of
Bengal

FRENCH
INDO-
CHINA

HONG
KONG

TAIWAN

⠿ Unoccupied China

Hainan

0   500 miles

© Facts On File, Inc.

0   500 km

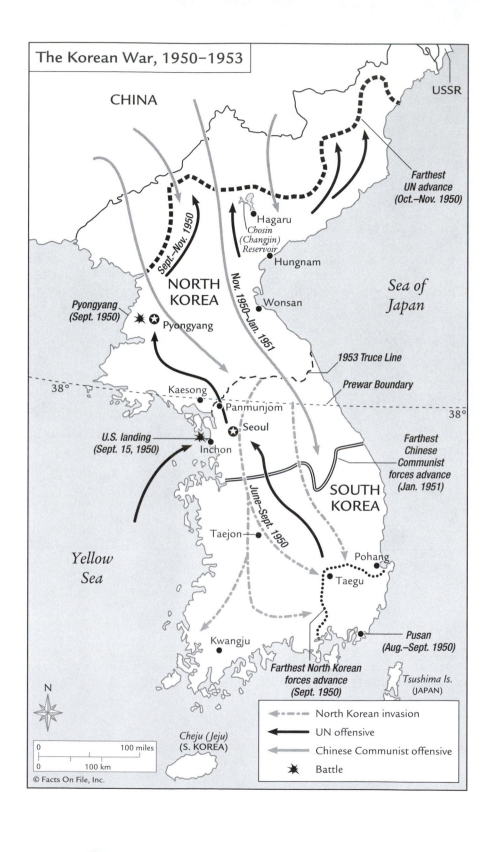

The Korean War, 1950–1953

CHINA

USSR

Farthest UN advance (Oct.–Nov. 1950)

Sept.–Nov. 1950

Hagaru
Chosin (Changjin) Reservoir

Hungnam

NORTH KOREA

Sea of Japan

Pyongyang (Sept. 1950)
Pyongyang

Nov. 1950–Jan. 1951

Wonsan

1953 Truce Line

38°

Kaesong

Prewar Boundary

Panmunjom

38°

U.S. landing (Sept. 15, 1950)
Seoul

Inchon

Farthest Chinese Communist forces advance (Jan. 1951)

SOUTH KOREA

June–Sept. 1950

Yellow Sea

Taejon

Pohang

Taegu

Kwangju

Pusan *(Aug.–Sept. 1950)*

Farthest North Korean forces advance (Sept. 1950)

Tsushima Is. (JAPAN)

N

Cheju (Jeju) (S. KOREA)

0   100 miles
0   100 km

© Facts On File, Inc.

North Korean invasion
UN offensive
Chinese Communist offensive
Battle

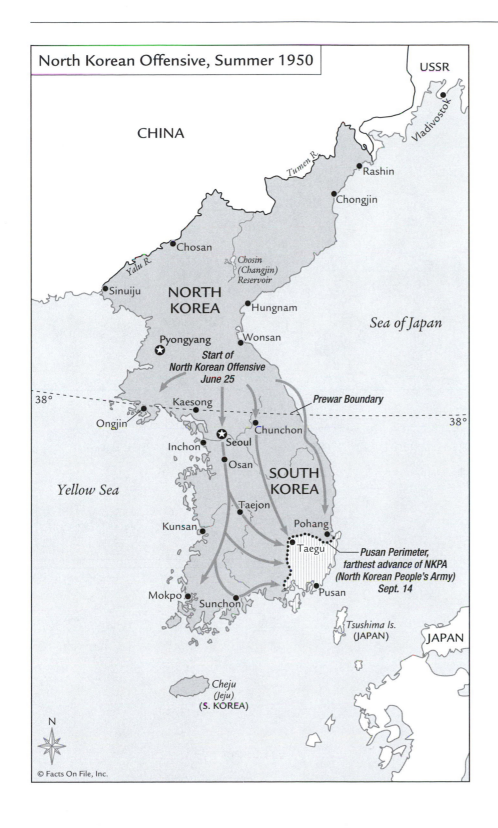

North Korean Offensive, Summer 1950

USSR

CHINA

Vladivostok

Tumen R.

Rashin

Chongjin

Chosan

Chosin
(Changjin)
Reservoir

Yalu R.

Sinuiju

**NORTH
KOREA**

Hungnam

Sea of Japan

Pyongyang

Wonsan

*Start of
North Korean Offensive
June 25*

38°

Kaesong

Prewar Boundary

Ongjin

Chunchon

38°

Inchon

Seoul

Osan

**SOUTH
KOREA**

Yellow Sea

Taejon

Pohang

Kunsan

Taegu

*Pusan Perimeter,
farthest advance of NKPA
(North Korean People's Army)
Sept. 14*

Mokpo

Pusan

Sunchon

*Tsushima Is.
(JAPAN)*

JAPAN

*Cheju
(Jeju)
(S. KOREA)*

N

© Facts On File, Inc.

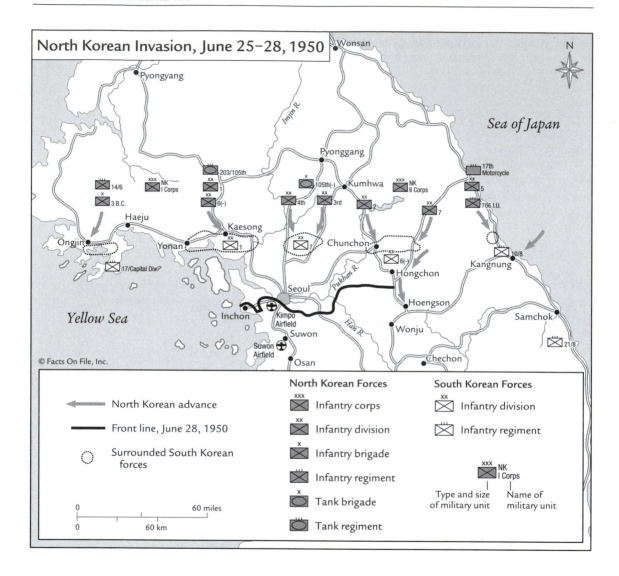

North Korean Invasion, June 25–28, 1950

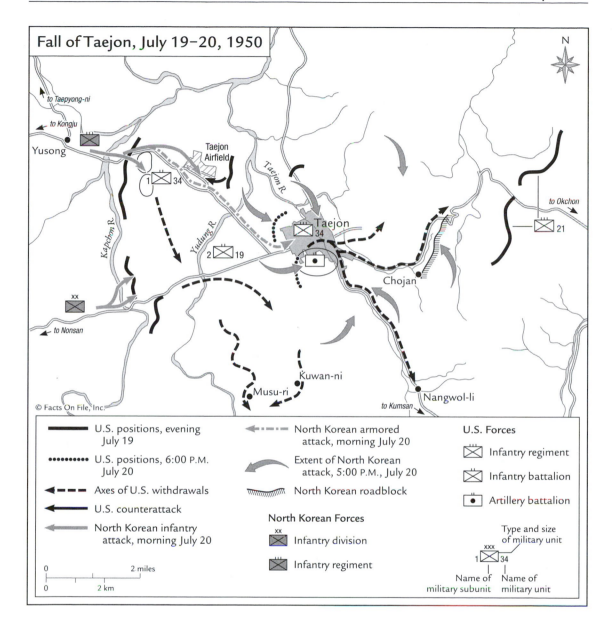

Fall of Taejon, July 19–20, 1950

to Taepyong-ni

to Kongju

Yusong

Taejon Airfield

Taejon R.

Kapchon R.

Yudung R.

1 34

2 19

XX

to Nonsan

Taejon 34

to Okchon

21

Chojan

Kuwan-ni

Musu-ri

Nangwol-li

to Kumsan

N

© Facts On File, Inc.

	U.S. positions, evening July 19		North Korean armored attack, morning July 20	**U.S. Forces**	

U.S. positions, evening July 19

U.S. positions, 6:00 P.M. July 20

Axes of U.S. withdrawals

U.S. counterattack

North Korean infantry attack, morning July 20

North Korean armored attack, morning July 20

Extent of North Korean attack, 5:00 P.M., July 20

North Korean roadblock

North Korean Forces

Infantry division

Infantry regiment

U.S. Forces

Infantry regiment

Infantry battalion

Artillery battalion

Type and size of military unit

XXX
1   34

Name of military subunit   Name of military unit

0   2 miles
0   2 km

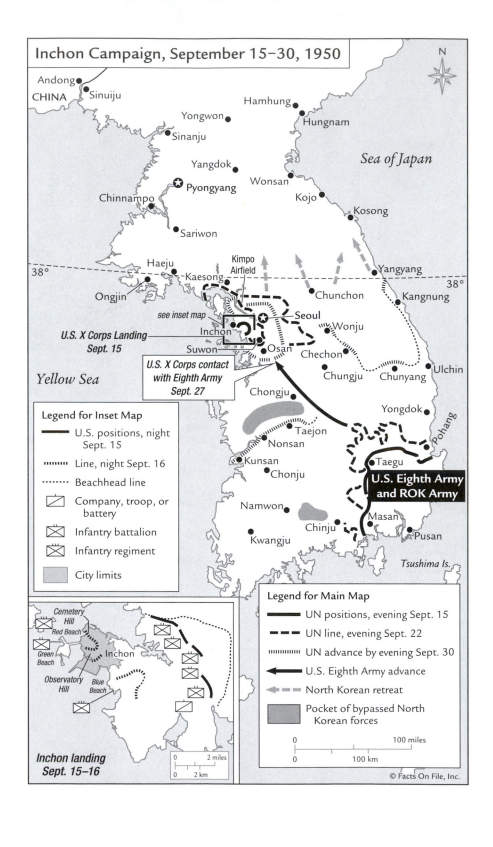

Inchon Campaign, September 15–30, 1950

Andong
CHINA
Sinuiju
Yongwon
Sinanju
Hamhung
Hungnam
Yangdok
Wonsan
Pyongyang
Kojo
Chinnampo
Kosong
Sariwon
Sea of Japan

38°
Haeju
Kaesong
Kimpo
Airfield
Yangyang
38°
Ongjin
Chunchon
Kangnung
see inset map
Seoul
U.S. X Corps Landing
Sept. 15
Inchon
Wonju
Suwon
Osan
Yellow Sea
U.S. X Corps contact
with Eighth Army
Sept. 27
Chechon
Chunyang
Chungju
Ulchin
Chongju
Yongdok
Pohang
Taejon
Nonsan
Kunsan
Taegu
Chonju
U.S. Eighth Army
and ROK Army
Namwon
Masan
Chinju
Pusan
Kwangju
Tsushima Is.

Legend for Inset Map
— U.S. positions, night Sept. 15
······· Line, night Sept. 16
···· Beachhead line
⊠ Company, troop, or battery
⊠ Infantry battalion
⊠ Infantry regiment
▨ City limits

Legend for Main Map
— UN positions, evening Sept. 15
--- UN line, evening Sept. 22
······· UN advance by evening Sept. 30
→ U.S. Eighth Army advance
⇢ North Korean retreat
▨ Pocket of bypassed North Korean forces

0   100 miles
0   100 km

© Facts On File, Inc.

Cemetery
Hill
Red Beach
Green
Beach
Inchon
Observatory
Hill
Blue Beach

Inchon landing
Sept. 15–16

0   2 miles
0   2 km

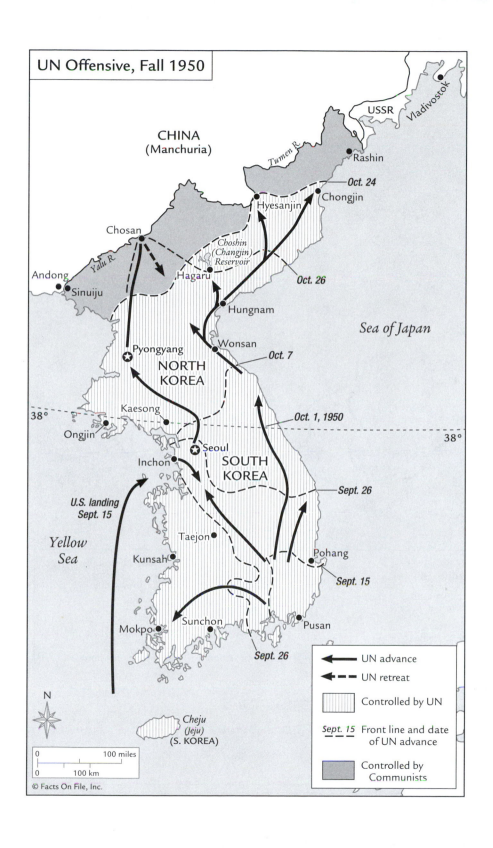

UN Offensive, Fall 1950

CHINA
(Manchuria)

USSR

Vladivostok

Tumen R.

Rashin

Oct. 24

Hyesanjin

Chongjin

Chosan

*Choshin
(Changjin)
Reservoir*

Andong

Yalu R.

Sinuiju

Hagaru

Oct. 26

Hungnam

Pyongyang

Wonsan

Oct. 7

NORTH
KOREA

Sea of Japan

38°

Kaesong

Oct. 1, 1950

38°

Ongjin

Seoul

SOUTH
KOREA

Inchon

Sept. 26

U.S. landing
Sept. 15

*Yellow
Sea*

Taejon

Kunsah

Pohang

Mokpo

Sunchon

Pusan

Sept. 15

Sept. 26

N

*Cheju
(Jeju)
(S. KOREA)*

←	UN advance
←- -	UN retreat
‖‖‖	Controlled by UN
Sept. 15 - - -	Front line and date of UN advance
▨	Controlled by Communists

0   100 miles
0   100 km

© Facts On File, Inc.

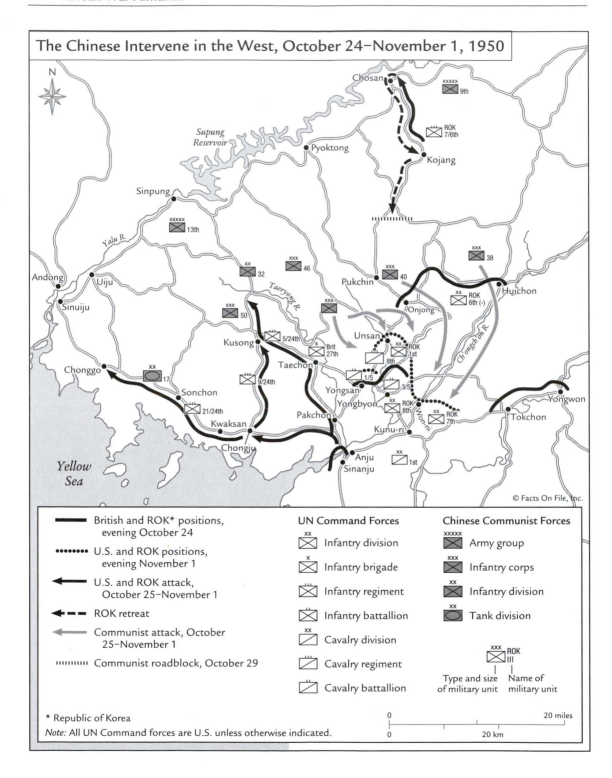

The Chinese Intervene in the West, October 24–November 1, 1950

Legend:

- ▬▬ British and ROK* positions, evening October 24
- •••••••• U.S. and ROK positions, evening November 1
- ◀▬ U.S. and ROK attack, October 25–November 1
- ◀‑‑‑ ROK retreat
- ◀▬ Communist attack, October 25–November 1
- ⅲⅲⅲ Communist roadblock, October 29

UN Command Forces

- ⊠ (xx) Infantry division
- ⊠ (x) Infantry brigade
- ⊠ (|||) Infantry regiment
- ⊠ (||) Infantry battalion
- ⊠ (xx) Cavalry division
- ⊠ (|||) Cavalry regiment
- ⊠ (||) Cavalry battalion

Chinese Communist Forces

- ⊠ (xxxxx) Army group
- ⊠ (xxx) Infantry corps
- ⊠ (xx) Infantry division
- ⊘ (xx) Tank division

⊠ (xxx / ROK / |||) — Type and size of military unit / Name of military unit

* Republic of Korea

Note: All UN Command forces are U.S. unless otherwise indicated.

0 ————— 20 miles
0 ————— 20 km

© Facts On File, Inc.

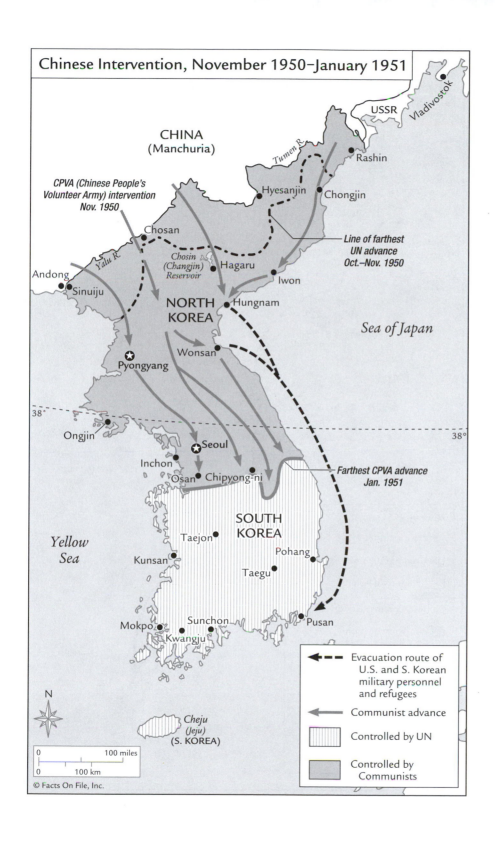

Chinese Intervention, November 1950–January 1951

CHINA
(Manchuria)

Tumen R.

USSR

Vladivostok

Rashin

CPVA (Chinese People's
Volunteer Army) intervention
Nov. 1950

Hyesanjin

Chongjin

Chosan

Line of farthest
UN advance
Oct.–Nov. 1950

*Chosin
(Changjin)
Reservoir*

Hagaru

Iwon

Yalu R.

Andong

Sinuiju

NORTH
KOREA

Hungnam

Sea of Japan

Wonsan

Pyongyang

38°

Ongjin

38°

Seoul

Inchon

Farthest CPVA advance
Jan. 1951

Osan

Chipyong-ni

SOUTH
KOREA

*Yellow
Sea*

Taejon

Pohang

Kunsan

Taegu

Mokpo

Sunchon

Pusan

Kwangju

N

*Cheju
(Jeju)
(S. KOREA)*

Evacuation route of
U.S. and S. Korean
military personnel
and refugees

Communist advance

Controlled by UN

Controlled by
Communists

0   100 miles

0   100 km

© Facts On File, Inc.

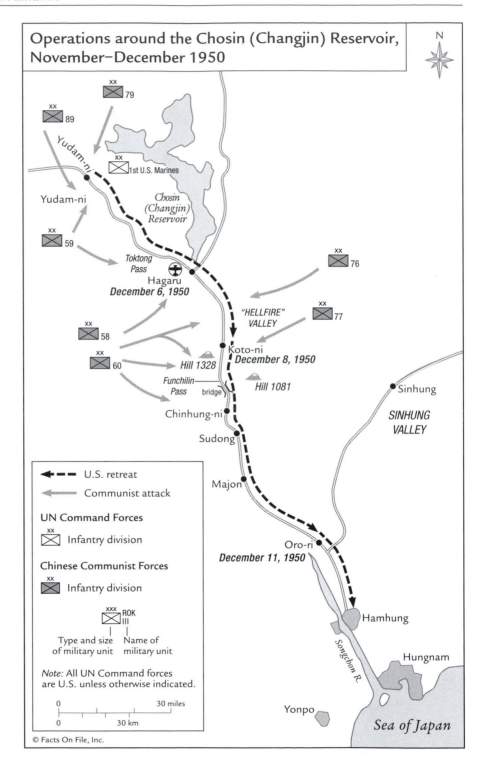

Operations around the Chosin (Changjin) Reservoir, November–December 1950

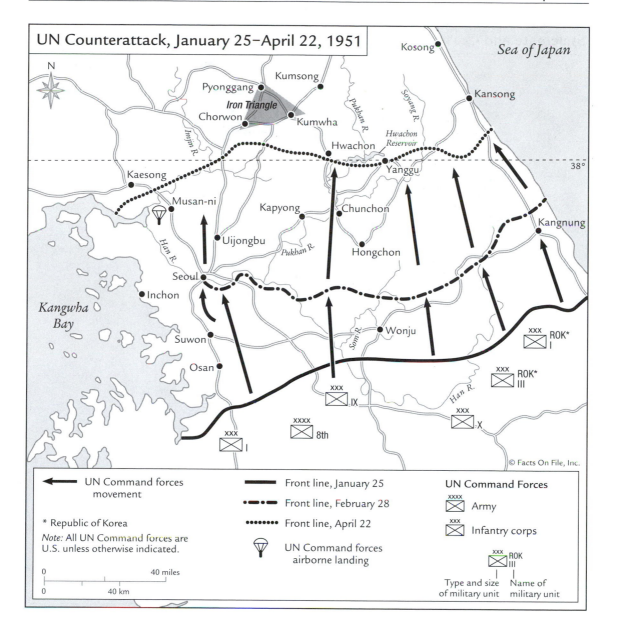

UN Counterattack, January 25–April 22, 1951

Sea of Japan

Kosong

Kumsong

Pyonggang

Iron Triangle

Chorwon

Kumwha

Kansong

Imjin R.

Pukhan R.

Soyang R.

Hwachon Reservoir

Hwachon

Yanggu

Kaesong

38°

Musan-ni

Kapyong

Chunchon

Kangnung

Han R.

Uijongbu

Pukhan R.

Hongchon

Seoul

Inchon

Kangwha Bay

Suwon

Som R.

Wonju

XXX ROK*
I

Osan

XXX ROK*
III

XXX
IX

XXX
X

XXXX
8th

XXX
I

© Facts On File, Inc.

Legend

UN Command forces movement

Front line, January 25

UN Command Forces

XXXX Army

* Republic of Korea

Front line, February 28

Note: All UN Command forces are U.S. unless otherwise indicated.

Front line, April 22

XXX Infantry corps

UN Command forces airborne landing

XXX ROK
III

Type and size of military unit   Name of military unit

0   40 miles

0   40 km

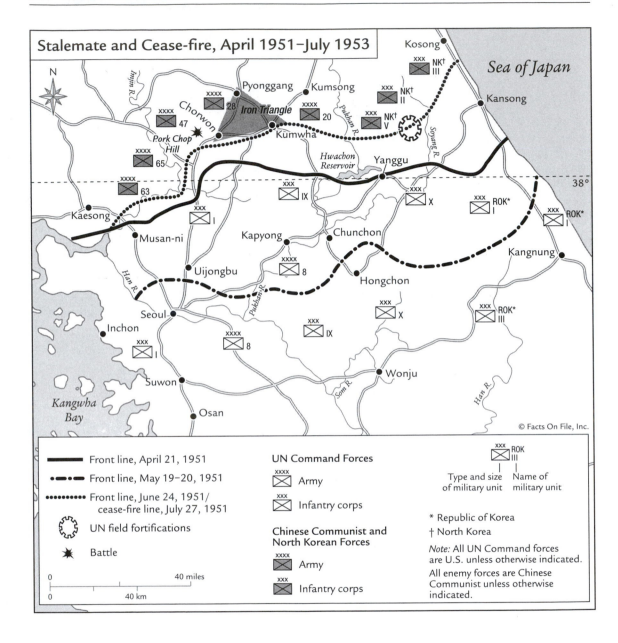

Stalemate and Cease-fire, April 1951–July 1953

Kosong

Sea of Japan

Kansong

Pyonggang   Kumsong

XXX NK† III

Chorwon   Iron Triangle

XXXX 28

XXX NK† II

XXXX 47

Pork Chop Hill

XXXX 20

Pukhan R.

XXX NK† V

XXXX 65

Kumwha

Hwachon Reservoir

Soyang R.

Yanggu

38°

XXXX 63

Kaesong

XXX IX

XXX X

XXX ROK* I

XXX ROK* I

XXX I

Musan-ni

Kapyong   Chunchon

Kangnung

Han R.

Uijongbu

XXXX 8

Hongchon

Pukhan R.

XXX X

XXX ROK* III

Seoul

XXX IX

Inchon

XXX I

XXXX 8

Wonju

Som R.

Han R.

Suwon

Kangwha Bay

Osan

© Facts On File, Inc.

	UN Command Forces		
▬▬▬ Front line, April 21, 1951	XXXX Army		
▬·▬·▬ Front line, May 19–20, 1951	XXX Infantry corps		
●●●●●● Front line, June 24, 1951/ cease-fire line, July 27, 1951	Chinese Communist and North Korean Forces		
⚙ UN field fortifications	XXXX Army		
✸ Battle	XXX Infantry corps		

XXX ROK III

Type and size of military unit   Name of military unit

* Republic of Korea
† North Korea

Note: All UN Command forces are U.S. unless otherwise indicated.

All enemy forces are Chinese Communist unless otherwise indicated.

0 _____ 40 miles
0 _____ 40 km

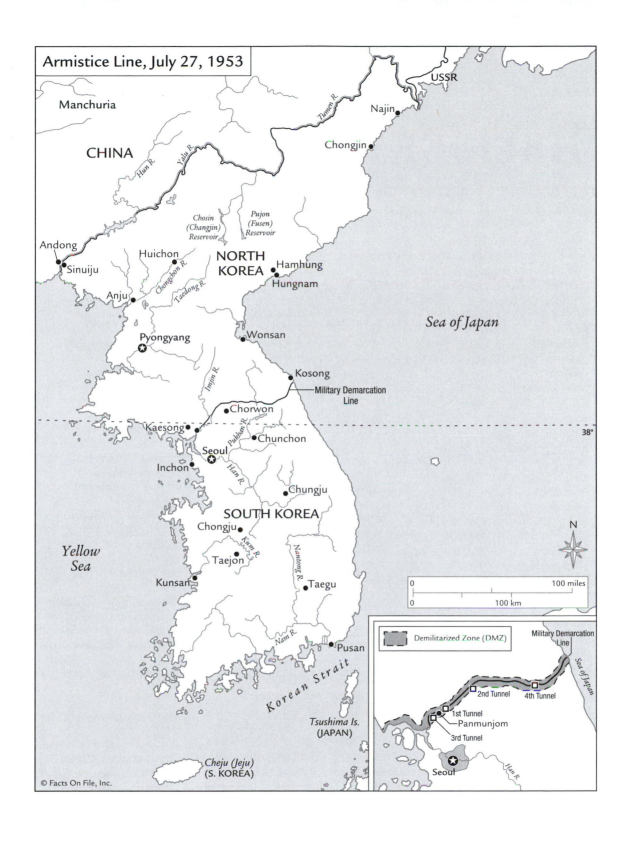

Armistice Line, July 27, 1953

Manchuria

CHINA

USSR

NORTH KOREA

Najin

Chongjin

Tumen R.

Yalu R.

Hun R.

Andong

Sinuiju

Huichon

Chosin (Changjin) Reservoir

Pujon (Fusen) Reservoir

Chongchon R.

Anju

Taedong R.

Hamhung

Hungnam

Sea of Japan

Pyongyang

Wonsan

Imjin R.

Kosong

Military Demarcation Line

Chorwon

Kaesong

Pukhan R.

Chunchon

38°

Seoul

Inchon

Han R.

Chungju

SOUTH KOREA

Chongju

Kum R.

Nantong R.

Taejon

Taegu

Yellow Sea

Kunsan

Nam R.

Pusan

Korean Strait

Tsushima Is. (JAPAN)

Cheju (Jeju) (S. KOREA)

N

| 0 | | 100 miles |
| 0 | | 100 km |

© Facts On File, Inc.

Demilitarized Zone (DMZ)

Military Demarcation Line

Sea of Japan

2nd Tunnel

4th Tunnel

1st Tunnel

Panmunjom

3rd Tunnel

Seoul

Han R.

BIBLIOGRAPHY

Acheson, Dean. *Present at the Creation: My Years in the State Department.* New York: Norton, 1969.

ACIG Korean War Team. "Soviet Air-to-Air Victories During the Korean War." www.acig.org/rtman/publish/article_314.shtml.

Alexander, Bevin. *Korea: The First War We Lost.* New York: Hippocrene Books, 1986.

Alexander, Joseph H., and Merrill L. Bartlett. *Sea Soldiers in the Cold War: Amphibious Warfare 1945–1991.* Annapolis, Md.: Naval Institute Press, 1995.

Anderson, R. C. B. *History of the Argyll and Sutherland Highlanders, 1st Battalion 1939–1954.* Edinburgh: Tate, 1956.

Angel, Raymond B. *From Segregation to Desegregation: Blacks in the Army 1703–1994.* Carlisle Barracks, Pa.: U.S. Army War College, 1990.

Appleman, Roy E. *East of Chosin: Entrapment and Breakout in Korea, 1950.* College Station: Texas A&M University Press, 1987.

———. *Escaping the Trap: The U.S. Army X Corps in Northeast Korea, 1950.* College Station: Texas A&M University Press, 1990.

———. *The United States Army in the Korean War: South to the Naktong, North to the Yalu.* Washington, D.C.: Office of the Chief of Military History, Department of the Army, 1987.

Archambault, A. H. *Soldiers of the Korean War.* Gettysburg, Pa.: Thomas Publications, 2000.

Archibald, Roger T. "History Is Not a Museum," *History News* 49, no. 3 (May–June 1994): 11.

Armstrong, Charles K. *The North Korean Revolution, 1945–1950.* Ithaca, N.Y.: Cornell University Press, 2003.

Ashley, David. *The Post Modern Condition.* Boulder, Colo.: Westview Press, 1997.

Atkins, E. L., H. P. Griggs, and Roy T. Seamans. *North Korean Logistics and Methods of Accomplishment.* Chevy Chase, Md.: Johns Hopkins University Press, 1951.

Bacahus, William A. "The Relationship between Combat and Peace Negotiations: Fighting While Talking in Korea, 1951–1953," *Orbis* (1962): 545.

Ballenger, Lee. *The Outpost War: U.S. Marines in Korea, Vol. 1: 1952.* Dulles, Va.: Brassey's, 2000.

———. *The Outpost War: U.S. Marines in Korea, Vol. 2: 1953.* Dulles, Va.: Brassey's, 2001.

Barclay, C. N. *The First Commonwealth Division, The Story of British Commonwealth Land Forces in Korea, 1950–1953.* Aldershot: Gale, 1954.

Barker, A. J. *Fortune Favours the Brave: The Battle of the Hook, Korea, 1953.* London: Leo Cooper, 1974.

Barris, Ted. *Deadlock in Korea: Canadians at War, 1950–1953.* Toronto: Macmillan, 1999.

Bartlett, Norman, ed. *With the Australians in Korea.* Canberra: Australian War Memorial, 1954.

Berebitsky, William. *A Very Long Weekend: The Army National Guard in Korea, 1950–1953.* Shippensburg, Pa.: White Mane, 1996.

Berger, Carl. *The Korean Knot: A Military and Political History.* Philadelphia: University Press, 1957, 1965, 1967.

Bernstein, Barton J., ed. *Politics and Policies of the Truman Administration.* Chicago: Quadrangle, 1970.

Biderman, Albert D. *March to Calumny: The Story of American POWs in the Korean War.* New York: Macmillan, 1963.

Biskind, Peter. *Seeing Is Believing: How Hollywood Taught Us to Stop Worrying and Love the Fifties.* New York: Pantheon Books, 1983.

Black, Robert W. *Rangers in Korea.* New York: Ivy Books, 1989.

Blair, Clay. *The Forgotten War: America in Korea, 1950–1953.* New York: Times Books, 1987.

Bland, Larry I., ed. *The Papers of George C. Marshall,* 4 vols. Baltimore: Johns Hopkins University Press, 1991.

Bodnar, John. *Remaking America: Public Memory, Commemoration, and Patriotism in the Twentieth Century.* Princeton, N.J.: Princeton University Press, 1996.

Bonnie, B. C., ed. *Korea under the American Military Government, 1945–1948.* Westport, Conn.: Praeger, 2002.

Breuer, William B. *Shadow Warriors: The Covert War in Korea.* New York: Wiley, 1996.

Brown, David. *The United States Air Force in Korea, 1950–1953.* Washington, D.C.: GPO, 1983.

Brown, Ronald J. *Counteroffensive: U.S. Marines from Pohang to No Name Line.* Washington, D.C.: Commemorative Series, U.S. Marine Corps Historical Center, 2001.

Brune, Lester H. *The Korean War: Handbook of the Literature and Research.* Westport, Conn.: Greenwood Press, 1996.

Bueschel, R. M. *Communist Chinese Air Power.* New York: Frederick A. Praeger, 1968.

Burning, John R. *Crimson Sky: The Air Battle for Korea.* New York: Brassey's Press, 1999.

Cagle, Malcolm W., and Frank A. Manson. *The Sea War in Korea.* Annapolis, Md.: U.S. Naval Institute Press, 1957.

Campigno, Anthony J. *A Marine Division in Nightmare Alley.* New York: Comet Press Books, 1958.

Carew, Tim. *Korea: The Commonwealth at War.* London: Cassell, 1967.

Catchpole, Brian. *The Korean War.* New York: Carroll & Graf, 2000.

Chace, James. *Acheson: The Secretary of State Who Created the American World.* New York: Simon and Schuster, 1998.

Chung, Henry. *The Russians Came to Korea.* Seoul: Korean Pacific Press, 1947.

Clare, Kenneth G. *Area Handbook for the Republic of Korea.* Washington, D.C.: Government Printing Office, 1969.

Clark, Ian. *Waging War.* Oxford: Clarendon Press, 1990.

Cleveland, William M. *Mosquitos in Korea.* New York: Mosquito Association, 1991.

Clodfelter, Michael. *Warfare and Armed Conflicts: A Statistical Reference to Casualty and Other Figures, 1618–1991.* Jefferson, N.C.: McFarland, 1992.

Collier, Rebecca L., comp. *Korean War Materials in the National Archives.* Washington, D.C.: National Archives and Records Administration, 2003.

Collins, J. Lawton. *War in Peacetime: The History and Lessons of Korea.* Boston: Houghton Mifflin, 1969.

Corr, Gerald H. *The Chinese Red Army.* New York: Schocken Books, 1974.

Correa, Edward L. *Logistics and the Chinese Communist Intervention during the Korean Conflict (1950–1953).* Carlisle Barracks, Pa.: U.S. Army War College, 1986.

Cotton, James, and Ian Neary, eds. *The Korean War in History.* Manchester, U.K.: Manchester University Press, 1989.

Cowart, Glenn C. *Miracle in Korea: The Evacuation of X Corps from the Hungnam Beachhead.* Columbus: University of South Carolina Press, 1992.

Crane, Conrad C. *American Air Power Strategy in Korea, 1950–1953.* Lawrence: University of Kansas Press, 2000.

Cumings, Bruce. *Child of Conflict: The Korean-American Relationship, 1943–1953.* Seattle: Washington University Press, 1983.

———. *Korea's Place in the Sun: A Modern History.* New York: W. W. Norton, 1997.

———. *The Origins of the Korean War, Vol. I, Liberation and the Emergence of Separate Regimes, 1945–1947.* Princeton, N.J.: Princeton University Press, 1981.

———. " 'Revising Postrevisionism,' or The Poverty of Theory in American Diplomatic History," *Diplomatic History* 17 (Fall 1993): 539–569.

———. *The Origins of the Korean War, Vol. II, The Roaring of the Cataract, 1947–1950.* Princeton, N.J.: Princeton University Press, 1990.

———. *War and Television.* London: Verso, 1992.

Cumings, Bruce, and Jon Halliday. *The Unknown War: Korea.* New York: Pantheon, 1988.

Cunningham-Boothe, Ashley, and Peter Farrar. *British Forces in the Korean War.* London: British Korean Veterans Association, 1988.

Dailey, Edward L. *MacArthur's X Corps in Korea: Inchon to the Yalu, 1950.* Paducah, Ky.: Turner Publishing, 1999.

Daskalopoulos, Ioannis. *The Greeks in Korea.* Washington, D.C.: Department of the Army, Office of the Assistant Chief of Staff for Intelligence, 1988.

Davidson, W. Phillips, and Jean Hungerford. *North Korean Guerilla Units.* Santa Monica, Calif.: RAND, 1951.

Davies, William J. *Task Force Smith: A Leadership Failure.* Carlisle Barracks, Pa.: U.S. Army War College, 1992.

Day, William W. *The Running Wounded: A Personal Memory of the Korean War.* Riverton, Wyo.: Big Ben Press, 1990.

Dayal, Shiv. *India's Role in the Korean Question.* New Delhi, India: Chand, 1959.

Department of Defense. *The Korean War: The Chinese Intervention.* Washington, D.C.: Chief of Military History, 2001.

———. *The Korean War: The Outbreak.* Washington, D.C.: Chief of Military History, 2001.

———. *The Korean War: Restoring the Balance.* Washington, D.C.: Chief of Military History, 2001.

———. *The Korean War: Years of Stalemate.* Washington, D.C.: Chief of Military History, 2001.

Detzer, David. *Thunder of the Captains: The Short Summer in 1950.* New York: Crowell, 1977.

DeWeerd, H. A. "Strategic Surprise in the Korean War," *Orbis* (1962): 435–452.

Diggins, John R. *The Proud Decade: America in War and in Peace, 1941–1960.* New York: Norton, 1988.

Dillie, John. *Substitute for Victory.* New York: Doubleday, 1954.

Dingman, Roger. "Atomic Diplomacy during the Korean War," *International Security* 13 (Winter 1998–1999): 61–89.

———. "Truman, Attlee, and the Korean War Crisis," In *The East Asian Crisis, 1945–1951, The Problem of China, Korea, and Japan: Papers.* London: International Center for Economics, and Related Disciplines. London School of Economics, 1982.

Dockrill, Michael, and John Young, eds. *British Foreign Policy, 1945–1956.* London: Macmillan, 1989; 16–148.

Doll, Thomas E. *USN/USMC over Korea: Navy and Marine Corps Air Operations over Korea.* Carrollton, Tex.: Squadron/Signal, 1988.

Dong-A, Ilbo. *Basic Documents on Security and Unification.* Seoul: Dong-A, 1971.

Drought, James. *The Secret.* Norwalk: Skylight Press, 1963.

Dunstan, Simon. *Armour of the Korean War, 1950–1953.* London: Osprey Publishing, 1982.

Ebbert, Jean, and Marie-Beth Hall. *Cross Currents: Navy Women from WWI to Tailhook.* Washington, D.C.: Brassey's, 1993.

Edwards, Paul M. *General Matthew B. Ridgway: A Bibliography.* Westport, Conn.: Greenwood Press, 1993.

———. *The Inchon Landing, Korea, 1950: An Annotated Bibliography.* Westport, Conn.: Greenwood Press, 1994.

———. *The Korean War: An Annotated Bibliography.* Westport, Conn.: Greenwood Press, 1998.

———. *The Korean War: A Documentary History.* Malabar, Fla.: Krieger Press, 2000.

Edwards, Richard. *The Korean War.* Hove, England: Wayland, 1988.

Eisenhower, Dwight D. *Mandate for Change.* Garden City, N.Y.: Doubleday, 1963.

Endicott, Stephen, and Edward Hagerman. *The United States and Biological Warfare: Secrets from the Early Cold War and Korea.* Bloomington: University of Indiana Press, 1998.

Ent, W. Uzal. *Fighting on the Brink: Defense of the Pusan Perimeter.* Paducah, Ky.: Turner Publishing, 1996.

Evanhoe, Ed. *Darkmoon: Eighth Army Special Operations in the Korean War.* Annapolis, Md.: Naval Institute Press, 1995.

Evens, Paul, and B. Michael Frolic, eds. *Reluctant Adversaries: Canada and the People's Republic of China, 1949–1970.* Toronto: University of Toronto Press, 1991.

Farrar-Hockley, Anthony. *The British Part in the Korean War, Vol. 1, A Distant Obligation.* London: HMSO, 1990.

———. *The British Part in the Korean War, Vol. 2, An Honourable Discharge.* London: HMSO, 1995.

———. *The Edge of the Sword.* London: Frederick Muller, Ltd., 1954.

Fehrenbach, T. R. *This Kind of War: A Study in Unpreparedness.* New York: Macmillan, 1963, 1994.

Feis, Herbert. *From Trust to Terror: The Onset of the Cold War, 1945–1950.* New York: Norton, 1970.

Field, James A., Jr. *History of the United States Naval Operations: Korea.* Washington, D.C.: Government Printing Office, 1962.

Fincher, Ernest. *The War in Korea.* New York: Franklin Watts, 1981.

Foot, Rosemary. "Making Known the Unknown War: Policy Analysis of the Korean Conflict in the Last Decade," *Diplomatic History* 15, no. 3 (Summer 1991): 411–431.

———. "Nuclear Coercion and the Ending of the Korean Conflict," *International Security* 13 (Winter 1988–89): 99–112.

———. *A Substitute for Victory: The Politics of Peacemaking and the Korean Armistice Talks.* Ithaca, N.Y.: Cornell University Press, 1990.

———. *The Wrong War: American Policy and the Dimensions of the Korean Conflict, 1950–1953.* Ithaca, N.Y.: Cornell University Press, 1985.

Fox, William J. *Inter-Allied Co-Operation during Combat Operations.* Washington, D.C.: Office of the Chief of Military History, Department of the Army, 1952.

Friedman, Edward, and Mark Selden. *American Asia: Dissenting Essays on Asian-American Relations.* New York: Pantheon, 1971.

Friedman, Norman. *Carrier Air Power.* Annapolis, Md.: Naval Institute Press, 1991.

Futrell, Robert F. *The United States Air Force in Korea, 1950–1953.* Rev. ed. Washington, D.C.: Office of Air Force History, 1983.

Gallaway, Jack. *The Last Call of the Bugle: The Long Road to Kapyong.* St. Lucia, Australia: University of Queensland Press, 1994.

Gardner, Lloyd C. *The Korean War.* New York: Quadrangle, 1972.

Gasston, Peter. *Thirty-Eighth Parallel: The British in Korea.* Glasgow, Scotland: A. D. Hamilton, 1976.

Geer, Andrew. *The New Breed: The Story of the U.S. Marines in Korea.* New York: Harper and Brothers, 1958.

George, Alexander L. *The Chinese Communist Army in Action.* New York: Columbia University Press, 1967.

Gilbert, Bill. *Ship of Miracles.* Chicago: Triumph Books, 2000.

Giusti, Earnest H. *The Mobilization of the Marine Corps Reserve in the Korean Conflict.* Washington, D.C.: Historical Branch, G-2, Division Headmasters, U.S. Marine Corps, 1967.

Goldstein, Warren. "Editorial," *The Chronicle of Higher Education,* April 10, 1998, p. A64.

Gorcharov, Sergei. "Stalin's Dialogue with Mao Zedong," *Journal of Northeast Asia Studies* 10, no. 4 (Winter 1991–92): 45–76.

Goncharov, Sergei N., John W. Lewis, and Xue Litai. *Uncertain Partners: Stalin, Mao, and the Korean War.* Stanford, Calif.: Stanford University Press, 1993.

Goodman, Allen E., ed. *Negotiating While Fighting: The Diary of Admiral C. Turner Joy at the Korean Armistice Conference.* Stanford, Calif.: Hoover Institution Press, 1978.

Gordon, Yefim, and Vladimir Rigmant. *MiG-15: Design, Development, and Korean War Combat History.* Osceola, Wis.: Motorbooks International, 1993.

Goulden, Joseph C. *Korea: The Untold Story of the War.* New York: Times Books, 1982.

Goulden, Terrence J. *U.S. Army Mobilization and Logistics in the Korean War.* Washington, D.C.: Government Printing Office, 1987.

Greenfield, Meg. "Missing World War II," *Newsweek,* June 6, 1994, p. 86.

Greer, Andrew. *The New Breed: The Story of the U.S. Marines in Korea.* New York: Harper & Row, 1952.

Grey, Jeffrey. *The Commonwealth Armies and the Korean War: An Alliance Study.* New York: Manchester University Press, 1988.

Griffith, Samuel B. *The Chinese People's Liberation Army.* New York: McGraw-Hill, 1967.

Gugeler, Russell A. *Combat Actions in Korea.* Washington, D.C.: Combat Forces Press, 1954.

Gupta, Karunakar. "How Did the Korean War Begin?" *China Quarterly* 52 (1972): 699–716.

Gurtov, Melvin, and Byong Moo Hwang. *China under Threat.* Baltimore: Johns Hopkins University Press, 1960.

Guttman, Allen. *Korea and the Theory of Limited War.* Boston: D. C. Heath, 1967.

Haas, Michael E. *Apollo's Warriors: United States Air Force Special Operations during the Cold War.* Maxwell AFB, Ala.: Air University Press, 1997.

Habesch, David. *The Army's Navy.* London: Chatham Publishing, 2001.

Hagiwara, Ryo. "The Korean War: The Conspiracies by Kim Il Sung and MacArthur." Typed manuscript located at the Center for the Study of the Korean War, n.p., n.d.

Halberstam, David. *The Fifties.* New York: Villard, 1993.

Halliday, Jon. "Air Operations in Korea: The Soviet Side of the Story," in *A Revolutionary War: Korea and the Transformation of the Postwar World.* Edited by William J. Williams. Chicago: Imprint Publications, 1993.

———. "The Korean War: Some Notes on Evidence and Solidarity," *Bulletin of Concerned Asian Scholars* 3 (November 1979): 2–18.

Halliday, Jon, and Bruce Cumings. *The Unknown War: Korea.* New York: Pantheon Books, 1998.

Hallion, Richard P. "Naval Air Operations in Korea," in *A Revolutionary War: Korea and the Transformation of the Postwar World.* Edited by William J. Williams. Chicago: Imprint Publications, 1993.

———. *The Naval Air War in Korea.* Baltimore: The Nautical and Aviation Publishing Company of America, 1986.

Hammel, Eric M. *Chosin: Heroic Ordeal of the Korean War.* New York: Vanguard Press, 1981.

Hankuk, Jon Jang. *The History of the Korean War,* 5 vols. Seoul: Hangrim, 1990, 1992.

Hass, Michael. *In the Devil's Shadow: U.N. Special Operations during the Korean War.* Annapolis, Md.: Naval Institute Press. 2000.

Hastings, Max. *The Korean War.* New York: Simon and Schuster, 1987.

Heinl, Robert D., Jr. *Victory at High Tide: The Inchon-Seoul Campaign.* Philadelphia: Lippincott, 1968.

Hermes, Walter. *Truce Tent and Fighting Front: United States in the Korean War.* Washington, D.C.: Center of Military History, 1966, 1991.

Hickey, Michael. *The Korean War: The West Confronts Communism.* New York: Overlook Press, 2000.

Higgins, Marguerite. *War in Korea: The Report of a Woman Combat Correspondent.* Garden City, N.Y.: Doubleday, 1951.

Hinshaw, Arned. *Heartbreak Ridge.* New York: Praeger, 1988.

Hopkins, William B. *One Bugle, No Drums: The Marines at Chosin Reservoir.* Chapel Hill, N.C.: Algonquin, 1986.

Hoyt, Edwin P. *The Bloody Road to Panmunjom.* New York: Stein & Day, 1985.

———. *The Pusan Perimeter: Korea 1950.* New York: Military Heritage Press, 1984.

———. *The Day the Chinese Attacked: Korea 1950.* New York: McGraw-Hill, 1990.

Hume, Edgar. "United Nations Medical Service in the Korean Conflict," *Military Surgeon* 109 (1951): 91–95.

Hunt, Michael H. "Beijing and the Korean Crisis, June 1950–June 1951," *Political Science Quarterly* 107, no. 3 (1992): 477.

Huston, James A. *Guns and Butter, Powder and Rice: U.S. Army Logistics of the Korean War.* Selinsgrove, Pa.: Susquehanna University Press, 1989.

———. *The Sinews of War: Army Logistics.* Washington, D.C.: Government Printing Office, 1966.

Ikle, Fred C. *Every War Must End.* New York: Columbia University Press, 1991.

Jackson, Robert. *Air War over Korea.* New York: Scribner's, 1973.

James, D. Clayton. *The Years of MacArthur: Triumph and Disaster, 1945–1964* (Vol 3). Boston: Houghton Mifflin, 1985.

James, D. Clayton, and Anne S. Wells. *Refighting the Last War: Command and Crisis in Korea, 1950–1953.* New York: Free Press, 1993.

Jin, Chul Soh. "Some Causes of the Korean War of 1950: A Study of Foreign Involvement in Korea (1945–1950)." Ph.D. dissertation, University of Oklahoma, 1963.

Kahn, Ely J. *The Peculiar War: Impressions of a Reporter in Korea.* New York: Random House, 1952.

Kaufman, Burton I. *The Korean War: Challenges in Crisis, Credibility, and Command.* Philadelphia, Pa.: Temple University Press, 1986.

Kemp, Robert F. *Combined Operations in the Korean War.* Carlisle Barracks, Pa.: U.S. Army War College, 1989.

Kennan, George F. *Memories, 1925–1950 and 1950–1963.* Boston: Atlantic, Little Brown, 1967, 1972.

Kerin, James, Jr. "The Korean War and American Memory." Ph.D. dissertation, University of Pennsylvania, 1994.

Khrushchev, Nikita. *Khrushchev Remembers and Khrushchev Remembers, the Last Testament.* Translated by Strobe Talbott. Boston: Little, Brown, 1974.

Kim Joungwoon Alexander. *Divided Kingdom: The Politics of Development, 1945–1972.* Cambridge, Mass.: Harvard University Press, 1975.

Kinkead, Eugene. *In Every War but One.* New York: Norton, 1959.

Knox, Donald. *The Korean War: Uncertain Victory.* San Diego: Harcourt Brace Jovanovich, 1988.

Kolko, Gabriel, and Joyce Kolko. *The Limits of Power: The World and United States Foreign Policy, 1945–1954.* New York: Harper, 1972.

Kublion, H. "The ROK Navy," *Naval Institute Proceedings* (October 1953): 1,134–1,135.

LaFeber, William. *America, Russia, and the Cold War, 1945–1975.* New York: Wiley, 1967.

Landsdown, John R. P. *With the Carriers in Korea: The Sea and Air War in SE Asia 1950–1953.* Wilmslow, Cheshire, U.K.: Crecy, 1997.

Langley, Michael. *Inchon Landing: MacArthur's Last Triumph.* New York: Times Books, 1979.

Lankov, Andrei. *From Stalin to Kim Il Sung: The Formation of North Korea, 1945–1950.* New Brunswick, N.J.: Rutgers University Press, 2002.

Launius, Roger D. *Task Paper in Airlift History.* Washington, D.C.: Office of History, Military Airlift Command, 1998.

Lawson, Don. *The United States in the Korean War.* New York: Abelard, 1964.

Leckey, Thomas. "Teaching History at High Noon: Letting the Lessons Emerge," *Commonweal* 118, (April 5, 1991): 22.

Leckie, Robert. *Conflict: The History of the Korean War.* New York: Da Capo, 1962, 1996.

———. *The March to Glory.* Cleveland: World, 1960.

Lee, Steven Hugh. *The Korean War.* Edinburgh, Scotland: Edinburgh Gate, 2001.

Leffler, Melvyn P. *A Preponderance of Power: National Security, The Truman Administration, and the Cold War.* Stanford, Calif.: Stanford University Press, 1992.

Levine, Steven I. "Soviet-American Rivalry in Manchuria and the Cold War," in *Dimensions of China's Foreign Relations.* Edited by Hsueh Chun-tu. New York: Praeger, 1977; 10–43.

Lewis, John W., Sergei N. Goncharov, and Xue Litai. *Uncertain Partners: Stalin, Mao, and the Korean War.* Stanford, Calif.: Stanford University Press, 1993.

Linklater, Eric. *Our Men in Korea.* London: Her Majesty's Stationery Office, 1952.

Lott, Arnold S. *Most Dangerous Seas.* Annapolis, Md.: Naval Institute Press, 1986.

Lowe, Peter. *The Origins of the Korean War.* London: Longman, 2000.

———. "The Significance of the Korean War in Anglo-American Relations." In *British Foreign Policy, 1945–1956,* edited by Michael Dockrill and John W. Young. London: Macmillan, 1989.

MacArthur, Douglas. *Reminiscences.* New York: Da Capo, 1964.

MacDonald, Callum A. *Korea: The War before Vietnam.* New York: Free Press, 1987.

———. "Rediscovering History: New Light on the Unknown War: Korea," *Bulletin of Concerned Asian Scholars* 244 (October 1992): 62.

MacGregor, Morris J., Jr. *Integration of the Armed Forces, 1940–1965.* Washington, D.C.: Center of Military History, 1981.

Malcolm, Ben S. *White Tigers: My Secret War in North Korea.* Washington, D.C.: Brassey's, 1995.

Malcolm, George I. *The Argylls in Korea.* London: Nelson, 1952.

Mansourov, Alexandre Y., tr. *Cold War International History Project,* "Stalin, Mao, Kim, and China's Decision to Enter the Korean War, September 16–October 15, 1950: New Evidence from Russian Archives." *Woodrow Wilson Cold War Center Bulletin* 3 (Fall 1993): 4–19.

Marshall, S. L. A. *Operation Punch and the Capture of Hill 440: Suwon, Korea, February 1951.* Chevy Chase, Md.: Johns Hopkins University Press, 1952.

———. *Pork Chop Hill.* New York: Jove Press, 1986.

———. *The River and the Gauntlet: Defeat of the Eighth Army by the Communist Chinese Forces, November 1950.* New York: Morrow, 1953.

Matray, James L. *Historical Dictionary of the Korean War.* Westport, Conn.: Greenwood Press, 1991.

———. "Korea's Partition: Soviet-American Pursuit of Reunification, 1945–1948," *Parameters* 28 (Spring 1998): 80–96.

———. *The Reluctant Crusade: American Foreign Policy in Korea, 1941–1950.* Honolulu: University of Hawaii Press, 1985.

McCormack, Gavan. *Cold War Hot War: An Australian Perspective on the Korean War.* Sydney: Hale and Iremonger, 1983.

McGibbon, Ian. *New Zealand and the Korean War, Vol. 2: Combat Operations.* Auckland: Oxford University Press, 1996.

McGuire, F. R. *Canada's Army in Korea.* Ottawa: Historical Section, Army General Staff, 1956.

Meid, Pat, and James M. Yinglin. *Operations in West Korea.* Washington, D.C.: U.S. Marine Corps Historical Branch, 1972.

Melady, John. *Korea: Canada's Forgotten War.* Toronto: Macmillan, 1983.

Merrill, John. *Korea: The Peninsular Origins of the War.* Newark: University of Delaware Press, 1989.

Mershon, Sherie, and Steve Scholssman. *Foxholes and Color Lines.* Baltimore, Md.: Johns Hopkins University Press, 1998.

Mersky, Peter B. *U.S. Marine Corps Aviation: 1912 to the Present.* Baltimore, Md.: Nautical & Aviation Publishing Company, 1997.

Meyers, Edward. *Thunder in the Morning Calm: The Royal Navy in Korea, 1950–1955.* St. Catharines, Ontario: Vanwell, 1991.

Middleton, Harry J. *The Compact History of the Korean War.* New York: Hawthorn, 1965.

Milano, James U., and Patrick Brogan. *Soldiers, Spies, and the Rat Line.* New York: Brassey's, 2000.

Miller, John, Owen J. Carroll, and Margaret E. Tackley. *Korea, 1951–1953.* Washington, D.C.: Office of the Chief of Military History, Department of the Army, 1956.

Millett, Allen. *Semper Fidelis: The History of the United States Marine Corps.* New York: Free Press, 1980, 1991.

Moeller, Susan D. *Shooting War: Photography and the American Combat Experience.* New York: Basic Books, 1991.

Montross, Lynn. *Cavalry of the Sky.* New York: Harper and Brothers, 1954.

———. *United States Marine Operation in Korea, 1950–1953,* 5 vols. Washington, D.C.: Historical Branch, G-3, Headquarters, U.S. Marine Corps, 1954–72.

Morton, Lois. "Willoughby on MacArthur: Myth and Reality," *Reporter* 11 (November 4, 1956): 46.

Mossman, Billy C. *Ebb and Flow, November 1950–July 1951: The United States in the Korean War.* Washington, D.C.: Center of Military History, 1990.

Mueller, John E. *War, Presidents, and Public Opinion.* New York: John Wiley & Sons, 1973.

Nalty, Bernard C. *Outpost War: U.S. Marines from the Nevada Battles to the Armistice.* Washington, D.C.: Commemorative Series, U.S. Marine Corps Historical Center, 2001.

———. *Stalemate: U.S. Marines from Bunker Hill to the Hook.* Washington, D.C.: Commemorative Series, U.S. Marine Corps Historical Center, 2001.

Nalty, Bernard C., and Morris J. MacGregor, eds. *Blacks in the Military.* New York: Free Press, 1986.

Neal, Arthur G. *National Trauma and Collective Memory.* London: M. E. Sharpe, 1998.

Odgers, George. *Across the Parallel: The Australian 77th Squadron with the United States Air Force in the Korean War.* Melbourne: Heinemann, 1952.

Oliver, Robert T. *Why War Came to Korea.* New York: Fordham University Press, 1950.

O'Ballance, Edgar. *Korea, 1950–1953.* London: Faber, 1969.

———. *The Red Army of China: A Short History.* New York: Praeger, 1963.

Omori, Frances. *Quiet Heroes: Navy Nurses of the Korean War, 1950–1953, Far East Command.* St. Paul, Minn.: Smith-House Press, 2000.

O'Neill, Robert. *Australia in the Korean War, 1950–1953, Vol. 1, Strategy and Diplomacy.* Canberra: Australian Government Publishing Service, 1981.

———. *Australia in the Korean War, 1950–1953, Vol. 2, Combat Operations.* Canberra: Australian Government Publishing Service, 1981.

Paige, Glen D. *The Korean Decision: June 24–30, 1950.* New York: Free Press, 1968.

Parry, Francis F. "Marine Artillery in Korea: Part I, Ready or Not," *Marine Corps Gazette* 71, no. 6 (June 1987): 47.

Paschall, Rod. *A Study in Command and Control: Special Operations in Korea, 1951–1953.* Carlisle Barracks, Pa.: U.S. Army Military History Institute, 1988.

Pearlman, Michael. "Korea: Fighting a War While Fearing to Fight One, the Specter of Escalation Management." Unpublished manuscript held in the Center for the Study of the Korean War.

Pelz, Stephen E. *America Goes to War, Korea, June 24–30: The Politics and Process of Decision.* Washington, D.C.: Woodrow Wilson Cold War Center, 1979.

Piehler, Guenter Kurt. *Remembering the War the American Way: 1783 to the Present.* Washington, D.C.: Smithsonian Institution, 1995.

Pimlott, John, ed. *British Military Operations, 1945–1984.* Greenwich, Conn.: Bison Books, 1984.

Poats, Rutherford M. *Decision in Korea.* New York: McBride Company, 1954.

Price, Scott T. *The Forgotten Service in the Forgotten War: The U.S. Coast Guard's Role in the Korean Conflict.* Annapolis, Md.: Naval Institute Press, 2000.

Purden, Wesley. "The New History Breeds Dunces," *Insight* (May 25, 1992): 17.

Quinn, Joseph. "Catching the Enemy off Guard," *Armor* 60, no. 4 (1951): 46.

Rees, David. *Korea: The Limited War.* New York: Macmillan, 1963.

Ridgway, Matthew B. *The Korean War*. New York: Doubleday, 1967.

Riley, John W., and Wilbur Schramm. *The Reds Take a City, The Communist Occupation of Seoul with Eye-Witness Accounts*. New Brunswick, N.J.: Rutgers University Press, 1951.

Roe, Patrick. *The Dragon Strikes: China and the Korean War, June–December 1950*. Novato, Calif.: Presidio, 2000.

Rose, Lisle A. *The Cold War Comes to Main Street: America in 1950*. Lawrence: University of Kansas Press, 1999.

Rottman, Gordon L. *Korean War Order of Battle: United States, United Nations, and Communist Ground, Naval and Air Forces, 1950–1953*. Westport, Conn.: Praeger Publishers, 2002.

Ruetten, Richard T. "General Douglas MacArthur's 'Reconnaissance in Force': The Rationalization of Defeat in Korea," *Pacific Historical Review* 36 (February 1967): 87.

Russell, George. "Defense on an Extended Front," *Infantry School Quarterly* 43, no. 2 (1953).

Russell, William C. *Stalemate and Standoff: The Bloody Outpost War*. DeLeon Springs, Fla.: W. Russell, 1993.

———. *Ten Days at White Horse*. Arlington, Va.: W. Russell, 1988.

Ryan, Mark A. *Chinese Attitudes toward Nuclear Weapons: China and the United States during the Korean War*. London: East Gate Book, 1989.

Sandler, Stanley. *The Korean War: No Victors, No Vanquished*. Lexington: University Press of Kentucky, 1999.

Sandler, Stanley, ed. *The Korean War: An Encyclopedia*. New York: Garland, 1995.

Sawyer, Robert K. *Military Advisors in Korea: KMAG in Peace and War*. Washington, D.C.: GPO, 1963.

Schaller, Michael. *Douglas MacArthur: The Far East General*. New York: Oxford University Press, 1989.

Schnabel, James F. *Policy and Direction: The First Year. The Official History of the United States Army in the Korean War*. Washington, D.C.: Department of the Army, 1972.

Schnabel, James F., and Robert J. Watson. *History of the Joint Chiefs of Staff*, Vol. 3, *The Korean War*. Washington, D.C.: Joint Chiefs of Staff, 1978.

"Secrets of the Korean War." *U.S. News and World Report*, August 9, 1993.

Severo, Richard, and Lewis Milford. *The Wages of War: When Americans Came Home: From Valley Forge to Vietnam*. New York: Simon and Schuster, 1997.

Sheldon, Walt. *Hell or High Water: MacArthur's Landing at Inchon*. New York: Macmillan, 1968.

Sherwood, John Darrell. *Officers in Flight Suits: The Story of American Air Force Fighter Pilots in the Korean War*. New York: New York University Press, 1996.

Sho, Kin Chull. "The Role of the Soviet Union in Preparation for the Korean War," *Journal of Korean Affairs* (January 3, 1974): 3–14.

Simmons, Edwin H. *Frozen Chosin: U.S. Marines at the Changjin Reservoir*. Washington, D.C.: Commemorative Series, U.S. Marine Corps Historical Center, 2001.

Simmons, Robert. *The Strained Alliance: Peking, Pyongyang, Moscow, and the Politics of the Cold War*. New York: Free Press, 1975.

Sleeper, Raymond S. "Korean Targets for Medium Bombardment," *Air University Quarterly Review* 4, no. 3 (Spring 1951): 21.

Smurthwaite, David, and Linda Washington. *Project Korea: The British Soldier in Korea, 1950–1953*. London: National Army Museum, 1988.

Soderbergh, Peter A. *Women Marines in the Korean War Era*. Westport, Conn.: Praeger, 1994.

Soffer, Jonathan M. *General Matthew R. Ridgway: From Progressivism to Reaganism, 1895–1993*. Westport, Conn.: Praeger, 1998.

Son-Yup, Paik. *From Pusan to Panmunjom*. Washington, D.C.: Brassey's, 1992.

Spanier, John W. *The Truman-MacArthur Controversy and the Korean War*. New York: W. W. Norton 1965.

Spurr, Russell. *Enter the Dragon: China's Undeclared War against the United States in Korea, 1950–1953*. New York: Newmarket Press, 1988.

Stairs, Dennis. *The Diplomacy of Constraint: Canada, the Korean War, and the United States*. Toronto: University of Toronto Press, 1974.

Stanton, Shelby L. *America's Tenth Legion: X Corps in Korea, 1950*. Novato, Calif.: Presidio Press, 1989.

Stearn, Peter N. *Meaning over Memory*. Chapel Hill: University of North Carolina Press, 1993.

Stelmach, Daniel S. "The Influence of Russian Armored Tactics on the North Korean Invasion, 1950." Ph.D. dissertation, Washington University, St. Louis, Missouri, 1973.

Stephanson, Anders. *Kennan and the Art of Foreign Policy*. Cambridge, Mass.: Harvard University Press, 1995.

Stewart, James T. *Airpower: The Decisive Force in Korea*. Princeton, N.J.: D. Van Nostrand Company, 1957.

Stockholm International Peace Research Institute. *The Problem of Chemical and Biological Warfare*, 6 vols. New York: Stockholm International Peace Research Institute, 1956.

Stokesbury, James L. *A Short History of the Korean War.* New York: William Morrow, 1988.

Stone, I. F. *Hidden History of the Korean War.* Boston: Little, Brown, 1952.

Stueck, William W., Jr. *The Korean War: An International History.* Princeton, N.J.: Princeton University Press, 1995.

———. *The Korean War in World History.* Lexington: University Press of Kentucky, 2004.

———. *The Road to Confrontation.* Chapel Hill: University of North Carolina Press, 1981.

Summers, Harry G., Jr. *Korean War Almanac.* New York: Facts On File, 1990.

Summers, Harry G., Jr. "The Korean War: A Fresh Perspective," *Military History* (April 1996): 1–8.

Swartout, Robert, Jr. "American Historians and the Outbreak of the Korean War: An Historiographical Essay," *Asian Quarterly* [Belgium] no. 11 (1979): 67–77.

Tang Tsou. *American Failures in China, 1941–1950.* Chicago: University of Chicago Press, 1963.

Tate, James H. "The First Five Months," *Army* 6, no. 3 (March 1951): 40.

Taylor, Maxwell D. *The Uncertain Trumpet.* New York: Harper, 1960.

Tepsurkayeu, Yuriy, and Leonid Krylou. "Combat Episodes of the Korean War: Three Out of a Thousand." Cookie Sewell, tr. www.kimsoft.com/2000/NK-af2.htm.

Terzibaschitsch, Stefan. *Escort Carriers and Aviation Support Ships of the U.S. Navy.* Annapolis, Md.: Naval Institute Press, 1981.

Thomas, Nigel, and Peter Abbot. *The Korean War, 1950–1953.* London: Osprey Publishing, 1986.

Thompson, Warren, and Jack C. Nicholls. *Korea: The Air War 1950–1953.* London: Osprey Aerospace, 1956.

Thorgrimsson, Thor, and E. C. Russell. *Canadian Naval Operations in Korean Waters: 1950–1953.* Ottawa: Queen's Printer, 1965.

Thorton, Richard C. *Odd Man Out: Truman, Stalin, Mao, and the Origins of the Korean War.* Novato, Calif.: Presidio, 2000.

Toland, John. *In Mortal Combat.* New York: William Morrow, 1991.

Tucker, Spencer C., ed. *Encyclopedia of the Korean War: A Political, Social, and Military History.* Santa Barbara, Calif.: ABC-CLIO, 2000.

UN Partisan Forces in the Korean Conflict, 1951–1952: A Study in Their Characteristics and Operation. Tokyo: Military History Detachment, 1954.

United States Operations Research Office. *Integration of ROK Soldiers into the U.S. Units (KATUSA).* Washington, D.C.: GPO, 1990.

Utz, Curtis A. *Assault from the Sea: The Amphibious Landing at Inchon.* Washington, D.C.: Naval History Center, Department of Navy, 1994.

Vatcher, William H. *Panmunjom, The Story of the Korean Military Armistice Negotiations.* New York: Frederick A. Praeger, 1958.

Voorhees, Melvin B. *Korean Tales.* New York: Simon and Schuster, 1952.

War History Compilation Committee. *The History of the United Nations Forces in the Korean War, Vol. 2.* Seoul: Ministry of National Defense, Republic of Korea, n.d.

Weathersby, Kathryn. "Attack or Not to Attack: Stalin, Kim Il Sung, and the Prelude to War," *Woodrow Wilson Cold War Center Bulletin* 5 (Spring 1995): 1, 2–9.

———. "Soviet Aims in Korea and the Origins of the Korean War, 1945–1950: New Evidence from the Russian Archives." *Cold War International History Project,* Working Paper no. 8 (November 1995).

Weathersby, Kathryn, tr. "New Findings on the Korean War," *Woodrow Wilson Cold War Center Bulletin* 3 (Fall 1993): 1, 14–18.

Weintraub, Stanley. *War in the Wards: Korea's Unknown Battle in a Prisoner-of-War Hospital Camp.* Garden City, N.Y.: Doubleday, 1968.

West, Philip. "Interpreting the Korean War," *American Historical Review* 94 (February 1989): 80–96.

Westover, John G. *Combat Support in Korea, U.S. Army in Action Series.* Washington, D.C.: Government Printing Office, 1955.

Wheeler, Michael O. *Nuclear Weapons and the Korean War.* McLean: Virginia Center for National Security Negotiations, 1994.

Whelan, Richard. *Drawing the Line: The Korean War, 1950–1953.* Boston: Little, Brown, 1990.

White, William L. *Back Down the Ridge.* New York: Harcourt Brace, 1963.

Whiting, Allen S. *China Crosses the Yalu: The Decision to Enter the Korean War.* New York: Macmillan, 1960.

Whitney, Courtney. *MacArthur: His Rendezvous with History.* New York: Alfred A. Knopf, 1956.

Willoughby, Charles A. *Intelligence in War: A Brief History of MacArthur's Intelligence Service, 1941–1951.* Tokyo: Dai-Nippon Printing Company, 1959.

Wilz, John Edward. "The MacArthur Hearings of 1951: The Secret Testimony," *Military Affairs* 39 (December 1975): 167.

———. "Did the United States Betray Korea in 1905?" *Pacific Historical Review* 44 (August 1985): 243–270.

Wood, Herbert Fairlie. *Official History of the Canadian Army: Strange Battleground. The Operations in Korea and Their Effects on the Defense of Canada.* Ottawa: Ministry of National Defense, 1966.

Woodrow Wilson Cold War Center. *Cold War Flashpoints.* Princeton, N.J.: Woodrow Wilson Cold War Center Bulletin, 1995.

Young, Gordon R., ed. *The Army Almanac: A Book of Facts Concerning the United States Army.* Harrisburg, Pa.: Stackpole Company, 1959.

Xi, Zhang. "China's Entry into the Korean War," *Chinese Historians* 6 (Spring 1993): 1–30.

Yergin, Daniel. *Shattered Peace.* Boston: Houghton Mifflin, 1977.

Xiaoming, Ahang. *Red Wings Over the Yalu: China, the Soviet Union, and the Air War in Korea.* College Station: Texas A & M University Press, 2002.

Yibo, Bo. "The Making of the 'Lean-to-One-Side' Decision." Translated by Zhai Qiang. *Chinese Historians* 5 (Spring 1992): 57–62.

Yu, Bin. "What China Learned from Its 'Forgotten War' in Korea," *Strategic Review* (Summer 1998): 4–16.

Zelman, Walter A. *Chinese Intervention in the Korean War.* Los Angeles: University of California Press, 1967.

Zhang, Shu Guang. *Mao's Military Romanticism: China and the Korean War, 1950–1953.* Lawrence, Kansas: University of Kansas Press, 1995.

Primary Collections

Army Plans and Operations Division, Record Group 319, National Archives, Suitland, Maryland

Center for the Study of the Korean War, Graceland University, Independence, Missouri

Central Plains Region, National Archives and Records Administration

Eisenhower Presidential Library, Abilene, Kansas

MacArthur Memorial Bureau of Archives, Norfolk, Virginia

Modern Military Records Branch, National Archives, Washington, D.C.

Naval Historical Center, Office of the Navy Historian, Washington, D.C.

Truman Presidential Museum & Library, Independence, Missouri

United National Archives (Readex Microprint Edition), 1978

United States Army Military History Institute, Carlisle Barracks, Pennsylvania

United States Marine Corps History (Division), Navy Yard, Washington, D.C.

Web Sites

The Forgotten Victory: www.theforgottenvictory.org

Cold War International History Project: http://cwihp.si.edu

Cold War Episodes: http://www.cnn.com

Korean War Site: www.korean-war.com

Soviet Air Activity: www.acig.org/rtman/publish/article_314.shtml

Korean War Information: www.koreanwar.org

Cold War Conflicts: www.britains-smallwars.com/korea

INDEX

Italic page numbers indicate illustrations. **Boldface** numbers denote biographies. In the Korean language, the following translit-erated suffixes (and others) denote specific geographical entities: *-do* (island or province), *-ri* (town or rural district), *-kun* (county), *-ni* (a variation of *-ri*, used after certain consonants). In English translations, these suffixes are commonly omitted.

A

Able Company 52, 66, 79, 81, 82, 90, 94, 102, 180, 202, 208, 213, 243, 254, 291, 302, 305, 313, 330, 331, 335, 344, 354, 364, 366, 375, 382, 421
"Able Dog." *See* Skyraider
Acheson, Dean G. 31, 33, 35, 111, 176, 200, 205, 209, 210, 212, 236, 282, **454**
Ae-do (North Korea) 139, 257
Agerholm, USS 199, 228, 329, 524
aircraft 500–511
Alacrity, HMS 177, 264, 267, 274, 523
Albatross (aircraft) 500
Albuquerque, USS 307, 312, 525
allied nations. *See also specific countries*
    military aid by 30, 31, 38, 514–525
    nonmilitary aid by 35, 38, 44, 512–513
    weapons used by 492–498, 500–510
Allison, John M. **454–455**
Almond, Edward Mallory 83, 84, 96, 103, 111, 113, 120, 133, 135, 138, 142, 147, 152, 154, 168, 401, **455**
Amethyst, HMS 246, 303, 309, 310, 312, 316, 317, 318
Amgak Island 253, 319
Amgak Peninsula 263, 265, 267, 269

Anchor Hill 350, 405
Anderson, Samuel E. 405, 409, *424*
Anderson, USS 199, 524
Andong (Dandong, China) 84, 111, 120, 127, 130, 131, 132, 136, 159, 162, 163, 164, 178, 189, 190, 215, 257, 329, 386, 415
Andong (South Korea) 57
Andrewes, William G. 66, 116, 155–156, 174, 187, **455**
Anju (North Korea) 63, 121, 122, 125, 127, 128, 138, 147, 155, 176, 215–217, 222, 241, 243, 246, 249, 251–255, 261, 263–265, 277, 313, 364, 375
Ansong (South Korea) 47, 319
antiaircraft weapons 495
Antietam, USS 249, 254, 272, 284, 285, 295, 331, 364, 401, 524
antitank rifles 499
Anui (South Korea) 62–63, 106
Anyang-ni (South Korea) 89, 90, 103
Anzac, HMAS 352
Apache, USS 271, 273, 277, 289
Apnok, ROKN 192, 224, 300
Argentina 512
Arisaka rifles 498
armistice/cease-fire talks
    on airfields 268, 272
    on cease-fire inspection 262

    on cease-fire line 231, 241
    China and 153, 161, 162, 210, 218–219, 222, *222*, 241, 243, 251, 260, 287, 316, 326, 328, 334, 341, 345, 370, 385, 394, 403, 411, 416, 418
    on demarcation line 258, 259
    DPRK and 218–219, 227, 251, 268, 278, 287, 316, 384, 394, 402, 406, 417, 452
    on economic issues 391
    and evacuation 409
    at Kaesong 219, 221, 222, *222*, 223, *223*, 227, 242
    new delegates at 274, 313, 324, 393
    at Panmunjom 247–248, 251, 252, *252*, 259, 263, 268, 278, 315, 370, *387*, 393, 394, 395, 397, *397*, 398, 400, 406, 412, 413, 416–417, 418, 421
    on political issues 270, 277
    on prisoners 156, 263, 266, 267, 268, 287, 314, 316, 334, 337, 341, 345, 370, 384, 385, 394, 397, *397*, 398, 402, 407, 411, 412, 416, 426
    proposals for 136, 149
    protest to *408*
    ROK and 218, 251, 287, 302, 393, 394, 395, 398,